MAN, SPACE, AND ENVIRONMENT

MAN, SPACE, AND ENVIRONMENT

CONCEPTS IN CONTEMPORARY HUMAN GEOGRAPHY

Edited by

Paul Ward English
University of Texas

Robert C. Mayfield
Boston University

New York
OXFORD UNIVERSITY PRESS
London   1972   Toronto

To our parents with admiration and affection

James and Mary English
Worcester, Massachusetts

Percy and Fay Mayfield
Abilene, Texas

✦✦✦✦✦✦✦✦✦✦✦✦✦✦✦✦✦✦✦✦✦✦✦✦✦✦✦✦✦✦✦

ACKNOWLEDGMENTS

In a project of this type the efforts of many contribute. First and foremost, our thanks to the authors and their publishers for graciously allowing us to reprint their materials; and to the University Research Institute of the University of Texas for financial support. Finally our gratitude to those who actually did the work while we sat back and thought about it: to Fred Bourque, Walter Greening, Rita Kilmer, Susan Polomé, and William TeBrake who worked on bibliography, translation, and editing; and to Annette Baker, Cris Beall, Curtis Jordan, Justine Marik, and William Smallwood of the Middle East Center and Earlayne Chance and Beverly Stoeltje of the Geography Department for their marvelous secretarial and organizational skills.

November 1970   *P.W.E.*
                                                         R.C.M.

CONTENTS

THE SPATIAL STRUCTURE OF HUMAN BEHAVIOR

✠✠✠✠✠✠✠✠✠✠✠✠✠✠✠✠✠✠✠✠✠✠✠✠✠✠✠✠✠

GENERAL INTRODUCTION

In the last fifteen years, the discipline of geography has experienced a renaissance. Like most periods of renewal, it has been marked by growth in both physical size and intellectual awareness, and by the development of a set of new approaches, techniques, and ideas. In this period, geography moved more deeply into the social sciences and extended its interest to encompass developing method-ologies in economics, political science, sociology, and related fields. But perhaps more important, it accelerated the development of its own conceptual frameworks, its own theoretical structures, to cope with major questions in the field. The step toward theory was most noticeably accompanied by an impatient and largely successful effort to achieve sophistication in analytical techniques. This demand for rigor took root in non-mathematical subfields as well, generating a renewed concern for the philosophical and conceptual underpinnings of all research in human geography. To be sure, the theoretical building blocks honed in this period have yet to be assembled into more general structures, but at least the foundation and corner-stones have been laid. Those who wish to work in the con-struction can find ready employment. With the dust settling a bit and, in particular, with the past decade of significant change in mind, we decided to prepare a reader for the beginning student of human geography which would not attempt a comprehensive review and appraisal of the discipline, but would try to identify the building blocks on which the future of the discipline will rest.

Our first purpose in this reader is to specify the major traditions in the discipline and those related conceptual frameworks which give coherence to contemporary human geography. Considering the rather baleful history of dichotomies in traditional geography (physical-human, systematic-regional, quantitative-qualitative: divisions recognized by neither editor), we found it somewhat dis-concerting to agree from the beginning on two central foci of theoretical development within the field, geography as the study of *man-environment systems* and geography as the study of *the spatial structure of human behavior.*

Within these two major research traditions, the next problem was to distinguish the conceptual frameworks used by geographers in attacking the central questions. In the study of *man-environment systems,* three were selected. The first and most traditional of these is the concept of the *cultural landscape,* the analysis of human interaction with the physical world through the study of man's tangible footprints on its surface. The second, *ecology,* focuses on processes of man-environment interactions rather than on form and content. The third, *environmental perception,* stresses man's "images" of his surroundings as a key to unraveling the nature of man-land transactions. Each of these frameworks provides a coherent working methodology for analyzing man-environment systems, but they differ in the identification of significant variables, the nature and sources of data collection, and the techniques of analysis employed.

Three frameworks were also identified within the broader tradition of geography as the *spatial structure of human behavior.* These are spatial diffusion, region, and spatial order. *Spatial diffusion* is concerned with locational changes of men, materials, and ideas through time, whether these shifts occur as spatially enveloping expansions from points of origin or as successive relocations that bypass many potential sites. The concept of *region* as a viable method of spatial delimitation facilitates the ordering of data from all geographical perspectives. *Spatial order* stresses the necessity of identifying patterns of order in the distributions of phenomena, distinguishing between underlying spatial patterns and those

culturally induced. The emphasis on form or process, content or flow, will vary by framework and scholar, but these approaches contribute to modern geographic methodology.

Our second purpose is to give the student insight into the strengths and weaknesses of each conceptual framework established. These may be biased by the assumptions of the researcher, by his priorities in the ordering of phenomena, in the structuring of his world. It is not accidental that anthropologists so often prove the importance of kinship in human affairs, while sociologists argue for social stratification and geographers for spatial organization. Each scholar perceives the world with a partial but finely ground lens. The techniques he brings to bear on research problems reinforce his predilections, and these techniques can rarely be challenged by the student. What can and should be understood and challenged are the underlying concepts, those philosophical premises which influence the writer's selection of problem and research technique.

Every scholar must order his views if he wishes to make a substantive contribution to knowledge. In this process of ordering, he develops his own model of reality, and models are to some degree self-fulfilling prophecies. If one takes a particular view of the world, the world responds with kindly conformity; this pliable response is the scholar's epistemological snare.

If one approaches, for example, the underdeveloped areas of the world as a student of *cultural landscapes,* then he will surely notice a variety of human imprints on the land. Iranian field patterns, settlement forms, and wooded shrine sites are, for him, significant cultural and spatial variables in the record of man's tenure in that region. Similarly, the granite-walled huts and granite-pillared fencerows of Southeastern Mysore will sharply define another tangible document of human occupance of the earth. If one brings to these same areas the conceptual thrust of *environmental perception*, however, one will closely examine the differing phenomenological precepts of nomad and peasant in Iran, variations in their cognitive environments, and differences in their perception of space and territory. In the villages of Mysore, this same observer would analyze the implications of local perceptions that nature is whimsical, vindictive, or both. "The rains have failed and only God knows why" or more pointedly "There is no rain because of corruption in the city, but we are paying the price in the village." A third view, that of *ecology* would attempt to integrate the desert hearth of central Iran, early irrigation technology, patterns of cooperation and conflict between nomad and peasant, prevailing forms of architecture and settlement, and the behavioral mandates of Islam into one functioning system to identify the host of processes that characterize the Iranian ecosystem. In Southeastern Mysore, this approach would delineate another similar ecosystem encompassing the same range of variables, although with very different data. Here, the scholar would attempt to identify common system characteristics in spite of the different cultural heritage and physical base, the complexities of the caste system and the monsoon, and interrelated patterns of land, labor, and technology.

The *spatial diffusionist*, by contrast, might be interested in the stage by stage relocation of the Zoroastrians, a minority religious faith in Iran, as they moved through the settlement hierarchy and ultimately assembled in the capital city, Teheran. In Mysore, his concern could be the contagious diffusion of a rumor that eating hybrid maize causes cholera, a rumor which swept three South Indian states in 1968. A *regional* viewpoint in Iran could lead to the examination of the limits of urban influence in the countryside, with the researcher piecing together the organizational network that binds village to town. In Mysore, the contiguity of two Dravidian languages might prompt the regionalist to delimit not a boundary line, but that zone in which the transition is effected by bilingualism. Finally, from the perspective of *spatial order*, the researcher in Iran might examine the possible relationships between the hierarchy of service centers to the hierarchical rank of pilgrimage centers. In Southeastern Mysore, he could analyze the spatial correlations between the settlement pattern, the distribution of abandoned villages, and the communication network as they related to the pattern of natural lakes and ponds in the area. In sum, the researcher follows his interests, and seeks problems congenial to his temperament and training. These predispositions should not go unnoticed by the student.

Having now cleverly implied that the editors of this volume are the only unbiased geographers in the profession by virtue of mastering all six conceptual frameworks, we discover the need to fill out the text with the writings of those scholars who have made these concepts so important in modern geography. In the following sections, these frameworks are presented as discrete approaches to common geographical problems in order to clarify for the student the fundamental philosophical and methodological assumptions that all writers bring to their research. But despite this separation, it is clear that there is considerable overlap among sections in both the questions asked and the methods followed. Several of the articles could appropriately appear under more than one heading. This overlap reflects the growing unity of the discipline and its recent progress toward identifying central questions which must be answered. The intellectual and methodological thrusts of landscape, ecology, perception, diffusion, region, and spatial order are applicable to the full spectrum of interests within modern geography. We hope that by identifying and presenting them in this way we will help the student gain insight into these important developments in contemporary human geography.

MAN AND ENVIRONMENT

1

THE CULTURAL LANDSCAPE

Cultural landscape, the study of human patterns on the earth, is one of the most enduring themes in the writings of European and American geographers, and virtually no landscape in the world has been left undescribed. This emphasis on landscape as a central focus in geography derives from two traditions in the discipline. In earlier times, many of the great explorers identified themselves as geographers, and in describing alien lands to the literate of Europe, they unveiled the broad contours of the landscapes and peoples of the New World, Asia, and Africa. Lately, professional geographers trained in the study of natural process have produced hundreds of detailed regional monographs. In these, emphasis lay on the concrete and the visible, on the formation of the physical landscape, and on the varied patterns of man's activities within each environment. The measure of these geographers and their writings is usually taken by historians and historical geographers, who must rely on the regionalist's faithful rendering of detail, his skill at observing and recording the essential facts of a people and their environment, to construct their own interpretations of man's tenure on earth. Most recently, the landscape theme in geography has been expressed in terms of man's role in changing the face of the earth,[1] man-environment systems,[2] and perception.[3] But whatever the terminology, there remains broad agreement in the profession and beyond that the study of landscapes is an essentially geographic concern, though few accept Sorre's statement that

1. The title and theme of a fine symposium volume edited by William L. Thomas, Jr., with the collaboration of Carl Sauer, Marston Bates, and Lewis Mumford. The volume is dedicated to George Perkins Marsh, one of the few voices raised in the nineteenth century against environmental determinism. See George Perkins Marsh, *Man and Nature: Or, Physical Geography as Modified by Human Action* (1864), edited by David Lowenthal, Cambridge: Harvard University Press, 1965.
2. Edward A. Ackerman, "Where Is the Research Frontier," *Annals, Association of American Geographers*, Vol. 53 (1963), pp. 429-40.
3. See section below, "The Aesthetic Landscape."

3

the "whole content of geography lies in the analysis of landscapes."[4]

The definition of landscape as a formal concept in modern geography emerged in Germany at the end of the nineteenth century and was introduced into American geography by Carl Sauer with the publication of his "Morphology of Landscape" in 1925.[5] Sauer was attempting, as Marvin Mikesell notes in the introductory selection, to provide a positive alternative to the then predominant philosophy of environmental determinism, and he found his inspiration in the *Landschaft* studies of German geographers. The determinists viewed environment as the active agency in man-environment interactions, relegating man to the position of a powerless, if adaptable, organism caught in the grip of powerful natural forces. Most determinists were well trained in the study of natural process and were capable of measuring even minute variations in the environment with competence. With the notable exception of Ellen Churchill Semple,[6] however, their grasp of cultural process was vague and instinctive. Thus, numerous studies of incredible naïveté were produced which explained such diverse cultural characteristics as the dourness of Scots, the Chinese world view, and the westward expansion of American settlement in terms of climate and landforms.

Landscape studies departed from this Darwinian view by stressing the role of man in reshaping the physical environment, in transforming physical landscapes into cultural landscapes. The job of the geographer was to bear witness to the creation and evolution of these cultural landscapes, to analyze the imprint of man on the surface of the earth. For Sauer, the cultural landscape was a region with a distinctive association of physical and cultural forms generated by the interplay of man and nature which, once identified, could be classified both spatially and genetically. In his classic study of the Santa Clara Valley in northern California, Jan Broek attempted to apply Sauer's methodology intensively to a small area.[7] Though the study failed to define a natural (as opposed to cultural) landscape, a pattern of careful reporting of observed facts on the distribution of people, dwellings, settlement, plant cover, and climate was set which marks the writings of geographers of the "Berkeley school" today.

The Visible Landscape

The cultural landscape, pursued through accurate, systematic description, stressed those visible, concrete elements associated with human occupation and utilization of the land. The emphasis was on facts more than theory, content more than context, and form more than process. Eventually, Sauer's rigorous definition of landscape as a region with distinctive forms was abandoned, and landscape took on the meaning of the "appearance of an area rather than the area itself."[8] Following this tradition, historical-

4. Max Sorre, "The Role of Historical Explanation in Human Geography," in Philip L. Wagner and Marvin W. Mikesell, eds., *Readings in Cultural Geography*, Chicago: University of Chicago Press, 1961, pp. 44-47.
5. Carl O. Sauer, "The Morphology of Landscape," *University of California Publications in Geography*, Vol. 2 (1925), pp. 19-54.
6. See, for example, her *Influences of Geographic Environment*, New York: Henry Holt, 1911.

7. Jan O. M. Broek, *The Santa Clara Valley, California: A Study in Landscape Change*, Utrecht: Oosthoek, 1932.
8. Methodological discussions of the landscape concept include Hans Bobek and Josef Schmithüsen, "Die Landschaft im logischen System der Geographie," *Erdkunde*, Vol. 3 (1949), pp. 112-20; J. B. Jackson, "The Meanings of Land-

cultural geographers of the Berkeley school[9] collected data on house types, barns, fences, place names, and other cultural forms, on irrigation systems, and patterns of plant and animal domestication and distribution. In the Middle West, geographers tended to study contemporary land-use patterns rather than culture history, and numerous articles on field patterns, farming systems, and settlement types were produced.[10] In each case, the collection of concrete facts through direct field observation was important, the ability to "observe," a curiosity about one's surroundings, and a talent for synthesizing information in map form were considered to be critical faculties.

The best works of these students of landscape are very good indeed. They are marked by historical perspective and an understanding of cultural and natural process that escape most well-intentioned students today. In these, the detailed collection of landscape facts is linked to broader themes in human history: the role of fire as a human tool of landscape change; the increasing power of man as an ecological dominant;[11] the influence of plant and animal domestication on the content of the cultural landscape and the quality of human life;[12] the diffusion of men and technology in culture change;[13] and always the search for origins, of agriculture and animal domestication, of terracing,[14] of settlement patterns,[15] and of individual forms in the landscape such as house types.[16]

But as Mikesell notes, the landscape approach to geography also had several major weaknesses.[17] First, Broek's Santa Clara Valley study demonstrated that all landscapes are, in practice, cultural landscapes because they have been impacted in differing degrees by human processes. Thus analyzing transitions from natural to cultural landscapes is virtually impossible. Second, classification of landscapes either genetically or descriptively has never been successfully accomplished, largely because of the enormous number of variables involved. Third,

scape," *Kulturgeografi*, No. 88 (1964), pp. 47-51; Josef Schmithüsen, "Was ist eine Landschaft?," *Erdkundliches Wissen*, Vol. 9 (1964), pp. 1-24.

9. For a critical view of the Berkeley school, see H. C. Brookfield, "Questions on the Human Frontiers of Geography," *Economic Geography*, Vol. 40 (1964), pp. 283-303.

10. A recent review of land-use studies can be found in J. W. Birch, "Rural Land Use: A Central Theme in Geography," pp. 13-28, in Dudley Stamp, ed., *Land Use and Resources: Studies in Applied Geography*, London: Institute of British Geographers, Special Publication, No. 1, 1968.

11. The most complete collection of articles on this theme is William L. Thomas, Jr., ed., *Man's Role in Changing the Face of the Earth*, Chicago: University of Chicago Press, 1956.

12. Carl O. Sauer, *Agricultural Origins and Disperals*, New York: American Geographical Society, 1956; David R. Harris, "New Light on Plant Domestication and the Origins of Agriculture: A Review," *Geographical Review*, Vol. 57 (1967), pp. 90-107; Erich Isaac, "On the Domestication of Cattle," *Science*, Vol. 137 (1962), pp. 195-204.

13. For example, Douglas Fraser, "Theoretical Issues in the Transpacific Diffusion Controversy," *Social Research*, Vol. 32 (1965), pp. 452-77.

14. J. E. Spencer and G. A. Hale, "The Origin, Nature and Distribution of Terracing," *Pacific Viewpoint*, Vol. 2 (1961), pp. 1-40.

15. Dan Stanislawski, "The Origin and Spread of the Grid-Pattern Town," *Geographical Review*, Vol. 36 (1946), pp. 105-20; Edward T. Price, "The Central Courthouse Square in the American County Seat," *Geographical Review*, Vol. 58 (1968), pp. 29-60.

16. Fred Kniffen, "Folk Housing: Key to Diffusion," *Annals, Association of American Geographers*, Vol. 55 (1965), pp. 549-77; Fred Kniffen and Henry Glassie, "Building in Wood in the Eastern United States," *Geographical Review*, Vol. 56 (1966), pp. 40-66; Wilbur Zelinsky, "Classical Town Names in the United States: The Historical Geography of an American Idea," *Geographical Review*, Vol. 57 (1967), pp. 463-95.

17. See also Paul Ward English, "Landscape, Ecosystem and Environmental Perception," *Journal of Geography*, Vol. 67 (1968), pp. 198-205.

intense preoccupation with the visible material landscape, with form rather than process, led to an unfortunate neglect of the less obvious, invisible forces which in some cases form cornerstones in the explanation of spatial patterns of human behavior. Thus in several studies of the geography of religion, the physical characteristics and distribution of religious buildings are described with only minor attention devoted to their social, political, and spiritual functions in society. Finally, though the best landscape studies are framed within a broader intellectual context, too many of them substitute diligence for intelligence, thereby contributing to what Mikesell calls the "episodic" quality of landscape research and, consequently, the minor contribution of landscape studies to theory-building in cultural geography.

Despite these shortcomings, landscape still remains a central concept of geography both in the profession and the popular mind. The selection by Carl Sauer demonstrates this. It links specific fact to general thesis, ranges effortlessly through time, views man and land as one interacting system, and demonstrates a remarkable sensitivity to and understanding of human communities, their way of life, and their cultural landscapes.

In "Homestead and Community on the Middle Border,"[18] written on the occasion of the centennial anniversary of the Homestead Act of 1862, Sauer describes the origins and evolution of rural farm life and landscape in the Middle West from its peopling in the nineteenth century to its decline in the twentieth. The first wave of settlement came primarily from Appalachia—Anglo-Saxon hunters and livestock raisers, who brought the log cabin, the long

18. An abbreviated version of this often overlooked article appeared in *Landscape*, Vol. 12 (1962), pp. 3-7.

rifle, and the American frontier to the plains. In the 1830's, German and Scandinavian farmers from the North migrated onto the plains, introducing plow agriculture, frame houses, and the work ethic to the region. Landscape and people are clearly focused in a single image: the simple houses with their neat fields and self-sufficient families, the town with its church and later its university, the mixture of ethnic and religious communities in the broader matrix of dispersed settlement on the township grid. But World War I intruded on this simple, austere, coherent way of life, attracting young men to the cities and bringing industrialization to the farm. Sauer laments the passing of this landscape and people; it was the life to which he was born and raised.

H. C. Darby approaches "The Changing English Landscape" from a different perspective than Sauer as he documents the impact of long-term social, economic, and political forces on the appearance and content of the English countryside. The Anglo-Saxon invasions mark, for Darby, the beginning of four major processes that played a significant role in creating the humanized landscape of modern England. These are the clearing of woodlands, the draining of marshes, reclamation of the heathlands, and changes in the extent and nature of agriculture. Economic forces and political motivations change from one period to the next, but the pace and pattern of landscape change persist. Woodlands cleared for arable land in early times, for example, are cleared in subsequent periods for lumber, charcoal, industry, and shipping. Marshes are drained first by windmill and later by pump; heathlands are reclaimed with the invention of crop rotations; agricultural land is enclosed by hedgerows and converted to pasture; landscape parks are designed; and finally the "dreary new industrial landscapes" of the Midlands and the North emerge, almost dividing England into "two countries." Darby's focus is on the visible landscape, on concrete elements of countryside, and on those forces which have altered the appearance of England.

The Aesthetic Landscape

For a number of geographers, the cultural landscape represents more than simply the visible, physical remains of human activity on the land; it provides insight into human value systems, defines complex relationships between environmental attitudes and environmental behavior, and documents the preferences of a people with respect to their surroundings. In this view, the aesthetic landscape is a symbolic creation, designed with care, whose form reflects a set of human attitudes. Those imprints which man has left on nature, therefore, reveal the thinking of a people about the world around them.

Several different approaches have been used to define the aesthetic and symbolic qualities of landscape.[19] Some writers have analyzed the changing attitudes of man to specific landscape elements such as mountains[20] or natural processes such as the hydrologic cycle.[21] Others have attempted to compare and contrast the world views held by different cultural groups, or alternatively to define landscape preference as revealed in art and literature.[22] For others, the aesthetic landscape is one element of the intellectual heritage of a people, reflecting changing views of man's relationship to nature and to God.[23] For all, however, the landscape is a document to be read as an intellectual, moral, and aesthetic statement of man as a human and a humane being.

In the selection from A. David Hill's *The Changing Landscape of a Mexican Municipio*, the tendency to view landscape in terms of aesthetic and symbolic meaning rather than content and form is demonstrated in the conceptions of physical environment held by the two cultural groups of the region, the Indians and the *ladinos*. These conceptions influence the perception and utilization of resources in Las Rosas. The Indians possess a greater intimacy with the flora, fauna, and surrounding countryside than do their modern counterparts; perhaps more important, Indians and *ladinos* bring a different set of values and beliefs to the landscape. The landscape possesses supernatural significance for the Indian, and tampering with it is viewed as unwise. Cultivation of corn in the *milpas* is the preferred way of life, being not only a means of subsistence but embodying participation in the religious and moral life of the community as

19. The best general statements of approaches to the aesthetic landscape are Paul Shepard, *Man in the Landscape: A Historic View of the Esthetics of Nature*, New York: A. Knopf, 1967, and Yi-Fu Tuan, "Attitudes Toward Environment: Themes and Approaches," pp. 4-17, in David Lowenthal, ed., *Environmental Perception and Behavior*, Chicago: University of Chicago, Department of Geography, Research Paper No. 109, 1967.
20. Marjorie Hope Nicolson, *Mountain Gloom and Mountain Glory: The Development of the Aesthetics of the Infinite*, Ithaca: Cornell University Press, 1959.
21. Yi-Fu Tuan, *The Hydrological Cycle and the Wisdom of God: A Theme in Geoteleology*, Toronto: University of Toronto, Department of Geography, Research Publication No. 1, 1968.
22. H. C. Darby, "The Problem of Geographical Description," *Transactions, Institute of British Geographer*, No. 30 (1962), pp. 1-14; Gerhard Hard, "Arkadien in Deutschland: Bemerkungen zu einem landschaftlichen Reiz," *Erde*, Vol. 96 (1965) pp. 21-41.
23. Clarence Glacken's remarkable book, *Traces on the Rhodian Shore*, Berkeley and Los Angeles: University of California Press, 1967, is the most complete and penetrating study of its kind.

well. By contrast, the *ladino* views the landscape and its resources as elements to be manipulated in the quest for wealth, power, and prestige. The artificial landscape created by these two resident cultures, then, differs not only in content and form, but in meaning as well. For Hill, the landscape exposes cultural values and beliefs as well as the footprints of man.

In the selection by Philip Wagner, this theme is pursued more fully. Landscape is considered not only as a passive embodiment of values and beliefs but as an active "medium of communication," a source of stimuli that influence human behavior in context. Through repeated interactions with local environments, men learn and judge, and ultimately each society defines those environments or environmental characteristics "conducive to the good life." The landscape becomes a subtle map and pattern of human behavior values, symbols, and behavior, whose complexity reveals the volume and variety of internal and external communications which contribute to its expressive value. The study of landscape then involves identification of the modes through which it communicates behavior clues, sets guidelines for observed behavior, and defines the daily ecology of human life.

For Yi-Fu Tuan, the cultural landscape provides the evidential base needed to examine the discrepancies between stated ideal and reality to determine how environmental attitudes relate to environmental behavior. Comparing Chinese and European attitudes toward nature, Tuan notes that Christianity, one of the most anthropocentric of world religions, replaced earlier beliefs in the holiness of landscapes and natural settings with a fundamentally new way of evaluating the environment, the environment as the servant of man. In the Christian world, however, man's power to transform nature remained

"an article of faith rather than fact" until population growth, administrative centralization, and the new technology of the scientific revolution emerged. In the Chinese world view as embodied in folklore and in the tenets of Taoism and Buddhism a more quiescent and adaptive approach to nature is proposed in which man is viewed as a component of nature, and harmony between man and environment is a desirable goal. The practice of geomancy, the art of siting structures so that they fit into the landscape rather than dominate it, is one example of this attitude translated into action. Despite these markedly different world views, Tuan notes that the landscapes of both Mediterranean Europe and China have been vastly transformed by man. The biotic mantle has been disturbed, forests destroyed; large-scale engineering projects have reshaped topography; erosion and clogged streams are common to both regions. Tuan gently explores this paradox, concluding that civilization, whether Chinese or European, is the exercise of human power over nature, but civilization in turn creates an aesthetic appreciation of nature expressed in world view. The evidence to support this thesis is found in the cultural landscape.

In "English Landscape Tastes," David Lowenthal and Hugh Prince treat the cultural landscape as a living expression of the values and tastes of a people. The landscape embodies a set of human preferences given form by those selected components of the countryside which the English have chosen to preserve and reproduce. In striking contrast with Darby's treatment of the same subject, Lowenthal and Prince are concerned with the symbolic significance of the English landscape, with the human attitudes and attributes it reflects, rather than with the underlying economic and political forces which contributed to its morphology. Using literature, painting, public hearings, and newspapers as source materials, a number of landscape preferences are identified: the English love of the bucolic and their view of England as a nation of the country not the city; their preference for picturesque, irregular, and complex scenes composed with care, depicting nature not as it is but as it might have been; their appreciation of deciduous trees as opposed to conifers, of order and neatness in scenery, of the use of façades to create an atmosphere of respectability and propriety. Landscape associations are used to document national attitudes—a rejection of the present, a fondness for the past; a preference for appearance at the expense of efficiency. For Lowenthal and Prince and, if they are correct, for the English as well, the landscape is "history made visible." It endows the present with "substance and durability."

In sum, the cultural landscape has been a focus of geographical concern for a substantial period of time. Despite the vast number of variables involved and certain methodological problems, this concept has retained an astonishing vitality in the profession over the years. This is perhaps less due to the intrinsic merits of landscape study than to the series of fine minds that have used it as a matrix for expressing their views on the nature of man and his world. In a sense its weaknesses are also its strengths. The concreteness of the visible landscape lends an idiosyncratic, static quality to many studies of the cultural landscape, yet as Houston has noted, it is the very concreteness of the landscape that enables observers to preserve the essential character and validity of the subject.[24] The emphasis on detailed field observation often emerges as pure description, yet in some cases it has contributed new evidence on major questions in culture history. In the end, however, it has been the flexibility of landscape scholars using the landscape concept that marks this body of literature, and judging by the recent attention being given to aesthetic landscapes, this will be the case for some time to come.

24. J. M. Houston, *The Western Mediterranean World: An Introduction to Its Regional Landscapes,* London: Longmans, Green, 1964, pp. 1-7, 706-8. Under Houston's editorship, a new set of volumes called "The World's Landscapes Series" is being published in this country by Aldine Publishing Company.

ᴕᴕᴕᴕᴕᴕᴕᴕᴕᴕᴕᴕᴕᴕᴕᴕᴕᴕᴕᴕᴕᴕᴕᴕᴕᴕᴕ

LANDSCAPE

Marvin W. Mikesell

In any discussion of the development of geography as a modern academic discipline, attention must be directed to the important concept of "landscape," for the identification, description, and interpretation of landscapes has long been a major geographic enterprise. Indeed, during the 1920s and 1930s several attempts were made to construct methodologies that made landscape study the essential, if not exclusive, task of

From the *International Encyclopedia of the Social Sciences* edited by David L. Sills, Vol. 8, pp. 575-80. Copyright © 1968 by Crowell Collier and Macmillan, Inc. Reprinted by permission.

geography.[1] While geographers are no longer preoccupied with landscape to this extent, there remains substantial agreement that landscape study is one of the important themes of geographic research, most notably in the subfield of cultural geography.[2] If a count were taken of technical terms used most frequently in geographic publications, the number of references to landscape would probably be exceeded only by those to area and region. Moreover, the same generalization can be made for the corresponding term in other languages, for example, *Landschaft* (German), *landskap* (Swedish), *landschap* (Dutch), *paysage* (French), *paesaggio* (Italian), and *paisaje* (Spanish).

Historical Development

The etymology of the common use of landscape is reasonably clear. In its Old English form (*landscipe*), the term was used in the Middle Ages to refer to a district owned by a particular lord or inhabited by a particular group of people. The modern forms of the word (landskip, landscape) date from the late sixteenth or early seventeenth century, when the influence of Dutch *landschap* painters encouraged a revival and redefinition of landscape to refer to representations of scenery, especially rural scenery, and then to scenery in general or a particular scene.[3]

The popular conception of landscape was well expressed by Philip Gilbert Hamerton, who wrote several books on landscape painting and landscape appreciation in the latter half of the nineteenth century. In a book entitled *Landscape* (1885), he wrote that the word could be used "in two senses— a general and a particular. In the general sense, the word 'landscape' without the article means the visible world, all that can be seen on the surface of the earth by a man who is himself upon the surface; and in the special sense, 'a landscape' means a piece of the earth's surface that can be seen at once; and it is always understood that this piece will have a certain artistic unity."[4]

This dual definition is reiterated in *Webster's New International Dictionary of the English Language*, where landscape is described as "a portion of land or territory which the eye can comprehend in a single view, including all the objects so seen, especially in its pictorial aspect." Moreover, both Hamerton and *Webster's* give the term a subjective connotation, for the reference is to area or scenery as viewed by a particular human observer. The dual popular meaning of landscape and its subjective overtones caused persistent difficulty when geographers spoke of the "objective reality" of landscape and tried to employ the term as a scientific concept.

The Influence of Sauer

The conception of geography as the scientific study of landscape is developed most completely in the American geographic literature in Carl Sauer's "The Morphology of Landscape,"[5] where the *Landschaft* stud-

1. Siegfried Passarge. *Vergleichende Landschaftskunde.* Berlin: Reimer, 1921-1930, 5 Vols.; Carl O. Sauer, "The Morphology of Landscape," *University of California Publications in Geography*, Vol. 2 (1925), pp. 19-54; Patrick W. Bryan. *Man's Adaptation of Nature: Studies of the Cultural Landscape.* London: University of London Press, 1933; Robert E. Dickinson, "Landscape and Society," *Scottish Geographical Magazine*, Vol. 55 (1939), pp. 1-15.
2. Philip L. Wagner and Marvin W. Mikesell, editors. *Readings in Cultural Geography*. Chicago: University of Chicago Press, 1962.
3. Preston E. James, "The Terminology of Regional Description," *Annals, Association of*

American Geographers, Vol. 24 (1934), pp. 78-86; J. B. Jackson, "The Meanings of Landscape," *Kulturgeografi,* Vol. 88 (1964), pp. 47-51.
4. Philip Hamerton. *Landscape.* Boston: Roberts, [1885] 1890, p. 10.
5. Carl O. Sauer, *op. cit.,* 1925.

ies of German geographers are reviewed and endorsed as an alternative to the philosophy then current in American geography. During the first quarter of the twentieth century American geographers moved away from their initial interest in physiography, and many redefined their concern as an attempt to trace causal relationships between elements of the natural environment and the activities or creations of man. To Sauer this development represented a denial of the proper task of the discipline, which was to establish a system embracing the "phenomenology of landscape." He argued that geography could not claim an independent status if it were preoccupied with a particular causal relationship and failed to claim a body of phenomena or "naively given section of reality" as its own. Just as the facts of history are time facts and their association gives rise to the concept of period, so the facts of geography could be regarded as place facts and their association could be expressed by the concept of landscape. According to this view, a landscape, defined as "an area made up of a distinct association of forms, both physical and cultural," has objective identity based on recognizable constitution, limits, and generic relation to other landscapes. Departing from the popular conception of the term, Sauer held that a landscape should not be regarded as an actual scene viewed by a particular observer but rather as a generalization derived from the observation of many individual scenes. Beginning with infinite diversity, the geographer should select salient and related features in order to establish the character of a landscape and place it in a system. Personal judgment in the selection of landscape content could be minimized by agreement on a logical, predetermined mode of inquiry. In other words, the underlying assumption of Sauer's argument was that the features thus studied would be characteristic and could be grouped into a pattern and that the landscape defined eventually by this inductive procedure could be described as belonging to a specific group in a general series. In addition, Sauer, following Krebs,[6] felt that landscapes should be studied genetically, that the structural units of a landscape should be placed in a developmental sequence, with the condition of the area prior to the introduction of man's activities as the datum line. The essential task of landscape study was thus to trace the development of a "natural landscape" into a "cultural landscape."

Sauer's statement had considerable influence in the development of American geographic thought, not only because it offered an alternative to "environmentalism" but also because he transmitted the ideas of several European geographers who were more advanced methodologically than their American counterparts at that time. However, the redefinition of geography as the study of landscape morphology proved to have serious practical and methodological difficulties, and Sauer repudiated many features of this initial programmatic statement in later publications.[7] Perhaps the most serious weakness of his argument of 1925 was the assumption that geographers should begin their inquiry by reconstructing the prehuman or natural condition of an area. In a world nearly devoid of undisturbed natural landscapes (Urlandschaften), the difficulties entailed in such a task are forbidding, and geographers concerned primarily with the present visible landscape were understandably reluctant to begin their studies in antiquity. Moreover, the genetic—

6. Norbert Krebs, "Natur- und Kulturlandschaft," *Zeitschrift der Gesellschaft für Erdkunde zu Berlin* [1923], pp. 81-94.
7. John Leighly, editor. *Land and Life: A Selection from the Writings of Carl Ortwin Sauer.* Berkeley and Los Angeles: University of California Press, 1963.

morphological method proved uncongenial to economic geographers whose studies tended to develop along generic and functional lines. Even in Broek's study of the Santa Clara Valley,[8] which is probably the most complete substantive application of Sauer's methodology, the datum line is not a reconstructed natural landscape but rather the "primitive" condition of the area when the first Europeans arrived. Similarly, studies of landscape development in Europe usually start not at the time of initial human occupation but rather at the period immediately preceding the great phase of forest clearing, draining of marshes, and reclamation of heathlands.[9] As geographers accumulated a comprehensive record of the effects of human activity on vegetation, soil, and surface features, they became increasingly wary of the concept of natural landscape.[10] The distinction most generally accepted today is between a "wild" or "primitive" landscape, in which features of the natural environment are altered but not eradicated or completely controlled, and "cultivated" or "artificial" landscapes.[11]

Geography as Landscape Science

The methodological objections raised against the definition of geography as landscape science centered on two issues, the vagueness of the term and certain philosophical difficulties.[12] Landscape had been employed by geographers to refer to the impression conveyed by an area, to the objects producing that impression, and to the area itself. In other words, the dual meaning of "scenery" and "area" was carried over from the popular use of the term "landscape." In German usage, *Landschaft* refers most commonly to a territorial unit and can usually be regarded as a synonym for "district," "area," or "region."[13] The ambiguity of *Landschaft* is enhanced by the fact that *Land* cannot be defined as the coincident areal expression of *Landschaft*, as in the case of the French terms *pays* and *paysage*, because a *Landschaft* is usually regarded as being smaller than a *Land*, as, for example, in the *Landschaften* of Rhineland or Siegerland. The German geographic literature also abounds in such expressions as *Kleinlandschaften* (small districts or tracts), *Grosslandschaften* (large areas or regions), *Landschaftsgruppe*

8. Jan O. M. Broek. *The Santa Clara Valley, California: A Study in Landscape Changes.* Utrecht: Oosthoek, 1932.
9. H. C. Darby, "The Changing English Landscape," *Geographical Journal*, Vol. 117 (1951), pp. 377-394.
10. William L. Thomas, editor. *Man's Role in Changing the Face of the Earth.* Chicago: University of Chicago Press, 1956.
11. Homer Aschmann, "The Evolution of a Wild Landscape and Its Persistence in Southern California," *Annals, Association of American Geographers* (Supplement), Vol. 49 (1959), pp. 34-46; H. R. Raup, "Transformation of Southern California to a Cultivated Land," *Annals, Association of American Geographers* (Supplement), Vol. 49

(1959), pp. 58-78; Howard J. Nelson, "The Spread of an Artificial Landscape over Southern California," *Annals, Association of American Geographers* (Supplement), Vol. 49 (1959), pp. 80-99.
12. Jan O. M. Broek, "The Concept of Landscape in Human Geography," *Comptes rendus, XVth International Geographical Congress, Amsterdam, 1938*, Vol. 2 (1938), pp. 103-109; Richard Hartshorne, "The Nature of Geography: A Critical Survey of Current Thought in the Light of the Past," *Annals, Association of American Geographers*, Vol. 29 (1939), pp. 173-658.
13. Kurt Bürger, "Der Landschaftsbegriff: Ein Beitrag zur geographischen Erdraumauffassung," *Dresdener geographische Studien*, Vol. 7 (1935), pp. 1-131; Hermann Lautensach, "Über die Erfassung und Abgrenzung von Landschaftsräumen," *Comptes rendus, XVth International Geographical Congress, Amsterdam, 1938*, Vol. 2 (1938), pp. 12-26; Josef Schmithüsen, "Was ist eine Landschaft?," *Erdkundliches Wissen*, Vol. 9 (1964), pp. 1-24; Otto Wernli, "Die neuere Entwicklung des Landschaftsbegriffes," *Geographica helvetica*, Vol. 13 (1958), pp. 1-59.

(groups of functionally related or morphologically similar areas or regions), *Landschaftsgürtel* (extensive belts or zones), and in such specific terms as *Stadtlandschaften* (urbanized areas), *Agrarlandschaften* (rural areas), and *historische Landschaften* (areas in which functional or morphologic unity is enhanced by the long continuation of an integrative force). Each of these terms refers to a general class of *Landschaften*. However, in the case of such expressions as *Alpenlandschaft* reference is made not only to the general characteristics of mountainous areas but also to the European Alps as a specific delimited area. Moreover, *Landschaftskunde* may refer to the study of particular *Landschaften* or to the regional differentiation of the entire globe. It is not surprising, therefore, that a substantial part of the methodological literature of German geographers deals with the problem of defining *Landschaft* and *Landschaften*,[14] and that the attempts to translate these terms compounded the inherent ambiguity of "landscape."

Current Usage

In addition to the semantic problem, many geographers felt that it could not be maintained that the study and interpretation of landscape is the exclusive preserve of the geographer or that landscape, however defined, contains all that is geographical. By the 1940s, the notion that landscape study should be regarded as the essential task of geography was generally discarded in favor of the view that landscape features consti-

tute merely one of several documents and points of reference in geographic research.

Features studied. The landscape features studied most often by geographers are those that have to do with the occupation and utilization of land.[15] Such features include the form and arrangement of settlement (houses and other buildings); field patterns, roads, paths, and other communication lines; crops and the "wild" or "tame" vegetation associated with settlements; irrigation works; and surface modifications—in short, the patterns and imprints of culture. Tangible, visible objects thus constitute the essential raw material of landscape study. However, the perspective of the geographer is not that of an individual observer located at a particular point on the ground. The geographer's work entails map interpretation as well as direct observation, and he makes no distinction between foreground and background.[16] The landscape of the geographer is thus very different from that of the painter, poet, or novelist. By means of survey, sampling, or detailed inventory, he achieves the comprehensive but synthetic perspective of a helicopter pilot or balloonist armed with maps, photographs, and a pair of binoculars. Indeed, it has been suggested that the geographic definition of landscape might be framed with reference to air photographs, both vertical and oblique, in which case the corresponding German term would not be *Landschaft* but rather *Landschaftsbild*.[17]

14. Siegfried Passarge, *op. cit.*, 1921-1930; Leo H. Waibel, "Was verstehen wir unter Landschaftskunde?," *Geographischer Anzeiger*, Vol. 34 (1933), pp. 197-207; Kurt Bürger, *op. cit.*, 1935; Hermann Lautensach, *op. cit.*, 1938; Hans Bobek and J. Schmithüsen, "Die Landschaft im logischen System der Geographie," *Erdkunde*, Vol. 3 (1949), pp. 112-120; J. Schmithüsen, *op. cit.*, 1964.

15. Carl O. Sauer, *op. cit.*, 1925; Patrick W. Bryan, *op. cit.*, 1933; Maximilien Sorre. *L'Homme sur la terre*, Paris: Hachette, 1961; James M. Houston. *The Western Mediterranean World: An Introduction to Its Regional Landscapes.* London: Longmans, Green and Co., 1964.
16. Camille Vallaux. *Les Sciences géographiques.* Paris: Alcan (new edition), 1929.
17. Richard Hartshorne. *Perspective on the Nature of Geography.* Chicago: Rand-McNally, AAG Monograph Series No. 1, 1959, p. 23.

However, landscape studies inevitably include consideration of cultural expressions that are invisible. If the rationale is to discover landscape features coincident with a culture area, then one may begin by delimiting the area according to linguistic or other nonmaterial phenomena. Moreover, without recourse to historical study there is no way to distinguish between what is ancient or recent, native or foreign. Culture history, accordingly, must enter strongly into any explanatory study of landscape.[18] Again, a landscape may be regarded not as an end in itself but merely as empirical data that can be employed to document culture change.[19] Most geographers who employ landscape data or seek to explain entire landscapes have ceased to be preoccupied (if indeed they ever were) with what is visible or invisible, material or non-material, for "there can be no finite limit placed upon the variety of data with which the regional cultural geographer must deal in his effort to depict the operation of man in his chosen landscape."[20]

A good indication of the scope of recent research is provided by a symposium dealing with the development of the agrarian landscape in northwestern Europe.[21] The subjects covered in this collection include (1) the prehistoric landscape and its connection with later development of settlement and field patterns, (2) medieval regulations of settlement and field patterns, (3) the influence of agrarian revolutions (e.g., the enclosure movement) on the landscape, and (4) recent changes in the agrarian landscape of industrialized and commercialized countries.

The virtues of an uninhibited approach to landscape study are perhaps most effectively illustrated by one early and three recent attempts to determine the effect of landscape tastes on landscape evolution.[22] In greater or lesser degree, landscapes always embody irrational creation. Accordingly, the origin, persistence, or disappearance of the concrete features of a landscape may be explained most adequately not by their form or function but by the idealized images and visual prejudices of human groups or of individuals.

Other Uses of the Concept

Finally, it must be noted that landscape is an important concept in several fields apart from geography. The origin of landscape as a painter's term has already been mentioned.[23] The reconstruction and interpretation of ancient landscapes is one of the essential tasks of archeology.[24] Novelists, poets, and travel writers employ landscape description either as an end in itself or as a

18. Philip L. Wagner and Marvin W. Mikesell, editors, *op. cit.*, 1962, pp. 1-24; Carl O. Sauer, *op. cit.*, 1963.
19. A. David Hill. *The Changing Landscape of a Mexican Municipio: Villa Las Rosas, Chiapas.* Chicago: University of Chicago, Department of Geography, Research Paper No. 91, 1964.
20. Joseph E. Spencer. *Asia, East by South: A Cultural Geography.* New York: John Wiley, 1954.
21. Staffan Helmfrid, editor. "Morphogenesis of the Agrarian Cultural Landscape (Papers of the Vadstena Symposium at the XIXth International Geographical Congress, (1960)," *Geografiska Annaler,* Vol. 43 (1961).

22. Robert Gradmann, "Das harmonische Landschaftsbild," *Zeitschrift der Gesellschaft für Erdkunde zu Berlin* [1924], pp. 129-147; David Lowenthal and Hugh C. Prince, "The English Landscape," *Geographical Review,* Vol. 54 (1964), pp. 309-346, "English Landscape Tastes," *Geographical Review,* Vol. 55 (1965), pp. 186-222; Gerhard Hard, "Arkadien in Deutschland: Bemerkungen zu einem landschaftlichen Reiz," *Erde,* Vol. 96 (1965), pp. 21-41.
23. Kenneth M. Clark. *Landscape into Art.* London: John Murray, 1949.
24. John Bradford. *Ancient Landscapes.* London: Bell, 1957.

way to establish a mood or set a scene.[25] In addition, a large critical literature on local and regional landscapes has been produced by architects, city planners, and others concerned with problems of landscape design.[26]

25. Benjamin F. Bart. *Flaubert's Landscape Descriptions.* Ann Arbor: University of Michigan Press, 1957; Lawrence Durrell, "Landscape with Literary Figures," *New York Times Book Review*, June 12, 1960.
26. Brenda Colvin. *Land and Landscape.* London: John Murray, 1948; Ian Nairn. *The American*

These several conceptions have been presented since 1952 in the magazine *Landscape*, published by J. B. Jackson of Santa Fe, New Mexico. Indeed, the diverse contributions to this magazine—from architects, ecologists, geographers, planners, and observers from many other backgrounds—provide an effective illustration of the continued value of landscape as an integrating concept in social science.

Landscape: A Critical View. New York: Random House, 1965.

‡‡‡‡‡‡‡‡‡‡‡‡‡‡‡‡‡‡‡‡‡‡‡‡‡‡‡‡‡‡‡

HOMESTEAD AND COMMUNITY ON THE MIDDLE BORDER

Carl O. Sauer

A public anniversary in the present American mood is likely to consider the date as a determinate point between the past and the future. The past thus is of interest chiefly because it shows what change has taken place and what its direction has been. The present is the base from which we project the future. Perhaps more than any other people, or at any other time, we are committed to living in a mundane future, confident we shall control it by anticipation, that is, by planning the march of the material progress desired.

The immediate instrument of change is provided by the spiraling advance of technics that appear to put limitless material possibilities in our hands, and it is of these that we think primarily. What we have gained, at least for the present, is the ability to produce many more goods of more kinds for

more people. We not only think to hold the horn of plenty but we believe we can and should pass it on to the rest of the world. Capacity to produce and capacity to consume form a reciprocating system that we desire to expand without end. Growth in material wants and in the ability to satisfy them and so to stimulate new wants is what we are agreed is progress. We measure progress by such things as gross national product, income per capita, standard of living (a term we have introduced to the world; perhaps it is the most widely known of all American phrases), level of employment, new construction, and other quantitative indices of an expanding economy. The system, insofar as we have seen it work, depends on continued acceleration and perhaps on being kept jogged by the stimuli of debt and taxes as well as of consumption and obsolescence. The American image is becoming that of the compulsive spender of neo-Keynesian doctrine. Thorstein Veblen formed his thesis of conspicuous waste too soon by a generation.

Output grows with input and so on, requiring more and more engagement of expert technicians. The objective of growth necessitates making and carrying out more and more decisions about public policy, which becomes an increasingly limited and coveted prerogative. For the individual and the community the choice as to how one would live becomes more restricted in the interest of the will and authority of what is proposed as the commonweal. Reducing the risks of livelihood we also diminish the diversity of purposes and ends of individual living, once richly present in rural America.

On this occasion we call to remembrance an event of a hundred years ago when American life differed greatly from the present in mode, mood, and meaning. We may take a look back over a formative span of our history which lasted for several generations, a long time as our history goes. In its first part we were a rural nation, the first major shift to city living coming as the result of the Civil War and its industrial mobilization. Thereafter, population flowed more and more from country to city but the ways and values of rural living continued for two more generations to have much the accustomed meaning and content. We are here in fact taking part in an Old Settlers Reunion, as descendants of those who left their previous places and conditions of life to take part in making a new West, the Promised Land which a chosen people came to possess. There was an Old Testament sense of fulfillment in the western migration which should not be forgotten.

The Homestead National Monument, situated where wooded valley met upland prairie, is a model geographic expression of the manner in which the West was settled. This first homestead as taken under the act lies well out into the farther and later part of the Midwest. Its specific location records still the original pioneer requirement of a living site with wood and water, requisites that the building of railroads soon made unnecessary. When this tract was taken up, only three young and raw towns were in the Territory of Nebraska, all of them on the Missouri River. Through them emigrant trails led to Oregon and California, bearing westward over prairie and wooded stream, in a land still ranged over by Indian, buffalo, antelope, and deer. In very short order the wild land was brought into cultivation and fully settled. By mid-century, the westward course of homesteading had begun to cross the Missouri line at the west, to be halted later by dryness farther on. In simple outline, I should like to direct attention to the peopling of that part of the interior we know as the Corn Belt. The Wheat Belt is another, though derivative, story. What sort of rural living was established on the Middle Border; what were its attainments and satisfactions, its lacks and failures?

The date of the Homestead Act marks conveniently for our recall a moment of significance in the mainstream of American history, the great westward movement of families seeking land to cultivate and own. This movement began from states of the eastern seaboard, swelled to surges across the wide basin of the Mississippi-Missouri and ebbed away in the High Plains. To the south and north there were other westward movements sufficiently different in kind and route as to be left out of present consideration. The Middle Border, as it has been named appropriately, was the wide, advancing wave of settlement that spread over the plains south of the Great Lakes and north of the Ohio River, making use of both waterways as approaches. Its advances made

Cleveland, Toledo, and Chicago northern gateways. At the south it gave rise to border cities on rivers, such as Cincinnati on the Ohio, St. Louis at the crossing of the Mississippi, and Kansas City on the great bend of the Missouri. The Mississippi was crossed in force in the 1830's, the Missouri River into Kansas in the border troubles prior to the Civil War. Although it did not begin as such this became the peopling of the prairies, the founding and forming of the actual Midwest.

The Homestead Act came pretty late in the settlement of the interior. Land had been given free of cost to many, as outlined in earlier chapters. It had been sold at nominal prices and on easy terms by public land offices and by canal and railroad companies. The squatter who settled without title was generously protected by preemption rights and practices that grew stronger. Many millions of acres had been deeded as homesteads before the act and many more continued to be acquired by other means afterwards. Land was long available in great abundance. The price in money of the wild land was the least cost of making it into a farm. Public land offices were set up to get land into private hands quickly, simply, and cheaply. Under the Graduation Act lands were reduced in price according to the length of time they had been on the market, the last cut being to twelve and one-half cents an acre. Canal and railroad lands were priced to sell. The railroads were well aware that revenue from farm traffic would be their largest return. The land seeker was induced to buy railroad land because he knew that he was given facility of transportation. The theme that land was a commodity for speculation is certainly true, yet it may be overstressed and oversimplified. The settler knew that the price of the farm was mainly in the work of all the family, in making out or doing without, in minimizing wants and spending. Largely our farms could not be reproduced from wild land at present prices, wages, and standards.

Advantage of location was of first importance in selecting the home site. The original entry of a tract was because of its immediate suitability as a homestead rather than because it would continue to be most desirable; locational advantages change as might productive capacity. Settlers were in process of regrouping themselves in neighborhoods of their liking. The drawbacks of one place having been experienced, a better location might be sought farther on. Property passed from one hand to another at a price reflecting, perhaps, the improvements made more than rise in land value. The term land speculation is not fully adequate or appropriate. The relinquisher was paid for the worth he had put in, the purchaser received a partially improved farm. The early succession of owners largely was a passing from weaker to stronger hands financially. The border was pretty fluid in its first years. Those who moved on are forgotten, or appear only as names of patentees and first conveyors of title. Those who remained and took root became the Old Settlers. There were various kinds and conditions of people who moved into or across the Middle Border, the restless and the sedentary, the overflow from older settlements farther east and the immigrants from Europe for whom this was a first opportunity to live on land of their own.

The famous frontier thesis of Professor Turner was adapted from a theory of social evolution that was popular late in the nineteenth century. According to it, mankind everywhere has gone through the same series of stages of progress from simpler to more advanced skills and societies. The succession is held to be the same, the rate to differ with the environment. It was an attractive, simple theory of history, not borne out by the facts anywhere. Turner picked up the general idea and thought to reproduce the whole supposed history of human experience in the short span of the American frontier. Thus he saw our frontier as a "field for comparative study of social development," beginning (1) with Indian and white hunter, followed by (2) the "disintegration of savagery by the entrance of the trader, the pathfinder of civilization," then by (3) the pastoral stage (4) the raising of unrotated crops of corn and wheat in sparsely settled farming communities (5) intensive agriculture, and finally (6) the industrial society. He saw each stage present "in the march toward the West, impelled by an irresistible attraction. Each passed in successive waves across the continent." This plot of a westward-moving pageant in six scenes was good drama but was not our history.

As corollary to this theory of cultural succession he proposed one of cultural regression, namely that whoever entered a new scene or stage reverted from his former ways to accept those of the "stage" he was joining. Thus, the wilderness "takes him from the railroad car and puts him in the birch canoe and arrays him in the hunting shirt and moccasin. It puts him in the log cabin of the Cherokee and Iroquois and runs an Indian palisade around him . . . he shouts the war cry and takes the scalp." A half truth. Every migrant group loses some of the elements of its previous culture in fitting itself into a new environment, whether wilderness or city. It may also introduce some traits of its own. The spell of a uniformly determinate course of social evolution as cast by the anthropologist Lewis Morgan and the sociologist Herbert Spencer took hold of Turner, who passed it on to his pupils.

The first three stages or waves of Turner did not exist in the Middle Border. The next two were not stages but the entry of differing cultures.

The American settler acquired learning that was important for his survival and well-being from the Indian, mainly as to agricultural ways. The settler was still a European in culture who had the good sense to make use of what was serviceable to him in the knowledge of the Indians of the eastern woodlands. This learning began at Jamestown and Plymouth and was pretty well completed before the Appalachians were crossed. It contributed Indian corn, along with beans and squash, as the basis of frontier sustenance. The seed corn the settler took west with him was dent corn from Indians of the Middle Seaboard and flint corn from those of the Northeast. Mainly he appears to have grown yellow dent, presumably acquired from Indians in Pennsylvania. A preferred parent in breeding our races of hybrid corn has been the Lancaster Surecropper, an old kind from eastern Pennsylvania. The Indian corn, beans, and squash of the East were well suited to western climate and soils until settlement got well beyond the Missouri River. The settler took over Indian ways of woodland clearing and planting. He prepared corn for his staple food in Indian ways, from succotash and hominy to corn cakes. He had learned back east to make maple syrup and sugar after the Indian fashion and continued thus to supply himself as far west as sugar maples grew. He brought with him the Indian art of dressing buckskins and making apparel. These were new learnings. Professor Turner possibly was right in attributing the stockade to Indian example but if so it too was learned from Indians of the Atlantic states. The Indians, of course, did not have log cabins.

Little seems to have passed from the Indians of the interior to the settlers. The Indian culture west of the Appalachians was still significantly based on cultivation, more largely so than is thought popularly to have been the case. Whether the western Indians contributed any strains of cultivated plants had little attention until we get much farther west, to the Mandans of the Upper Missouri and the Pueblo tribes of the Southwest. The Pawnee were a numerous village-dwelling people living toward the western margin of the humid country. One might expect that some strains of plants they cultivated passed on to the white settlers. Did their earth lodges suggest the dugout house of the pioneer, a curious and unusual form of dwelling? The Caddoan tribes to which the Pawnee and Wichita Indians belonged were anciently established farmers as well as hunters living between the prairies and high plains (witness the Coronado expedition) and might have had something to add to the trans-Missouri frontier.

The American entry into the Mississippi Valley encountered the Indian tribes in an advanced condition of disturbance, dislodgement, and dissolution. In most of our early accounts they are described in terms of disdain, deprecation, and disgust, without awareness that what was being witnessed was the breakdown of a native society. The Delawares, Wyandots, and Shawnees had been driven far from their homes. The Spanish government in Upper Louisiana invited them to a haven west of the Mississippi. Briefly they built and occupied farming villages there, but the Louisiana Purchase soon dislodged them again to drift west beyond the borders of Missouri. The Illini tribes were broken early, beginning with Iroquois raids that stemmed from French and English rivalries. American penetration about the Great Lakes pushed Pottawatomis, Kickapoos, Sacs, and Foxes to pressing upon tribes that lived beyond the Mississippi. The old resident tribes did not like the new ones, the whites liked neither. The Missourians in particular, carrying on the Indian hating of the Kentuckians and Tennesseans would

have none of them. The remnants of a score of tribes were piled west beyond the Missouri line, some from as far east as Pennsylvania and New York. In the territories that were to become Kansas and Nebraska they were given reservations between the native Osages, Kansas, and Pawnees until most of them in a last remove were taken into the Indian Territory. (The original Kansas City, Kansas, was named Wyandot and began as a village of those Indians.)

Dispossessed of title to home, deprived of their economy, and losing hope that there might be another start, many were reduced to beggary or lived as pariahs about the white settlements. Their debauch was completed by alcohol, a thing wholly foreign to their ways, which became for them a last escape. Objects of despair to each other, and of contempt and annoyance to the whites, the time was missed when the two races might have learned from each other and lived together.

The French settlements, nearly all in river villages, were the meager reality of a vast colonial design of a New France that was planned to reach from the St. Lawrence to the Gulf of Mexico. The French habitants contributed little to the ways of the Middle Border. Some of their villages remained as enclaves in the American land. They were indifferent farmers. Despite the rich alluvial lands by the side of which they lived, they were often short of food. Some were fur traders in season, ranging far up the rivers, and instructing a few Americans in the fur trade, but this had precious little to do with the settlement of the interior. Some showed Americans, such as Moses Austin, a very primitive way to mine and smelt lead. The Americans got the word "prairie" from them to replace the name "barrens," which had been given to grassy uplands in Kentucky and was still used in Missouri around the time of the Louisiana Purchase. The French were easygoing, amiable people who did a little of various things and some of these well but they were not the pathfinders of a French, much less an American, civilization, nor did they think of themselves as such. The romantic attribution to the trader of being the pathfinder has its proper place in the western mountains and beaver streams, not in the interior prairies and woodlands.

Most of the earlier American pioneers of the Mississippi Valley came by a southerly approach. They were known as Virginians and Carolinians, later as Kentuckians and Tennesseans, and in final attenuation as Missourians. They came on foot and horseback across the Cumberlands and Alleghanies, usually to settle for a while in Kentucky or Tennessee and thence to move on by land or river and cross the Ohio and Mississippi rivers. The relocations of the Lincoln and Boone families are familiar examples. Turner's stages are not properly descriptive of the order or manner of their coming. By his scheme they would need to be distributed through his four first stages, least apparent in the second. Actually, they do not sort out as such separate waves.

The border had an element that came in for unfavorable comment in almost every early account, of persons who had taken to the backwoods because they did not fit into an ordered society, because of their indolence, perhaps for some misdemeanor or crime. They were the shiftless and the reckless, sometimes called drifters in the language of the West, the flotsam carried on the advancing wave of settlement, but not the first, nor a distinct wave. Violence was not marked in the history of this border except for Kansas where ruffians enjoyed a license through the approaching civil conflict. Some such "out" groups became lodged permanently in the poor corners of the Midwest. But largely they drifted on into the farther Southwest and Far West. Some got stranded on the overflow lands of the Missouri and Mississippi, others in the "hollers" of the hill lands adjacent. They were early in the history of settlement and chose to live segregated from the rest, usually marrying among their own kind. Of all settlers these were the most fully self-sufficient. A patch of cleared ground was in the woman's care; a litter of hogs ranged free. The men fished and hunted and loafed and kept hound dogs. In the steamboat days money could be had by cutting and loading firewood. When the railroads came there were ties to be hacked. They would work to sell something when they wanted money, employment they avoided. They were indifferent to increasing their income or to owning property. Some were defectors from civilization; I knew two of the most famous names of Virginia among them. They were considered to be predominantly a farther fringe of the Southern poor whites, usually bearing English surnames, in part a residue from the least fit part of those shipped to the Colonies. I do not think that Turner's view of cultural regression on the frontier applies; the frontier gave room for antisocial elements as well as for the builders of society.

The main contingent of pioneer settlers were a different breed. Theodore Roosevelt hailed them as Scotch-Irish, Mencken stressed their Celtic tone and temperament, Ellen Semple saw them as Anglo-Saxons of the Appalachians. Whatever their origins, and they were multiple, those were the backwoodsmen who brought and developed the American frontier way of life. They were woodland farmers, hunters, and raisers of livestock in combination, and very skilled in the use of axe and rifle. Trees were raw material for their log cabins and worm fences, and also an encumbrance of the ground, to be deadened, burned, or felled.

The planting ground was enclosed by a rail fence, the livestock ranged free in wood or prairie. When the New Englander Albert Richardson reported life in eastern Kansas in the time of border troubles *(Beyond the Mississippi)* he said he could tell the home of a settler from Missouri by three things: The (log) house had the chimney built on the outside and at the end of the house; the house was located by a spring which served for keeping food in place of a cellar, and one was given buttermilk to drink. He might have added that there would be corn whiskey on hand and that if the family was really Southern the corn bread would be white.

This colonization was early and massive, beginning by 1800 and having the new West almost to itself until into the 1830's. At the time of the Louisiana Purchase American settlers already held Spanish titles to a million acres in Missouri alone, mainly along the Mississippi and lower Missouri rivers. They moved up the northern tributaries of the Ohio River as far as these were wooded; they filled the river valleys of Illinois and those of eastern Iowa and even penetrated north somewhat into Wisconsin and Minnesota. Their homes and fields were confined to wooded valleys, their stock pastured on the upland prairies. Nebraska alone of the mid-continent remained almost wholly beyond the limits of their settlement.

Viewed ecologically, their occupation of the land was pretty indifferent to permanence. Trees were gotten rid of by any means, the grasslands were overgrazed, game was hunted out. They were farmers after the Indian fashion of woods deadening, clearing, and planting, and made little and late use of plow or wagon. The impression is that they gave more heed to animal husbandry than to the care of their fields or to the improvement of crops. Central and northwest Missouri for example, the best flowering of this "Southern" frontier, developed the Missouri mule early in the Sante Fe trade, and later bred saddle, as well as trotting, horses, and beef cattle. I do not know that it contributed anything to crop improvement, unless it was in bluegrass pastures.

There was self-sufficiency of food to this frontier but also there was a well-marked commercial side. It had things to sell or exchange for merchandise, above all tobacco, not a little corn whiskey, hogs on the hoof, in some cases hemp or cotton, all items that could be put on boat or horseback or driven to more or less distant markets. The settlers brought with them knowledge as to how tobacco should be grown, harvested, cured, and packed for shipment.

Corn and tobacco were the two crops planted in the new clearings in the woods, and they continued to be grown on the same land so long as its fertility lasted. Several acres of tobacco gave the needed purchasing power to the small farmer. Tobacco growing also attracted slave-owning planters north across the Ohio and especially west across the Mississippi, beginning with the Spanish government that freely granted land and sanction of slavery. From the beginning, the backwoods farmer, the hunter of the long rifle, and the slave-holding planter mingled in this stream of American Colonists; they might indeed be the same individuals. When the corn and tobacco fields began to fail under the clean cultivation these crops required, more virgin woodland was at hand or farther on. The effects of soil exposure to slope-wash by continued planting of corn and tobacco in early days may still be seen from the Muskingum Valley across Missouri to the Kansas border in surfaces of light color and tight texture that reveal the loss of the original top soil (A horizon).

This migration of the early nineteenth century came without benefit of constructed facilities of transportation, of public or private capital, or of most of the products of the newly begun machine age, except for the river steamboat. The people came in bands of kindred and friendship to settle in contiguity that was less than close clustering and more than wide dispersal. Their locations bore the name of a "settlement" quite properly, identified perhaps by the name of the leader, or of the stream along which their homesteads were strung. Thus, the group Daniel Boone led to Missouri was known both as the Boone Settlement and as the Femme Osage Settlement, the French name of the principal creek. The colony of families the senior Bollinger led from North Carolina across the Mississippi to Missouri was known by his name and as the Whitewater Settlement. Largely such transplanted communities were of kith and kin that maintained close connections even though each household lived on its own homestead. The lonely family cabin, removed far from and isolated from its neighbors is mostly a myth, even as to Daniel Boone himself. Sociability, not aloofness, was the quality of life sought. Much of the work was done by mutual aid; leisure time was time for meeting, a word of special meaning in the vernacular of the frontier. Such were the people and the life that Mark Twain knew so well and portrayed with affection. They enjoyed discourse in all forms and on all occasions, respected those who excelled in it, and produced an able lot of politicians, lawyers, ministers of the gospel, and schoolteachers.

The great northern immigration began in the 1830's and depended from the beginning on improved transportation, the Erie Canal, steamships on the Great Lakes, stout and capacious wagons. It continued to demand internal improvements (the term of the time for public aid to communication), first canals and soon railroads, only rarely, constructed and surfaced roads. Wagon transport, however, was important and a wagon-making industry sprang up in the hardwoods south of the Great Lakes. It may be recalled that the automobile industry later took form in the same centers and by using the same skills and organization of distribution. Canals, most significantly the Illinois and Michigan Canal completed in 1848, linked the Great Lakes to rivers of the Mississippi system for shipping farm products to the East. Railroads were first projected as feeder lines to navigable waters. The first important construction, that of the Illinois Central, was chartered in 1850 to build a railroad from Cairo, at the junction of the Ohio and Mississippi rivers, to La Salle, on the Illinois and Michigan Canal and on the Illinois River. It was given a grant by Congress of two million acres of land. Its principal early support was by the sale of lands, in tracts from forty acres up, its continued success depended on the produce of the farms and the goods needed to be shipped in. The pattern was adopted and given an East-West orientation by other rail lines that quickly spread their ribbons of steel westward, often in advance of the farm homesteads.

This last great movement of land settlement was out onto the prairies and it differed largely in manner of life and kind of people from the settlement of the woodlands. It depended on industry and capital for the provision of transportation. It was based from the start on plow farming, cast-iron or steel plows to cut and turn the sod: plows that needed stout draft animals, either oxen or heavy horses. By 1850, agricultural machinery had been developed for cultivating corn and harvesting small grains and was responsible for the gradual replacement of oxen by horses as motive power.

The prairie homestead differed from that of the woodlands in the first instance by depending on plow, draft animals, and wagon. It, too, grew corn as the most important crop. In part the corn was used for work stock but largely it was converted into meat and lard by new, large breeds of swine developed in the West. Stock was penned and fed. Fences were needed, not to fence stock out of the fields but to confine it. The livestock was provided with feed and housing. The farm was subdivided into fields, alternately planted to corn, wheat, oats, clover, and grass, arranged in a rotation that grew the feed for the work animals and for the stock to be marketed. A barn was necessary for storage and stables. This mixed economy, its cash income from animals and wheat, spread the work time through the seasons, and maintained the fertility of the land. It was a self-sustaining ecologic system capable of continuing and improving indefinitely and it was established by the process of prairie settlement. There was no stage of extractive or exhaustive cultivation.

By the time of the Civil War—in a span of twenty years or so—the prairie country east of the Mississippi, the eastern half of Iowa, and north Missouri were well settled. Some counties had reached their highest population by then. My native Missouri county had twice its current population in 1860. More people were needed to improve the land and to build the houses and barns than it took to keep the farms going. Some of the surplus sought new lands farther west, much of it went into building the cities. These people who settled the prairies were farmers, born and reared, out of the Northeast or from overseas, first and in largest number Germans and thereafter Scandinavians. They knew how to plow and work the soil to keep it in good tilth, how to care for livestock, how to arrange and fill their working time. They needed money for their houses and barns, which were not of logs but frame structures with board siding. The lumber was mainly white pine shipped in from the Great Lakes, long the main inbound freight source.

These settlers needed money, as well as their own labor, to dig wells and drain fields. The price of the land again was the lesser part of the cost of acquiring a farm. The hard pull was to get enough capital to improve and equip the homestead and this was done by hard labor and iron thrift. This is a sufficient explanation of the work ethic and thrift habits of the Midwest, often stressed in disparagement of its farm life. In order to have and hold the good land it was necessary to keep to a discipline of work and to defer the satisfactions of ease and comforts. The price seemed reasonable to the first generation who had wrested a living from scant acres in New England or to those who had come from Europe where land of one's own was out of reach.

Dispersed living, the isolated family home, became most characteristic of the "Northern" folk on the frontier. In Europe, nearly everyone had lived in a village or town; in this country, the rural village disappeared or never existed. Our farmers lived in the "country" and went to "town" on business or pleasure. The word "village," like "brook" was one that poets might use; it was strange to our western language. The nature of frontier life has often been ascribed to the ways of the Scotch-Irish who have been credited with or held responsible for almost anything that took form or place there. Thus, the dispersed farmsteads have been credited to the fact that some lived on small tracts in Scotland, as so-called cotters. Over here, they were conspicuous in the forward fringe of settlement but it cannot be said that it was the Scotch-Irish who broke the conventionally ordered pattern of rural living in villages. The nucleated New England town early acquired outlying farm homes in number. The Pennsylvania German settlements early included farm as well as village habitation. Land was available to the individual over here in tracts of a size beyond any holdings he might ever have had overseas. The village pattern was retained almost only where religious bonds or social planning prescribed living in close congregation.

Normally, the land holding was the place where the family lived and this identification became recognized in the establishment of title. The act of living on the occupied land was part of the process of gaining possession. As time went on, prior occupation and improvement of a tract gave more and more weight to preemption rights; living on the land protected against eviction and gave a first right to purchase or contract for warranty of ownership. The Homestead Act was a late extension of the much earlier codes of preemption by which possession by residence on the land and improvement could be used to secure full and unrestricted title.

The General Land Survey established the rectangular pattern of land description and subdivision for the public domain. Rural land holdings took the form of a square or sums of squares, in fractions or multiples of the mile-square section of land. The quarter section gradually came into greatest favor as the desired size of a farm and became the standard unit for the family farm in the Homestead Act. Thus, four families per square mile, a score or so of persons, were thought to give a desirable density of rural population. The reservation of one school section out of the thirty-six in a township, for the support of primary public schools, provided an incentive for the only kind of public building contemplated in the disposal of public lands. Four homes to the square mile and about four schools to the six-mile-square townships gave the simple general pattern for the rural geography of the Midwest. The pattern was most faithfully put into effect on the smooth upland prairies. Here the roads followed section lines and therefore ran either north-south or east-west and the farmsteads were strung at nearly equal intervals upon one or the other strand of the grid. It is curious that this monotony was so generally accepted, even a clustering of homes at the four corners where the sections met (and giving the same density) being exceptional.

Little attention has been given to the site where the house was placed, or to the assemblage of the structures that belonged to the farm. The choice of location was greatly important, as in exposure to wind and sun, for example. We may take a largely forgotten instance, malaria. Presumably, malaria came with the French, carried up the Mississippi from the south. The French were subject to chills and fever but kept on living in the river bottoms. The Americans also suffered thus, but soon began to select their living sites accordingly. The general idea was that the sickness came from the miasmas forming from stagnant water, the answer was to build the house on a ridge where the wind would sweep the miasmatic air away. The river bottoms long had a bad reputation. The Illinois Valley was malarial through most of its length, the early settlement of Bureau at the southward bend of the upper river for instance having been relocated for that reason. It would be of interest to determine the distribution of malaria at various times, the flare-ups and gradual recession, and the effects on living sites.

The logistics of home location is an attractive and hardly investigated field of study, as is indeed the whole question of the rural landscape and its changes. The location of house and farm buildings involved conservation of energy in the work on the farm, cultural preferences of different colonizing groups, micro-climatic adjustments, and esthetic satisfactions. The relation of water, drainage, and sanitation was unrecognized, the toll paid in typhoid and "summer complaint."

Building was starkly utilitarian and unadorned. Neither the log cabin of the woodlands, nor the box-shaped frame house of the prairies, nor yet the sod house of the Transmissouri country (made possible by the sod-cutting plow) was more than compact and economical shelter, varying but little in each form. Ready-cut houses of standard simple patterns were already offered by railroads to buyers of their land, an early form of tract housing. Quality of house and quality of land seem to be in no relation. The embellishment of the home and the planting of the yard were left mostly to the second generation, for country town as well as farm. The history of the dissemination of ornamental trees and shrubs might be revealing, perhaps to be documented through the nurseries that sprung up from Ohio to Nebraska (mainly post Civil War?).

The economy from its beginnings was based on marketing products, but it also maintained a high measure of self-sufficiency. Smokehouse, cellar, and pantry stored the food that was produced and processed on the farm. The farm acquired its own potato patch, orchard, berry and vegetable gardens, diversified as to kind from early to late maturity, for different flavors and uses, selected for qualities other than shipping or precocious bearing. The farm orchards now are largely gone and the gardens are going. Many varieties of fruits that were familiar and appreciated have been lost. A family orchard was stocked with diverse sorts of apple trees for early and midsummer applesauce, for making apple butter and cider in the fall, for laying down in cool bins in the cellar to be used, one kind after another, until the russets closed out the season late in winter. The agricultural bulletins and yearbooks of the past century invited attention to new kinds of fruits and vegetables that might be added to the home orchard and garden, with diversification, not

standardization in view. Exhibits in the county and state fairs similarly stressed excellence in the variety of things grown, as well as giving a prize for the fattest hog and the largest pumpkin.

The Mason jar became a major facility by which fruit and vegetables were "put up" for home use in time of abundance against winter or a possible season of failure in a later year. The well-found home kept itself insured against want of food at all times by producing its own and storing a lot of it. The family, of ample size and age gradation, was able to provide most of the skills and services for self-sufficiency by maintaining diversified production and well-knit social organization. This competence and unity was maintained long after the necessity had disappeared. As time is measured in American history the life of this society, and its vitality, was extraordinary.

Looking back from the ease of present days these elder days may seem to have been a time of lonely and hard isolation. It was only toward the end of the period that the telephone and rural mail delivery were added. The prairie lacked wet-weather roads. In the hill sections, ridge roads might be passable at most times, on the plains, winter was likely to be the season of easiest travel, spring, that of immobilization by mud. The country doctor was expected to, and did rise above any emergency of weather. Life was so arranged that one did not need to go into town at any particular time. When the weather was bad the activities of the family took place indoors or about the farmyard. In our restrospect of the family farm as it was, we may incline to overstress its isolation. The American farmstead did not have the sociality of the rural villages of Europe or of Latin America, but the entire family had duties to learn and perform and times of rest and diversion. It depended on a work morale and competence in which all participated and in which its members found satisfaction. Perhaps it suffered fewer social tensions and disruptions than any other part of our society.

Though living dispersed, the farm families were part of a larger community which might be a contiguous neighborhood or one of wider association. The community, in some cases, got started on the Boone pattern of a settlement of kith and kin. A sense of belonging together was present to begin with or it soon developed. The start may have been as a closed community; it was likely to continue in gradual admission of others by some manner of acceptance. Consanguinity, common customs, faith, or speech were such bonds that formed and maintained viable communities through good times and bad. The Mennonite colonies are outstanding examples. The absence of such qualities of cooption is shown in the Cherokee strip, opened as a random aggregation of strangers.

The bond of common customs and language showed up strongly in the German settlements made between 1830 and the Civil War, and in the Scandinavian settlements of somewhat later origin. Both were attracted to districts where some of their people had chanced to locate and tended to increase about such nuclei. This clustering, a partial segregation, gave protection from cultural alienation and loss and afforded time to adjust and contribute to the common ways of life. Although the Germans were sharply divided as to confession, they were drawn into areas where German speech was used, however strong the difference in creed or dialect. Most of their settlement took place before 1870 and included people not only from the states that were to join the German empire, but from Switzerland, Austria, and later from Russia.

The country church played a leading part in social communication, differing again according to the particular confession. Catholic and Lutheran communicants perhaps had more of their social life determined by their church than did the others. Their priests and pastors were most likely to remain in one community and to exercise and merit influence on it. Parochial schools extended the social connections. Church festivals were numerous and attractive. Sunday observance was less austere. The Methodist church on the other hand shifted its ministers, usually every two years. In a half century of service my grandfather was moved through a score of charges in five states. The high periods of the Methodist year were the winter revival meetings and the camp meetings in summer after the corn was laid by. For some, these were religious experiences, for others, especially for the young people, they were sociable times, particularly the camp meeting, held in an attractive, wooded campground where one lived in cabins or tents on an extended picnic. Almost everyone belonged to some church and in them found a wide range of social contacts and satisfaction.

The churches also pioneered higher education, founding colleges and academies across the Middle West from Ohio into Kansas before the Civil War and before the Morrill Act fathered the tax-supported colleges. These church-supported small colleges, about fifty of which still exist, first afforded education in the liberal arts to the youth of the prairie states and they did so by co-education. Their students were drawn by their church affiliations, not only from nearby but from distant places. In these colleges, humane learning was cultivated and disseminated. Their campuses today are the Midwest's most gracious early monuments of the civilization aspired to by its pioneers.

Country and town were interdependent, of the same way of life, and mostly of the same people. By a tradition that may go back to the town markets of Europe, Saturday was the weekday for coming to town to transact business (note the pioneer implications in the term "to trade") and to visit. The town provided the services, goods, and entertainment which the farm family required. In time, it also became home for the retired farmer. Farmstead and its particular town were linked in community by factors beyond the one of economy of distance. When the railroads were building across the prairie, they laid out what seemed a most rational spacing of town sites for shipping and trading centers. Some grew, some withered away, and some never got started. Quantitative measurement of radius of trade never has been enough. The choice of direction and destination in going to town had other reasons than economy of energy expended. One liked it better in one town than in another, a matter of social values and affinities which are ponderable but not measurable.[1]

The era of the Middle Border ended with World War I. Hamlin Garland introduced the name in 1917 in his *Son of the Middle Border,* a retrospect he made in middle age. Willa Cather, growing up on the westernmost fringe of Nebraska, drew its life in quiet appreciation in her two books written before the war. Then she saw her world swept away. Some of us have lived in its Indian summer, and almost no one was aware how soon and suddenly it was to end.[2] A quarter section was still a good size for a family farm and the farm was still engaged in provisioning itself as well as in shipping grain and livestock. It was still growing a good crop of lusty offspring. The place of the family in the community was not significantly determined by its income, nor had we heard of standard of living.

The outbreak of the war in 1914 brought rapidly rising demand and prices for supplies to the Allies and to American industry. Our intervention in 1917 urged the farmer to still more production: "Food will win the War" —in the war that was to end all wars. He made more money than ever before, he had less help, he was encouraged to buy more equipment and more land. The end of the war saw a strongly industrialized country that continued to draw labor from the rural sections. Improved roads, cars, tractors, and trucks made the horse unnecessary and thereby the old crop rotation broke down. Farming became less a way of life and more a highly competitive business for which the agricultural colleges trained specialists, engineers, chemists, economists, to aid fewer and fewer farmers to produce more market goods, to widen their incomes against the rising cost of labor, taxes, and capital needs. This became known as "freeing people from the land," so that now we have about a tenth of our population living on farms (among the lowest ratios in the world) and these are not reproducing themselves.

The Middle Border now belongs to a lost past, a past in which different ways and ends of life went on side by side. We have

---

1. Lewis Atherton, *Mainstreet of the Middle Border* (1960) has a large documentation and itemization of life in the country towns. His composite picture is later and less attractive than are my own recollections. He stated that he was not relying on his own memories or family tradition. I, however, have done so, not knowing a nearer approach to objectivity than by putting such recall to reflective scrutiny. This is not sociologic method but do systems of analysis bring enough understanding of what we are, or of what we were? A literary genre in disparagement of rural life and country town originated towards the end of the period with its ugly geography of Winesburg, Spoon River, Zenith, and Main Street.

2. I made field studies in northern Illinois and in Missouri from 1910 to 1914, when rural life was much more like that of Civil War time than of the present.

since defined the common welfare in terms of a society organized for directed material progress. For the present at least, we control the means to produce goods at will. We have not learned how to find equivalent satisfactions in jobs well done by simple means, and by the independent judgment that gave competence and dignity to rural work. The family farm prepared youth well for life—there or elsewhere. It enriched the quality of American life and it will be missed.

★★★★★★★★★★★★★★★★★★★★★★★★★★★★★

THE CHANGING ENGLISH LANDSCAPE

H. C. Darby

It was William Cowper the poet who once wrote that "God made the country and man made the town," a sentence that reads strangely to anyone who thinks about the English landscape. It is true that there is much about the English scene that is non-human; Lord Avebury began his delightful book on "The scenery of England" (1902) by saying that "the scenery of any country so greatly depends on the structure and arrangement of the rocks of which it is composed, that it cannot be described without some reference to geological causes." It is to the geologist, and not least to the geomorphologist, that we look for an explanation of the foundations of our landscape, for the English scene as we view it today represents a collection of legacies from the past, and many of these legacies are from geological time. But not all; some are more recent in origin, and it is of them that I wish to speak. It was Vidal de la Blache who said that "geography is the science of places," but he meant places as modified by man and not as they were on the first morning of creation. Art as well as Nature has gone into the making of our "sweet especial English scene."

But at this point a question naturally arises. Where shall we begin in our search for the origins of this humanized landscape? The answer to this is fairly clear; the coming of the Anglo-Saxons opened a new chapter in the history of the settlement and land-use of Britain, and the Anglo-Saxons were followed in the north and east by the Scandinavians. Both groups of invaders, with a fine eye for country, covered Roman Britain with their new villages and, in so doing, sketched the pattern of our English human geography. The Anglo-Saxons did not come into an empty land, and many contributions from pre-Saxon days have entered into the making of England. But even so, as far as there ever is a new beginning in history the coming of the Anglo-Saxons was such a beginning. Since then an immense and unceasing struggle has resulted in the clearing of the woodlands, the draining of the marshes and the reclamation of the heathlands. Not only have the limits of agriculture been extended, but its character has been changed and its field systems altered. And, even as the cultivated land was being extended, it was also being encroached upon by the rising tide of industrial development. The black satanic land-

From *The Geographical Journal,* Vol. 117 (1951), pp. 377-98. Reprinted by permission.

scapes of the Midlands and the North are in their way as awe-inspiring as any in the realm of Nature. Finally, we must not forget that while much of the landscape—rural as well as urban—has grown from man's necessities, some of it is the result of a sense of pleasure. The landscape garden is a peculiarly English manifestation.

Clearing the Wood

Perhaps the most important factor in the evolution of our countryside has been the clearing of the wood which once clothed the greater part of it. In spite of the activity of successive prehistoric peoples, and in spite of the mark left by four centuries of Roman civilization, it is certain that when the Romans left Britain in A.D. 410 it was still very largely a wooded country. The distribution of wood marked on the Ordnance Survey Map of Roman Britain, and repeated on that of Britain in the Dark Ages, has been

Dense Woodland
Open Woodland

Figure 1. The woodlands of England and Wales from the Ordnance Survey map of Roman Britain.

criticized in detail but at any rate it does serve to indicate the order of magnitude involved when we speak of the woodland of Roman Britain.

The early Anglo-Saxon records are filled with the struggles of the Anglo-Saxon states and with the Anglo-Danish conflict. But behind the clash of warfare, clearing went steadily on. Many of the quiet villages of the English countryside were at one time pioneer settlements battling to reduce the wood and thicket around them. The lumberman with his axe and his pick became the ploughman with his oxen. New farms and hamlets sprang up until by the time of the Domesday Book most of the villages we see today had come into being. It is not surprising that the Anglo-Saxon described the ploughman as the "grey-haired enemy of the wood." The success of this expansion into wooded country is shown by many of the place-names of today. Names with such endings as -ley, -hurst and -holt show the existence either of wood or of clearings in woodland. Sometimes a placename tells its own story by embodying the memory of a personal name. Thus the village name of Knowsley in Lancashire is derived from a man named Cynewulf, while Chorley, found in Lancashire and elsewhere, was originally the clearing of the *ceorls* or peasants.

The relevance of place-names to a reconstruction of former woodland is well illustrated by the distribution of different types of names in Middlesex. Upon the light soils of the south of the county, names which do not indicate wood are common, *e.g.* those ending in -ing and -ton. The wood names, on the other hand, lie on the intractable London Clay in the north of the county; here was a great expanse of wood, and the names register a stage in the process of clearing it. Even in the twelfth century much of this area could still be described as "a great forest with wooded glades and lairs of wild beasts, deer both red and fallow, wild boars and bulls." How different is the scene today, but some memory of past conditions is preserved by the name Enfield Chase.

Some of the effects of the Anglo-Saxon and Scandinavian settlements were summed up in the Domesday Survey of 1086. Normally, the amount of wood was recorded in one of two ways. For some counties the measurements were in terms of acres or in terms of length and breadth. For other counties the wood was measured in terms of the swine it could feed, for swine formed an important element in the economy of the time and they fed upon acorns and beech mast. The sum total of the evidence leaves us in no doubt about the wooded nature of large tracts of England. Essex for example was still a very wooded county; it had many villages with wood for over 1000 swine, and some with sufficient even for 2000. When the Domesday evidence for all England has been assembled we shall be able to perceive a number of such heavily wooded tracts, separated by areas cleared since the fifth century.

The records of the Middle Ages and later times contain abundant evidence that the clearing begun so vigorously in Anglo-Saxon times was continued throughout the length and breadth of the land. The demands made upon the woodland were various. One important need was for ordinary domestic purposes and for the building of castles, churches and bridges. It was not a very spectacular destruction but, in total, the amount of wood consumed in this way must have been considerable. Another demand upon woodland was that of the expanding arable. Mr. H. S. Bennett has described the role of the clearing in the life of a medieval village: "For a family burdened with more children than their shares in the common fields would warrant, such assart land was a god-send. Here they could utilise their spare

labour, and produce something to help fill the many hungry mouths at home." [1] The medieval records of every county tell their own story of spreading cultivation but much of the work must have escaped mention in any document.

The clearing continued in post-medieval years. In the seventeenth century that famous agricultural writer, Walter Blith, mentioned woods that had become what he called "gallant cornfields," and the woods he had in mind were scattered through a variety of counties. It was the same in the eighteenth century. In Gloucestershire for example we are told that "in every year many acres of beechwood are destroyed, and given up to the plough." [2] In the nineteenth century the process continued; in about 1851 what remained of the Forest of Hainault was converted into arable land. A manufacturer of steam-ploughs entered into a contract to clear the land, and he did so in six weeks by attaching anchors to the roots of the old oaks and tearing them out. Epping Forest nearly disappeared in the same way.

A third cause of the disappearing woodland was the demand of industry. Lead, copper and tin mines all needed wood for pit-props and for charcoal; glass-making and many other industries involved what a seventeenth-century writer called a "continuale spoile of woods." But of all the industries that consumed wood the most devouring was the iron industry and we hear much of the cutting down of wood in the iron centres of the Forest of Dean and the Weald. The solution to the problem raised by the increasing scarcity of wood was to find a substitute. In 1709, after the experiments of the sixteenth century, Abraham Darby was smelting with coke at Coal-

1. H. S. Bennett, "Life on the English Manor," p. 51 (Cambridge, 1937).
2. T. Rudge, "General view of the agriculture of the county of Gloucester," p. 243 (London, 1813).

brookdale, and by the middle of the eighteenth century the use of coal had become common.

There was a fourth demand upon wood. The expansion of England's mercantile marine, and the development of the English navy from the Tudor age onwards, depended upon an adequate supply of oak for the hulls of ships. The Dutch wars of the seventeenth century, the maritime wars of the eighteenth and the Napoleonic Wars, were a heavy and continuous drain upon suitable English oak. Samuel Pepys, in the middle of the Dutch wars, could only say "God knows where the materials can be had." During the Napoleonic Wars, Lord Collingwood used to carry a pocketful of acorns to drop at intervals, but this was an indication of the urgency of the problem, not a solution. English timber never recovered from the strain of the wars with France. The problem remained acute until, in the American Civil War, the Battle of Hampton Roads on 9 March 1862 demonstrated the superiority of the iron-clad. Within a few months the whole problem of naval construction had to be revised. But although the timber problem soon became only a memory it had left a permanent mark on the English countryside.

Draining the Marsh

The marsh that confronted the Anglo-Saxon invaders disappeared far more slowly than the woodland. Many alluvial valleys were originally marshy, or at any rate subject to floods, and have been drained by the embankment and regulation of parts of their streams. The history of these small and local transformations has for the most part been lost, but they must be borne in mind when picturing the countryside of the fifth and sixth centuries. Along many streams the transformation is still far from complete.

An interesting phase in the story of the taming of many streams was the construc-

tion of artificial water meadows subject to controlled flooding. They are said to have been first made in England by that curious Elizabethan figure, Sir Horatio Pallavacini, who lived at Babraham to the south of Cambridge. The cult of the water meadow reached its height in the eighteenth century, and it was most important in the southern counties of Wiltshire, Hampshire, Gloucestershire and Dorset. With changing farming conditions the water meadow ceased to be a familiar feature of rural economy, though it has not altogether disappeared today.

When we speak of the marshes of England, we usually think not of these valley strips but of the great stretches that give a special character to some countrysides. The largest is the expanse of the Fenland itself, but there are other tracts of considerable size—the levels of Somerset, the warplands of the Isle of Axholme, Yorkshire and Nottinghamshire, the carrs of the Ancholme valley, the marshes of Holderness, and the mosslands of Lancashire; to these must be added the coastal marshes of the lower Thames and elsewhere. It would be impossible to describe all these changes; each story is an epic in itself.

Of these stretches of marsh, that of the great Fenland provided the most spectacular transformation. The southern peat area of the Fenland was drained in the seventeenth century. But technical difficulties of various kinds have since jeopardized this success more than once. Windmill pumps saved the situation in the eighteenth century, but by 1800 disaster was again abroad and the cultivated land was relapsing to "waste and water." The advent of the steam engine again brought relief, but the Fenland long remained a watery countryside. At the middle of the century the great copper butterfly was not yet extinct; nor the ague against which the fenmen indulged in brandy drinking and took opium pills. But the steam

engine was gaining ground; at the great Exhi-
bition of 1851 one of the sights which
"astonished the visitors" was Appold's
Centrifugal Pump, and it was with the aid of
one of these new pumps that the last remaining large stretch of water in the Fenland
was drained. Thus disappeared Whittlesea
Mere; "the wind, which, in the autumn of
1851 was curling the blue water of the lake,
in the autumn of 1853 was blowing in the
same place over fields of yellow corn."[3] Yet
in spite of the potency of Appold's pump
and its successors, the fen floods still affirm
their challenge, as we know only too well.

The draining that took place in Lancashire was very different in character. Here
was no large continuous stretch of marsh,
but scattered areas called "mosses" or
"mosslands"; something of their former
extent can be seen from the present-day
distribution of peat below 600 feet. These
scattered areas were drained in a piecemeal
fashion in the eighteenth and nineteenth
centuries and the progress of the work was
summed up with pride by W. J. Garnett in
1849. Even then Chat Moss, one of the
largest stretches, was still but incompletely
drained. As Garnett confessed, "there is still
much of the moss in its natural state; but it
is to be hoped that, lying as it does in the
heart of a populous district, and traversed by
a railway connecting together the two most
important towns of the kingdom, it will not
long continue so."[4] Today the traveller on
the Liverpool-Manchester line can see on
either hand a fertile, cultivated countryside.

In addition to the greater marshes of the
kingdom there were many lesser ones and
the story of one of them must stand for the
others. The 4000 acres of Ot Moor, to the

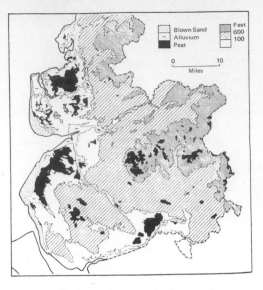

Figure 2. The Lancashire mosslands (peat below
600 feet).

north-east of the city of Oxford, were described once as a dreary and extensive waste,
"subject to perpetual inundations."[5] It
provided common pasture for the cattle and
geese of seven villages around and was an
unhealthy, ague-ridden spot, the haunt of
the wild duck and the heron. Proposals to
drain the area met with opposition from the
commoners who raised the cry "Ot Moor for
ever." At length, under an Act of 1815, it
was drained and enclosed, but not without
much rioting.

Reclaiming the Heath

Generally speaking, the reclamation of the
heathlands started later than the clearing of
the woodland and the draining of the
marshes. The dry light soils of many parts of
lowland England were inherently infertile,
and their development had to await the

3. W. Wells, "The Drainage of Whittlesea Mere," *J.
Roy. Agric. Soc.* 21 (1860) 141.
4. W. J. Garnett, "Farming of Lancashire," *J.
Roy. Agric. Soc.* 10 (1849).

5. John Dunkin, "Oxfordshire: The history and
antiquities of the Hundreds of Bullington and
Ploughley," vol. i, p. 119 (London, 1823).

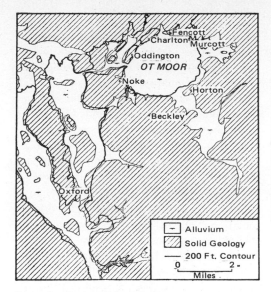

Figure 3. The location of Ot Moor.

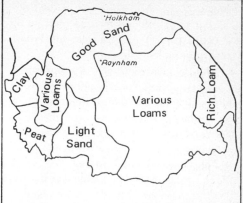

Figure 4. The soil of Norfolk (after Arthur Young, 1804).

coming of new crops and new methods of husbandry. The full value of sheep to arable farming could not be realized until the introduction of rotations involving such crops as turnips, clover and artificial grasses. When the sheep were folded on these crops it was said that "the foot of the sheep turned sand into gold." The new ideas advocated by the agricultural writers of the sixteenth and seventeenth centuries increased the technical mastery that made reclamation possible.

The reward was reaped in the eighteenth century, and on the light soils of western Norfolk there were remarkable changes. Here at the beginning of the century great expanses of warren met the eye, where "two rabbits struggled for every blade of grass." It was to Raynham that the second Viscount Townshend retired in 1730 from the disappointments and vexations of politics, and the rest of his life was given up to the development of his estate. In particular, he devoted himself to advocating the famous "Four Course System" in which wheat, turnips, barley and clover followed one

another in rotation. The success of his effort was spectacular, and within a few years the warrens around Raynham were converted into productive arable land.

Some twelve miles to the north lay the village of Holkham, the home of the Coke family, and here in the middle of the eighteenth century there was a similar transformation. Others also shared in the rewards to be gained from the "Norfolk Husbandry," and Arthur Young, writing in 1768, was loud in its praise:

All the country from Holkham to Houghton was a wild sheep-walk before the spirit of improvement seized the inhabitants; and this glorious spirit has wrought amazing effects; for instead of boundless wilds, and uncultivated wastes, inhabited by scarce anything but sheep; the country is all cut into inclosures, cultivated in a most husbandlike manner. [6]

To this north-western area of Norfolk, Arthur Young gave the name of "Good Sand"; good in contrast to the "light" or poor sandy country that adjoined it to the south. But there were limits even to the wonders of the Norfolk husbandry, and in the southern sandy country these limits were

6. A. Young, "A six weeks' tour through the southern counties," pp. 21-2 (London, 1768).

reached. This area, later known as the Breckland, remained for another 150 years, in the words of Arthur Young "a tract which deserves to be called a desert."

From the eighteenth century onwards there was a periodic outcry about the waste lands of Britain. The fate of these tracts varied; some were reclaimed after the manner of western Norfolk, some were afforested, others have remained in an open condition up to the present day.

One area that became arable was the Lincolnshire Wolds, a land of warren and gorse and rabbits. The greatest achievement in the life of Tennyson's *Northern Farmer* (which he remembered with pride upon his deathbed) had been the "stubbing of Thorganby waste," high up on the Wolds. In 1851 J. A. Clarke recapitulated the story of the reclamation: "The gorse has been grubbed, the rough sward burned, and all the warrens, with one or two exceptions, have been brought into good cultivation." [7] A similar transformation took place on the heaths of the oolitic limestone that stretches north and south of the city of Lincoln. The character of the Yorkshire Wolds was changed too, largely through the work of Sir Christopher Sykes. It would not be difficult to find many other tracts of arable land that owe their character to the hand of the eighteenth century improver.

To the more sterile heathlands afforestation gave a new value; the Breckland landscape has been completely altered since 1921 by the planting of conifers. The same is true of the Suffolk Sandlings, the Dorset heathlands, the Bagshot country and Cannock Chase. The contrast in the last area between the Greenwoods' map of 1828 and the Ordnance Survey I-inch map of 1946 is remarkable; the southern part of the heath-

land has disappeared under the spread of industrialization, and in the north there has been extensive planting. Yet afforestation has not wholly covered what the demands of agriculture left empty, and many stretches of heath and common remain as inliers of an older, wilder landscape surrounded by improvement. A number of these areas have been used as military training grounds and some have been adapted for golf courses, but many still appear as open tracts of *Calluna* and *Erica*. Daniel Defoe thought that such countrysides were "horrid and frightful to look upon" and other writers have found them bleak and desolate, but time has given them a new value. In 1823 Cobbett spoke of "those miserable tracts of heath and fern and bushes and sand called Ashdown Forest and Saint Leonard's Forest," but in 1894 Lord Eversley could describe Ashdown Forest as "an exceedingly beautiful and valuable open space," thus demonstrating the truth that beauty is in the eye of the beholder. London is fortunate in having so great a number of these open tracts nearby—on the Bagshot Series, the Lower Greensand, the Hastings Beds and, to a less extent, on the Blackheath Beds. The struggle for the preservation of these open spaces, and others elsewhere in the realm, forms an interesting chapter in the history of the countryside during the nineteenth century.

The Changing Arable

For the greater part of its history, the agricultural land of England would have looked strange to us. Over much of the countryside each village was surrounded by those great stretches of arable land known as open fields, for of the 8500 parishes which existed at the time of the Reformation some 4500 seem to have been cultivated in this way. In the remainder, open-field cultivation either had never existed or had disappeared silently during the Middle Ages. By the sixteenth

---

7. J. A. Clarke, "On the farming of Lincolnshire," *J. Roy. Agric. Soc.* 12 (1851) 330.

century, it was certainly not characteristic of the south-east, the south-west, the west and the north. Over the rest of the country, and chiefly in the Midlands, the open fields remained unenclosed for another three centuries. The complexities of the enclosure movement by which they disappeared are many and controversial, but we can at any rate say that from about 1450 to 1750 enclosure took place privately, and that after 1750 it was continued by various Acts of Parliament until, by about 1850, open fields had disappeared from all but a few rare villages. Dr. Gilbert Slater's well-known Enclosure map shows the later or parliamentary phase of the movement. [8]

Much attention has been given to the social consequences of enclosure but the effects were also geographical, for the face of the countryside was greatly altered. To our eyes the unenclosed landscape would have appeared bare; there was little or nothing to break the sweep of the wind across the ploughed earth. In 1822 Cobbett was still able to find near Royston "those very ugly things, common-fields, which have all the nakedness, without any of the smoothness, of Downs." To him this naked countryside appeared "dreary" and "bleak and comfortless," and it cheered him as he left Royston to see enclosed fields "divided by quick-set hedges." The fences around the enclosed fields were made by planting "quick" or live cuttings, usually of hawthorn, and so was spread the ubiquitous English hedgerow.

In many people's eyes it is to the hedgerow that the English landscape owes its peculiar charm. One result of their construction was to give the countryside the appearance of being much more wooded than it really is; but an airman sees little to remind him of the great woodlands that confronted the Anglo-Saxons when they first arrived in Britain. What he does see is sometimes said to resemble a chequer-board or a patchwork quilt.

The hedgerow was not the only consequence of enclosure. The disappearance of open-fields was frequently accompanied in the sixteenth century by the conversion of arable into pasture, and much of England came to look greener than before. From this period date the majority of the deserted villages described by Mr. M. W. Beresford and Dr. W. G. Hoskins. One example must stand for all these changes; it was on a December day in 1495 that Sir Ralph Shirley turned the arable of the Leicestershire village of Willowes into sheep and cattle pastures and "thirty persons departed in tears and have perished." [9] Willowes was but one of some sixty villages in Leicestershire to suffer this fate. There was depopulation on a similar scale in other counties— Warwickshire, Yorkshire and Lincolnshire for example. Yet we must not exaggerate; not all enclosures meant conversion to pasture and not all conversions to pasture brought about the obliteration of a village. It was not until the eighteenth century that enclosure really gave the Midland countryside its present character. As Arthur Young wrote in 1774:

The fact is this; in the central counties of the kingdom, particularly Northamptonshire, Leicestershire, and parts of Warwic, Huntingdon and Buckinghamshires, there have been within 30 years large tracts of the open field arable under that vile course, 1. fallow, 2. wheat, 3. spring corn, inclosed and laid down to grass, being much more suited to the wetness of the soil than corn. [10]

---

8. *Geogr. J.* 29 (1907) 40.

9. W. G. Hoskins, "Essays in Leice~ ~ire History," p. 100 (Liverpool, 1950). See also M. W. Beresford, "The lost villages of medieval England," *Geogr. J.* 117 (1951) 129-49.
10. A. Young, "Political Arithmetic," p. 148 (London, 1774).

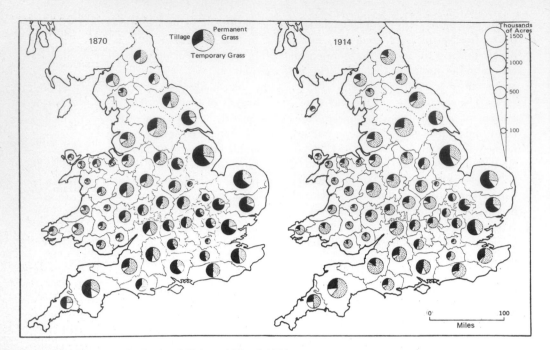

Figure 5. Land use in England and Wales, 1870 and 1914.

Of all the Midland countries, the changes in Leicestershire were as outstanding as in any. It was, noted William Marshall in 1790, "not long ago an open arable-county including a proportion of cows and rearing cattle; now a continued sheet of greensward. A district of grazing grounds." [11]

But the Midland arable did not disappear without leaving traces of itself and today anyone who travels through the Midlands can see the ridges and furrows that are regarded by many as relics of the former open-field system. The old pattern of cultivation remains visible through the new pattern of field and hedgerow that has been imposed upon it. By the time the enclosing impulse was over the broad distinction between the arable and the grazing districts of England had been drawn, and the result was summed up in Caird's generalization of 1850. His map shows the contrast between what he called "the chief Corn Districts" of the south and east and "the principal Grazing, Green Crop and Dairying Districts" of the Midlands and the West. [12]

Since 1850 the changes of agricultural history have modified but not obliterated the distinction that Caird drew. During the generation that followed the repeal of the Corn Laws in 1846 a variety of factors sustained arable farming, and the full effects were not felt for another thirty years. The year 1879 marked the end of a golden age in English farming; the crash was accentuated by a succession of bad harvests and was as overwhelming as it was sudden. Since then the decline of the arable acreage of England has often been discussed. It was most ap-

11. W. Marshall, "Rural economy of the midland counties," p. 193 (London, 1790).

12. J. Caird, "English agriculture in 1850-51," frontispiece (London, 1852).

parent on the heavier soils where grass and milk replaced wheat and beans, and the *Journal of The Royal Agricultural Society* began to fill with papers on the best method of laying land down to grass. The green was spreading from the west and from the Midlands, but only too often the expense of laying down was so great that stretches of arable were allowed to "tumble down" to rough pasture and to thistles and thorns. It should be pointed out that the total area affected was less than the outcry about it might suggest; in many parts of eastern England soil and climate forbade large-scale conversion. Even so, the countryside generally began to assume a neglected appearance; uncleared ditches, untrimmed hedges and unmended barns told their own story.

From 1866 onwards, the returns of the Board of Agriculture enable us to set the contemporary accounts against a statistical background, and conditions in 1870 and 1914 are compared in Figure 5. The decline of the arable was interrupted by the ploughing-up campaign of the 1914-18 war, but after 1918 conversion to grassland proceeded even more rapidly than before; the situation did not change until the events of the last war. The effects of wartime changes upon English agriculture have been discussed by Professor Stamp,[13] by 1945, as he showed, the arable acreage once more equalled that of 1879. The plough had returned to many of the grassland fields of Leicestershire and the Midlands generally, but even so the total area under cultivation in 1945 (tillage, rotation grass and permanent grass) was still below that in 1879.

The Landscape Garden

When towards the end of the seventeenth century Celia Fiennes toured England on a side-saddle, she found a large number of newly built houses surrounded by gardens and parks. A park with "fine rows of trees" was coming to be regarded as a necessary element in the dignity of a country seat. Stimulated by John Evelyn's "Sylva" (1664), people were planting not only for utility but for ornament. Early in the next century Defoe was struck by this new addition to the variety of the English landscape; the new estates he said gave a "kind of character to the island of Great Britain in general."[14]

The gardens that were thus coming into being were of a very formal character. André le Nôtre who planned the lay-out at Versailles had many pupils in England, and the influence of his geometrical designs was very evident. Avenues and walks were laid out in straight lines, frequently radiating from one point, parterres were arranged in stiff and symmetrical patterns and trees were cut and clipped with precision. Art held Nature uncompromisingly at bay. Some of these formal lay-outs are well seen in the engravings of Joannes Kip. But early in the eighteenth century there was much criticism of this formality, and the complaints were symptoms of a new inspiration in garden design. The restrictions of the formal style were soon broken down, and the new irregular garden was in turn to develop into the landscape park. The three great gardeners of the eighteenth century were William Kent (1685-1748), Lancelot Brown (1715-83) and Humphrey Repton (1752-1818). The cult of the landscape garden was part of a wider artistic and literary movement which drew much of its inspiration from the work of the great landscape painters of the age—Claude, Poussin and Salvator Rosa. The aim of the landscape gardener was to display the quali-

---

13. L. Dudley Stamp, "Wartime changes in British agriculture," *Geogr. J.* 109 (1947) 39-57.

14. Daniel Defoe, "A tour through England and Wales," vol. i, p. 167 (Everyman's edition).

ties emphasized by these painters of natural scenery. Horace Walpole expressed this aim by saying that "an open country is but a canvass on which a landscape might be designed."[15] The making of a landscape garden thus became a study in composition; building against a background of trees with a foreground of grass and tree-clumps, the whole reflected in an irregular sheet of water.

Although William Kent's object was to make a garden resemble the landscape of Nature itself, there was still a considerable element of formality in his style. One feature of his designs was the planting of trees in clumps, and the clump became a characteristic element in the eighteenth century park. The facts of Nature were made to conform to the necessities of composition. Horace Walpole said that "the living landscape was chastened or polished" by Kent, but that he sometimes went so far as to imitate Nature even in her faults, and in Kensington Gardens planted dead trees to give an air of verisimilitude to the scene.

As the eighteenth century advanced, the urge of the Romantic Movement was reflected in the fashion for an increasingly irregular lay-out—not Nature "chastened or polished" but Nature herself. Many great avenues were now replaced by meandering paths, and the desire for informality was carried a step further under the leadership of Lancelot Brown. When consulted he had the habit of saying "I see great *capability* of improvement here" and became known as "Capability Brown." Under his influence the park was allowed to encroach upon the garden, right up to the walls of the house itself; he believed that scenery should be as

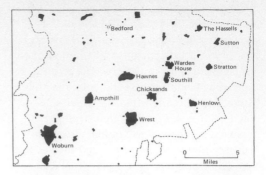

Figure 6. The parks of central Bedfordshire (after Bryant, 1826).

natural as possible and that there should be what he called "no disgusting display of art." He had many critics but, whatever his faults, his influence up and down the country was enormous.

In the latter years of the century many people thought that landscapes should not merely imitate Nature but imitate Nature in the raw, and that parks and gardens should display what William Gilpin called "the bold roughness of nature." With this went a predilection for ruins, to be constructed if they did not already exist, and for such things as garden temples, grottoes, hermitages, rustic pavilions and pagodas. Amidst much contending criticism the third great gardener of the century, Humphrey Repton, tried to steer a middle path between formalism and Romanticism. It was he who executed the designs for Regent's Park and for the gardens of Russell Square.

Whatever the artistic differences among the landed gentry and professional gardeners of the eighteenth century, the consequences of their work were very great for the English landscape. As Uvedale Price wrote in 1794, these embellishments were giving "a new and peculiar character to the general face of the country."[16] The effect was to be seen not

15. Horace Walpole, "The history of the modern taste in gardening." It first appeared in 1771. See J. W. U. Chase, "Horace Walpole: gardenist," p. 37 (Cincinnati, 1943).

16. Uvedale Price, "An essay on the picturesque," p. 1 (London, 1794).

only around the great palaces of the realm—
Blenheim, Chatsworth, Stowe and the like—
but also around what the county gazetteers
were in the habit of calling "a neat mansion
pleasantly situated in a park." Small men as
well as great had followed Joseph Addison's
advice and made "a pretty landskip" of their
possessions. [17] The county maps of the time
bear witness to the widespread distribution
of these parks; in Bedfordshire for example
they were numerous (Fig. 6), but not more
numerous than in many other counties. The
nineteenth and twentieth centuries were to
see many changes in taste and in economic
circumstance, but there are still stretches of
countryside where the traveller encounters
one great landscape garden after another.

Towns and the Seats of Industry

In the year 1696 Gregory King estimated the
population of England and Wales at about
five and a half millions. The eighteenth
century saw a considerable increase and the
first Census, in 1801, revealed a population
of just under nine millions. This was to become nearly eighteen millions by 1851, and
thirty-six millions by 1911. There is much
that is controversial about this growth, but it
is clear that the main factor in the extraordinary increase was a decline in the death
rate as a result of improving medical knowledge and sanitary control. Even more striking than this increase of population was its
concentration on the coalfields. By 1700
almost all the coalfields with which we
are familiar were beginning to be worked,
but they were not yet centres of population.
The main lines of the distribution of population were still upon the medieval pattern,
and the most populous tract of England lay
on either side of a line joining London and
Bristol. By 1801 the pattern had altered and

---

17. *The Spectator*, No. 414 (25 June 1712).

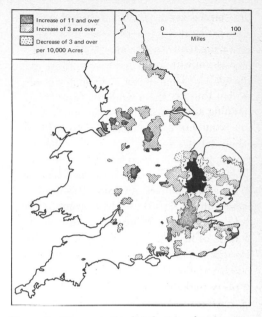

Figure 7. Changes in the distribution of emigrants
from Cambridgeshire, 1851-61.

the most densely populated counties, outside the London area, were now Lancashire,
Warwick, the West Riding and Staffordshire.
As Arthur Young wrote in 1791 "all the
activity and industry of this kingdom is fast
concentrating where there are coal pits." It
is difficult to estimate from the Census Returns the exact proportion of urban to rural
dwellers, or of industrial to agricultural
population, but it is clear that not only was
the population becoming urban but becoming so at a fast rate. Some index of this is
provided by the fact that in 1801 about 17
per cent. of the population of England and
Wales lived in towns of over 20,000 inhabitants. By 1851 the figure was 35 per cent.
and by 1901 it had reached 55 per cent.

The main cause of this concentration was
migration from the countryside and from
Ireland. It is an astounding fact that in 1851,
in almost all the great towns, immigrants
from elsewhere outnumbered the people

born in the town. Dr. Redford has however shown that it is incorrect to envisage this movement as a cataclysmic shift from the counties of the south and east to those of the Midlands and north. "The majority of the migrants to the town came from the immediately surrounding counties, their places in turn being taken by migrants from places farther away." [18] But while this was generally true, it is also a fact that there was some long-distance migration; for example, many of the natives of Cambridgeshire who left it between 1851 and 1861 seem to have gone direct to the rising centres of industry and to London.[19] The net result of all these complicated movements throughout the countryside was to produce six conurbations, each formed by the expansion and coalescence of neighbouring towns and villages, and each with over a million inhabitants—Greater Manchester, Merseyside, West Yorkshire, Greater Birmingham, Tyneside and, in a class by itself, Greater London.[20]

The dreary character of these new industrial landscapes has often been described—the cotton towns, the woollen towns, the iron towns, and the coalfields in general. Houses were huddled along unpaved streets amid unspeakable conditions of sanitation. Towering above many of these back-to-back streets, the tall chimneys of the textile factories were at one time rising almost annually. It was in 1844 that Friedrich Engels drew in words his picture of an urban prospect in Manchester, and a grim picture it is. In the mining areas fields disappeared beneath slag heaps and pit banks and, as the

scene of intense activity moved from one locality to another, the scars of derelict land were left behind. A contemporary writing of the east Durham plateau in 1841 could say: "Within the last ten or twelve years an entirely new population has been produced. Where formerly there was not a single hut of a shepherd, the lofty steam engine chimneys of a colliery now send their volume of smoke into the sky, and in the vicinity a town is called as if by enchantment, into immediate existence." [21] In 1843 Thomas Tancred gave a graphic picture of the growing conurbation of Birmingham: "The traveller appears never to get out of an interminable village. . . . In some directions he may travel for miles, and never be out of sight of numerous two-storied houses, so that the area covered by bricks and mortar must be immense. These houses . . . are interspersed with blazing furnaces, heaps of burning coal in process of coking . . . heaps of the refuse of the mines or of slag from the blast furnaces." [22]

The formation of these five great continuous urban groups by no means accounts for all the urban growth of the nineteenth century. There were many other growing areas, as obvious in the landscape of England as they were important in its economy, Sheffield and Bristol, and the Five Towns where history was revolutionized when Josiah Wedgwood opened his pottery there in 1759. Nottingham and Hull are now also above the 300,000 mark. But we must remember that not less rapid has been the growth of other towns of a different character. The Census Report of 1851 computed the rate of growth of some 220 representative towns, and it is interesting to note that

18. A. Redford, "Labour migration in England, 1800-50," p. 158 (Manchester, 1926).
19. H. C. Darby, "The movement of population to and from Cambridgeshire between 1851 and 1861," Geogr. J. 101 (1943) 118-25.
20. C. B. Fawcett, "Distribution of the urban population in Great Britain 1931," Geogr. J. 79 (1932) 100-116.

21. "Report of the Child Employment Commission," Appendix I, p. 143 (1841).
22. Thomas Tancred in the introduction to the "Report of the Midland Mining Commission" (1843).

the highest rate of growth was that of watering places: [23]

Number	Category	Increase per cent 1801-1851
15	Watering Places	254
51	Manufacturing towns	224
28	Mining and Hardware towns	217
26	Sea-ports (excluding London)	196
1	London	146
99	County towns (excluding London)	122
220		176

Four of these watering places have since
passed the hundred thousand mark, and well
passed it if their satellites be included—
Brighton, Southend, Bournemouth and
Blackpool. Some of these places of health
and pleasure had reputations long before the
railway age. Others were new; Bournemouth
now stands where in 1830 there were some
half dozen houses and a wild heath on which
the bustard and hen-harrier bred.

Finally, in this urban catalogue, comes
London itself. In 1724, Defoe was amazed at
its "prodigy of buildings," and at that time
it must have been a city of some half a
million people. By 1801 it had nearly
doubled. To Cobbett, early in the nineteenth
century, it was a monstrosity, the "great
wen" that he so often derided. Shelley
summed up some of its characteristics by
saying that "Hell is a city much like
London." But even as these complaints were
being written the "great wen" was spreading
over country village and low-lying marsh
alike. J. P. Malcolm, writing in 1803,
thought it almost easier to "describe the
varying form of a summer cloud, than to
trace from year to year the outline of

London." [24] Later developments were to
make it even less easy. Perhaps the simplest
way to compress the story of its vast spread
is to say that in Defoe's day roughly one
citizen out of every ten in England and
Wales lived in London. In 1801 the figure
was one in nine; by 1880 it was one in six.
Today it is one in five. These figures are not
comparable in the sense that they do not
refer to the same area at different dates; but
they do serve to indicate the spreading tide
of bricks and mortar that was blotting out
the countryside.

Dr. Thomas Sharp has summed up the
impact of the nineteenth century upon the
English landscape by saying that "henceforward England became almost two
countries. The Midlands and the North advanced grimly along a hideous road of in-
dustrialism, while the South (in which, significantly, was situated the capital city)
slumbered fitfully in the tree-folded parks
and the half-dead small towns and villages of
its 'improved' landscape." [25] This does
emphasize the distinction that Mackinder
drew between "industrial" and "metropolitan" England. But it is a statement that
must be qualified; there are many rural areas
in the North—comfortable farming dales as
well as open solitudes where the curlew cries
over the ling and the bent. Conversely, a
comparison of the Census Reports for 1921
and 1931 shows an appreciably greater increase of population in the Home Counties
than elsewhere. The preliminary figures of
the 1951 census show that this increase has
continued, but at a relatively slower rate. He
who walks abroad in the South may see on
either hand the marks of this latest phase in
the changing English landscape.

23. "Census of Great Britain, 1851: Population
Table I," p. xlix (London, 1852).

24. J. P. Malcolm, *Londinium Redivivum*, vol. i, p.
5 (London, 1803).
25. Thomas Sharp, "English panorama," p. 58
(London, 1936).

⚓⚓⚓⚓⚓⚓⚓⚓⚓⚓⚓⚓⚓⚓⚓⚓⚓⚓⚓⚓⚓⚓⚓⚓⚓⚓⚓⚓

THE PROCESS OF LANDSCAPE CHANGE: BICULTURAL IMPLICATIONS

A. David Hill

The realization that most men subsist at levels of material comfort far below those of others has posed the problem, particularly attacked by economists, of economic underdevelopment. The idea that cultures change in the face of contact with others has held the attention of anthropologists. These two interests underlie this paper, but it focuses principally upon the changing character of the cultural landscape—that composite of features, visible on the earth's surface, which gives evidence of man's occupancy. The idea that the landscape reflects significant cultural conditions, thereby evincing "the areal importance and character of man's activity" has gained, in American geography, its greatest momentum from Professor Carl O. Sauer at the University of California. This study offers no substantial modifications of that idea. However, it suggests that the interpretation of the cultural landscape offers an additional means, geographically-oriented, by which economic and cultural change may be studied. The landscape under consideration in this study is located in the Chiapas Highlands of Southeastern Mexico, an area which is, in many ways, representative of underdeveloped regions in Latin America.

Changes in the landscape arise because of the new spatial relationships caused by increased accessibility and by other environmental, cultural, and economic stimuli. Modern introductions tend to accumulate in particular places because the encroaching commercial economy chooses to develop only those sites which can be accommodated to a modern system of resource exploitation. Elsewhere, the traditional aspects of the landscape remain because the Indian perceives the natural environment differently than does the commercially-oriented segment of the population. Furthermore, the Indian's separate and unique code of values and system of resource use, strongly reinforced by social sanctions and traditions, present further barriers to change. In addition, the Indian's meager capital, simple technology, inferior social status in the bicultural community, and lack of understanding of the complexities of the modern commercial system preclude him from fully participating in or benefitting from the developing commercial culture. Indeed, it appears that the initial stages of economic development in this area have been detrimental to the economic position of the Indian relative to the non-Indian.

That the new features of the cultural landscape are largely products of stimuli imposed from beyond the region cannot be denied, but the "modern" elements are localized because the outside stimuli have well developed foci. They are both countered and aided by internal forces. In fact, it is a conclusion of a recent exhaustive study on the process of economic develop-

From *The Changing Landscape of a Mexican Municipio: Villa Las Rosas, Chiapas*, Research Paper No. 91, Department of Geography, University of Chicago, 1964. Reprinted by permission.

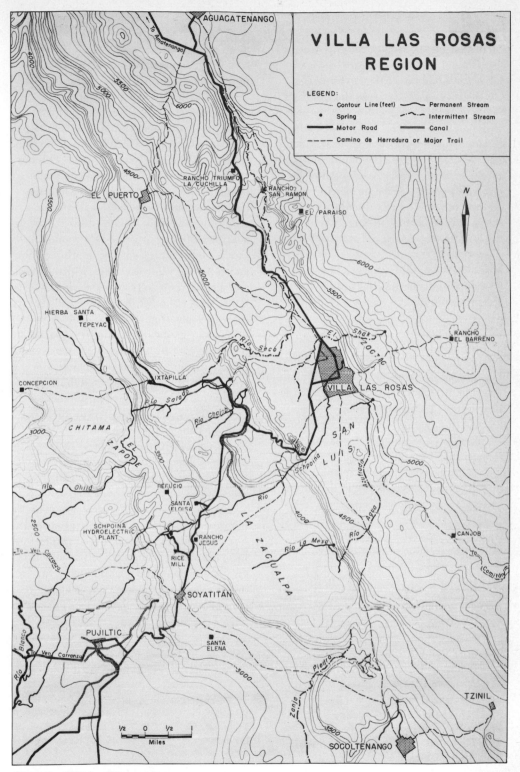

Figure 1. Villa Las Rosas region.

ment that "both the barriers to [economic] growth and the causes of growth seem to be largely internal rather than external."[1]

The process of change in the Las Rosas region is taking place within the context of a society which has a basic cultural duality, i.e., two different cultural groups—Indians and *ladinos*—comprise the population. Cultural factors in large measure control the rate at which the landscape is being altered and the economic and cultural differences of the bicultural society are largely responsible for both the dynamics and statics of the process.

Conceptions of the Physical Environment

Cultural heritage provides a traditional design for life. Tradition is relevant to the interpretation of the cultural landscape because it is the basis for the perception of a set of natural features as resources and also provides the technology, equipment, tools, and institutions for resource exploitation.[2] Differential perception of the habitat through two basically different cultural "lenses" is relevant to our explanation of the process of landscape change in the study region for, as we have seen, a people's estimation of their own needs and their capabilities to use natural features largely determines the ultimate manner in which those features are exploited. Spoehr has suggested that the basic contrasts in the interpretation of natural resources lie "at the root of the change that takes place [when preliterate societies] come in contact with Western

industrial civilization."[3] It is thus necessary to attempt to set down the two contrasting views of the physical environment held by the Indian and the *ladino*.

One approach to understanding man's conception of his physical milieu is to note the natural features which he utilizes and the manner in which he exploits them. This has been attempted for some of the most important and constant resource-using activities in the study area, such as irrigation, crop production, and wood-gathering for fire and for building purposes. Less economically significant activities, such as hunting, fishing, and gathering wild vegetables, fruits, berries, and insects, are also resource-using practices in the area, although these are usually relegated to spare-time activities and are most often associated with the Indians; indeed, the gathering of wild products is strictly an Indian practice. Without recourse to a detailed tally, it may be suggested that the Indian utilizes a much greater number and variety of natural features within the area than does the *ladino*. The wealthy *ladino*'s diet is varied with imported and factory-processed foods, whereas the Indian often eats wild items which have been gathered, shot, or caught in the mountains, fields, canals, and streams of the local area. This use of wild products implies a very special knowledge of the habitat. For example, with little effort one young Indian was able to give either Tzeltal or Spanish names to ninety-six specific places such as hills, springs, caves, plains, and streams in an area within a radius of about 5 miles of Las Rosas.

A description of the use of natural resources may not tell much about the basis

1. Everett E. Hagen, *On the Theory of Social Change: How Economic Growth Begins* (Homewood, Ill.: The Dorsey Press, Inc., 1962), p. 55.
2. A classic treatment of this theme is C. Daryll Forde's *Habitat, Economy and Society: A Geographical Introduction to Ethnology* (London: Methuen & Co. Ltd., 1934).

3. Alexander Spoehr, "Cultural Differences in the Interpretation of Natural Resources," in William L. Thomas (ed.), *Man's Role in Changing the Face of the Earth* (Chicago: University of Chicago Press, 1956), p. 99.

upon which resource conceptions are founded. In order to be able to explain why the Indian conceives of the habitat differently from the *ladino* and, therefore, exploits it differently, one must understand that Indian culture in Las Rosas functions with a set of beliefs and values which are very unlike those of the *ladino*, especially the cosmopolitan *ladino*. The Indian design for life (and perhaps peasant culture everywhere) is not oriented toward improvisation. The agriculture of peasants "is a livelihood and a way of life, not a business for profit," [4] as it is with the cosmopolitan *ladinos*. Maize for the Indian is not merely a cereal which provides the bulk of his diet and a product to sell but rather it has such deep and underlying significance in Indian life that Emundo Flores has been prompted to write:

Maize is the product of greatest importance in the kitchen, the mythology, and the politics of the Mexican. It is a basic necessity, a mother-image, a phallic symbol, a dietary obsession, and for the Secretary of Agriculture, a nightmare. It is as though the ancestral hunger of the Mexicans could only express itself in terms of maize. Wherever there are Mexicans and water there is maize. With respect to its location, one can say it is ubiquitous. [5]

The above characterization may be somewhat overdrawn—it certainly is for the cosmopolitan *ladino*—but in the Las Rosas region one can expect that, as long as Indian culture remains, *milpas* will be an important feature of the landscape because to be an Indian is to be a *milpero*. There is no work more essential to identity and prestige in Indian culture than the work in the *milpa*. It is "best" for a man to work his own *milpa*

because, culturally defined, that is man's work. And, having observed the pride with which Indians show their *milpas*, one might add that the *milpa* is the *raison d'être* for their lives. Even if a man can support his family by means other than his *milpa*, he will invariably choose to work also in the maize. As was implicit in Flores' remarks, this "compulsion" about maize is not exclusively an Indian trait in Mexico, for Federal soldiers stationed in Las Rosas in 1961 worked their own *milpas*.

Perhaps the working of a *milpa* is a resource practice which is not always "gainful," to use Firey's term (i.e., not always "efficient in realizing culturally defined sustenance needs"), but it is always "culturally consistent." [6] Redfield "knew some men [in a Maya village who] continued to practice agriculture, although economically disadvantageous, because to plant a cornfield was essential to participating in the moral and religious life of the community." [7]

In Las Rosas at the present time, however, there is some evidence to indicate that work on one's own land may not be disadvantageous, and there is some question as to whether available wage opportunities in the area are decisively compensatory. Wage labor is only a last resort when emergency cash is needed, and if an Indian leaves his village to work for wages it is often because he has no land of his own—a condition which may be the greatest single reason for out-migration. This is not a unique situation. For example, Moore has observed in Mexico that "for many workers industrial employment is a temporary expedient of unusual ad-

---

4. Robert Redfield. *The Peasant Society and Culture* (Chicago: University of Chicago Press, 1956), p. 18.

5. Edmundo Flores. *Tratado de Economía Agrícola* (México, D.F.: Fondo de Cultura Económica, 1961), p. 388.

6. Walter Firey, *Man, Mind and Land: A Theory of Resource Use* (Glencoe, Ill.: The Free Press, 1960), pp. 30-33.

7. Redfield, *The Peasant Society. . .* , p. 64. See also Margaret Mead (ed.), *Cultural Patterns and Technical Change* (New York: Mentor Book, 1955), p. 181.

versity."[8] Since, as previously noted, the
level of local wages is approximately equal
to a *milpero*'s productivity, the wage laborer
has no considerable economic advantage
over the peasant who has sufficient land, and
the peasant perceives greater security in his
mode of activity even though he may believe
that wage work offers more cash. For example, when it was suggested to one Indian
that he might make more money working
for wages on the highway than he does with
his *milpa*, he answered:

If a man is working on the highway, and he gets
sick, then he can't work and he has no money to
buy food for his family. But if he has his own
milpa, the work can wait for a little, while he re-
covers, and he still has his *milpa* to feed his family.

The most important locus for wage labor
in the region lies in *tierra caliente*, but, as
one Indian put it, "it is better to stay here
[Las Rosas] and work for 3 or 4 pesos a day
than to go there [Pujiltic] and work for 7 or
10 because there one cannot sleep well and
one gets sick." Yet many Las Rosas men go
to Pujiltic, mainly because there are more
jobs available but also because the wages are
slightly higher than in the immediate vicinity
of Las Rosas. The rationalizations about
"sleep" and "getting sick" usually hold only
for a man with land to work or one without
need of emergency cash. (The reader should
note that a large majority of the Pujiltic
field workers are boys and young men.) The
apparent ambiguity is thus largely explain-
able by the fact of necessity. Greaves has
pointed out that

It may seem worth while to refuse wages which
are higher than the cash return to independent
production when there is no particular need of that
extra increment of cash, for the variability of productive effort depends for the most part upon the
elasticity of the worker's demand schedule, and it

is when the money character of the native's wants
increases that the cash value of his output assumes
a greater importance.[9]

Indian culture imbues the physical environment with a mystical quality so powerful and compelling as to discourage the individual from conceiving of tampering with
it beyond the bounds which tradition ascribes. The habitat to the Indian is not
merely objective reality or a set of physical
phenomena as it is to the cosmopolitan
ladino. On the contrary,

The cosmos of the Pinola [Las Rosas] Indian is
populated with spirits. . . . The hills and caves are
the residences of the spirits of ancestors and of
living men who are old and powerful. In the water
holes, Thunder abides; *nawals* [animal souls of
men] roam about the forest. A man, unless he is
reaffirmed in the possession of a powerful spirit
and *nawals*, does not intrude in those places because his *chulel* [ethereal spirit] might be retained
by its residents.[10]

The Indian does not *ultimately* interpret the
outcome of his interactions with the habitat
in terms of his own technical capacities or
fluctuations of natural conditions, but rather
in terms of supernatural beliefs. He has "no
other explanation for his success or failure. . . . He lives in a world populated with
powerful spirits which both protect and
attack him. His behavior is a continuous
search for harmony with those forces."[11]
Thus, according to the Indian view, the
exploitation of the habitat cannot ultimately
bring about satisfaction or disappointment
in life because that is due to mystical forces
beyond man's puny control. He can at best
hope to cope with these forces by adhering

8. Wilbert E. Moore. *Industrialization and Labor:
Social Aspects of Economic Development* (Ithaca,
N.Y.: Cornell University Press, 1951), p. 115.

9. Quoted in Moore, *op. cit.*, p. 43, from I. C.
Greaves, *Modern Production Among Backward
Peoples* (London: George Allen and Unwin, 1935),
pp. 62-63.
10. M. Esther Hermitte. "Social Mobility in a
Chiapas Bicultural Town" (Chicago: Unpublished
Master's Thesis, Department of Anthropology,
University of Chicago, 1962), p. 34.
11. *Ibid.*

to the traditional way of life—that pattern which has previously sustained life.

The Indian, as opposed to the *ladino*, possesses a "pre-capitalist" ethic. Power and prestige within the Indian group come to the individual not from wealth but from his strict conformance to the Indian norms and from the power of his supernatural spirits.

> Respect for older men, economic equality, reciprocity, and cooperation instead of competition are highly valued in the moral code [of Las Rosas Indians]. But the reward for compliance with the norms follows particular channels. The person who proves himself worthy of his group will find, at the end of the long and hard life, a place among the powerful ones if consensus is reached that he possesses a good spirit. In this other-worldly oriented culture the summit of prestige is reached only by acquisition of supernatural powers.[12]

Despite the numerous overt dissimilarities between Indians and *ladinos*, the belief in the supernatural as construed by Indian culture may, in the final analysis, be the most singularly meaningful criterion for cultural differentiation.

The Indian's perception of his own capacity to direct his destiny is further restricted by his feelings of inferiority, especially relative to *ladinos*. It has been shown that the Indian equates himself with the poor man, and attention has been called frequently to the general truth of this view. Furthermore, Indians consider themselves ignorant compared to *ladinos*; they often relate stories about how they have been duped in one way or another by *ladinos*. It has been observed that Las Rosas Indians are more timid and insecure than some other Indian groups in the general area[13] which perhaps is due in part to the fact that these other groups have

enjoyed greater isolation from the *ladino*.[14] Perhaps the constant discrimination, derision, and abuse which Indians receive from *ladinos* in Las Rosas has engendered a type of "group inferiority complex." The Las Rosas Indian even portrays himself as the poor fool, compared to other Indian groups, in his stories or myths. One which the author heard "explained" the origin of the tough grass which has invaded the communal land north of Las Rosas as follows: "Pinoltecos went to Amatenango to buy wheat seed, but were given grass seed instead, and planted it thinking it to be wheat."

The following comments provide a final illustration of how Indians and *ladinos* have viewed the exploitation of the natural environment. According to an Indian,

> Several years ago the *ladinos* tried to make a coffee plantation on the communal Zoctic lands. They elected an Indian leader of the group—the *ladinos* were using him in order to get the cooperation of the Indians. The people [Indians] were discontent and rose up directed by the *alcalde*. They opposed the planting of coffee on Zoctic because it is the only place where one can get *bejuco* to make houses; coffee cultivation would have left us without material for buildings.

A cosmopolitan *ladino*, when asked about the use of Zoctic for coffee, remarked that it would be foolish "since the price of coffee is so low" and he thought the land was *"only useful for cattle."*

In sum, the Indian views the habitat as changeable only within the context that tradition ascribes, and he reckons to have no ultimate power over nature because sole and

---

12. *Ibid.*
13. Personal communication with Marcelo Díaz de Salas.

14. This idea was expressed in the author's paper, "The Land Question as a Factor in Explaining Culture Change: The Case of San Bartolomé and Pinola in Chiapas, Mexico," delivered at 57th Annual Meeting of the Association of American Geographers and abstracted in *Annals*, Association of American Geographers, LII, No. 3 (September, 1962), 337.

ultimate authority is vested in supernatural forces. John Gillin has said that

> The principal and fundamental goal of Indian cultures is to effect a peaceful adjustment or adaptation of men to the universe. In contrast, the main goal of Ladino culture is to effect control of the universe by man. The Indian wishes to come to terms with the universe, the Ladino wishes to dominate it.[15]

The *ladino* subscribes to the view that he can manipulate the physical milieu to turn a profit which brings him wealth, power, and prestige; he is the undaunted innovator who believes that, with his own will, he can change the habitat to extract profit if only he has sufficient capital or technology or if market or labor conditions are propitious. For the *ladino*, "the world is his oyster"—a view which stimulates change in the cultural landscape of the Las Rosas region; the Indian's view militates against change.

Participation in the Modern System

Man, in mediating with his natural environment, creates various "artificial environments" which reflect his natural milieu as well as his system of economy, social organization, and technology; the resulting "artificial landscape" of a place thus represents the type or combination of types of systems possessed by that place's inhabitants—past and/or present.[16] New artificial features of the landscape of the Las Rosas area connote the imposition of the system of modern Mexican culture, locally represented in the population by the cosmopolitan *ladino*. Participation in this system requires, for example, the use of cash, the use of manufactured products of Western industry, the

production of commercial crops, and the utilization of modern technology. The beneficiary of the system must, in competition with other participants, rationalize his productive effort in order to gain the greatest possible profit which, of course, is interpreted by the system to mean the greatest possible material wealth.

In juxtaposition to the modern system is the traditional one of the illiterate Indian—technologically less complex and designed to satisfy an entirely different set of values and goals. The virtually self-sufficient Indian *milpero* is the typical participant in this system. In reality, there are probably no Indians who do not participate to some extent in the more complex modern system, for to do so has become a necessity. The modern system has been imposed upon the Indian by the *ladino* world, and in order to subsist, he must interact economically with the *ladino*. To the Indian money has become a necessity and thus he produces cash crops and/or works for wages. The extent to which he participates in such aspects of the modern system is variable and manifests the considerable changes he has already made to accommodate to it.

That much of the region's cultural landscape is still very "Indian" reflects the fact that, despite the changes which the Indian has made, he is still merely a marginal participant in the modern system and, as a corollary, he is at the most only a marginal beneficiary. In a sense the Indian is a "defensive participant"—he only moves here or there to defend himself. He never takes the initiative, the offensive, because he does not understand the new system. It is as though he were an actor who does not know his lines. He cannot compete with the *ladino* because he does not know "the rules of the game." He merely goes through the motions without knowing why the game is being played. The spirits of the Indian *Meiltatiles*,

---

15. John Gillin, "Ethos and Cultural Aspects of Personality," in Sol Tax *et al.*, *Heritage of Conquest* (Glencoe, Ill.: The Free Press, 1952), p. 196.
16. This is the principal theme of Philip Wagner's *The Human Use of the Earth* (Glencoe, Ill.: The Free Press, 1960).

the most powerful men in the supernatural hierarchy, fly over the town to guard the Indian community. But they do not watch the new road—it is the *ladino's* road and not a part of the Indian system.

The marketing of maize exemplifies both the differential participation of *ladinos* and Indians in the modern system and the resulting benefits which accrue to both groups. Maize brokerage was entirely a private enterprise in Central Chiapas before the introduction of the warehouses of Almacenes Nacionales de Déposito, S.A. (ANDSA) in Tuxtla in 1956 and in San Cristóbal and Comitán in 1961. *Ladino* middlemen would purchase maize at low prices in small amounts from Indians and transport it to San Cristóbal or other centers, thereby reaping large, if not excessive, profits; they would buy maize during the harvest season and store it in their houses for resale at high prices during periods of scarcity. The purchase of an Indian's crop before it was harvested and in some cases even before it was planted *(compras en cosecha)* was another tactic.

All of these practices continue in the Las Rosas region. The system of *compras en cosecha* functions as a mechanism of credit for the poor peasant: The wealthy *ladino* offers to buy the peasant's crop before harvest at a time when the peasant is in need of emergency cash. The purchase price is considered a loan until the buyer has received the crop which, when he disposes of it, usually earns him a very high rate of interest on his loan.[17]

The federal government, via the agency of ANDSA, has attempted to impose its control over the maize market in order to counter supply imbalances throughout the nation, to stabilize prices, and to remedy the evils of large profit-taking by individual maize brokers. Discussion of the latter two objectives is germane to this study. If an individual wants to sell maize to ANDSA, the following procedure is required:

a. The seller must make a *solicitud*, i.e., send a photograph of himself, certify that the land on which he grows the maize belongs to him (it can be private, communal, *ejido*, or rented), and state where the land is located.
b. An inspector is then supposed to verify the information given in the *solicitud*.
c. The seller gets his authorization and at the same time deposits money to pay for henequen sacks *(costales)* which he can then pick up. The *costales* must be new and meet ANDSA specifications; ANDSA sold them for 5 pesos each in 1961.
d. Maize is taken to the warehouse in *costales* (10 or 11 to 1 metric ton) where it is checked and graded. If the maize is acceptable, the seller gets a ticket which is negotiable at a bank in Tuxtla.'

The minimum amount of maize which ANDSA will buy is 1 metric ton at 800 pesos per ton (1961 prices). The agency in turn sells maize at 850 pesos per ton in minimum amounts of 1 *costal* (between 80 and 100 kilograms). An individual may buy maize from the warehouse and resell it in the open market, but the government's relatively high selling price usually inhibits excessive

17. The system has its historical roots in the debt peonage of the *hacienda* system—the implications of which have been analyzed by many authors. For example, see Eric R. Wolf, *Sons of the Shaking Earth* (Chicago: University of Chicago Press, 1959), chapter 10, and Nathan L. Whetten, *Rural Mexico* (Chicago: University of Chicago Press, 1948), chapter 5. Debt peonage, of course, has had

broad historical implications. See Hans Bobek's discussion of "Rent Capitalism" in "The Main Stages in Socio-Economic Evolution from a Geographical Point of View," in Philip L. Wagner and Marvin W. Mikesell (eds.), *Readings in Cultural Geography* (Chicago: University of Chicago Press, 1962), pp. 233-40.

profit-taking in such ventures. Individual peasants may cooperate to sell maize to ANDSA in order to have the requisite minimum lot of 1 ton. This, however, is rarely done; the foreman at the warehouse in San Cristóbal reported to the author that he remembered only two cases of such cooperative selling during the 1960-61 season.

The government pays the full guaranteed price of 800 pesos per ton only if rigid specifications are met: (1) the maize must be "free of odor"; (2) the moisture-content must be less than 13 per cent; (3) impurities must be less than 2 per cent; and (4) it must be free of diseases. If these conditions are not met, deductions in price are made according to a pre-determined scale.

The ANDSA program has various effects and, although it attempts to constrain the unscrupulous middleman, it appears, in the Las Rosas region, to favor the larger operator at the expense of the peasant. From the standpoint of the wealthy *ladino*, the program may stimulate greater maize production, given the fact that prices are guaranteed, thereby reducing the risk of growing maize. However, the system is overtly opposed by the cosmopolitan *ladino* who calls it "excessive government control." But perhaps it is attacked most because it imposes *de jure* restrictions on profit-taking activities. For example, an individual may not privately store maize which he himself has not grown nor may he store more than what he needs for his family's requirements. Obviously these stipulations are extremely difficult, if not impossible, to enforce without a huge staff of inspectors and, consequently, abuses are commonplace.

From the standpoint of the Las Rosas Indian, the program is ineffective, if not detrimental. Indeed, only a few peasants have any knowledge of the program, and even it it were understood, it is doubtful that the Indians would take advantage of it.

The peasant normally has no surplus maize to sell and if he does he rarely has an entire ton which, the reader will note, is a reasonably good yield from 1 hectare. If the peasant does have the requisite ton, he must pay a *ladino* trucker to haul it to the warehouse but the costs are often beyond the reach of the individual peasant.

Lacking a ton of maize, the peasant is unable to sell to ANDSA individually, and cooperative buying and selling by peasants, and especially Indians, is unheard of in Las Rosas.[18] Since the Indian has virtually no possibility of selling to ANDSA, he regularly sells to the wealthy *ladino*, oftentimes *en cosecha*. Thus the ANDSA program has left unsolved the local problem of the profiteering middleman. Indeed, it appears that the system acts as a stimulus to increase the economic inequality between the *ladino* and the Indian. (One might suggest that the *total* modern system has this effect.) With his trucks, land, money, "know-how," and influence the *ladino* can easily amass large quantities of maize, transport it to the government warehouses, and receive appreciable profits. (Las Rosas prices for maize during 1961 averaged about 600 pesos per ton, while the government was paying 800 pesos.) While *ladino* maize brokers previously extracted large profits, they were nevertheless at the mercy of fluctuating market prices; now often carrying on their activities extralegally, they are able to sell

18. The Instituto Nacional Indigenísta (INI) has helped some Indians in Chamula and elsewhere to acquire trucks, but the author does not know the extent to which they combine their harvests for sale at the government's guaranteed price. INI has no such programs to aid Las Rosas Indians. The influence of INI has been strongest in all-Indian communities, perhaps because *ladinos* have used their hegemony to prevent INI's work within the *ladino*-dominated localities. Aguacatenango and Amatenango, both entirely Indian villages, have cooperative stores established by INI.

for relatively high, guaranteed prices. The individual Indian is usually helpless due to his ignorance of the program and his lack of cooperative economic organization.

The ANDSA program does not preclude the peasant from buying and selling maize. However, small-scale ventures of independent production and distribution are not always profitable as witness the following example of one Las Rosas Indian's trip to San Cristóbal to sell maize in September, 1961: Taking 2 *fanegas* (1 *fanega* = about 120 kilograms) and selling them to Zinacantecos[19] for 125 pesos per *fanega*, his expenses and receipts were as follows:

Transport by Truck of 2 *Fanegas*	16	pesos
Personal Round-Trip Fare	12	pesos
Food in San Cristóbal	2	pesos
Total Expenses of Trip	30	pesos
Receipts from Sale of 2 *Fanegas*	250	pesos
"Profit" from Trip	220	pesos

However, he would have received 230 pesos for his maize had he sold it in Las Rosas and, thus, as a result of his trip, he incurred a loss of 10 pesos. It is notable that the maize price in the above example (125 pesos per *fanega* or about 1,037 pesos per ton) is much higher than the government price. Records at the San Cristóbal warehouse in 1961 showed that virtually all maize was bought by ANDSA during the surplus-period, January-April. It appears that the ANDSA prices are attractive only during this period and that in periods of scarcity during the year most maize is exchanged outside the ANDSA system.

---

19. These Indians operate widely and openly in this sphere of activity. When the author questioned ANDSA personnel about this, they replied that nothing is done to prevent the Zinacantecos from such dealings since they buy and sell in "such small quantities." There apparently is not, however, any regulation stating the minimum amounts of maize which may be exchanged outside the government system.

As the example of maize marketing illustrates, the modern system is highly complex—usually beyond the Indian's comprehension—and so demanding of capital that the Indian is virtually excluded from full participation and benefit. The Indian knows well the lesson that *el dinero va a abundar cada vez mas* ("money makes money"), not from his own experience, but from observing the *ladino*. The example also indicates that the absence of a spirit of economic cooperation among peasants in Las Rosas severely limits their capabilities to compete in the modern system. Even *ejidatarios* do not operate joint economic ventures. According to the 1950 *Censo Agrícola, Ganadero y Ejidal*, there were no Las Rosas *ejidatarios* who belonged to any *ejido* associations for credit or agricultural production. The president of the Ejido Villa Las Rosas told the author that for *ejido* members to sell cooperatively on a large scale would require an organization the size and complexity of which they do not possess. Indians frequently mention the absence of cooperation in various contexts. For example,

The communal lands north of town are now being invaded by the cattle belonging to Manuel Diaz. The people aren't sufficiently united to take measures such as fencing the land or combining forces to keep the cattle out. *Bienes Comunales* never does anything effectively.

The "lack of knowledge" among Las Rosas Indians and their "inability to cooperate" was discouraging to one Indian who had returned to Las Rosas after having been "outside" for many years learning about the modern system:

I never became an *agrarista* [*ejido* member] because I don't like it. On the coast [Pacific coast of Chiapas] it was very different. There you appoint a president of a committee and have a meeting and they don't all talk at the same time like they do here. Here they have no order to talk. Nobody can hear. The people here don't know how to discuss anything. On the *fincas* [on the coast] a person has to ask permission from the president of the committee to talk. On the *fincas* I was a union member. I have always like organizations. Here in Pinola [Las Rosas] there are no unions. Tomas Solis and Jose de la Cruz wanted to start a union for *panela* but I believe it can't be done because the union has to be organized. Besides the *panela* is only seasonal and not year around activity like on the *fincas*. And it would be difficult to cover the expenses here. And besides, how could we force the rich *ladinos* to buy *panela* from us. There is no law for that. What would be good here is a cooperative store. When several people get together and each one puts up 100 or 200 pesos and they buy things for a little store and then sell and share the benefits, then you have a cooperative. Here it couldn't be done because the people don't understand.

There's a need to divide up more communal land, but it can't be done due to the lack of cooperation among the people. The people aren't going to help. Nobody is going to take money out of his pocket to help.[20]

In contrast to the general absence of effective economic cooperation among Indians, wealthy *ladinos*, especially within their families, characteristically pool their resources, most conspicuously their capital goods, which reflect their considerably diverse activities. Even the upper-class *ladino* women engage in large entrepreneurial ventures. Members of perhaps the wealthiest *ladino* family in Las Rosas own trucks, maize mills, ranches, stores, pool-halls, theaters, and other real estate and equipment. Although their several trucks are

owned individually, they are shared or exchanged within the family to meet specialized needs, thereby affecting considerable "internal economies."

Ladinos form cooperatives to buy and sell maize and to receive credit from banks such as the Banco Nacional de Crédito Agrícola and the Financiera de Oaxaca—institutions which prefer creditors to form societies whose members have "unlimited liability." Large investment loans, generally at between 9 and 12 per cent per annum, are usually taken from banks provided collateral is available. Normally, credit up to one-third the value of the property is extended with the remission of the deed. To the author's knowledge, no Indians have obtained credit from recognized banking institutions. Most small loans are made by local individuals who charge rates which are considerably higher than those of banks, although some local *ladinos* borrow from one another for as little as 1 1/2 per cent per month. Most *ladinos* will lend to other *ladinos* for about 2 or 3 per cent per month, but Indians pay 5, 10, and even 20 per cent per month when borrowing from local *ladinos*. Such usurious discrimination is but another factor which widens the economic gulf between *ladinos* and Indians.

Since there is no appreciable economic cooperation among the Indians, it is virtually axiomatic that none occurs between Indians and *ladinos*. The *ladino*-Indian interaction in the economic sphere does not constitute cooperation in the sense of planned benefit to all interacting parties. Both *ladinos* and Indians accept the fact of economic interdependence, but mutual suspicion characteristically accompanies situations in which they meet.

In economic interaction as well as in all other types of bicultural contact, the Indian is always cast in the subordinate role—hardly a propitious situation for cooperative action.

---

20. This trait suggests a parallel with Edward Banfield's "society of amoral familists" in which "no one will further the interest of the group or community except as it is to his private advantage to do so" and "organization (i.e., deliberately concerted action) will be very difficult to achieve and maintain." There are, however, too many inconsistencies, too numerous to relate here, to grant a general similarity between Las Rosas society and the Italian peasant society described by Banfield. Edward C. Banfield. *The Moral Basis of a Backward Society* (Glencoe, Ill.: The Free Press, 1958), pp. 85-89.

The social distance between Indians and *ladinos* is particularly great in informal and unorganized situations in which individuals meet and, even on more "structured" occasions such as *ejido* meetings or the community celebrations of national holidays, the *ladinos* "perform the role of indulgent patronizers."[21] Even in legal matters, the Indian's position is jeopardized by the usurpation of the authority of the *alcalde* by the *presidente municipal*—an office which usually has been occupied by *ladinos*; the last Indian *presidente*, although not born in Las Rosas, was shot in the plaza in the 1930's.

The *ladino's* ethnic prejudice against Indians is a serious barrier to the integration of the community. The Indian's disenchantment and suspicion resulting from this discrimination has instilled in him a kind of protective "rugged individualism," the manifestations of which are not aggressiveness but rather passivity and uncooperativeness—traits which are exemplified in the following comment by an Indian:

> Don Jorge Ruiz, a past *presidente municipal*, worked well, and began the highway. But not everybody cooperated because they knew that the President of the Republic says one doesn't have to help if one isn't paid. I helped but only once for 3 days and when the *presidente* asked me I said I wasn't an *ejidatario* and that I was very poor. So he pardoned me. The people didn't want to make the highway because the owners of the trucks make the most business. Anyway, do I go free anywhere on the road? I go because I have the money, and if I don't have it, I don't go. So the people had a good reason for not wanting to give their service.

In sum, although the Indian segment of the community has a cultural cohesion reinforced by its own moral and social sanctions (about which more will be said later), there is no effective moral solidarity of the bicultural community as a whole. Clearly this condition is an important impediment to community-wide cooperative efforts (such as working on the road) which are designed to bring about "modernization" or economic and social change.

The egalitarian norm of the Indian culture promotes the cultural solidarity of the Indian community, but it also militates against material progress for the community as a whole and fosters economic inequality between Indians and *ladinos*. Contrary to a basic tenet of *ladino* ideology, the Indian code opposes "excessive" personal acquisitiveness which may cause economic disequilibrium within the group. This is not to say that individual Indians do not strive to better their economic positions. The Indian rationalizes his economic effort but the resulting wealth is channelled away from capital savings by features of the social organization.[22] Calling an Indian a hard worker is tantamount to calling him a good man. Cooperation for economic advancement between peasant families rarely extends beyond the form of labor exchange *(prestar mano)*. Within Indian families there is considerable pooling of goods to advantage, but the generally low level of wealth and the social sanctions and organization reinforcing equality impede progress.

What are some of the important organizational features and social sanctions of Indian culture which help to maintain the egalitarian norm? Nash has pointed out that the "inheritance mechanism tends to fragment such estates as are accumulated,"[23] but this mechanism also operates in *ladino* society. The argument that one's obligations to

21. Hermitte, *op. cit.*, p. 37.

22. Manning Nash, "The Social Context of Economic Choice in a Small Society," *Man*, LXI, Art. 219 (November, 1961), 186-91.

23. Manning Nash, "The Small Scale Economy: The Context of Economic Choice," in Report on the "Man-in-Nature" (Project of the Departments of Anthropology and Geography, University of Chicago, 1959), III, 9. (Hectographed.)

members of the "extended family" are a serious barrier to capital saving has been attacked by Nash,[24] and for Las Rosas, too, it appears that other impediments are far more serious. Indeed, "extended families may be important in the initial aggregation of capital and also in the channelling of investment."[25] In Las Rosas, however, this appears to be generally true only for nuclear or closely related families of both *ladinos* and Indians. Frank Cancian, from his studies among the Zinacantecos, reports that the same families have for several generations held the highest and most expensive offices of the Indian civil-religious hierarchy.[26] One might conclude that, although these public offices which require large personal expenditures act as an economic levelling mechanism, they do not, at least in Zinacantan, dissipate wealth to the point that a family cannot retain its relatively high economic position in the community.

Las Rosas Indians no longer climb the expensive ladder of public office—the Indian religious hierarchy disappeared at least thirty years ago and the influence of the civil hierarchy has greatly diminished. However, if an Indian succeeds in accumulating a little capital, there remain informal but nevertheless culturally-sanctioned methods of public expenditure. For example, one wealthy Las Rosas Indian celebrates his "Saint's Day" every year with a "lavish" fiesta which is attended by the Indian community. In fact, the people expect this man to hold his fiesta because he is able to do so; if he did not, he likely would be accused of greed or would be envied, which usually results in witchcraft. Indians often tell of an Indian man who accumulated 5,000 pesos and then used it to buy a bell for the church. Such "informal" acts probably enable relatively rich men to maintain their status within the Indian community without having to fear witchcraft.

Supernatural sanctioning is perhaps the most important factor operating to maintain the egalitarian norm among Las Rosas Indians.[27] Clearly an Indian may accumulate capital and invest it in animals or *sitios*, but there are limits of "conspicuous consumption"[28] beyond which he dare not go. The reader will note that it is fear of envy and witchcraft[29] and not necessarily lack of money which prevents the Indian from building a house like a *ladino's*. Esther Hermitte writes that

Adherence by the Indians to the norms of the Tzeltal community is reinforced by supernatural sanctions. The power to punish by witchcraft, attributed to men of strong spirit, is the most effective means of social control in this area.[30]

Nash has suggested that witchcraft is the largest and most formidable obstacle to economic growth among Chiapas Indians.[31]

---

24. Manning Nash, "Some Social and Cultural Aspects of Economic Development," *Economic Development and Cultural Change*, VII, No. 2 (January, 1959), 143.

25. *Ibid.*

26. Personal communication, 1961. See Frank Cancian, "Informant Error and Native Prestige Ranking in Zinacantan," *American Anthropologist*, LXV, No. 5 (October, 1963), 1069; and also his "Economics and Prestige in a Maya Community: A Study of the Religious Cargo System in Zinacantan, Chiapas, Mexico" (unpublished Ph.D. dissertation, Harvard University, 1962).

27. For a detailed analysis of the operation of supernatural controls in Las Rosas, see Hermitte, *op. cit.*

28. I use this term in the general sense in which Veblen introduced it.

29. In Amatenango, for example, "at least one man is killed every two months for being a practitioner of witchcraft." Nash, "The Social Context . . . ," p. 191.

30. Hermitte, *op. cit.*, pp. 27-28. For a description of the operation of witchcraft and a trial of a witch-slayer, see Manning Nash, "Witchcraft as Social Process in a Tzeltal Community," in Report on the "Man-in-Nature" Project, *op. cit.*

31. Nash, "The Small Scale . . . ," p. 13.

It helps to "inhibit economic expansion of any given unit within the society under the threat of expulsion or sacral retribution," and therefore helps to insure the perpetuation of a "democracy of poverty."[32]

The Indian still lives in accordance with his own cultural system—historically speaking, an amalgam of indigenous culture and of traits assimilated through 400 years since the Conquest. Very recently, a new wave of cultural alternatives has broken upon the Las Rosas region bringing about a weakening of the traditional system. But until the Indian more completely adapts to the modern system, he will remain only a marginal participant and beneficiary of that system. The modern system places heavy demands for dramatic change upon the Indian. History provides a clue as to what may be the Indian's future if he cannot accommodate and adapt quickly enough to the rapidly encroaching system:

The Indian [in the United States] had to go. Unable, unwilling to use more than 1 per cent of the continental resources, he had to yield to the race which was willing and able to exploit, con-

sume, waste or dissipate, in two centuries, the accretion of the historic and geologic past. . . .

The Indian lost two-thirds of his reservation lands largely because he could not adapt his culture and economy fast enough to conform to the white methods of exploiting the continental natural resources. Where he made the adaptation, where he proceeded to exploit the natural resources in his possession commercially by and for himself, there he retained possession of his lands.[33]

The culture of modern Mexico has been advancing into the Las Rosas region, particularly during the past decade along the road it built to gain quick passage. The evidences of this advance are reflected in the changing cultural landscape. The landscape which once bore only the imprint of traditional Indian culture, modified by that of the Spaniard, now is beginning to suggest the mark of a very different society. Landscape changes, intimately linked to cultural processes, portray, and perhaps portend, man's changing design for life.

32. *Ibid.*, p. 9.

33. Quoted by Morton H. Fried in "Land Tenure, Geography and Ecology in the Contact of Cultures," in Wagner and Mikesell, *op. cit.*, p. 304, from Walter V. Woelke, "Indian Land Tenure, Economic Status and Population Trends," *Report on Land Planning*, Part X (Washington, D.C.: U.S. Government Printing Office, 1935), p. 2.

✦✦✦✦✦✦✦✦✦✦✦✦✦✦✦✦✦✦✦✦✦✦✦✦✦✦✦✦✦

CULTURAL LANDSCAPES AND REGIONS: ASPECTS OF COMMUNICATION

Philip L. Wagner

Environment in Communication
The cultural divisions of the world, however we delimit them, have evolved through communication of ideas—from father to son; among neighbors; through emigrants and traders; by way of pictures, songs, and books. Properly we study culture history, as we call the greater outlines of the origins and

To appear in the forthcoming *Geoscience and Man*, Vol. V, the Kniffen volume, edited by Bob F. Perkins. Printed by special arrangement with Louisiana State University Press.

dispersals of cultural ideas. With reason, too, we seek to understand the regularities of process by which a given innovation may diffuse through spatial fields. For communication reaches to the core of cultural geography.

Great stress is justly placed, of late, upon "spatial perception," by which is mostly meant what given environmental exposures communicate to specific human groups. Environment communicates; indeed, all communication has to reach its human target through his sensory (environmental) field. The problem of environment's capacity to transmit what we may call ideas in fact includes and transcends the lesser one of any particular recipient's perceptions of them. Consideration of environments—landscapes and societies—in this respect again reveals communication reaching to the core of cultural geography.

Artifact morphologies akin to those of cultural geography, especially in the case of fine and minor arts, have always had to do pre-eminently with heavily expressive subject matters. Although the immediately expressive element in artifacts is often clear, geographers have seldom given it its due, preferring—when, indeed, they did advance beyond mere formalism—sometimes to connect morphology with more abstract (and often dubiously relevant) ideological themes, and sometimes to confine their interest to perceptual responses. The expressive qualities of environments and their component parts, rooted in human aspiration and intention, are certainly now ripe for geographic study, and once again, represent communication at the core of cultural geography.

Recent advances in so-called "multi-media" techniques attest the not astonishing discovery by communications specialists, educators, artists, and advertisers that environments embody more than one communication channel, in fact a great and vari-

able multitude of them, and that some or all may operate together in a harmonious way. This should have struck geographers a long time since. If "the medium is the message," then any man's environment is in turn a great and variegated, synergetic medium. The term, "medium of communication," in this context, implies only the immediate source of sense stimuli, however; backing up and feeding into any such immediate environmental source of stimuli, a chain of connections often runs away into distant space and times forgotten. A whole unique geography and history as well belong to each communicating element of an individual's environment. This particular sort of geography itself may claim to participate in the core of the cultural discipline.

Presumably, it would be worthwhile to distinguish among those elements of any environment that are intentionally expressive, those only conventionally expressive (e.g., sunsets and "majestic" mountains), and those not expressive in themselves at all. Likewise, communicative elements may be discriminated according to their connections with various external systems—their origins or contemporary linkages. The environmental manifold of communication thus breaks down into various components, each to be examined in its own right when desired. Certainly some analytic approach is necessary if the implications of communication for the cultural situation are to be grasped.

In a special but important sense, all interaction with environment can be regarded as communication. "Information" (in its modern technical sense) is generated by the interaction of organism with habitat. This point is far from trivial, and in fact deserves to monopolize the following section.

Environmental Learning

At the outset, let us set the notion of human "activity" apart from that of human "behavior." The first may be described in strictly physical terms; the second may not. Activity belongs to all animate, and at least some inanimate, nature. Behavior, however, consists of acts; and acts have meaning; and meaning is engendered and maintained exclusively within and by some system of communication. Human beings can learn activities and they can learn behavior.

It is uncomfortable to write about learning, because the topic formicates with controversies. But we can say that an individual, by learning, acquires enough mastery of a given pattern of activity or behavior that he can initiate and carry it through quite readily and independently of supervision. He learns what we here call an activity by trial and error interaction with his physical surroundings, the latter acting as his coach and critic in that they respond in such a way as to inhibit, or enhance and facilitate, his efforts. In the course of the individual's learning, the environment he has been learning in may itself become somewhat modified to accommodate his activity.

If the learning involves what we call behavior, then it invokes and responds to the critical and guiding influences of communication with other humans—actual or imaginary—as well as physical constraints. As an individual learns behavior, the society, or communicating group of human beings in whose care he learns, also may be modified somewhat, accommodating to his presence and behavior.

Learning thus described is nothing less than repeated, formative communication between an individual and his environment, to some extent affecting and reshaping both. Trial and error is the main procedure, and a kind of environmental selection operates upon what man attempts.

What can be said of the activity or behavior learned by individuals in trial and error interaction with environments may

possibly be said as well of that of whole societies operating in a concerted way. Human social units, too, discover for themselves as units the limits of the physically possible, and also test out and adjust to unitary roles within a yet larger social universe. Societies may be held to "learn," insofar at least as they are affected and reshaped by interaction with environments, and their repertory of behavior is influenced accordingly. Not "environment," but dialectic interaction with environment, is decisive for them.

There are thus potentially two avenues of approach to the study of aggregate behavior in societies, as adjusted with environments. On the one hand, the society itself, or the lesser social groups, may well display, in the forms and practices of ordinary life, results of the "learning" speculatively here suggested—what earlier geographers might well have designated "adaptation to environment." On the other hand, the one identical environment of many individuals, affording closely similar experiences in trial and error, may produce a high degree of similarity among its denizens. Either one or both of these effects may contribute to phenomenon we call culture, which, significantly, is notoriously areal in nature.

"Culture" implies, among other things, something such as "the usual observed behavior of a group of people sharing in the same environment"—qualified as to degree, of course. It also suggests, to be sure, "learned behavior," with certain further qualifications, and this again leads back toward environment. The concepts of culture and of environment, both eminently and necessarily areal, can hardly avoid contracting some close relationship.

"Trial and error learning" is too rudimentary a notion, for the "trials" involved are manifestly not random, unintentional, and empty of any significance of their own.

They rest on motives, i.e., "something makes them happen." Since the subject of motivation is at least as fluctuous a study as learning itself, however, we shall do best simply to allege that the motives of most trials involved in learning are overwhelmingly communicated socially. This comes close to an assertion that by far the greater part of what men try and learn is behavior, rather than mere activity, according to our previous distinction. Man is very "cultural."

The learning process here so crudely summarized proceeds toward a readjustment among surrounding local forces—physical or social—and the individual. Its outcome is inherently local and particular, in effect enabling the individual to fit into a certain specialized ecological niche. Through communication, however, the ecology of learning becomes enormously more complex. A person tries and learns to live in his own little setting largely on the basis of outside ideas. Furthermore, habits learned in one locality are carried with him elsewhere, and passed on to others. (The term "idea" somehow connotes such a distillate of habit or behavior, actual or potential, thus released from its immediate material context, free to roam and change men's ways.)

It may seem odd to think of localities, as such, affecting each other. Yet if we allow that local circumstances do condition learning, by communication one place gives the pattern for another. I venture to call this one of the two key points of cultural geography. Half our subject is the export-import trade in human experience.

Geographers now vaguely sense an excess in their holy zeal against environmentalism. It is clearly time to say that our environments constrain, select, and shape activity and behavior. Man proposes, God disposes. Otherwise we all should live in purest fantasy-land. Geographical adjustments (which are nothing but experience in context) are the stuff of culture. Once we cease to conceive the "social" as disconnected from all the rest of our experience, "culture" loses its peculiarly incorporeal and extramundane aura, and comes down to earth where it belongs. Through the effects of learning—and learned behavior is pretty much what we mean by culture—human beings do "respond" and "adapt" to environment: not simply to the environment of the moment, though, but to all those countless local environments in which they have learned in the past, and in which those who taught them have learned (and so on back forever).

The venerable notion that environment teaches and forms society has never disappeared, despite geography's demurrers. In a surprisingly crude guise, it dominates the policy and practice of many influential architects and planners now. Almost all the great contemporary architectural theorists have been enthusiastic environmental determinists. Their faith deserves our notice, and suggests a lesson.

The Morality of Landscape

The melioristic vision of the architects calls for the improvement of the material, moral, and aesthetic quality of human life through improvement in environmental design. This point of view is not too different from the Marxist-Leninist faith in the transformation of nature as the key to human betterment, except that it presumably leans more on learning. It is to be noted that in both accepted doctrines, not merely the momentary lot of man is bettered, but a moral transformation results in the human being himself through the influence of his superior environment. I should like to venture the suggestion that all societies tend to hold and to actualize a somewhat similar conception of the man-environment relation, i.e., that peoples everywhere and throughout history have regarded some particular sort of environment as uniquely conducive to the good life, and have labored to create it.

Cultural geographers may view a landscape as imperfectly substantiating a society's ideal environment. Its forms, proportions, orientation, and properties are meant to be the very map and pattern for correct, harmonious behavior, and to give the model by which such behavior may be learned. It is hard, even for a stranger, not to fall into the prescribed routes and rhythms, and rapidly to trim his ways to local property and propriety as symbolized all round him. Words need hardly intervene. Even so, and more so, does a child acquire behavior in familiar milieux. Yet coming upon the empty stage we often miss the sense of the drama; we try in vain to guess, to feel the import of the local life when visiting the vacant scenes of its performances. A place or a landscape declares its underlying intent, and its ideal meaning, when living people activate it and actualize it. Otherwise it may be nearly mute.

It is probably the rule that communities conceive behavior with its time and place ordained; consider, for example, worship, lovemaking, or feasting in North American societies. The seasons, furthermore, are known according to their tasks and joys, all having proper situation; and even lifetimes are divided according to succeeding phases of residence and occupation. Likewise, each place and parcel of land is the scene of expected performances, in work or amusement, by a stated company at due times. The very "person," moreover, amounts largely to an individual configuration that has been compounded of the places, times, and actions of a life. It is only in connection with declared rituals, apparently, that we accord full recognition to this intimate fourfold relationship that binds together time, place, act, and man—making each, in good

degree, the function and expression of the other three reciprocal determinants. Yet every culture's ideal maps inscribe these complex designations on imaginary landscapes that foreshadow real ones. And such assignments of identity and intention are at least partially echoed and repeated in the multiple media of the place names; visual symbolisms; attendant instruments and structures; associated popular usages, customs, and observances; and even evidence like weeds, of the brute response of nature to disturbance of its realms. The forms of landscape and the norms of behavior are congruent.

The very intricacy of a long-developed landscape, subtle and complex, may well defy and frustrate productive study. How is one to grasp it and explain it? Sometimes, when a man is fortunate enough to gain full admittance into a culture not his own, he may sense all of a sudden the eloquence of every previously-neglected gesture, and see the portent of all the things that, heretofore unnoticed, now surround him with a world of delicate and varied meanings. But can experience like this ever be transmitted to a stranger? Alas, research must do more than merely transmute the ineffable into the inane.

Cultural geographers may taste as private pleasures all the involutions of a living landscape, and find delight in intimations of the ideal order they obey. The common task, however, is to learn and teach whatever is of general significance and use about particular communities, landscapes, and cultures. A local folk, their home and ways, with due respect, must stand for more than quirks and whims. The cultural process of learning and teaching, rather than the peculiar (and momentary) cultural content should, I propose, always be the major focus of the cultural geographer's investigations.

Such a stricture need not annul all in-

terest in the rich suggestiveness of landscapes. Quite the contrary: the roles of landscape content in symbolic discourse, and as
part of what defines behavior, are of major
consequence. Landscape, like and with behavior, instructs and informs. The most
attractive objects of all for geographic study
are expressive landscape features, and the
structures of exterior connection feeding
into them. Such, with the people themselves,
are sources of culture.

Features and Structures of Communication

An organism in its habitat acquires activity
patterns conforming to its own genetic potentials and accommodated to environmental forces and constraints. Thus also
man's activities develop. The child of man,
however, is early caught up in an intense and
continual sensory interchange with other
human beings that will last his life long, and
which soon takes over his behavioral development. The early genesis and foundation
of his behavior and his culture can be
sought, first of all, among those human
beings with whom he is so soon and so long
in communication face to face. The circle of
impinging persons widens, initially from
parents to the kin, and neighbors, then as
the child's mobility increases, his direct
encounters multiply and diversify. His behavior becomes more versatile accordingly.
But those with whom he lives and plays and
later works—who in most societies even yet
are still his nuclear family and nearest kin—
continue to communicate most amply with
him and to dominate his learning.

Such we may imagine to have been, until
quite recent centuries, the usual structure of
communication and the source of culture for
most people, as it is today for those in the
many small, remote, and isolated communities that still survive. As even now, in former
times expressive artificial features of environment played a part as well in education;
but their range and reference was of vastly
different magnitude. The settlement itself,
the fields and gardens, houses, tools and
weapons, costumes and paraphernalia, ampli-
fying learning, brought the individual into
contact with the work of vanished craftsmen
and builders, the ancestors, whose presence
thus, and through renown, weighed heavily
upon the living.

Whoever travels, or is visited with frequency by strangers, may of course enjoy
expanded opportunities for learning. A village some of whose inhabitants often venture abroad is opener to new ideas, as is a
place much frequented by traders. Geographically and culturally, the degree of
isolation, or its reciprocal, the intensity of
intercourse with the outside, is of the greatest moment. It is, to be sure, not merely the
magnitude but also the character of extrinsic
influence that count. For any one community, its relative degree of isolation being
given, a geography of influential intercourse
is implied, and with it an associated history.
Particular connections count, and have particular consequences for culture and landscape.

Artifacts from afar can hardly fail to play
a part in imparting something to a culture.
Their function therein may depart altogether
from the implicit intentions of their
makers, or even their importers, yet often
enough they will continue to express a sense
implanted into them deliberately. Any discussion of such communicative artifacts,
indeed, must take account of quantitative
variations in the content of deliberate expression in them. Artistic creations, as well
as all representational design and literary
material, heavily loaded with intentional
significance, have special potency as agents
of communication, as well as being highly
durable. The inventory of such products in a
community's environment indicates its

further cultural capacities—interpreted in light of the given structure of communication. The cultural and geographic implications of such a topic as community literacy, or the role of formal schools, are recognizably enormous. In this instance, too, the character as well as the magnitude of influence is crucial.

A communicative situation and the potential cultural development of a country, a community, or even an individual, may be assessed more or less realistically on the basis of face-to-face encounters, intrinsic expression in material environment, and extrinsic influences manifested either directly through environmental features (artifacts) or mediated by other individuals. But what will diagnose the cultural base-line, the instantaneous state of communications, at which we must begin to measure change? Persons and societies are already formed and functioning when first we come upon them. Perhaps established patterns in the landscape, and customary patterns of behavior, may present themselves with adequate fidelity and frequency to give a start for observation. Eventually those patterns, by the methods of the culture historian, may themselves be scrutinized for traces of their earlier careers within a different universe of communication, and antecedent patterns also reconstructed.

Many different agencies usually take part simultaneously in communication, varying in impact and importance, within advanced communities. The resulting complexity raises crucial and far-reaching geographic problems. Modern artifactural surrogates for face-to-face encounter—television, radio, and cinema in particular—come as eloquent, imposing strangers whom one can hear without reply. Their spell and potency are notorious; their uniqueness lies in being at one time both institutional and intimate. The geographical relationships of these

media are wildly askew, making havoc of any accepted principles of spatial contiguity or continuity. And such media, operating in conjunction with all the other kinds, carry their share and sector of the message traffic as part of innumerable, ever-recombining segments of systems or hybrid chains of varied media. A stolen letter begets a broadcast that begins a whispered rumor that arouses a parade of protest-placards.

Roughly speaking, every sort of medium thus may form a segment of a greater chain, combined with like or unlike others instantaneously. A host of pathways, variously selected and combined, may be in operation at a given moment, all picked out by circumstances from the great interconnecting network of internodal links of all sorts.

No need here to detail the actual technical facilities of communication, which are in the main well known, nor to recount their particular geographies. The social geographic structure of communication does, however, call for more discussion.

Social Geography of Communication

The whisper rather than the shout epitomizes man's communication patterns. Communication among men tends to be selective, directed, and contextual. The image of a broadcast, or indiscriminate diffusion of messages, is largely a misrepresentation. As a speaker addresses a definite listener and chooses an appropriate occasion, so most communication is channeled straight from originator to recipient, and transmitted with due consideration of the circumstances. Even a broadcaster has a definite audience in mind. Established habit ordains certain preferential pairs and groups to function in communication linkage, and established precedence assigns the initiative and discretion in the process to some participants while denying them to others. The system generally is hierarchical, and this confers on it directional properties. A given party, subordinate to another, may be permitted only to receive messages, and (as in the case of radio, for example) may be sufficiently equiped technically only to do so, whereas a sender controls the content entirely. Even with technical parity, the relationship is commonly uneven or asymmetrical in this fashion.

Almost all social institutions are agencies of communication. Their functions in communication are adjusted to the geographic pattern of their territorial structure and jurisdiction. Thus such social units as national or local governments, business organizations, and armies occupy themselves very largely with communication, and even institutions like the family, age-set, and work gang are equally absorbed in that function. Even the smaller, spatially restricted systems operate in a highly differentiated way. Some specific members, usually centrally located, give the orders, conduct the inquiries, make the proclamations in the name of the group.

A "directed" network (as the corresponding graph would be called), such as the above sort, links the individuals of an institution in communication. The links ("edges" of the graph) between members of the social group ("vertices" or nodes) can consist of any of many different technical devices, and not all need by any means be similar. Every conceivable mechanism of communication may function as part of one great network; an idea first set out in a diplomatic conversation may proceed to its effect by way of coded cable, airmail pouch, and muleback courier in order to compose a minor boundary disagreement. Every new transmission may select a fresh unprecedented pathway over the infinite variety of linkages.

Any community except the most remote or primitive is caught in the many nets of different and often uncoordinate institutional communication, and almost any in-

dividual is similarly connected into many separate lines of communication. What a ravel of geographies this is, and how hard to disentangle! The less isolated is a place or person, of course, the greater the multiplicity of alternate communication linkages available to it or him, and the more flexible their combinations. Probably, too, some pronounced effects upon behavior follow from decrease of isolation. Hypothetically, a series of important relationships might seem to apply:

The volume of communication incoming to a place or person should be roughly inverse in proportion to the isolation (in fact this is a postulate for measuring isolation, apart from mere physical remoteness).

The variety of communications reaching a person or place should increase as nearly a direct function of volume.

The diversity of behavior patterns among the whole population of a place, or in the repertory of a person, should express some positive relationship with variety of communications, and thus be correlated directly with their volume, and inversely with isolation. This should pertain, *inter alia*, to the specialized division of labor.

Furthermore, allowing that behavior implies norms, the degree of homogeneity of landscape features in a place, or the relative monotony of an individual's possessions and material surroundings, should be directly proportional to their isolation. This might likewise affect the breadth of resource use, and derivatively, wealth, as well.

Through any short interval of time, the rate of cultural change should express in some fashion a direct relation with the existing volume and variety of communication.

In the longer historical perspective, cultural and geographic change should correlate inversely with degree of isolation.

Such propositions may seem like truisms, but they remain contingencies rather than tautologies. They contain certain implicit premises of dubious validity. These relationships have of course often been asserted for concrete instances, but probably never subjected to adequate logical formulation and empirical verification. Given an acceptable set of physical measures of isolation, it should be possible, with suitable controls, to test them.

One has good reason to suspect a dangerous oversimplification in the foregoing hypotheses, however. In empirical ethnography, their implication of cultural impoverishment and monotony as concommitants of isolation is not consistently borne out. Analogously, a reclusive individual need not, as well we know, be undereducated, indigent, or stereotyped in manner. These hypotheses, therefore, ought not to be hastily and uncritically embraced, for they conceal at least one major fallacy: the hidden and ridiculous premise that a place can be isolated from itself.

Communities of even modest size may undergo largely endogenous development with impressive results, just as individuals on occasion can achieve a high degree of cultivation and versatility privately at home. The native heritage, communicated down through time unbroken, may to a large degree supplant exogenous sources of initiative. No doubt we ought to count tranquility, or rather continuity in peace, as on occasion just as favorable a circumstance as wide communication for the flowering of culture.

Internal evolution of a culture, a society, or a landscape, of course, proceeds while interchange goes on externally. Conflicting tendencies are likely to arise in this situation, expressing what have long been recognized in geography as centrifugal and centripetal forces.

Some Dialectical Processes

An imbalance of functions inheres in the disparity of roles in all acts of communication. The various tensions and stresses commonly resulting therefrom offer to cultural geography some of its most arresting problems, to which we may allude here briefly.

The very medium of communication, such as a natural language, itself is not infrequently the subject or the content of communication. More precisely, linguistic norms tend to be propagated expressly, over various networks or channels of communication. In the rather common case in which a national elite attempts to spread and impose a uniform literary or colloquial standard for a language, divergent regional forms, derived from independent dialects or from *ad hoc* recasting of the standard patterns, or from both sources, often survive and compete successfully in at least certain social circles and speech contexts. The key to this persistent rivalry lies in the use, by the proponents of the respective norms, of different if parallel communication vehicles. The standard language usually is disseminated in the schools, the press and electronic media, the courts, the military service, and similar institutions of a national, centralizing tendency in general, while the local vernacular continues to be imparted in the home, the playground, the market, and other such situations of informal face-to-face contact among local people. Given that this contrast and resulting differentiation of the speech forms takes place everywhere and all the while, every language will develop slang and dialects a little differently everywhere until a host of recognizably distinct usages, and with time a set of separate languages, comes into being; the standard, formalized and assiduously maintained, may persist so long and well as to outlive by far its last native speakers and become a purely literary or liturgical language, as have Latin, Attic Greek, and Sanskrit. Thus we see the implication of the ceaseless warfare in the classroom, pitting teacher-talk against the living language of the schoolyard.

The geographical consequence of such linguistic tensions is that even if no extraneous speech communities intruded themselves into an area, as has periodically occurred almost everywhere, the language map would become diversified in time by this decay and local drift. When speakers of descendant dialects then subsequently move around, and re-settle elsewhere carrying in their speech the evidence of earlier affiliation, they can rather easily be identified. The first-instanced kind of linguistic diversification takes place, almost certainly, as a purely space-dependent phenomenon. The rate of drift away from the initial homogeneous pattern is apparently everywhere essentially the same, and the direction taken is presumably quite random for each change, and surely altogether independent of gross influences of the physical environment. We may therefore consult it as a specially convenient paradigm of cultural development in general, which can be modified in accord with the selectivity of physical environments and the massive circulation of ideas to which any community is in some degree exposed as it communicates with the outside. Even dialect development is far from a purely endogenous evolution, but it is a suggestive approximation of one.

A second example of a tension expressing itself in striking geographic form occurs in the domain of religions. In this case, local physical and social circumstances do undoubtedly exert a major influence on rustic provincial cults that in time come to distort and even directly contradict the nominal pure faith. Ancient local gods may reappear as assimilated saints, although perhaps uncanonized and only regional. Tribal medicine men upon their death become elevated to saintly status, and their tombs attract pilgrimages. Soothsayers and magicians corrupt the rituals in copying them, and turn the liturgy to awesome spells. Religious reformers and monkish bureaucrats are always railing and crusading against analogous impurities of faith and worship in the realms of any of the world religions. The detailed geographic picture of the sects and local cults of any great religion — still to be filled in — would surely show effects of both the secular decay exemplified in language areas, and the powerful impact of local nature and ancestral custom, in diversifying religious ideas and usages.

Both linguistic and religious tensions of the sorts described ordinarily result in an accommodation among diverse parties, rather than total victory for one of the contenders. The standard language thus becomes the dialect appointed for use by certain persons in given situations, and the strict canonical religion becomes the expected doctrinal position and ritual practice of the religious professionals and a few derided purists. Here the dialectical principle can be interpreted concretely as the assimilation of the conflict into the manifold of environment, composed of integral complexes of place, time, act, and man.

A like divisive tendency plagues political institutions. Local interests and powers grow apart from national rulers; segments of the bureaucratic structure inveterately exploit their ambiguous position to enlarge their own autonomy. These problems plague especially the newer, less robust states, which are further handicapped, for the most part, in lacking any pretence of united ethnic foundations for nationhood. Geographical fragmentation in some of these cases may *de facto* prove so great as to promote secessions and rebellions and foredoom the state.

The political example is useful as an indication of another principle. It illustrates the relationship of geographical scale to the maintenance of unified communities, under various circumstances of communication. Rival communication systems are at the base of regional dissidence and separatism in many precariously stable countries. Differences of language play a major role. Even more perhaps does the almost universal preponderance of rather rustic face-to-face connections at the local scale over those inherent in either the more centralizing technical communication media or a reasonable dense and regular internal traffic defeat large-scale integration. The geography of their communications is the crux of the crisis in such countries.

The classical dichotomy between nature and culture, although in some respects perhaps invalid, does point up a genuine and fateful dialectic. In Nature we perceive endogenous and native forces, and in Culture those that are exogenous and alien. They are ever at war, and a landscape is their dubious truce. Man creates by encroaching on Nature and enslaving her processes, and Nature works to assimilate or annihilate what man creates. It is culture that make man a stranger in the world wherever he lives. His ways are at odds with all his surroundings, and he must hold these at bay and force them to yield to his will or he perishes. Mankind's power in this struggle lies in the cultural sharing of experience, inherited and communicated freely.

The master theme of all human geography is man's transformation of environment, with all its promises and perils. We seek not only to describe it as it appears in its countless local guises, but with proper caution to evalute it and predict its consequences. Today, of course, this corresponding ecological concern becomes most timely. But the theme of human geographic

transformations has commonly been treated from the standpoint of entire communities and large culture areas. It may with equal reason be developed at the level of the individual person, for indeed all geographic change must ultimately rest upon the personal aspirations and initiatives of individuals. Accordingly, through seeking an appreciation of the personal use of environments we can discern a new significance in the elements of landscape.

Expressive Environment

A keystone for this argument is the notion, previously introduced, that manmade features of environment possess expressive value. This principle is uncontested in the case of the plastic and pictorial arts, and even with regard to decoration. A certain recognized component of human vitality resides in all design, standing apart from nature. The expressive power of manmade things, and the intensity of their vital communication, obviously vary tremendously — but all together, artificial objects make up a closed company, a separate universe that always asserts a claim to special meanings. It is characteristic that the "message" of an artifact seldom can be isolated from its context, much less translated clearly into some other medium like language. Artifacts stand as presences in their own right, like persons themselves, in their own inimitable idiosyncrasy and entirety. They differ of course from man himself in their usual immobility and unmoved permanence, thus forming a sensibly different realm — allied and related to man, derived from and representative of man, and deeply involved in his life.

Like words, artifacts do not duplicate or merely serve as vehicles for ideas: they are ideas. Their perfection is their own. And as in the case of words, what they communicate has its autonomous value. It is fatuous to suppose that if the meaning of some imposing human creation cannot be put into so many words it does not mean anything. Seeing landscape only in verbal terms is as silly as evaluating music or paintings purely in terms of their "story." It is meanings immanent in the surroundings and revealing themselves as experience that fix much of culture in landscapes.

Environment, as here conceived, includes all material surroundings accessible to sense. The human community and the actions of its members are surely as eloquent as objects. But artifacts, which are as someone said, "fossilized gestures," and their spatial arrangement that records movements, constitute a kind of permanent record and guide. Of all that may be imparted by the living gesture and posture, by speech and all attendant signals, and by motions and locomotions, it is probably only the most substantial and consequential content that an individual or group will trouble to implant in artifacts.

All behavior is potentially communication. Elaborate behavior toward material results, that modifies environment, commands a special eloquence. It objectifies the self and person.

Being intensely absorbed, according to the nature of their species, in a constant business of communication, human beings individually and collectively always devote a very large part of their time and energy to self display and self assertion. The Self itself is probably man's invention, and its emergence in prehistory was no doubt the very point at which humanity turned human. Human beings, through their behavior and their possessions, notoriously represent themselves, and even more are their personal creations, like their living offspring, treated as their full and fitting representatives. Every landscape man has altered therefore is littered with the by-

products of creative life, attesting bygone personalities and ethnic identities, even as contemporary occupants continue to embellish it with further vital signs. We should not take this to suggest a jumble of clashing egotisms immortalized in junk, however. A personality is a self refined and shaped by life within community, as community itself is adjusted by its life within the habitat.

Man's individual person, as was earlier suggested, cannot be fully detached from a matrix of times, places, and acts in which it becomes manifested and realized. These associations of a man can hardly be inadvertent, or indifferent emotionally. On the contrary, either introspection or observation can lead us to the safe conclusion that a major care of human life is the manifestation of the personality through selection, improvement, and management of the personal environmental display, artifactual and behavioral.

Given such constant intimations of a deeply personal import in landscapes, we may visualize environments as eloquently communicating ideals and models of personal and group life, and as imparting rather detailed and concrete instructions for established ways to succeeding generations. Undoubtedly what is thus registered in landscape and also in custom does represent the most agreed, evolved, and adjusted principles of living in the given place and group, for the given material expression must emerge as outcome of uncertain struggles in society and nature. Expressive landscape thus developed fosters security and continuity, promulgating the tried and the true in object lessons.

Still change goes on, by slow accretions as the generations add their increment of personal and ethnic declaration, and as extrinsic elements penetrate the area and become in varying degree naturalized. Migration adds its influence, so that discontinuities in occupation occur, and many of the lessons of the land are lost, while new ways slowly work their way into the setting by trial and error. When an area is repeopled, the former inhabitants' expression in the landscape may persist, not merely to brood over the new-comers, but to insinuate something of the older ways into their patterns of living. Forms continue to suggest adjusted norms, unless the former are too nearly impercepti-ble or the latter too incompatible with the new culture.

Study of Landscapes and Regions

From a practical point of view, it is desirable to investiage just how forms and norms are related, and to learn to study the actual processes by which a landscape expresses and communicates behavior clues. Such a concern will dictate a close attention to the daily ecology of human actions within the community, seeking regularities, and a con-centration on the differentiating formal elements in environment that serve to set guidelines for observed behavior. Not merely the crude observation of people confining their walking to roads and paths, their work to their own land, their sleeping to their own beds, will suffice, although such common-places dimly indicate the kind of correla-tions — infinitely finer in discrimination — that are needed. Certain symbolisms may be interpreted through indicators that duplicate them, such as the great mass of written or rote-spoken rules of behavior and design which, in many societies, parallels and il-luminates much of environmental expres-sion. And in some extreme cases, like Oriental cities and our own highways, an inordinate amount of written matter is in-scribed all over visual environments, offering explicit guides for behavior. Perhaps the most elusive, yet one of the most essential, features of a landscape is that peerless dec-

laration of individuality and integrity, style. The term defies exact verbal definition, but we all know it as an over-whelmingly vital property of individuals, artifacts, and places. We may rest our hopes for understanding behavioral cues upon our sense of order only until we stumble onto style, for style escapes from order. Yet the cultivation of expressive personal style is very likely far more nearly central to the human use of landscape and to life than is any more mundane and reason-able search for a cozy, safe adjustment with material environment. Perhaps like so many things whereof we cannot speak, style must simply be confronted and contemplated. And the mere experience of style may yet yield more of understanding of the world and of ourselves then all our principles. Still, we wish to grasp it in our discipline as best we can.

Cultural geography may profit greatly from close attention even just to the process of communication of styles in itself — for it is therein that behavior sometimes becomes most visibly disciplined and directed by the subtleties of form. Furthermore, style in landscape features and in acts connotes, undoubtedly, a wealth of affect, and in consequence may reveal a good deal about social relationships and sentiments that otherwise might go undetected. We note, for example, that the "exploitative," "un-creative," "impersonal," and "rootless" feel of modern living seems to find a clear ex-pression in the style of mass-consumption artifacts and entertainments, and also that alternative styles in dress, decoration, and deportment readily symbolize rebellion against these patterns and a search for more congenial life styles, on the part of youth. What every novelist knows about the elo-quence of style can help the cultural geog-rapher in reaching deeper insight into land-scapes and societies.

Changing structures of communication

also enter into many current problems in North American societies. The "ghetto," for example, is an isolated, ingrown place, and its calls for help are heard as tragically distant and unclear. The so-called "gap" that sunders generations, and the reputed "silence" of a vague majority bear witness to rival channels of communication used by various elements of the society, that used to maintain close dialogue. To a considerable extent, even problems like these express themselves in definite changes in social geographic patterns. The several groups of people concerned in each such separation come to frequent different places, and heed new and incompatible sources and systems of communication, until at last they are, to echo the typical complaint, "talking different languages." Here, then, is some indication of the scope of this cultural geographic problem of the structure of communication, in the very immediate contemporary context.

A welcome opportunity for growth in practical relevance thus arises; but the study of structures and features of communication as a central aspect of the cultural region, and the corresponding study of expressive elements of the cultural landscape, promise even more significant general advance in cultural geography.

The traditional interests of the discipline already long portended this direction. As they grow, too, the pioneering present concerns with "spatial diffusion" and "spatial perception" are likely to develop toward a more communication-oriented conception of the subject. A revitalized and richer cultural geography is in the making.

♣♣♣♣♣♣♣♣♣♣♣♣♣♣♣♣♣♣♣♣♣♣♣♣♣♣♣♣♣♣♣

DISCREPANCIES BETWEEN ENVIRONMENTAL ATTITUDE AND BEHAVIOR: EXAMPLES FROM EUROPE AND CHINA

Yi-Fu Tuan

Discrepancy between stated ideal and reality is a worrisome fact of our daily experience: in the political field one learns to discriminate between an orator's fulsome profession and what he can or will, in fact, carry out. The history of environmental ideas, however, has been pursued as an academic discipline largely in detachment from the question of how—if at all—these ideas guide the course of action, or how they arise out of it. Needless to say, there are many paradigmatic views of nature, such as those of science, that have great explicatory power and may, once they are applied, affect the lives of many people; but in themselves they do not enjoin a specific course of action. In contrast, the acceptance of certain specific environmental ideas can have a definite effect on decision and on behavior. If it is widely held, for example, that a dry and sunny climate is a great restorer of health, we may suppose that an appreciable number of people will seek out these areas for health. But what of less specific ideas? We may

From the *Canadian Geographer*, Vol. 12 (1968), pp. 176-91. Reprinted by permission.

believe that a world-view which puts nature in subservience to man will lead to the exploitation of nature by man; and one that regards man as simply a component in nature will entail a modest view of his rights and capabilities, and so lead to the establishment of a harmonious relationship between man and his natural environment. But is this correct? And if essentially correct, how direct or tenuous is the link? These are some of the questions I wish to explore with the help of examples from Europe and China. The discrepancies are noted here; their resolution must await another occasion.

To the question, what is a fundamental difference between the European and the Chinese attitude towards nature, most people with any opinion at all will probably make some such reply: that the European sees nature as subordinate to him whereas the Chinese sees himself as a part of nature. Taken as a broad generalization and with a grain of salt there is much truth in this distinction; a truth illustrated with diagrammatic force when one compares the formal European garden of the seventeenth century with the Chinese naturalistic garden. The geometric contrast reflects fundamental differences in environmental evaluation. The formal European garden in the style of the Le Nôtre was designed to produce a limited number of imposing prospects. It can be appreciated to the full only at a limited number of favored spots where the onlooker is invited by the garden's design to gaze at distant vistas. Or, seen in another way, the European garden is a grandiose setting for man; in deference to him, nature is straitjacketed in court dress. The Chinese garden, on the other hand, is designed to produce almost constantly shifting scenes: there are no set prospects. The nature of the garden requires the perceiver to move along a winding path and to be more than visually

involved with the landscape. It is not nature that is required to put on court dress in deference to man: rather, it is man who must lay aside his formalistic pretensions in order to enter nature.

This widely recognized distinction is valid and important. On the other hand, by the crude test of the total tonnage of earth removed there may not be so very much difference between the European formal and the Chinese naturalistic garden. Both are human artifacts. It is not widely known that some of the famous scenic areas of China are works of man rather than of geologic processes. The West Lake of Hang-chou, for example, was celebrated by T'ang and Sung poets and it remains to this day an adornment of China. To the casual visitor, the West Lake region may appear to be a striking illustration of how the works of man can blend modestly into the magistral context of nature. However, the pervasiveness of nature is largely an illusion induced by art. Some of the islands in the lake are man-made. Moreover, the lake itself is artifical and has to be maintained with care. In the thirteenth century, military patrols, under the command of specially appointed officials, looked after its policing and maintenance; it was forbidden, for example, to throw any rubbish into it or to plant in it lotuses or water-chestnuts. Peasants were recruited to clear and enlarge the lake, to keep it from being cluttered up by vegetation and silt.[1] Hang-chou's environs, then, owe much of their calm, harmonious beauty to human art and effort. The sense of open nature in Hang-chou is enhanced by its scale: the West Lake region is a cluster of public and semi-public parks. In the much smaller compass of the private garden the illusion of pervasive nature is far more difficult to achieve: never-

1. Jacques Gernet, *Daily Life in China on the Eve of the Mongol Invasion 1250–1276* (London, 1962), pp. 51–52.

theless the aim of the Chinese gardener was to achieve it with cleverly placed, water-worn limestone whose jagged outlines denoted wildness, and by means of winding footpaths that give the stroller an illusion of depth and space. In this line the Oriental's ultimate triumph is symbolized by the miniature garden, where wild nature is reduced to the scale of a dwarf landscape that can be fitted into a bowl. Complete artifice reigns: in the narrow confines of a bowl, shrubs are tortured by human skill into imitating the shape and posture of pines, the limbs of which may have been deformed by winds that swept the China Seas.

I have begun with a contrast and then proceeded to suggest that, from another perspective, the contrast is blurred. The publicized environmental ethos of a culture seldom covers more than a fraction of the total range of environmental behavior. It is misleading to derive the one from the other. Simplifications that can mislead have at times been made. For example, Professor Lynn White has recently said: "What people do about their ecology depends on what they think about themselves in relation to things around them. Human ecology is deeply conditioned by beliefs about our nature and destiny—that is, by religion."[2] He goes on to say that the victory of Christianity over paganism was the greatest psychic revolution in Western culture. In his view, despite all the talk of "the post-Christian age" and despite evident changes in the forms of modern thinking, the substance often remains amazingly akin to that of the Christian past. The Western man's daily habits of action are dominated by an implicit faith in perpetual progress which was unknown either to Greco-Roman antiquity

or to the Orient. It is rooted in, and is indefensible apart from, Judeo-Christian teleology. Peoples of the Western world continue to live, as they have lived for about 1700 years, very largely in a context of Christian beliefs. And what has Christianity told people about their relations with the environment? Essentially that man, as something made in God's image, is not simply a part of nature; that God has planned the universe for man's benefit and rule. According to White, Christianity is the most anthropocentric religion the world has seen. It has not only established a dualism of man and nature but has also insisted that it is God's will that man exploit nature for his proper ends.[3]

To press the theme further, it is said that Christianity has destroyed antiquity's feeling for the holiness of landscapes and of natural things. The Greek religious tradition regarded the land not as an object to be exploited, or even as a visually pleasing setting, but as a true force which physically embodied the powers that ruled the world. Vincent Scully, the architectural historian, has argued that not only were certain landscapes regarded by the ancient Greeks as holy and expressive of specific gods, but also that the temples and the subsidiary buildings of their sanctuaries were so formed in themselves and so placed in the landscapes and to each other as to enhance, develop, and complement the basic meaning of the landscape.[4]

Martin Heidegger, a modern philosopher whose insights have been greatly influenced by early Greek philosophy, characterized the Greek temple as disclosing the earth on which it stands. The whiteness of the temple discloses the darkness and the strength of the rock underneath; it reveals the height

2. Lynn White, "The Historical Roots of our Ecologic Crisis," *Science*, CLV (1967), 1205.

3. *Ibid.*
4. Vincent Scully, *The Earth, The Temple, and The Gods* (New Haven, 1962), p. 3.

and blueness of the sky, the power of the storm and the vastness of the sea.[5] In the Christian tradition, on the other hand, holiness was invested not in landscapes but in man-made altars, shrines, churches, and basilicas that dominated the landscapes. Constantine and Helen are said to have built basilicas over caves in the Holy Land to celebrate the triumph of Christianity over the "cave cultus" of the pagan world. In the Christian view it was not emanation from the earth but ritual that consecrated the site; man not nature bore the image of God and man's work, the hallowed edifice, symbolized the Christian cosmos. In pagan antiquity, at the level of the common people, each facet of nature had its own guardian spirit. Before one ventured to cut a tree, mine a mountain, or dam a brook, it was important to placate the spirit in charge of that particular situation, and to keep it placated. By destroying animistic beliefs, Christianity made it possible to exploit nature in a mood of indifference to the feeling of natural objects.

Much of this is now Western folklore and Lynn White is among the more recent writers to give it eloquent expression. The thesis, then, is that Christianity has introduced a fundamentally new way of evaluating the environment, and that this new evaluation has strongly affected Western man's traffic with the natural objects around him. The generalization is very useful, although one should take note of facts that appear to contradict it. As Clarence Glacken has demonstrated, in the ancient world there was no lack of interest in natural resources and their quick exploitation. Economic activities such as mining, the various ways of obtaining food, canal building, and drainage are clear proof of man's incessant restless-

ness in changing the earth about him.[6] Glacken points out that in Sophocles' *Antigone* there are lines which remind one of the eulogies of science in the eighteenth century, and of contemporary enthusiasm for man's control over nature. At one point in the play the chorus declares how the earth has felt man's ungentle touch:

Oh, Earth is patient, and Earth is old,
And a mother of Gods, but he breaketh her,
To-ing, froing, with the plough teams going,
Tearing the soil of her, year by year.[7]

The tearing of soil has led to erosion. In Plato's *Critias* there is the well-known passage in which he describes how the soils of Attica have been washed down to the sea. "And, just as happens in small islands, what now remains compared with what then existed is like the skeleton of a rich man, all the fat and soft earth have wasted away, and only the bare framework of the land being left." Plato then describes the former arable hills, fertile valleys, and forested mountains "of which there are visible signs even to this day." Mountains which today have food only for bees could, not so long ago, grow trees fit for the largest buildings. Cultivated trees provided pasturage for flocks, and the soil was well watered and the rain was "not lost to it, as now, by flowing from the bare land to the sea."[8] Plato's comments sound remarkably modern; they remind us almost of the lamentations of latter-day conservationists.

If there is evidence of man's awareness of his power to transform nature—even destructively—in the time of Sophocles and Plato, there is evidence of much greater awareness

---

5. Vincent Vycinas, *Earth and Gods: An Introduction to the Philosophy of Martin Heidegger* (The Hague, 1961), p. 13.

6. Clarence Glacken, *Traces on the Rhodian Shore* (Berkeley and Los Angeles, 1967), p. 118.
7. Sophocles, *Antigone*, transl. by Gilbert Murray in Arnold Toynbee, *Greek Historical Thought* (New York, 1952), p. 128.
8. Plato, *Critias*, transl. by Arnold Toynbee in *Greek Historical Thought*, pp. 146–47.

Figure 1. The growing "second nature" in antiquity. In spite of a passive or adaptive attitude toward nature (suggested by the importance of the "environmental theory" in philosophy and by respect for the *genius loci* of natural object in folk religion), the ancient landscapes have been markedly transformed by man. Figure 1 shows how nature can even be dominated by man's engineering achievements. Reproduced from Clarence Glacken, *Traces on the Rhodian Shore.*

of the almost limitless capabilities of man in Hellenistic times. Agriculture and related occupations such as cattle-breeding were then the most important source of wealth in the ancient world. Land reclamation was not a haphazard affair but one based on the science of mechanics and on practical experience with canal-digging, irrigation, and swamp drainage. It was a time of faith in progress. But far more than the Greeks, the Romans have imposed their will on the natural environment (Fig. 1). And perhaps the most dramatic example of the triumph of the human will over the irregular lineaments of nature is the Roman grid method of dividing up the land. As Bradford puts it, centuriation well displayed the arbitrary but methodical qualities in Roman government. With absolute self-assurance and great technical competence, the Romans have imposed the same formal pattern of land division on the well-watered alluvium of the Po Valley as on the near-desert of Tunisia. Even today

the forceful imprint of centuriation can be traced across some thousands of square miles on both sides of the central Mediterranean, and it can still stir the imagination by its scale and boldness.[9]

Against this background of the vast transformations of nature in the pagan world, the inroads made in the early centuries of the Christian era were relatively modest. Christianity teaches that man has dominion over nature. St. Benedict himself had cut down the sacred grove at Monte Cassino because it was a survival of pagan worship. And the story of how monks moved into the forested wilderness, and by a combination of work and prayer, had transformed them into cloistered "paradises" is a familiar one. But for a long time man's undisputed power over nature was more a tenet of faith than a fact of experience: to become a realized fact

9. John Bradford, *Ancient Landscapes* (London, 1957), p. 145.

Europe had to wait for the growth of human numbers, for the achievement of greater administrative centralization and for the development and wide application of new technological skills. Fields that were cleared in heavy forests testified to the mediaeval farmer's great capacity for changing his environment: it was a change, however, that must continually be defended against the encroachments of nature (Fig. 2). Farmsteads and arable lands multiplied through the Middle Ages at the expense of forest and marshes, but these man-made features lacked the permanence, the geometric order, and the prideful assertion of the human will that one can detect more readily in the Roman road system, aqueducts, and centuriated landholdings. The victory of Christianity over paganism may well have been, as Lynn White says, the greatest psychic revolution in Western culture; but for lack of real, as distinct from theologically postulated, power the full impact of that revolution on ecology was postponed.

As to China, Western humanists commonly show bias in favor of that country's Taoist and Buddhist traditions. They like to point out the virtues of the Oriental's quiescent and adaptive approach towards nature in contrast to the aggressive masculinity of Western man. Support for the quiescent view is easily found in the Taoist classics. The *Tao Tê Ching*, for example, has a rather cryptic message of seven characters *(wei wu wei, tzu wu pu chih)* which James

Figure 2. A fifteenth-century print showing a mediaeval scene. Foreground: ploughing team and field; midground: water mill; background: castle. Technological innovations, such as the heavy plough and the water mill, appear to have given man a position of dominance vis-à-vis nature, from about the ninth century onward, that he lacked in the earlier Christian centuries.

Legge has translated as: "When there is this abstinence from action, good order is universal." And Joseph Needham has recently interpreted it to mean: "Let there be no action (contrary to Nature), and there is nothing that will not be well regulated."[10] It is easy to see how these words might appeal to the modern man, who finds in his own environment the all-too-evident consequences of human action "contrary to nature." In another influential Taoist book of much later date *(T'ai shang kan ying p'ien)*, one finds the belief that "even insects and crawling things, herbs and trees, may not be injured." These Taoist texts have been much translated into European languages; the latter, with its injunction against injuring even insects and crawling things, is believed to have had some influence on the thought of Albert Schweitzer.[11]

Another aspect of Chinese attitude towards nature, which has found favor among some Western humanists, is embodied in the concept of *feng-shui* or geomancy. This concept has been aptly defined as "the art of adapting the residences of the living and the dead so as to co-operate and harmonize with the local currents of the cosmic breath."[12] If houses and tombs are not properly located, evil effects would injure the inhabitants and the descendants of those whose bodies lay in the tombs. On the other hand, good siting would favor wealth, health, and happiness. Good siting involves, above all, taking proper note of the forms of

hills and directions of watercourses since these are themselves the outcome of the molding influences of winds and waters, that is, of *feng-shui*; but in addition one must also consider the heights and forms of buildings, the directions of roads and bridges. A general effect of the belief in *feng-shui* is to encourage a preference for natural curves—for winding paths and for structures that seem to fit into the landscape rather than to dominate it; and at the same time it promoted a distaste for straight lines and geometrical layouts. In this respect it is of interest to note the short life of China's first railway. This was built in 1876 and connected Shanghai with its port of Wu-sung. Although the venture was at first well received, the mood of the local people turned sour after a native was killed by the locomotive. The people in their hostility thought that the railway had offended the principle of *feng-shui*. On 20 October, 1877, the Chinese government closed the railway, and so a symbol of Western progress was temporarily sacrificed to the local currents of the cosmic breath.[13]

An adaptive attitude towards nature has ancient roots in China. It is embodied in folklore, in the philosophical-ethical precepts of Taoism, and later, Buddhism, and it draws support from practical experience: the experience that uncontrolled exploitation of timber, for example, brings hurtful results. In ancient literature one finds here and there evidence of a recognition for the need to regulate the use of resources. Even as early as the Eastern Chou period (eighth century— third century B.C.), deforestation necessitated by the expansion of agriculture and the building of cities seems to have led to an appreciation of the value of trees. In that ancient compendium of songs the *Shi Ching*,

10. Joseph Needham, *Science and Civilisation in China*, vol. II (Cambridge, 1956), p. 69.
11. E. H. Schafer, "The Conservation of Nature under the T'ang dynasty," *Journ. Econ. and Soc. Hist. of the Orient*, v (1962), 282.
12. H. Chatley, "Feng shui" in *Encyclopaedia Sinica*, ed. by S. Couling (Shanghai, 1917), p. 175. See also Andrew March, "An Appreciation of Chinese Geomancy," *Journ. Asian Studies*, XXVII (1968), 253–67.

13. *Encyclopaedia Sinica*, p. 470.

we find the sentiment expressed in lines such as these:

On the hill were lovely trees,
Both chestnut-trees and plum trees.
Cruel brigands tore them up;
But no one knew of their crime.

Trees were regarded as a blessing. As another poem put it,

So thick grow those oaks
That the people never look for firewood.
Happiness to our lord!
May the spirits always have rewards for him.[14]

In the *Chou Li*—a work which was probably compiled in the third century B.C., but may well include earlier material—we find mentioned two classes of officials whose duties were concerned with conservation. One was the *Shan-yu*, inspector of mountains, and the other the *Lin-heng*, inspector of forests. The inspectors of mountains were charged with the care of forests in the mountains. They saw to it that certain species were preserved, and in other ways enforced conservation practices. Thus trees could only be cut by the common people at certain times; those on the south side in the middle of winter and those on the north side in the middle of summer. At other seasons the people were permitted to cut wood in times of urgent need, such as when coffins had to be made or dykes strengthened, but even then certain areas could not be touched. The inspectors of forests (in the *Lin-heng* office) had similar duties. Their authority covered the forests that lay below the mountains.[15] Another ancient literary reference to conservation practice was in the *Mencius*. The sage advised King Huai of Liang that he would not lack for wood if he allowed the people to cut trees only at the proper time.[16]

Through Chinese history perspicacious officials have from time to time warned against the dire consequences of deforestation. A scholar of the late Ming dynasty reported on Shan-hsi, a province in North China: "At the beginning of the reign of Chia-ching" (1522–66), he wrote, "people vied with each other to build houses, and wood from the southern mountains were cut without a year's rest. The natives took advantage of the barren mountain surface and converted it into farms. . . . If heaven sends down a torrent, there is nothing to obstruct the flow of water. In the morning it falls on the southern mountains; in the evening, when it reaches the plains, its angry waves swell in volume and break embankments causing frequent changes in the course of the river."[17]

Deforestation was deplored by the late Ming scholars not only because of its effect on stream flow and on the quality of the soil in the lowlands, but also—interestingly enough because of their belief that the forests on mountain ridges were effective in slowing down the horse-riding barbarians. As one scholar put it, "I saw the fact that what the country relies on as strategically important is the mountain, and what the mountain relies on as a screen to prevent advance are the trees."[18] There was also recognition of the aesthetics of forested mountains. Wu-tai mountains in northern Shan-hsi, for example, were famous everywhere. But the question was asked: since they have become almost bare, what remained to keep them famous?

These brief notes suggest that there existed in China an old tradition of forest

14. *Shi Ching,* transl. by Arthur Waley as *The Book of Songs* (New York, 1960), pp. 138, 213.
15. *Chou Li,* transl. by E. Biot as *Le Tcheou-li* (Paris, 1851), vol. I, 371–74.
16. *Mencius,* Bk. I, pt. 1, 3:3.

17. Ch'ao-ting Chi, *Key Economic Areas in Chinese History* (New York, 1963), p. 22.
18. Gazetteer (1596) written by Chen Teng and translated by W. C. Lowdermilk, and D. R. Wickes, *History of Soil Use in the Wu T'ai Shan Area,* Monog., Roy. Asiatic Soc., NCB, 1938, p. 8.

care. Officials encouraged the practice but the people engaged in it on their own initiative when it did not conflict with the urgent needs of the moment. Nearly forty years ago, the American conservationist W. C. Lowdermilk noted how thousands of acres in An-hui and Ho-non were planted with pine from local nurseries, a practice he recognized as ancient and independent of the modern forestry movement. Lowdermilk also found that the North China plain "actually exports considerable quantities of logs of *Paulownia tomentosa* to Japan and poplar (*Populus tomentosa*) to match factories. It is true that no forests are to be found in this plain, but each village has its trees, which are grown according to a system."[19]

In Communist China trees are extensively planted to control soil erosion, in answer to pressing economic needs but also for aesthetic reasons. Roadside planting, a practice dating back to the Eastern Chou period, uses the "traditional" trees *(Populus simonii, Pinus tabulaeformis, Salix babylonica, S. matsudana, Aesculus chinensis, Ulmus parvifolia)*, but in particular the poplars. Afforestation proceeds in villages, and most conspicuously, in cities, new suburbs, and industrial districts where the trees hide a great deal of the raw ugliness of new construction.[20]

Thus far I have sketched what may indeed be called the "official" line on Chinese attitude towards environment; it is widely publicized and commonly accepted. There is however another strain: the enlightened memorials to the emperor on the need for the conservation of resources are in themselves clear evidence of the follies that have

already been committed. Unlike the Western man of letters the geographer is usually aware of China's frequent mistreatment of nature. He perceives that country, not through the refined sentiments of Taoist philosophy, Neo-Confucianism, and Oswald Siren, but through the bleak reports of Mallory, Lowdermilk, and Thorp. Deforestation and erosion on the one hand, the building of cities and rice terraces on the other are the common foci of his attention rather than landscape painting or poetry contests in the cool precincts of a garden. The two images of reality complement each other: in an obvious but not trite sense, civilization is the exercise of human power over nature, which in turn may lead to the aesthetic appreciation of nature. Philosophy, nature poetry, gardens, and orderly countryside are products of civilization, but so equally are the deforested mountains, the clogged streams, and, within the densely packed, walled cities, the political intrigue.

If animistic belief and Taoist nature philosophy lie at the back of an adaptive attitude towards nature, what conceptions and ideals—we may ask—have encouraged the Chinese, through their long history, to engage in gigantic transformation of environment—whether this be expressed positively in huge works of construction or negatively in deforested mountains? Several ancient beliefs and conceptions may be recognized and they, individually or together, have allowed the Chinese to express the "male" principle in human nature. Consider, for example, the fact that one of the greatest culture heroes of China was Yu, the legendary founder of the Hsia dynasty. He was famed primarily for his magnificent deeds: He "opened up the rivers of the Nine Provinces and fixed the outlets of the nine marshes"; he brought peace and order to the lands of Hsia and his achievements were of an enduring kind which benefited succeeding

19. W. C. Lowdermilk, "Forestry in Denuded China," *Ann., Amer. Acad. Pol. Soc. Sci.*, CLII (1930), 137.
20. S. D. Richardson, *Forestry in Communist China* (Baltimore, 1966), pp. 152–53.

dynasties.[21] Chinese rulers were bidden to imitate the ancient culture heroes, and one way to imitate them was to ensure order and prosperity by large-scale engineering works. Another ancient idea of importance to the "male" principle of dominance was to see in the earthly environment a model of the cosmos. The regular motions of the stars were to be translated architecturally and ritually to space and time on earth. The walled city oriented to the cardinal directions, the positioning of the twelve city gates, the location of the royal compound and the alignment of the principal axial street were given a geometric pattern that reflected the order to be found in heaven. The key concept was built on the related notions of rectilinearity, order, and rectitude. This key concept acquired architectural and social forms which were then imposed on earth, for the earth itself lacked paradigms of perfect order. Indeed the experience of mountains and waters has led to such unaggressive prescriptions as the need to observe and placate the spirits of the earth, the need for man to understand the balance of forces in nature, to contemplate this harmony and to adapt himself to it. By contrast, the observation of the stars has inspired such masculine attitudes as geometric order, hierarchy, and authoritarian control over earth and men.

The two outlooks—celestial and terrestrial, masculine and feminine—are not easy to reconcile. Events in heaven affect events on earth but not in any obvious or dependable way: abnormal floods and droughts have traditionally been taken as warnings by those who derive their power from astronomy. Tension, if not contradiction, is also revealed when these two ideas find architectural and geographical substance. The construction of Ch'ang-an in the

Sui and T'ang dynasties illustrates the triumph of the cosmic principle of order and rectilinearity over the earth principle of complex harmony and natural lines (Fig. 3). Ch'ang-an was laid on new ground and on an unprecedented scale. The site in the Wei Ho valley was chosen for functional reasons but also because of its great historical links: the site received the sanction of the great men and deeds in the past. Geomantic properties of the site were studied; however, unlike villages and rural roads the topographical character of the region seems to have made little impact on the city's fundamental design. Astronomers had an important role in the laying out of the city: they measured the

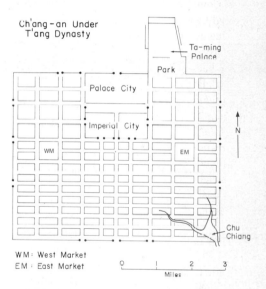

Figure 3. The cosmic paradigm in Chinese city-building as exemplified by Ch'ang-an during the T'ang dynasty. The city grid reflects the super-position of a regular cosmic pattern on the irregularities of the earth. The curves of Taoist nature are represented mainly by Chu Chiang park in the southeastern corner of the city and by the gardens of the wealthy and of monasteries, but the rectilinear geometry of the city streets and enclosed wards dwarfs these manifestations of terrestrial nature. The imposing, rather lifeless, north-south avenues are more than 400 feet wide.

---

21. Ssu-ma Ch'ien, *Shi Chi*, chap. 29.

shadow of the noon sun on successive days and observed the North Star by night in order to arrive at accurate alignments of the city walls to the four directions.[22] In the course of building Ch'ang-an, which had an enclosed area of 31 square miles, villages were levelled and trees uprooted; broad straight avenues were laid out and then rows of trees planted. Thus, despite the geomantic gestures, in Ch'ang-an the superposition of man's and heaven's order on natural terrain was complete. Or rather not quite complete, if we accept the charming story of why one great old locust tree was not in line. It had been retained from the old landscape because the chief architect had sat under it as he supervised the construction, and a special order from the emperor in honor of his architect spared it from being felled.[23]

The natural environment of both Mediterranean Europe and China has been vastly transformed by man: constructively in the building of cities and roads, in the extension of arable land and the introduction of new crops; destructively in deforestation and erosion. Of any long-settled, thoroughly civilized part of the world, we can draw up a list of forces and the motives for their use that would more or less account for the transformation of the biotic mantle. Such lists may well agree in fundamentals: fire is widely used to clear vegetation; the forest is cleared to create more grazing and arable land; timber is needed for the construction of palaces, houses, and ships, for domestic and industrial fuel, or as raw material for paper mills. Then again the forest is pushed back because it may shelter dangerous wild animals or provide hiding places for bandits. Naturally, the means at hand and the motives for using them vary from region to region: in contrast to the Mediterranean world, for example, China's vegetation suffered less from sheep and goats, and less from the enormous demands of shipbuilding which flourished with the Mediterranean maritime powers. China's forests, on the other hand, suffered more from the demands of city building and the need for domestic fuel.

To illustrate further the kinds of force that work against conservation practices in China, consider some of the causes of deforestation. One is the ancient practice of burning trees in order to deprive dangerous animals of their hiding places. There exists a passage in the *Mencius* of how in ancient times the luxuriant vegetation sheltered so many wild beasts that men were endangered. The great minister Shun of legendary repute ordered Yih to use fire, and "Yih set fire to, and consumed the forests and vegetation on the mountains and in the marshes, so that the birds and beasts fled away to hide themselves."[24] Even in the early decades of the twentieth century non-Chinese tribes in Kuang-hsi and Kuei-chou provinces are known to burn forests to drive away tigers and leopards; and in North China, in such long-settled areas as central Shen-hsi province, fires were ostensibly started by Chinese farmers for no other purpose. It is not always easy to establish the real reason for setting fire to forest. When asked, the farmers may say that it is to clear land for cultivation, although the extent of burning far exceeds the need for this purpose; or it is to leave fewer places in which bandits may hide; or to encourage the growth of small-sized sprouts in the burnt over area, which would then save the farmers the labor of

22. A. F. Wright, "Symbolism and Functions: Reflections on Changan and Other Great Cities," *Journ. Asian Studies*, XXIV (1965), 670.
23. N. I. Wu, *Chinese and Indian Architecture* (New York, 1963), p. 38.

24. *Mencius*, Bk III, pt. 1, 4:7.

splitting wood![25] The last reason tends to upset any residual illusion we may have of the Chinese farmer's benign attitude towards nature. A fire can of course also be started accidentally. A risk that is special to the Chinese is the forest fire caused by the burning of paper money at the grave mounds, which, in the rugged parts of the South, are commonly located beyond the fields and at the edge of the forested hills.

Forests in North China were depleted in the past for the making of charcoal as an industrial fuel. Robert Hartwell has shown how, from the tenth century onward the expanding metallic industries had swallowed up many hundreds of thousands of tons of charcoal each year, as did the manufacture of salt, alum, bricks, tiles, and liquor.[26] By the Sung dynasty (960–1279 A.D.) the demand for wood and charcoal as both household and industrial fuel had reached a level such that the timber resources of the country could no longer meet it; the result was the increasing substitution of coal for wood and charcoal.

An enormous amount of timber was needed in the construction of the old Chinese cities, probably more than that required in building Western cities of comparable size. One reason for this lies in the dependence of traditional Chinese architecture on timber as the basic structural material. Mountains may be stripped of their cover in the construction of a large palace.[27] And if a large palace required much timber,

a whole city would require much more, especially if it were of the size of Ch'ang-an, capital of T'ang dynasty, and Hang-chou, capital of the southern Sung dynasty. Both had populations of more than a million people. The great expansion in the size of Hang-chou in the thirteenth century led to the deforestation of the neighboring hills for construction timber. The demand for timber was such that some farmers gave up rice cultivation for forestry.[28] Cities in which houses were so largely made of wood ran the constant danger of demolition by fire; and this was especially true of the southern metropolises where the streets tended to be narrow. The necessity of rebuilding after fire put further strain on timber resources. But of even greater consequence than the accidental burning of parts of cities was the deliberate devastation of whole cities in times of upheaval, when rebels or nomadic invaders toppled a dynasty. The succeeding phase of reconstruction was normally achieved in quick time by armies of men who made ruthless inroads upon the forest.

The theme we have yet to trace is the involved interplay between environmental attitude and environmental behavior, between the philosophy identified with a people and the actions that people may undertake. Besides the more glaring contradictions of professed ideal and actual practice, there exist also the unsuspected ironies: these derive from the fact that the benign institutions of a complex society, no less than the exploitative, are not always able to foresee all the consequences of their inherent character and action. For example, Buddhism in China is at least partly responsible for the preservation of trees around temple compounds, for the islands of green

25. Reported by A. N. Steward and S. Y. Cheo in "Geographical and ecological notes on botanical explorations in Kwangsi province, China," *Nanking Journ.*, V (1935), 174.
26. R. Hartwell, "A Revolution in the Chinese Iron and Coal Industries during the Northern Sung, 960–1126 A.D.," *Journ. Asian Studies*, XXI (1962), 159.
27. See L. S. Yang, *Les aspects économiques des travaux publics dans la Chine impériale*, Collège de France, 1964. p. 37.

28. Gernet, (n. 1), p. 114.

Figure 4. Temple trees protected within the precincts of a village. This scene of northern Shan-hsi province in China shows a deforested and badly denuded landscape. Under pressure from rising population for more land, religion can do no more than save a few scattered groves. From Lowdermilk and Wickes.

in an otherwise denuded landscape (Fig. 4); on the other hand, Buddhism introduced to China the idea of the cremation of the dead; and from the tenth to the fourteenth century the practice of cremation was sufficiently common in the southeastern coastal provinces to have had an effect on the timber resources of that area.[29] The researches of E. H. Schafer provide us with another illustration of irony in Chinese life; for it would seem that the most civilized of arts was responsible for the deforestation of much of North China. The art was that of writing which required soot for the making of black ink. The soot came from burnt pine. And, as Schafer put it, "Even before T'ang times, the ancient pines of the mountains of Shantung had been reduced to carbon, and now the busy brushes of the vast T'ang bureaucracy were rapidly bringing baldness to the T'a-hang Mountains between Shansi and Hopei."[30]

I began by noting the contrast between the European formal garden and the Chinese naturalistic garden, and then suggested that these human achievements probably required comparable amounts of nature modification. To compare artworks and construction projects on the basis of the quantitative changes made on the environment is a useful exercise in so far as we wish to emphasize the role of man as a force for change along with other geophysical forces; but it is only the beginning in the interpretation of the meaning of these works and how they reflect cultural attitudes. It seems to me valid to see the European garden as an extension of the house: in the development of the European garden some of the formality and values of the house are taken outdoors in the form of

29. A. C. Moule, *Quinsai* (Cambridge, 1957), p. 51.

30. Schafer, (n. 11), pp. 299–300.

courtyards, terraces, formal parterres, and avenues, and now the smooth, carpet-like lawn. The lawn displays the house; its sloping surfaces are a pedestal for the house. The Chinese garden, on the other hand, reflects a totally different philosophy from the orthogonal rectitude of the traditional Chinese house. In stepping through a circular gate, from the rectangular courtyard into the curvilinear forms of the garden, one enters a different world. Perhaps something of the difference in attitude towards outdoor spaces is retained to the present day. Simone de Beauvoir notes how a French family picnic is often an elaborate affair involving the transportation of a considerable portion of the household goods outdoors: it is not always a harmonious event for whatever tension that may exist in the house is carried to the less organized natural environment where it is exacerbated by entanglement with flies, fishing rods, and spilled strawberry jam. In Communist China, de Beauvoir spent an afternoon (1955) in the playgrounds of the Summer Palace outside Peking. She captures the peace of the scene with an anecdote: "In the middle of the lake I see a little boat: in it a young woman is lying down peacefully asleep while two youngsters are frisking about and playing with the oars. Our boatman cups his hands. 'Hey!' he calls. 'Look out for those kids!' The woman rubs her eyes, she smiles, picks up the oars, and shows the children how they work."[31]

31. Simone de Beauvoir, *The Long March* (Cleveland, 1958), p. 77.

* *

ENGLISH LANDSCAPE TASTES

David Lowenthal and Hugh C. Prince

Landscapes are formed by landscape tastes. People in any country see their terrain through preferred and accustomed spectacles, and tend to make it over as they see it. The English landscape, as much as any other, mirrors a long succession of such idealized images and visual prejudices. What we describe here as characteristically English landscape taste is not necessarily what a majority of the English people would select, favor, or even understand. We have abstracted no sample, taken no poll, sought no national norm. We have examined only a small fraction of the published notes and comments on the landscape attitudes herein discussed. But the points of view that we deal with are expressed again and again in literature, in speeches, at public hearings, in newspaper articles, and in letters. If they are not the attitudes of the common man, they are, we think, representative of that minority who have been most active in creating English landscape taste and in molding the landscape itself.

The types of landscape the English prefer, preserve, and reproduce they regard as uniquely English, embodying the past and present virtues of the inhabitants. Few of these traits are in fact exclusively English; they are distinctive, however, in the sense

From the *Geographical Review*, Vol. 55 (1965), pp. 186-222. Copyright © 1965 by the American Geographical Society of New York. Reprinted by permission.

that they occur throughout the realm but not generally elsewhere.

Among a people so appreciative of their landscape,[1] the range of taste is bound to be great. Inevitably, some preferences conflict with others; the diversity of views prompted an American ambassador to observe that "it's all true about England, everything you've ever heard."[2] Of many characteristically English preferences, we limit ourselves here to a consideration of a few prominent and well-loved aspects of the countryside.

The Bucolic

"God made the country, and man made the town," wrote Cowper.[3] He was manifestly mistaken. No landscape is more intimately man-made than the English countryside as a whole; indeed, the lineaments of Cowper's own village had just been transformed by a parliamentary enclosure. But Cowper's real aim was to glorify the country and defame the town, and most of his countrymen still echo his prejudice.

"The English are town-birds through and through," as D. H. Lawrence declares. "Yet they don't know how to build a city, how to think of one, or how to live in one."[4] They abominate city life and regard towns as prisons to flee from at every opportunity. Townsmen though they are, they still think of rural England as home, the countryside as the essential nation. The London factory hand visualized the England he had fought to save not as London, "not his own street, but as Epping Forest, the green place where he had spent Bank Holidays."[5] The same bucolic fancy enthralled one who should have known better, the son of a Midland ironmaster: "To me, England is the country, and the country is England," confessed Stanley Baldwin in 1924, between terms as Prime Minister. "The sounds of England, the tinkle of the hammer on the anvil in the country smithy, the corncrake on a dewy morning, the sound of the scythe against the whetstone, and the sight of a plough team coming over the brow of a hill, . . . the one eternal sight of England"[6] (Figs. 1 and 2). But the whole picture of a pastoral England was already a travesty in 1924: village smithies were going out of business, the corncrake was becoming a rare bird,[7] and the tractor had doomed the plow team to extinction. Yet schoolchildren still are taught that

> whoever wakes in England
> Sees, some morning, unaware,
> That the lowest boughs and the brushwood sheaf
> Round the elm-tree bole are in tiny leaf,
> While the chaffinch sings on the orchard bough
> In England—now![8]

Passion for the countryside is perhaps strongest where the cities are most bleak— the industrial encampments of the Midlands and the north. Folk in Bradford, Priestley

1. See David Lowenthal and Hugh C. Prince: "The English Landscape," *Geogr. Rev.*, Vol. 54, 1964, pp. 309-346. This article raised the queries, and provided the stimulus, for much of the present paper.
2. Walter Hines Page, as quoted in Christopher Salmon: "The Merry-Go-Round," *Listener*, Nov. 19, 1953, pp. 849-850; reference on p. 849.
3. William Cowper: "The Task," Book i, "The Sofa," line 749, in *Poems* (2 vols.; London, 1814), Vol. 2, p. 40.
4. D. H. Lawrence, as quoted in Asa Briggs: *Victorian Cities* (London, 1963), p. 8.

5. H. V. Morton: *In Search of England* [1927] (Harmondsworth, Middlesex, 1960), p. 14.
6. Stanley Baldwin: "England" [address to the Royal Society of St. George, May 6, 1924], in *On England, And Other Addresses* (London, 1926), pp. 1-9; reference on pp. 6-7.
7. "Cautious Ways of the Corncrake," *The Times*, London, Aug. 11, 1964, p. 8.
8. Robert Browning: "Home Thoughts, from Abroad," in *The Poetical Works of Robert Browning* (17 vols.; New York, 1894), Vol. 6, p. 95.

Figure 1. "The Hay Wain" (1821), by John Constable, exemplifies English devotion to rustic life and landscape. (The National Gallery, London)

recalls, "did not care very much if our city had no charm, for it was simply a place to go and work in, until it was time to set out for Wharfedale or Wensleydale again."[9]

The Englishman traditionally longs to be "Master of a small House and a Large Garden."[10] His hobbies are overtly and actively bucolic. In the summer thousands of street-bred Londoners join the shepherds in Hyde Park to watch the national sheep-dog trials.

Stay-at-homes see the Royal International Horse Show at the White City on television. To follow such events calls for a fair knowledge of country lore. But beyond the traditional bucolic pursuits—gardening, shepherding, riding—most townsmen know little about country life. Urban love of the countryside is in most respects "unrealistically sentimental, totally uninstructed."[11]

Seaside resorts excepted, there are few things in England for which a rural setting is not generally preferred. Windsor and Hampton Court are monuments to the notion that royalty belongs in the country. Whatever the reality, universities are imagined as green havens of peace. Cathedrals are found in

9. J. B. Priestley: *English Journey* (London, 1934), p. 174.

10. Abraham Cowley: "The Garden," in *The Works of Mr. Abraham Cowley* (11th edit.; 2 vols.; London, 1710), Vol. 2, pp. 731-732. A London Transport poster of 1924 quotes this phrase with approval as a reason to "Move to Edgware" (frontispiece in Peter Hall: London 2000 [London, 1963]).

11. "The Death of a Village," *The Times*, July 29, 1964, p. 5.

Figure 2. "Strayed Sheep" (1853), by William Holman Hunt, is an idealization of pastoral felicity on the downs. (The Tate Gallery, London)

many large cities, and many cathedrals are urban foci; but the popular image of them conforms to the genre of painting that shows Salisbury Cathedral behind lush meadows. The countryside is the proper frame for the profane as well as for the sacred. On the advice of the Royal Fine Art Commission, the height of a new hotel in Ascot was reduced so as to preserve the feeling of a forest setting for the racecourse.[12]

Moreover, the traditional English city is countrified. London above all is conceived as essentially rural; Londoners cherish easy access to places where the urban scene is hardly visible. It is the threat to this camou-flage, more than the actual appearance of the buildings, that disturbs Londoners about skyscrapers. Henry James observed with delight that "you may traverse this immense distance [from Notting Hill to Whitehall] . . . altogether on soft, fine turf, amid the song of birds, the bleat of lambs, the ripple of ponds, the rustle of admirable trees."[13] And the Royal Fine Art Commission would prohibit high buildings at the western end of Kensington Gardens "to retain the feeling that this green space still leads towards the more open areas in the west."[14]

12. *Eighteenth Rept. Royal Fine Art Commission. September 1960—August 1962*, London, 1963 (*[Parliamentary Command Paper] Cmnd. 1927*), p. 10.

13. Henry James: *Essays in London and Elsewhere* (New York, 1893), p. 16.
14. *Seventeenth Rept. Royal Fine Art Commission, September 1959—August 1960*, London, 1961 (*[Parliamentary Command Paper] Cmnd. 1336*), p. 7.

Spacious greenery is not all that gives London a rural air. The city is in a sense an archipelago of villages, whose names are inscribed on the urban map and whose inhabitants think parochially of their shops and "locals." Thus Marylebone, a resident writes, "still has a High Street that curves and narrows as it picks its way among the ghosts of dead farms and forgotten private properties."[15] Where villages did not exist, they were invented. In the 1800's St. John's Wood was developed as a secluded hamlet of rustic villas, and Nash's most durable contributions to the urban scene were two park villages set on the edge of a dell in a far corner of the Regent's Park estate. Today increasing numbers of city dwellers like to give the impression that they are in fact villagers. *The Times* envisages even the residents of Westminster as forgetting the Abbey and the Houses of Parliament to "announce themselves as the village folk of Minster-in-the-Marsh."[16]

English fondness for the bucolic is as old as English topographical writing. But it was mainly in reaction to nineteenth-century industrial building and overcrowding that the English countryside became an object of veneration. Urban brutalization inspired Patrick Geddes to admire the small community, William Morris to sentimentalize handicrafts, and Ebenezer Howard to create Garden Cities. But those who could afford to do so fled the city entirely. From rustic villas in Surrey and Cheshire the well-to-do moved ever farther from the sight and sound of the advancing town. The motor age has greatly accelerated the urban exodus to still unspoiled villages beyond the Green Belts. But the traditional character of these villages—a rural way of life, close family ties, distinctive

design and period architecture—can be maintained only by the most stringent restrictions on development.

The Picturesque

England has its nature lovers who disdain the domesticated and swear by the wild fells of Westmoreland or Kipling's Sussex, where

> No tender-hearted garden crowns,
> No bosomed woods adorn
> Our blunt, bow-headed, whale-backed Downs,
> But gnarled and writhen thorn—
> Bare slopes where chasing shadows skim.[17]

But the countryside beloved by the great majority is tamed and inhabited, warm, comfortable, humanized. Unimpressed by the storm-wracked Hebrides, an English excursionist complained on her return to London that "there was nothing but scenery up there."[18] Scenes of natural grandeur lack those qualities which make landscapes picturesque: an intimate, lived-in appearance, or a desuetude inspiring romantic melancholy.

The favored landscape is what Turner denoted "elegant pastoral" as distinct from merely "pastoral[19];" it calls to mind traditional upper-class tastes and pursuits. What is considered "essentially English" is a calm and peaceful deer park, with slow-moving streams and wide expanses of meadowland studded with fine trees.[20] The scene should

15. Patrick O'Donovan: London '64: "Fine Village to Live In," *Observer*, Mar. 29, 1964.
16. "Village Life," *The Times*, Feb. 16, 1963, p. 9.
17. Rudyard Kipling: Sussex [1902], in *Rudyard Kipling's Verse* (definitive edit.; New York, 1940), p. 214.
18. Miss Gertrude Usher, in the *News Chronicle* (London), as quoted in *This England: Selections from the "New Statesman" This England Column 1957-60* (London, 1960), p. 26.
19. W. G. Rawlinson: Turner's *Liber Studiorum: A Description and a Catalogue* (London, 1878), pp. iv-v.
20. *Third Rept. Royal Fine Art Commission*, London, 1928 (*[British Command Paper] Cmnd. 3238*), pp. 5-6.

Figure 3. Saltram House and grounds, Plympton, Devon. An eighteenth-century classical façade masks the remains of a large Tudor house; cattle graze under beech trees in the landscaped park. (The National Trust; Photo Precision Ltd., copyright reserved)

include free-ranging domestic animals, since "the sight of grazing cattle . . . [is] one of the traditional delights"[21] (Fig. 3). When it is arable land, hedgerows and small fields are usually obligatory.[22] Like the Vale of St. Albans in Defoe's description, picturesque England is "all a planted garden. . . . The inclos'd corn-fields made one grand parterre,

the thick planted hedge rows, like a wilderness or labyrinth, divided in espaliers; the villages interspers'd . . . In a word, it was all nature, and yet look'd all like art."[23]

Picturesque taste is essentially a preference for the irregular, the complex, the intricate, the ornate (Fig. 4). The English like landscapes compartmented into small scenes furnished with belfried church towers, half-timbered thatched cottages, rutted lanes, rookeried elms, lich gates, and

21. *Thirty-Sixth Ann. Rept. Council for the Preservation of Rural England, 1961-1962*, Vol. 17, No. 4, p. 7.
22. *Thirteenth Rept. National Parks Commission, for the Year Ended September 30, 1962*, London, 1962, pp. 14-15; Brian Hackett: "Design in Rural Landscape," *Planning Outlook*, Vol. 1, No. 3, Autumn, 1949, pp. 22-38.

23. Daniel Defoe: *A Tour through England & Wales, Divided into Circuits or Journies* [1724-1726] (2 vols.; Everyman's Library, Nos. 820 and 821; London [1928]), Vol. 2, pp. 8-9.

Figure 4. Gazebo in the rustic style at Nymans Gardens, Sussex, built as a dovecote in 1923. (Photograph: The Countess of Rosse and the National Trust)

stiles—in short, "the intimate and appealing beauty which our forbears impressed upon it." [24] The devotee of the picturesque dislikes what is formal, geometrical, anticipated, too evidently planned or dictated. With Rupert Brooke, he resents the regimented tulip beds of Berlin and yearns for an unkempt hedge where blows "an English unofficial rose." [25]

English towns traditionally shun monu mental Beaux-Arts layouts. "City Saved from Utopia Planners," heralds a report of Leicester's decision to keep its open marketplace. [26] Leicester thus retains a sense of mystery and informality akin to what James admired in Chester, "a perfect feast of crookedness—of those random corners, projections and recesses, odd domestic interspaces charmingly saved or lost, those innumerable architectural surprises and caprices and fantasies . . . infinite accident and infinite effect." [27] As Casson suggests for seaside resorts, "a glimpse of the sea down a

24. [Lord Strang:] Opening Address by the Chairman of the National Parks Commission at the Conference of Park Planning Authorities at Windermere on May 19 and 20, 1960 [mimeographed], pp. 11-12.
25. Rupert Brooke: "The Old Vicarage, Grantchester," in *The Collected Poems of Rupert Brooke* (New York, 1915), p. 155.

26. Ian Nairn, in the *Daily Telegraph*, London, Apr. 16, 1963.
27. Henry James: *English Hours* (2nd edit.; New York, 1960), p. 39.

side street can be just as exciting and evocative as a full view from a promenade frontage."[28]

The prime example of the picturesque, as
of the bucolic, is London. "The essential
qualities of the City," Pevsner writes of the
business center, "are closeness, variety, and
intricacy, and the ever-recurring contrasts of
tall and low, of large and small, of wide and
narrow, of straight and crooked, the closes
and retreats and odd leafy corners."[29]
Picturesque intimacy and irregularity similarly prevail in other quarters.

After the 1666 fire Evelyn, Wren, and
others planned to rebuild London as a regular, symmetrical city, with grand boulevards
and long vistas down straight avenues, formal parks and promenades, houses uniformly spaced and sized. None of these
materialized; and in contrast with the slow,
wide panoramas of Paris, London unfolds a
rapid succession of small new vistas. St.
Paul's Cathedral provides the classic illustration of picturesque taste. Two decades ago
the Royal Fine Art Commission rejected an
open geometrical layout so that the great
dome might continue instead to be glimpsed
"in a hundred different views"[30] (Fig. 5).
Current planning likewise eschews a head-on
confrontation for several partial, oblique,
transitory vistas, keeping the precinct of the
cathedral small enough "to maintain its
involvement with everyday life."[31] This

scheme has its critics, but most of them
object to the incongruity and ugliness of the
new buildings hard by rather than to the
general notion of hidden intimacy.

From the condemnation of planning and
regimentation, one might well suppose the
picturesque to be a series of happy accidents, and conclude that the desired impression of roughness and irregularity was entirely fortuitous. Nothing is further from the
truth; the picturesque is contrived and composed with as much care as any geometrical
layout. The laws of the picturesque are
strict; one enthusiast explains at length why
at least three cows are needed for a picturesque grouping,[32] another learnedly debates
whether there should be an odd or even
number of trees in a clump.[33] Picturesque
landscapes are modeled on images and ideas
received from the arts; hence—however their
creators strive to conceal their handiwork—
they are inherently artificial.

The consummate achievement of picturesque art is the landscape garden of the
eighteenth century. The English landowner
molded terrain, planted trees, and sited
buildings to create scenes resembling, not
real nature, but the idealizations of nature
depicted in the paintings of certain artists,
notably Claude Lorrain, Gaspard Poussin,
and Salvator Rosa. "Nature was frequently
scarcely seen at all, for the lover of the picturesque was bent upon discovering not the
world as it is, but the world as it might have

28. Sir Hugh Casson: "Seaside Sense" [paper
delivered at the Conference on the Future Development of Holiday Resorts, London, November 13,
1962; mimeographed], p. 6.
29. Nikolaus Pevsner: London, Vol. 1: *The Cities
of London and Westminster* (The Buildings of
England, BE12; Harmondsworth, Middlesex,
1957), p. 105.
30. "Observations on the City of London's Report
on Post-War Reconstruction" (Royal Fine Art
Commission, London, 1945), p. 7.
31. "St. Paul's," *Architectural Rev.*, Vol. 119,
1956, pp. 295-298; Michael Manser: "Common

Sense about St. Paul's," *Observer*, July 12, 1964,
p. 23.
32. William Gilpin: *Observations, Relative Chiefly
to Picturesque Beauty, Made in the Year 1772, on
Several Parts of England; Particularly the Mountains, and Lakes of Cumberland, and Westmoreland* (2 vols.; London, 1786), Vol. 2, p. 258.
33. Humphry Repton: "Observations on the
Theory and Practice of Landscape Gardening"
[1803], in *Landscape Architecture of the Late
Humphry Repton, Esq.* (edited by J. C. Loudon;
London, 1840), pp. 117-320; reference on p. 170.

Figure 5. St. Paul's Cathedral, London, from Watling Street (1930). (The Royal Commission on Historical Monuments; Crown copyright reserved)

been had the Creator been an Italian artist of the seventeenth century."[34] Guidebooks recommended visits to the Lake District during the wet months, when clouds, mists, and moving vapors gave the landscape a luminous softness most like a wash drawing or an aquatint.

To see landscapes as pictures, the traveler of the period stood with his back to the view and looked into a Claude glass, a plano-convex mirror about four inches in diameter, tinted to conjure up the illusion of golden distance. With the landscape thus reduced to the size of a postcard and extraneous detail lost, shape, balance, and perspective could be seen at a glance. Assemblages of rocks, trees, houses, and stretches of water were judged by their suitability for paintings.

Painters of the period found the actual English landscape wanting in picturesque interest. Asked to paint Lord Hardwicke's park, Gainsborough declined, asserting that "with regard to *real views* from Nature in this country, he has never seen any place that affords a subject equal to the poorest imitations of Gasper [Poussin] or Claude."[35] A "grand" scene in Scotland interested Gilpin's imagination, "but not the eye," because it was too formless to make a picture.[36] Criticized for a virtually unrecognizable landscape sketch, a character in a satire of the period retorts: "If it is not like what it *is*, it is what it *ought* to be. I have only made it picturesque."[37]

The esthetic impact of a picturesque scene was supposed to be a means to an end: to stimulate moral reflection, to appeal to emotion. Followers of Inigo Jones thought the dim interiors of medieval churches suited to "the bigotted inhabitants of the convent and the cloister"; they preferred the Greek style because "light is cheerful, and cheerfulness is the disposition of innocence."[38] Devotees of the Gothic condemned classical taste as artificial and contrived, but they themselves were not more natural or spontaneous. In the Lake District they admired cliffs, crags, mists, and storms because these called to mind awe-inspiring landscapes painted by Salvator Rosa and described in novels by Mrs. Radcliffe. Such scenes induced reflections about puny man confronted by the force of the Creation. Melancholy was aroused by the silent pool, the deep dark grotto, the gloom of overhanging branches, the falling ruin.[39]

The ruin was a landscape feature especially favored by lovers of the picturesque—and here picturesque taste joins hands, as we shall shortly see, with façadism and antiquarianism. Old things are apt to be wrinkled, variegated, accidented; above all, weathering has harmonized them with the rest of the landscape (Fig. 6). "A piece of Palladian architecture may be elegant in the last degree," Gilpin advised. "But . . . should we wish to give it picturesque beauty, . . . we must beat down one half of it, deface the other, and throw the mutilated members

34. Samuel H. Monk: *The Sublime: A Study of Critical Theories in XVIII-Century England* (Ann Arbor, Mich., 1960), p. 204.
35. Gainsborough, as quoted in Kenneth Clark: *Landscape into Art* (Pelican Books, A 369; Harmondsworth, Middlesex, 1956), p. 48.
36. William Gilpin: *Observations, Relative Chiefly to Picturesque Beauty, Made in the Year 1776, on Several Parts of Great Britain; Particularly the High-Lands of Scotland* (2nd edit.; 2 vols.; London, 1792), Vol. 1, p. 172.
37. [James Plumptre:] *The Lakers: a Comic*

Opera, in Three Acts (Act I, Scene 2) (London, 1798), p. 20.
38. Vicesimus Knox: "Cursory Considerations on Architecture," Essay 79, in *Essays, Moral and Literary* (2 vols.; London, 1782), Vol. 1, pp. 340-351; reference on p. 348.
39. B. Sprague Allen: *Tides in English Taste (1619-1800): A Background for the Study of Literature* (2 vols.; Cambridge, Mass., 1937), Vol. 2, pp. 151-158.

Figure 6. The church at Netley Abbey, Hampshire. This thirteenth-century Cistercian abbey, dissolved in 1536, is now owned by the Ministry of Public Buildings and Works. (The Ministry of Public Buildings and Works; British Crown Copyright)

around in heaps. In short, from a *smooth* building we must turn it into a *rough* ruin."[40] Deliberate destruction for picturesque effect is no longer the mode, but the English still appreciate a good ruin, however achieved. The bomb that destroyed St. Faith's in Stroke Newington in 1944 is said to have created "a spectacle of incredible grandeur . . . out of a church of very moderate artistic stature."[41]

The Deciduous

A special aspect of English taste for the picturesque is a decided preference for bushy-topped, broad-leaved, deciduous trees. "German conifer-worship," to use Hyams' term, is "shared in Britain only by the Forestry Commission."[42]

The British are particularly prone to identify themselves with "native" trees. Objecting to the phrase "tough as teak" (a foreign tree), a correspondent recommends that sports writers "refer to such timbers as ash, oak, beech, birch, when they want to

40. William Gilpin: *Three Essays: On Picturesque Beauty; On Picturesque Travel; and On Sketching Landscape* (London, 1792), pp. 7-8.
41. John Summerson: *Heavenly Mansions and Other Essays on Architecture* (New York, 1963), p. 238.

42. Edward Hyams: "The Countryside," *New Statesman*, Dec. 20, 1963, p. 923.

emphasize the toughness of some of our British manhood."[43] Broad-leaved trees generally—including the horse chestnut, the London plane, and the English walnut, introduced from abroad as recently as the seventeenth century[44] —tend to be thought of as indigenous, and most conifers as exotic.

Deciduous trees please the English because they are delicately patterned, softly outlined, varied in form and color, scumbled in texture, seasonal in foliage, tolerant of undergrowth, and generally older than conifers. "The seasonal colour changes, the depths of light and shade of the varying foliage of native broadleaved trees, are an essential ingredient" in the landscape, notes the Council for the Preservation of Rural England.[45] By contrast, "the immovable and immutable conifer blanket is foreign to our experience."[46] And the brown, pine-needled floor is a barren substitute for the ferns, grasses, and mosses of the hardwood forest.

Conifers are considered gloomy, harsh, and oppressive, partly because many of them are strictly commercial. The long lines of evergreens behind barbed-wire fences are not unjustly condemned as "Sitka slums," "jerry-planting," and "scenic claustrophobia." The Forestry Commission's coniferous plantation at Thetford Chase, in the Breck-

land, has been termed "a 36,000-acre eyesore, a vast timber-factory as deadly as any industrial squalor of the 19th century";[47] amenity groups exhort the Commission to replace conifers with birch and ash, to soften blocks of pine and spruce by interspersing hardwoods, or at least to conceal them behind hardwood screens. The Commission hopes, however, that time will alter taste; "the decried coniferous plantations of today may be the prized possession of future generations."[48] As soon as people begin to look at them "we need not fear that the russet brown of the Japanese larch in winter, or the silvery sheen of Sitka spruce or noble fir, will be regarded with any less delight than . . . the golden autumnal tints of the birch and the aspen."[49]

But most English people continue to prefer what forest economists scorn as "ye olde worlde pixie woods,"[50] as opposed to the "numbing . . . predictability," the "endless precision of trunks and bottle-green foliage," and other "trance-inducing effects" of serried ranks of conifers.[51] One landowner charges that this preference exemplifies "that last infirmity of the urban mind— belief that the countryside exists to indulge contemporary taste in the picturesque."[52] But only a deciduous medley really suits

43. Letter in the *Manchester Evening News,* as quoted in *This England* [see footnote 18 above], p. 11.
44. H. L. Edlin: *Trees, Woods & Man* (London, 1956), pp. 224-225; Edward Hyams: "The Countryside," *New Statesman,* Nov. 26, 1960, p. 853.
45. Memorandum submitted to the Government Working Party on Forestry Policy, November 13, 1962 [first draft, mimeographed], p. 3.
46. "The Case for Control of Afforestation of Open Land in National Parks" (Standing Committee on National Parks of the Councils for the Preservation of Rural England and Wales and the Joint Action Group for the Protection of Dartmoor and Exmoor, London, 1961), p. 16.

47. Geoffrey S. Kelly: "Afforestation v. Landscape," *Architectural Rev.,* Vol. 120, 1956, pp. 387-390.
48. Country Landowners' Association: "Landowners and the Future," in *The Countryside in 1970:* Proceedings of the Study Conference held at Fishmongers' Hall, London, E.C.4, 4-5 November 1963 (London, 1964), pp. 223-235 (Paper No. 12); reference on p. 223.
49. Edlin, *op. cit.* [see footnote 44 above], p. 168.
50. Lord Lytton for the Country Landowners' Association, quoted in "Efforts to Save Exmoor Trees," *The Times,* June 7, 1961, p. 7.
51. Roy Perrott: "A Nice Place to Get Lost In," *Observer,* Apr. 26, 1964, p. 5.
52. Lord de L'Isle: "Trees to Be Felled" [letter of Nov. 12], *The Times,* Nov. 15, 1958, p. 9.

that sweet confusion so characteristic of the English landscape.

The Tidy

If confusion, irregularity, and even "wild obscurity and rude neglect"[53] are admired and cultivated, the English landscape is also an exemplar of order and neatness. Seemliness and propriety are respected; untidiness, however prevalent,[54] is felt to be ill-mannered and offensive; demarcations are clearcut. Neatness is a matter of boundaries as well as of areas. Roadside verges, hedgerows, fences, and railroad rights-of-way are trim, distinct, unambiguous. A strikingly tidy feature of the English landscape is its rivers and canals, whose channels and borders are almost everywhere tended and smooth.

Turf is admired above all; the vast extent of grassland is an English phenomenon. Seldom is it fanatically prim. What people want is countryside easy to walk in and to look at, a rough carpet kept free of messy undergrowth. Trees, if any, are to be neatly grouped or trimmed so as not to detract from the grassy expanse.

Most downland and much other pastureland in England share with private gardens and landscape parks this amalgam of clarity, order, and accessibility (Figs. 2, 3, and 6). The scraggly growths of briar and bramble, the motley ground cover, the untended seedlings that clutter backyards, roadsides, and derelict agricultural lands in America would be tolerated by few English landowners, private or public. "Every piece of land which has been removed from the care

of nature must be adopted by someone if it is not to become derelict," an English landscape architect concludes.[55] For neatness, land must be used, not left alone. Without grazing sheep, grass loses its creeping habit, and the surface becomes ragged and unkempt. On Salisbury Plain, where the War Department has ousted the shepherd, close-cropped turf has given given way to rank, soggy, almost colorless grass. The farmer is seen as the nation's unpaid landscape gardener.[56] To eradicate scrub on Coombe Hill, a famous beauty spot and viewpoint in the Chilterns, the National Trust plans to clear the land and return it to grazing.[57]

Neatness usually proscribes rather than prescribes, however. "Best-Kept Village" campaigns place greater emphasis on removing litter and concealing the unsightly than on new embellishments of the local scene. Weary of the "lifeless tidiness" usual in such competitions, one critic wondered "what would happen to the unfortunate cow which passed through the prize-winning streets at the wrong moment."[58]

Even litter is different in England. The organization that combats it is called the "Keep Britain Tidy Group"—*tidy*, not clean, safe, healthy, or beautiful. The Country Code[59] for urban visitors stresses order and decorum, everything in its proper place.

53. Richard Payne Knight: *The Landscape: A Didactic Poem in Three Books Addressed to Uvedale Price, Esq.* (Book II, line 191) (London, 1794), p. 32.
54. "Dirt and untidiness had become a national trait" (Shelagh McCormick: The Mousetrap in the Kitchen, *Daily Telegraph,* Aug. 1, 1964, p. 6).
55. Sylvia Crowe: *Tomorrow's Landscape* (London, 1956), p. 137.
56. By L. Dudley Stamp: "Land Classification and Agriculture," in *Greater London Plan 1944* (by Patrick Abercrombie; London, 1945), pp. 86-96; reference on p. 95.
57. *News Letter,* The National Trust for Places of Historic Interest or Natural Beauty, London, Spring, 1961, p. 11.
58. W. G. Hoskins: "The Heritage and an Historical Account of Its Disfigurement," *Journ. Royal Soc. of Arts,* Vol. 105, 1956-1957, pp. 78-84; reference on p. 79.
59. National Parks Commission: *The Country Code for Visitors to the Countryside* (London, 1951).

Tidiness is continually emphasized in the schools; it is not nature lovers alone who organize litter removal. To the English, the absence—or at least the concealment—of disfigurement and squalor often matters more than the presence of beauty.

Façadism

Whether or not beauty is at stake, appearances do count. The English want things to look right and go to considerable trouble to secure what they consider an appropriate façade. The bucolic, the picturesque, the tidy, are all aspects of this penchant for dressing up the landscape. Landscape and building façades are like costumes or vestments, stressing the respectability, propriety, and aspirations of the wearers. Conventional and imitative, façades are employed to conceal structure, to disguise function, to palliate the unpleasant, to camouflage the crude.

Façades also help create the atmosphere considered appropriate to specific activities: jollity in the glittering gin palace, security in the bank, seclusion in the cathedral close, and, on a broader scale, neighborliness in the village, scholarly fellowship in the college court, respectability at Bournemouth and Cheltenham, pleasure at Brighton and Blackpool. The façades lining Blackpool's Golden Mile underscore the mood of holiday gaiety. The labyrinthine dazzle of colored illuminations portraying fairy tales and Pickwickian revels, the blaring amusement arcades, the gypsy fortunetellers and trick photographers, the gargantuan displays of food and drink, all proclaim that Blackpool is FUN. In contrast, Bournemouth is tree-shaded, slow-paced, stately, with the hush of old age and good manners over its trim, wide-spaced villas. In Blackpool or Bournemouth, in Salford or Salisbury, the shape, size, style, fabric, and setting of buildings instruct the visitor how to approach them and remind the resident how to behave.

To induce the proper frame of mind in the spectator, a place should be properly attired. Regardless of structure, houses, pubs, shops, hospitals, schools, and post offices have each their special style. Good architecture was exclusively classical in Georgian England, but churches and universities continued to be built in the Gothic style because "it was still the natural way of building a church or a college,"[60] the proper expression of religious and scholastic sentiment. For banks and government buildings, on the other hand, the appropriate style was classical, and despite the Gothic Revival they remained classical well into the nineteenth century. When a habitual style is departed from or traditional decor is omitted, the English public is apt to feel uncomfortable and out of place.

Façades in England are employed to restrain more than to adorn, to conceal rather than to advertise. The acme of good appearance is invisibility, as Sir Albert Richardson characterized his Neo-Georgian council offices at Ampthill: "My building, like all good-looking things, *will not be noticed*; it will creep up on you."[61] People tend to prefer things to look unrelated to their structure and function. Above all, the English are averse to blatant commercialism. Decent folk are not in trade; business is best subdued and muted, as in Savile Row, where tailors display bolts of cloth without price labels (no *garments* are exhibited). The better shops look austere and retiring, seeming to apologize for their very existence.

What the spectator sees matters much

---

60. Kenneth Clark: *The Gothic Revival: An Essay in the History of Taste* (Pelican Books, A687; Harmondsworth, Middlesex, 1964), p. 9.
61. Sir Albert Richardson, as quoted in "Professor Defends His Neo-Georgian Council Offices," *Guardian*, Sept. 22, 1962. (Italics ours.)

more than how the resident lives. Interior comfort, convenience, and attractiveness are readily sacrificed to obtain a desired exterior effect. Blenheim Palace presents a magnificent façade of pavilions, towers, and balustrades, but as Pope pointed out, it was unlivable:

'tis very fine,
But where d'ye sleep, or where d'ye dine?
I find, by all you have been telling,
That 'tis a house, but not a dwelling.[62]

Appearance held such priority over use that the American Ambassador half a century ago judged that the English "frantically resent conveniences. They build their great law court building . . . so as to provide an entrance hall of imposing proportions which they use once a year; and to get this fine hall they have to make their court rooms, which they must use all the time, dark and small and inaccessible."[63]

Just as exteriors are more important than interiors, so fronts matter more than backs. The front presented to the world sets the tone of the place; when fashions change, it is the front that is stuccoed. A half-timbered house with an overhanging upper story may be given a classical look by putting a Queen Anne front on its Mary Ann back. The screen-wall at Ashridge was built purely as a façade to give the house the longest frontage in Hertfordshire. This is a sham comparable with the false bridge at Kenwood, fashioned in wood to look like stone, a white-painted, two-dimensional representation of balustrading.

In real stone, cement, and plaster is Nash's London terrace scenery (Fig. 7). North from Carlton House Terrace, up Regent Street into Regent's Park, it culminates in the exuberant carpentry of Cumberland Terrace, furnished with false pediments, screens, and hollow columns. Current concern for façades is exemplified in the treatment of Clarence Terrace and Sussex Place, two of the Nash terraces bordering Regent's Park. Once elegant residences, these buildings had deteriorated into offices and then to virtual abandonment. Their dangerously dilapidated façades were maintained by periodic applications of paint, but the walls behind them were crumbling, and the flimsy structures were collapsing on their insecure foundations. Declining rentals made maintenance increasingly unprofitable after the war, and the Crown, which owns the buildings, adopted plans for complete rebuilding. For three years the London County Council insisted that the buildings be preserved as they were. This the contractors considered impracticable; and they were backed by the Royal Fine Art Commission, which favored retention of the façades in replica rather than in reality. That the façades should be preserved was never in question; rather, as Banham put it, "top brains in architecture [were] arguing whether it is morally better to patch up the facades . . . or pull them down and rebuild them exactly as they were." In the end the latter view prevailed.[64] So important are these buildings as scenery that the developers are required to keep an arrangement of rooms, inconveniently small for modern purposes, that will enable the passerby looking through windows to see walls at proper distances

62. Alexander Pope: "Upon the Duke of Marlborough's House at Woodstock, Epigrams and Inscriptions," in *Works* (edited by Whitwell Elwin and W. J. Courthope; 10 vols.; London, 1871-1889), Vol. 4 (1882), p. 451.
63. Walter Hines Page to Woodrow Wilson, 1914, in *The Life and Letters of Walter H. Page* (by Burton J. Hendrick; 3 vols.; New York, 1925), Vol. 1, p. 173.

64. Reyner Banham: "The Embalmed City," *New Statesman*, Apr. 12, 1963, pp. 528-530, reference on p. 528; "Change of Mind on Nash Terraces," *The Times*, Feb. 20, 1963, p. 5.

Figure 7. Cumberland Terrace, Regent's Park, London, by John Nash (1826). (The Royal Commission on Historical Monuments; British Crown Copyright)

inside the rooms; he must not be outraged by too much or too little depth.

Façadism is no recent fad, but an ancient English tradition. "England was the first country to break the unity of interior and exterior and wrap buildings up in clothes not made for them but for buildings of other ages and purposes," writes Pevsner.[65] English enthusiasm for adopting one style after another is based partly on infatuation with the landscapes and architecture of other countries, partly on a firm belief in native artistic deficiency. The imitation of Continental work goes back to the Norman Conquest. English Norman is borrowed Romanesque, Early English follows Continental Gothic, English Decorated follows French Flamboyant, Elizabethan and Jacobean are

imitations of Rhenish Renaissance, and the Baroque finds expression in the works of Wren, Hawksmoor, and Vanbrugh.

With Palladianism, a style entirely dependent on measured proportions and exterior effects, function and structure were completely subordinated to façades. The houses of Burlington, Kent, and Colen Campbell were built simply to be looked at. Their proportions, their exact symmetry, their axial vistas through halls and chambers and from inside to outside, their windows, entrances and exits, steps and porticoes, were designed as pure scenery (Fig. 3). The open, airy Palladian plan, well suited to the climate of central Italy, was a misfit in the damp, cold, blustery English countryside. High walls and deep porticoes designed to exclude the glare of the Italian sun deprived English occupants of light and views. Rooms

65. Nikolaus Pevsner: *The Englishness of English Art* (London, 1956), p. 29.

were dark and drafty, chimneys smoked, kitchens were far from dining rooms. The Palladian house Lord Burlington designed for General Wade was so inconvenient that "he could not live in it," but so elegant that he planned to buy the house opposite in order to look at it.[66]

Despite the discomforts it frequently entails, façadism has remained the fashion ever since. Half a century ago architects were taken to task for producing "what looked domestic, or looked farmlike, or looked ecclesiastical . . . –things that looked like things but that were not the things themselves."[67] Lancaster judged that in the 1920's "the old English fondness for disguising everything as something else now attained the dimensions of a serious pathological affliction."[68]

The commonest disguises are those intended to make new objects look old, to harmonize with their surroundings. Fresh woodwork is stained and varnished, ivy and creeping plants cover bare new walls, and the Devon County Council urges that corrugated asbestos roofs be coated with farmyard manure to promote a "natural" growth of lichen and moss.[69] But English concern for age and antiqueness deserves a section to itself.

Antiquarianism

At the base of a statue outside the National Archives building in Washington, D. C., is carved the inscription "What Is Past Is Prologue," or as a taxi driver is said to have explained it to a puzzled visitor, "You ain't seen nothin' yet." Nothing could be more typical of the way Americans view their place in time or less so of the English. "We follow an inverted Coué system," explains Marcus Cunliffe, "according to which every day, in every way, things are getting worse and worse."[70] It is in the past that England's importance and glory are seen to lie. "To me and millions more," a correspondent writes, " 'England' is a beautiful word that conjures up the glories of our history."[71]

Rejection of the Present

So strong a hold has the past that the English often find it more substantial than the present. "What is characteristically British is superannuated," Kingsley Amis fears. "Some British people of all classes may be beginning to love themselves for their quaintness."[72] This is not to say that history is neglected in other parts of the world. Millions of Americans make pilgrimages to Mount Vernon and Williamsburg. And it is to Americans, not to their own countrymen, that two Englishmen have contracted to sell sixteen-square-yard lots of "history-impregnated land"—at one hundred dollars a lot.[73] Nor do the English normally display the reverent zeal shown by the Poles, who have rebuilt the medieval center of war-bombed Warsaw to look exactly as it was. But historical attachments in-

66. Lord Chesterfield, as cited by Horace Walpole in a letter to George Montagu, May 18, 1748, in *Yale Edition of Horace Walpole's Correspondence* (edited by W. S. Lewis and Ralph S. Brown, Jr.), Vol. 9 (New Haven, 1941), p. 56.
67. William Richard Lethaby, in the *Architectural Journ.*, Vol. 17, 1910, p. 482.
68. Osbert Lancaster: *Here, of All Places* (Boston, 1958), p. 160.
69. "Dartmoor: Building in the National Park" (published for the Devon County Council, Exeter; London, 1955), p. 48.

70. Marcus Cunliffe: "The Comforts of the Sick-Bay," *Encounter*, Vol. 21, No. 1, 1963, pp. 96-99; reference on pp. 98-99.
71. Letter in the *Daily Telegraph*, quoted in "This England," *New Statesman*, Jan. 18, 1963, p. 68.
72. Kingsley Amis: "What's Left for Patriotism?" *Observer*, Jan. 20, 1963, p. 21.
73. "Ye Olde Englishe Historie for Sale," *Sunday Times*, Apr. 14, 1963, p. 12.

spire the English in a fashion and to a degree to be found among no other people.

Love of the past complements English devotion to the open air. The signs of antiquity stir imagination and excite feeling. As Thomas Gray could not look at the Cam without seeing

High Potentates, and Dames of royal birth
And mitred Fathers in long order go,[74]

so the "crumbling courts" of Cambridge colleges mellowed by the "grace of antiquity" recall for A. C. Benson "the old tradition of multifarious humanity that has century by century entwined itself with the very fabric of the place." [75]

This habit of seeing landscapes through past associations, this valuation of places according to their connections with a presumed or inferred history, is best described as antiquarianism. It is a distinctively English stance. Antiquarianism emerges now as a nostalgic desire to put the clock back to any or every era, now as an urge to commemorate the past by preserving all relics of former times.[76] "It is not a question of retaining a few old buildings," a planner notes, "but of conserving . . . a major part of the heritage of the English-speaking world, of which this country is the guardian." [77] Many still

believe, with Ruskin, that there is "no question of expediency or feeling whether we shall preserve the buildings of past times or not. *We have no right whatever to touch them.* They are not ours." [78]

Any past is better than none. Fortheringay Castle, where Mary Queen of Scots was beheaded, and the Bloody Tower are as jealously guarded as any village Maypole or Temple of Fortune. In America the past is loved only when it was glorious; relics of shame and dishonor are ignored or whitewashed. Because Jay Gould "was a robber baron, not a great American," the village of Tarrytown did not want his Hudson Valley estate made a national historic site.[79] But in England commemoration does not imply moral endorsement; the whole stream of history, good, bad, and indifferent, has its place in the landscape.

This blanket approval of everything past has its critics, to be sure. "Some seem to admire indiscriminately whatever has been long preserved," Samuel Johnson remarked apropos of the passion for ruins, "without considering that time has sometimes co-operated with chance." [80] But to the antiquarian time lends enchantment to everything. "If the design be poor," wrote Ruskin, time "will enrich it; if overcharged, simplify it; if harsh and violent, soften it." [81] The concept that architectural structures had a natural life-span led the architect John Soane to sketch buildings as they would look not only in youth but in a state

74. Thomas Gray: "Ode for Music" [1769], in *The Poetical Works of Gray and Collins* (edited by Austin Lane Poole; London, 1917), p. 113.
75. Arthur C. Benson: *From a College Window* (London, 1906), p. 15.
76. "Monuments Threatened or Destroyed: A Select List, 1956-1962" (Royal Commission on Historical Monuments [England], London 1963). (An annotated list of more than 800 hallowed buildings from Roman to Edwardian times.)
77. "Traffic in Towns, A Study of the Long Term Problems of Traffic in Urban Areas: Reports of the Steering Group and Working Group Appointed by the Minister of Transport [Buchanan Report]" (London, 1963), p. 197.

78. John Ruskin: *The Seven Lamps of Architecture* (New York, 1961), p. 186.
79. George B. Case, as quoted in "Tarrytown Urging U. S. to Cancel Law for a Gould Shrine," *New York Times*, Sept. 16, 1964, p. 33.
80. Samuel Johnson, as quoted in John Gloag: *The English Tradition in Architecture* (London, 1963), p. 215.
81. [John Ruskin:] *Modern Painters* (5 vols.; New York, 1886), Vol. 1, p. 105 (Part II, Sect. 1, Chap. 7, § 26).

of ruin.[82] Today the patina of age endows the nineteenth-century factory and even the slag heap with a nostalgic aura. The National Trust feels that "the time has now come to add industrial monuments" to its list of cherished inheritances redeemed.[83]

Even Dartmoor Prison has its admirers. Some lovers of rural England take comfort in the prospect that "this grim relic will no longer dishonour the landscape,"[84] but "if the Dartmoor we have known and loved is to be preserved," the advocate maintains, "the prison must be preserved too. It is now part of Dartmoor's tradition, history, appeal, fascination, and character."[85] As a commentator aptly remarks, "If any institution survives long enough in England, someone is sure to love it."[86]

The charm of much of the English scene is like that of the fictitious pub which "covered all periods from Thomist to Edwardian, and rejected nothing but the malaise of the present."[87] English resistance to change, English reluctance to disturb relict landscape or townscape, stems from a positive aversion to the contemporary—a present made up, as one architect put it, of "nylon, pylon and skylon."[88] The chairman of a House of Commons committee to select a design for a proposed extension to the Houses of Parliament bluntly confessed that "I can't think of a single modern building I like."[89] Everything connected with the past is valued above anything in the present or in any probable future. "Hardly a decent thing," a planner complains, "seems to have been done in the landscape here for wellnigh a hundred years."[90] So pervasive is this hankering after the past that *The Field* can hardly be censured for advertising a Cotswold residence with "large garage, converted into coach house."[91]

To reiterate the superiority of the past is to dismiss the possibility of progress. When a proposed new office block for Peterborough is condemned as "yet another modern monstrosity [that] will mar the character of this ancient city,"[92] we do not need to know what either the new office block or old Peterborough looks like; all that matters is that the former is new and the latter old. Antiquarian defeatism is patent in the confession that the Royal Fine Art Commission often try to preserve "buildings of no more than second-rate importance, possibly even third-rate. . . . The uppermost consideration in our minds is really fear as to what will take their place."[93] No wonder modern architecture in London seems "but a wheel-

---

82. John Piper: *Buildings and Prospects* (London, 1948), p. 89.

83. *Rept. 1962-63*, The National Trust for Places of Historic Interest or Natural Beauty, London, 1963, p. 5.

84. *Thirty-Fifth Ann. Rept. Council for the Preservation of Rural England, 1960-1961*, Vol. 17, No. 3, p. 38.

85. Article in *The Times*, quoted in *This England* [see footnote 18 above], p. 34.

86. Peter Green: "Tree Feller," *Listener*, Apr. 4, 1963, p. 608.

87. Nigel Dennis: *Cards of Identity* (New York, 1960), pp. 161-162.

88. Sir Albert Richardson, as quoted in "Sir Albert Richardson Is Dead; Championed the Georgian Era," *New York Times*, Feb. 4, 1964, p. 33.

89. Selwyn Lloyd, as quoted in William Hickey: "No, I am *NOT* a Mod, Says Selwyn, So He Wants Parliament Left Alone," *Daily Express*, London, May 9, 1964, p. 3.

90. Thomas Sharp: "The North-East—Hills and Hells," in *Britain and the Beast* (edited by Clough Williams-Ellis; London, 1938), pp. 141-159; reference on p. 142.

91. Quoted in the *New Yorker*, Sept. 5, 1964, p. 105.

92. "Peterborough Monstrosity? Office Block to Adjoin Church," *Guardian*, Feb. 9, 1963, p. 4.

93. Hoskins, *op. cit.* [see footnote 58 above], p. 82.

barrow full of cuttings grown in a rich compost of history." [94]

Devotion to the past is not a primeval English trait; "there was no Saxon Society for the Preservation of Roman Villas," *The Times* observes.[95] But even before 1600 John Leland and William Camden were searching the byways of Tudor England for Roman antiquities and looked with appreciative eyes at the remains of the Ancient Britons. With the classical revival the passion for the past became widespread. As early as 1628 John Earle excoriated that "unnaturall disease to bee enamour'd of old age and wrinckles, and loves of all things . . . the better for being mouldy and wormeeaten." [96] Avid for Roman relics, Anthony à Wood complained that the fellows of Merton at Oxford "would not let me live in the College for fear I should pluck it down to search after Antiquities." [97] In the eighteenth century Horace Walpole and his contemporaries restored the Middle Ages to favor; in the nineteenth Pugin and Ruskin raised "Gothic" from an expression of barbarity to the pinnacle of civilized taste. Later antiquaries have continued to add to the list of meritorious periods and imitable styles.

Rejection of the Sensuous

"Certainly, we love old buildings," writes Piper, "but we love them for what they stand for rather than for what they look like." [98] Antiquarianism is essentially nonesthetic. Critics apply different standards of judgment to the old and the new. What is condemned as crude, banal, or vulgar in a modern creation is likely to be defended as unsophisticated, primitive, or bold in an antique. Of contemporary architectural guidebooks, Pevsner alone emphasizes esthetic considerations over "quaintness, oldness or association." [99]

Historical preferences, unlike most visual choices, have to be consciously learned. The Englishman likes what he thinks conforms with canons of criticism. Denying that he knows anything about art, he accepts what he thinks educated, knowledgeable people would approve—"our English way," as Ruskin puts it, "of liking nothing, and professing to like triglyphs." [100] Immediate impressions are suspect, for good taste is formed only by long acquaintance with the work of masters and a knowledge of history; spontaneous enthusiasm is ignorant or ill-bred. These inhibitions, according to one critic, have made the Englishman "devoid of natural taste, . . . valuing things for their 'antiqueness' . . . instead of for their looks and suitability; awkward and uncomfortable at the very mention of the word beauty." [101]

The criterion of good taste in building, and to a smaller extent in landscape generally, is: from what does it derive, and how closely does it follow that model? Burlington's Palladian villa at Chiswick is deemed admirable because it is a faithful replica of

94. Lewis Mumford: "The Sky Line: The Liveliness of London," *New Yorker*, Sept. 19, 1953, pp. 98-103; reference on p. 99.
95. "Ancient Sights," *The Times*, Mar. 14, 1956, p. 11.
96. John Earle: "An Antiquary," in *Microcosmographie or, A Piece of the World Discovered in Essayes and Characters* [1628] (London, 1928), p. 13.
97. "The Life of Anthony à Wood from the Year 1632 to 1672, Written by Himself," in *The Lives of Those Eminent Antiquaries John Leland, Thomas Hearne, and Anthony à Wood* (2 vols.; Oxford, 1772), Vol. 2, pp. 253-254.
98. Piper, *op. cit.* [see footnote 82 above], p. 90.

99. Geoffrey Grigson, in the *Observer*, as quoted on back cover of Pevsner, London [see footnote 29 above].
100. John Ruskin: *The Stones of Venice* (3 vols.; New York, 1886), Vol. 1, p. 44 (Chap. 2, § 13).
101. Geoffrey M. Boumphrey: "Shall the Towns Kill or Save the Country?" in *Britain and the Beast* [see footnote 90 above], pp. 101-112; reference on p. 104.

the Rotonda at Vicenza; we applaud Burlington's scholarly virtuosity, not his architectural imagination. The Hammonds found the secret of eighteenth-century charm not "in any special beauty or nobility of design or expression, but simply in an exquisite fitness."[102] Fitness implied faithful adherence to the standards of one's betters.

That appreciation of the past has little to do with esthetic judgment is evident, too, from the omnivorous appetites of preservationists. However disregarded before, a thing is no sooner threatened with extinction than strenuous efforts are made to save it. Canals have rare qualities to offer, including scenery, solitude, and silence, but "it was not these charms which drove on those who wished to revive the Stratford canal. It was the fact that the canal was derelict."[103] Beauty and harmony are not at issue in the clamor to preserve some of the bulbous brick bottle ovens—now being replaced by electric kilns—that for a century darkened the skies of the Potteries and made Stoke on Trent the smokiest place in Britain.[104] The imminent closure of many railway lines and stations has rekindled nostalgia for gaslights, for Evercreech Junction as evoked by Betjeman, and for the quaint lunacies of Rowland Emmett's trains.

Rejection of the Functional

Offered a decision between something new and something old, or between something beautiful and something old, the English seldom consider it a hardship to choose the old. However, to reject something useful for something old usually demands a sacrifice of comfort, a conscious self-denial. A resident of Thurloe Square in South Kensington, for instance, is forbidden to replace her old studded front door with a new one that would keep out the cold winds.[105]

The dictates of antiquarianism are basically incompatible with those of function. The distinction is underscored in a recent government decision to retain the old lamp standards in Birdcage Walk alongside their replacements: "The new lights are to provide the illumination, and the old ones to provide the charm and interest."[106] In humbler surroundings the distinction is accepted without question; as a contemporary novelist puts it, working-class families with two downstairs rooms "lived in one and kept the other as a museum: this was England."[107] Stringent restrictions on land use are widely imposed—and accepted—in the name of the past; profit and efficiency are subordinated to historical context and flavor. Thus the headquarters of a leading national bank remain antiquated because the Minister of Housing and Local Government considers the building so fine a specimen of Victoriana, occupying so important a place in the City of London, that "he would be most unwilling to concur in its destruction."[108]

If useful in no other sense, the past is often said to have pedagogical value: one learns from the visible witnesses of history. Appreciative envy of past ways of life is felt to enlarge the range of experience. The luxurious appurtenances of English country houses provided a liberal education for C. E.

102. J. L. Hammond and Barbara Hammond: *The Village Labourer* [1911] (Guild Books, Nos. 239 and 240; 2 vols.; London, 1948), Vol. 2, p. 129.
103. "Towpath Message for a Nation," *The Times*, July 16, 1964, p. 13.
104. John Wain: "Portrait of Stoke-on-Trent," *Geogr. Mag.*, Vol. 33, 1960-1961, pp. 35-46; Kenneth Hudson: *Industrial Archaeology: An Introduction* (London, 1963), pp. 108-111.

105. "An Open-and-Shut Case," *New York Times*, Apr. 13, 1964, p. 32.
106. Lord Silkin in the House of Lords, as reported in the *Observer*, July 26, 1964, p. 11.
107. John Wain: *Hurry On Down* (Harmondsworth, Middlesex, 1960), p. 183.
108. Sir Keith Joseph, as quoted in "City Bank Building to Stay," *The Times*, Aug. 8, 1964, p. 4.

Montague: "You would be worse off to-day if you were without the idea you get from these things of the measure of man's iron will and versatile power to give himself a good time."[109]

At some country houses historical education is spiced with up-to-date popular entertainment. The Duke of Bedford maintains a zoo, a shooting gallery, and a miniature golf course at Woburn Abbey; Lord Montagu has a motor museum and a collection of traction engines at Beaulieu, and holds jazz festivals there. But vulgar showmanship spoils the lesson, Richardson protests: "If people want that kind of thing, they can go to a town and indulge in a saturnalia, but in the country to bring these vulgarities to rural scenes would be entirely wrong."[110] And many owners share his misgivings. "My Home [Blenheim Palace] is an education, not an entertainment," says the Duke of Marlborough. "If you inherit an historical place from your ancestors, it is a pity to turn it into a fun fair."[111]

Associations

But when all is said, the educational argument does not explain why the English prefer the old to the useful, the past to the present; it presupposes that history is worth having, even at the cost of comfort and beauty. Personality, not pedagogy, is the mainspring of English antiquarianism; the supreme value of relict landscapes and old buildings lies in their associations with historical events and persons. The English have a collector's eye for authorship, period, and authenticity; they take pride in distinguish-

ing Neolithic from early Bronze Age trackways, in discovering whether ridge-and-furrow in a field is medieval or modern, in determining whether the vaulting of a church aisle is Early English or Decorated. Like other collectors, they want to know whether particular details are rare, typical, or commonplace; above all, whether genuine or fake.

Archeologist or tourist, the English traveler takes a taxonomic interest in the landscape. For him, Ian Nairn writes, "an Historical Attraction" is "something to be looked at pedantically and individually and not seen whole as part of the landscape."[112] Preservationists "recognize any sash-windowed brick box as 'Georgian' but cannot see the true Georgian essence of a group of houses combined into a single architectural unity and related to a designed landscape."[113] Instead they compile an inventory of parts, listing sashes and chimneypieces, pediments and door knockers, in *catalogues raisonnés*. "Finished" cities like Bath and Cambridge, with complete sets of crescents or colleges, receive some attention as entities, but to a historical taxonomist a place like Gloucester or Colchester seems only an incongruous medley.

Places are linked most of all with persons: a creator, designer, or author; a possessor, patron, or heir; an individual associated, either causally or fortuitously, by historical events or literary allusions. "The olde oak beam is treasured because Henry VIII once cracked his skull on it; one's reactions to a baronial castle, eighth or nineteenth century, are inevitably coloured by the way you feel

109. C. E. Montague: *The Right Place: A Book of Pleasures* (London, 1924), p. 171.
110. Sir Albert Richardson, as quoted by Lord Strang [see footnote 24 above], p. 4.
111. Quoted by Atticus, *Sunday Times*, Apr. 14, 1963, p. 9.

112. Ian Nairn: "Outrage" (London, 1955; reprint of the June, 1955, Special Number of the *Architectural Review*), p. 407.
113. R. Furneaux Jordan: "SPAN: The Spec Builder as Patron of Modern Architecture," *Architectural Rev.*, Vol. 125, 1959, pp. 109-112 and 119-120; reference on p. 112.

about the people who built it."[114] Works by acknowledged masters rate higher than anonymous period pieces. Any landscape garden attributed to "Capability" Brown ranks above masterpieces such as Brocket or Wivenhoe created by Richard Woods or Shardeloes laid out by the virtually unknown Richmond. Possessions of great patrons and cognoscenti acquire distinction by connection, and are admired more as belongings than as works of merit in their own right.

In their associations, some antiquities were born great, some achieved greatness, others had greatness thrust upon them. It is the third category with which Englishmen are most passionately concerned—the innumerable inns where some king ate or drank, the "priest's hole" without which no self-respecting estate agent will sell a Tudor mansion, the well-worn seat in the "Cheshire Cheese" in Fleet Street where Dr. Johnson conversed with literary friends, the green on Plymouth Hoe where Drake is said to have played bowls as the Spanish Armada sailed up the English Channel. These are things that whet the antiquarian appetite. Visitors interviewed at Clandon Park and Hardwick Hall were less moved by the appearance of these great houses than by the thrill of direct contact with past events and characters associated with them.[115] Portraits, not porticoes, are the most popular attractions of country mansions.

These were just Vanbrugh's reasons for preserving the ancient manor houses at Woodstock two and a half centuries ago: "They move more lively and pleasing Reflec-tions . . . On the Persons who have Inhabited them; [and] On the Remarkable things which have been transacted in them."[116] No building is really precious, as Ruskin declares, "till it has been entrusted with the fame, and hallowed by the deeds of men, till its walls have been witnesses of suffering, and its pillars rise out of the shadows of death . . . Better the rudest work that tells a story or records a fact, than the richest without meaning."[117]

Historical associations are not a peculiarly English preoccupation, and even in England such interests are by no means exclusively English: Stratford on Avon attracts mainly Americans.[118] To American visitors, however, Shakespeare is more than a mortal, he is a symbol; Stratford and the Bard epitomize Old England, and any mention of them, however incongruous, has this Olde Worlde connotation. It is not for the English that the Shakespeare Hotel calls one of its bars "Measure for Measure" and a double bedroom "As You Like It," or that there is a Wimpy Bar named "The Judith Shakespeare Tearooms."[119] The English shrug off Stratford as "a hostage to Tourism" and generally regard the past displayed there as bogus.[120] A reconstructed birthplace only faintly

---

114. Katharine Whitehorn: "Thrown to the Joneses," *Observer Weekend Rev.*, Feb. 2, 1964, p. 33.

115. National Trust Survey conducted for the British Travel and Holidays Association by the Gallup Poll, September, 1961, p. 5 and Tables 17 and 19.

116. [To the Duchess of Marlborough] June 11, 1709, in *The Complete Works of Sir John Vanbrugh* (edited by Bonamy Dobrée and Geoffrey Webb; 4 vols.; London, 1927-1928), Vol. 4, p. 29.

117. Ruskin, *The Seven Lamps of Architecture* [see footnote 78 above], pp. 177 and 174 respectively.

118. The pattern is long established. "The American tourist usually comes straight to this quarter of England—chiefly for the purpose of paying his respects to the birthplace of Shakespeare" (James, *English Hours* [see footnote 27 above], p. 132).

119. "An Attic, a Chapel, and a Legend," *Sunday Times*, Mar. 17, 1963, p. 8.

120. Nairn, "Outrage" [see footnote 112 above], p. 408.

resembling the supposed original, a mulberry tree "*supposed* to have grown from a cutting from the tree *reputedly* planted by Shakespeare"[121]—such relics may content overseas visitors, but natives dismiss them with derision.

Nothing so vague or imprecise satisfies the English. Apart from the names of public houses commemorating monarchs and a few heroic or legendary figures—Nelson, Marlborough, Dick Whittington, Robin Hood—associations are intensely and preciously local. The connections that matter are those between specific places, people, and events, however insignificant the place, unimportant the person, or trivial the event. Thus the tiny driftwood hut of an obscure nineteenth-century balladist-vicar, R. S. Hawker, gains interest as a historical monument and makes the Cornish village of Morwenstow memorable by association with the poet and his strange dwelling.[122] At the other extreme, Westminster Abbey sheds its glory impartially on nonentities and men of distinction; but his memorial in the Poets' Corner of the Abbey does not evoke the personality of a poet such as Thomas Gray—for that one must visit the scene of his "Elegy," the country churchyard at Stoke Poges, and the monument nearby. Practically every parish church contains some such evocative memorial or tomb; practically every village or street is known as the birthplace or residence of someone or other. London Transport posters advertise houses and districts for their period and personal flavor. Hastings boasts its proximity to a decisive battle of the Norman Conquest, Wallsend on Tyne proclaims its situation at the eastern termi-

nus of Hadrian's Wall (Fig. 8). Hundreds of villages and streets are known mainly for quite adventitious connections with events and persons, real or fictional; the image of Baker Street owes more to Sherlock Holmes than to any actual resident. With nothing else to invoke, a town may embroider a minor incident into a legend of the kind that Lady Godiva's ride made Coventry famous for.

Some two dozen National Trust houses are preserved principally because famous people lived or worked in them, and such associations dominate the display in many of the rest.[123] Public money is spent to repair an early model farm because it was "probably inspired by experiments of Prince Albert."[124] Even Geoffrey Grigson, who admits that associations "have long viciously and sentimentally interfered with seeing what *is*, on its own account," wants signposts to the Vale of Clwyd because Hopkins wrote poems there, to Somersby in Lincolnshire because Tennyson grew up there, and to Little Skirrid near Abergavenny because Henry James climbed it.[125] Few literate Englishmen are ignorant of such associations. Ever since Thomas Fuller's "History of the Worthies of England" (1662) biographical gazetteers have flooded the island. A recent example of this genre links some 350 writers with 800 British scenes: Kenilworth Castle with Sir Walter Scott, the Old Curiosity Shop with Dickens, Aldeburgh with George Crabbe, and so on.[126]

The English seldom merely *see* a land-

---

123. "National Trust Properties" (London, 1963), p. xix.
124. "Grant for Historic Playground," *The Times*, Aug. 13, 1964, p. 12.
125. Geoffrey Grigson: "Travel with a Bookcase," *New Statesman*, Jan. 18, 1963, pp. 74 and 76.
126. John Freeman: *Literature and Locality: The Literary Topography of Britain and Ireland* (London, 1963).

---

121. "On the Bard Beat: A Report from Shakespeare Country, Part II," *Evening Standard*, London, Apr. 14, 1964, p. 10.
122. W. A. Trevener: Trust Hut (letter), *Daily Telegraph*; John Betjeman: *Cornwall: A Shell Guide* (London, 1964), pp. 86-88.

Figure 8. Hadrian's Wall from Hotbank Crags, looking east toward Housesteads Fort, Northumberland. (National Parks Commission; British Crown Copyright)

scape; they see it as delineated in famous books and paintings. Not only are poets and painters known by their special landscapes, they have made these landscapes their own. So "Grantchester belongs to Rupert Brooke," and "the steep meadows and copses behind Brawling Parva belong, not by law of possession but by right of brush, to Gilbert Spencer."[127] Summary descriptions of the English scene invariably evoke the Lake District in terms of Wordsworth, Dorset as depicted by Hardy, Suffolk in Constable's cornfields, and over Norfolk the blustery skies of Crome. The most obscure

artists enrich the vision of some observers. "Who can look at a Cotswold manor, the distinct stones, the hollyhock spire, the clipped box, without running his gaze down the flag-stones to the bottom right-hand corner where he will expect to find, written on a scroll among the snapdragon, F. L. GRIGGS? Who does not see in Merrion Square on Henrietta Street the Guinness-brown brick, the green, etched-in ironwork, the silver-grey stone of a Malton aquatint?"[128] Betjeman's questions are purely rhetorical; they clearly imply that anyone who does not think of Griggs or Malton is only half seeing these landscapes.

127. R. C. Robertson-Glasgow: "Poets and Places," *Sunday Times Weekly Rev.*, Oct. 6, 1963, p. 41.

128. John Betjeman: *First and Last Loves* (London, 1960), p. 23.

Books matter more than pictures. "The English genius in the arts has been, above all, literary," writes Pritchett; "it has fed on the associations of the mind rather than on the delights of the eye."[129] Painters themselves readily acknowledge their debt to landscape literature. Reynolds counted it no virtue in Gainsborough that he saw nature with the eye of a painter rather than with that of a poet.[130] Poetic insight and historical evocation were the touchstones of esthetic satisfaction; poets were largely insensitive to what they saw with their own eyes. When Pope writes of

> Pan with flocks, with fruit Pomona crowned, Here blushing Flora paints the enamelled ground,

we feel, with Allen, that "he is indifferent to the beauty of fruit and flowers,"[131] and that his inspiration springs from mental associations, not from visual delights. An English proverb asserts, and London Transport reiterates, that "almost every picture tells a story."[132] We might add as a corollary that almost every landscape recalls a history.

For the inveterate antiquarian, associations survive all visible vestiges. Thus a character in Nigel Dennis's novel is told that he has "sole right to the faggots of Holborn Common. Fleet Street now occupies the site, but if you wish to assert your claim, not Beaverbrook himself can stop you." And he replies, "The claim is warmth enough for me."[133] Truth outdoes fiction; until a few months ago a special Picquet of Guards marched daily through the City and took up overnight positions in the Bank of England because an earlier bank building had been threatened during the Gordon Riots of 1780.[134] The English everywhere rejoice in latent or fictional associations sanctioned and superscribed by "time immemorial." That appearances so hallowed may be deceptive they are also aware. The past is more significant visually than it is socially. But the English derive comfort from known anachronisms. The preponderance of the past in the English landscape suggests "that even the most radical things we have done might still be continuous with what our forefathers did. And this surely would be a source of strength."[135] History made visible endows the present with substance and durability.

Although everything has a past, the past is as evanescent as the present. Left unprotected, the past crumbles to dust and finally vanishes. But before it disappears its character changes; "at a certain point in time even the greatest architecture ceases to be completely architecture and becomes partially landscape."[136] Stonehenge and

129. V. S. Pritchett: *London Perceived* ([London and] New York, 1962), p. 85.
130. Joshua Reynolds: "Fourteenth Discourse" [1788], in *Discourses Delivered to the Students of the Royal Academy by Joshua Reynolds, Kt.* (edited by Roger Fry; London, 1905), pp. 373-397; reference on p. 381.
131. Allen, *op. cit.* [see footnote 39 above], Vol. 1, p. 129, including quotation from Alexander Pope's "Windsor Forest."
132. "Roundabout: A Selection of Items of Curiosity and Interest Reprinted from London Transport's Series of Roundabout Posters" (London [1962?]), last page.

133. Dennis, *op. cit.* [see footnote 87 above], p. 153.
134. Watching the ceremony in 1914, Walter Hines Page commented, "Nothing is ever abolished, ever changed" (to Woodrow Wilson, May 11, 1914, in *The Life and Letters of Walter H. Page* [see footnote 63 above], Vol. 1, p. 168), but the congestion of rush-hour traffic has forced the march to be abandoned, and the Picquet now arrives at the bank in an army vehicle.
135. Christopher Salmon: "Prospect of Britain," *Listener*, Nov. 12, 1953, pp. 803-804.
136. Osbert Lancaster: "The Future of the Past: Some Thoughts on Preservation," *Cornhill Magazine*, No. 1040, Summer, 1964, pp. 122-132; reference on p. 127.

Hadrian's Wall have passed almost entirely into landscape (Fig. 8); St. Pancras Station in London, just a century old, is valued more as a skyline feature than as architecture. Appreciation of such resultant landscapes, as distinct from the original structures, characterizes English taste. Mocking such preferences in her satirical "History of England," Jane Austen alleges that Henry VIII dissolved the monasteries, leaving them "to the ruinous depredations of time," principally in order to improve the English landscape[137] (Fig. 6).

It is as a part of the landscape that the Foreign Office building today is considered indispensable. Even the Victorian Society does not pretend that it is a great building; "the importance of Whitehall is geographical, not architectural,"[138] and its proposed demolition jeopardizes what Hussey describes as "a composition of landscape architecture unsurpassed in the world."[139]

Those who regard present-day life as an intrusion on the scenes of the past view things quite differently from those who prefer the past to be peopled. For the former, a minimum of modernity can dispel historical atmosphere. A crumbling ruin, a deserted medieval village, a haunted house, are affecting because they are no longer occupied; no present function obscures the imagined past. A ruin eliminates "the psychological barrier between 'spectator' and 'user,'" Summerson maintains; "the building is free—everybody's building, nobody's building."[140] An eighteenth-century windmill is more evocative than a cotton mill of the same period because it is more obviously useless, more remote from our times. Old buildings still in use did not interest Gilpin, but he thought abandoned relics delightful additions to the scene. Religious prejudice buttressed his esthetic argument: "Where popery prevails, the abbey is still intire and inhabited; and of course less adapted to landscape."[141]

But the English today increasingly prefer historic places to look lived in, rather than to be labeled and ossified as at Williamsburg and other American reproductions. They can enjoy the spirit of the past without banishing motorcars, shops, and television. "We don't want a Blackpool here," commented a Lake District parish councillor about a proposed development, "but we don't want a museum."[142] The National Trust avoids museumization by having its showplaces tenanted, if possible by families long associated with them, as, for example, at Knole, Cliveden, Coughton Court, Sizergh Castle, and Wightwick Manor.[143] To retain or create the desired lived-in look, the Trust often disregards period purity and abstract beauty to include well-loved but frankly ugly objects and arrangements such as "stuffed vermin" and "peacock's tails" and other "old favourites, like the armchair made from the skin and hoofs of the late Lady Hoare's pony." As a Trust adviser puts it, "a discreet intermingling of homely rubbish with works of art may provide a salu-

---

137. Jane Austen: *Love and Friendship, and Other Early Works* (London, 1922), pp. 85-97; reference on p. 89.
138. Diana Rowntree: "The F.O.," *Guardian*, Jan. 7, 1964, p. 7.
139. Christopher Hussey: Plans for Foreign Office (letter), *The Times*, Nov. 25, 1963, p. 11.
140. Summerson, *op. cit.* [see footnote 41 above], p. 236.

141. Gilpin, *Observations . . . [on] the Mountains, and Lakes of Cumberland, and Westmoreland* [see footnote 32 above], Vol. 1, p. 13.
142. *Thirteenth Rept. National Parks Commission* [see footnote 22 above], p. 73.
143. J. F. W. Rathbone: "The National Trust: Its Growth and Its Problems," in *The Preservation and Development of Ancient Buildings and Historical or Artistic Sites* (Council of Europe, 1963), pp. 65-71; reference on p. 66.

tary and not contemptible relief to the visitor in search of atmosphere."[144]

Current taste favors keeping historical buildings in use, however remote from their original function. Swansea Castle was formerly set apart as a monument, quarantined against the everyday life of the town center; the decision was overruled, and the castle is now occupied by a local newspaper office.[145] To the English in general, continuity is more important than verisimilitude. Instead of Williamsburg or Mystic Seaport they have Windsor, whose "pretensions to genuineness would hardly deceive a four-year-old," but which has become, as Lancaster notes, an integral part of the surrounding landscape;[146] unlike American historical reconstructions, Windsor is a real place.

But some love the past as it was and wish it restored to its pristine appearance; others enjoy it as it has become with all the accretions from time and weather. These opposing views were sharply focused in the controversy over the cleaning of St. Paul's. Those who favored cleaning argued that the cathedral should be seen as Wren originally built it, and that the grime and sediment of centuries not only obscured and ultimately destroyed decorative details but spoiled the general configuration of the building, the pattern of weathering disturbing its unity of effect. Opponents objected that washing the soft stone might efface sculptural detail. But they were mainly concerned lest cleaning rob St. Paul's of the weight of history, the dimension of time conveyed by the weathered stone and its patterns of light and shade; the building was more than Wren's creation, it was organic. Moreover, thrown into relief against the dark buildings around it, the whitened cathedral might endanger the living harmony of the whole precinct.[147]

But appreciation of grime goes beyond this. As pioneers of the Industrial Revolution, the English regard themselves as to some extent the special caretakers of that era; thus the soot-encrusted façades of the Foreign Office courtyard make it "a monument to the age of smoke."[148] No other people seem to consider deposits of dirt worth preserving for their own sake.

The toleration of grime as a valid relic is only one example of the general English feeling that the whole of the past is worth preserving. No single era, however ancient, takes precedence over the entire palimpsest of time; later additions all contribute to the historical character of a place. Thus at Avebury a medieval tithe barn straddles the earthworks of the prehistoric stone circle; when the barn roof was about to collapse, it was restored by public subscription, so that its unique combination with the earlier relic continues to enhance the general historical landscape.

Abundant though they are, genuine relics in the landscape do not suffice English nostalgia for the past. Eighteenth-century landowners created illusions of antiquity by stuffing their gardens with dovecotes, grottoes, towers, temples, arches, obelisks, columns, and sham ruins (Fig. 9), some of

144. James Lees-Milne: "Thoughts on Preserving Country Houses," *News Letter, The National Trust for Places of Historic Interest or Natural Beauty*, London, Spring, 1962, pp. 3-5.
145. "Swansea Castle, Glam.," *Architectural Rev.*, Vol. 122, 1957, p. 347.
146. Lancaster, "The Future of the Past" [see footnote 136 above], p. 129.

147. For example, Peter Rawstorne: "Leave St. Paul's Alone!" *Observer Weekend Rev.*, Nov. 25, 1962, p. 23; and Michael Manser: "Why Stop at St. Paul's?" *ibid.*, Jan. 5, 1964, p. 22.
148. Rowntree, *op. cit.* [see footnote 138 above]. "Only a man who loves the industrial revolution can really see what Britain looks like" (Ronald Bryden: "Scousiad," *New Statesman*, Oct. 2, 1964, p. 508).

Figure 9. Fillingham Castle Gateway, Lincolnshire, by Sir Cecil Wray (*c.* 1760), sham Gothic. (Photograph by C. Ogden, The Royal Commission on Historical Monuments; British Crown Copyright)

them tenanted with hired hermits and shepherds. Intended effect varied with architectural style. Classical ruins were meant to sadden the spectator by reminding him of the victory of the barbarians over civilization, whereas ruins in the Gothic style represented merely the triumph of time over strength.[149]

Artificial relics no longer stir such emotions. English folk today are shocked, according to a historian of art, when they discover "that a seeming castle is only a disguised cowshed. It is a sham; it is telling a lie."[150] Barring deliberate deceit, however, antiquarian taste still dominates the human landscape. The English continue to embellish the countryside with monuments and other memorials to historical figures and episodes, and to make new houses look like old ones. To advertise a house as "period style" is almost a sufficient guarantee of its attractions. A paint company offers "Authentic Period Colours" for William and Mary, Queen Anne, Early and Late Georgian, and Regency interiors. Local authorities regularly give preference to period reproductions over buildings in a modern style.

The mania for remodeling "in keeping" with a historical style has gone to such lengths in certain cities that many of their streets have more fake than real Georgian buildings.[151] When Reigate's Town Planning Committee decided that a new shop in the High Street should be "in Tudor or Georgian style to harmonize with the general tone and atmosphere," a critic wondered what they wore at the meeting—"buckles and periwigs, or simply doublet and hose?" Thanks to this "desperate slavering after the past," Reigate was already "three-quarters spoiled by gen-

149. Allen, *op. cit.* [see footnote 39 above], Vol. 2, pp. 169-172.
150. Clark, *The Gothic Revival* [see footnote 60 above], p. 44.

151. "Chichester, Sussex," *Architectural Rev.,* Vol. 123, 1958, p. 208. See also Peter Moro: "Faking the Past," *Twentieth Century,* Vol. 171, 1962, pp. 88-90.

tility and characterless fakes." [152] For John
Wain the whole of "Sussex, with its fabulous
beauty, its groomed cottages in Hollywood
black and white, its glossy cows and immense trees, was . . . a stage set, a fake." [153]

A building may be "mock" or "pseudo,"
however, without being bad. In many milieus the best course is to "carry on where
the past left off, carefully and accurately
reproducing their personal style, and cou-
rageously plead guilty to charges of
'pastiche.' " [154] As the word pastiche implies, the English are seldom permitted to
take the past too seriously. Expressions of
ridicule for antiquarianism everywhere en-
liven the landscape. Scores of follies poke fun
at the preserver or builder of ruins. [155] Pilt-
down man is only the most famous of many
historical hoaxes. A stone inscribed by
eighteenth-century wits in supposed commemoration of Hardicanute's death from
overdrinking was solemnly identified and
attributed to the eleventh century by the
then Director of the Society of Antiquaries. [156] In such ways the fanatic antiquarian is daunted and history put in its
proper place. Whether a place is old or new,
sham or true, matters less, in the final analysis, than that it is truly itself, a real place
distinct from all others.

Genius Loci

"Consult the genius of the place in all,"
urged Pope. [157] Ever since, it has been an
English axiom that the character of a site, its
local geography and history, should govern
its lineaments. The goal is not localism but
specificity; each place is assumed to be
unique. Individuality is valued for its own
sake.

At the root of the disposition to admire
what gives a place its special character lies a
preference for the concrete and specific as
against the abstract and the general. English
architecture has long exhibited this trait. [158]
English seaside resorts, for example, have
many elements in common and may at first
glance seem much alike. But the regularities
are superficial. Each town, as Casson remarks, "has buried somewhere a personality
of its own, a personality composed less often
perhaps of buildings than of other qualities—contours, street pattern, drama, colour,
cosiness, surprise, intimacy, stock, smells,
noises." The resident is exhorted to discover,
protect, and enrich this character, "whatever
it is that makes Whitley different from Mar-
gate, or Eastbourne from Ilfracombe." [159]

Genius loci takes several forms. One is to
build structures and alter landscapes to fit in
with local contours and vegetation. Made of
local materials, buildings should also be
shaped, colored, and sited in conformity
with the natural landscape. Houses on Dartmoor, the Devon County Council recommends, ought to be long in relation to their
width, dark in color, seen against a natural
background rather than silhouetted against
the sky, and "sit firmly and securely on the
ground and seem to grow naturally out of
it" [160] (Fig. 10). Millstone Grit villages in

152. Ian Nairn: "The Dilemma of 'Amenity,' "
Architectural Rev., Vol. 125, 1959, pp. 285-286;
reference on p. 285.
153. Wain, *op. cit.* [see footnote 107 above],
p. 198.
154. Osbert Lancaster: "Parliament Stays 'Trad,' "
Daily Express, May 6, 1964, p. 10.
155. See Sir Hugh Casson, edit.: *Follies* (London,
1963).
156. Allen, *op. cit.* [see footnote 39 above], Vol.
2, p. 91.
157. Alexander Pope: "Epistle IV, To Richard

Boyle, Earl of Burlington, on the Use of Riches,"
in *Works* [see footnote 62 above], Vol. 3 (1881),
p. 176.
158. Pevsner, *The Englishness of English Art* [see
footnote 65 above], pp. 26-27.
159. Casson, "Seaside Sense" [see footnote 28
above], p. 6.
160. "Dartmoor" [see footnote 69 above], pp.
18, 22, and 24.

Figure 10. Lake Farm, Sourton, Devon, harmonizes with the slope, scale, and texture of the Dartmoor uplands. (From *Dartmoor: Building in the National Park*, Architectural Press Ltd.)

Figure 11. Milldale village in the Peak District, Derbyshire, looking east. (National Parks Commission; British Crown Copyright)

the Peak District are, like their environs, angular, rough in texture, somber in hue (Fig. 11). Each locale has its own set of rules to which honor is paid.

In another guise, genius loci is anti-esthetic. Places are to be accepted as they are; they may be admirable even though ugly; if not *because* they are ugly. It was no local booster but an able town planner who compared the "gloomy grandeur . . . [of] the grime of Manchester or the pall of smoke over lower Sheffield . . . to the eruption of a volcano or the burst of a thunderclap," and admired them as "thoroughly typical of the strength of these cities."[161] Huddersfield

and Stoke on Trent are now frequently praised for their local character, and some cite even Slough and Staines as exemplars of genius loci.

Two conflicting tendencies, both predominantly nonesthetic, dominate English landscape taste. One is to accept as good what the authorities say is good, to see and to judge on the basis not of feeling or direct response but of historical and other associations. Even façadism is an interest in appearance for the sake of ideas. The other tendency is to shun "good" taste and external standards in favor of a nostalgic but firm commitment to the old, the tried, the worn, and at times the ugly—in short, to whatever is, as long as it is uniquely and unyieldingly itself.

---

161. Sir Patrick Abercrombie: *Town and Country Planning* (3rd edit.; The Home University Library of Modern Knowledge, No. 163; London, 1959), p. 105.

🙚🙚🙚🙚🙚🙚🙚🙚🙚🙚🙚🙚🙚🙚🙚🙚🙚🙚🙚🙚🙚🙚🙚🙚🙚🙚🙚🙚

BIBLIOGRAPHY

The Cultural Landscape

ASCHMANN, HOMER, "The Evolution of a Wild Landscape and Its Persistence in Southern California," *Annals, Association of American Geographers,* Vol. 49 (1959), pp. 34-46. An analysis of the early impact of man on the vegetation, and the persistence, of a wild landscape in southern California.

BOBEK, HANS, and J. SCHMITHÜSEN, "Die Landschaft im logischen System der Geographie," *Erdkunde,* Vol. 3 (1949), pp. 112-20. A penetrating methodological discussion of the landscape as a basis for geographical study.

BROEK, JAN O. M., *The Santa Clara Valley, California: A Study in Landscape Changes,* Utrecht, Netherlands: Oosthoek, 1932. This classic study traces the evolution of a cultural landscape.

BROEK, JAN O. M., "The Concept Landscape in Human Geography," Vol. 2, section 3a, pp. 103-9 in International Geographical Congress, Fifteenth, Amsterdam (1938), *Comptes rendus,* Leiden: Brill, 1938. A methodological description of the strengths and weaknesses of the landscape concept in geography.

CRARY, DOUGLAS, "A Geographer Looks at the Landscape," *Landscape,* Vol. 9 (1959), pp. 22-25. Landscapes possess spatial and temporal properties and are the products of physical and human processes.

DARBY, H. C., "The Problem of Geographical Description," *Transactions, Institute of British Geographers,* No. 30 (1962), pp. 1-14. The totality and meaning of a landscape is rarely captured in the prose of geographical description. Darby examines several methods of incorporating explanation into geography.

FRANCAVIGLIA, RICHARD V., "The Mormon Landscape: Definition of an Image in the American West," *Proceedings of the Association of American Geographers,* Vol. 2 (1970), pp. 59-61. By using ten Mormon cultural elements the author maps the extent of the Mormon cultural landscape.

HARD, GERHARD, "Arkadien in Deutschland: Bemerkungen zu einem landschaftlichen Reiz," *Erde,* Vol. 96 (1965), pp. 21-41. The charm that central European moors and forests held for German geographers can be attributed to the region's similarity to the "classical world" of the South.

HARVEY, D. W., "The Analysis of Land Use Patterns," *Transactions, Institute of British Geographers*, Vol. 33 (1963), pp. 123-44. The processes of locational change explain distributions of production better than initial locational decisions.

HILL, A. DAVID, *The Changing Landscape of a Mexican Municipio: Villa Las Rosas, Chiapas*, Chicago: University of Chicago, Department of Geography, 1964. A monograph on the impact of modern forces on the people and landscape of a region in Mexico.

ISAAC, ERICH, "Religion, Landscape and Space," *Landscape*, Vol. 9 (1959-60), pp. 14-18. Space is accorded symbolic meaning and is commonly altered to conform with religious or ideological beliefs.

LEMON, JAMES T., "The Agricultural Practices of National Groups in Eighteenth-Century Southeastern Pennsylvania," *The Geographical Review*, Vol. 56 (1966), pp. 467-96. The belief that German immigrants were better farmers than their British and Irish counterparts is examined through analysis of settlement and landscape.

LEWIS, PIERCE F., "The Geography of Old Houses," *Earth and Mineral Sciences*, Vol. 39 (1970), pp. 33-37. House-types provide perspective in the study of the landscape expressions of urban processes and culture change.

LOWENTHAL, DAVID, "Is Wilderness 'Paradise Enow'?: Images of Nature in America," *Columbia University Forum* (1964), pp. 34-40. The paradise of one generation is not that of another. Lowenthal examines historical trends in American environmental attitudes and landscape preferences.

LOWENTHAL, DAVID, "Nature and the American Creed of Virtue," *Landscape*, Vol. 9 (1959-60), pp. 24-25. The conservation ethic has gained popularity due to nostalgia for the simplicity of nature.

LOWENTHAL, DAVID, "The American Scene," *The Geographical Review*, Vol. 58 (1968), pp. 61-88. The American cultural landscape is evidence of the collective aspirations and environmental values of those who create it.

LOWENTHAL, DAVID, and HUGH C. PRINCE, "The English Landscape," *Geographical Review*, Vol. 54 (1964), pp. 309-46. A discussion of salient elements in the English landscape as a reflection of human preferences.

MEINIG, D. W., "The Mormon Culture Region: Strategies and Patterns in the Geography of the American West, 1847-1964," *Annals, Association of American Geographers*, Vol. 55 (1965), pp. 191-220. The varied landscape expression of the Mormon subculture is discussed.

MIKESELL, MARVIN, "Deforestation in Northern Morocco," *Science*, Vol. 132 (1960), pp. 441-48. Mikesell documents the impact of human processes on the landscape of northern Morocco.

MUMFORD, LEWIS, "The Social Function of Open Spaces," *Landscape*, Vol. 10 (1960-61), pp. 1-6. City and suburb alike should contain a landscape and garden as an integral part of urban life.

NELSON, HOWARD J., "The Spread of an Artificial Landscape over Southern California," *Annals, Association of American Geographers*, Vol. 49 (Supplement, 1959), pp. 80-99. A description of the development of an urban-industrial landscape in southern California.

RAUP, H. R., "Transformation of Southern California to a Cultivated Land," *Annals, Association of American Geographers*, Vol. 49 (Supplement, 1959), pp. 58-78. The historical evolution of the agricultural landscape of southern California from the mission period to modern times.

SAUER, CARL O., *Land and Life: A Selection from the Writings of Carl Ortwin Sauer*, Berkeley: University of California Press, 1963. A collection of the major writings of the leading contemporary cultural geographer in America.

SAUER, CARL O., *The Early Spanish Main*, Berkeley: University of California Press, 1966. A case of mistaken identity led to Spain's disastrous colonial policy in the new world. Sauer traces the history of the expedition, with emphasis on Columbus's impact on the organization and subjugation of the new lands.

SAUER, CARL O., "The Morphology of Landscape," in John Leighly, ed., *Land and Life: A Selection from the Writings of Carl Ortwin Sauer*, Berkeley: University of California Press, 1963, pp. 315-50. A classic methodological statement proposing the comparative analysis of landscapes as an important area of geographical inquiry.

SCHMITHÜSEN, JOSEF, "Was ist eine Landschaft?" *Erdkundliches Wissen*, Vol. 9 (1964), pp. 1-24. A lengthy discussion of various definitions of landscape.

SHEPARD, PAUL, JR., *Man in the Landscape: A Historic View of the Esthetics of Nature*, New York: Alfred A. Knopf, 1967. A personal investigation of the variable sentimental position of man in his environment.

SHEPARD, PAUL, JR., "The Cross Valley Syndrome," *Landscape*, Vol. 10 (1961), pp. 4-8. Water gaps have captured the attention of adventurers, artists, and writers because of the suggestiveness of unique landforms.

SPENCER, J. E., and G. A. HALE, "The Origin, Nature, and Distribution of Agricultural Terracing," *Pacific Viewpoint*, Vol. 2 (1961), pp. 1-40. The authors describe the origin and distribution of several terracing techniques as evidence of man's ability to alter the natural landscape.

THOMAS, WILLIAM L., ed., *Man's Role in Changing the Face of the Earth*, An International Symposium under the Co-chairmanship of Carl O. Sauer, Marston Bates, and Lewis Mumford. Chicago: University of Chicago Press, 1956. Fifty-three prominent scholars from a variety of academic disciplines discuss the salience and magnitude of the human imprint on the landscape.

TUAN, YI-FU, "Topophilia," *Landscape*, Vol. 11 (1961), pp. 29-32. Geographers should join the poet and artist by revealing their personal landscape experiences.

WAGNER, PHILIP, *The Human Use of the Earth*, New York: The Free Press, 1960. A discussion of the artificial landscape, the visible expression of man's interaction with the physical environment.

WAGNER, PHILIP, "The Path, the Road, the Highway," *Landscape*, Vol. 10 (1960), pp. 36-40. Three distinct cultures inhabit rural Mexico, each with its own unique landscape.

2
ECOLOGICAL PERSPECTIVES

Most research and writing in human geography have implicitly embodied an ecological perspective, although until recently few geographers explicitly identified themselves with this methodology.[1] Yet points of contact between man and environment, interactions between cultural systems and their surroundings, have stubbornly remained the central content of the discipline, whether defined as the study of man-environment systems or as the spatial structure of human behavior. Ecological concern underlies the earth-bound view of students of landscape and the varied approaches to environmental perception; it is latent in studies of innovation diffusion, regional systems, and even the recondite literature on spatial order. One can trace the laborious history of ecological interest among geographers from the early determinists, through possibilism, to areal differentiation;[2] ecological viewpoints continue to exist as tacit assumptions in the work of most modern geographers.

The current ubiquitous interest in "ecology," not only in the field of geography but throughout the social sciences, has been encouraged by the flexibility and elasticity of the term in the hands of various writers.[3] Few words have more

---

1. One exception is Harlan Barrow's presidential address to the Association of American Geographers, which pleaded with geographers to define their discipline as "human ecology." See H. H. Barrows, "Geography as Human Ecology," *Annals, Association of American Geographers,* Vol. 13 (1923), pp. 1-14. As Ackerman notes, "the hint given by Barrows was never seriously followed by his colleagues." Edward A. Ackerman, "Where Is the Research Frontier?," *Annals, Association of American Geographers,* Vol. 53 (1963), pp. 429-40.
2. An excellent survey of this literature is Harold and Margaret Sprout, *The Ecological Perspective on Human Affairs,* Princeton: Princeton University Press, 1965.
3. In addition to the volume by the Sprouts cited above, the variety of definitions of "ecology" is treated in: Andrew P. Vayda and Roy A. Rappaport, "Ecology, Cultural and Non-cultural," pp. 477-497, in James A. Clifton, *Introduction to Cultural Anthropology,* Boston: Houghton Mifflin, 1968; Marvin W. Mikesell,

definitions; consequently, few are so loosely defined—ecology has become a notion for all seasons. The term was first proposed by the Swiss biologist, Ernst Haeckel to refer to the relationships among organisms living within a defined space and their patterns of adaption to their environment;[4] and as used by plant and animal ecologists, major stress was placed on the measurable biological effects of these interactions. When the basic concepts of ecology, such as community, ecological niche, competition, succession, interdependence, differentiation, and dominance, were applied by analogy to human populations, however, a new emphasis was placed on man-environment interactions *per se* rather than on the effects of these interactions. In sociology, for example, human ecology quickly moved from this biological orientation to defining human ecology as "the study of the spatial and temporal relations of human beings as effected by environmental forces," or alternatively as "the study of the form and development of the human community."[5] By extension, similar redefinitions of ecology found a place in the literature of

anthropology, psychology, political science, and geography. In geography today, two major thrusts in the broad and varied ecologic literature are most relevant. These are cultural ecology and ecosystem.

Cultural Ecology

Cultural ecology studies the interactions of societies with one another and with the natural environment in order to comprehend those processes of adaption and transformation that operate to alter social institutions, human behavior, and environment. Ideally, the entire range of social and natural phenomena are comprehended in a single "ecosystem" (discussed below), thus disposing of the artificial separation of man and nature. In fact, the "holistic" ecological approach is fraught with so many inherent complications that most cultural ecologists concentrate on specific sets of relationships, for example, between population density and subsistence patterns, or alternatively technology and environment, with the intent of expanding the investigation to other components and ultimately gaining insight into the total man-environment system. In all cases, studies in cultural ecology tend to stress process more than form, to articulate what is happening in a system rather than its content. This emphasis is particularly noticeable in the writings of the anthropologist Julian Steward, one of culture ecology's most articulate spokesmen. [6]

In "The Concept and Method of Cultural Ecology" Steward defines cultural ecology as the study of those processes by which a society adapts to its environment. Reacting to the emphasis which other scholars have placed on specific cultural histories or unique cultural patterns as explanations for

"Cultural Ecology," to be published in *Focus on Geography: Key Concepts and Teaching Strategies* (41st Yearbook, National Council for the Social Studies, 1971); and the relevant articles in the *International Encyclopedia of the Social Sciences.* Of the readers available on ecology, the most varied and reflective is Paul Shepard and Daniel McKinley, editors, *The Subversive Science: Essays Toward an Ecology of Man,* Boston: Houghton Mifflin, 1969.
4. Ernst Haeckel, *The History of Creation,* translated by E. R. Lankester, New York: Appleton, 1876, 2 vols.
5. That is, from the viewpoint expressed by Park to that of McKenzie and Hawley. See Robert Ezra Park, "Human Ecology," *American Journal of Sociology,* Vol. 42 (July 1936), pp. 1-15; Roderick D. McKenzie, "The Scope of Human Ecology," *Publications of the American Sociological Society,* Vol. 20 (1926), pp. 141-54; Amos H. Hawley, *Human Ecology: A Theory of Community Structure,* New York: Ronald, 1950.

6. His major work is *Theory of Culture Change: The Methodology of Multilinear Evolution,* Urbana: University of Illinois Press, 1955.

the origin of cultural features and cultural change, Steward stresses processes of adaption to local environments as a source of change in social institutions and human behavior. But he is not an environmental determinist. For Steward, man is an ecological dominant by virtue of his cultural capacities, but no universal statement can be made concerning the relationships of man and nature; detailed specific investigation of these interactions must be the basis for theory building. Thus, Steward's "method" of cultural ecology stresses analyses of the relationships between environment and the exploitative technology, those patterns of human behavior involved in environmental exploitation, and the relationships between these behavioral patterns and other aspects of culture. By defining in such a discriminating way those aspects of the society (his "culture core") that merit empirical investigation, Steward avoids the gross generalizations that placed similar research in disrepute previously.[7]

This discriminating selection of critical aspects of human behavior for intensive analysis in defining patterns of human adaption to environment is also evident in the study by Vayda, Leeds, and Smith, "The Place of Pigs in Melanesian Subsistence." Here, the authors present the hypothesis that the ritual slaughter of pigs on a large scale in Melanesia actually functions as a homeostatic mechanism to maintain the long-term balance between human populations and environmental resources.[8] Reject-

ing earlier suppositions that ritual pig-killing represented an example of resource mismanagement, of the economic inefficiency of primitive societies, the authors suggest that these rituals constitute a continuing check on a too-rapid expansion of the pig population which, given the pig's talents for scavenging, could create a situation where pigs would overrun the countryside and menace cultivated fields and gardens. Since these festivals are held only after discussion and careful assessment of available resources, this study provides a convincing example of a rational adaptation of specific patterns of human behavior to local environmental conditions.

Porter's study, "Environmental Potentials and Economic Opportunities," also attempts to identify critical relationships between environment and subsistence forms by using the concept of subsistence risk. Framed within the context of an extensive interdisciplinary exploration of cultural adaptation to environment,[9] Porter defined the environmental potential for exploitation by man of two typical environmental settings in East Africa, one with a steep altitudinal gradient, the other gentle, in terms of the degree of uncertainty or risk each environment possesses for subsistence farmers and pastoralists. He found not simply two environments (one for hoe-farmers, one for herders) but a continuum of microenvironments, which, excepting the most extreme, were susceptible of human manipulation. By stressing the need for careful delineation of relevant environmental parameters, and the role of man as a causative agent of environmental

7. Curiously, by being so specific, he has been criticized by some for reducing "ecology to something akin to a research technique." Amos A. Hawley, "Human Ecology," pp. 328-37, in *International Encyclopedia of the Social Sciences*, New York: Macmillan, 1968.
8. For a fully developed study of the critical role of pigs in Melanesian ecosystems, see Roy A. Rappaport, *Pigs for the Ancestors: Ritual in the*

Ecology of a New Guinea People, New Haven: Yale University Press, 1967.
9. "The Culture and Ecology Project in East Africa" directed by Walter Goldschmidt of UCLA. A summary of its findings is published in Walter Goldschmidt *et al.*, "Variation and Adaptability of Culture: A Symposium," *American Anthropologist*, Vol. 67 (1965), pp. 400-447.

change, Porter's study is consistent not only with the principles of cultural ecology enunciated by Steward but with other broad frameworks of research in human geography.

Gould's paper, "Man Against His Environment: A Game Theoretical Framework," pursues the idea of environmental uncertainty and subsistence risk by introducing game theory as a conceptual framework and tool of research to probe human strategies used to overcome environmental problems. In the first example, various crop combinations available to farmers in Western Ghana are evaluated in terms of their payoff in wet and dry years to define those strategies which will, in the long run, minimize risk, avoid famine, and maximize productivity. The second example examines the climatic uncertainties of driving cattle to market in Ghana. Here, five possible rainfall conditions from very wet to dry govern the best long-run strategy for marketing the cattle. By utilizing this broad conceptual construct, Gould succeeds in identifying the range of potential decisions available to these primary producers and suggests a measure of the degree of economic rationality involved in decision-making processes in traditional societies. In so doing, he suggests that game theory may provide insight into the fundamental focus of cultural ecology, patterns and processes of human adaptation to environment.

Ecosystem

A second major development in the broad field of "ecology" relevant to modern geography is the study of ecosystems, which can be defined as "functioning interacting systems composed of one or more living organisms and their effective environment" [10] or, when applied to man, the study of biological and cultural man living in and interacting with his environment. The study of ecosystems, that is of entire wholes, has long attracted scholars, and although the term itself was introduced in the mid-thirties,[11] the analytic techniques and mathematical descriptions necessary to handle such complexity did not become available until recently. The great advantages of a systems approach in ecology and geography are obvious: it delineates the hierarchy of organizational units, the quality of stability, and the gestalt properties of complex man-environment transactions within a single framework, thus making possible the delineation of principles of form and process. Stoddart discusses the significance of systems analysis, specifically ecosystems, in modern geography.

Ecology can provide, in Stoddart's view, a methodology for modern geography of "sufficient power to lead to new insight and new approaches." The major advantages of ecosystems, as compared with other organizational concepts such as region or landscape are four: first, they treat man and environment within a single framework; second, they are structured in a rational way; third, they analyze the functioning of systems not simply their form; and finally, they are a special type of general systems with all that implies. But despite the wide applicability of the ecosystem approach to topics of geographical concern, there have been few specific studies which can be cited as examples demonstrative of its potentiality. One of the finest has been written by Geerts.[12]

---

10. F. R. Fosberg, editor, *Man's Place in the Island Ecosystem,* Honolulu: Bishop Museum Press, 1963,

p. 2. Also see F. C. Evans, "Ecosystem as the Basic Unit in Ecology," *Science,* Vol. 123 (1956), pp. 1127-28.
11. By Tansley. See A. G. Tansley, "The Use and Abuse of Vegetational Concepts and Terms," *Ecology,* Vol. 16 (1935), pp. 284-307.
12. Clifford Geertz, *Agricultural Involution: The Processes of Ecological Change in Indonesia,*

In "Two Types of Ecosystems," Clifford Geertz describes the two basic agricultural systems of Indonesia—*swidden*, slash and burn cultivation, and *sawah*, terraced rice farming. Using an ecosystem framework Geertz treats the interaction between specific variables of culture and environment to identify the processes by which these interactions are regulated, and to relate these concepts to the functioning of the system—in this case Indonesia—as a whole. Swidden agriculture is a multicrop system with a highly diverse regime, a cycling of nutrients between living forms, a closed-cover architecture, and a delicate equilibrium. By contrast, terraced rice farming *(sawah)* is an open-field monocrop with a highly specialized regime, a heavy dependence on water-borne minerals for nutrition, a reliance on man-made irrigation systems, and a stable equilibrium. By analyzing these ecosystems in detail, Geertz is able to associate their basic characteristics with the uneven distribution of population in Indonesia and with the derivative set of social and economic quandaries that have beset Indonesia for a century.

In his discussion of island ecosystems, Rappaport traces the evolution of "pristine ecosystems" into "human ecosystems" as they are altered by or come under the control of man. Migrating human populations introduced new plants and new organisms into the islands of the Pacific, altering the composition of local ecosystems intentionally in some cases, inadvertently in others. The extent of impact varied; occasionally pre-existing species were replaced or eliminated, more often the biological complexity of the system was simply enriched. The high islands by and large were most susceptible to human alteration, the coral atolls less, and the reef-lagoon systems least.

Berkeley: University of California Press, 1963.

Throughout the discussion, Rappaport suggests the range of possible conditions generated by human modification of existing island systems, and thereby identifies the importance of viewing these interactions within an ecosystem framework in order to gain insight and avoid error.

Mabogunje's development of a systems model to explain why people move, the tenor and thrust of rural-urban migration, provides one final example of the usefulness of this conceptual framework in elucidating major geographical problems. His purpose is to treat rural-urban migration as a dynamic spatial process; his goal is to develop a comprehensive understanding of the structure and operation of this system and its relationships to other systems. Using rural Africa as a base, Mabogunje delineates major social and economic processes that act as environmental parameters to shape the decision to migrate; among these are the decline of rural isolation and self-sufficiency, increased transportation and communication links, and the movement from a status to a market economy. The family and the village community are identified as control sub-systems in rural areas; residential and occupational forces operate in similar fashion in the cities. Reacting to earlier studies that viewed migration in terms of push-pull factors, Mabogunje demonstrates that the use of systems concepts such as energy, feedback, equifinality, flow, and growth can contribute incisiveness and breadth to this complex problem.

Of the three conceptual frameworks geographers have utilized in their efforts to probe the relationships of man and environment, the ecological approach is at once the simplest and most complex, the most fascinating and the most difficult to accomplish. Whereas landscape relies on man's footprints, and perception examines images to identify salient man-nature processes, ecology attempts to attack the processes frontally and thus faces the problem of an overwhelming set of variables and forces, which, lacking a well-trained interdisciplinary team, tend to resolve themselves into a description of those few facets of the environment or human behavior the researcher has mastered. Thus, while scores of studies urge an ecological approach for everything from mental health to childhood dreams, few studies have actually been completed. That geographers should pursue this methodology is clear, for perhaps no other framework encompasses so succinctly the traditional focus and thrust of the discipline.

☙☙☙☙☙☙☙☙☙☙☙☙☙☙☙☙☙☙☙☙☙☙☙☙☙☙☙

THE CONCEPT AND METHOD OF CULTURAL ECOLOGY

Julian H. Steward

Objectives in Ecological Studies

At the risk of adding further confusion to an already obscure term, this paper undertakes to develop the concept of ecology in relation to human beings as an heuristic device for understanding the effect of environment upon culture. In order to distinguish the present purpose and method from those implied in the concepts of biological, human, and social ecology, the term *cultural ecology* is used. Since cultural ecology is not generally understood, it is necessary to begin by showing wherein it differs from the other concepts of ecology and then to demonstrate how it must supplement the usual historical approach of anthropology in order to determine the creative processes involved in the adaptation of culture to its environment.

The principal meaning of ecology is "adaptation to environment." Since the time of Darwin, environment has been conceived as the total web of life wherein all plant and animal species interact with one another and with physical features in a particular unit of territory. According to Webster,[1] the biological meaning of ecology is "the mutual relations between organisms and their environment." The concept of adaptive interaction is used to explain the origin of new genotypes in evolution; to explain phenotypical variations; and to describe the web of life itself in terms of competition, succession, climaxes, gradients, and other auxiliary concepts.

Although initially employed with reference to biotic assemblages, the concept of ecology has naturally been extended to include human beings since they are part of the web of life in most parts of the world. Man enters the ecological scene, however, not merely as another organism which is related to other organisms in terms of his physical characteristics. He introduces the super-organic factor of culture, which also affects and is affected by the total web of life. What to do about this cultural factor in ecological studies has raised many methodo-

1. *New International Dictionary* (2nd ed., unabridged, 1950).

From *Theory of Culture Change*, Urbana, University of Illinois Press, 1955, pp. 30-42. Reprinted by permission.

logical difficulties, as most human and social ecologists have recognized.[2] The principal difficulty lies in the lack of clarity as to the purpose of using the concept of ecology. The interaction of physical, biological, and cultural features within a locale or unit of territory is usually the ultimate objective of study. Human or social ecology is regarded as a subdiscipline of its own right and not as means to some further scientific end. Essentially descriptive, the analysis lacks the clear objectives of biology, which has used ecology heuristically to explain several kinds of biological phenomena. If human or social ecology is considered an operational tool rather than an end in itself, two quite different objectives are suggested: first, an understanding of the organic functions and genetic variations of man as a purely biological species; second, a determination of how culture is affected by its adaptation to environment. Each requires its own concepts and methods.

The first, or biological objective, involves several somewhat different problems, all of which, however, must view man in the web of life. Since man is a domesticated animal, he is affected physically by all his cultural activities. The evolution of the Hominidae is closely related to the emergence of culture, while the appearance of *Homo sapiens* is probably more the result of cultural causes than of physical causes. The use of tools, fire, shelter, clothing, new foods, and other material adjuncts of existence were obviously important in evolution, but social customs should not be overlooked. Social groups as determined by marriage customs as well as by economic activities in particular environments have undoubtedly been crucial in the differentiations of local populations and may even have contributed to the emergence of varieties and subraces of men.

2. Milla Aissa Alihan, *Social Ecology*. New York: Columbia University Press, 1938.

The problem of explaining man's cultural behavior is of a different order than that of explaining his biological evolution. Cultural patterns are not genetically derived and, therefore, cannot be analyzed in the same way as organic features. Although social ecologists are paying more and more attention to culture in their enquiries, an explanation of culture per se has not, so far as I can see, become their major objective. Culture has merely acquired greater emphasis as one of many features of the local web of life, and the tools of analysis are still predominantly borrowed from biology. Since one of the principal concepts of biological ecology is the community—the assemblage of plants and animals which interact within a locality—social or human ecology emphasizes the human community as the unit of study. But "community" is a very general and meaningless abstraction. If it is conceived in cultural terms, it may have many different characteristics depending upon the purpose for which it is defined. The tendency, however, has been to conceive of human and biological communities in terms of the biological concepts of competition, succession, territorial organization, migration, gradients, and the like. All of these derived fundamentally from the fact that underlying biological ecology is a relentless and raw struggle for existence both within and between species—a competition which is ultimately determined by the genetic potentials for adaptation and survival in particular biotic-environmental situations. Biological co-operation, such as in many forms of symbiosis, is strictly auxiliary to survival of the species.

Human beings do not react to the web of life solely through their genetically-derived organic equipment. Culture, rather than genetic potential for adaptation, accommodation, and survival, explains the nature of human societies. Moreover, the web of life of any local human society may extend far beyond the immediate physical environment and biotic assemblage. In states, nations, and empires, the nature of the local group is determined by these larger institutions no less than by its local adaptations. Competition of one sort or another may be present, but it is always culturally determined and as often as not co-operation rather than competition may be prescribed. If, therefore, the nature of human communities is the objective of analysis, explanations will be found through use of cultural historical concepts and methods rather than biological concepts, although, as we shall show, historical methods alone are insufficient.

Many writers on social or human ecology have sensed the need to distinguish between biological and cultural phenomena and methods, but they have not yet drawn clear distinctions. Thus, Hollingshead recognizes a difference between an "ecological order [which] is primarily rooted in competition" and "social organization [which] has evolved out of communication."[3] This attempt to conceptualize competition as a category wholly distinct from other aspects of culturally determined behavior is, of course, artificial. Bates,[4] a human biologist, recognizes the importance of culture in determining the nature of communities, but he does not make clear whether he would use human ecology to explain the range of man's biological adaptation under environ-

mental-cultural situations or whether he is interested in man's culture. The so-called Chicago school of Park, Burgess, and their followers were also primarily interested in communities of human beings, especially urban communities. Their methodology as applied to Chicago and other cities treat the components of each as if they were genetically determined species. In analyzing the zoning of a modern city, such categories as retail businesses, wholesale houses, manufacturing firms, and residences of various kinds, and even such additional features as rate of delinquency, are considered as if each were a biological species in competition with one another for zones within the urban area. Such studies are extremely enlightening as descriptive analysis of spatial distributions of kinds of activities within a modern Euro-American city. They do not, however, necessarily throw any light on world-wide ecological urban adaptations, for in other cultures and periods city zoning followed very different culturally prescribed principles. For example, most of the cities of ancient civilizations were rather carefully planned by a central authority for defensive, administrative, and religious functions. Free enterprise, which might have allowed competition for zones between the institutions and subsocieties arising from these functions, was precluded by the culture.

A fundamental scientific problem is involved in these different meanings attached to ecology. Is the objective to find universal laws or processes, or is it to explain special phenomena? In biology, the law of evolution and the auxiliary principles of ecology are applicable to all webs of life regardless of the species and physical environments involved. In social science studies, there is a similar effort to discover universal processes of cultural change. But such processes cannot be conceptualized in biological terms. The social science problem of explaining the

---

3. A. B. Hollingshead, "Human Ecology and Human Society," *Ecological Monographs*, Vol. X (1940); C. C. Adams, "The Relations of General Ecology to Human Ecology," *Ecology*, Vol. XVI (1935), pp. 316–335, and "Introductory Note to Symposium on Relation of Ecology to Human Welfare," *Ecological Monographs*, Vol. X (1940), pp. 307–311.
4. Marston Bates, "Human Ecology," in *Anthropology Today: An Encyclopedic Inventory*, edited by A. L. Kroeber. Chicago: University of Chicago Press, 1953, pp. 700–713.

origin of unlike behavior patterns found among different societies of the human species is very different from the problems of biological evolution. Analyzing environmental adaptations to show how new cultural patterns arise is a very different matter than seeking universal similarities in such adaptation. Until the processes of cultural ecology are understood in the many particulars exemplified by different cultures in different parts of the world a formulation of universal processes will be impossible.

Hawley, who has given the most recent and comprehensive statement of social ecology,[5] takes cultural phenomena into account far more than his predecessors. He states that man reacts to the web of life as a cultural animal rather than as a biological species. "Each acquisition of a new technique or a new use for an old technique, regardless of the source of its origin, alters man's relations with the organisms about him and changes his position in the biotic community." But, preoccupied with the totality of phenomena within the locale and apparently with a search for universal relationships, Hawley makes the local community the focus of interest.[6] The kinds of generalizations which might be found are indicated by the statement: "If we had sufficient knowledge of preliterate peoples to enable us to compare the structure of residence groups arranged in order of size from smallest to largest, we should undoubtedly observe the same phenomena—each increment in size is accompanied by an advance in the complexity of organization." [7] This is the kind of self-evident generalization made by the unilinear evolutionists: cultural progress is manifest in increasing popula-

tions, internal specialization, over-all state controls, and other general features.

Hawley is uncertain in his position regarding the effect of environmental adaptations on culture. He states: "The weight of evidence forces the conclusion that the physical environment exerts but a permissive and limiting effect," [8] but he also says that "each habitat not only permits but to a certain extent necessitates a distinctive mode of life." [9] The first statement closely conforms with the widely accepted anthropological position that historical factors are more important than environmental factors, which may be permissive or prohibitive of culture change but are never causative. The second is nearer to the thesis of this paper that cultural ecological adaptations constitute creative processes.

Culture, History, and Environment

While the human and social ecologists have seemingly sought universal ecological principles and relegated culture in its local varieties to a secondary place, anthropologists have been so preoccupied with culture and its history that they have accorded environment only a negligible role. Owing in part to reaction against the "environmental determinists," such as Huntington and Semple, and in part to cumulative evidence that any culture increases in complexity to a large extent because of diffused practices, the orthodox view now holds that history, rather than adaptive processes, explains culture. Since historical "explanations" of culture employ the culture area concept, there is an apparent contradiction. The culture area is a construct of behavioral uniformities which occur within an area of environmental uniformities. It is assumed that cultural and natural areas are generally

5. Amos H. Hawley, *Human Ecology: A Theory of Community Structure.* New York: The Ronald Press, 1950.
6. *Ibid.*, p. 68.
7. *Ibid.*, p. 197.

8. *Ibid.*, p. 90.
9. *Ibid.*, p. 190.

coterminous because the culture represents an adjustment to the particular environment. It is assumed further, however, that various different patterns may exist in any natural area and that unlike cultures may exist in similar environments.

The cultural-historical approach is, however, also one of relativism. Since cultural differences are not directly attributable to environmental differences and most certainly not to organic or racial differences, they are merely said to represent divergences in cultural history, to reflect tendencies of societies to develop in unlike ways. Such tendencies are not explained. A distinctive pattern develops, it is said, and henceforth is the primary determinant of whether innovations are accepted. Environment is relegated to a purely secondary and passive role. It is considered prohibitive or permissive, but not creative. It allows man to carry on some kinds of activities and it prevents others. The origins of these activities are pushed back to a remote point in time or space, but they are not explained. This view has been best expressed by Forde, who writes:

Neither the world distributions of the various economies, nor their development and relative importance among the particular peoples, can be regarded as simple functions of physical conditions and natural resources. Between the physical environment and human activity there is always a middle term, a collection of specific objectives and values, a body of knowledge and belief: in other words, a cultural pattern. That the culture itself is not static, that it is adaptable and modifiable in relation to physical conditions, must not be allowed to obscure the fact that adaptation proceeds by discoveries and inventions which are themselves in no sense inevitable and which are, in any individual community, nearly all of them acquisitions or impositions from without. The peoples of whole continents have failed to make discoveries that might at first blush seem obvious. Equally important are the restrictions placed by social patterns and religious concepts on the utilization of certain resources or on adaptations to physical conditions.[10]

The habitat at one and the same time circumscribes and affords scope for cultural development in relation to the pre-existing equipment and tendency of a particular society, and to any new concepts and equipment that may reach it from without.[11]

But if geographical determinism fails to account for the existence and distribution of economies, economic determinism is equally inadequate in accounting for the social and political organizations, the religious beliefs and the psychological attitudes which may be found in the cultures based on those economies. Indeed, the economy may owe as much to the social and ritual pattern as does the character of society to the economy. The possession of particular methods of hunting or cultivating, of certain cultivated plants or domestic animals, in no wise defines the pattern of society. Again, there is interaction and on a new plane. As physical conditions may limit the possibilities of the economy, so the economy may in turn be a limiting or stimulating factor in relation to the size, density and stability of human settlement, and to the scale of the social and political unit. But it is only one such factor, and advantage may not be taken of the opportunities it affords. The tenure and transmission of land and other property, the development and relations of social classes, the nature of government, the religious and ceremonial life—all these are parts of a social superstructure, the development of which is conditioned not only by the foundations of habitat and economy, but by complex interactions within its own fabric and by external contacts, often largely indifferent to both the physical background and to the basic economy alike.[12]

Cultural Ecology

Cultural ecology differs from human and social ecology in seeking to explain the origin of particular cultural features and

10. C. Daryll Forde, *Habitat, Economy and Society*. London: Methuen and Company, 1949, p. 463.
11. *Ibid.*, p. 464.
12. *Ibid.*, p. 90.

patterns which characterize different areas rather than to derive general principles applicable to any cultural-environmental situation. It differs from the relativistic and neo-evolutionist conceptions of culture history in that it introduces the local environment as the extracultural factor in the fruitless assumption that culture comes from culture. Thus, cultural ecology presents both a problem and a method. The problem is to ascertain whether the adjustments of human societies to their environments require particular modes of behavior or whether they permit latitude for a certain range of possible behavior patterns. Phrased in this way, the problem also distinguishes cultural ecology from "environmental determinism" and its related theory "economic determinism" which are generally understood to contain their conclusions within the problem.

The problem of cultural ecology must be further qualified, however, through use of a supplementary conception of culture. According to the holistic view, all aspects of culture are functionally interdependent upon one another. The degree and kind of interdependency, however, are not the same with all features. Elsewhere, I have offered the concept of *cultural core*—the constellation of features which are most closely related to subsistence activities and economic arrangements. The core includes such social, political, and religious patterns as are empirically determined to be closely connected with these arrangements. Innumerable other features may have great potential variability because they are less strongly tied to the core. These latter, or secondary features, are determined to a greater extent by purely cultural-historical factors—by random innovations or by diffusion—and they give the appearance of outward distinctiveness to cultures with similar cores. Cultural ecology pays primary attention to those features which empirical analysis shows to be most closely involved in the utilization of environment in culturally prescribed ways.

The expression "culturally prescribed ways" must be taken with caution, for its anthropological usage is frequently "loaded." The normative concept, which views culture as a system of mutually reinforcing practices backed by a set of attitudes and values, seems to regard all human behavior as so completely determined by culture that environmental adaptations have no effect. It considers that the entire pattern of technology, land use, land tenure, and social features derive entirely from culture. Classical illustrations of the primacy of cultural attitudes over common sense are that the Chinese do not drink milk nor the Eskimo eat seals in summer.

Cultures do, of course, tend to perpetuate themselves, and change may be slow for such reasons as those cited. But over the millenia cultures in different environments have changed tremendously, and these changes are basically traceable to new adaptations required by changing technology and productive arrangements. Despite occasional cultural barriers, the useful arts have spread extremely widely, and the instances in which they have not been accepted because of pre-existing cultural patterns are insignificant. In pre agricultural times, which comprised perhaps 99 per cent of cultural history, technical devices for hunting, gathering, and fishing seem to have diffused largely to the limits of their usefulness. Clubs, spears, traps, bows, fire, containers, nets, and many other cultural features spread across many areas, and some of them throughout the world. Later, domesticated plants and animals also spread very rapidly within their environmental limits, being stopped only by formidable ocean barriers.

Whether or not new technologies are valuable is, however, a function of the society's cultural level as well as of environmental potentials. All pre-agricultural societies found hunting and gathering techniques useful. Within the geographical limits of herding and farming, these techniques were adopted. More advanced techniques, such as metallurgy, were acceptable only if certain pre-conditions, such as stable population, leisure time, and internal specialization were present. These conditions could develop only from the cultural ecological adaptations of an agricultural society.

The concept of cultural ecology, however, is less concerned with the origin and diffusion of technologies than with the fact that they may be used differently and entail different social arrangements in each environment. The environment is not only permissive or prohibitive with respect to these technologies, but special local features may require social adaptations which have far-reaching consequences. Thus, societies equipped with bows, spears, surrounds, chutes, brush-burning, deadfalls, pitfalls, and other hunting devices may differ among themselves because of the nature of the terrain and fauna. If the principal game exists in large herds, such as herds of bison or caribou, there is advantage in co-operative hunting, and considerable numbers of peoples may remain together throughout the year.[13] If, however, the game is nonmigratory, occurring in small and scattered groups, it is better hunted by small groups of men who know their territory well.[14] In each case, the cultural repertoire of hunting

devices may be about the same, but in the first case the society will consist of multi-family or multilineage groups, as among the Athabaskans and Algonkians of Canada and probably the pre-horse Plains bison hunters, and in the second case it will probably consist of localized patrilineal lineages or bands, as among the Bushmen, Congo Negritoes, Australians, Tasmanians, Fuegians, and others. These latter groups consisting of patrilineal bands are similar, as a matter of fact, not because their total environments are similar—the Bushmen, Australians, and southern Californians live in deserts, the Negritoes in rain forests, and the Fuegians in a cold, rainy area—but because the nature of the game and therefore of their subsistence problem is the same in each case.

Other societies having about the same technological equipment may exhibit other social patterns because the environments differ to the extent that the cultural adaptations must be different. For example, the Eskimo use bows, spears, traps, containers and other widespread technological devices, but, owing to the limited occurrence of fish and sea mammals, their population is so sparse and co-operative hunting is so relatively unrewarding that they are usually dispersed in family groups. For a different but equally compelling reason the Nevada Shoshoni[15] were also fragmented into family groups. In the latter case, the scarcity of game and the predominance of seeds as the subsistence basis greatly restricted economic co-operation and required dispersal of the society into fairly independent family groups.

In the examples of the primitive hunting, gathering, and fishing societies, it is easy to show that if the local environment is to be exploited by means of the culturally-derived techniques, there are limitations upon the

13. Julian H. Steward, *The Methodology of Multilinear Evolution.* Urbana: University of Illinois Press, 1963, chapter 8.
14. *Ibid.*, chapter 7.

15. *Ibid.*, chapter 6.

size and social composition of the groups involved. When agricultural techniques are introduced, man is partially freed from the exigencies of hunting and gathering, and it becomes possible for considerable aggregates of people to live together. Larger aggregates, made possible by increased population and settled communities, provide a higher level of sociocultural integration, the nature of which is determined by the local type of sociocultural integration.[16]

The adaptative processes we have described are properly designated ecological. But attention is directed not simply to the human community as part of the total web of life but to such cultural features as are affected by the adaptations. This in turn requires that primary attention be paid only to relevant environmental features rather than to the web of life for its own sake. Only those features to which the local culture ascribes importance need be considered.

The Method of Cultural Ecology

Although the concept of environmental adaptation underlies all cultural ecology, the procedures must take into account the complexity and level of the culture. It makes a great deal of difference whether a community consists of hunters and gatherers who subsist independently by their own efforts or whether it is an outpost of a wealthy nation, which exploits local mineral wealth and is sustained by railroads, ships, or airplanes. In advanced societies, the nature of the culture core will be determined by a complex technology and by productive arrangements which themselves have a long cultural history.

Three fundamental procedures of cultural ecology are as follows:

First, the interrelationship of exploitative or productive technology and environment must be analyzed. This technology includes a considerable part of what is often called "material culture," but all features may not be of equal importance. In primitive societies, subsistence devices are basic: weapons and instruments for hunting and fishing; containers for gathering and storing food; transportational devices used on land and water; sources of water and fuel; and, in some environments, means of counteracting excessive cold (clothing and housing) or heat. In more developed societies, agriculture and herding techniques and manufacturing of crucial implements must be considered. In an industrial world, capital and credit arrangements, trade systems and the like are crucial. Socially-derived needs—special tastes in foods, more ample housing and clothing, and a great variety of appurtenances to living—become increasingly important in the productive arrangement as culture develops; and yet these originally were probably more often effects of basic adaptations than causes.

Relevant environmental features depend upon the culture. The simpler cultures are more directly conditioned by the environment than advanced ones. In general, climate, topography, soils, hydrography, vegetational cover, and fauna are crucial, but some features may be more important than others. The spacing of water holes in the desert may be vital to a nomadic seed-gathering people, the habits of game will affect the way hunting is done, and the kinds and seasons of fish runs will determine the habits of riverine and coastal tribes.

Second, the behavior patterns involved in the exploitation of a particular area by means of a particular technology must be analyzed. Some subsistence patterns impose very narrow limits on the general mode of life of the people, while others allow considerable latitude. The gathering of wild vegetable

---

16. *Ibid.*, chapters 9 to 12.

products is usually done by women who work alone or in small groups. Nothing is gained by co-operation and in fact women come into competition with one another. Seed-gatherers, therefore, tend to fragment into small groups unless their resources are very abundant. Hunting, on the other hand, may be either an individual or a collective project, and the nature of hunting societies is determined by culturally prescribed devices for collective hunting as well as by the species. When surrounds, grass-firing, corrals, chutes, and other co-operative methods are employed, the take per man may be much greater than what a lone hunter could bag. Similarly, if circumstances permit, fishing may be done by groups of men using dams, weirs, traps, and nets as well as by individuals.

The use of these more complex and frequently co-operative techniques, however, depends not only upon cultural history—i.e., invention and diffusion—which makes the methods available but upon the environment and its flora and fauna. Deer cannot be hunted advantageously by surrounds, whereas antelope and bison may best be hunted in this way. Slash-and-burn farming in tropical rain forests requires comparatively little co-operation in that a few men clear the land after which their wives plant and cultivate the crops. Dry farming may or may not be co-operative; and irrigation farming may run the gamut of enterprises of ever-increasing size based on collective construction of waterworks.

The exploitative patterns not only depend upon the habits concerned in the direct production of food and of goods but upon facilities for transporting the people to the source of supply or the goods to the people. Watercraft have been a major factor in permitting the growth of settlements beyond what would have been possible for a foot people. Among all nomads, the horse has

had an almost revolutionary effect in promoting the growth of large bands.

The third procedure is to ascertain the extent to which the behavior patterns entailed in exploiting the environment affect other aspects of culture. Although technology and environment prescribe that certain things must be done in certain ways if they are to be done at all, the extent to which these activities are functionally tied to other aspects of culture is a purely empirical problem. I have shown elsewhere[17] that the occurrence of patrilineal bands among certain hunting peoples and of fragmented families among the Western Shoshoni is closely determined by their subsistence activities, whereas the Carrier Indians are known to have changed from a composite hunting band to a society based upon moieties and inherited statuses without any change in the nature of subsistence. In the irrigation areas of early civilizations[18] the sequence of socio-political forms or cultural cores seems to have been very similar despite variation in many outward details or secondary features of these cultures. If it can be established that the productive arrangements permit great latitude in the sociocultural type, then historical influences may explain the particular type found. The problem is the same in considering modern industrial civilizations. The question is whether industrialization allows such latitude that political democracy, communism, state socialism, and perhaps other forms are equally possible, so that strong historical influences, such as diffused ideology— e.g., propaganda—may supplant one type with another, or whether each type represents an adaptation which is specific to the area.

The third procedure requires a genuinely holistic approach, for if such factors as

17. *Ibid.*, chapters 6, 7, 10.
18. *Ibid.*, chapter 11.

demography, settlement pattern, kinship structures, land tenure, land use, and other key cultural features are considered separately, their interrelationships to one another and to the environment cannot be grasped. Land use by means of a given technology permits a certain population density. The clustering of this population will depend partly upon where resources occur and upon transportational devices. The composition of these clusters will be a function of their size, of the nature of subsistence activities, and of cultural-historical factors. The ownership of land or resources will reflect subsistence activities on the one hand and the composition of the group on the other. Warfare may be related to the complex of factors just mentioned. In some cases, it may arise out of competition for resources and have a national character. Even when fought for individual honors or religious purposes, it may serve to nucleate settlements in a way that must be related to subsistence activities.

The Methodological Place of Cultural Ecology

Cultural ecology has been described as a methodological tool for ascertaining how the adaptation of a culture to its environment may entail certain changes. In a larger sense, the problem is to determine whether similar adjustments occur in similar environments. Since in any given environment, culture may develop through a succession of very unlike periods, it is sometimes pointed out that environment, the constant, obviously has no relationship to cultural type. This difficulty disappears, however, if the level of socio-cultural integration represented by each period is taken into account. Cultural types therefore, must be conceived as constellations of core features which arise out of environmental adaptations and which represent similiar levels of integration.

Cultural diffusion, of course, always operates, but in view of the seeming importance of ecological adaptations its role in explaining culture has been greatly over-estimated. The extent to which the large variety of world cultures can be systematized in categories of types and explained through cross-cultural regularities of developmental process is purely an empirical matter. Hunches arising out of comparative studies suggest that there are many regularities which can be formulated in terms of similar levels and similar adaptations.

✶✶✶✶✶✶✶✶✶✶✶✶✶✶✶✶✶✶✶✶✶✶✶✶✶✶✶✶✶✶✶✶

THE PLACE OF PIGS IN
MELANESIAN SUBSISTENCE[1]

Andrew P. Vayda, Anthony Leeds, and David B. Smith

The use of pigs in Melanesia would appear to be one of those "cherished examples of the ideological and organizational mismanagement of food production" to which Harris[2] has recently alluded. It seems that the religious concomitants of the husbandry and slaughter of pigs in Melanesia and the strong sentiments that individuals attach to the animals have led observers to underestimate or even to ignore the importance of pigs in the subsistence of the human populations of Melanesia. Bunzel,[3] for instance, has cited the pig feasts of the Mafulu people in New Guinea as evidence of "economic inefficiency" in primitive societies. Deacon,[4] writing of Malekula in the Hew Hebrides, has asserted that the importance of the domesticated pig is "sociological" rather than "economic." And Linton,[5] in a discussion of Oceanic cultures, has depicted the keeping of pigs as a "luxury occupation" and a "form of ostentatious waste."

We do not accept the above views. Unfortunately, there are large gaps in what is known about Melanesian economy and ecology; quantitative data, for example, are appallingly deficient. Nevertheless, a fresh look at what information is available suggests some interpretations of the place of pigs in Melanesian subsistence that differ strikingly from Linton's and the others cited above. Our general hypothesis is

---

1. Since the original publication of this article in 1961, Roy A. Rappaport (in *Pigs for the Ancestors*, New Haven: Yale University Press, 1967, pp. 63ff.) has shown the inapplicability of some of our interpretations to New Guinea highland areas where meteorological vicissitudes are not as significant as in certain Melanesian lowland regions. Rappaport (*ibid.*, pp. 84-87) has, however, suggested that pig-keeping in these highland areas has other adaptive functions, which have been summarized as follows in a recent article by Vayda ("An Ecological Approach in Cultural Anthropology," *Bucknell Review*, Vol. XVII (1969), No. 1, pp. 112-19): ". . . pigs intended for slaughter in the festivals are disposed of earlier if misfortunes or emergencies so require. That is to say, if people are suffering from certain severe illnesses or injuries or if warfare is about to be undertaken, then various spirits must be immediately placated by being presented with the souls of pigs. The flesh of the sacrificial animals is retained for consumption by the individuals suffering from illness or injury or otherwise undergoing stress and . . . is probably important for counteracting the stress-induced increase in these individuals' catabolization of protein; the negative nitrogen balancing resulting from this increase, if not offset by the ingestion of high-quality proteins, may impair the healing of wounds and the production of antibodies and have other physically harmful consequences for people on low-protein diets."

2. Marvin Harris, "The Economy Has No Surplus?" *American Anthropologist*, Vol. LXI (1959, p. 194.

3. Ruth Bunzel, "The Economic Organization of Primitive Peoples," in *General Anthropology*, Franz Boas, editor. New York: D. C. Heath, 1938, p. 331.

4. A. Bernard Deacon, *Malekula, A Vanishing People in the New Hebrides.* London: Routledge, 1934, pp. 16ff., 202.

5. Ralph Linton, *The Tree of Culture.* New York; Knopf, 1955, pp. 98ff.

From *Proceedings of the American Ethnological Society,* Spring 1961, edited by Viola E. Garfield, Seattle, University of Washington Press, 1961. Reprinted by permission.

that pigs are, in fact, vitally important to the management of subsistence by Melanesian populations. Lack of space makes it impossible for us to present all the relevant data. But we can provide the reasoning and some key facts in support of our interpretations.[6] Further, we can perhaps suggest pathways to guide the collection of data and the more satisfactory testing of hypotheses in the future.

It must be emphasized, first, that pork, regardless of the circumstances of its consumption, provides nutriment and that the nutriment from pork may well be important in the diets of many Melanesian populations. Some observations by ethnographers are suggestive. For example, Bell,[7] working on Boieng Island in the Tanga group of the Bismarck Archipelago, has noted that "pork is quite an ordinary item in the Tangan diet." The number of occasions for killing and eating pigs listed by Luzbetak,[8] suggests that the New Guinea highlanders of the Middle Wahgi region have pork quite often and quite regularly. Thurnwald,[9] describing a Bougainville people in the Solomon Islands, has said: "In the life of the Buin people there is no incident which cannot serve as an occasion for feasting upon pigs and pudding." Similarly, Ross,[10] writing of

the Mt. Hagen tribes of the New Guinea highlands, has reported: "Pork is eaten very often, for every imaginable ceremonial affair. . . ." It should be noted also that even in parts of Melanesia where the consumption of pork seems to be less frequent, pigs may nevertheless be important in the local diet as sources of animal protein otherwise hardly available.[11]

Within the large area of Melanesia there are, of course, many different social and ceremonial contexts in which pigs are slaughtered and pork consumed. Pigs are used in both the large and small feasts that follow or accompany ceremonies and sacrifices to spirits and ghosts, life-crisis rites, trading between communities, various construction projects, distributions of property, and the prestige competitions among local "big men." Each of these somewhat diverse occasions constitutes a formally recognized time for the congregation of people. In the context of our argument, an important thing about these people is simply that they eat; the guests at a feast consume their share of pork either immediately or within a few days after the feast. Because meat generally spoils quickly under Melanesian conditions, it would often be impractical to slaughter a pig for consumption by a single nuclear family. By bringing together considerably more people than those in a nuclear family, the feasts provide a solution to the problem of using all of the flesh of an animal after it has been killed. Feasts are, of course, given

6. Our data in the paper are drawn both from standard sources and from answers to questions sent by us to anthropologists who have worked in Melanesia. For their generous assistance in providing information, we are indebted to Ralph Bulmer, Ann Chowning, Anthony Forge, Ward Goodenough, Diamond Jenness, Mervyn Meggitt, Philip Newman, Leopold Pospisil, Marshall Sahlins, and Richard Salisbury. Not all of these persons agree with our interpretations and point of view.
7. F. L. S. Bell, "Report on Field Work in Tanga," *Oceania*, Vol. IV (1934), p. 295.
8. Louis J. Luzbetak, "The Middle Wahgi Culture: A Study of First Contacts and Initial Selectivity," *Anthropos*, Vol. LIII (1958), p. 68.
9. Richard C. Thurnwald, "Pigs and Currency in Buin," *Oceania*, Vol. V (1934), p. 124.
10. Rev. William A. Ross, "Ethnological Notes on

Mt. Hagen Tribes (Mandated Territory of New Guinea)," *Anthropos*, Vol. XXXI (1936), p. 350.
11. This, according to M. J. Meggitt, "The Enga of the New Guinea Highlands: Some Preliminary Observations," *Oceania*, Vol. XXVIII (1958), pp. 286ff., is the situation among Enga-speaking New Guinea highlanders. The paucity of animal protein sources in the New Guinea highlands has been noted also by H. A. P. C. Oomen, "Poor-Food Patterns in New Guinea," *Nieuw-Guinea Studiën*, Vol. III (1959), pp. 41ff.

by people who can collect sufficient pigs and vegetal resources for the occasion. Guests who partake are more or less obligated to reciprocate, but usually may wait to do so until they have both an appropriate ceremonial occasion and, more importantly, sufficient foodstuffs for requiting their erstwhile host; alternatively, reciprocation may take the form of contributions of goods and services when the host is planning another large feast.[12] The distributions of pork and vegetal foods thus tend in general to be made by those best able to make them at particular times. The effect of this tendency is to reduce the inequalities in food consumption which may occur from time to time and from place to place.

The part that pigs play in Melanesian subsistence may be further illuminated by a consideration of Liebig's law of the minimum, described by Bartholomew and Birdsell[13] as one of the most firmly established ecological generalizations.[14] It states

that biological reactions are controlled not so much by the *average* amounts of essential factors in the environment as by *extremes* in the presence of these factors. Bartholomew and Birdsell[15] illustrate this by noting that population in a semidesert area having many fruitful years in succession may be restricted to an otherwise inexplicably low density by a single drought year occurring but once in a human generation. Unfortunately, the fieldworker who spends some months or even a year or more in a Melanesian community is seldom able (and too often not even inclined) to record significant temporal differences in the availability of food supplies. An ethnographer staying in one community for as long as a year can get some idea of at least the seasonal variations, but he can hardly assess the magnitude of year-to-year fluctuations. We think that there is a great need for quantitative data on temporal variations in the availability of food resources and especially of vegetal produce, since these are the variations which seem to us to make pigs crucial in Melanesian subsistence.

But even if the quantitative data are deficient, evidence of significant variations is at hand. From most parts of Melanesia, we have some reports of food shortages due mainly to meteorological factors, especially those leading to drought.[16]

12. Feast-giving and its reciprocation are discussed by Ann Chowning, Personal Communication, June, 1960; Tom Harrisson, *Savage Civilization*. London: Macmillan, 1937, pp. 33ff.; Louis H. Luzbetak, *op. cit.*, 1958, pp. 68ff.; M. J. Meggitt, *op. cit.*, 1958, pp. 287, 288, 297ff.; Douglas Oliver, "The Solomon Islands," *Natural History*, Vol. L (1942), pp. 177ff.; Douglas Oliver, *A Solomon Island Society*. Cambridge: Harvard University Press, 1955, pp. 364ff.; J. A. Todd, "Report on Research Work in South-West New Britain, Territory of New Guinea," *Oceania*, Vol. V (1934), p. 201.
13. George A. Bartholomew and Joseph B. Birdsell, "Ecology and the Protohominids," *American Anthropologist*, Vol. LV (1953), p. 488.
14. Lee R. Dice, *Natural Communities*. Ann Arbor: University of Michigan Press, 1952, pp. 217ff.; Charles H. Lowe, "Contemporary Biota of the Sonoran Desert: Problems," in *The University of Arizona Arid Lands Colloquia*. Tuscon; University of Arizona Press, 1958-59, pp. 56ff.; Walter P. Taylor, "Significance of Extreme or Intermittent Conditions in Distribution of Species and Management of Natural Resources, with a Restatement of Liebig's Law of Minimum," *Ecology*, Vol. XV (1934), pp. 374-379.

15. George A. Bartholomew, and Joseph B. Birdsell, *op. cit.*, p. 488.
16. The places from which such reports are available include the Loyalty Islands (E. Hadfield, *Among the Natives of the Loyalty Group*. London: Macmillan, 1920, p. 48), the New Hebrides (John Layard, *Stone Men of Malekula*. London: Chatto and Windus, 1942, p. 170), the Solomon Islands (Beatrice Blackwood, *Both Sides of Buka Passage*. Oxford: Clarendon Press, 1935, p. 288; A. I. Hopkins, *In the Isles of King Solomon*. London; Seeley, Service and Co., 1930, p. 232; Walter G. Ivens, *The Island Builders of the Pacific*. London: Seeley, Service and Co., 1930, p. 273; Douglas Oliver, *op. cit.*, 1955, p. 30), New Britain (J. A. Todd, *op. cit.*, p. 194), the Schouten Islands (H.

We refer to such reports not so much as evidence of food shortages per se but rather as evidence that the quantity of available food supplies is subject to important temporal variation related especially to meteorological vicissitudes. A way in which Melanesian populations are able to adjust to such unpredictable variation is through the practice of trying to plant more crops every

---

Ian Hogbin, "Tillage and Collection: A New Guinea Economy," *Oceania*, Vol. IX [1938], p. 130; Camilla H. Wedgwood, "Report on Research in Manam Island, Mandated Territory of New Guinea," *Oceania*, Vol. IV [1934], p. 391), the Trobriands (Leo Austen, "The Trobriand Islands of Papua," *Australian Geographer*, Vol. III [1936], p. 19; Leo Austen, "The Seasonal Gardening Calendar of Kiriwana, Trobriand Islands," *Oceania*, Vol. IX [1939], p. 251; H. Ian Hogbin, *Social Change.* London: Watts, 1958, p. 197, Bronislaw Malinowski, *Coral Gardens and Their Magic*, 2 vols., London: George Allen and Unwin, 1935, Vol. 1, pp. 160-164 , Vol. II, pp. 119-122), the d'Entrecasteaux Islands (R. F. Fortune, *Sorcerers of Dobu.* London: Routledge, 1932, pp. 131ff.; D. Jenness, and A. Ballantyne, *The Northern d'Entrecasteaux.* Oxford: Clarendon Press, 1920, pp. 31-33), the New Guinea lowlands (J. A. Forge, Personal Communication, June, 1960; Ross, cited in Abraham L. Gitlow, "Economics of the Mount Hagen Tribes, New Guinea," *Monographs of the American Ethnological Society*, No. 12. Locust Valley: J. J. Augustin, 1947, pp. 20ff.; F. E. Williams, *Orokaiva Magic.* London: Oxford University Press, 1928, pp. 112ff.), the New Guinea highlands (Robert M. Glasse, "Revenge and Redress among the Huli: A Preliminary Account," *Mankind*, Vol. V [1959], p. 275; M. J. Meggitt, "The Valleys of the Upper Wage and Lai Rivers, Western Highlands, New Guinea," *Oceania*, Vol. XXVII [1956], pp. 125, 128; M. J. Meggitt, "The Ipili of the Porgera Valley, Western Highlands District, Territory of New Guinea," *Oceania*, Vol. XXVIII [1957], p. 36; M. J. Meggitt, *op. cit.*, 1958, pp. 261ff., 282, 295; H. A. P. C. Oomen, *op. cit.*, p. 44; K. E. Read, "The Gahuku-Gama of the Central Highlands," *South Pacific*, Vol. V [1951], p. 155), and Frederik Hendrik Island (Bureau for Native Affairs, Hollandia, Netherlands New Guinea, "Anthropological Research in Netherlands New Guinea Since 1950," *Oceania*, Vol. XXIX [1958], p. 138).

year than can be or need to be consumed by the planters in a year not appreciably disturbed by adverse weather.[17] Planting what will be more than enough should the weather be good is a means of ensuring that there will be enough and possibly just barely enough should the weather be bad. In this connection, it must be noted that the root crops which are the staples of most Melanesian populations can be stored at best for only a limited time.[18] Therefore, in the times of bad weather and poor harvests, little reliance can be placed on stores of these crops from previous years.

If, then the size of the human population is limited by the times of minimal yield, the vegetal surpluses of normal years become available for the feeding of livestock. Indeed, the literature is rich in examples consistent

---

17. Some implications of the practice are discussed also by Marvin Harris, *op. cit.*, p. 192, and by Marshall D. Sahlins, "Political Power and the Economy in Primitive Society," in *Essays in the Science of Culture in Honor of Leslie A. White*, G. Dole and R. Carneiro, editors. New York: Thomas Y. Crowell, 1960, p. 407. Further evidence, especially quantitative data on production and consumption, would be useful for establishing just how widespread and how effective the practice is.
18. Bronislaw Malinowski, *op. cit.*, 1935, Vol. I. p. 160; New Guinea Nutrition Survey Expedition, *Report.* Canberra, Department of External Territories, 1947, p. 24; H. A. P. C. Oomen, *op. cit.*, p. 41; Harry M. Raulet, "Some Ecological Determinants of Social Structure in Northwest Melanesia," unpublished Ph.D. dissertation, Columbia University, New York, 1960, pp. 59ff., 62n., 89n.; Marshall D. Sahlins, Personal Communication, November 12, 1960. In the limited areas where sago rather than any root crop is the staple, some different kinds of adjustments may be found.
19. Information on these practices is given by Beatrice Blackwood, *op. cit.*, p. 292; Ann Chowning, *op. cit.*; J. A. Forge, *op. cit.*; Louis J. Luzbetak, *op. cit.*, 1958, p. 69; M. J. Meggitt, Personal Communication, April 5, 1960; Douglas Oliver, *op. cit.*, 1955, p. 136; and Marie Reay, "Individual Ownership and Transfer of Land Among the Kuma," *Man*, Vol. LIX (1959), p. 78.

with the view that surpluses are so used by Melanesians. We may read, for example, that pigs commonly are fed parings and sub-standard tubers and are allowed to root in old gardens for unharvested taro or yams.[19] The practice of feeding vegetal surpluses to the pigs in the years of normal and maximal crop yields is described as "banking" in Oliver's account[20] of a Solomon Island culture, and the term seems appropriate, for the pigs are indeed food reserves of the hoof.[21]

In years of minimal yield when the garden produce has to be used entirely for the support of the local human population, attempts may be made to trade away or cere-monially to give away the pigs to distant and better-supplied communities or else to have the pigs agisted at such places.[22] If these

attempts are unsuccessful, the pigs must subsist on what they can forage for them-selves. This is under all but the most extreme circumstances not very hard for them to do. The animals are omnivorous. They eat rinds, peels, and other garbage; they eat feces; in the forests, they eat wild roots, leaves, grasses, berries, seeds, and even the flesh of frogs, small lizards, snakes, and insects.[23] Moreover, in the years of minimal yield, not only can the mature pigs in most cases take care of their own subsistence but they can also be a vital source of food for human beings, who may hunt and eat some of the pigs that have gone wild or simply slaughter and eat some of those that have remained relatively tame.[24]

---

20. Douglas Oliver, *op. cit.*, 1955, p. 470.
21. New Guinea Nutrition Survey Expedition, *op. cit.*, p. 24; Douglas Oliver, "A Case of Change in Food Habits in Bougainville, British Solomon Islands," *Applied Anthropology*, Vol. I (1942), No. 2, p. 35.
22. The trading chains that sometimes extend through a long series of communities in highland New Guinea and involve movements of pigs in return for more durable stores of value such as shells, stone axes, and rings may be a means of adjusting the supply of pigs to the resources avail-able locally for the support of pigs and for the support of men (G. A. M. Bus, "The *Te* Festival or Gift Exchange in Enga (Central Highlands of New Guinea)," *Anthropos*, Vol. XLVI [1951], pp. 813-824; A. P. Elkin, "Delayed Exchange in Wabag Sub-District, Central Highlands of New Guinea, with Notes on the Social Organization," *Oceania*, Vol. XXIII [1953]; M. J. Meggitt, *op. cit.*, 1958, pp. 288ff.; M. J. Meggitt, *op. cit.*, 1960; Leopold Pospisil, "Kapauku Papuans and Their Law," *Yale University Publications in Anthropology* 54. New Haven: Yale University Press, 1958, pp. 121ff.). This kind of adjusting, whether in years of minimal yield or at other times, is probably more feasible in large and ecologically varied areas such as the island of New Guinea than in relatively restricted areas such as the Trobriand archipelago. While the Trobriand people are also involved in a geographi-cally extensive trading system (Bronislaw

Malinowski, "Kula; The Circulating Exchange of Valuables in the Archipelagoes of Eastern New Guinea," *Man*, Vol. XX [1920]; Bronislaw Malinowski, *Argonauts of the Western Pacific*. London: Routledge, 1922), apparently they cannot move goods as readily (and with as little advance preparation) between a number of dif-ferent ecological regions as can the New Guinea highlanders. Within Melanesia, there doubtless are important variations in what people do, and can do, with pigs; these variations should of course be investigated further.
23. The place of such items in the diets of Melanesian pigs is noted by Diamond Jenness, Personal Communication, March 30, 1960; Louis J. Luzbetak, *op. cit.*, 1958, p. 69; and M. J. Meggitt, *op. cit.*, 1960.
24. J. A. Todd, *op. cit.*, p. 194, writing of south-west New Britain, says: "Fish and reef products provide a rather inadequate flesh supply [for the people]. This is augmented now and then with pigs killed for ceremonial purposes, *and in the lean season with pigs, wild and domestic, killed simply for food*" (italics ours). M. J. Meggitt, *op. cit.*, 1956, pp. 128, 133, mentions that in times of food shortage the Aruni and Kandep people of the New Guinea highlands kill and cook pigs on the dance grounds. Regarding the Aruni ceremony, M. J. Meggitt, *ibid.*, p. 128, observes: "[It] seems simply aimed at maintaining group morale, and there appear to be no spells or invocations to ancestral ghosts. Quite importantly, it adds protein to the diet at a time this is needed." More data from all of

It may be concluded then that if, as we have indicated, pigs are continually important in the diets of Melanesian populations and may be vitally important at certain critical times, and if they serve as repositories for surplus vegetal produce that might otherwise be unavailable for consumption by people, it is hardly warranted to regard Melanesian pig-keeping as a "luxury occupation" and a "form of ostentatious waste."[25] On the contrary, it may be concluded that pigs appear, from a materialistic standpoint, to be a good thing for Melanesian populations. One remaining matter, however, needs to be discussed. The pigs of the Melanesians apparently are in the category of those good things of which there can be too much.[26]

In this connection it must be noted first of all that although pigs in general breed quickly,[27] their deaths from natural causes and their frequent slaughter for the big and small feasts that are, as we have already discussed, a feature of many occasions, constitute a continuing check on the too-rapid expansion of the total pig population of any of the Melanesian territories within which pigs are regularly circulated from community to community. Nevertheless, if the growth of the crops and wild plants that constitute major sources of food for the pigs is favorable throughout much of a large territory for a succession of years, and no bad times intervene, the pig population may then increase to such an extent as to become more and more a menace to the people's gardens.[28] Among New Guinea highlanders and some other Melanesians, the fact of having a large pig population on hand is the "trigger" for holding great festivals in the course of which so many hundreds and sometimes even thousands of pigs are slaughtered that some of the pork becomes inedible or is eaten in sickening and ex-

---

Melanesia on what happens to pigs during bad times would be desirable.

25. Pigs may of course be important not only as a source of meat but also as a source of dung for manuring. Enga-speaking New Guinea highlanders, according to M. J. Meggit, *op. cit.*, 1958, p. 291, often turn pigs into garden lands and believe that the dung of pigs enhances soil fertility by "putting grease back into the land." The use of dung for manure may well be more important where cultivation is not "slash-and-burn" but rather almost permanent, as in a few parts of the New Guinea highlands. It would be desirable to have more data from all of Melanesia regarding the uses to which pig dung is put.

26. We regard it important that this category should be recognized and investigated by anthropologists. Elsewhere, one of us has suggested that Maori slaves in *pre*contact times (A. P. Vayda, "Maori Warfare," *Polynesian Society Maori Monographs,* No. 2. Wellington: Polynesian Society, 1960, pp. 106ff.) and Northwest Coast wealth in *post*contact times (A. P. Vayda, "A Re-examination of Northwest Coast Economic Systems," *Transactions of the New York Academy of Sciences,* April, 1961), were also "good things of which there could be too much." Do the horses of the Plains Indians also belong in this category? This question has been raised by Harold Hickerson, *Personal Communication,* May 1961 who points out that one means whereby particular Plains

Indian groups could avoid having too many horses for too long was by becoming the targets of the horse-stealing raids of other groups. The subject seems to us to merit a great deal of further investigation.

27. Vital statistics of Melanesian pigs in particular have been received in personal communications from Forge, Meggitt, Pospisil, and Salisbury. Additional data on the population dynamics of Melanesian pigs would be very useful, and it is hoped that future fieldworkers will note such things as: the number of shoats per sow; the number per litter; the number that survive infancy; the number, sex, and age of piglets dying or getting killed prior to sexual maturity; the number of boars castrated and their ages at the time of castration; the number and age of mature animals slaughtered; and the proportions of tried sows, unbred sows, boars, and castrated males slaughtered.

28. Paula Brown, and H. C. Brookfield, "Chimbu Land and Society," *Oceania,* Vol XXX (1959), p. 22.

cessive quantities.[29] Whether intended as such or not by the people themselves, these massive slaughters are a way of keeping the land from being overrun with pigs. Enough animals, however, seem always to be spared from the slaughters to ensure that any pigs needed will be around later on.

Our statement that having a large pig

29. Louis H. Luzbetak, "The Socio-Religious Significance of a New Guinea Pig Festival," Parts I and II, *Anthropological Quarterly*, N. S., Vol II (1954), p. 113, describing a festival in the course of which the Nondugl people of the Middle Wahgi region of the New Guinea highlands slaughtered more than 2,000 pigs, mentions that "sometimes a native, whose stomach had been filled to capacity [with pork], caused nausea by smelling a certain variety of the rhododendron plant and thus emptied his stomach only to be able to fill it again." At this festival, there was, according to Luzbetak, much sickness as a result both of overeating and of eating dirty and partly decayed meat.
30. Paula Brown, and H. C. Brookfield, *op. cit.*, p. 46; G. A. M. Bus, *op. cit.*, p. 816; Louis J. Luzbetak, *op. cit.*, 1954, pp. 62ff.; K. E. Read, "Nama Cult of the Central Highland, New Guinea," *Oceania*, Vol. XXIII (1952), p. 17.

population on hand triggers the great festivals may require some explication. The statement is based on the fact that getting the pigs together for a massive slaughter is evidently no simple matter of collecting all the pigs within a given territory whenever people decide that it would be agreeable to gain prestige or other incorporeal rewards by the means of holding a great festival. On the contrary, meetings are called and assessments are made of available resources, and the indications are that there are many times when a festival might be agreeable and yet no festival is held because the number of pigs on hand is simply not sufficient.[30] To have a sufficient number of pigs for a major festival may well mean having very considerably more pigs than are required to be retained in order to have animals as stores for surplus vegetal produce and in order to have pork for consumption throughout the year. The massive slaughters at the festivals help to maintain a long-term ecological balance between Melanesian man and the crops and fauna from which he draws his sustenance.

✛✛✛✛✛✛✛✛✛✛✛✛✛✛✛✛✛✛✛✛✛✛✛✛✛✛✛✛✛✛

ENVIRONMENTAL POTENTIALS AND ECONOMIC OPPORTUNITIES: A BACKGROUND FOR CULTURAL ADAPTATION

Philip W. Porter

My task in this cooperative research has been to examine environment and to express the varieties of environment as potentials for different subsistence uses. The environment

is thus seen as a potential for exploitation by man, and at a further remove, a potential for the shaping of culture. In order to relate environment and subsistence forms to one

From *American Anthropologist*, Vol. 67, No. 2 (1965), pp. 409-20. Reprinted by permission of the American Anthropological Society.

another in a meaningful way we use the concept of subsistence risk. In outline, first we discuss environmental parameters in East Africa and explain subsistence risk; second, we examine two environmental gradients, a steep one in Pokot, and a gentle one in Kamba country; and third, we conclude with some suggestions as to what these environmental types and gradients mean for economic exploitation and cultural adaptation.

Environmental Parameters

The environmental setting with which we are concerned is equatorial highland and lowland. The Pokot of west-central Kenya and the Wakamba also of Kenya in the area east of Nairobi lie within a degree of the equator, the Pokot to the north, the Wakamba to the south. The elevations of settlements range from 10,000 to 3,000 ft. in Pokotland; from 7,000 to 2,500 in Ukambani. There is a clear relationship between rainfall and elevation in East Africa (see Fig. 1). It increases with altitude with such regularity that a simple regression equation allows fairly precise calculation of rainfall from elevation. An important feature of the rainfall is its distribution through the year, which is most closely tied to the equinoctial overhead passage of the sun, and precipitation resulting from local convectional storms in the

Generalized Altitudinal Profile

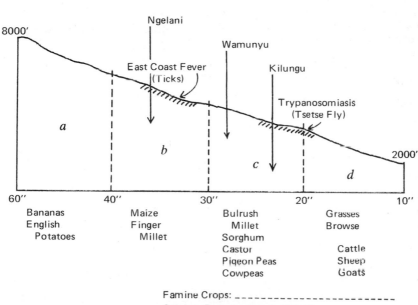

Figure 1. Generalized altitudinal profile in East Africa showing relationships among rainfall, elevation, and crops. The relationships may be summarized as follows:

1. The higher, the wetter.
2. The lower, the hotter.
3. The less the mean annual rainfall, the greater the variability.
4. The importance of the bimodal rainfall regime increases with decreases in altitude.
5. The bimodal regime merges into a single maximum with increases in latitude.

train of this overhead passage (see Fig. 2). Where rainfall is ample these peaks may not be important, but as rainfall amounts decline, the concentration of precipitation in the bimodal peak periods, and the spacing of the maxima with respect to one another, do become important. Still another variable is the reliability of rainfall, which generally can be said to decrease as the amount of rainfall decreases.

Granting that technology can extend the range of a subsistence activity, we can see (Fig. 1) that there is a zone in which the growing of bananas would be possible (the requirements are over 44 inches of rainfall per annum, evenly distributed); next comes a zone in which the growing of grains, finger millet and maize, is favored. These are water demanding crops if they are to do well. Moving on to drier areas it becomes necessary to rely more heavily on quick-maturing water-conservative plants such as bulrush millet, sorghum, castor, pigeon peas, and

Water Balance Diagram

Machakos, Av. Rf. 35.5"

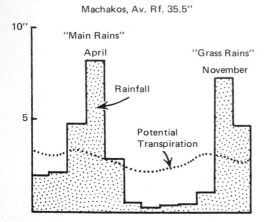

Figure 2. Water balance diagram for Machakos, Ukambani. The rainfall has a bimodal regime which is characteristic of areas close to the equator. The year is thus divided into four alternating periods of rainfall surplus and deficit. The moisture deficit is partly met by moisture stored in the soil.

cowpeas, as well as tuberous famine corps like sweet potatoes and cassava. At some point even these drought resistant plants cannot be relied upon, and subsistence becomes based on the grasses and browse plants which can sustain livestock in very dry environments.

Now to add another variable to this altitudinal profile: we must remember that temperature as well as rainfall has been changing with altitude, at about 3.5° f. per thousand feet. The interrelations of heat and moisture provide zones in which the vectors of two important livestock diseases can flourish. Roughly, one can say that well-watered areas between 4,000 and 7,000 ft. are both warm and moist enough to support tick populations, the vector of East Coast Fever. There is a tendency for livestock diseases to be associated with particular kinds of vegetation. In the case of East Coast Fever in Kenya it is with combretaceous woodland and forest. The other great livestock menace, trypanosomiasis, is found in areas suited to the tsetse fly. The necessary habitat involves heat, moisture, and shade, all in close proximity, and accordingly moist lowlands and drier plains areas of thicket and dense *Acacia* thorn scrub near perennial streams are commonly tsetse infested. Since livestock disease is associated with vegetation types, the boundaries between infested and free areas are often sharp. The Pokot and Wakamba know which areas are infested and the times of year it is unsafe to run livestock there. The environmental limits for crops, however, are seldom so clearly stated in nature, a point to which we will presently return.

We can, I hope, see that this over-all gradient in rainfall, heat, and the presence or absence of livestock diseases represents a continuum or profile of environmental types wherein differing subsistence activities are possible depending on the technology and will of the people. But these types merge, one into the other, and we are hard pressed to know where to draw boundaries between types. By tampering with the slope of the altitudinal profile, I now introduce another variable, one that is peculiarly spatial (Fig. 3). It is a distance factor, related to the range of movement of people under normal primitive circumstances. An abrupt change in elevation, on the order of two to three thousand feet in a few miles, can effectively collapse or eliminate certain environments and place very different environmental types so close to one another as to be within walking distance. It is reasonable to expect that the subsistence economy in an area of environmental diversity would differ from that in a zone of environmental uniformity.

Subsistence Risk

All human activities involve risk. Men have devised individual and institutional strategies to cope with these dangers. The uncertainties connected with farming and herding in East Africa are proverbial. The Masai lost 400,000 head of cattle from drought during 1961, when our field season was just starting. In large measure, subsistence uncertainty can be traced to vagaries of climate. Tick populations, pests such as army worms, stalk borers and dioch-bird swarms are related to climatic conditions. Agricultural (as well as pastoral) risks are not everywhere the same. It is, I feel, in a geography of subsistence risks that a meaningful link can be forged between subsistence economies and environmental potentials. Subsistence risk is not given in nature, it is a settlement negotiated between an environment and a technology. Just how much risk an individual or a community can tolerate, how often a failure of crops or decimation of herds can be borne, is a problem that each culture must solve. A community has institutional and technical means of coping with risk. It can tighten its belt, develop surpluses, or raid neighboring territory. Danger to the individual can be decreased by sharing out risks, through dispersal of fields, timing of harvests, cattle deals, and the like. We may assume that in the degree to which the

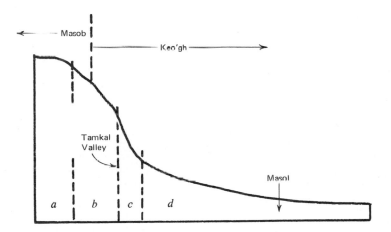

Figure 3. A steep altitudinal profile in West Pokot District places different environmental zones close to one another.

situation is tenuous, adjustment to risk is the essential element in the articulation of subsistence with environment.

The way in which I thought the geography of subsistence risk could be subjected to rigorous analysis was to map rainfall probabilities. We can describe this as a method for determining water need/water supply relationships for various agricultural seasons. Water need, the term which measures the transpiration requirement of incoming radiant energy, has been based on the work of Penman and Thornthwaite.[1] The calculation of rainfall probabilities is patterned after studies by Manning, Glover, Robinson and McCulloch[2] except that they generally deal in rainfall *per se*, rather than its relationship to plant transpiration requirements.

Against the water need was compared the water supply (rainfall) over a number of years. The number of years in which a season showed a positive water balance, divided by the total number of years, gives the probability of transpiration demands

being met. Where the water balance is a negative value, that is, need exceeds supply, it is argued that plants wilt and die, and crops consequently fail or the harvest is severely reduced.

By studying the temporal as well as spatial variability of environment we at last touch the reality of what is going on between people and environments. We see a way of grasping and using process, of taking into account secular change. We find, in short, a way of coping with that flux which people term "ecology."

The Pokot. Pokotland shows an extremely steep environmental gradient. Basically there is *keo'gh*, the hot country, and *masob*, the cold country; but within these climates are several explicitly named and managed zones: valley bottoms, steep lower hill slopes, and land higher up on a bench at about 7,000 ft. (Figs. 3 and 4). There are specific crops, irrigation, and other agricultural techniques for each zone. People are organized within the *korok*, which geo-politically is a space laid out to include these several zones. People commonly have farms in all zones. The timing of planting, weeding, irrigating and harvesting is carefully worked out so that there is a constant movement between zones and no intolerable peak load of work in any month. In the Pokot view, life in

1. H. L. Penman, "Natural Evaporation from Open Water, Bare Soil and Grass," *Proceedings of the Royal Society of London* (A), Vol. 193 (1948), pp. 120-145; "Vegetation and Hydrology," *Technical Communication* No. 53. Harpenden: Commonwealth Bureau of Soils, 1963, pp. 40-43. C. W. Thornthwaite, "An Approach Toward a Rational Classification of Climate," *Geographical Review*, Vol. 38 (1948), pp. 55-94. C. W. Thornthwaite and J. R. Mather, "Instructions and Tables for Computing Potential Evapotranspiration and the Water Balance," C. W. Thornthwaite Associates, Laboratory of Climatology, *Publications in Climatology*, Vol. 10 (1957), No. 3, pp. 181-311. C. W. Thornthwaite and J. R. Mather, editors, "Average Climatic Water Balance Data of the Continents," Part I, "Africa," C. W. Thornthwaite Associates, Laboratory of Climatology, *Publications in Climatology*, Vol. 15 (1962), No. 2.
2. J. Glover and J. S. G. McCulloch, "The Empirical Relation Between Solar Radiation and Hours of Sunshine," *Quarterly Journal of the Royal Meteorological Society*, Vol. 84 (1958), pp.

172-175. J. Glover, P. Robinson, and J. P. Henderson, "Provisional Maps of the Reliability of Annual Rainfall in East Africa," *Quarterly Journal of the Royal Meteorological Society*, Vol. 80 (1954), pp. 602-609. Joan M. Kenworthy and J. Glover, "The Reliability of the Main Rains in Kenya," *East African Agricultural Journal*, Vol. 23 (1958), pp. 267-271. H. L. Manning, "The Statistical Assessment of Rainfall Probability and Its Application in Uganda Agriculture," *Research Memoirs*, No. 23. London: Empire Cotton Growing Corporation, 1956, pp. 460-480. P. Robinson and J. Glover, "The Reliability of the Rainfall Within the Growing Season," *East African Agricultural Journal*, Vol. 19 (1954), pp. 137-139.

Tamkal could hardly be contemplated except as one based on the use of several zones.

Much of the work is communally shared. Large fields (called *parahgomucho*) involving even 30 people are cut from bush, burned,

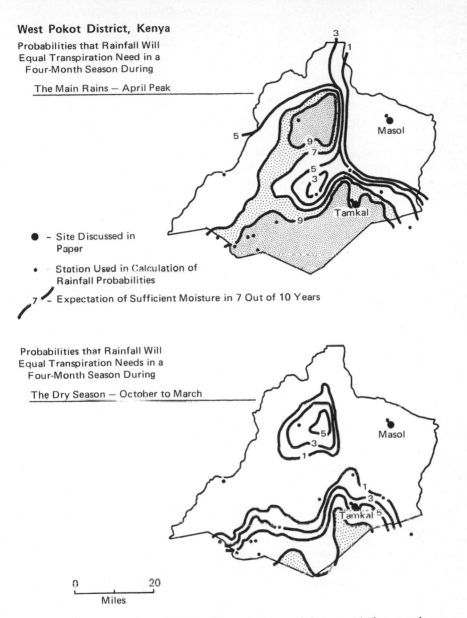

West Pokot District, Kenya

Probabilities that Rainfall Will Equal Transpiration Need in a Four-Month Season During

The Main Rains — April Peak

● – Site Discussed in Paper

• Station Used in Calculation of Rainfall Probabilities

7 – Expectation of Sufficient Moisture in 7 Out of 10 Years

Probabilities that Rainfall Will Equal Transpiration Needs in a Four-Month Season During

The Dry Season — October to March

0   20
Miles

Figure 4. Maps showing the probability of transpiration needs being met in four-month crop seasons during the main rains and during the dry season in West Pokot District. The isolines describe the certainty a farmer has of obtaining sufficient moisture for crops for particular seasons and places. Note the steep gradient between Tamkal and the plains to the northeast.

fenced, irrigated and protected from birds and animals on a communal basis. Year by year there is a constant recurrence of opening new farms and letting used fields revert to bush. This creates a kaleidoscopic involvement of kin and neighbors, for the personnel of one *parahgomucho* is different from the next. Since the head of a household will have 4 to 6 fields in crop and 20 others in fallow, this means that his fortunes and risks are inextricably enmeshed with those of the community at large.

The use of multiple environments does not stop at having farms at different elevations. Abutting on the escarpment walls are wide plains covered with poor thorn *Acacia*. Although tsetse infested along the perennial rivers, the Masol plains elsewhere are marginally suitable for livestock. There can be no question of agriculture here. These dry plains are less than a day's walk from farming communities in the adjacent hills. A long established trade in milk, livestock, and grain flourishes between the two sectors. A mutually beneficial specialization of economic activity exists along this steep environmental gradient. Because of the abruptness of the environmental change, the Pokot have not been in a position to argue with nature; subsistence adaptations here are explicit and successful. The probability of agricultural success or failure changes so precipitously that it is a discontinuity, not really a gradient.

Ukambani. We turn now to the Wakamba. Here our interest centers on the gradual transition in rainfall probabilities from the high potential areas in the west, which change imperceptibly with loss of altitude to the southeast (Figs. 1, 5 and 6). We will examine three points along this gradient, the two extremes being the communities in which Dr. Oliver worked. In the time available, I have no choice but to adopt a telegraphic even stream-of-consciousness

delivery by which to create an image of the subsistence and its technology.

Ngelani. The farming community is in the western hills at elevations of 5,500 to 6,500 ft. Rainfall exceeds 35 inches and is bimodal, being concentrated into the November-December grass rains, and the March-May main rains (Fig. 2). The probability of obtaining adequate moisture to satisfy transpiration needs is 0.8 in four months in the grass rains (Fig. 5), and over 0.9 in four months in the main rains (Fig. 6). Population density is high, some sub-locations achieving values of 1,600 people per square mile. Land is individually owned, sold and inherited. Land values in this area are about 2,000 shillings per acre; this compares with the average annual income in the district for a man—about 1,600 shillings. Land transactions are the subject of much litigation and secrecy.

The typical farmer has from 4 to 7 acres in crop. The crops are few, but water demanding: maize, beans, peas, and Irish (English) potatoes. Yields are high. Technology involves ox-drawn steel plows, cultivators, terraced land, use of manure and insecticides. Seed selection, planting, and weeding are done with reasonable care, but without specific concern for drought and moisture conservation. Livestock are owned, but generally kept elsewhere, on lower adjacent plains.

Wamunyu. Wamunyu represents a zone of medium potential along the gradient. Elevations are here all within a few hundred feet of 4,000 ft. The rainfall is nearly 30 inches and shows the same marked concentration into two seasons. The probability of water supply equalling water need for four months in the grass rains is about 0.85; in the main rains, only 0.3 (Figs. 5 and 6). The density of population is between 150 and 300 persons per square mile. The crops here are more numerous and increasingly of a sort

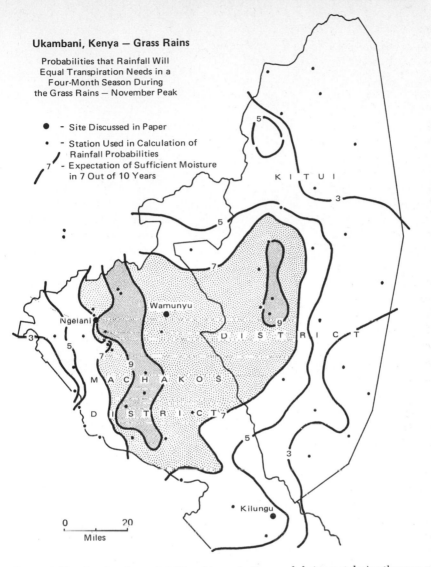

Ukambani, Kenya — Grass Rains

Probabilities that Rainfall Will
Equal Transpiration Needs in a
Four-Month Season During
the Grass Rains — November Peak

● - Site Discussed in Paper

• - Station Used in Calculation of
Rainfall Probabilities

7 - Expectation of Sufficient Moisture
in 7 Out of 10 Years

K I T U I

Wamunyu

Ngelani

D I S T R I C T

M A C H A K O S

D I S T R I C T

Kilungu

0   20
Miles

Figure 5. Map showing the probability of transpiration needs being met during the grass rains (November peak) in Ukambani, Kenya. The isolines describe the certainty a farmer has of obtaining sufficient moisture for crops. Note the gentleness of the probability gradient between Ngelani and Kilungu.

that do well in dought: maize and beans, of course, but also sweet potatoes, pigeon peas, cowpeas, bulrush millet, and cassava. Livestock are much more heavily depended on. Commonly one brother in a family will assume responsibility for the cattle of every-

one, for the livestock must be driven great distances for graze.

The farmer who uses bench terraces and manure, who plants early and weeds early (to reduce transpiration and conserve soil moisture) obtains good and nearly certain

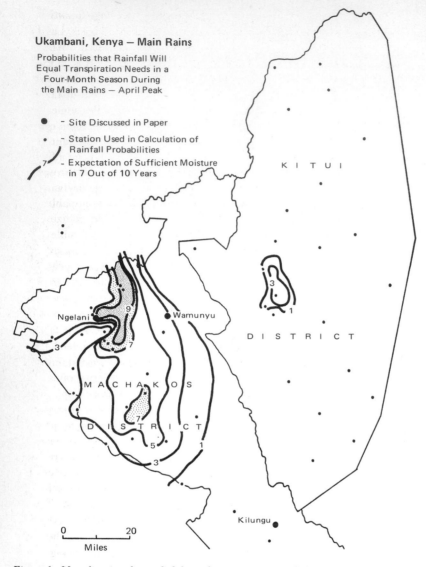

Figure 6. Map showing the probability of transpiration needs being met during the main rains (April peak) in Ukambani, Kenya. The isolines describe the certainty a farmer has of obtaining sufficient moisture for crops. Note that although the gradients have steepened over those shown for the grass rains (Fig. 5), the gradient is still more gentle than in the area cited in West Pokot District (Fig. 4).

yields. Most farmers, however, do poorly. They plant maize because it is easier than the traditional bulrush millet and is not susceptible to bird damage, like millet and sorghum. Their yields are poor; the second season maize usually fails altogether. This part of the district has some of the worse *mangalata*, or devastated land, in Africa—the result of overgrazing and planting row corps (maize) on easily gullied slopes. Grazing beyond the carrying capacity of the land denudes it of vegetation, prevents the annual grass firing to keep back the bush, and this allows rain to etch out gullies, which in turn lowers the water table and makes the re-establishment of a grass cover difficult. This is an area of chronic crop failure and famine. From 1943 to 1961 the district had to import maize in 15 out of 19 years, and in 7 of these years there was severe famine.

In describing the environmental parameters earlier, we left out what is perhaps the most important one—man. Machakos District, the western and populous portion of Ukambani, in the past 44 years increased its population fourfold, from 120,000 to 570,000, an annual increase of 3 percent. As a consequence, an agriculture that worked well in the moist hills in the west has been successively pushed out into areas where the chances of failure are greatly increased, with devastating effects on the environment, as we have seen. There is great fluidity and uncertainty in the Wakamba use of environment in this area. The environmental gradient is gentle; the agricultural limits are not clear; and despite various tactics to spread risk and create a viable subsistence, the people have not yet found a workable solution.

Kilungu. The third, and most pastoral, site lies at an elevation of about 2,500 ft. The rainfall averages just under 25 inches and is very unreliable. The rainfall profile is again bimodal, but the November-December grass rains are definitely better. The likelihood of having enough rainfall to meet transpiration needs in four months in the grass rains is a little better than even, about 0.65 (Fig. 5); but for the main rains, less than 0.1 (Fig. 6). Population density is between 50 and 150 around Kilungu; but by and large the *Acacia-Commiphora* and *Acacia tortilis* areas of Ukambani support densities under 25 people per square mile.

The Mkamba here uses huge quantities of land on a shifting cultivation basis. Land is owned, but not sold or inherited. "Who would want his father's land? It is all used up and worthless." New bush is there for the taking. Fields are deployed great distances from one another, over 10 miles sometimes. A multitude of crops, many of them quick-maturing, hardy and drought-resistant, is sown in what appears to have been a fit of temporary insanity. Seeds are all thrown together and worked into large dryland clearings that are virtually unmappable. Here is a list of crops from one field: maize, beans, cowpeas, groundnuts, red millet, sorghum, castor, bulrush millet, cassava, pumpkins, calabashes, and pigeon peas. Six kinds of millet are grown here. The great number of crops, mixed sowing, placement of fields far apart—all are attempts to reduce the risk the individual takes. Care is taken to plant before or with the rains; indeed the second planting is done amongst standing unharvested crops from the grass rains. This second crop is usually a forlorn hope. Early weeding is done; timing is most important. The tools are simple, there being no plow, no use of draft animals, almost no manuring or terracing. The basic implements are: hoe, panga, ax, and over large parts of Kitui District, the digging stick. Agriculture is insufficient of itself as a subsistence base. The people are heavily involved with livestock; indeed, they think of themselves as herders. In the community studied, the average family holding in stock was 20 cattle, 9 sheep, and 28 goats. The drier the realm, the greater becomes the dependence on livestock. There is greater emphasis also on gathering and hunting, as evidenced by the importance of honey, gum arabic and poaching in the local economy.

In this paper we have examined some East African environments in three ways: (1)

according to the variety in types of environment, (2) according to their spatial arrangement, that is, the steepness of gradient between types, and (3) according to their inherent secular variability. By way of conclusion we make six assertions:

1. It is evident that there are not two types of environment in East Africa—one for farmers and one for herders—but many, each having its own peculiar set of subsistence possibilities and problems. A complex pattern in which agricultural and pastoral activities are either symbiotic, competitive, excluded, or integrated is therefore to be expected.

2. A steep environmental gradient provides positive advantages by allowing people to use multiple environments and even to form specialized reciprocal economies as a means of combatting the uncertainties of nature.

3. In semi-arid uniform environments a greater premium is placed on mobility. This favors pastoralism as a subsistence mode, but even agriculture may reflect it by a greater dispersion of fields. People will attempt to be more internally self-sufficient; their subsistence mode may be unstable because the environmental limits are not clear.

4. An effective adjustment of agricultural subsistence to the environmental demands of semi-arid areas can be achieved only by the most meticulous management of the available resources. The constraints of a rigorous agricultural timetable tend to restrict movement and other activities. This may be competitive with pastoral pursuits.

5. Where environmental potentials are high and subsistence risks are minimal or absent, the population increases, densities become high, settlements are permanent, and internal disputes over land become likely.

6. A model which seeks to describe culture as adaptive, through subsistence, to environmental potential cannot ignore man himself as a causative agent of environmental change. The circuitry of the model should allow for reciprocal energy flows, for feedback. In saying this we confirm rather than deny the value of the truly ecologic approach, and highlight the need to proceed historically in any study of a specific culture.

We would claim that the study of environmental potential is enhanced by an appreciation of the spatial arrangement and temporal variability of environmental types. We therefore suggest that the use of rainfall probability gradients and the involvement of subsistence risks offer a promising way to relate environment realistically to actual subsistence technologies, and thereby to the kinds of life that people fashion for themselves.

★★★★★★★★★★★★★★★★★★★★★★★★★★★★★

MAN AGAINST HIS ENVIRON-
MENT: A GAME THEORETIC
FRAMEWORK

Peter R. Gould

Without cataloging the many and various definitions of human geography by professional geographers over the past few decades, it is safe to say that most have included the words *Man* and *Environment*. Traditionally, geographers have had a deep intellectual curiosity and concern for the face of the earth and the way it provides, in a larger sense, a home for mankind. Much of what we see upon the surface of the earth is the work of Man, and is the result of a variety of decisions that men have made as individuals or groups. Unfortunately, we have all too often lacked, or failed to consider, conceptual frameworks of theory in which to examine Man's relationship to his environment, the manner in which he weighs the alternatives presented, and the rationality of his choices once they have been made. Underlining a belief that such theoretical structures are desirable, and that they sometimes enable us to see old and oft-examined things with new eyes, this paper attempts to draw the attention of geographers to the Theory of Games as a conceptual framework and tool of research in human geography.[1] Upon its initial and

formal appearance in 1944,[2] a reviewer stated: "Posterity may regard this . . . as one of the major scientific achievements of the first half of the twentieth century," and although the social sciences have been relatively slow in considering the Theory of Games, compared to the widespread application of all forms of decision theory throughout engineering, business, and statistics, its increasing use in our sister disciplines of economics, anthropology, and sociology indicates a sure trend, fulfilling the extravagant praise heaped upon it at an earlier date.

The Theory of Games, despite its immediate connotation of amusements of a frivolous kind, is an imposing structure dealing,

---

1. References to Game Theory in geographic literature are almost nonexistent. What few references there are usually appear as peripheral points to a larger discussion on linear-programming solutions, for example: William L. Garrison, "Spatial Structure of the Economy II," *Annals,* Association of American Geographers, Vol. 49, No. 4 (December,

ber, 1959), pp. 480-81. It should be noted, parenthetically, that much of the mathematics used in Game Theory is the same as that used in linear programming, and one of the hopeful things about the new ways of looking at old problems is that a common mathematics underlies many of the same theoretical structures. In terms of efficiency, a key made from a little modern algebra may often open many doors.

2. The basic work, now revised, is John von Neumann and Oskar Morgenstern, *Theory of Games and Economic Behavior* (Princeton: Princeton University Press, 1953) Excellent introductions are J. D. Williams, *The Compleat Stratygyst* (New York: McGraw-Hill Book Co., 1954), Anatol Rapoport, *Fights, Games and Decisions* (Ann Arbor: University of Michigan Press, 1961); while a complete critique and survey is R. Duncan Luce and Howard Raiffa, *Games and Decisions* (New York: John Wiley and Sons Inc., 1958).

From the *Annals* of the Association of American Geographers, Vol. 53, (1963), pp. 290-97. Reprinted by permission.

in essence, with the question of making rational decisions in the face of uncertain conditions by choosing certain strategies to outwit an opponent, or, at the very least, to maintain a position superior to others. Of course, we do not have to think in terms of two opponents sitting over a chessboard; we may, as geographers, think in terms of competition for locations whose value depends upon the locational choices of others,[3] or, perhaps more usefully, in terms of man choosing certain strategies to overcome or outwit his environment. A good example of the latter is a Jamaican fishing village,[4] where the captains of the fishing canoes can set all their fishing pots close to the shore, all of them out to sea, or set a proportion in each area. Those canoes setting pots close to the shore have few pot losses, but the quality of the fish is poor so that the market price is low, particularly when the deep-water pots have a good day and drive the price of poor fish down still further. On the other hand, those who set their pots out to sea catch much better fish, but every now and then a current runs in an unpredictable fashion, battering the pots and sinking the floats, so that pot losses are higher. Thus, the village has three choices, to set all the pots in, all the pots out, or some in and some out, while the environment has two strategies, current or no-current. Game Theory has successfully predicted the best

choice of strategies and the proportion each should be used, a proportion very close to that arrived at by the villagers over a long period of trial and error.

Man continually finds himself in situations where a number of different choices or strategies may be available to wrest a living from his environment. Indeed, without soaring to those stratospheric heights of philosophical, or even metaphysical, discussion, to which all discourse in the social and physical sciences ultimately leads, let it be said that to be Man rather than Animal is, in part, to be able to recognize a variety of alternatives, and in a *rational* manner, reasoning from those little rocks of knowledge that stick up above the vast sea of uncertainty, choose strategies to win the basic struggle for survival. The perception that alternatives exist, and the recognition that their specific value, or utility, for a given time and place may depend upon an unpredictable environment, about which Man has only highly probabilistic notions based upon past experience, is clearly central to any discussion of man-environment relationships within a game theoretic framework. Thus, growing concomitantly with, and, indeed, embedded in, the Theory of Games, is a theory of utility intuitively raised, axiomatically treated, and experimentally tested in the real world.[5]

The Barren Middle Zone of Ghana (Fig. 1), a belt which, for environmental and historical reasons, has a very low population density, has one of the severest agricultural

3. W. L. Garrison, *Annals*, Association of American Geographers, Vol. 49, pp. 480-81, reviewing Tjalling C. Koopmans and Martin Beckmann, "Assignment Problems and the Location of Economic Activities," *Econometrica*, Vol. 25 (January, 1957), pp. 53-76.
4. William Davenport, "Jamaican Fishing: A Game Theory Analysis," *Yale University Publications in Anthropology*, No. 59 (1960); an excellent case study drawn from detailed anthropological field work which provided the basis for assigning actual monetary values to the various choices presented to the village as a whole.

5. The barbarous treatment of utility theory by those who fail, or refuse, to see the difference between a man declaring a preference because of the supposedly existing greater utility, rather than assigning a higher utility to a man's preference after it has been declared, did much damage at one time in the field of economics. The latter must always be kept in mind to avoid confusion; see Luce and Raiffa, *op. cit.*, p. 22.

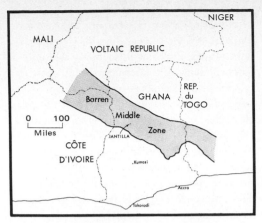

Figure 1. The Barren Middle Zone of Ghana of low population density and extreme variability of rainfall.

			Wet Years	Dry Years
			Environment Moisture Choices	
		Yams	82	11
Farmers of Jantilla	Crop Choice	Maize	61	49
		Cassava	12	38
		Millet	43	32
		Hill Rice	30	71

Figure 2. Payoff matrix for two-person-five-strategy-zero-sum game; crop choices against moisture choices.

climates in West Africa,[6] with heavy precipitation followed by the extreme aridity of the Harmatten, which sweeps south from the Sahara. A further problem is that the high degree of variability of the precipitation makes it difficult for the farmers to plan effectively.[7]

Let us assume that the farmers of Jantilla, a small village in Western Ghana, may use the land to grow the following crops, each with different degrees of resistance to dry conditions, as their main staple food: yams, cassava, maize, millet, and hill rice.[8] In Game Theory terms the cultivation of these crops represents five strategies. In the same terms, and to simplify this initial example, let us make the somewhat unrealistic assumption that the environment has only two strategies; dry years and wet years. These strategies may be put into matrix form (Fig. 2), called the payoff matrix, and represent a two-person-five-strategy-zero-sum game, in which the values in the boxes represent the average yields of the crops under varying conditions, perhaps in calorific or other nutritional terms. For example, if the farmers of Jantilla choose to grow only yams, they will obtain a yield of eighty-two under wet year conditions, but the yield will drop to eleven if the environment does its worst. It should be noted that the values in the boxes have been chosen simply to provide an example of Game Theory, but this, in turn, emphasizes the close relationship of these methods to direct field work, for only in this way can we obtain these critical subcensus data. In a very real sense, our tools are outrunning our efforts to gather the necessary materials. We might also note, parenthetically, that extreme accuracy of data, while always desirable, is not essential in order to use Game Theory as a tool, since it can be shown that payoff matrices subjected to a fairly high degree of random shock by injecting random error terms still give useful approximations and insights upon solution.[9]

6. Walter Manshard, "Land Use Patterns and Agricultural Migration in Central Ghana," *Tijdschrift voor Economishe en Sociale Geografie* (September, 1961), p. 225.

7. H. O. Walker, *Weather and Climate of Ghana*, Ghana Meterological Department, Departmental Note No. 5 (Accra, 1957), p. 37, map (mimeographed).

8. Manshard, "Land Use Patterns . . .," pp. 226-29. See also Thomas T. Poleman, *The Food Economies of Urban Middle Africa* (Stanford: Food Research Institute, 1961).

9. In linear-programming terms this would follow from the notion that the boundary conditions

A payoff matrix in which one opponent has only two strategies can always be reduced to a two-by-two game which is the solution for the complete game, in this case a five-by-two. We may, if time is no object, and we like dull, tedious work, take every pair of rows in turn and solve them for the maximum payoff to the farmers; but, fortunately, we also have a graphical solution which will point to the critical pair at once (Fig. 3). If we draw two scales from zero to one hundred, plot the values of each

---

would have to change quite drastically, in most cases, in order for there to be a change in the minimax point which would alter, in turn, the choice of strategies (see Fig. 3).

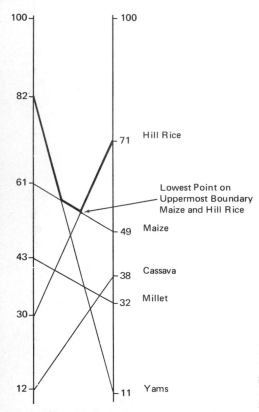

Figure 3. Graphical solution to assign critical pair of strategies in two-person-five-strategy-zero-sum game.

of the farmer's strategies on alternate axes, and connect the points, then the lowest point on the uppermost boundary will indicate which crops the farmers should grow to maximize their chances of filling their bellies.[10] Now we can take this pair of strategies, maize and hill rice (Fig. 4), and by calculating the difference between each pair of values and assigning it, regardless of sign, to the alternate strategy, we can find the proportion each strategy should be used. Thus, maize should be grown 77.4 per cent of the time and hill rice 22.6 per cent of the time, and if this is done the farmers can assure themselves the maximum return or payoff over the long run of fifty-four.

These proportions immediately raise the question as to how the solution should be interpreted. Should the farmers plant maize 77.4 per cent of the years and hill rice for the remaining 22.6 per cent, mixing the years in a random fashion;[11] or, should they plant these proportions each year? As Game Theory provides a conceptual framework for problems where choices are made repeatedly, rather than those involving choices of the unique, once-in-history variety, the cold-blooded answer is that *over the long haul* it makes no difference. However, when men have experienced famine and have looked into the glazed eyes of their swollen-bellied children, the long run view becomes somewhat meaningless. Thus, we may conclude that the farmers will hold strongly to the short-term view and will plant the proportions *each year* since the truly cata-

---

10. This is simply the graphical solution to the basic linear-programming problem. The values, and the resulting slopes, have been deliberately exaggerated for the purposes of illustration.

11. For a discussion on the necessity of a random mix of strategies see R. B. Braithwaite, *Scientific Explanation: A Study of the Function of Theory, Probability and Law in Science* (Cambridge: The University Press, 1955), pp. 236-39.

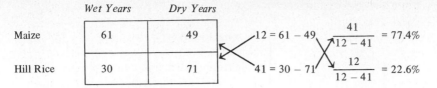

Figure 4. Solution of two-by-two payoff matrix to achieve most efficient choice of crop proportions

strophic case of hill rice and wet year could not then occur.

It is interesting to note, simply as an aside, that solving this two-by-two matrix vertically tells us that over the long run we may expect dry years 58.5 per cent of the time (Fig. 5), if we assume the environment to be a totally vindictive opposing player trying to minimize the farmers' returns.

The solution of this little game raises some interesting questions for the geographer. Does the land-use pattern approach the ideal? And if not, why not? If the land-use pattern does not approach the ideal, does this imply a conscious departure on the part of the people, or does their less-than-ideal use of the land reflect only the best estimate they can make with the knowledge available to them, rather than any degree of irrationality? Do the farmers display rational behavior in our Western sense of the term

despite all the warnings of the anthropologists about the illusory concept of economic man in Africa? If one were in an advisory position, would this help to make decisions regarding the improvement of agricultural practices? If the solution exceeds the basic calorific requirements of the people, is it worth gambling and decreasing the proportion of one or both crops to achieve a better variety of foods—if this is desired by the people? How far can they gamble and decrease these proportions if inexpensive, but efficient, storage facilities are available, either to hold the surpluses of one year to allay the belt-tightening "hungry season" of the next, or to sell in the markets of the south when prices are high? Thus, the usefulness of the tool is not so much the solving of the basic problem, but the host of questions it raises for further research.

A further example from Ghana will make this clear (Fig. 6). For centuries the people living south of the great Niger arc have raised cattle and have driven them along the old cattle trails to the markets of Ghana.[12] The driving of cattle is a chancy business because, while Man can overcome cattle diseases such as rinderpest with modern veterinary medicines, he cannot yet predict the very dry years in this area of high rainfall variability through which the cattle have to be driven to market. Let us assume that the

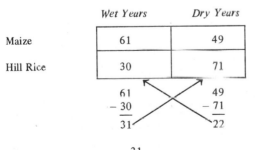

Dry Years Expected $\frac{31}{53}$ = 58.5 per cent

Figure 5. Vertical solution of two-by-two payoff matrix to yield proportion of dry years expected.

12. Peter R. Gould, *The Development of the Transportation Pattern in Ghana* (Evanston: Northwestern University Studies in Geography, No. 5, 1961), p. 137.

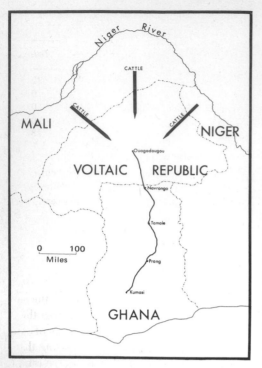

Figure 6. Areas of cattle production and main route to traditional cattle markets.

further assume that Nature, or the environment, also has five strategies ranging from years with intensely dry conditions to unusually wet years. Thus, the strategies available to the cattle traders and the environment form a two-person-five-by-five-zero-sum game and may be represented by a five-by-five matrix which indicates, for example, the average price of an animal in various markets under different conditions (Fig. 7). The matrix indicates that a trader may gamble upon the season being a very wet one, in which case he would drive all his animals to Kumasi; but, if he guessed wrong, and the season was a less than average one, cattle would die or lose a great deal of weight on the way and he would get much less in Kumasi than if he had sold them in another market such as Ouagadougou.[13] This, of course, is a deliberate simplification, for we are not taking into account the possibility of varying demands, the question of alternative local supplies at some of the markets, nor the probability of Ghanaian consumers substituting one source of protein

northern cattle traders of the Voltaic Republic, Mali, and Niger have the choice of selling their cattle in five markets: Ouagadougou, Navrongo, Tamale, Prang, and Kumasi. Each market thus represents a strategy and the traders may choose any one, or a mixture, of these in which to sell their animals. Let us

13. It has been suggested by Professor William Garrison that this problem might be readily handled in a practical sense by a standard linear-programming approach; a suggestion that would confirm Luce's and Raiffa's evocative comment on the Theory of Games that "... one can often discover a natural linear programming problem lurking in the background," *op. cit.*, p. 18.

| | | | *Environment* *Available Moisture Choices* | | | | |
			Very *Wet*	*Above* *Average*	*Average*	*Below* *Average*	*Intense* *Drought*
Cattle Traders	Markets	Ouagadougou	15	20	30	40	50
		Navrongo	20	15	15	20	5
		Tamale	40	30	20	15	10
		Prang	60	50	40	20	15
		Kumasi	80	70	40	25	10

Figure 7. Payoff matrix in two-person-five-by-five-zero-sum game; market choices against available moisture choices.

Environment
Available Moisture Choices

						1	2	3	4	....	59	60	Total
Ouagadougou	15	20	30	40	50	15	65	115*	165*	....	2,060	2,110*	32
Navrongo	20	15	15	20	5	20	25	30	40	....	870	875	0
Tamale	40	30	20	15	10	40	50	60	70	....	2,045	2,055	0
Prang	60	50	40	20	15	60	75	90	105	....	1,875	1,890	0
Kumasi	80	70	40	25	10	80*	90*	100	110	....	2,065	2,075	28
	15*	20	30	40	50								
	95	90	70	65	60*								
	175	160	110	90	70*								

Ouagadougou   32 $\dfrac{32}{60}$ = 53.4 per cent

Kumasi   28 $\dfrac{28}{60}$ = 46.6 per cent

2,190 2,250 1,880 1,845 1,830
etc.

Figure 8. Solution by iteration of payoff matrix.

for another, for example, fresh fish from the coast or dried Niger perch.[14] It might be possible to gather data to fill payoff matrices for other suppliers, but the situation would become much more difficult since we would be in the realm of non-zero-sum games that are, both conceptually and computationally, much more complex.[15]

Given the above strategies, what are the best markets the cattle traders can choose, and what are the best proportions?—"best" in the sense that over the long run the traders selling certain proportions of their cattle in these markets will get the maximum payoff. The solution of a five-by-five matrix

in a zero-sum game is not as easy as the case where one opponent has two, or even three, choices. We do have, however, ways of choosing the strategies and *estimating* the proportions that should be used, the estimation being based upon a relatively simple iteration which converges upon the solution and which may be carried to any degree of required accuracy (Fig. 8). In the above example, the iteration has been carried out sixty times, and by counting the number of asterisks in each row of a market, which mark the maximum figure in each column of the estimating process, we can calculate that the traders should sell thirty-two sixtieths, or 53.4 per cent, of their cattle in Ouagadougou and then drive the remainder right through Navrongo, Tamale, and Prang to the Kumasi market (Fig. 9).

Let us pose the question, now, of what might happen if a really strong transportation link were forged between Tamale and Navrongo, such as the remaking and tarring of a road, so that upon arrival at the Voltaic-Ghanaian border cattle would no longer have to make their way on the hoof, but could be driven in trucks to the southern

14. Peter Garlick, "The French Trade de Nouveau," Economic Bulletin of the Department of Economics, University of Ghana (mimeographed), p. 19.
15. Zero-sum games are so called because upon choosing a particular strategy one competitor's gain (+) becomes the opponent's loss (−), the gain and loss summing to zero. Non-zero-sum games are those cases where an alteration in strategic choice *may* raise or lower the payoff for both players. Two-person-non-zero-sum games can be handled using the notion of imaginary side payments. N-person-non-zero-sum games may best be described as computationally miserable.

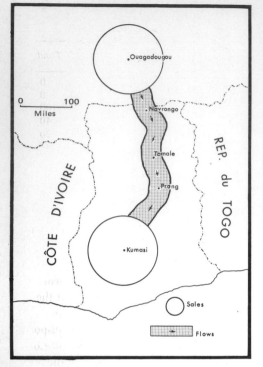

Figure 9. Proportional sales and flows of cattle prior to road improvements and trucking.

markets arriving in much better condition even in the very driest of seasons (Fig. 10). The payoff matrix would obviously change, and we might expect very much higher prices to prevail in Tamale, Prang, and Kumasi for the fat, sleek animals, rather

than the bags-of-bones that often stumbled into these markets in former years. Again, the payoff matrix can be solved using the iterative method 160 times on this occasion (Fig. 11), to produce completely different choices and proportions from the previous example. Now it is no longer worthwhile for the traders to sell cattle in the Ouagadougou or Navrongo markets, but sell instead 62.5 per cent in Tamale, 25 per cent in Prang, and 12.5 per cent in Kumasi. Thus, an improved road link, a visible sign on the landscape of a technological improvement, changes Man's perception and evaluation of the same choices available to him before, and as a result changes the patterns of flows and sales (Fig. 12). Now the flow has increased over the northern portion of the route, and it has become desirable to sell portions of the herds in the Tamale and Prang markets, the increases at these markets coming from former sales at Ouagadougou and Kumasi. Again, solving the payoff matrix points up some interesting questions for the geographer. First, it raises the whole question of estimating the effects of improving a transportation link—what will the flows be before and after? Can we obtain payoff values from one part of West Africa and use them to estimate changes of flows in other parts? Secondly, the question, again: how close does the behavior of the cattle traders approach that required to obtain the maximum

			Environment				
			Available Moisture Choices				
			Very Wet	*Above Average*	*Average*	*Below Average*	*Intense Drought*
		Ouagadougou	15	20	30	40	50
Cattle Traders	Markets	Navrongo	20	15	15	20	5
		Tamale	80	80	70	70	80
		Prang	100	100	90	80	70
		Kumasi	130	130	120	90	60

Figure 10. New payoff matrix indicating price changes in markets as a result of new road link between Tamale and Navrongo.

Environment
Available Moisture Choices

						1	2	3	4	160	Total
Ouagadougou	15	20	30	40	50	50	100	150	190		0
Navrongo	20	15	15	20	5	5	10	15	35		0
Tamale	80	80	70	70	80	80*	160*	240*	310*....... .		100
Prang	100	100	90	80	70	70	140	210	290		40
Kumasi	130	130	120	90	60	60	120	180	270		20
	130	130	120	90	60*						
	210	210	190	160	140*						

$$\text{Tamale } \frac{100}{160} = 62.5\%$$

$$\text{Prang } \frac{40}{160} = 25.0\%$$

$$\text{Kumasi } \frac{20}{160} = 12.5\%$$

etc.

Figure 11. Solution by iteration of new payoffs matrix.

payoff over the long run? Thirdly, what would be the effect of increasing the speed of communication so that cattle traders who started early in the season could inform others on the trail to the north about the conditions they find? And, finally, we should note the way an improved transportation link in effect extends the influence of one or more markets over others as the effect of distance is broken down allowing the demands of one center to impinge upon another.

By taking two examples from the traditional economy of Ghana, this paper has tried to point out the possible utility of the Theory of Games as a tool of research and as a conceptual framework in human and economic geography. That such frameworks are needed is evident, for without these broad conceptual constructions in which to place our facts and observations it becomes an almost impossible task to raise and tackle, in a meaningful and lasting fashion, questions of Man's equilibrium with his environment, his perceptions and judgments about it, and the rules by which he reacts at different points in time and space. The work of Man is all around us upon the face of our earth, and is the result of men perceiving a variety of alternatives, subsequently limiting the range of choices according to their idea

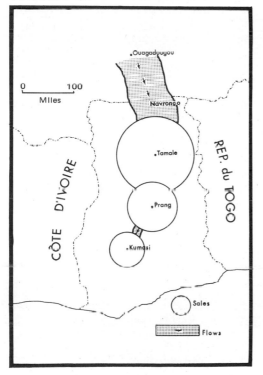

Figure 12. Proportional sales and flows of cattle after road improvements and trucking.

of what is useful and good, and *deciding* upon certain strategies to gain those ends. Thus, the whole body of decision theory, of which the Theory of Games is but one part, has an increasingly important role to play. Perhaps, in the same way that information theory has illuminated old problems of

central-place structure, linear-programming solutions have helped our understanding of shifting flows and boundaries, and the theory of queues is throwing light upon problems ranging from those of the Ice Age to those of livestock production, the Theory of Games may also have a role to play.

✦✦✦✦✦✦✦✦✦✦✦✦✦✦✦✦✦✦✦✦✦✦✦✦✦✦✦✦✦✦

GEOGRAPHY AND THE ECOLOGICAL APPROACH: THE ECOSYSTEM AS A GEOGRAPHIC PRINCIPLE AND METHOD

D. R. Stoddart

Dr. Eyre's brief but interesting paper on "Determinism and the ecological approach in geography"[1] seeks to demonstrate that by adopting an ecological viewpoint, geographers will rid themselves of naïve determinism and misinterpretation in both physical and human geography. This theme is, however, of wider importance than Eyre would indicate, for the significance of the ecological approach in geography is not merely that studies of vegetation and soils add "cohesion and distinctiveness" to geographical work, nor that "a more ecological approach enhances the prestige of geographers within the academic world."[2] but that ecological concepts provide a research method which geography so sadly lacks. Geography, as derived by Hettner and Hartshorne from the writings of Kant, occupies

what Schaefer[3] calls an "exceptionalist" position, that of a branch of knowledge with a unique integrating function, synthesizing more specialized fields in space as history does in time. With this idea Eyre apparently agrees; for him, "geography either stands or falls as an integrating discipline."[4] Schaefer's paper a decade ago marked the beginning of the retreat from this aloof and rather superior position; recent workers, from Ackerman to Bunge, take the position that geography in its aims and methods is essentially no different from other branches of science, and that it is precisely because of its Kantian heritage that the subject has managed to isolate itself from virtually every major development in the field of scientific thought since 1859.

---

1. S. R. Eyre, "Determinism and the ecological approach to geography," *Geography*, vol. 49, 1964, pp. 369-76.
2. *Op. cit.*, p. 374.

3. F. K. Schaefer, "Exceptionalism in geography: a methodological examination," *Annals of the Association of American Geographers*, vol. 43, 1953, pp. 226-49.
4. S. R. Eyre, *op. cit.*, p. 376.

From *Geography*, Vol. 50 (1965), pp. 242-51. Reprinted by permission.

The fundamental contribution of ecology to the geographer, therefore, is in providing a methodology. British geographers, in their quest for the region and its spirit, exemplified in the work of Herbertson,[5] held up as an ideal a concept which defies rational analysis and which should have died with the biological vitalism which inspired it. American geographers, following Hartshorne in his quest for "areal differentiation," committed themselves to what was, at worst, an exercise in the classification of areas, involving as an afterthought problems of organization and function. Neither view of geography provided an analytical tool of sufficient power to lead to new insights and new approaches. In recent years, geographers have become aware of the potentialities of the *ecosystem concept* in geographical work. The idea of the ecosystem is implicit in much of Eyre's paper; this note briefly outlines the properties and applications of the ecosystem idea in geography, and indicates some of the great potentialities which the concept possesses as a research tool in geography.

Properties

The term *ecosystem* was formally proposed by the plant ecologist Tansley in 1935,[6] as a general term for both the biome ("the whole complex of organisms—both animals and plants—naturally living together as a sociological unit" [7]) and its habitat. "All the parts of such an ecosystem—organic and inorganic, biome and habitat—may be regarded as interacting factors which, in a mature ecosystem,

are in approximate equilibrium: it is through their interactions that the whole system is maintained." [8] Fosberg[9] has developed the definition as follows:

An ecosystem is a functioning interacting system composed of one or more living organisms and their effective environment, both physical and biological. . . . The description of an ecosystem may include its spatial relations; inventories of its physical features, its habitats and ecological niches, its organisms, and its basic reserves of matter and energy; its patterns of circulation of matter and energy; the nature of its income (or input) of matter and energy; and the behaviour or trend of its entropy level.

Properties of biological ecosystems have been recently outlined by Evans,[10] Whittaker,[11] and Odum[12] while the whole terrestrial ecosystem has been termed the *ecosphere*, derived from ecosystem and biosphere, by Cole.[13]

The ecosystem concept has four main properties which recommend it in geographical investigation. First, it is *monistic*: it brings together environment, man, and the plant and animal worlds within a single framework, within which the interaction between the components can be analysed. Hettner's methodology, of course, emphasizes this ideal of unity, and some synthesis was achieved in the regional monographs of the French school, but the unity here was aesthetic rather than functional, and correspondingly difficult to define. Ecosystem analysis disposes of geographic dualism, and

5. A. J. Herbertson, "The higher units: a geographical essay," *Scientia*, vol. 14, 1913, pp. 203-12.

6. A. G. Tansley, "The use and abuse of vegetational concepts and terms," *Ecology*, vol. 16, 1935, pp. 284-307.

7. A. G. Tansley, *Introduction to Plant Ecology*, London, 1946, p. 206.

8. *Op. cit.*, p. 207.

9. F. R. Fosberg. "The island ecosystem," in F. R. Fosberg, editor, *Man's Place in the Island Ecosystem, a Symposium*, Honolulu, 1963, pp. 1-6, reference on p. 2.

10. F. C. Evans, "Ecosystem as the basic unit in ecology," *Science*, vol. 123, 1956, pp. 1127-8.

11. R. H. Whittaker, "Ecosystem," *McGraw-Hill Encyclopaedia of Science and Technology*, vol. 4, New York, 1960, pp. 404-8.

12. E. P. Odum, *Ecology*, New York, 1963.

13. L. Cole, "The ecosphere," *Scientific American*, vol. 198, no. 4, April, 1958, pp. 83-92.

with it the problem of determinism which Eyre discusses; the emphasis is not on any particular relationship, but on the functioning and nature of the system as a whole. Thanks very largely to the work of Hartshorne, the monism—dualism controversy is no longer a live issue in the west, but in the U.S.S.R., where Anuchin[14] has attempted to put forward monistic ideas on the unity of geography, he has been violently attacked.[15]

Secondly, ecosystems are *structured* in a more or less orderly, rational and comprehensible way. The essential fact here, for geography, is that once structures are recognized they may be investigated and studied, in sharp contrast to the transcendental properties of the earth and its regions as organisms or organic wholes.[16] Much geographical work in the past has been concerned with the framework of systems, and the current concern with geometry of landforms, settlement patterns and communication networks may be interpreted on this level. As an example of a structural investigation in biology, reference may be made to the work of Hiatt and Strasburg[17] on the food web and feeding habits of over 200 species of fish in coral reefs of the Marshall Islands in the Pacific. Observation showed

that the fish could be classified into five trophic groups, which were related in a rather complex manner. These relationships formed the structure shown in Figure 1, which includes all levels from plankton and algae to sharks and other carnivores.

Thirdly, ecosystems *function;* they involve continuous through-put of matter and energy. In geographic terms, the system involves not only the framework of the communication net, but also the goods and people flowing through it. Once the framework has been defined, it may be possible to quantify the interactions and interchanges between component parts, and at least in simple ecosystems the whole complex may be quantitatively defined. Odum and Odum[18] in a pioneering study, again on a Marshall Island coral reef, attempted to quantify the major trophic stages in the coral reef community—the primary producers, the herbivores and the carnivores. Figure 2A shows a biomass pyramid for a measured quadrat near the seaward edge of a reef; Figure 2B is a mean biomass pyramid generalized from quadrats across a whole reef flat. While the details of the interpretation, particularly the trophic status of the corals, is open to question, the Odums have certainly demonstrated the possibility of quantifying the gross structural characteristics of small ecosystems. Equally remarkable is Teal's study[19] of a salt marsh ecosystem in Georgia. Teal constructed a food web for the salt marsh, and then measured standing crop, production and respiration for each of its components. Figure 3 shows in diagrammatic form the energy flow through this

14. V. A. Anuchin, *Teoreticheskiye Problemy Geografii,* Moscow, 1961; reviewed by N. N. Baranskiy, *Soviet Geography,* vol. 2, no. 8, 1961, pp. 81-4.
15. S. V. Kalesnik, "About 'monism' and 'dualism' in Soviet geography," *Soviet Geography,* vol. 3, no. 7, 1962, pp. 3-16.
16. P. Vidal de la Blache, "Le principe de la géographie générale," *Annales de Géographie,* vol. 5, 1895-6, pp. 129-42; A. J. Herbertson, *op. cit.;* A. Stevens, "The natural geographical region," *Scottish Geographical Magazine,* vol. 55, 1939, pp. 305-17.
17. R. W. Hiatt and D. W. Strasburg, "Ecological relationships of the fish fauna on coral reefs of the Marshall Islands," *Ecological Monographs,* vol. 30, 1960, pp. 65-127.

18. H. T. Odum and E. P. Odum, "Trophic structure and productivity of a windward coral reef community on Eniwetok Atoll," *Ecological Monographs,* vol. 25, 1955, pp. 291-320.
19. J. M. Teal, "Energy flow in the salt marsh ecosystem of Georgia," *Ecology,* vol. 43, 1962, pp. 614-24.

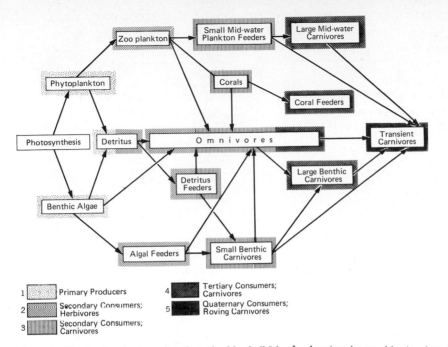

Figure 1. The food web of coral reefs in the Marshall Islands, showing the trophic structure in a qualitative manner. After Hiatt and Strasburg.

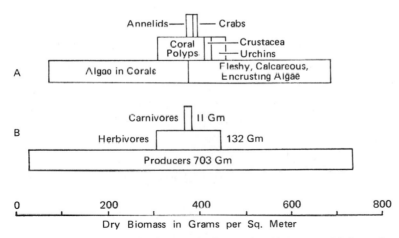

Figure 2. Biomass pyramids, showing the dry weight of living materials in quadrats on the reef of Eniwetok Atoll in the Marshall Islands. A—a quadrat on the reef edge; B—average biomass for the reef. Gross trophic structure is here shown in a quantitative way. After Odum and Odum.

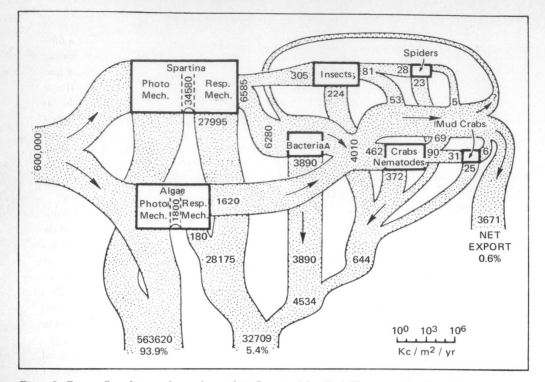

Figure 3. Energy-flow diagram for a salt marsh in Georgia. After Teal. The numerals refer to kcal/sq. m./yr.

ecosystem, and the part played by each component of the web, with an energy input (light) of 600,000 kcal/sq.m./yr.

Fourthly, ecosystems are a type of general system, and the ecosystem possesses the attributes of the general system. In general system terms, the ecosystem is an open system tending towards a steady state and obeying the laws of open-system thermodynamics. Many of the properties of such systems have been implicitly recognized in the past—for example, the idea of climax in vegetation, of maturity in soils, and of grade in geomorphology—but most of these conceptions have been, in effect, the application of classic thermodynamic ideas to closed system situations. With the development of open system thermodynamics,[20] many of

these older ideas are being reinterpreted in a dynamic rather than a static manner. Whittaker[21] has thus revised Clements' views on succession and climax; Jenny, and more recently Nikiforoff,[22] have done the same for soils; and Chorley[23] and others have reinterpreted landforms in open system terms. Ecosystems in a steady state possess the property of self-regulation (action and reaction), and this is similar in principle to a wide range of mechanisms such as homeo-

20. K. G. Denbigh, *The Thermodynamics of the Steady State*, London, 1951.

21. R. H. Whittaker, "A consideration of climax theory: the climax as a population and pattern," *Ecological Monographs*, vol. 23, 1953, pp. 41-78.
22. H. Jenny, *Factors of Soil Formation*, New York, 1941; C. C. Nikiforoff, "Reappraisal of the soil," *Science*, vol. 129, 1959, pp. 186-96.
23. R. J. Chorley, "Geomorphology and general systems theory," *Professional Paper*, United States Geological Survey, no. 500-B, 1962.

stasis in living organisms, feedback principles in cybernetics, and servomechanisms in systems engineering.[24] Systems such as ecosystems, moreover, can be conceived on different levels of complexity, and it is the task of the geographer to search out aspects of reality which are significant at the level at which the system is conceived. Systems, in fact, possess many of the structural properties of theoretical models, and a first approximation to system structure may be reached in a model-building manner, by selection, simplification, and ordering of data at a series of levels.[25] Thus systems may be built at the framework level (e.g., settlement hierarchies or transport nets) or as simple cybernetic systems (e.g., the mechanism of supply and demand, and of Malthus' doctrine), or at the more complex level of social systems and living organisms. Often in the case of more complex systems, a system has been conceived at a very much lower level of complexity, in the hope of gaining insight into problems where the data are too involved or the techniques inadequate. In geography, for example, the study of human groups, highly complex systems, has often been carried out on the level of "clockwork" systems, such as simple deterministic, cause-effect relationships. The potential value of a system clearly depends on the correct selection of components when the system is structured, and this normally presupposes considerable experience with the problems or data involved.[26]

Applicability

The ecosystem concept is in origin a biological idea, and most of its applications, including those already quoted, have been from the non-human world. Some attempts have been made, however, to describe fairly complex ecosystems in which man may play some part. Fosberg,[27] for example, after many years' work on coral atolls, attempted a general qualitative description of the coral atoll ecosystem, in terms of the media involved, the inflow of energy, primary productivity and successive elaboration, transformation and decomposition of its animal and plant community, excretion and accumulation of matter, and total turnover of matter and energy. Fosberg subsequently convened a symposium[28] to discuss the rôle of man in the isolated ecosystems of islands, in which the discussion ranged from man's own appraisal of his ecological status to more detailed discussion of the effects of overpopulation on island life. Islands in fact provide small laboratories for the testing and analysis of relatively simple and well-defined ecosystem structures. Thus Sachet[29] has described the effects of the introduction of pigs on the ecology of Clipperton Island; vegetation was severely checked by crabs until men introduced pigs, which ate crabs and allowed the vegetation to grow again. The pigs have recently been killed, and the ecological readjustments are awaited. In a similar situation, Stoddart[30] has shown how

24. N. Wiener, "Cybernetics, or control and communication in the animal and the machine," *Actualités scientifiques et industrielles*, vol. 1053, 1948, pp. 1-194.

25. R. J. Chorley, "Geography and analogue theory," *Annals of the Association of American Geographers*, vol. 54, 1964, pp. 127-37.

26. On the levels of systems, K. Boulding, "General systems theory—the skeleton of science," *General Systems*, vol. 1, 1956, pp. 11-17.

27. F. R. Fosberg, "Qualitative description of the coral atoll ecosystem," *Atoll Research Bulletin*, no. 81, 1961, pp. 1-11; also in *Proceedings, Ninth Pacific Science Congress*, vol. 4, 1962, pp. 161-7.

28. F. R. Fosberg, editor, *Man's Place in the Island Ecosystem, a Symposium*, Honolulu, 1963.

29. M.-H. Sachet, "History of change in the biota of Clipperton Island," in J. L. Gressitt, editor, *Pacific Basin Biogeography, a Symposium*, Honolulu, 1963, pp. 525-34.

30. D. R. Stoddart, "Storm conditions and vegetation in equilibrium of reef islands," *Proceedings,*

coral islands in the Caribbean are in equilibrium with major storms, and are even built up during hurricanes, but when man replaces the natural vegetation by coconut plantations, the storms begin to cause catastrophic erosion. A classic study of an island ecosystem involving man is that of Thompson[31] on the interaction of man, plants and animals in Fiji.

Most ecosystems involving man are more complex than the salt marsh and coral reef systems already described (Figures 1-3), and attempts to describe ecosystems at such complex levels are likely to be difficult until experience is gained with relatively simple or restricted systems. Fosberg's focus on islands is one way out of this problem; another, which has received considerable attention recently, is to concentrate on primitive human and sub-human groups, in the hope of obtaining insight into the structure and function of more complex organizations. For example, Schaller's extraordinary study[32] of the mountain gorilla, *Gorilla gorilla berengei*, its territoriality, population structure, ecology and behaviour, and DeVore's[33] of the baboon, demonstrate the intriguing possibilities of primate geography. Among geographers, Sauer has been pre-eminent in the study of the ecology of man in the Pleistocene, and Daryll Forde, in a classic volume, studied the ecology of some two dozen modern primitive peoples.[34] Most of these studies, however, were con-

ducted on traditional lines, and not within an explicit system framework; with some of the simpler groups it should be possible to delineate ecosystems with as much precision as in the non-human world.

The power of ecosystem analysis to pose new problems in geography, and hence to seek new answers, is demonstrated by Clifford Geertz's discussion of shifting cultivation and wet rice cultivation in Indonesia.[35] Geertz points out that most discussions of shifting cultivation emphasize its negative characteristics,[36] but that it is more profitably viewed in its system characteristics in relation to the tropical forest it replaces. Both are highly diverse systems, in which matter and energy circulate rapidly among the vegetation components and the topmost soil layer; the soil itself plays little part in this energy flow, and may often be impoverished. Burning is seen as a means of channelling the nutrients locked up in the vegetation into certain selected crop plants; the general ecological efficiency is lowered, but the yield to man increased. In a well-developed shifting cultivation system both structure and functions are comparable to those in the tropical forest, but the equilibrium is more delicately poised. By contrast, in wet rice cultivation, the ecosystem structure is quite different, the productivity is high, and the system equilibrium is more stable. The analysis is given in qualitative terms, but points the way to several lines of quantitative investigation, with clear import for land-use planning and rural reform programmes.

Apart from Geertz's work, there are few specific system-building studies in geography. The ecologist Dice, after working on natural communities, has produced a survey

Ninth Conference on Coastal Engineering (Lisbon), New York, 1964, pp. 893-906.
31. L. Thompson, "The relations of man, animals and plants in an island community (Fiji)," *American Anthropologist*, vol. 51, 1949, pp. 253-67.
32. G. B. Schaller, *The Mountain Gorilla: Ecology and Behavior*, Chicago, 1963.
33. I. DeVore and S. L. Washburn, "Baboon ecology and human evolution," in F. C. Howell and F. Bourlière, editors, *African Ecology and Human Evolution*, London, 1964, pp. 335-67.
34. C. Daryll Forde, *Habitat, Economy and Society*, London 1934.

35. C. Geertz, *Agricultural Involution; the Process of Ecological Change in Indonesia*, Berkeley, 1963.
36. P. Gourou, *The Tropical World*, London, 1953.

of ecosystem properties which may serve as a programme for human ecosystem research;[37] Chorley has carried systems analysis into geomorphology;[38] systems theory is being used in many branches of land-use planning, for example in the study of water resources;[39] Brookfield has briefly noted the potential of ecosystem studies;[40] but only Ackerman, in a major paper,[41] has pointed to systems analysis as geography's great research frontier.

Problems

It may be objected that the study of ecosystems in geography is either *(a)* not new, or *(b)* "not geography." In a sense, it is true, the study of systems is implicit in most geographic work; in economics system-building goes back to Smith and Ricardo, and in human and physical geography elements of systems are even older. The study of the ecosystem, however, requires the explicit elucidation of the structure and functions of a community and its environment, with the ultimate aim of the quantification of the links between the components. The ecosystem is a type of general system, defined as a "set of objects together with relationships between the objects and between their attributes."[42] Partaking in general system

theory, the ecosystem is potentially capable of precise mathematical structuring within a theoretical framework, a very different matter from the tentative and incomplete descriptions of highly complex relationships which too often pass for geographical "synthesis." The charge that ecosystems study is "not geography" lies in the fact, presumably, that the ecosystem definition does not explicitly define the earth's surface as a field of operation. "Ecology is the study of environmental relationships; geography is the study of space relationships," states Davies,[43] but he goes on to add that "what is not clear is where the one stops and the other starts." The study of space relationships, if it is to be more than mere nominal-scale classification of areas, must involve system building, while the limits of the ecosystem may be set at any desirable areal extent. So flexible is the ecosystem concept, moreover, that it may be employed at any level from the drop of pond water to the universe, and is currently being employed in the study of the artificial ecosystem within space capsules and interplanetary rockets.[44] Within any areal framework the ecosystem concept will give point to enquiry, and thus highlight both form and function within a spatial setting. Simplistic ideas of causation and development, or of geographic dualism, are in this context clearly irrelevant; ecosystem analysis gives the geographer a tool with which to work.

Potentialities

The value of systems analysis lies not only in its emphasis on organization, structure and functional dynamics. By its general system

37. L. R. Dice, *Natural Communities*, Ann Arbor, 1952; L. R. Dice, *Man's Nature and Nature's Man: the Ecology of Human Communities*, Ann Arbor, 1955.
38. R. J. Chorley, *op cit.*, 1962.
39. R. N. McKean, *Efficiency in Government through Systems Analysis, with emphasis on Water Resources Development*, New York, 1958.
40. H. C. Brookfield, "Questions on the human frontiers of geography," *Economic Geography*, vol. 40, 1964, pp. 283-303.
41. E. A. Ackerman, "Where is the research frontier?," *Annals of the Association of American Geographers*, vol. 53, 1963, pp. 429-40.
42. A. D. Hall and R. E. Fagen, "Definition of system," *General Systems*, vol. 1, 1956, pp. 18-28.
43. J. L. Davies, "Aim and method in zoogeography," *Geographical Review*, vol. 51, 1961, pp. 412-7, reference on p. 415.
44. E. B. Konecci, "Space ecological systems," in K. E. Schaefer, editor, *Bioastronautics*, New York, 1964, pp. 274-304.

properties, it brings geography back into the realm of the natural sciences, and allows us to participate in the scientific revolutions of this century from which the Kantian exceptionalist position excluded us. Perhaps the most significant implication of the ecosystem approach in geography is that systems may be linked with information theory, and thus with the whole new world of cybernetics, communications, and related mathematical techniques. Ecosystems are ordered arrangements of matter, in which energy inputs carry out work. Remove the energy input and the structure will break down until the components are randomly arranged (maximum entropy), which is the most probable state. Brillouin[45] has shown that order, or negative entropy, in systems, corresponds to information. First attempts have been made, as a result, to apply information theory to ecosystem analysis[46] and to interpret ecosystems in terms of cybernetics,[47] but the geographical implications of this have yet to be assessed. New mathematical techniques are being applied to geographical problems—for example, Gould's use of game theory in economic development studies in Ghana[48] and Kansky's application of network analysis to transportation patterns.[49] These are, however,

essentially tools; they do not provide a methodology. This systems analysis does, and using it, geography can no longer stand apart in its isolated "integrating" position.

Geography therefore stands to-day in much the same position as in 1859, following the publication of *On the origin of species.* In the century which has elapsed geography has borrowed many diverse ideas from biology, and attempts have been made to re-state the nature of geography in ecological terms, most notably by Barrows in 1923.[50] Barrows, however, stated his position in deterministic terms, and succeeded in frightening off both geographers and sociologists, leaving the field which he delineated in the possession of neither.[51] Many of the insights gained from biology were applied in geography in an oversimplified and incautious way, and soon lost their power to stimulate fresh insight. The emergence of the ecosystem idea as a tight-knit interacting complex of man and nature—clearly enough stated in the third chapter of Darwin's *Origin*—awaited the development of the growing body of systems theory. In the last few years it has begun to be applied by geographers both as a research tool, and as a methodological instrument offering an alternative to that of Kant and Hettner. It links geography with the mainstream of modern scientific thought, in systems analysis and related disciplines, and opens up as yet unexplored possibilities in the application to geography of the whole field of information theory and communication techniques. In the ecosystem concept ecology makes its most profound and powerful contribution to geography.

45. L. Brillouin, *Science and Information Theory,* New York, 1962; L. Brillouin, *Scientific Uncertainty, and Information,* New York, 1964.
46. D. R. Margalef, "Information theory in ecology," *General Systems,* vol. 3, 1958, pp. 36-71.
47. B. C. Patten, "An introduction to the cybernetics of the ecosystem: the trophic-dynamic aspect," *Ecology,* vol. 40, 1959, pp. 221-31.
48. P. R. Gould, "Man against his environment: a game theoretic framework," *Annals of the Association of American Geographers,* vol. 53, 1963, pp. 290-7.
49. K. J. Kansky, "Structure of transportation networks: relationships between network geometry and regional characteristics," *Research Papers,* Department of Geography, University of Chicago, vol. 84, 1963.

50. H. H. Barrows, "Geography as human ecology," *Annals of the Association of American Geographers,* vol. 13, 1923, pp. 1-14.
51. L. F. Schnore, "Geography and human ecology," *Economic Geography,* vol. 37, 1961, pp. 207-17.

⚓⚓⚓⚓⚓⚓⚓⚓⚓⚓⚓⚓⚓⚓⚓⚓⚓⚓⚓⚓⚓⚓⚓⚓⚓⚓⚓⚓⚓

TWO TYPES OF ECOSYSTEMS

Clifford Geertz

Inner vs. Outer Indonesia

A handful of mere statistics of the most routine, humdrum sort can sketch a picture of the basic characteristics of the Indonesian archipelago as a human habitat with more immediacy than pages of vivid prose about steaming volcanoes, serpentine river basins, and still, dark jungles. The land area of the country amounts to about one and one-half million square kilometers, or about that of Alaska. Of this only about one hundred and thirty-two thousand square kilometers are in Java, the rest making up what are usually called "the Outer Islands"—Sumatra, Borneo (Kalimantan), Celebes (Sulawesi), the Moluccas, and the Lesser Sundas (Nusa Tenggara). But the country's total population (1961) is around ninety-seven million, while Java's population alone is about sixty-three million. That is to say, about 9 percent of the land area supports nearly two-thirds of the population; or, reciprocally, more than 90 percent of the land area supports approximately one-third of the population. Put in density terms, Indonesia as a whole has about 60 persons per square kilometer; Java has 480, and the more crowded areas of the central and east-central parts of the island more than a thousand. On the other hand, the whole of Indonesia minus Java (i.e., the Outer Islands) has a density of around twenty-four per square kilometer. To summarize: all over, 60; the Outer Islands, 24; Java, 480: if ever there was a tail which

wagged a dog, Java is the tail, Indonesia the dog.[1]

The same plenum and vacuum pattern of contrast between Java and the Outer Islands appears in land utilization. Almost 70 percent of Java is cultivated yearly—one of the highest proportions of cropland to total area of any extensive region in the world— but only about 4 percent of the Outer Islands. Estate agriculture aside, of the minute part of the Outer Islands which is cultivated, about 90 percent is farmed by what is variously known as swidden agriculture, shifting cultivation, or slash-and-burn farming, in which fields are cleared, farmed for one or more years, and then allowed to return to bush for fallowing, usually eventually to be recultivated. On Java, where nearly half the smallholder's crop area is under irrigation, virtually no swidden agriculture remains. In the irrigated regions, field land is in wet-rice terraces, about half of them double-cropped, either with more wet rice or with one or several secondary dry crops. In the unirrigated regions, these dry crops (maize, cassava,

1. S. Sumaniwata, *Sensus Penduduk Republik Indonesia*, 1961 (preliminary report). Djakarta, Central Bureau of Statistics, 1962. Madura is included with Java in the calculations but the transitional area of West New Guinea (Irian) is not included. For a useful general summary of Indonesian demographic realities, see "The Population of Indonesia," *Edonomi dan Keuangan Indonesia*, Vol. 9 (1956), pp. 1-27.

From *Agricultural Involution: The Processes of Ecological Change in Indonesia*, University of California Press, 1963, pp. 12-37. Reprinted by permission of the Regents of the University of California.

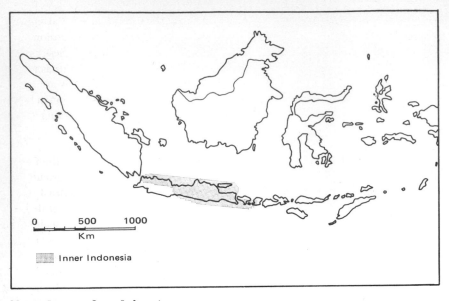

Map 1. Inner vs. Outer Indonesia.

sweet potatoes, peanuts, dry rice, vegetables, and others) are grown in a crop-and-fallow regime. Production statistics present, of course, the same picture: in 1956 approximately 63 percent of Indonesia's rice, 74 percent of her maize, 70 percent of her cassava, 60 percent of her sweet potatoes, 86 percent of her peanuts, and 90 percent of her soya beans were produced in Java.[2]

Actually, this fundamental axis of ecological contrast in Indonesia is not altogether accurately demarcated when one phrases it, following the received practice of the census takers, simply in terms of Java (and Madura) versus the Outer Islands, because in fact the "Javanese" pattern is found in southern Bali and western Lombok as well, and is but weakly represented in the southwestern corner of Java (South Bantam and South Priangan) where a pattern more like that of the Outer Islands, including a certain amount of swidden, is found. Thus, we might better refer to the contrast as one between "Inner Indonesia"—northwest, central, and east Java, south Bali, and west Lombok; and "Outer Indonesia"—the rest of the Outer Islands plus southwest Java, which do in fact form more or less of an arc pivoted on central Java. (See Map 1.) Such a division is, in any case, a gross one which needs modification in detail: patches of relatively intensive irrigation agriculture are found at either tip, around Lake Toba, and in the western highlands in Sumatra as well as in the southwest arm of the Celebes, for example, and eastern Madura deviates somewhat from the Javanese norm.[3] But it does lead, in a broad and general way, to a fruitful discrimination of two different sorts of ecosystems with two different sorts of

2. J. Metcalf, *The Agricultural Economy of Indonesia,* Monograph 15. Washington, D.C.: U.S. Department of Agriculture, 1952; *Statistical Pocketbook of Indonesia.* Kjarkarta: Biro Pusat Statistik, 1957, p. 51.

3. G. J. A. Terra, "Farm Systems in South-East Asia," *Netherlands Journal of Agricultural Science,* Vol. 6 (1958), pp. 157-181.

dynamics—one centering on swidden agriculture, one on wet-rice agriculture—in terms of which the striking differences in population density, modes of land use, and agricultural productivity can be understood.

Swidden

As Conklin has pointed out, much of the inadequate treatment swidden agriculture has received in the literature is a result of the fact that characterizations of it have tended to be negatively phrased.[4] Thus, Gourou outlines as its four most distinctive features: (1) it is practiced on very poor tropical soils; (2) it represents an elementary agricultural technique which utilizes no tool except the axe; (3) it is marked by a low density of population; and (4) it involves a low level of consumption.[5] Similarly, Pelzer says that it is marked by a lack of tillage, less labor input than other methods of cultivation, the nonutilization of draft animals and manuring, and the absence of a concept of private landownership.[6] For Dobby, it represents "a special stage in the evolution from hunting and food gathering to sedentary farming," this specialness evidently consisting of such null traits as nonrelation to pastoral pursuits and the production of very little which is of trading or commercial significance.[7] And for many, by far its most outstanding feature is that singled out by

Spate—namely, that its practice is "attended by serious deforestation and soil erosion."[8] Aside from the fact that most of these depreciatory statements are dubious as unqualified generalizations (and a few are simply incorrect), they are not of much help in understanding how swidden farming systems work.

In ecological terms, the most distinctive positive characteristic of swidden agriculture (and the characteristic most in contrast to wet-rice agriculture) is that it is integrated into and, when genuinely adaptive, maintains the general structure of the pre-existing natural ecosystem into which it is projected, rather than creating and sustaining one organized along novel lines and displaying novel dynamics. In the tropics, to which, for reasons we may postpone considering, this form of cultivation is today largely confined, the systemic congruity between the biotic community man artificially establishes on his swidden plot and that which exists there in stable climax independent of his interference (in the main, some variety of tropical forest) is striking. Any form of agriculture represents an effort to alter a given ecosystem in such a way as to increase the flow of energy to man: but a wet-rice terrace accomplishes this through a bold reworking of the natural landscape; a swidden through a canny imitation of it.

The first systemic characteristic in which a swidden plot simulates a tropical forest is in degree of generalization. By a generalized ecosystem is meant one in which a great variety of species exists, so that the energy produced by the system is distributed among a relatively large number of different species,

---

4. H. Conklin, *Hanunóo Agriculture in the Philippines.* Rome: Food and Agricultural Organization of the United Nations, 1957, p. 149.
5. P. Gourou, "The Quality of Land Use of Tropical Cultivators," in W. R. Thomas, Jr., editor, *Man's Role in Changing the Face of the Earth.* Chicago: University of Chicago Press, 1956, pp. 336-349.
6. K. J. Pelzer, *Pioneer Settlement in the Asiatic Tropics.* New York: Institute of Pacific Relations, 1945, pp. 16ff.
7. E. H. G. Dobby, *Southeast Asia.* London: University of London Press (4th ed.), 1954, pp. 347-349.

8. O. H. K. Spate, "The Burmese Village," *The Geographical Review,* Vol. 25 (1945), p. 527, quoted in E. Leach, *Political Systems of Highland Burma.* Cambridge: Harvard University Press, 1954, p. 22.

each of which is represented by a relatively small number of individuals. If, on the contrary, the system is one with a relatively small number of species, each of which is represented by a relatively large number of individuals, it is said to be specialized. Put somewhat more technically, if the ratio between number of species and number of organisms in a biotic community is called its *diversity index*, then a generalized ecosystem is one characterized by a community with a high diversity index, a specialized one by a community with a low diversity index. Natural communities tend to vary widely in their degree of generalization, or the size of their diversity index: a tropical forest, and in particular a rain forest, is a very generalized, very diverse community, with an enormous variety of plant and animal species sporadically represented; a tundra is characterized by a very specialized, uniform community, with relatively few species but, at least in the sub-arctic, a large number of clustered individuals.[9]

Much of the most effective human utilization of the natural habitat consists of changing generalized communities into more specialized ones, as when natural ponds containing a wide variety of green plants, aquatic animals, and fishes are transformed into managed ones in which the number of types of primary plant producers is sharply reduced to those which will support a few select types of fish edible by man. The rice terrace, which can, in these terms, be viewed as a sort of slowly drained, managed pond focused on an edible plant, is an outstanding example of artificially created specialization. The reverse process, increased generalization, also occurs, of course, as when man introduces into a temperate grassland area (for

example, the American prairie) a wide variety of interrelated domestic plants and animals, which, though they constitute a much more diverse community than that indigenous to the area, nonetheless prove to be viable within it.

Still other human adaptations, however, attempt to utilize the habitat not through altering its diversity index, but through more or less maintaining its over-all pattern of composition while changing selected items of its content; that is, by substituting certain humanly preferred species for others in functional roles ("niches") within the pre-existing biotic community. This is not to say that such adaptations do not seriously alter the indigenous ecosystem (as, in a gross sense, most hunting and gathering adaptations do not), or that their general effect on the balance of nature may not sometimes be a radical one; but merely that they alter the indigenous ecosystem by seeking to replace it with a system which, although some of its concrete elements are different, is similar to it in form, rather than by a system significantly more specialized or more generalized. Large-scale cattle herding during the nineteenth century on the previously buffalo-dominated southern and western plains is an example of this type of adaptation within a specialized system. Swidden agriculture is certainly an example of it within a generalized one.

The extraordinarily high diversity index of the tropical forest, the kind of natural climax community which still characterizes the bulk of Outer Indonesia, has already been mentioned. Though there are probably more floral species in this region than any other of comparable size in the world (van Steenis has estimated that between twenty and thirty thousand species of flowering plants, belonging to about 2,500 families, can be found in the archipelago), continuous stands of trees or other plants are rare, and

9. These concepts are taken from E. P. Odum, *Fundamentals of Ecology*. Philadelphia and London: Saunders, 1959, pp. ii, 50-51, 77, 281-283, 316, and 435-437.

the occurrence of as many as thirty different species of trees within a hundred square yards is not at all uncommon.[10] Similarly, on about a three-acre swidden plot in the Philippines (detailed field studies are lacking for Indonesia as such) Conklin has seen as many as forty different sorts of crops growing simultaneously, and one informant drew an ideal plot containing at one time forty-eight basic kinds of plants. The people of the area, the Hanunóo of Mindoro, distinguish more than sixteen hundred different plant types (which is a finer classification than that employed by systematic botanists), including the astounding number of four hundred thirty cultivates.[11] Conklin's vivid

description of what a Hanunóo swidden in full swing looks like gives an excellent picture of the degree to which this agriculture apes the generalized diversity of the jungle which it temporarily replaces:

Hanunóo agriculture emphasizes the inter-cropping of many types of domesticated plants. During the late rice-growing seasons, a cross section view of a new [plot] illustrates the complexity of this type of swidden cropping (which contrasts remarkably with the type of field cropping more familiar to temperate zone farmers). At the sides and against the swidden fences there is found an association dominated by low, climbing or sprawling legumes (asparagus beans, sieva beans, hyacinth beans, string beans, and cowpeas). As one goes out into the center of the swidden, one passes through an association dominated by ripening grain crops but also including numerous maturing root crops, shrub legumes and tree crops. Pole-climbing yam vines, heart-shaped taro leaves, ground-hugging sweet potato vines, and shrublike manioc stems are the only visible signs of the large store of starch staples which is building up under-ground, while the grain crops fruit a meter or so above the swidden floor before giving way to the more widely spaced and less rapidly maturing tree crops. Over the first two years a new swidden produces a steady stream of harvestable food in the form of seed grains, pulses, sturdy tubers, and underground stems, and bananas, from a meter below to more than 2 meters above the ground level. And many other vegetable, spice and non-food crops are grown simultaneously.[12]

The second formal characteristic common to the tropical-forest and swidden-agriculture ecosystems is the ratio of the quantity of nutrients locked up in living forms (that is, the biotic community) to that stored in the soil (that is, the physical substratum): in both it is extremely high. Though, as with the tropical forest itself,

10. G. van Steenis, "Maleische Vegetatieschetsen," *Tijdschrift v. d. Nederlandsche Aardijkskundig Genootschap* (1935), pp. 25-67, 171-203, 363-398; and E. H. G. Dobby, *op. cit.*, p. 61. This floral diversity is paralleled by an equally great wealth of fauna: the industrious as well as famous naturalist A. R. Wallace found 200 species of beetles in a square mile of Singapore forest and brought back a total of more than 125,000 animal specimens from the general Malaysian region. C. Robequain, *Malaya, Indonesia, Borneo and the Philippines* (trans. E. D. Laborde). New York: Longmans, Green, 1954, pp. 38-59. For a general ecological analysis of tropical forest plant diversity, see P. W. Richards, *The Tropical Rain Forest.* Cambridge, Cambridge University Press, 1952, pp. 231-268. More popular accounts, but which include some discussion of fauna as well, are M. Bates, *Where Winter Never Comes.* New York: Scribners, 1952, pp. 175-211; and W. B. Collins, *The Perpetual Forest.* Philadelphia and New York: Lippincott, 1959.
11. H. Conklin, "An Ethnoecological Approach to Shifting Agriculture," *Transactions of the New York Academy of Sciences*, Series II, Vol. 17 (1954), pp. 133-142. Other valuable field studies of swidden in Malaysia include J. D. Freeman, *Iban Agriculture.* London: Her Majesty's Stationery Office, 1955 (on diversity, pp. 51-54); and W. R. Geddes, *The Land Dayaks of Sarawak.* London: Her Majesty's Stationery Office, 1954 (on diversity, pp. 64-65). A brief description of swidden-making in East Indonesia can be found in P. R. Goethals, *Aspects of Local Government in a*

Sumbawan Village, Modern Indonesia Project Monograph Series. Ithaca: Cornell University Press, 1961, pp. 25-29.
12. H. Conklin, *op. cit.*, 1957, p. 147. Conklin estimates that in the first and most active year of the swidden cycle up to 150 specific crop types may be planted at one time or another.

much variation is found, tropical soils are in general extensively laterized. As precipitation in most of the humid, rain-heavy tropics greatly exceeds evaporation, there is a significant downward percolation through the soil of relatively pure, lukewarm water, a type of leaching process whose main effect is to carry away the more highly soluble silicates and bases, while leaving behind a dreary mixture of iron oxides and stable clays. Carried to an extreme, this produces ferralite, a porous, crumbly, bright-red, acidic soil which, however excellent the Indonesians find it for making bricks without straw, is of much less value from the point of view of the support of plant life. Protected to a certain extent by the shielding effects of the thick vegetation cover, most tropical soils have not developed such a serious case of what Gourou has called pedological leprosy.[13] But the great majority of them, having been exposed to these ultra-stable climatic conditions over very long periods of time, are markedly leached, and thus seriously impoverished in minerals requisite to the sustenance of life.[14]

This apparent and oft-remarked paradox of a rich plant and animal life supported on a thin soil is resolved by the fact that the cycling of material and energy among the various components of a tropical forest is both so rapid and so nearly closed that only the uppermost layers of the soil are directly and significantly involved in it, and they but momentarily. The intense humidity and more or less even distribution of rainfall, the equable, moderately elevated temperatures, the small month-to-month variations in day length and amount of sunlight—all the monotonous constancies of the tropics—are conducive to a high rate of both decomposition and regeneration of animal and vegetable material. Speedy decomposition is insured by the multiplication of bacteria, fungi and other decomposers and transformers which the humid conditions favor, as well as by the multitude of herbiverous animals and insects who are so ravenous that, as Bates remarks, virtually "every fruit and every leaf [in the tropical forest] has been eaten by something."[15] An enormous amount of dead matter is thus always accumulating on the forest floor—leaves, branches, vines, whole plants, faunal remains and wastes; but their rapid decay and the high absorptive capacity of the luxuriant vegetation means that the nutrients in this dead organic matter are reutilized almost immediately, rather than remaining stored to any great extent or for any great length of time in the soil where they are prey to the leaching process.

The role of humus in creating a topsoil storehouse of nutrient materials in colloidal form to be drawn upon gradually as needed, which looms so prominently in ecosystems at higher latitudes, is here minimized; organic materials rarely extend in significant quantity more than a few inches beneath the forest floor, because the nutrients set free by the rapid decay of dead matter are quickly taken up again by the shallow, splayed root systems of the intensely competitive plants. Thus, despite the heavy rains, loss of nutrients due to runoff in this process of transfer is very slight, so that quite marginal additions of energy from outside the system through nitrogen fixing in leguminous trees

---

13. P. Gourou, *The Tropical World* (trans., E. D. Laborde). New York: Longmans, Green, 1953, p. 21.

14. This paragraph and those immediately following are based mainly on P. W. Richards, *op. cit.*, pp. 203-226; E. H. G. Dobby, *op. cit.*, pp. 74-84; and P. Gourou, *The Tropical World* (trans. E. D. Laborde). New York: Longmans, Green, 1953, pp. 13-24. However, much remains to be learned about soil factors in the tropics.

---

15. M. Bates, *op. cit.*, p. 209.

and adsorption of minerals released by rock decomposition are themselves enough to compensate for it. The climax community, once established, through still imperfectly understood processes of ecological succession, is thus virtually self-perpetuating. By maintaining most of its energy in the form of living things most of the time, the tropical-forest ecosystem is able to prevent any significant escape of energy across its boundaries and to circumvent the problem of impoverished soil conditions by feeding largely upon itself.

Swidden agriculture operates in essentially this same supernatant, plant-to-plant, direct cycling manner. The burning of the slashed plot is at base a means both of accelerating the process of decay and of directing that process in such a fashion that the nutrients it releases are channeled as fully as possible into certain selected food-producing plants. A significant proportion of the mineral energy upon which swidden cultivates, and especially the grains, draw for their growth comes from the ash remains of the fired forest, rather than from the soil as such, so that the completeness with which a plot is burnt is a crucial factor in determining its yield, a fact of which probably all swidden cultivators are aware.[16] A good burn, in turn, is dependent on the one hand upon the care and thoroughness with which the vegetation has been cut, and on the other upon the dryness of the weather during the cutting-planting period. Over the thoroughness of the cutting the cultivators

have a high degree of control and, though different groups of swidden agriculturalists, as any other type of farmers, vary widely in their skills, yet their felling, slashing, trimming techniques, as well as their actual firing methods, are commonly well developed. Over the weather they have, of course, no control (though they are usually adept at estimating it), and intense ritual activity is commonly directed toward preventing rain, or at least maintaining confidence, during the anxious, all-important few weeks between cutting and sowing. At any rate, the primary function of "slash and burn" activities is not mere clearing of the land (the use of the term "clearing," with respect to swiddens is actually somewhat misleading) but rather the transfer of the rich store of nutrients locked up in the prolific vegetation of the tropical forest to a botanical complex whose general ecological productivity, in the sense of the total energy flow in the system, may be substantially smaller but whose yield to man is a great deal larger.[17]

General ecological productivity is lower because this transfer is less efficient than that which takes place under natural conditions of decay and regeneration. Here, a large amount of energy does escape across the boundaries of the system. Gourou estimates that between six and nine hundred pounds of nitrogen alone go up in smoke in the burning of a single acre of forest; and, despite the utmost shrewdness in judging the weather and the greatest speed in firing and planting, much ash is inevitably washed

---

16. For example, among the Mandaya of eastern Mindanao, those cultivating over 1,700 feet where burning is impossible because of the absence of a dry period harvest about 10 to 15 cavans of rice per hectare, while those cultivating in lower areas where burning is possible average 30-35; Aram A. Yengoyan, personal communication. In general, however, the precise effect of firing as a fertilizing mechanism remains to be investigated experimentally, like so much else about swidden.

17. This analysis is based on the descriptions of swidden techniques given in H. Conklin, *op. cit.*, 1957, pp. 49-72; J. D. Freeman, *op. cit.*, pp. 40-48; and C. Hose and W. MacDougal, *The Pagan Tribes of Borneo*. London, Macmillan, 1912. For the distinction between ecological productivity and yield to man, see G. Clarke, *Elements of Ecology*. New York: John Wiley, 1954, pp. 482-500.

away by the rains before it can be utilized by the cultivates, fast growing as they tend to be.[18] Further, as the cultivates are less woody in substance than those indigenous to the forest, they do not form a very appropriate material for the technique of accelerating and channeling nutrient transfer through the deliberate production of ash, and so the firing process is not continuously repeatable. The result is, of course, the well-known drop in fertility on swidden plots (rice output of south Sumatran plots is known to drop as much as 80 percent between a first and second cropping), and the surrender of the plot to natural regeneration.[19]

But, despite the fact that secondary forest growth is, at least in the earlier phases of regeneration, notably less luxuriant than primary, if the period of cultivation is not too long and the period of fallow long enough, an equilibrated, nondeteriorating and reasonably productive farming regime (productive in the sense of yield to man) can be sustained, again to a significant degree irrespective of the rather impoverished soil base on which it rests.[20] The burned forest provides most of the resources for the cultivates; the decaying cultivates (nothing but the edible portions of plants is removed from the plot) and the natural processes of secondary succession, including invasions from the surrounding forest within which plots are usually broadly dispersed rather than tightly clustered, provide most of the resources for the rapidly recuperating forest. As in the undisturbed forest, "what happens" in an adapted swidden ecosystem

happens predominantly in the biotic community rather than in the physical substratum.

Finally, a third systemic property in which the tropical forest and the swidden plot tend to converge is general architecture: both are "closed-cover" structures. The tropical forest has often been compared to a parasol, because of the effectiveness with which the tall, closely packed, large-crowned, evergreen trees both deflect the rain and shut out the sun so as to protect the soil against the worst effects of the leaching process, against baking, and against erosion. Photosynthesis takes place almost entirely at the very top of the forest, from a hundred to a hundred and fifty feet up, and so most of the growing things (as well as much of the faunal life) reach desperately toward this upper canopy seeking their small place in the sun, either by climbing, as the thousands of woody lianas and other vines, by finding an epiphytic perch, as the orchids and ferns, or by mere giantism, as the dominant trees and the bamboos, leaving the darkened floor relatively free of living plants.[21] In a swidden, this canopy is, of course, radically lowered, but much of its umbrella-like continuity is maintained, in part by planting cultigens not in an open field, crop-row manner, but helter-skelter in a tightly woven, dense botanical fabric, in part by planting shrub and tree crops of various sorts (coconuts, areca, jakfruit, banana, papaya, and today in more commercial areas rubber, pepper, abaca, and coffee), and in part by leaving some trees standing. In such a way, excessive exposure of the soil to rain and sun is minimized and weeding, exhausting task in any case, is brought within reasonable proportions because light penetration to the

18. P. Gourou, *The Tropical World* (trans. E. D. Laborde). New York: Longmans, Green 1953, p. 26.

19. K. J. Pelzer, *op. cit.*, 1945, p. 16.

20. H. Conklin, *op. cit.*, 1957, p. 152; E. Leach, *op. cit.*, 1954, p. 24; and W. R. Geddes, *op cit.*, pp. 65-68.

21. M. Bates, *op. cit.*, 1952, pp. 200-203.

floor is kept down to a much lower level than in an open-field system.[22]

In sum, a description of swidden farming as a system in which "a natural forest is transformed into a harvestable forest" seems a rather apt one.[23] With respect to degree of generalization (diversity), to proportion of total system resources stored in living forms, and to closed-cover protection of an already weakened soil against the direct impact of rain and sun, the swidden plot is not a "field" at all in the proper sense, but a miniaturized tropical forest, composed mainly of food-producing and other useful cultivates. Yet, as is well known, though less well understood, the equilibrium of this domesticated form of forest system is a great deal more delicate than that of the natural form. Given less than ideal conditions, it is highly susceptible to breakdown into an irreversible process of ecological deterioration; that is, a pattern of change leading not to repeated forest recuperation but to a replacement of tree cover altogether by the notorious *imperata* savannah grass which has turned so much of Southeast Asia into a green desert.[24]

Swidden cultivation may turn thus maladaptive in at least three ways: by an increase in population which causes old plots to be recultivated too soon; by prodigal or inept agricultural practices which sacrifice future prospects to present convenience; and by an extension into an insufficiently humid environment in which the more deciduous forests have a much slower recovery rate and in which clearing fires are likely to burn off accidentally great stands of timber.[25] The population problem has been much discussed, though exact figures are difficult to obtain. Van Beukering has put the population ceiling for swidden in Indonesia over-all at about 50 per square kilometer, Conklin estimates that the Hanunóo area can carry 48 per square kilometer without deterioration, and Freeman calculates 20-25 as the maximum in his central Sarawak region; but it is not known to what degree the various local population densities in Outer Indonesia now exceed critical limits and are producing grassland climaxes as a result of the need for more rapid recultivation.[26] With the population of the region now increasing at 2 percent or more annually, however, the

---

22. For an excellent description of the concurrent employment by recent immigrant Javanese farmers of an open-field system and by indigenous farmers of a closed-field one in the Lampong area of south Sumatra, and of the essential defeat of the former by the weeding problem, see Kampto Utomo, *Masjarakat Transmigran Apontan Didaerah W. Sekampung (Lampung)*. Djakarta: P. T. Penerbitan Universitas, 1957, pp. 127-132. Some forms of partial swidden-farming—i.e., where swidden is auxiliary to other forms of cultivation—are, however, open-field systems; while integral systems— i.e., where swidden is the sole form of cultivation— commonly are not. I owe this point to Harold Conklin.
23. Kampto Utomo, *op. cit.*, p. 129.
24. P. Gourou, *L'Asie*. Paris: Hachette, 1953, p. 288, estimates that about 40 percent of the Philippines and 30 percent of Indonesia are

covered with *imperata*, presumably nearly all of it caused by man. These figures may be somewhat high, however. K. J. Pelzer, *op. cit.*, 1945, p. 19, estimates the Philippine grassland percentage at 18.
25. A full consideration of the factors relating to the breakdown of the swidden cycle into a deflected grassland succession would need, of course, to consider topographical and edaphic variables, the role of animal husbandry, associated hunting practices, and so on. For such a micro-analysis, see H. Conklin, "Shifting Cultivation and the Succession to Grassland," *Proceedings, 9th Pacific Science Congress* (1957), Vol. 7 (1959), pp. 60-62.
26. J. A. van Beukering, *Het Ladangvraagstuk, een Bidrijfs- en Sociaal Economische Probleem*. Batavia: Mededeelingen v. h. Departement v. Economische Zaken in Nederlandsch-Indie, No. 9, 1947; H. Conklin, *op. cit.*, 1957, pp. 146-147; J. D. Freeman, *op. cit.*, pp. 134-135. These various figures are all somewhat differently calculated.

problem seems likely to become overtly pressing in the not too distant future; glib references to Outer Indonesia as "grossly underpopulated" constitute a simplistically quantitative and ecologically naive view of demography.

The fact that wasteful or inept methods may be destructive to the long-run equilibrium of swidden agriculture not only underscores the wide variation in proficiency with which different groups of shifting cultivators operate, but, even more important, demonstrates that cultural, social, and psychological variables are at least as crucial as environmental ones in determining the stability of human modes of adaptation. An example of such a thriftless use of resources by swidden farmers is provided by Freeman who says that the Iban have been less shifting cultivators than *mangeurs de bois*.[27] Located in a primary forest area into which they have fairly recently expanded at the expense of indigenous tribes, the Iban are well below maximum population densities. But they nevertheless seriously overcultivate, often using a single plot three years in succession or returning to a fallowed one within five years, and thereby causing widespread deforestation. The reasons for this overcultivation are various, including an historically rooted conviction that there are always other forests to conquer, a warrior's view of natural resources as plunder to be exploited, a large village settlement pattern which makes shifting between plots a more than usually onerous task, and, perhaps, a superior indifference toward agricultural proficiency. But, again, to what degree such prodigality exists among the swidden agriculturalists of Outer Indonesia is virtually unknown.

As for the climatic factor, the most highly generalized, evergreen, closed-cover tropical forest, commonly specified as "rain forest" is chiefly characteristic of equatorial lowland areas where a marked dry season is absent; as one moves toward higher-latitude areas with a marked dry season, it shades off, more or less gradually, into a shorter, more open, less diverse, and at least partly deciduous variety of tropical forest, usually called "monsoon forest."[28] The delicacy of swidden equilibrium increases at equal pace with this transition toward a more subtropical environment because of the steadily diminishing power of the natural community rapidly to reconstitute itself after human interference. The greater ease, and uncontrollability, with which such drier woodlands burn, fanned often by stronger winds than are common in the rain forest areas, only increases the danger of deterioration to grassland or scrub savannah and, in time, by erosion to an almost desert-like state. The southeast portion of the Indonesian archipelago, the Lesser Sundas, where the parching Australian monsoon blows for several months a year, has been particularly exposed to this general process of ecological decline, and in some places devastation is widespread.[29] All in all, the critical limits within which swidden cultivation is an adaptive agricultural regime in Outer Indonesia are fairly narrow.

Sawah

The micro-ecology of the flooded paddy field has yet to be written. Though extensive and detailed researches into the botanical

---

27. J. D. Freeman, *op. cit.*, pp. 135-141.

28. E. H. G. Dobby, *op. cit.*, pp. 62, 65-70. Variation in tropical forest composition is also affected by altitude, soil, and local land mass configurations. For a full discussion, see P. W. Richards, *op. cit.*, pp. 315-374.
29. See F. J. Ormeling, *The Timor Problem.* Groningen, Kjakarta and s'Gravenhage: Wolters and Nijhoff, 1956.

characteristics of wet rice, its natural requirements, the techniques of its cultivation,
the methods by means of which it is
processed into food, and its nutritional value
have been made, the fundamental dynamics
of the individual terrace as an integrated
ecosystem remain unclear.[30] The contrast
between such a terrace—an artificial,
maximally specialized, continuous-cultiva-
tion open-field structure to a swidden plot
could hardly be more extreme; yet how it
operates as an organized unit is far from
being understood. Knowledge remains on
the one hand specialized and technical, with
developed, even experimental, analyses of
breeding and selection, water supply and
control, manuring and weeding, and so on,
and, on the other, commonsensical, resting
on a vast, unexamined accumulation of
proverbial, rice-roots wisdom concerning
similar matters. But a coherent description
of the manner in which the various ecological
components of a terrace interrelate to form
a functioning productive system remains
noticeable by its absence. So far as I am
aware, a genuinely detailed and circumstantial analysis of any actual wet-rice field
(or group of fields) as a set of "living
organisms and nonliving substances interacting to produce an exchange of material
between the living and the non-living parts"
does not exist in the literature.[31]

The most striking feature of the terrace as
an ecosystem, and the one most in need of
explanation, is its extraordinary stability or
durability, the degree to which it can continue to produce, year after year, and often
twice in one year, a virtually undiminished

yield.[32] "Rice grown under irrigation is a
unique crop," the geographer Murphey has
written,

> . . . soil fertility does affect its yield, as does
> fertilization, but it does not appear to exhaust the
> soil even over long periods without fertilization,
> and in many cases it may actually improve the soil.
> On virgin soils a rapid decline in yield usually takes
> place, in the absence of fertilization, within the
> first two or three years, but after ten or twenty
> years the yield tends to remain stable more or less
> indefinitely. This has been borne out by experi-
> ments in various parts of tropical Asia, by in-
> creased knowledge of the processes involved, and
> by accumulated experience. On infertile soils and
> with inadequate fertilization the field stabilizes at a
> very low level, as is the case now in Ceylon and
> most of South Asia, but it does stabilize. Why this
> should be so is not yet entirely understood.[33]

The answer to this puzzle almost certainly lies in the paramount role played by
water in the dynamics of the rice terrace.
Here, the characteristic thinness of tropical
soils is circumvented through the bringing of
nutrients onto the terrace by the irrigation
water to replace those drawn from the soil;
through the fixation of nitrogen by the
blue-green algae which proliferate in the
warm water; through the chemical and bac-
terial decomposition of organic material,
including the remains of harvested crops in
that water; through the aeration of the soil
by the gentle movement of the water in the
terrace; and, no doubt, through other ecological functions performed by irrigation
which are as yet unknown.[34] Thus, al-

---

30. For an encyclopedic summary of such researches, see D. H. Grist, *Rice*. London: Longmans,
Green (3rd ed.), 1959.
31. The quotation is the formal definition of an
ecosystem given in E. P. Odum, *op. cit.*, p. 10.

32. P. Gourou, *The Tropical World* (trans. E. D.
Laborde). New York: Longmans, Green, 1953, p.
100; and P. Gourou, *L'Asie*. Paris: Hachette, 1953,
p. 74.
33. R. Murphey, "The Ruin of Ancient Ceylon,"
Journal of Asian Studies, Vol. 16 (1957), pp.
181-200.
34. In addition to the mentioned Grist (esp. pp.
28-49), Gourou, and Murphey references, useful, if
unsystematic, material on the micro-ecology of
irrigated rice can be found in K. J. Pelzer, *op. cit.*,
1945, pp. 47-51, and especially in T. Matsuo, *Rice*

though, contrary to appearances, the paddy plant actually requires no more water than dry-land crops for simple transpirational purposes, "the supply and control of water . . . is the most important aspect of irrigated paddy cultivation; given an adequate and well-controlled water supply the crop will grow in a wide range of soils and in many climates. It is therefore more important than the type of soil."[35]

This primary reliance on the material which envelops the biotic community (the "medium") for nourishment rather than on the solid surface in which it is rooted (the "substratum"), makes possible the same maintenance of an effective agricultural regime on indifferent soils that the direct cycling pattern of energy exchange makes possible on swiddens.[36] Even that soil quality which is of clearest positive value for paddy growing, a heavy consistency which irrigation water will not readily percolate away, is more clearly related to the semi-aquatic nature of the cultivation process than to its nutritional demands, and paddy can be effectively grown on soils which are "unbelievably poor in plant nutrients."[37] This is not to say that natural soil fertility has no effect on wet-rice yields, but merely that, as "paddy soils tend to acquire their own special properties after long use," a low natural fertility is not in itself a prohibitive factor if adequate water resources are available.[38] Like swidden, wet-rice cultivation is essentially an ingenious device for the agri-cultural exploitation of a habitat in which heavy reliance on soil processes is impossible and where other means for converting natural energy into food are therefore necessary. Only here we have not the imitation of a tropical forest, but the fabrication of an aquarium.

The supply and control of water is therefore the key factor in wet-rice growing—a seemingly self-evident proposition which conceals some complexities because the regulation of water in a terrace is a matter of some delicacy. Excessive flooding is often as great a threat as insufficient inundation; drainage is frequently a more intractable problem than irrigation. Not merely the gross quantity of water, but its quality, in terms of the fertilizing substances it contains (and thus the source from which it comes) is a crucial variable in determining productivity. Timing is also important: paddy should be planted in a well-soaked field with little standing water and then the depth of the water increased gradually up to six to twelve inches as the plant grows and flowers, after which it should be gradually drawn off until at harvest the field is dry. Further, the water should not be allowed to stagnate but, as much as possible, kept gently flowing, and periodic drainings are generally advisable for purposes of weeding and fertilizing.[39] Although with traditional (and in some landscapes, even modern) methods of water control the degree to which these various optimal conditions can be met is limited, even at its simplest, least productive, and most primitive this form of cultivation tends to be technically intricate.

And this is true not only for the terrace itself, but for the system of auxiliary water works within which it is set. We need not

Culture in Japan. Tokyo: Yokendo, 1955, pp. 109-112.

35. D. H. Grist, *op. cit.*, pp. 28-29.

36. For the distinction between "medium" and "substratum," see G. Clarke, *op. cit.*, pp. 23-58, 59-89.

37. R. L. Pendleton, "The Formation, Development and Utilization of the Soils of Bangkok Plain," *Natural History Bulletin 14*, 1947; quoted in D. H. Grist, *op. cit.*, p. 11.

38. R. Murphey, *op. cit.*

39. D. H. Grist, *op. cit.*, pp. 28-32. One of the primary functions, aside from nutrition, of irrigation water is, in fact, the inhibition of weed growth.

accept Karl Wittfogel's theories about "hydraulic societies" and "oriental despotisms" to agree that while the mobility of water makes it "the natural variable *par excellence*" in those landscapes where its manipulation is agriculturally profitable, its bulkiness makes such manipulation difficult, and manageable only with significant inputs of "preparatory" labor and at least a certain amount of engineering skill.[40] The construction and maintenance of even the simplest water-control system, as in rainfall farms, requires such ancillary efforts: ditches must be dug and kept clean, sluices constructed and repaired, terraces leveled and dyked; and in more developed true irrigation systems dams, reservoirs, aqueducts, tunnels, wells and the like become necessary. Even such larger works can be built up slowly, piece by piece, over extended periods and kept in repair by continuous, routine care. But, small or large, waterworks represent a level and kind of investment in "capital equipment" foreign not only to shifting cultivation but to virtually all unirrigated forms of premodern agriculture.

This complex of systemic characteristics— settled stability, "medium" rather than "substratum" nutrition, technical complexity and significant overhead labor investment—produce in turn what is perhaps the sociologically most critical feature of wet-rice agriculture: its marked tendency (and ability) to respond to a rising population through intensification; that is, through absorbing increased numbers of cultivators on a unit of cultivated land. Such a course is largely precluded to swidden farmers, at least under traditional conditions, because of the precarious equilibrium of the shifting regime. If their population increases they

must, before long, spread out more widely over the countryside in order to bring more land into cultivation; otherwise the deterioration to savannah process which results from too rapid recultivation will set in and their position will become even more untenable. To some extent, such horizontal expansion is, of course, possible for traditional wet-rice agriculturalists as well, and has in fact (though more slowly and hesitantly than is sometimes imagined) occurred. But the pattern of ecological pressures here increasingly encourages the opposite practice: working old plots harder rather than establishing new ones.

The reasons for this introversive tendency follow directly from the listed systemic characteristics. The stability of the rice terrace as an ecosystem makes the tendency possible in the first place. Because even the most intense population pressure does not lead to a breakdown of the system on the physical side (though it may lead to extreme impoverishment on the human side), such pressure can reach a height limited only by the capacity of those who exploit it to subsist on steadily diminishing per capita returns for their labor. Where swidden "overpopulation" results in a deterioration of the habitat, in a wet-rice regime it results in the support of an ever-increasing number of people within an undamaged habitat. Restricted areas of Java today—for example, Adiwerna, an alluvial region in the north-central part of the island—reach extraordinary rural population densities of nearly 2,000 persons per square kilometer without any significant decline in per-hectare rice production. Nor does there seem to be any region on the island in which wet-rice growing was employed effectively in the past but cannot now be so employed due to human over-driving of the landscape. Given maintenance of irrigation facilities, a reasonable level of farming technique, and no autoge-

40. K. Wittfogel, *Oriental Despotism.* New Haven: Yale University Press, 1957, p. 15.

nous changes in the physical setting, the *sawah* (as the Javanese call the rice terrace) seems virtually indestructible.

Second, the "medium-focused" quality of the regime limits it fairly sharply to those areas in which topography, water resources, and soluble nutrients combine to make the complex ecological integration of sawah farming (whatever that may turn out in detail to be) possible. All agricultural regimes are, of course, limited by the environmental conditions upon which they rely. But wet-rice cultivation, particularly under premodern technological conditions, is perhaps even more limited than most and, within Indonesia, certainly more than swidden, which can be carried out over the greater part of the archipelago, including, as it once was, most of those parts now pre-empted by sawah. Swidden can be pursued on rugged hillsides, in wet lowland forests, and in relatively dry monsoon country where, at least without the assistance of modern methods of water control, conservation, and regulation, sawah cannot. Exact data are difficult to obtain but the great extension of irrigated rice-farming in Indonesia and the rest of Southeast Asia during the last hundred years or so as a result of the application of Western technology ought not to obscure the fact that before the middle of the nineteenth century such farming was restricted to a few, particularly favorable areas. In 1833, when Java was just on the eve of her most disastrous period of social change, the island, which today has about three and a half million hectares of sawah had only slightly more than a third that much.[41]

Yet there is another introversive implication of the technical complexity aspect of traditional wet-rice cultivation. Because productivity is so dependent on the quality of water regulation, labor applied to the improvement of such regulation can often have a greater marginal productivity than that same labor applied to constructing new, but less adequately managed, terraces and new works to support them. Under premodern conditions, gradual perfection of irrigation techniques is perhaps the major way to raise productivity not only per hectare but per man. To develop further water works already in being is often more profitable than to construct new ones at the established technical level; and, in fact, the ingenious traditional water-control systems of Java and Bali can only have been created during a long period of persistent trial-and-error refinement of established systems. Once created, an irrigation system has a momentum of its own, which continues, and even increases, to the point where the limits of traditional skills and resources are reached. And, as the gap between the first rainfall, stream-bank, or swamp-plot sawah and those limits is usually great, economic progress through step-by-step technological advance within a specifically focused system can be an extended process, as shown in the following description of a Ceylonese system:

> . . . The Kaläwewa canal system—now has a giant tank at its head which leads into a fifty-five mile long watercourse, which in turn feeds into three large tanks which provide water for the ancient capital of Anuradhapura. It all looks like a colossal and highly organized piece of bureaucratic planning, the work of one of Wittfogel's idealised Oriental Despots. But if so, the planning must have been done by a kind of Durkheimian group mind! The original Tissawewa tank at the bottom end of the system was first constructed about 300 B.C. The Kaläwewa tank at the top end of the system was first constructed about 800 years later and elaborations and modifications went on for at least another 600 years.[42]

---

41. The contemporary figure is from *Statistical Pocketbook of Indonesia, op. cit.,* p. 46; the 1833 figure (1,270,000 ha.) from J. J. van Klaveren, *The Dutch Colonial System in Indonesia.* Rotterdam (?), no publisher, 1955, p. 23.

---

42. E. Leach, "Hydraulic Society in Ceylon," *Past and Present,* Vol. 15, 1959, pp. 2-25.

However, as mentioned, it is not only with respect to ancillary waterworks that wet-rice agriculture tends toward technical complexity, but on a more microscopic level with respect to the individual terrace itself. In addition to improving the general irrigation system within which a terrace is set, the output of most terraces can be almost indefinitely increased by more careful, finecomb cultivation techniques; it seems almost always possible somehow to squeeze just a little more out of even a mediocre sawah by working it just a little bit harder. Seeds can be sown in nurseries and then transplanted instead of broadcast; they can even be pregerminated in the house. Yield can be increased by planting shoots in exactly spaced rows, more frequent and complete weeding, periodic draining of the terrace during the growing season for purposes of aeration, more thorough ploughing, raking, and leveling of the muddy soil before planting, placing selected organic debris on the plot, and so on; harvesting techniques can be similarly perfected both to reap the fullest percentage of the yield and leave the greatest amount of the harvested crop on the field to refertilize it, such as the technique of using the razor-like hand blade found over most of inner Indonesia; double cropping and, in some favorable areas, perhaps triple cropping, can be instituted. The capacity of most terraces to respond to loving care is amazing. As we shall see, a whole series of such laborabsorbing improvements in cultivation methods have played a central role in permitting the Javanese rural economy to soak up the bulk of the island's exploding population.

Finally, independently of the advantages of technical perfection, the mere quantity of preparatory (and thus not immediately productive) labor in creating new works and bringing them up to the level of existing ones tends to discourage a rapid expansion of terraced areas in favor of fragmentation

and more intensive working of existing ones. In developed systems, this is apparent; a people who have spent 1,400 years in building an irrigation system are not likely to leave it readily for pioneering activities, even if the established system becomes overcrowded. They have too much tied up in it, and at most they will gradually create a few new terraces on the periphery of the already well-irrigated area, where water resources and terrain permit. But this reluctance to initiate new terrace construction because of the heavy "overhead" labor investment is characteristic even of areas where irrigation is still undeveloped, because of the inability or the unwillingness of peasants to divert resources from present production. In contemporary Laos, for example,

> Most villages are only semi-permanent and forest land is still available. The irrigated rice fields have become fragmented because their yields are more reliable than those of the [swidden]. The creation of new [sawahs] is not easily done, for it involves the extension of irrigation ditches and major investment of labor. This labor must be hired or supplied by the family itself, and implies existing fluid capital or a large extended family containing a number of able-bodied workers. Neither of these situations commonly occurs among Lao peasants, and therefore the progressive division of existing [wet rice] land and cultivation of [swidden] which requires less initial labor.[43]

Therefore, the characteristics of swidden and sawah as ecosystems are clear and critical: On the one hand a multicrop, highly diverse regime, a cycling of nutrients between living forms, a closed-cover architecture, and a delicate equilibrium; on the other, an open-field, monocrop, highly specialized regime, a heavy dependency on water-borne minerals for nutrition, a reliance on manmade waterworks, and a stable equilibrium. Though these are not the only two tradi-

---

43. J. M. Halpern, "The Economies of Lao and Serb Peasants: A Contrast in Cultural Values," *Southwestern Journal of Anthropology*, Vol. 17 (1961), pp. 165-177.

tional agricultural systems in Indonesia, they are by far the most important and have set the framework within which the general agricultural economy of the country has developed. In their contrasting responses to forces making for an increase in population—the dispersive, inelastic quality of the one and the concentrative, inflatable quality of the other—lies much of the explanation for the uneven distribution of population in Indonesia and the ineluctable social and cultural quandaries which followed from it.

⚘⚘⚘⚘⚘⚘⚘⚘⚘⚘⚘⚘⚘⚘⚘⚘⚘⚘⚘⚘⚘⚘⚘⚘⚘⚘⚘⚘⚘

ASPECTS OF MAN'S INFLUENCE UPON ISLAND ECOSYSTEMS: ALTERATION AND CONTROL[1]

Roy A. Rappaport

I

This paper will first be concerned with components of prehuman Pacific island ecosystems, and with the cultural and noncultural elements likely to have been introduced by human agency in pre-European times. Then, some of the possible alterations in these ecosystems subsequent to and resulting from human introductions will be discussed; and suggestions will be made concerning possible implications for human social organization of man's participation in the various kinds of ecosystem.

For the sake of convenience, we shall refer to the prehuman ecosystems as the "pristine ecosystems." Their reconstruction is no easy task. Many essential data have not yet been provided by paleoecological investigations, and the inferences that may be made from existing island ecosystems are limited. In those ecosystems in which man has had a place, pristine conditions have presumably been obscured by man himself as well as by continuing physiographic and climatological processes, and the few islands without permanent populations may, by their nature, have special characteristics and therefore cannot be used uncritically as models for reconstructions of prehuman ecosystems in general. Nevertheless, some tentative characterizations of the pristine ecosystems can be made. Zimmerman, earlier in this symposium, outlined for us in some detail the characteristics of the pristine terrestrial ecosystems of high islands. It would be well to review some of these characteristics briefly.

Owing to the difficulty of transportation across open sea, these systems were generally characterized by the presence of few genera.

1. This paper, originally presented in the symposium by A. P. Vayda and R. A. Rappaport, has been revised by Rappaport in light of the discussions and is published under his sole authorship. The author is indebted to Dr. Vayda for invaluable advice and editorial assistance, and to H. E. Maude for suggestions, corrections, and amplifications. These were included in the paper which he, as discussant, prepared for presentation at this symposium. Many of his suggestions have been incorporated into the present version of this paper. The points of view presented, however, are the responsibility of the author alone.

From *Man's Place in the Island Ecosystem*, edited by F. R. Fosberg, Honolulu, Bishop Museum Press, 1963, pp. 155-170. Reprinted by permission.

The relative number of genera in the various situations was roughly in inverse proportion to the distance from the large masses of Australia and Melanesia, the points of origin for most of the forms, although some plants and animals did arrive in various islands from other directions. Members of many large taxonomic groupings were able to arrive only rarely if at all; thus, for instance, very few terrestrial vertebrates became established in, and mammals were totally absent from, large portions of the island world. The forms which did establish themselves, however, frequently did so in the absence of those biotic and edaphic features which had kept them in check in their earlier habitats, and often found "ecological vacuums" in their new homes. These two factors made for rapid, sometimes explosive, population expansion. Indeed, conditions on the high islands, which are characterized by great meteorological and physical variety within restricted space, encouraged rapid and prolific speciation. (Thus, in Hawaii, 1,200 or more species of land snails in nine families have arisen from possibly no more than twenty-four ancestral stocks.) Many of the adaptations associated with this speciation were extreme and narrow, however, and were possible only in the absence of forms better able to exploit the same sets of resources. Thus, as new immigrants arrived there was frequent replacement of forms, and it is unlikely that equilibria were ever approached.

While the biotic elements in the pristine high islands were taxonomically restricted, those on the low islands were even more so. The indigenous vegetation of uninhabited Rose Atoll, for instance, included only three vascular species in as many genera.[2] While

this example is extreme, similar data may be found concerning larger inhabited islands. Hatheway[3] studied the vegetation of Canton Island some 20 years after the arrival of relatively permanent residents. Of the approximately 160 vascular plant species present at the time of his study, he regarded only 14 species in as many genera to be indigenous. On the same island, Van Zwaluwenburg[4] found only 93 species of insects, not all of which were indigenous.[5] On Kapingamarangi, an island peopled a relatively long time ago, Niering[6] found 98 vascular plant species, 58 of which had been introduced by man.

Several factors combine to make the terrestrial biota of the atoll among the world's most restricted. Fosberg has suggested that in addition to the factor most pertinent in high islands, that of difficulty of transportation across open water, the relatively short period of time during which dry land has been exposed on coral atolls is of primary importance. He points also to the lack of topographic or altitudinal diversity which was crucial in the processes of speciation in the high islands, and finally, to special edaphic conditions such as high salinity and calcareousness prevailing on atolls.[7]

2. Marie-Hélène Sachet, *A Summary of Information on Rose Atoll*, Atoll Research Bulletin 29. Washington, D.C.: National Research Council, 1954, p. 15.

3. William Hatheway, *The Natural Vegetation of Canton Island, an Equatorial Pacific Atoll*, Atoll Research Bulletin 43. Washington, D.C.: National Research Council, 1955, p. 2.
4. R. H. Van Zwaluwenburg, *The Insects and Certain Arthropods of Canton Island*, Atoll research Bulletin 42. Washington, D. C.: National Research Council, 1955, p. 11.
5. O. Degener and E. Gillaspy, *Canton Island, South Pacific*, Atoll Research Bulletin 41. Washington, D.C.: National Research Council, 1955, p. 48.
6. William A. Niering, *Bioecology of Kapingamarangi Atoll, Caroline Islands: Terrestrial Aspects*, Atoll Research Bulletin 49. Washington, D.C.: National Research Council, 1956, p. 4.
7. F. R. Fosberg, *Vegetation of Central Pacific Atolls: A Brief Summary*, Atoll Research Bulletin

It is possible, however, that despite the lack of diversity in the low island biota, equilibria were more closely approximated on atolls than on the high islands, for conditions were so special that the introduction of most new forms was in large measure prohibited. Those floral elements which did become dominant were highly adapted for both water-borne dispersal and for survival under the forbidding conditions offered by the atoll. Consequently they were almost invulnerable to displacement by other forms. It is interesting to note that none of the 150 floral species recently brought to Canton by man has shown any tendency to invade the still undisturbed areas of the island, which continue to be dominated by indigenous forms.[8]

Reef-lagoon biota, found in association with both coral atolls and high islands, may be regarded as belonging to distinct ecosystems which contrast strikingly with those on dry land. Considerable stability and great taxonomic variety in reef-lagoon ecosystems is indicated by some recent investigations such as Hiatt and Strasburg's study[9] of 233 of the approximately 600 species of fish judged to be present in Marshall Islands reef communities. The 233 species belonged to 127 genera and 56 families, and it should not be forgotten that the biota included many organisms in addition to fish. Odum and Odum,[10] who studied the reef community of Eniwetok Atoll in the Marshall

Islands, also discuss the variety and richness of reef-lagoon ecosystems. Moreover, they point out that the Eniwetok reef-lagoon system seemed to sustain itself; the primary producers were members of the community and apparently there was little derived from exotic plankton. To Odum and Odum this seemed a "true climax community" with little or no variation in living biomass. Similarly, Hiatt and Strasburg[11] refer to reef ecosystems as "steady state equilibria," self-adjusted and apparently fluctuating in composition very little, if at all, from year to year. The stability of these reef-lagoon systems, despite the exploitation to which they have been subjected for considerable time, gives some grounds for supposing that the difference between observed and pristine conditions is probably much less in reef-lagoon than in terrestrial ecosystems.

II

Pacific island ecosystems were eventually entered by human populations, together with their associated mutuals, parasites and commensals. Information concerning the biotic associations arriving at the various islands is scanty, but it is clear that a simple reconstruction of an early Pacific cultigen inventory would only mark the range of *possible* introductions into any particular island. While the range of Pacific cultigens was limited, it was broad enough to insure that no human group transported the full inventory, and the range of organisms associated with either the humans or the domesticates and cultigens in relationships of commensalism or parasitism was even broader. It must be assumed, therefore, that each island in the Pacific received a set of organisms that differed to a greater or lesser degree from the sets introduced into other islands.

23. Washington, D.C.: National Research Council, 1953, p. 5.
8. William Hatheway, *op. cit.*, 1955, p. 2.
9. R. W. Hiatt and D. W. Strasburg, "Ecological Relationships of the Fish Fauna on Coral reefs of the Marshall Islands," *Ecological Monographs*, Vol. 30 (1960), pp. 65-127.
10. Howard T. Odum, and Eugene P. Odum, "Trophic Structure and Productivity of a Windward Coral Reef Community on Eniwetok Atoll," *Ecological Monographs*, Vol. 25 (1955), pp. 291-320.

11. R. W. Hiatt, and D. W. Strasburg, *op. cit.*, p. 66.

The migrating human populations should be seen as units comparable to other animal populations being introduced into the island ecosystems. A population, human or not, may be defined as an aggregate of organisms that belong to the same species, occupy a common habitat, and have in common certain distinctive means whereby they exploit one or more niches in one or more ecosystems. Needless to say, human populations rely most heavily upon extra-biological (that is cultural) means in exploiting niches in ecosystems; but there is no advantage, for ecological inquiry, in treating cultures as entities to be separated from the culture carriers. Particular means may be regarded as attributes of particular populations, particular cultural means as attributes of particular human populations.

Considerable diversity must have obtained among human founding populations in the Pacific islands. Even in such restricted areas of the island world as Polynesia, the circumstances of settlement were such that we cannot assume common human traits, both biological and cultural, to have been brought equally to all islands. A multiplicity of points of embarkation is indicated by linguistics and stratigraphic archaeology.[12] Furthermore, immigrant groups, which often seem to have comprised only a few people,[13] no doubt represented chance samples of their ancestral populations. They brought with them neither the whole gene pools nor the entire cultures of those populations.[14]

Continuing investigations should elucidate some of the variations, particularly in technology, which pertained among human founding populations. Questions concerning differences in tool inventories will, to some extent, be answered by stratigraphic archaeology. But while it is already evident that there were marked differences among the forms of tools even in the inventories of groups as closely related historically as the Polynesian populations, the functional differences between these forms are not clear. While it may be possible to do anything with a tangless adz that can be done with a tanged adz, for example, it is less likely that the variety of fish that can be taken on two-piece hooks corresponds exactly to that which can be taken on one-piece hooks. In eastern Polynesia both one- and two-piece hooks are found, whereas in western Polynesia only two-piece hooks are known. Archaeology has yet to decide for us whether these differences are differences in the hook inventories of the immigrant groups, or whether they are a result of subsequent differentiation from initially similar bases, a less likely possibility. If the latter is the case, we may have an example of technological "adaptive differentiation." If the former, we have an initial difference which may have made for slightly different impacts on more or less similar marine ecosystems.

It is extremely unlikely that the biological variation among different founding populations can ever be fully known; but studies of differences among contemporary populations may help to illuminate the possible importance of biological variation in the ability of particular populations to participate in particular ecosystems. In this symposium Maude tells us ". . . while I could

12. Kenneth P. Emory, Personal Communication, 1961; Ward Goodenough, "Oceania and the Problem of Controls in the Study of Cultural and Human Evolution," *Journal of Polynesian Society*, Vol. 66 (1957), pp. 146-155; George W. Grace, "Austronesian Linguistics and Culture History," *American Anthropologist*, Vol. 63 (1961), pp. 359-368; Roger C. Green, Personal Communication, 1961.
13. A. P. Vayda, "Polynesian Cultural Distributions in New Perspective," *American Anthropologist*, Vol. 61 (1959), pp. 817-828.

14. Ward Goodenough, *op. cit.*

scarcely drink the well water in many Gilbertese villages, particularly in times of drought, the people of Bangai on Tabiteuea, situated on a remote sandy islet, have apparently become accustomed to drinking water so brackish that even the Gilbertese, when visiting them, are reported to bring their own bottled supplies." It cannot be asserted, of course, that the ability to use resources which others cannot use indicates genetic difference. It is probable that the people of Bangai had, through lifelong use, simply become conditioned to water which others were unable, or preferred not, to tolerate. However, the possible biological basis of this ability, genetic or not, does merit investigation. Answers to this and similar questions, particularly those concerning the dietary requirements of various populations, may demonstrate that inter-population biological differences may be significant variables in the interaction of men and ecosystems.

We should also consider differences between founding populations in those portions of their cultures which comprised the means for ordering elements in the ecosystems into meaningful categories. To be noted here are such questions as: what was immediately recognized as food and what was not; what restrictions, if any, were placed upon the exploitation of various portions of the biota, or on specific practices of exploitation; how close a correspondence there was between what were *seen* to be the critical relationships pertaining among biotic elements and the operational relationships which did, *in fact*, pertain among the same elements.

To deal with these questions, it may be useful to make a distinction between the "operational environment" of a population and what could be termed its "cognized environment." The term operational environment was originally proposed by Marston

Bates,[15] who quotes a definition of environment constructed earlier by Mason and Langenheim:

> The environment of any organism is the class composed of the sum of those phenomena that enter a reaction system of the organism or otherwise directly impinge upon it to affect its mode of life at any time throughout its life cycle as ordered by the demands of the ontogeny of the organism or as ordered by any other condition of the organism that alters its environmental demands.

The cognized environment may be seen as the class composed of the sum of the phenomena ordered into meaningful categories by a population. The operational and cognized environments will include many of the same elements, but they may differ extensively in the structuring of relationships between elements.

It is probable that in the case of human populations in small Pacific islands no operational nor cognized environment is, or ever was, coterminous with a particular ecosystem. Both the cognized and operational environments of such populations include elements best seen as components of several distinct ecosystems; that of the dry land, and those of the sea. On the other hand, it is clear that no cognized environment will ever include all of the elements in any ecosystem, and it is possible that some elements in an ecosystem will be so remote, functionally, from a population in the same ecosystem that these elements may be considered to be outside that population's operational environment.

As in the case of their biological components, it will never be possible to reconstruct the cognitive systems of founding populations in the Pacific, much less map their cognized environments. However, the analysis of contemporary folk taxonomies in

---

15. Marston Bates, "Ecology and Evolution," in Sol Tax, editor, *Evolution After Darwin*. Chicago: University of Chicago Press, 1960, Vol. I, p. 554.

such areas as ethnobotany and ethno-
zoology, a study already pioneered by
Conklin and others, should yield important
insights into the roles played by distinctive
cognitive capacities and limitations, in structuring the interaction of particular populations with particular ecosystems.

III

Among the numerous and varied elements of
the established island ecosystems and the
elements introduced into them an almost
infinite number of specific interactions is
conceivable. The data are deficient on the
interactions that actually took place, but it
is evident that not all exotic forms could
find a place in the islands to which they
were conveyed. Among the forms that might
be rejected were human beings themselves.
There are islands in the Pacific which were
reached by people in pre-European times but
seem never to have supported permanent
human populations. In some, such as
Phoenix Island, it was probably the terrestrial, rather than the reef-lagoon system
which was inhospitable to man. We have no
evidence to indicate that the reef-lagoon
system of Phoenix Island differed markedly
from those of nearby inhabited atolls, but
we do know that Phoenix was considerably
smaller than its inhabited neighbors; too
small, according to Maude, to provide a
home for a sufficient number of humans to
form a viable community. Further, and
associated with its small size and local
atmospheric conditions, there was quite
possibly a deficiency of fresh water on
Phoenix. Rainfall was slight and irregular,
and when, in 1937, Maude dug six wells to a
depth of twelve feet, he was unable to find a
fresh water lens.[16]

16. H. E. Maude, "The Colonization of the
Phoenix Islands," *Journal of Polynesian Society*,
Vol. 61 (1952), p. 77.

While it is probable that in most uninhabited low islands deficiencies in terrestrial
rather than in reef-lagoon systems were
crucial, it is clear that not all reef-lagoon
systems are equally utilizable by humans. It
seems, in fact, that factors in some reef-
lagoon systems have severely hindered, or
even prevented, human colonization. The
recent history of the Gilbertese colony on
Sydney Island in the Phoenix group is an
example. While the size of the island was
sufficient for a viable colony, and while
coconut cultivation was possible, Maude in
this symposium writes that "the configuration of the shore-line afforded no adequate
lee for the deep sea fisherman, and with
many of the reef fish toxic . . . and no fish in
the lagoon . . . the colony had to be abandoned after 20 years." The sea channel into
the lagoon, according to Maude, had dried
up, resulting in a level of salinity in the
lagoon too high to maintain marine biota.

Maude also suggests that some islands
were differentially hospitable to different
immigrant populations:

> . . . there existed many environments so un-
> congenial to some immigrants that sooner or later
> they prefered to risk all the perils of the deep
> rather than remain; whereas on these same islands
> others more accustomed to making the best use of
> strictly limited ecosystems were later able to es-
> tablish comfortable and permanent homes. . . . The
> more limited the environmental potentialities, the
> fewer and more specialized the human populations
> willing to add themselves to the establishment.

The importance of possible interpopulation
cognitive and perhaps biological variation is
suggested here.

On other islands, conditions permitted
the establishment of humans, but excluded
certain of the species associated with them.
Thus, certain plants such as sweet potatoes
and kava, widely cultivated in Polynesia,
could not be grown on many atolls. Certain
commensals and parasites conveyed inadvertently by man may likewise have failed to

become established. This may have been especially true of weeds associated with food crops that came to be cultivated in new ways and under new conditions.

It may be useful to regard certain classes of cultural means as also subject to rejection. Existing stone tools could not be replaced on isolated islands lacking suitable stone; other materials, generally shell, had to be utilized on many of the coral atolls. Dugout canoes could not be built on islands which neither had large trees nor received appropriate drift logs.[17] Also subject to rejection was some of the knowledge pertaining to subsistence procedures not feasible in the new settings. Knowledge of techniques of swidden agriculture, for example, might be lost within a few generations on a coral atoll. Moreover, such social features as the organization of personnel for specific subsistence procedures might also be rejected.

Of the exotic forms *not* rejected, some were established less easily and less extensively than others. On coral atolls, for instance, the establishment of introduced root crops, most commonly taro-like plants, generally required painstaking modification of the cultivation sites. Also, certain arboreal forms were not readily established in coral atolls. Whereas the cultivation of breadfruit was possible there, it was limited by calcareous soils[18] and by the sensitivity of the trees to salt water in the form of spray or occasional inundation.[19] That there could be difficulty in establishing and maintaining even that important and widely distributed food plant, the coconut, is suggested by its reported near-absence from a number of

atolls prior to the advent of the copra trade.[20] The limiting factor probably was drought.

On the other hand, some animals, after being brought by man to certain islands, apparently became established readily and were by no means confined to areas modified by human activities. Most notable of such animals were rats. Cook[21] found rats on uninhabited Palmerston in 1777. An abundance of the animals was noted by Mayor in 1920 on Rose Atoll, which has never been inhabited,[22] and Sharp[23] states that at least five Polynesian islands had rats but no people at the time of European discovery. Certain insects probably were transported by people. On uninhabited Alona islet in Ant Atoll, Marshall[24] found swarms of cockroaches. The ability of some animals to establish themselves without much help from man is indicated also by the fact that on some islands, especially the larger ones, domesticated animals have escaped and have maintained themselves in the "wild." In Moorea in the Society Islands, "wild" pigs and chickens have become established in the mountainous and more or less inaccessible interior, and have recently been joined by "wild" goats and cattle as well. There are interesting examples from lower and smaller islands too. Maude[25] found rabbits on un-

17. On Easter Island, see Marshall Sahlins, "Esoteric Efflorescence on Easter Island," *American Anthropologist*, Vol. 57 (1955), p. 1050.
18. René L. H. Catala, *Report on the Gilbert Islands: Some Aspects of Human Ecology*, Atoll Research Bulletin 59. Washington, D.C.: National Research Council, 1957, p. 11.
19. F. R. Fosberg, *op. cit.*, pp. 5, 8.

20. Bengt Danielsson, *Work and Life on Raroia.* Stockholm: Saxon and Lindstroms, 1955, pp. 64-65.
21. James Cook, *A Voyage to the Pacific Ocean . . . Performed . . . in the years 1776 . . . 1780.* London: Nicol and Cadell, 1784, Vol. I p. 217.
22. Marie-Hélène Sachet, *op. cit.*, p. 20.
23. Andrew Sharp, *Ancient Voyagers in the Pacific*, Polynesian Society, Mem. 32. Wellington, N.Z.: 1956, p. 136.
24. J. T. Marshall, Jr., *Atolls Visited During the First Year of the Pacific Islands Rat Ecology Project*, Atoll research Bulletin 56. Washington, D.C.: National Research Council, 1957, p. 5.
25. H. E. Maude, *op. cit.*, pp. 76-77.

inhabited Phoenix in 1937, and Green[26] has seen goats on Kamaka, an uninhabited island in the Mangarevan Islands.

Man himself as an exotic biotic element in island ecosystems must not be forgotten. Like many other immigrant species populations, humans found ecological vacuums in the ecosystems they entered. Population growth must frequently have been explosive. A model proposed by Birdsell[27] suggests that populations in "open" environments are likely to double, at least initially, in each generation. Densities exceeding 1,000 per square mile were eventually reached on some islands.

It seems probable that, generally, the flora transported inadvertently and introduced by pre-European human populations did not become dominant. Merrill[28] believes that in 1769, when Banks and Solander made their collections in Tahiti, there were relatively few introduced weeds and that the flora had not been greatly altered as to constituent species. It may be that, in general, the establishment of most introduced floral elements was restricted in pre-European times to sites modified by human activities. This seems so for the important food plants, of which all except pandanus were introduced by man. The same kind of restriction for weeds is suggested by Merrill's interpretation, but the data are deficient.

While it is possible, as Maude suggests, that many islands were congenial to some human immigrants and not to others, immigrant populations were rarely confronted with kinds of ecosystems about which they knew nothing. For example, since most high islands have fringing reefs, often with coral islets on them, atolls would not have been entirely strange even to many immigrant high islanders[29]. Nevertheless, no two Pacific islands have ever been alike in all important respects; elements apparently similar in two islands might turn out to differ significantly. Thus, some fish, especially red snappers, groupers, jacks and barracuda, are toxic within rather narrow geographical limits, harmless in nearby areas[30]. This means that the occurrence of toxicity or non-toxicity, even among recognized fish, could not be taken for granted by immigrant groups.

The classifications and reclassifications that humans made of both flora and fauna had a bearing upon the interaction between themselves and island ecosystems. Edible plants and such fauna as sharks and sea-slugs might be utilized, depending upon whether they had been classified as edible or otherwise in the islands from which the people came. There might have been some reclassifications. An emergency food, for example, might have been reclassified as a staple. This was true of *Portulaca oleracea* (purslane) among Gilbertese settlers of the Phoenix Islands.[31] On occasion, people were confronted with plants that they did not know at all. Cumberland tells us that the principal staple vegetable food of the Maoris was the starchy root of the *Pteridium esculentum*, a

26. Roger Green, Personal Communication, 1961.
27. Joseph Birdsell, "Some Population Problems Involving Pleistocene Man," *Cold Spring Harbor Symposium of Quantitative Biology*, Vol. 22 (1957), pp. 47-68.
28. Elmer Drew Merrill, "The Botany of Cook's Voyages and Its Unexpected Significance in Relation to Anthropology, Biogeography and History," *Chronica Botanica*, Vol. 14 (1954), p. 212.

29. Ward Goodenough, *op. cit.*, pp. 151-152.
30. A. H. Banner, "Fish Poisoning Reports Wanted for University of Hawaii Study," *South Pacific Communications Quarterly Bulletin*, Vol. 9 (1959), p. 31.
31. I. G. Turbott, "Diets, Gilbert and Ellice Islands Colony," *Journal of Polynesian Society*, Vol. 58 (1949), pp. 36-46; I. G. Turbott, "Portulaca: A Specialty in the Diet of the Gilbertese in the Phoenix Islands, Central Pacific," *Journal of Polynesian Society*, Vol. 63 (1954), pp. 77-85.

fern that must have been unknown to the first settlers of New Zealand.

Occasionally, man's introductions resulted in the complete elimination and replacement of certain pre-existing forms, or more frequently, the range and numbers of those forms were reduced. Such reductions were not always directly due to man. In Hawaii the rat played an important part in bringing some plants and certain ground-nesting birds to the brink of extinction (Zimmerman, in this symposium). But human activities in many cases did have a direct influence. Certain plants and animals were eliminated or substantially reduced, not because they were pests, nor because, being useful, they were overexploited, but simply because they were in the way. This must have been true in localities where sedentary horticulture was instituted. In most areas of tropical Polynesia and Micronesia where swidden agriculture was being practiced, secondary forest usually replaced virgin forest. On Moala Island in Fiji, however, where the lands around long-established villages were deforested as a result of swiddening, replacement was by a thick cover of reed[32]. Some plant and animal populations were undoubtedly eliminated or reduced through direct over-exploitation. This may have been the reason for moa extinction in New Zealand, although, as Sharp[33] suggests in a speculative reconstruction, rats and dogs may also have been responsible for the extinction of these birds. Certain shellfish, particularly the more accessible or more visible ones on reefs or close to shorelines, may have been brought to near extinction through overexploitation. Pertinent information on this should become available with the publication of the midden

analyses of recent archaeological excavations in Mangareva and in the Society and Hawaiian islands.

Some plants or animals were the victims of human activities directed against other plants or animals. The use of fire in connection with the hunting of wild fauna could destroy much natural vegetation, and Cumberland indicates that many acres of forests in New Zealand may have been eliminated in this manner in Moa-hunter times. A more recent example is available from tropical Polynesia. Some years ago, when Tahitians began to use fire for hunting pigs in the highlands, large portions of Tahitian uplands were burned. These areas are now covered by weeds largely of American origin, rather than by indigenous arboreal vegetation.

Man's activities sometimes provided new opportunities for certain indigenous species. Coconut groves planted by man were, for instance, an attractive habitat for a number of indigenous plants. Certain of these, such as morinda and pandanus, may so flourish under coconut trees as to threaten to choke out the plantations.[34]

Nonliving components of the ecosystems were also significantly affected by man. When sea-birds were frightened away by human settlements on coral atolls, the soils could no longer be replenished with the phosphate and nitrate contents of guano.[35] In modern times, additional phosphate has been lost from island ecosystems through the export of large quantities of phosphorous-rich copra.[36] In the Tahitian uplands, where human activities have recently affected a replacement of arboreal

---

32. Marshall Sahlins, "Land Use and the Extended Family in Moala, Fiji," *American Anthropologist*, Vol. 59 (1957), pp. 458-459.
33. Andrew Sharp, *op. cit.*, p. 136.

34. F. R. Fosberg, *op. cit.*, p. 11.
35. Ibid., p. 3; William Hatheway, *The Land Vegetation of Arno Atoll, Marshall Islands*, Atoll Research Bulletin 16. Washington, D.C.: National Research Council, 1953, p. 61.
36. F. R. Fosberg, *op cit.*, p. 11.

flora, the water-retaining capacity of the soil has been seriously impaired; streams that previously flowed all the time are now dry for part of the year.

IV

Man's introductions affected levels of productivity and the organization of biotic communities differently in each of the three kinds of Pacific island.[37]

The terrestrial systems of high islands were probably the most vulnerable to processes resulting in changed productivity and changed community organization. In general, these systems were extremely hospitable to most new organisms; and there was, no doubt, substantial change in the organization of some biotic communities simply concomitant to the introduction of new species. These introductions increased organic diversity, on the genus level at least, but it is improbable that in themselves they had an important effect upon the general productivity of the ecosystems. Much more important changes, particularly involving processes lowering productivity, could have resulted directly from human activities. Evidence of such processes in pre-European Polynesia and Micronesia are generally lacking, but in Melanesia such degradation is clear. In the latter area, indeed, Barrau[38] usually credits the formation of grassland,

scrub, savannah, and savannah woodland, at the expense of forest, to human activity: "In most areas, man is responsible for spreading these herbaceous formations, which have developed as a result of damage caused to the original vegetation by shifting agriculture or by burning for hunting purposes. Burning was also used in some places to facilitate foraging. . . ."

First, the replacement of forest by grassy cover affected the water supply. Barrau suggests[39] that the development of a definite dry season in large areas of Melanesia was a result of the replacement of arboreal by herbaceous formations. Such replacement of forest over hilly areas too limited in size to affect the rainfall regime might still reduce the effective water supply over larger regions. A recent case observed in Tahiti has been mentioned above, and elsewhere in this symposium Gourou notes a similar case in nineteenth century Mauritius. Second, the replacement of forest by other vegetation on slopes may have brought about soil erosion.

It is possible that the replacement of arboreal by herbaceous climaxes was not unknown in pre-European tropical Polynesian and Micronesian high islands. The lack of evidence, however, suggests that in those areas in which primary forests were removed, they were usually replaced by secondary forest rather than by nonarboreal covers. The productivity rates of these fast growing secondary forest formations were probably not at great variance with those prevailing in the primary forests and, further, the long-range tendency toward re-establishment of the original climax was not destroyed. It would seem that on the high islands of Micronesia and Melanesia serious degradation of the terrestrial ecosystems was not frequently or widely induced by human populations, despite their

---

37. "Basic of primary productivity of an ecological system, community, or any part thereof, is defined as the rate at which energy is stored by photosynthetic and chemosynthetic organisms (chiefly green plants) in the form of organic substances which can be used as food materials. . . . The rates of energy storage at consumer and decomposer trophic levels are referred to as secondary productivities." Eugene P. Odum, *Fundamentals of Ecology*. Philadelphia: Saunders (2nd ed.), 1959, p. 68.

38. Jacques Barrau, *Subsistence Agriculture in Melanesia*, B. P. Bishop Museum Bulletin 219. Honolulu: Bishop Museum Press, 1958, p. 19.

39. *Ibid.*, p. 25.

size and density, occupancy of one to three millenia, and removal of primary forest cover from large areas. This is in marked contrast to some larger and less densely populated regions in Melanesia.

The terrestrial systems of atolls were less vulnerable to change induced by pre-European man. While there was possibility of drastic reduction of productivity rates on high islands through the replacement of climax forest by scrub, weed, or grass, the agricultural possibilities presented by atolls precluded such extensive degradation. The cultivation of root crops on atolls was not only restricted to areas under which the water table was relatively low in salinity, but restricted to sites which had been pains-takingly modified by excavating and com-posting. The areas thus transformed were generally small, relative to total island size. Furthermore, it is probable that primary productivity in taro pits was higher than in any unmodified portion of the escosystem. Great emphasis on tree cultivation is largely recent; a response to the European demand for copra. Nevertheless, it can be assumed that on many atolls cultivated trees, particu-larly coconut and to a lesser extent bread-fruit, were significant in pre-European eco-systems. Tree cultivation necessitated at least partial replacement of indigenous arborescent forms, but trees were replaced by trees. Changes in community structures were, therefore, less profound than in those high islands on which trees were replaced by very different vegetations. Furthermore, since coconut groves sometimes sheltered a lower story of indigenous species such as pandanus and morinda, it is doubtful whether pre-European tree cultivation in itself served to lower levels of primary pro-ductivity. It must be noted, however, that cultivated trees were more vulnerable to drought than the indigenous varieties, and that during periods of water shortage

primary productivity must have decreased more markedly in cultivated groves than in areas of indigenous vegetation. Furthermore, the cultivation and consumption of coconut has induced depletion of phosphorus in atoll soils, contributing to long-run lowering of productivity. This has become serious on some atolls in recent times, but to what extent it was a problem in pre-European times is uncertain.

Atoll water supplies, while more pre-carious than those of high islands, were less vulnerable to damage by man. Derived mainly from a hydrostatic lens under a rela-tively flat surface they were generally un-affected by human activity.

Reef- lagoon ecosystems were least af-fected by human participation. Community structure and productivity rates probably always remained, as they still do, quite con-stant. There is no clear-cut evidence of either the introduction of new organisms into pristine reef-lagoon systems by man or of the complete elimination of any of the con-stituent species populations by man, al-though both may have occurred.[40] Quite possibly the numbers of certain species dropped drastically from time to time, and it is even possible that occasionally the total biomass of the faunal components of some communities was reduced significantly be-cause of human activities. Such events, how-ever, must have been of short duration, for the primary producers of the reef-lagoon community, in contrast to those of terres-trial systems, could hardly be affected by man. Essentially calcareous algae and zooxanthellae, these primary producers could not be utilized directly as food by

---

40. An exception to this may be pointed out in the Palmyra Island lagoon, where the ecological conditions and the biota were completely modified when free circulation of ocean water was cut off. See E. Y. Dawson, *Pacific Naturalist*, Vol. I (1959), No. 2, pp. 1-51.

man, nor could the space they occupied be turned by man to other uses. Therefore species or whole faunas which had been temporarily reduced could always find the nutriment with which to regenerate their numbers.

V

The kinds of communities emerging from interactions between pristine ecosystems and introduced elements, including man, may be broadly categorized according to man's place in them. On the reef, in the lagoon, and in the sea there continued to be relatively un- modified communities, composed of generally the same elements in generally the same relationships as those that obtained prior to man's arrival. The ecological niche or niches exploited by human populations belonging to such communities depended mainly upon the biotic elements present before the advent of man; the presence, location, and quantity of these elements were subject to little or no control by human beings.

Within Pacific island terrestrial eco- systems, there emerged rather different kinds of biotic communities, which may be designated as "anthropocentric." In such communities, both the presence of the main biotic elements, particularly the primary producers, and the decisive relationships among them depended upon the ecological niches that human beings had arranged for themselves according to their criteria of self-interest. The nature and composition of the communities were the result of attempts by human populations to construct and dominate simplified ecosystems consisting of short food chains.

These anthropocentric communities were delicate. Because they usually did not ex- tend over all of a locality in which similar climatic and edaphic conditions prevailed, the territory of anthropocentric com-

munities might be subject to reconquest by the unmodified biota at community borders. Within the anthropocentric communities were weeds and animal pests that threatened either to subvert the entire communities or, at least, to divert substantial organic matter from food chains leading to man. Moreover, the perpetuation of the anthropocentric communities depended upon the continuing presence of a large class of things not within the "cognized" environment of the human population; nitrogen-fixing bacteria and trace elements, for example. The functional requisites of even known elements were not necessarily clearly understood and might at times fail to be provided by appropriate human action. Thus the disruption of anthropocentric communities might come about through too great a difference be- tween the structures of the cognized and the operational environments.

Human intraspecies competition placed anthropocentric communities in jeopardy. During warfare the human population might be unable to burn the bush or to plant cultigens at the proper times, and enemy plantations might be deliberately destroyed. This is said to have been true of the native wars of such Polynesian high islands as Tahiti, Hawaii, Samoa, and Mangaia.[41] Regarding Tuamotuan coral atolls, Lucett[42] wrote in the middle of the nineteenth cen- tury that warriors from the island of Anaa "some years ago . . . overran nearly every island in the group . . . rooting up and de- stroying every cocoa-nut tree standing,

41. A. P. Vayda, "Maori Warfare," unpublished Ph.D. dissertation, Columbia University, New York, 1956, p. 240; Robert W. Williamson, *Essays in Polynesian Ethnology*, Ralph Piddington, editor. Cambridge: Cambridge University Press, 1939, pp. 36-38.
42. Edward Lucett, *Rovings in the Pacific, from 1837 to 1849*. London: Longmans, Brown, Green, and Longmans, 1851, p. 260.

which accounts for their scarcity at the other islands."

VI

I have already noted that the perpetuation of the anthropocentric community depended upon a degree of control[43] by humans over the presence, location, and quantity of the principal biotic elements. The biotic elements of the relatively unmodified communities of the reef, lagoon, and sea were subject, for the most part, to man's control only after they had been removed from their habitats and converted into economic goods, but the essential elements of the anthropocentric communities could be and were controlled while still in their habitats. Concomitant to these differences in controllability are certain differences in possibilities for human social organization. While in both kinds of communities there could be large social units for the *distribution* of economic goods, it seems to me that in the Pacific in anthropocentric communities only were continuing permanent social units needed and that there could be large-scale and elaborate units for *production* and extraction as well.

Among anthropocentric communities themselves there were contrasts in the factors limiting human populations which also may have had significance for human social organization. On the atolls, food yields derived from anthropocentric communities were particularly vulnerable to reduction by natural events, such as tsunamis, typhoons, and droughts. They therefore fluctuated uncontrollably, unpredictably, and sometimes disastrously. On the

high islands, the food yields derived from anthropocentric communities were much less subject to reduction by catastrophe, but were more vulnerable to decline from general degradation of the ecosystems brought about by human activity. Since such degradations are not widely evidenced in pre-European tropical Polynesia and Micronesia, there is reason to believe that high island populations in these areas were limited by finite but stable food resources. It may be that the relatively large-scale production, extraction, and distribution organizations found on these islands served to protect the inherently unstable ecosystems from the kind of degradation observed in Melanesia, where no such large-scale organizations occurred. I suggest further that these large-scale, stratified, and sometimes centralized organizations were, in fact, a managerial development in response to the need of large and perhaps expanding populations to derive stable or increasing food supplies from the anthropocentric communities of spatially limited ecosystems in which man's activities could easily induce degradation.

On the other hand the uncontrollable and unpredictable fluctuations in the food yields of atoll anthropocentric communities were not amenable to amelioration by any degree of management. This, combined with the generally greater reliance upon foods derived from the uncontrollable reef-lagoon system, may be an important reason for the general absence of such large-scale production and extraction organizations from atolls.

An attempt has been made to view human populations as neither more nor less than populations of a generalized and flexible species, for in the most fundamental respects man hardly differs from other animals. His populations participate in ecosystems, as do the populations of other species; they occupy particular positions in food webs as do others; and they are limited

---

43. For our purposes, a degree of control is present when sufficient of the elements in an event, series of events, or process can be manipulated to such an extent that there is a better than chance opportunity to achieve a predicted result.

by factors little different from those that limit others. Man is sometimes able to devise and control biotic communities, but when he does he becomes bound by the demands of his own living invention. In the detail of man's commitment to, and participation in, the biotic communities in which he has his being there is much to illuminate his social and political organization. The study of man, the culture bearer, cannot be separated from the study of man, a species among other species.

✠✠✠✠✠✠✠✠✠✠✠✠✠✠✠✠✠✠✠✠✠✠✠✠✠✠✠✠

SYSTEMS APPROACH TO A THEORY OF RURAL-URBAN MIGRATION

Akin L. Mabogunje

In the growing literature on the study of migration, two theoretical issues have attracted the greatest attention, namely, why people migrate and how far they move. A simple model for explaining the reasons why people move has been formulated in terms of the "pull-push" hypothesis.[1] This has been elaborated variously to take account of internal migration movements of the rural-rural, rural-urban, or urban-urban types and international migrations. The issue of how far people move has, in turn, given rise to the formulation of a surprisingly large number of models of varying degrees of statistical or mathematical sophistication. In most of these models the distance covered is treated as either the sole independent variable or as one of many independent variables explaining the number of migrants moving to particular destinations. Morrill[2] has provided a valuable summary of these models and suggests that they can be classified broadly into deterministic and probabilistic models.

Most of these theoretical formulations have been applied to conditions in the developed countries of the world and especially to urban-to-urban migrations. Their relevance for handling migratory movements from rural to urban areas and particularly in the circumstances of underdeveloped countries has hardly been considered. Yet, it is these areas of the world where rural-urban migrations are presently taking place that afford the best opportunity for testing theoretical notions about this class of movements.

It is suggested that Africa in particular, is a unique area from which to draw important empirical evidence about this type of movements. Similarly valuable data, however, can also be derived from examining the history of some of the advanced countries of the

1. R. Herberle, "The Causes of Rural-Urban Migration: a Survey of German Theories," *American Journal of Sociology*, 43 (1938), pp. 932-950; J. C. Mitchell, "Migrant Labour in Africa South of the Sahara: the Causes of Labour Migration," *Bulletin of the Inter-African Labour Institute*, 6 (1959), pp. 8–46.

2. R. L. Morrill, "Migration and the Spread and Growth of Urban Settlement," *Lund Studies in Geography*, Ser. B, 26 (1965).

From *Geographical Analysis*, Vol. 2 (1970), pp. 1-18. Copyright ©1970 by the Ohio State University Press. All rights reserved. Reprinted by permission.

world. It is, of course, true that in Africa attention to date has been focussed to a disproportionate extent on seasonal and other non-permanent transfers of population from rural to urban areas, that is, on what has been referred to as a "constant circulatory movement" between the two areas.[3] But, it will be shown that this type of movement represents a very special case of rural-urban migration. To make the point clear, it is necessary to offer a definition of the latter. Essentially, rural-urban migration represents a basic transformation of the nodal structure of a society in which people move from generally smaller, mainly agricultural communities to larger, mainly non-agricultural communities. Apart from this spatial (or horizontal) dimension of the movement, there is also a socioeconomic (or vertical) dimension involving a permanent transformation of skills, attitudes, motivations, and behavior patterns such that a migrant is enabled to break completely with his rural background and become entirely committed to urban existence. A permanence of transfer is thus the essence of the movement.

Rural-urban migration also represents an essentially spatial concomitant of the economic development of a region. Indeed, it has been suggested that one of the basic goals of economic development is to reverse the situation wherein 85 per cent of the population is in agriculture and lives in rural areas while only about 15 per cent is in non-agricultural activities and lives in the cities.[4] Rural-urban migration represents the spatial flow component of such a reversal. It

is a complex phenomenon which involves not only the migrants but also a number of institutional agencies, and it gives rise to significant and highly varied adjustments everywhere in a region.

It can be urgued with a great deal of justification that few of the theoretical models provided so far have considered migrations, especially rural-urban migration, as a spatial process whose dynamics and spatial impact must form part of any comprehensive understanding of the phenomenon. It is the main contention of this paper that such an understanding can best be achieved within the framework of General Systems Theory.[5] This approach demands that a particular complex of variables be recognized as a system possessing certain properties which are common to many other systems. It has the fundamental advantage of providing a conceptual framework within which a whole range of questions relevant to an understanding of the structure and operation of other systems can be asked of the particular phenomenon under study. In this way, new insights are provided into old problems and new relationships whose existence may not have been appreciated previously are uncovered. In this paper no attempt is made to define major components and relationships in a formal, mathematical manner. The emphasis here is on a verbal analysis of the ways in which the system operates. This, it is hoped, will enable us to identify areas where present knowledge is fragmentary and where future research may be concentrated with some profit.

---

3. J. C. Mitchell, "Wage Labour and African Population Movements in Central Africa," in *Essays on African Population*, ed. K. M. Barbour and R. M. Prothero. New York, 1962. p. 232.
4. W. A. Lewis, *Theory of Economic Growth.* London, 1955. p. 333.

5. L. von Bertalanffy, "An Outline of General System Theory," *British Journal of the Philosophy of Science* 1 (1950), pp. 134-165; ———. "General System Theory," *General Systems Yearbook*, 1 (1956), pp. 1-10; ———. "General System Theory—a Critical Review," *General Systems Yearbook*, 7 (1962), pp. 1-20.

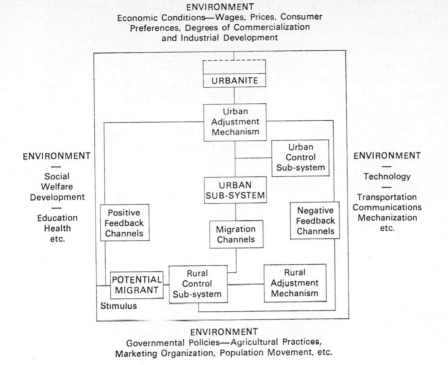

Figure 1. A system schema for a theory of rural-urban migration.

Defining the System of Rural-Urban Migration

A system may be defined as a complex of interacting elements, together with their attributes and relationships.[6] One of the major tasks in conceptualizing a phenomenon as a system, therefore, is to identify the basic interacting elements, their attributes, and their relationships. Once this is done, it soon becomes obvious that the system operates not in a void but in a special environment. For any given system, this environment comprises "the set of all objects a change in whose attributes affects the system, and also those objects whose attributes are changed by the behaviour of the

system."[7] Thus, a system with its environment constitutes the universe of phenomena which is of interest in a given context.

Figure 1 indicates the basic elements in the rural-urban migration system as well as the environment within which the system operates. It shows that a systems approach to rural-urban migration is concerned not only with why people migrate but with all the implications and ramifications of the process. Basically, the approach is designed to answer questions such as: why and how does an essentially rural individual become a permanent city dweller? What changes does he undergo in the process? What effects have these changes both on the rural area from which he comes and on the city to which he moves? Are there situations or institutions

---

6. A. D. Hall and R. E. Fagen, "Definition of System," *General Systems Yearbook*, 1 (1956), p. 18.

7. A. D. Hall, and R. E. Fagen, *op. cit.*, p. 20.

which encourage or discourage the rate of movement between the rural area and the city? What is the general pattern of these movements, and how is this determined? These, and other such questions, define the problems for which we require a theory of rural-urban migration.

It can be shown theoretically that areas with isolated and self-sufficient villages such as were found in many parts of Africa until recently, are not likely to experience rural-urban migration, since, in any case there would be hardly any cities in such areas. The fact that today such movements characterize many parts of the continent and are lately assuming spectacular proportions means that rural areas are in general no longer isolated or self-sufficient. It is therefore relevant to ask: what forces have contributed and continue to contribute to the decline in these conditions of isolation and self-sufficiency in the rural areas? They are, in the main, forces set in motion by increasing economic development. In most African countries, this was brought about initially by the colonial administrations and further reinforced in recent years by the activities of the new African governments. Decreasing isolation means not only improvement in transportation and communication links but also greater integration of the rural economy into a national economy. Such integration makes the rural economy more responsive to changes in wages and prices, consumer preferences, and the overall demand pattern within the country. It also subjects it to a wide range of governmental legislations or official policies over which, in many cases, the rural community has little or no control. Decreasing isolation also means greater social and cultural integration of rural and urban areas such that levels of expectations in both areas begin to converge towards a recognizable national norm of what is the "good life." The breakdown of isolation brings the rural areas within the orbit of one or more urban centers and sharpens the awareness and desire of villagers for the ever increasing range of goods and services which the urban centers have to offer. To acquire these, the villagers have to produce more agricultural goods and enter into an exchange relation with the city. Alternatively, they may move into the city to sell their labor direct in exchange for wages with which to buy goods and services.

This then is the environment within which the system of migration from rural to urban areas operates. This is the environment which stimulates the villager to desire change in the basic locale and rationale of his economic activities and which, in consequence, determines the volume, characteristics, and importance of rural-urban migration. Moreover, it is an environment which is constantly changing, and these changes affect the operation of the system. Hence, for any theory of rural-urban migration to be of value it must take into account this dynamic aspect of the problem.

The basic elements in the system of migration are shown in Figure 1. It identifies first the potential migrant who is being encouraged to migrate by stimuli from the environment. Few studies have concerned themselves with the universe of potential migrants. More often, the tendency has been to study only those who successfully made the move. Even for these, attention is given mainly to classificatory characteristics such as age, sex, religion, education, and ethnic or racial origin rather than to an analysis or understanding of the background to their move.[8] There is, of course, no doubt that what this variety of information is meant to indicate is the pattern of distribution of the

8. A. Diop, "Enquête sur la migration toucouleur à Dakar," *Bulletin de l'Institut Français d'Afrique Noire, Ser. B,* 22 (1960), pp. 393-418.

"propensity to migrate" within the rural population. But this is neither explicitly stated nor formulated. Moreover, an equally valuable concept which this variety of information might have been used to explore is that of "migration elasticity."[9] This relates not so much to the propensity to migrate but to how long impulses or stimuli from the environment must be transmitted to a potential migrant before he makes the desired move.

Within the systems framework, attention is focussed not only on the migrant but also on the various institutions (sub-systems) and the social, economic, and other relationships (adjustment mechanisms) which are an integral part of the process of the migrant's transformation. The two most important sub-systems are the rural and the urban control sub-systems. A control sub-system is one which oversees the operation of the general system and determines when and how to increase or decrease the amount of flow in the system. A simple example is provided by the thermostat which controls the amount of heat that flows within a given   área. If we accept the existence of control sub-systems in this type of migration movement, the problem then is to identify which institutions operate in this manner both in the rural and the urban areas.

In the rural areas, a true control sub-system would, of course, be the family, both nuclear and extended. In the first place, it is the family that holds back potential migrants until they are old enough to under take the move. Even when they are of an age to move, the family still acts as a control sub-system in many ways. In some places, it enables members of both sexes to move out; in others, members of one sex tend to get away more easily than those of the other. Where the potential migrant is marrried, the issue of whether he can move alone or with his wife and children may depend on the customary role of the sexes in agricultural activities, the age at which marriage is encouraged, and the circumstances and age at which a young man may expect to be economically independent of his parents. More important as a control mechanism is the relation of family members to the family land, especially as this relation is expressed through the lineage system and the inheritance law. An inheritance law that encourages most of the land to go into the hands of the first child (the primogeniture rule) will tend to stimulate more migration of the other children[10] compared to one based on the equality of access (partible inheritance rule) by all the children. In either case, the size of the farmland, the nature of the major agricultural products, and the prevailing prices for these would also be of decisive significance.

Apart from the family, the village community itself may act as a control sub-system. Its controlling role is not often direct but is obvious in either a positive or negative way in the various activities which it sponsors or encourages. Thus, a village community which attempts to improve its economic conditions, for instance, through co-operative farming or marketing, may discourage, at least in the short-run, permanent migration. On the other hand, a village community which puts emphasis on social betterment, for example, through education, may inadvertently stimulate migration to the city through training the younger generation to be more enlightened and more highly motivated. A pertinent aspect of the study of rural-urban migration is thus to assess how

9. J. Wolpert, "Migration as an Adjustment to Environmental Stress," *Journal of Social Issues*, 22 (1966), pp. 92-102.

10. C. M. Arensberg, *The Irish Countryman, an Anthropological Study*. New York, 1937.

different rural communities react to migration away from the village. Such assessment should involve more than the opinion survey of the older generations. It should include an investigation of village activities and administration, and of the degree of cohesiveness in the community.

The urban control sub-system operates at the opposite end of the migrant's trajectory to encourage or discourage his being absorbed into the urban environment. Absorption at this level is of two kinds: residential and occupational. Basically, the control sub-system here can be identified with the city administration and other employment agencies operating under national laws and statutes. The city administration can ensure availability of relatively cheap and adequate housing in quantities which could make the transition of the rural migrant either difficult or easy. Apart from housing, the activities of the city administration in providing reception centers as well as various amenities and services may be a vital factor in gradually inducing a migrant to commit himself to the urban way of life.

A major factor in this commitment is, of course, the securing of an employment. In the city, there are numerous employment agencies offering, at any one time, very limited opportunities for the migrant. A pressing problem in the control sub-system is how to bring together and make known these disparate, but sometimes impressive, lists of vacancies. In some urban communities, this function of collation is left entirely to the press and their advertising columns. In others, a labor exchange is provided. The effectiveness with which these organizations function can be crucial for the inflow of migrants. However, once the migrant has secured an employment, a number of other factors determine his final commitment. Among these are: the type of job he secures, whether seasonal or permanent, the oppor-

tunity the job offers for improvement in his skill and for advancement in his status, the provisions available for security against the normal hazards of industrial life, and his eventual retirement due to old age.

At both the village and the city level, the decision of the migrant to move from or to move into the community sets in motion a series of adjustments. With regard to the village community, the mechanism for these adjustments should operate in such a way as to lead to an increase in the *per capita* income of the community. At least theoretically, the loss of one of the productive units in the village should lead to an increase of the productive capacity available to the remaining units; otherwise such losses from the rural area would eventually lead to a significant drop in agricultural production, to food shortage, and to famine. That these do not occur in many places means that some adjustments do take place to maintain aggregate productivity from these areas. The Ardeners[11] in their study of the Hsu of the Cameroons, for instance, point out that, in spite of the fact that as much as 40 per cent of the adult male population in the village was absent, food production did not show any significant drop. Studies of other communities in Africa have indicated similar observations.[12] However, what is involved in the adjustment to rural-urban migration is more than the minor arrangements by which the farmlands belonging to seasonal or short-term migrants are tended in their absence by their wives, their friends or other members of their families. What is involved here are the ways and methods by which rural communities permit migrants to re-

11. E. Ardener, Shirley Ardener, and W. A. Warmington. *Plantation and Village in the Cameroons.* London, 1960. pp. 211-229.
12. R. M. Prothero, "Migratory Labour from North-Western Nigeria," *Africa,* 27 (1957), p. 250.

nounce partially or wholly their rights to productive resources in the rural areas.

One of the major research frontiers in rural-urban migration studies is the understanding of how this renunciation is accomplished. In Africa, for instance, such renunciation must be seen against the background of a complex land tenure situation and the fact that sale of land is regarded as basically a foreign concept. There is some evidence that one of the implications of rural-urban migration is to encourage a growing individualization of land-holding (with or without enclosuring) and a disposition to treat land as a marketable commodity. In the Eastern Region of Nigeria, for instance, rural-urban migration has been leading to a new pattern of land distribution and ownership. This is especially so in those areas not too far from the major urban centers.[13] It would appear, however, that initially it is the usufruct (or right to beneficial usage) on the land and not ownership that is regarded as negotiable. As a result, leasehold or annual rental of agricultural land has become widespread in many parts of West Africa and serves as a means of re-allocating land which would otherwise remain unutilized because its owners have migrated to the cities. In some other cases, it is the right to exploit tree crops such as the oil-palm, cocoa, or rubber that is exchanged for monetary considerations either by outright payment or by share-cropping arrangement. In all cases, the effect of the renunciation of the migrant's claims on land or other resources is to enable some members of the village community to increase their net income by the expenditure of their often under-utilized labor. The more

complete the renunciation by the migrant, the greater the acceptance of the idea of outright sale or alienation of land. Renunciation, by providing increased capacity in land or other resources, also encourages attempts at production for a market, diversification of crop production on individual farms, and a reduction in the subsistence sector of the village economy.

Sometimes, however, this process of adjustment is induced by government and has the effect of widely stimulating migration from the rural areas. This was in fact, what happened in Britain in the 18th and 19th centuries with the various Enclosure Acts. In Africa, especially in East and Central Africa, the same process can be witnessed today. Thus, in Rhodesia, the Native Land Husbandry Act of 1951 individualized agricultural holdings and occasioned the loss by many farmers of their right to cultivate former family land. This disenfranchisement, as was only to be expected, gave rise to a flood of migrants most of whom had no alternative but to become permanently committed to wage employment and psychologically attuned to surviving in an urban environment.

In the urban areas, the mechanism of adjustment is basically one of incorporating the migrant into a new frame of reference more relevant to his needs in the city. In this respect, a city can be described as an assemblage of interacting interest groups. Part of the process of becoming a member of such a community would thus be to identify closely with one or more of these groups. The mechanism of incorporation in the urban areas, in contrast to the adjustment process in the rural areas, has been the subject of a number of studies. In particular, attention has been called to the role of ethnic unions and various voluntary organizations such as the church, trade unions, occupational associations, and recreation societies in helping

---

13. N. I. Ndukwe, "Migration, Agriculture and Trade in Abriba Town." Unpublished Mss., Department of Geography, University of Ibadan, 1964; A. I. Onwueke, "Awka Upland Region, the Land of Migrant Farmers." Unpublished Mss., Department of Geography, University of Ibadan, 1966.

the rural migrant to adjust to his new environment.[14]

Finally, of the various elements of the system, there is the city *qua* city, seen as part of an urban sub-system. What aspects of urban life and activities are relevant for the understanding of rural-urban migration? To answer this question, it is important to visualize the city as comprising a hierachy of specializations. In other words, a city is a place where everyone is trying to sell specialized skill. The more specialized the skill, the greater the demand for it, and hence the higher the price it commands on the market. Within this conceptual framework, the illiterate, unsophisticated rural migrant is seen as belonging to the lowest level of the hierachy. A corollary is that the higher a person moves up within the hierachy, the greater his commitment to the urban way of life and the less the probability of his reversion to rural existence. This is one reason why the type of job which a rural migrant secures in the city can be so crucial to how soon he becomes committed to urban life. This is also one reason why those countries, such as Rhodesia, which are anxious to ensure that the African does not become an urban resident, pursue a discriminatory policy with regard to his acquistion of skill in urban employment. Yet, as Masser pointed out, even in Rhodesia the propensity to return to the village after migrating to the city decreases with the minimal rise in the skill of the migrant.[15]

---

14. M. Banton, *West African City*. London, 1957;————. "Social Alignment and Identity in a West African City," in *Urbanization and Migration in West Africa*, ed. Hilda Kuper. Los Angeles, 1956, pp. 131-147; K. Little, *West African Urbanization*. London, 1965.
15. F. I. Masser, "Changing Pattern of African Employment in Southern Rhodesia," in *Geographers and the Tropics: Liverpool Essays*, ed. R. W. Steel and R. M. Prothero. London, 1964. p. 229.

Another interesting aspect of this concept of the city is that upward mobility within the hierarchy of specializations is often accompanied by changes in residential location within the city. This is no doubt a function of rising income, but is is also closely related to the length of stay in the city and the increasing commitment of a migrant to spend the remaining part of his working life there. There have been many studies of the residential pattern and varying length of stay of migrants in urban areas. Unfortunately, a good number of these studies have been concerned more with indicating the ethnic basis of this pattern than with investigating the dynamic factor of skill differentiation and status advancement which is operating to blur out the importance of ethnicity. As a result, this rather crucial dimension of rural-urban migration has tended to be neglected. Its investigation should yield some rather interesting results.

One final aspect of the examination of cities as a hierarchy of specializations relates to the significance of size. What effect has the size of a city on the type of migrants attracted to it? Clearly, small urban centers have fewer tiers of specializations and more restricted employment opportunities than the larger ones. Yet, competition for positions in them may be less intense. Are certain types of migrants attracted to such centers first and then able to "leap-frog" gradually to bigger and bigger centers? What type of migrants would make direct for the larger cities? Does rural-urban migration into the larger cities take place in the manner of "a series of concentric migratory contractions" suggested by Ashton[16] for Britain in the 18th century? According to Ashton, the larger industrial centers attracted a number

---

16. T. S. Ashton, *An Economic History of England: The Eighteenth Century*. London, 1966 ed., pp. 15-17.

of workers and their families who were living in the larger market towns on their perimeters. These towns in turn made good their losses from the surrounding villages, the villages from the hamlets, and the hamlets from the farms. In this way, there was no sharp discontinuity in the pattern of life with which the migrant was familiar. Are there conditions, for instance, the nature of the transportation network and development, which would make such a pattern of migration appropriate for Britain of the 18th century but not for Africa in the 20th century? Or, does this pattern reflect stable human reaction to a permanent spatial dislocation of existing networks of social contacts?

The Energy Concept in Systems Analysis

A system comprises not only matter (the migrant, the institutions, and the various organizations mentioned) but also energy. In the physical sense, energy is simply the capacity of a given body to do work. It can be expressed in a number of ways, but two forms of it are relevant here. There is "potential energy" which is the body's power of doing work by virtue of stresses resulting from its relation either with its environment or with other bodies. The second form is "kinetic energy" which is the capacity of a body to do work by virtue of its own motion or activity.

In a theory of rural-urban migration, potential energy can be likened to the stimuli acting on the rural individual to move. What is the nature of these stimuli? As pointed out earlier, a number of studies have tried to identify why people migrate and have come up with a variety of answers generally subsumed under the push-and-pull hypothesis. This suggests that people migrate from rural areas to the cities because of one of two general causes: overpopulation and

environmental deterioration in the rural areas (the push factor) or the allurement or attraction of the city (the pull factor or the so-called "bright-light theory"). The push factor, it is claimed, explains migrations directed to earning extra income to pay the annual tax or to take a new bride or to buy a few manufactured articles or to escape oppressive local mores. The pull factor, on the other hand, explains migrations undertaken as a modern form of initiation ceremony to adult status or as the basis for later receiving preferential admiration of the village girls or as the product simply of an intense curiosity about the city.

These explanations, to the extent that they have any theoretical validity at all, are relevant only at the aggregate level. These are notwithstanding the results from completed questionnaire surveys requiring individuals to indicate the reason or reasons for their migration into the city. But, as Richards[17] and Gulliver[18] stress, the battery of questions usually asked of migrants hardly ever reveals anything about why they moved. In Africa, the great number of temporary migrants to the cities on whom most studies have been concentrated, are involved in making no major decisions other than on the length of time they can or have to be away from home. The reasons for their migration are very often manifold and usually not easy to articulate in a few, simple sentences. What the questionnaire does, in fact, is to suggest to the migrant a set of equally plausible reasons, besides the obvious one of coming to earn extra income.

Within the systems framework, the explanation of why people migrate must be in terms of differential individual responses to

17. A. I. Richards, ed., *Economic Development and Tribal Change.* Cambridge, 1954. p. 66.
18. P. Gulliver, "Nyakyusa Labour Migration," *Rhodes-Livingstone Journal*, 21 (1957), p. 59.

the stimuli both from the environment and from within the system. It differs from the pull-and-push hypothesis in putting the emphasis at the individual level, not on why people migrate from particular areas but why any person from any village would want to migrate to the city. The stimulus to migrate is related to the extent of the integration of rural activities into the national economy, to the degree of awareness of opportunities outside of the rural areas, and to the nature of the social and economic expectations held by the rural population not only for themselves but also for their children. Indeed, the notion of "expectations" or "aspirations" is central to an understanding of the ways in which the stimulus from the environment is transmitted to individuals, and for that reason it is a crucial variable in the theory of rural-urban migration. What determines the variation in the level of individual expectations in rural areas and conditions individual responses to the stimulus to migrate? Clearly, for a given cohort in any rural area, one can, at least theoretically, conceive of individuals who respond promptly to the stimulus and others who take a much longer time to respond. One may in fact ask whether there is a threshold below which the stimulus cannot be expected to act and an upper limit beyond which its impact is no longer felt? How are these limits defined—by age, wealth, natural alertness, or family position? In short, two problems in the theory of rural-urban migration which still require resolution concern the nature and significance of rural expectations and their relation to the differential effectiveness of the stimulus to migrate.

Once an individual has been successfully dislodged from the rural area, we can assume that he is translating his "potential energy" into its "kinetic form." The major issues concern not only the act of moving but also the cost, the distance, and the direction of movement. These three variables clearly determine the crisscross channels of migration as well as their destinations. Again, as already indicated, this aspect of migration studies has received considerable theoretical attention. Starting with Ravenstein's laws of migration[19] which try to establish the relation between distance and the propensity to move, there have been various attempts to seek understanding through using the gravity model,[20] and the intervening opportunities model.[21] There have also been other studies which have tried to understand the pattern of migration channels through probabilistic models.[22]

As soon as a migrant has moved from the rural to the urban area, his role in the system is greatly amplified. Basic to an understanding of this amplified role is the concept of "information," a central notion in the theory of communications. Information can be defined simply as bits of messages in a system which lead to a particular set of actions. Thus, one can easily assume that the first migrant from a village to a city would soon start to transmit back to the village information about his reception and progress in the city. Ignoring for the moment the question of "information content," it can be shown that the level of information can be

19. E. G. Ravenstein, "The Laws of Migration," *Journal of the Royal Statistical Society*, 48 (1885), pp. 167-235; 52 (1889), pp. 242-305.
20. S. C. Dodd, "The Interactance Hypothesis: A Gravity Model Fitting Physical Masses and Human Groups," *American Sociological Review*, 15 (1950), pp. 245-256; J. W. Stewart, "Demographic Gravitation: Evidence and Applications," *Sociometry*, 11 (1948), pp. 31-57.
21. S. A. Stouffer, "Intervening Opportunities: A Theory Relating Mobility and Distance," *American Sociological Review*, 5 (1940), pp. 845-67; ———. "Intervening Opportunities and Competing Migrants," *Journal of Regional Science*, 2 (1960), pp. 1-26.
22. G. Kulldorf, "Migration Probabilities," *Lund Studies in Geography*, Ser. B, 14 (1955).

measured in terms of decisions.[23] A particular set of decisions can be compared with the random choice from a universe of equally probable decisions. Its deviation from the latter becomes a measure of the level of information. It also represents a statement of the level of order or organization existing within the system. Information is thus a crucial feature of the operation of a system since it determines at any point of time the state of organization of the system.

Of equal importance is the notion of "feedback" which has been the focus of the field of Cybernetics. This can be explained quite simply in terms of stimulus-response behavior. A stimulus affects a receptor which communicates this message to some controlling apparatus and from this to an effector which gives the response. In feedback, the effector's activity is monitored back to the receptor with the result that the system's behavior is in some way modified by the information. The feedback process can have one of two effects. It can further amplify the deviation (in this case by stimulating further migration), or it may counteract the deviation by encouraging a return to the initial situation. Deviation-amplifying feedbacks are regarded as positive; deviation-counteracting feedbacks as negative.

The notion of a "most probable or random state" is one that needs further clarification. Imagine a situation in which migrants from a village are lost to their communities as soon as they move out and send back no information on their reactions to the cities to which they moved. Later migrants then, not knowing where the first set of migrants went to might choose any city in the system, almost in a random manner. Over time, the distribution of migrants from individual villages may come to approximate a situation in which the number of migrants from any village to a city is proportional to the size of that city. This is the most probable state in which no order or organization is evident in the system. Conceptually, it can be seen as a state of maximum disorder, or a state of maximum "entropy."

Yet, the general experience is that migrants are never lost in this sense to their village or origin but continue to send back information. If the information from a particular city dwells at length on the negative side of urban life, on the difficulties of getting jobs, of finding a place to live, and on the general hostility of people, the effect of this negative feedback will slow down further migration from the village to this city. By contrast, favorable or positive feedback will encourage migration and will produce situations of almost organized migratory flows from particular villages to particular cities. In other words, the existence of information in the system encourages greater deviation from the "most probable or random state." It implies a decrease in the level of entropy (or disorder) or an increase in negative entropy (negentropy). The result is greater differentiation in the pattern of migration which reflects some form of organization. Thus, experience of rural-urban migration in many parts of the world emphasizes this organized nature of the moves. In many North African cities, for instance, it is not uncommon for an entire district or craft occupation in a city to be dominated by permanent migrants from one or two villages.[24] Furthermore, this element of "organization" resulting from the operation of feedback in the system underlies the varying rate of population growth among cities.

---

23. L. von Bertalanffy, *op. cit.*

24. J. I. Clarke, "Emigration from Southern Tunisia," *Geography*, 42 (1957), pp. 99-101; G. Marty, "A Tunis: éléments allogènes et activités professionnelles," *Revue de l'Institut des Belles Lettres Arabes*, Tunis (1948), pp. 159-188.

A major area of research into rural-urban migration thus concerns the flow of information between the urban and the rural areas. Considerable work on this question has been undertaken in Europe and the United States and some of the results are of great interest. Hägerstrand, for instance, insists that we must distinguish between "active" and "passive" migrants.[25] The former are those who seek out suitable destinations which, in their eyes, guarantee future prosperity; the latter are those who follow impulses (feedbacks) emanating from persons of their acquaintance, primarily those who had made "fortunate" moves. One implication of this distinction is that in a theory of rural-urban migration, the crucial moves which we need to understand and explain are those of the active migrants. In the aggregate, these moves are likely to be complex and not easily explained in terms of a few choice variables.

A number of other studies have concentrated on the measurement of the information field of a potential migrant as a means of understanding the general pattern of his behavior in space.[26] Individual information fields may be aggregated to produce community mean information fields, and these have been used in studies which attempt to predict the volume and pattern of migratory movements.[27]

25. T. Hägerstrand, "Migration and Area: Survey of a Sample of Swedish Migration Fields and Hypothetical Considerations on their Genesis," in "Migration in Sweden, a Symposium," ed. D. Hannerberg et al., *Lund Studies in Geography, Ser. B*, 13 (1957), p. 132.
26. D. F. Marble, and J. D. Nystuen, "An Approach to the Direct Measurement of Community Mean Information Fields," *Papers and Proceedings, Regional Science Association*, 11 (1962), pp. 99-109; R. L. Morrill, and F. R. Pitts, "Marriage, Migration and the Mean Information Field: a Study in Uniqueness and Generality." *Annals of the Association of American Geographers*, 57 (1967), pp. 401-422.
27. R. L. Morrill, *op. cit.*

Relation Between a System and Its Environment

Systems can be classified into three categories depending on the relationship they maintain with their environment; first, the isolated systems which exchange neither "matter" nor "energy" with their environment; second, the closed systems which exchange "energy" but not "matter"; third, the open systems which exchange both "energy" and "matter." The distinction between the categories, however, is largely one of scale and depends on which elements are regarded as belonging to the system and which to the environment. Thus, if the scale was to be reduced significantly, an open system could become an isolated system.

Given the system in Figure 1, it can be seen that rural-urban migration is an open system involving not only an exchange of energy but also of matter (in this case, persons) with the environment. The persons concerned would be defined as all those, who having migrated into cities, have become involved in making local decisions or formulating national policies and legislations on economic and other matters which do affect the volume, character, and pattern of migration. The energy exchange has to do with the increasing economic activities resulting from rural-urban migration and affecting the overall economic and social conditions of the country.

One major implication of viewing rural-urban migration as an open system is the fact that it enables us to explore the principle of equifinality in so far as it applies to this phenomenon. This principle emphasizes that the state of a system at any given time is not determined so much by initial conditions as by the nature of the process, or the system parameters. In consequence, the same results may spring from different origins or, conversely, different results may be produced by the same "causes." In either case, it is the nature of the process which is determinate, since open systems are basically independent of their initial conditions. This principle is of considerable importance in studying rural-urban migration in different parts of the world since there has been a tendency to regard this movement in countries such as in Africa and Asia as a special kind different from elsewhere in the world. There is, of course, no doubt that initial conditions in Africa today are vastly different from what they were in countries such as Britain and the United States at the times of the massive migrations there of people from the rural areas into the cities. But, according to the principle of equifinality, as long as we keep in mind the particular system's parameters, an understanding of the migration process as it affected and continues to affect those developed countries may throw considerable light on what is currently happening in many parts of the underdeveloped world.

Growth Process in the System

From what has been said so far, it must be assumed that one of the concomitants of the continued interaction between the system and its environment will be the phenomenon of growth in the system. This will be indicated by, among other things, a rise in the volume of migration from the rural to the urban areas. Within a system framework, this phenomenon involves more than a simple growth or increase in the number of people moving from one area to another. It is much more complex, involving not only the individual components of the system but also the interaction between them and the system as a whole.

Boulding[28] has indentified three types of growth processes that may occur in a system. The first is "simple growth" and in-

volves the addition of one more unit of a given variable such as a migrant, a farm, a vehicle, or a retail establishment. The second type is "population growth," a process which involves both positive and negative additions. In general, this type of growth depends on the surplus of births (positive additions) over deaths (negative additions) and applies to variables which have an age distribution and regular rates of births and deaths. The third type is "structural growth," the growth process of an aggregate with a complex structure of interrelated parts. This process often involves a change in the relation of the components since the growth of each component influences and is influenced by the growth of all other components in the system. Structural growth shades imperceptibly into structural change since, in most cases, it is not only the overall size of the structure that grows but also its complexity.

In viewing rural-urban migration as a system, growth, in the form of structural growth, is an important dimension for more detailed investigation and study. What effects have an increase in the volume of migration on the character of the cities? What effects have the growth in the size and complexity of the cities on the types of migrants, on villages and their spatial distribution, on farms and their areal extent, on the crops grown and their qualitative importance, on the types of equipment used and on the average income of families in the rural areas? What effects have changes or growth in these variables on the volume and characteristics of migrants and on further growth and complexity in the urban areas?

It may be argued, of course, that to conceive of a theory of rural-urban migration in this broad, systematic framework is to suggest a catchall embracing a wide range of changes taking place in a country at any given time. In a sense, this is deliberate since part of the object of this paper is to call attention to the paramount importance of

28. K. Boulding, "Toward a General Theory of Growth," *General Systems Yearbook*, 1 (1956), pp. 66-75.

"flow phenomena" in the spatial processes modifying the character of any country. Thus, just as the flow of water acts as a major sculpturing agent in the physical geography of any area of the world, the flow of persons (migration), of goods and services (trade and transportation), and of ideas (communication) is a crucial agency in shaping the human geography of a country.

More than this, there is the fact that growth in such "flow phenomena" creates form. Growth in the flow of rural-urban migrants affects the pattern of population distribution, the areal size and internal configuration of cities, the types of buildings in rural areas, the size and arrangements of farms, and the number, size, and network density of rural roads. These, in a sense, are simply the results of the way the system tries to adjust to growth processes. However, as Boulding has pointed out, there is a limit to the extent to which the system can go on making these adjustments. "Growth," states Boulding, "creates form; but form limits growth. This mutuality of relationship between growth and form is perhaps the essential key to the understanding of structural growth."[29]

This paper has tried to show how a theory of rural-urban migration can gain in incisiveness and breadth by being construed within a General Systems Theory framework. The conceptualization of the problem in this way emphasizes the structural congruencies or isomorphy with other problems. Further, one of the major attractions of this approach is that it enables a consideration of rural-urban migration no longer as a linear, uni-directional, push-and-pull, cause-effect movement but as a circular, interdependent, progressively complex, and self-modifying system in which the effect of changes in one part can be traced through the whole of the system. Such a circularity gives special prominence to the dynamic nature of rural-urban migration and allows the process to remain as one of considerable interest over an indefinite period of time. In other words, it emphasizes rural-urban migration as a continuous process, occurring in most countries all the time though at different levels of complexity. In this respect, the systems approach also serves as a normative model against which one can seek to explain obvious deviations. If the movement of people from the rural to the urban areas is not generating the set of interconnected effects which the theory leads us to expect, we may ask why. We may then investigate the various elements in the system to ascertain which of them is not functioning in the proper way. Alternatively, we may examine critically the politico-economic environment (such as, for example, the situation in those areas of the world where discriminatory policies exist based on race or caste) in order to appreciate those features that do impair the efficient operation of the system. In either case, the basic systems approach would provide the most important insight to the many dimensions of the problem. More than that, it would emphasize the crucial role of rural-urban migration as one of the most important spatial processes shaping the pattern of human occupance of the earth's surface.

29. K. Boulding, *op. cit.*, p. 72.

****

BIBLIOGRAPHY

Ecological Perspectives

ABU-LUGHOD, JANET, "The City Is Dead—Long Live the City: Some Thoughts on Urbanity," *American Behavioral Scientist*, Vol. 10 (September 1966), pp. 3-5. The author discusses old and new approaches in the study of social ecology and warns against overlooking significant life-style differences that appear between and within urban units.

ALEXANDER, CHRISTOPHER, "A City Is Not a Tree," *Architectural Forum*, (April 1965), pp. 58-62; (May 1965), pp. 58-61. Planned cities compare unfavorably with "natural" cities because of the designer's naïve interpretation of urban organizational complexity.

BARTHOLOMEW, GEORGE A., JR, and JOSEPH BIRDSELL, "Ecology and the Protohominids," *American Anthropologist*, Vol. 55 (1953), pp. 481-98. The authors discuss man's development and early distribution in terms of food supply and population equilibrium.

BLAUT, JAMES M., "The Ecology of Tropical Farming Systems," *Revista Geográfica*, Vol. 28 (1961), pp. 47-67. The author offers a definition of the environmental role in tropical farming systems and challenges the traditional environmentalist approach to these ecosystems.

BOULDING, KENNETH E., "Economics and Ecology," in F. Fraser Darling and John P. Milton (eds.), *Future Environments of North America: Transformation of a Continent*, Garden City, New York: Natural History Press, 1966, pp. 225-34. Boulding notes the common ground between economics and ecology, as well as very striking differences.

BURTON, IAN, *Types of Agricultural Occupance of Flood Plains in the United States*, Chicago: University of Chicago, Department of Geography, Research Paper No. 75, 1962. Burton uses both theoretical and empirical approaches to develop a typology of agricultural occupance of flood plains in the United States.

CARSON, D. H., "The Interactions of Man and His Environment," *School Environments Research: Environmental Evaluation*, Ann Arbor, Michigan: University of Michigan Press, 1965, pp. 13-52. Studies should emphasize the interrelations rather than the distinction between man and environment.

COE, MICHAEL D., and KENT V. FLANNERY, "Microenvironments and Meso-American Prehistory," *Science*, Vol. 143 (1964), pp. 650-54. Fine-scale ecological analysis of archeological evidence and contemporary ethnology clarify the processes of domestication and urbanization in early Meso-America.

DUCKHAM, A. N., "Agricultural Perspectives: Short-Term Climate Change and the Farmer," *Institute of Biology, Symposia*, No. 14 (1965), pp. 193-201. The effects of weather variation on food production and consumption are discussed using an ecosystem model.

EYRE, S. R., "Determinism and the Ecological Approach to Geography," *Geography*, Vol. 49 (1964), pp. 369-76. Eyre suggests that the proper focus of geography is its role as integrater of physical and human terrestrial phenomena.

FIREY, WALTER, "Sentiment and Symbolism as Ecological Variables," *American Sociological Review*, Vol. 10 (1945), pp. 140-48. An analysis of Boston suggests that sentiment distorts the economic relationship between locational activity and space.

FOOTE, DON C., and BRYN GREER-WOOTEN, "An Approach to Systems Analysis in Cultural Geography," *Professional Geographer*, Vol. 20 (1968), pp. 86-91. An application of systems methodology to the Eskimos of northwest Alaska.

FOSBERG, F. R., "The Island Ecosystem," in F. R. Fosberg (ed.), *Man's Place in the Island Ecosystem: A Symposium*, Honolulu: Bishop Museum Press, 1963, pp. 1-6. This introduction discusses the mechanics and behavior of ecosystems in general and certain peculiarities of island ecosystems.

FRAKE, C. O., "Cultural Ecology and Ethnography," *American Anthropologist*, Vol. 64 (1962), pp. 53-59. A major methodological statement for the field of ethnoecology.

GLACKEN, CLARENCE J., *Traces on the Rhodian Shore*, Berkeley: University of California Press, 1967. A classic volume tracing changing concepts of man and nature through time.

GLACKEN, CLARENCE J., "This Growing Second World Within the World of Nature," in F. R. Fosberg (ed.), *Man's Place in the Island Ecosystem: A Symposium,* Honolulu: Bishop Museum Press, 1963, pp. 75-100. A historical account of Western man's view of his place in the natural hierarchy.

GLACKEN, CLARENCE J., "Reflections on the Man-Nature Theme as a Subject for Study," in Fraser Darling and John P. Milton (eds.), *Future Environments of North America: Transformation of a Continent,* Garden City, New York: Natural History Press, 1966, pp. 355-71. A discussion of some of the problems posed by historical studies of environmental attitudes.

KELLMAN, M. C., "Some Environmental Components of Shifting Cultivation in Upland Mindanao," *The Journal of Tropical Geography,* Vol. 28 (1969), pp. 40-56. Fallowing, runoff, and erosion are discussed in terms of site deterioration or ecological imbalance resulting from traditional agricultural practices.

KEYFITZ, NATHAN, "Population Density and the Style of Social Life," *Bioscience,* Vol. 16 (1966), pp. 868-73. Keyfitz attempts a historical explanation of the difference between the life-styles of developed and underdeveloped societies as functions of population density.

KUNKEL, J. H., "Some Behavioral Aspects of the Ecological Approach to Social Organization," *American Journal of Sociology,* Vol. 73 (July 1967), pp. 12-29. Kunkel constructs a behavioral model of man based on activities of individuals as they are limited by ecological characteristics.

LOWENTHAL, DAVID, "Daniel Boone Is Dead," *Natural History,* Vol. 77, No. 7 (1968), pp. 8-16, ff. Lowenthal takes a gentle swipe at hardy naturalists and advocates a more personal communion with nature in all of its various forms, rural and urban.

MARK, H., and K. P. SCHWIRIAN, "Ecological Position, Urban Central Place Function, and Community Population Growth," *American Journal of Sociology,* Vol. 73 (1967), pp. 30-41. The authors suggest that central place function plays only a small part in the growth of small communities and that proximity to large urban areas is now, at least in the developed Western world, a more important criterion for their continued growth.

MARQUIS, STEWART, "Ecosystems, Societies, and Cities," *American Behavioral Scientist,* Vol. 11 (1968), pp. 11-15. Marquis discusses natural ecosystems and man's artificial ecosystem, the city.

MOHOLY-NAGY, SIBYL, "The Four Environments of Man," *Landscape,* Vol. 17 (1967), pp. 3-9. Four distinct spatial patterns have dominated urban history.

MOSS, R. P., and W. B. MORGAN, "The Concept of the Community: Some Applications in Geographical Research," *Transactions, Institute of British Geographers,* No. 41 (1967), pp. 21-32. A functional approach to the study of geographical systems emphasizing the usefulness of the concept of community.

PIÓRO, Z., "Ecological Interpretation of Settlement Systems," *International Social Science Journal,* Vol. 18 (1966), pp. 527-38. Pióro advocates an ecological approach, employing its theoretical framework, methodology, and techniques, in settlement surveys when planning is the research goal.

SANDERS, WILLIAM T., "Cultural Ecology of Nuclear Mesoamerica," *American Anthropologist,* Vol. 64 (1962), pp. 34-44. An examination of the roles of culture and environment in the development of pre-Iron Age civilization in the New World.

SCHWARTZ, DAVID C., "On the Ecology of Political Violence: 'The Long Hot Summer' as a Hypothesis," *American Behavioral Scientist,* Vol. 11 (1968), pp. 24-28. Schwartz investigates the supposed relationship between violence and climatological factors, revealing significant differences between urban and rural-based violence.

SEWELL, W. A. DERRICK (ed.), *Human Dimensions of Weather Modification,* Chicago: University of Chicago, Department of Geography, Research Paper No. 105, 1966. The discussions revolve around approaches to weather modification and its physical and economic implications.

SIMMONS, I. G., "Ecology and Land Use," *Transactions, Institute of British Geographers,* No. 38 (1966), pp. 59-72. Definition of systems concepts as applied to land-use and the balance between man and nature.

STODDART, D. R., "Organism and Ecosystem as Geographical Models," in Richard J. Chorley and Peter Haggett (eds.), *Models in Geography,* London: Methuen, 1967, pp. 511-48. Discussion of alternate paradigms for geographical study.

STRAUSZ-HUPE, R. (ed.), "Society and Ecology," *American Behavioral Scientist,* Vol. 11 (1968), pp. 1-48. The authors feel that technological growth is a fact of life, and it is only the uses to which increasing energy reserves are to be put that is in doubt.

SWEET, L. E., "Camel Raiding of North Arabian Bedouin: A Mechanism of Ecological Adaptation," *American Anthropologist,* Vol. 67 (1965), pp. 1132-50. Camel raiding is a response to certain environmental imperatives and is a homeostatic mechanism which promotes a balanced camel pastoral economy.

TUAN, YI-FU, *The Hydrologic Cycle and the Wisdom of God: A Theme in Geoteleology,* Toronto: University of Toronto, Department of Geography, Research Publication No. 1, 1968. For at least one hundred and fifty years, the concept of the hydrological cycle was derived from natural theology as much as natural philosophy.

UHLIG, HARALD, "Hill Tribes and Rice Farmers in the Himalayas and South-East Asia: Problems of the Social and Ecological Differentiation of Agricultural Landscape Types," *Transactions, Institute of British Geographers* (September 1969), pp. 1-23. A comparative examination of Asian agricultural landscape types employing socio-economic and ecological parameters.

WHITE, LYNN, JR., "The Historical Roots of Our Ecologic Crisis," *Science,* Vol. 155 (1967), pp. 1203-7. White blames Christianity and the merging of science and technology in the late nineteenth century for our present ecologic crisis.

****

3
ENVIRONMENTAL PERCEPTION AND BEHAVIOR

The empirical study of the objective world through descrip-
tion, categorization, and analysis of specific phenomena is
one of the strongest traditions of post-Renaissance
Western scholarship. The accomplishments of this approach
have been many; the sophisticated analytical techniques
and instrumentation used by scientists to explore the
natural world and its derivative technology saturate the
fabric of modern life. In academia, this empiricism
governed the departmentalization of knowledge so that
students became specialists in particular objects, that is,
geologists, botanists, and chemists, despite the fact that
most scholars recognized that academic disciplines should
be defined by their laws, principles of order, and concep-
tual frameworks and not by specific content. This trend in
scholarship posed a problem for geographers because their
studies encompassed too many discrete phenomena, and
divisions emerged in the field when physical geographers
confined their attention to one set of objects, economic
geographers another.[1] Ultimately, a number of these
specialists defected from the mother field leaving behind a
bewildering discussion as to the nature of geography, a
determined search for unity in a field spanning both man
and environment, and most recently the problem of
generating a coherent analysis of environmental
problems in an intellectual world entrenched in
narrow trenches.

That this intellectual ambience born of the scientific
revolution strongly influenced the work of human geog-
raphers is understandable, particularly since many were
trained in the physical sciences. These men approached the
world of man with tools honed in the exploration of
nature, and sought rigor in the categorization and accurate
description of the "elements of human geography." For

---

1. This problem is recognized in one of the early discussions of
behavioralism in geography. See William Kirk, "Problems of
Geography," *Geography*, Vol. 48 (1963), pp. 357-71.

Vidal de la Blache, the greatest of the French school, these elements were man's tools and raw materials, his means of sustenance, human establishments, building materials, and transportation patterns.[2] In America, human geographers studied house types and field patterns, described and classified settlement types, and traced the diffusion of individual plants, animals, and items of material culture. Man was examined principally by studying the objects around him; objects were surrogates for man. Thus, farmers were explored through their barns and fields, rather than through their decisions, values, or behavior unless these more humane attributes rearranged nearby objective phenomena. The spread of settlement was interpreted through analyzing the climate, soils, and vegetation of frontier regions with little attention beyond identification directed to the experience, aspirations, and perceptions of the settlers. In reaction to this tradition and in response to the development of a behavioral approach to man in the social sciences, human geographers recently have experimented with a more human and in a sense less geographic approach to human geography by studying men and not objects. Much of this recent research is subsumed under the rubric of *environmental perception*.

Geographers approach the concept of environmental perception in a variety of ways, some quite simple, others complex. At the simplest level, environmental perception assumes that each man has an "image" of the world and that his preferences, evaluations, decisions, and subsequent behavior are based on these pictures in his head rather than on the world of objective reality (if

such exists).[3] Given this premise, man's behavior with respect to environment becomes the central nexus of the research problem and those forces which contribute to environmental and spatial behavior such as past experience, available information, physiological and psychological condition, philosophical traditions, social constraints, and communication spheres become the legitimate concern of the geographer. It is here that the complexity begins and problems emerge.

The inquiries of human geographers into perception embrace larger arenas than the precise physiological definitions of perception proposed by thirty years of clinical psychology or the carefully circumscribed delineations of several generations of philosophers. The entire process from physiological response to stimulus, through subsequent evaluation and decision-making, to overt behavior is encompassed within the recent literature but no body of theory or even methodology comprehends so complex a process, and the assumptions which underlie such studies lie hidden. If, for example, one attempts to examine the scope and intensity of those individual or group perceptions of a city which influence urban spatial behavior, the full range of environmental as well as human complexity becomes relevant. The physical patterning of the city, its streets and pathways, its neighborhoods and central cores, must be identified and analyzed, first purely as morphological entities and then in terms of the operational environments within which men work, the perceptual environments they identify, and the behavioral environments which elicit responses from them.[4] But this

---

2. As defined in his posthumous text, *Principes de géographie humaine*, and in the work of his students.

3. The term "image" derives from Kenneth E. Boulding's clear and penetrating volume, *The Image*, Ann Arbor: University of Michigan Press, 1956.

4. See Sonnenfeld selection.

information must be deciphered to expose the influence of man's cognitive structuring of space (geometric or nodal), the pattern of cultural symbolization reflected in all human structures, the weight of past decision-making in circumscribing both acceptable behavior and the environment in which the present behavior occurs, and the complex of social and cultural configurations implicit in the use of terms like neighborhood, community, or node of social interaction. Identification of significant variables lies open to a wide range of interpretation. If race influences spatial behavior in modern American cities, can one assume that cultural dominance will circumscribe minorities similarly given different traditions of social patterning? Or are there age similarities in perceiving environment which lie deeper than modern racial tensions such that analysis of the process of spatial learning and symbolization among children would provide critical data in evaluating adult behavior? The identification and selection of meaningful behavioral acts, preferences and decisions from the array of human behavior available for study is extremely perplexing.

An early and excellent statement of the complexity and breadth of geographical interest in the field of man's perception of his world is provided in the introductory selection by David Lowenthal, whose major concern lies with "the relation between the world outside and the pictures in our heads."[5] In Lowenthal's view, the universe of geographical discourse is not confined to geographers but is expressed in the differing world views held by all men. While there is consensus concerning the broad outlines of a shared world view, not all men agree, and even the consensus view will change through time. Men after all perceive partial views of the world, restricted both physically and biologically, conditioned by their culture and society. Such basic elements as direction, distance, and physical space are perceived in a personal, a cultural, and a consensual way. The degree of fit between the outside world and our views of it, both personally and culturally, need to be investigated, according to Lowenthal, and patterns of visual perception, spatial organization, and language relating to these world views merit detailed examination by human geographers.

Obviously, a broad sweep of knowledge is required to cope with such intricate questions, and the point need not be belabored; once human geographers seriously study humans and their spatial perceptions and behavior the entire range of problems which bedevil other social scientists become their concern as well. Having recognized the complexity of the entire social system and lacking the theoretical structures, inferences, predictions, or perceptual apparatus and instrumentation necessary to penetrate with sensitivity, human geographers have experimented with a variety of discernible but overlapping approaches to the problem. All share an interest in spatial behavior, environmental preferences, and environmental decision-making, but research designs vary depending on whether primary interest is focused on individual or group responses to environment, whether the analysis focuses on specific environmental components or on images of total environments, whether the research is conducted in a laboratory setting or the real world, and whether the researcher is attempting to explain spatial behavior or the decision process.

5. David Lowenthal, "Geography, Experience, and Imagination: Towards a Geographical Epistemology," *Annals, Association of American Geographers,* Vol. 51 (1961), pp. 241-61. For a more recent statement and bibliography, see Thomas F. Saarinen, *Perception of Environment,* Washington, D.C.: Association of American Geographers, Commission on College Geography Resource Paper No. 5, 1969.

Spatial Behavior

Space, in a philosophical sense, is empty. It requires bounding and identification by an individual, an interaction between self and environment, to be recognized. These interactions are defined early in life, biologically and culturally, when men as children learn to organize and perceive environmental patterns and to charge certain of these with meaning, both symbolic and practical. In a sense, each individual possesses a unique and ineluctably personal view of the world, and his responses to specific environments or environmental components will depend on that complex of personal preferences, physiological capacities, and past experiences peculiar to him. In other words, he sees his world in subtly different ways than others. But interpretation and recognition of social and environmental patterns are learned, so that members of the same learning group can reasonably be expected to share similar responses to salient elements of the environment.[6] Thus, there is hope of identifying certain generalized patterns of spatial behavior which, if not universal, are at least shared within cultures. The primary thrust of research in spatial behavior has this objective—to discover those shared characteristics which might provide clues in developing methodological and theoretical insights through analysis of the perception, evaluation, learning, and response of individuals to their environment.

In order to simplify the problem of defining man's perception of his environment, many authors have focused their attention on those critical spheres of environment that impinge directly on the individual. Nearly a decade ago, the British geographer William Kirk, influenced by work in Gestalt psychology and particularly that of Kurt Lewin, suggested the term "behavioral environment" to define the values, configurations, and cultural contexts which men attribute to the objective world as distinct from the world of objects *per se*, which he identified as the "phenomenal environment." [7] More recently, Julian Wolpert has used the term "action space" for the immediately perceived environment and "decision environment" to encompass the degree of information, perception, uncertainty, and threat surrounding locational decision-makers when they select strategies to cope with the environment and accomplish goals.[8] The objectives of these definitions are to penetrate the behavioral process and focus clearly on the relevant stimuli.

In his discussion of this problem, Sonnenfeld delimits four distinct environments of progressively more limited scope, the *geo-*

---

6. At least two immediate danges are presented here. First, identifying individual as opposed to aggregate behavior and attempting to explain the latter by simply grouping behavioral information about individuals is dangerous because the behavioral process for individuals does not extend to groups. Second, there is a temptation of assuming causal explanations for behavioral regularities when statistical explanations are more appropriate.

7. Kirk, *op. cit.*, pp. 364 ff. Lewin used the term "life space" to encompass the individual, and the totality of his psychological environment, real and perceived. Kurt Lewin, *Field Theory in the Social Sciences*, New York: Harper and Row, 1951.
8. Julian Wolpert, "Behavioral Aspects of the Decision To Migrate," *Papers of the Regional Science Association*, Vol. 15, (1965), pp. 159-69; "Departures from the Usual Environment in Locational Analysis," *Annals, Association of American Geographers*, Vol. 60, (1970), pp. 220-29. In a similar vein, see Peter Gould, "The Measurement of Spatial Perception," *University of Bristol, Geography Seminar Series A*, No. 8 (1967); R. M. Downs, "Approaches to and Problems in the Measurement of Geographic Space Perception," *University of Bristol, Geography Seminar Series A*, No. 9, (1967); and Robin M. Haynes, *Behavior Space and Perception Space: A Reconnaissance*, University Park: Pennsylvania State University, Papers in Geography, No. 3, 1969, mimeographed.

graphical environment, the *operational environment,* the *perceptual environment,* and the *behavioral environment,* to distinguish and separate those factors most relevant to individual behavior from the more inert total setting in which it occurs. At the most inclusive level, the geographical environment comprehends the total universe external to man, far and near, whether it impinges on him directly, indirectly, or not at all. The operational environment, on the other hand, is limited to his immediate surroundings, quite literally it is the environment in which he operates. The perceptual environment includes only those elements in the operational environment of which man is aware, whereas the behavioral environment requires not only awareness of a particular facet of the environment but a behavioral response as well. In presenting these definitions, Sonnenfeld is encouraging human geographers to view the environment in a more discriminating and precise way. The application of this typology in cross-cultural behavioral research could be quite fruitful.[9]

Personal Space. Yet the most detailed and exact research in the realm of man's perception of environment and spatial behavior lies not in the field of human geography, but in a growing interdisciplinary frontier of knowledge that has attracted the attention of psychologists, anthropologists, designers, and architects, which Edward Hall, one of its leading proponents, calls "proxemics": the study of man's use of space as a specialized elaboration of culture.[10] The fundamental concepts in this body of literature derive from early work in ethology, specifically that of Lorenz, Howard, Wynne-Edwards, and others recently popularized in Robert Ardrey's *The Territorial Imperative.*[11] Here, territory and behavior are treated as a system of some complexity. Variations in available space lead to alterations in animal behavior, such that in addition to conditioning patterns of population density, selective breeding, and conflict resolution, territory also influences dominance behavior, sexual activity, social order, and status. Beyond the immediate territory of the individual, patterns of spatial organization in the form of irregular concentric zones regulate interactions between and within species. Among these flight distance (a measure of interspecies approachability), critical distance (the zone separating flight distance from attack distance), personal distance (the normal spacing of non-contact animals), and social distance (nearness to other members of the same species) are the most commonly mentioned.

Proxemics, or the study of personal space, has established that each individual possesses an analogous spatial envelope and a set of personal distances that quite literally are extensions of his personality as well as expressions of his culture. These spatial zones vary in dimension with context, but behavioral responses record their perimeters

9. See, for example, Sonnenfeld's "Variable Values in Space Landscape: An Inquiry into the Nature of Environmental Necessity," *Journal of Social Issues,* Vol. 22 (1966), pp. 71-82; "Environmental Perception and Adaption Level in the Arctic," in David Lowenthal, ed., *Environmental Perception and Behavior,* Chicago: University of Chicago, Department of Geography, Research Paper No. 109, 1967, pp. 42-59; "Equivalence and Distortion of the Perceptual Environment," *Environment and Behavior,* Vol. 1 (1969), pp. 83-99.

10. Hall's two basic volumes are *The Silent Language,* Garden City, New York: Doubleday, 1959; and *The Hidden Dimension,* Garden City, New York: Doubleday, 1966.

11. The references here are Konrad Lorenz, *On Aggression,* New York: Harcourt, Brace, and World, 1963; H. E. Howard, *Territory in Bird Life,* London: Murray, 1920; V. C. Wynne-Edwards, *Animal Dispersion in Relation to Social Behavior,* New York: Hafner, 1962; and Robert Ardrey, *The Territorial Imperative,* New York: Atheneum, 1966.

when invasion, crowding, or spatial restruc-
turing occurs. This patterning has been
principally explored in laboratory-like
microsettings such as hospital wards, office
buildings, and classrooms.[12] How do seating
arrangements influence propensity for conversation or patterns of leadership? To what
degree do spatial arrangements in offices and
classrooms, meeting halls and churches,
expose hidden regularities in man's organization and use of space which derive from
inarticulated culturally defined sets of social
and personal distances.

This subject is explored in the selection
from Robert Sommer's book, *Personal
Space,* which identifies some of the invisible
boundaries which protect and compart-
mentalize each man, and the dangers and
discomfort of infringing on another's personal space or having your own penetrated.
Distinguishing between individual distance,
the characteristic spacing of the species, and
personal distance, Sommer examines their
proportions in a variety of contexts by measuring psychological, physiological, and
behavioral responses to closeness and crowding. The remainder of his book is primarily
devoted to a detailed analysis of four man-
environment systems, the hospital, school,
tavern, and dormitory, in terms of the relations of design problems, traditional patterns
of spatial behavior, and spatial arrangements.

The work of Edward Hall, mentioned
above, is less concerned with the immediate
problems of designing microspaces, although
he has defined four zones of personal
distance based on response to sensory
stimuli for middle-class white Americans,
ranging from intimate (contact to eighteen
inches) to public (twenty-five feet or more),
and has urged that these proxemic patterns
should be integrated into the designs of

architects and urban planners.[13] The central
thrust of his research has been to demonstrate clearly that personal space varies
cross-culturally. By exploring the similarities
and differences from culture to culture, Hall
has attempted to "shed light on our own
out-of awareness patterns" of spatial behavior and to improve the possibilities of
intercultural understanding. His clear exposition of cross-cultural variations in proxemics
identifies the importance of spatial relationships in non-verbal communication and
significant cultural differences in the definition of concepts such as privacy and
crowding.

Environmental Preferences and Decision-Making

Human geographers have tended to work in
broader settings and with larger populations
than researchers in proxemics and personal
space, concerning themselves primarily with
environmental preferences and decisions that
effect either resource utilization or locational patterns. The questions asked are
classically geographic in nature; why do men
live where they do; why do they use their
environment as they do; how do they perceive other environments; and how do these
perceptions influence environmental and
locational decision-making? But the approach is more rigorous and more behavioral. Mental images of space and perceptual surfaces are determined. Factors such as
stress, partial information, risk, and hazard
are considered in examining the decision
process. Perhaps most important, these geographers no longer assume that automatic or
uniform perceptions or responses to sets of
environmental factors exist, thus the search
for explanation and ultimately theory
probes much more deeply into the nature of
man as a locational being rather than, as has

12. For an example by a geographer, see David
Stea, "Space, Territory and Human Movements,"
Landscape, Vol. 15 (Autumn 1965), pp. 13-16.

13. *The Hidden Dimension,* Chapter 10.

been the case in the past, seeking insights into human behavior through reconnaissance in the natural world.

Peter Gould's "On Mental Maps" represents one of the behavioral approaches to the definition and analysis of perceptual environments.[14] The objective of his study is to devise a technique which will measure the ways in which people in the United States perceive and evaluate geographical space in terms of residential desirability. These perceptions or "mental maps" that men hold of their environment are critical, in Gould's opinion, in the formation of those decisions which restructure the human landscape, decisions such as where to settle, where to locate industry, and what to grow. And these decisions vary with the experience, knowledge, and aspirations of each individual. In adopting this approach, Gould's paper departs from earlier writings in the behavioral literature which assumed a rather narrow normative model of "economic man" in which each decision-maker was blessed with perfect knowledge, powers of prediction, and economic rationality.[15] Instead, a model of "satisficing" behavior in which men are assumed to act with finite knowledge, imperfect perceptions, and a complex of goals is used, and this allows for a much broader continuum of human responses and more realistic insights into the behavioral process.

In order to examine spatial images in the American mind and to identify residential preferences, Gould sampled the attitudes of students at four major universities, in Alabama, California, Minnesota, and Pennsylvania, by asking them to provide rank order listings of their preferences for each state. These Gestalt impressions were then converted into maps of residential desirability as viewed by each student group, and these maps formed the basis for discussion of the degree to which environmental images are shared, the ways in which they influence human decisions, and the theoretical implications of environmental preferences in the analysis of spatial behavior. Although the data base for this study is tentative, the implications of "mental maps" and derivative approaches for research in human geography are clear.

A second approach developed by human geographers relates concepts in behavioral science to the perception and utilization of resources, and the broader question of the quality of the environment, specifically in terms of the ways in which resource managers and users respond to natural hazards.[16] These studies integrate intensive analysis of components in the physical

---

14. After writing this article, Gould applied the "mental map" construct intensively in a detailed regional study of the locational preference of British school pupils. See P. R. Gould and R. R. White, "The Mental Maps of British School Leavers," *Regional Studies,* Vol. 2 (1968), pp. 161-82, reprinted in *General Systems,* Vol. 14 (1969), pp. 51-66. See also footnote 8 above.
15. Discussed more fully as applied to a spatial context in Julian Wolpert, "The Decision Process in Spatial Context," *Annals, Association of American Geographers,* Vol. 54, (1964), pp. 537-58.

16. Among the best-known of these studies are Ian Burton, *Changes in the Urban Occupance of Flood Plains in the United States.* Chicago: University of Chicago, Department of Geography, Research Paper No. 57, 1961; Ian Burton and Robert W. Kates, "The Floodplain and the Seashore," *Geographical Review,* Vol. 54 (1964), pp. 366-85; Robert W. Kates, *Hazard and Choice Perception in Flood Plain Management,* Chicago: University of Chicago, Department of Geography, Research Paper No. 78, 1962; "Perceptual Regions and Regional Perception in Flood Plain Management," *Papers of the Regional Science Association,* Vol. 11 (1963), pp. 217-27; Thomas Frederick Saarinen, *The Perception of Drought Hazard on the Great Plains,* Chicago: University of Chicago, Department of Geography, Research Paper No. 106, 1966; Gilbert F. White, *Choice of Adjustment to Floods,* Chicago: University of Chicago, Department of Geography, Research Paper No. 93, 1964.

environment with detailed examination of human attitudes and responses to stimuli such as hazards. How do men cope with the uncertainties generated by natural catastrophes such as floods, droughts, and earthquakes? What factors contribute to the marked differences in one man's definition of wilderness as opposed to another's?[17] In each study, human attitudes toward resources are seen as intervening variables in the man-environment system. Once again the search is for behavioral regularities, regularities that might contribute to theory-building and to intelligent policy decisions with respect to resource utilization.

The article by Burton and Kates, "The Perception of Natural Hazards in Resource Management" demonstrates the impact of variations in human perceptions of, and adjustments to, natural hazards on the use of resources. The authors begin by defining and classifying natural hazards by their principal causal agent, thus including fog but excluding smog. While the frequency and magnitude of various hazards can be defined with some precision, considerable variation in human attitudes to and perception of hazards exists. Even among technical and scientific personnel, differences in perception exist despite their greater access to records and broader knowledge, at least partially because of the difficulties inherent in predicting disasters such as tornadoes, droughts, or floods. If the experts disagree, the same is true of resource users directly affected by hazards who differ in sensitivity to hazard, attitudes toward nature, and future expectations. In probing the range of human responses to hazards, both within and among groups, Burton and Kates grapple with the full range of complexity, both human and environmental, which must be examined in behavioral research in the real world.

Direct analysis of the decision-making process is a third approach human geographers have used to investigate spatial behavior. A variety of decision models developed in the social sciences have been applied to locational decision-making, viewing the sets of choices among existing alternatives not only within an economic framework but also in terms of the knowledge, attitudes, and anticipations of the decision-makers. Certain facets of the decision process have attracted more attention than others: first, decision objectives and goals, particularly in the location of public facilities and in planning; second, the degree of rationality in the decision process as gauged by the concepts of adaptively rational behavior and bounded rationality; and third, the impact of stress and threat as environmental factors present in the decision environment.

In "Departures from the Usual Environment in Locational Analysis," Julian Wolpert examines behavioral factors in the decision-making process relating to the location of controversial facilities, where "unusual" components in the decision environment such as threat and conflict contribute to stress conditions. Using the expansion of a metropolitan university into the neighboring community as a specific example, Wolpert discusses the role of "public interest," confrontation with local interest groups, and stress responses to threat as forces contributing to potentially dysfunctional or maladaptive behavior on the part of the policy-makers.[18] Since loca-

---

17. Robert Lucas, "Wilderness Perception and Use: The Example of the Boundary Waters Canoe Area," *Natural Resources Journal*, Vol. 3 (1964), pp. 394-411.

18. Elsewhere he has applied three behavioral concepts, place utility, search behavior, and life cycle to the problem of migration. See "Behavioral Aspects of the Decision To Migrate." *Papers and Proceedings, Regional Science Association*, Vol. 15 (1965), pp. 159-69.

tional decision-making in urban areas such as the placement of sewage facilities, expressways, and urban renewal projects often generates considerable tension, behavioral decision models of this type should have wide applicability. More broadly, Wolpert's suggestion that the location of controversial facilities rarely represents the most rational or efficient solution to problems, that knowledge of the decision atmosphere is essential to interpreting artifacts in the landscapes, casts doubt on historical research which interprets urban landscapes as the product of rational economic behavior.

The literature on environmental perception marks the accelerating movement of geography into the social sciences, and the initial steps in a more behavioral approach to traditional geographical concerns. Though as yet little more than a nascent impulse, these studies are characterized by an appreciation of the techniques, ideas, and concepts currently circulating in the behavioral sciences. Implicit in each study is a deep concern for what is perhaps the oldest and most central theme in geography, the interrelationships between man and his environment. The freshness of approach to this essentially epistemological question lies in their intense and subtle probing of human behavior. This development is not only important for framing research questions, but in the added dimensions of understanding that could be generated by human geographers who have the background and training to analyze human beings. For these reasons, more studies of environmental perceptions and behavior are likely to be forthcoming.

✚✚✚✚✚✚✚✚✚✚✚✚✚✚✚✚✚✚✚✚✚✚✚✚✚✚✚✚✚

GEOGRAPHY, EXPERIENCE, AND IMAGINATION: TOWARDS A GEOGRAPHICAL EPISTEMOLOGY [1]

David Lowenthal

"The most fascinating *terrae incognitae* of all are those that lie within the minds and hearts of men." With these words, John K.

Wright concluded his 1946 presidential address before the Association of American Geographers. This paper considers the nature of these *terrae incognitae*, and the relation between the world outside and the pictures in our heads.[2]

1. This is an expanded version of a paper read at the XIXth International Geographical Congress, Stockholm, August, 1960. For encouragement, advice, and criticism, I am grateful to George A. Cooper, Richard Hartshorne, William C. Lewis, William D. Pattison, Michael G. Smith, Philip L. Wagner, William Warntz, J. W. N. Watson, and John K. Wright. Richard F. Kuhns, Jr., has kindly read and commented on several drafts of the manuscript, and I am indebted to him for numerous suggestions and references.

2. John K. Wright, "Terrae Incognitae: the Place of the Imagination in Geography," *Annals,* Association of American Geographers, Vol. 37 (1947), pp. 1-15, on p. 15. The phrase "The World Outside and the Pictures in Our Heads" is the name of the first chapter in Walter Lippmann, *Public Opinion* (New York: Macmillan, 1922). As my subtitle

From the *Annals,* Association of American Geographers, Vol. 51, No. 3 (1961), pp. 241-260. Reprinted by permission.

The General and the Geographical World View

Neither the world nor our pictures of it are identical with geography. Some aspects of geography are recondite, others abstruse, occult, or esoteric; conversely, there are many familiar features of things that geography scarcely considers. Beyond that of any other discipline, however, the subject matter of geography approximates the world of general discourse; the palpable present, the everyday life of man on earth, is seldom far from our professional concerns. "There is no science whatever," wrote a future president of Harvard, a century and a half ago, "which comes so often into use in common life." [3]

This view of geography remains a commonplace of contemporary thought. More than physics or physiology, psychology or politics, geography observes and analyzes aspects of the milieu on the scale and in the categories that they are usually apprehended in everyday life. Whatever methodologists think geography ought to be, the temperament of its practitioners makes it catholic and many-sided. In their range of interests and capacities—concrete and abstract, academic and practical, analytic and synthetic, indoor and outdoor, historical and contemporary, physical and social—geographers reflect man generally. "This treating of cabbages and kings, cathedrals and linguistics, trade in oil, or commerce in ideas," as Peattie wrote, "makes a congress of geographers more or less a Committee on the Universe." [4]

suggests, this is not a study of the meaning or methods of geography, but rather an essay in the theory of geographical knowledge. Hartshorne's methodological treatises analyze and develop logical principles of procedure for geography as a professional science, "a form of 'knowing,'" as he writes, "that is different from the ways in which we 'know' by instinct, intuition, *a priori* deduction or revelation" (Richard Hartshorne, *Perspective on the Nature of Geography* [Chicago: Rand McNally, for Association of American Geographers, 1959], p. 170). My epistemological inquiry, on the other hand, is concerned with *all* geographical thought, scientific and other: how it is acquired, transmitted, altered, and integrated into conceptual systems; and how the horizon of geography varies among individuals and groups. Specifically, it is a study in what Wright calls *geosophy:* "the nature and expression of geographical ideas both past and present . . . the geographical ideas, both true and false, of all manner of people—not only geographers, but farmers and fishermen, business executives and poets, novelists and painters, Bedouins and Hottentots" ("Terrae Incognitae," p. 12). Because geographers are "nowhere . . . more likely to be influenced by the subjective than in their discussions of what scientific geography ought to be" (*ibid.*), epistemology helps to explain why and how methodologies change.
3. Jared Sparks, MS. in Sparks Collection (132, Misc. Papers, Vol. I, 1808-14), Harvard College Library: quoted in Ralph H. Brown, "A Plea for Geography, 1813 Style," *Annals*, Association of

American Geographers, Vol. 41 (1951), p. 235. For similar nineteenth-century views see my "George Perkins Marsh on the Nature and Purpose of Geography," *Geographical Journal*, Vol. 126 (1960), pp. 413-17.
4. Roderick Peattie, *Geography in Human Destiny* (New York: George W. Stewart, 1940), pp. 26-27. "In the broadest sense," Richard Hartshorne notes, "all facts of the earth surface are geographical facts" (*The Nature of Geography: a Critical Survey of Current Thought in the Light of the Past* [Lancaster, Pa.: Association of American Geographers, 1939], p. 372). On the interests and capacities of geographers, see J. Russell Whitaker, "The Way Lies Open," *Annals*, Association of American Geographers, Vol. 44 (1954), p. 242; and André Meynier, "Réflexions sur la spécialisation chez les Géographes," *Norois*, Vol. 7 (1960), pp. 5-12.

Most of the physical and social sciences are, both in theory and in practice, more generalizing and formalistic than geography. The exceptions are disciplines which, like geography, are in some measure humanistic: notably anthropology and history. The subject-matter of anthropology is as diversified as that of geography, and more closely mirrors the everyday concerns of man; but anthropological research still concentrates predominantly on that small and remote fraction of mankind— "primitive" or nonliterate, traditional in culture,

Geographical curiosity is, to be sure, more narrowly focused than mankind's; it is also more conscious, orderly, objective, consistent, universal, and theoretical than are ordinary queries about the nature of things. Like geography, however, the wider universe of discourse centers on knowledge and ideas about man and milieu; anyone who inspects the world around him is in some measure a geographer.

As with specifically geographical concepts, the more comprehensive world of ideas that we share concerns the variable forms and contents of the earth's surface, past, present, and potential—"a torrent of discourse about tables, people, molecules, light rays, retinas, air-waves, prime numbers, infinite classes, joy and sorrow, good and evil." [5] It comprises truth and error, concrete facts and abstruse relationships, self-evident laws and tenuous hypotheses, data drawn from natural and social science, from

history, from common sense, from intuition and mystical experience. Certain things appear to be grouped spatially, seriated temporally, or related causally: the hierarchy of urban places, the annual march of temperature, the location of industry. Other features of our shared universe seem unique, amorphous, or chaotic: the population of a country, the precise character of a region, the shape of a mountain. [6]

Universally Accepted Aspects of the World View. However multifarious its make-up, there is general agreement about the character of the world and the way it is ordered. Explanations of particular phenomena differ from one person to another, but without basic concurrence as to the nature of things, there would be neither science nor common sense, agreement nor argument. The most extreme heretic cannot reject the essence of the prevailing view. "Even the sharpest dissent still operates by partial submission to an existing consensus," reasons Polanyi, "for the revolutionary must speak in terms that people can understand." [7]

Most public knowledge can in theory be verified. I know little about the geography

---

homogeneous in social organization—whose ways of life and world views are least like our own (Ronald M. Berndt, "The Study of Man: an Appraisal of the Relationship between Social and Cultural Anthropology and Sociology," *Oceania*, Vol. 31 [1960], pp. 85-99). More particularistic, more concerned with uniqueness of context than geography, history also comprehends more matters of common interest (especially the acts and feelings of individuals); but because the whole realm of history lies in the past, more historical data is secondary, derivative. Although "geography cannot be strictly contemporary" (Preston E. James, "Introduction: the Field of Geography," in *American Geography: Inventory and Prospect* [Syracuse University Press, for Association of American Geographers, 1954], p. 14), geography is usually *focused* on the present; direct observation of the world plays a major role in geography, a trifling one in history. In theory, at least, the remote in space is everywhere (on the face of the earth) personally accessible to us, the remote in time accessible only through memories and artifacts.
5. W. V. Quine, "The Scope and Language of Science," *British Journal for the Philosophy of Science*, Vol. 8 (1957), pp. 1-17, on p. 1.

6. For various combinations of geographical facts and relationships, see John K. Wright, " 'Cross-breeding' Geographical Quantities," *Geographical Review*, Vol. 45 (1955), pp. 52-65. For the varieties of data that comprise knowledge in general, see Rudolph Carnap, "Formal and Factual Science," in Herbert Feigl and May Brodbeck, eds., *Readings in the Philosphy of Science* (New York: Appleton-Century-Crofts, 1953), pp. 123-128; Karl R. Popper, *The Logic of Scientific Discovery* (New York: Basic Books, 1959), appendix x, pp. 420-441; Friedrich Waismann, "Analytic-Synthetic," *Analysis*, Vol. 11 (1950-51), pp. 52-56; J. W. N. Watkins, "Between Analytic and Empirical," *Philosophy*, Vol. 32 (1957), pp. 112-131.
7. Michael Polanyi, *Personal Knowledge: Towards a Post-Critical Philosophy* (Chicago: University of Chicago Press, 1958), pp. 208-209.

of Sweden, but others are better informed; if I studied long and hard enough I could learn approximately what they know. I cannot read the characters in Chinese newspapers, but hardly doubt that they convey information to the Chinese; assuming that there is a world in common, other peoples' ways of symbolizing knowledge must be meaningful and learnable.

The universe of geographical discourse, in particular, is not confined to geographers; it is shared by billions of amateurs all over the globe. Some isolated primitives are still ignorant of the outside world; many more know little beyond their own countries and ways of life; but most of the earth's inhabitants possess at least rudiments of the shared world picture. Even peoples innocent of science are privy to elements of our geography, both innate and learned: the normal relations between figure and ground; the distinctive setting of objects on the face of the earth; the usual texture, weight, appearance, and physical state of land, air, and water; the regular transition from day to night; the partition of areas by individual, family, or group.

Beyond such universals, the geographical consensus tends to be additive, scientific, and cumulative. Schools teach increasing numbers that the world is a sphere with certain continents, oceans, countries, peoples, and ways of living and making a living; the size, shape, and general features of the earth are known by more and more people. The general horizon of geography has expanded rapidly. "Until five centuries ago a primal or regional sense of space dominated human settlements everywhere"; today, most of us share the conception of a world common to all experients.[8]

The General Consensus Never Completely Accepted. The whole of mankind may in time progress, as Whittlesey suggests, to "the sense of space current at or near the most advanced frontier of thought." But no one, however inclined to pioneer, visits that frontier often, or has surveyed more than a short traverse of it. "Primitive man," according to Boulding, "lives in a world which has a spatial unknown, a dread frontier populated by the heated imagination. For modern man the world is a closed and completely explored surface. This is a radical change in spatial viewpoint."[9] But the innovation is superficial; we are still parochial. "Even in lands where geography is part of a compulsory school curriculum, and among people who possess considerable information about the earth," Whittlesey points out, "the world horizon is accepted in theory and rejected in practice."[10]

The "dread unknowns" are still with us. Indeed, "the more the island of knowledge expands in the sea of ignorance, the larger its boundary to the unknown."[11] Primitive world views were simple and consistent enough for every participant to share most of their substance. Within Western scientific society, no one really grasps more than a small fraction of the public, theoretically communicable world view. The amount of information an individual can acquire in an instant or in a lifetime is finite, and miniscule compared with what the milieu presents; many questions are too complex to describe, let alone solve, in a practicable length of time. The horizons of knowledge are expanding faster than any person can keep up with. The proliferation of new sci-

8. Derwent Whittlesey, "The Horizon of Geography," *Annals*, Association of American Geographers, Vol. 35 (1945), pp. 1-36, on p. 14.

9. Kenneth E. Boulding, *The Image* (Ann Arbor: University of Michigan Press, 1956), p. 66.
10. Whittlesey, *op. cit.*, pp. 2, 14.
11. L. S. Rodberg and V. F. Weisskopf, "Fall of Parity," *Science*, Vol. 125 (1957), pp. 627-33; on p. 632.

ences extends our powers of sense and thought, but their rigorous techniques and technical languages hamper communication; the common field of knowledge becomes a diminishing fraction of the total store.[12]

On the other hand, we tend to assume things are common knowledge which may not be; what seems to me the general outlook might be mine alone. The most devoted adherents to a consensus often mistake their own beliefs for universal ones. For a large part of our world view, we take on faith much of what we are told by science. But we may have got it wrong; as Chisholm points out, "we are all quite capable of believing falsely at any time that a given proposition is accepted by the scientists of our culture circle."[13] In our impressions of the shared world view we all resemble the fond mother who watched her clumsy son parade, and concluded happily, "Everyone was out of step but my Johnnie."

The World View Not Shared by Some. The most fundamental attributes of our shared view of the world are confined, moreover, to sane, hale, sentient adults. Idiots cannot suitably conceive space, time, or causality. Psychotics distinguish poorly between themselves and the outside world. Mystics, claustrophobics, and those haunted by fear of open space (agoraphobia) tend to project their own body spaces as extensions of the outside world; they are often unable to delimit themselves from the rest of nature. Schizophrenics often underestimate size and overestimate distance. After a brain injury, invalids fail to organize their environments or may forget familiar locations and symbols. Impairments like aphasia, apraxia, and agnosia blind their victims to spatial relations and logical connections self-evident to most. Other hallucinatory sufferers may identify forms but regularly alter the number, size, and shape of objects (polyopia, dysmegalopsia, dysmorphopsia), see them always in motion (oscillopsia), or locate everything at the same indefinite distance (porrhopsia).[14]

12. Polanyi, *Personal Knowledge*, p. 216; Rafael Rodriguez Delgado, "A Possible Model for Ideas," *Philosophy of Science*, Vol. 24 (1957), pp. 253-269, on p. 255. "The organism has a definite capacity for information which is a minute fraction of the physical signals that reach the eyes, ears, and epidermis" (Colin Cherry, *On Human Communication: a Review, a Survey, and a Criticism* [New York: Wiley, 1957], p. 284). See also George A. Miller, "The Magical Number Seven, Plus or Minus Two: Some Limits on Our Capacity for Processing Information," *Psychological Review*, Vol. 63 (1956), pp. 81-97; Henry Quastler, "Studies of Human Channel Capacity," in Colin Cherry, ed., *Information Theory; Papers Read at the Third London Symposium*, 1955 (New York: Academic Press, 1956), pp. 361-371.
13. Roderick M. Chisholm, *Perceiving: a Philosophical Study* (Ithaca: Cornell University Press, 1957), p. 36. Personal surprise and disappointment are evidence to most of us that our private worlds are not, in fact, identical with the common world view (R. E. Money-Kyrle, "The World of the Unconscious and the World of Commonsense," *British Journal for the Philosophy of Science*, Vol. 7 [1956], pp. 86-96, on p. 93). G. A. Birks, "Towards a Science of Social Relations," (*ibid.*, Vol. 7 [1956], pp. 117-128, 206-221) shows what happens when private ideas about the world have to be adjusted to conform with the consensus.

14. For the effects of various types of illness and injury on perception and cognition of the milieu see Otto Fenichel, *The Psychoanalytic Theory of Neurosis* (New York: W. W. Norton, 1945), p. 204; C. O. de la Garza and Philip Worchel, "Time and Space Orientation in Schizophrenics," *Journal of Abnormal and Social Psychology*, Vol. 52 (1956), pp. 191-194; T. E. Weckowicz and D. B. Blewett, "Size Constancy and Abstract Thinking in Schizophrenia," *Journal of Mental Science*, Vol. 105 (1959), pp. 909-934; H. J. Eysenck, G. W. Granger, and J. C. Brengelmann, *Perceptual Processes and Mental Illness*, Institute of Psychiatry, Maudsley Monographs No. 2 (London: Chapman and Hall, 1957); G. W. Granger, "Psychophysiology of Vision," in *International Review of Neurobiology*, Vol. 1 (1959) [New York: Academic Press], pp. 245-298; Andrew Paterson and

A fair measure of sensate function is also prerequisite to the general view of the common world. No object looks quite the way it feels; at first sight, those born blind not only fail to recognize visual shapes but see no forms at all, save for a spinning mass of colored light. They may have known objects by touch, but had nothing like the common conception of a space with objects in it. A purely visual world would also be an unreal abstraction; a concrete and stable sense of the milieu depends on synesthesia, sight combined with sound and touch.[15]

To see the world more or less as others see it, one must above all grow up; the very young, like the very ill, are unable to discern adequately what is themselves and what is not. An infant is not only the center of his universe, he *is* the universe. To the young child, everything in the world is alive, created by and for man, and endowed with will: the sun follows him, his parents built the mountains, trees exist because they were planted. As Piaget puts it, everything seems intentional; "the child behaves as if nature

were charged with purpose," and therefore conscious. The clouds know what they are doing, because they have a goal. "It is not because the child believes things to be alive that he regarded them as obedient, but it is because he believes them to be obedient that he regards them as alive." Asked what something is, the young child often says it is *for* something—"a mountain is for climbing"— which implies that it has been *made* for that purpose.[16]

Unable to organize objects in space, to envisage places out of sight, or to generalize from perceptual experience, young children are especially poor geographers. To learn that there are other people, who perceive the world from different points of view, and that a stable, communicable view of things cannot be obtained from one perspective alone, takes many years. Animism and artificialism give way only gradually to mechanistic outlooks and explanations. "No direct experience can prove to a mind inclined towards animism that the sun and the clouds are neither alive nor conscious"; the child must first realize that his parents are not all-powerful beings who made a universe centered on himself. Piaget traces the development in children of perceptual and conceptual objectivity, on which even the most primitive and parochial geographies depend.[17]

Again in old age, however, progressive

O. L. Zangwill, "A Case of Topographic Disorientation Associated with a Unilateral Cerebral Lesion," *Brain*, Vol. 68 (1945), pp. 188-212; A. R. Luria, "Disorders of 'Simultaneous Perception' in a Case of Bilateral Occipito-Parietal Brain Injury," *Brain*, Vol. 82 (1959), pp. 437-49.

15. "From a perception of only 3 senses . . . none could deduce a fourth or fifth" (William Blake, "There is No Natural Religion: First Series, " in *Selected Poetry and Prose of William Blake* [New York: Modern Library, 1953], p. 99); the congenital deaf-mute does not know how music sounds even though he knows that tones exist. For the effects of sensory deprivation, see Felix Deutsch, "The Sense of Reality in Persons Born Blind," *Journal of Psychology*, Vol. 10 (1940), pp. 121-140; Kai von Fieandt, "Toward a Unitary Theory of Perception," *Psychological Review*, Vol. 65 (1958), pp. 315-20; Géza Révész, *Psychology and Art of the Blind* (London: Longmans, Green, 1950); J. Z. Young, *Doubt and Certainty in Science: a Biologist's Reflection on the Brain* (Oxford: Clarendon Press, 1951), pp. 61-66.

16. Jean Piaget, *The Child's Conception of the World* (Paterson, N. J.: Littlefield and Adams, 1960), pp. 248, 357.

17. *Child's Conception of the World*, pp. 384-385; *Construction of Reality in the Child* (New York: Basic Books, 1954), pp. 367-369. Piaget and his associates have worked chiefly with schoolchildren in Geneva. How far their categories and explanations apply universally or vary with culture and milieu remains to be determined. Margaret Mead ("An Investigation of the Thought of Primitive Children, with Special Reference to Animism," *Journal of the Anthropological Institute*, Vol. 62 [1932], pp. 173-190) found that Manus children

loss of hearing, deficiencies of vision, and other infirmities tend to isolate one from reality and to create literally a second geographical childhood.[18]

Different as they are from our own, the perceived milieus, say, of most children of the same age (or of many schizophrenics; or of some drug addicts) may closely resemble one another. But there is little communication or mutual understanding of a conceptual character among children. No matter how many features their pictures of the world may have in common, they lack any *shared* view of the nature of things.

Mutability of the General Consensus. The shared world view is also transient: it is neither the world our parents knew nor the one our children will know. Not only is the earth itself in constant flux, but every generation finds new facts and invents new concepts to deal with them. "You cannot step twice into the same river," Heraclitus observed, "for fresh waters are ever flowing in upon you." Nor does anyone look at the river again in the same way: "The vision of the world geographers construct must be created anew each generation, not only because reality changes but also because human preoccupations vary."[19]

Because we cherish the past as a collective guide to behavior, the general consensus alters very slowly. Scientists as well as laymen ignore evidence incompatible with their preconceptions. New theories which fail to fit established views are resisted, in the hope that they will prove false or irrelevant; old ones yield to convenience rather than to evidence. In Eiseley's phrase, "a world view does not dissolve overnight. Rather, like . . . mountain ranges, it erodes through long centuries."[20] The solvent need not be truth. For example, in the seventeenth century many scholars believed that the earth—the "Mundane Egg"—was originally

---

rejected animistic explanations of natural phenomena. They were more matter-of-fact than Swiss children (and Manus adults) because their language was devoid of figures of speech, because they were punished when they failed to cope effectively with the environment, because their society possessed no machines too complex for children to understand, and because they were barred from animistic rites until past puberty. In Western society, on the other hand, "the language is richly animistic, children are given no such stern schooling in physical adjustment to a comprehensible and easily manipulated physical environment, and the traditional animistic material which is decried by modern scientific thinking is still regarded as appropriate material for child training" (p. 189). (Indeed, books written for children show clearly that adults think children *ought* to be animists.) Elsewhere, however, child animism appears to be significant and tends to decline with age and maturity (Gustav Jahoda, "Child Animism: I. A Critical Survey of Cross-Cultural Research," *Journal of Social Psychology*, Vol. 47 [1958], pp. 197-212).

18. The decline of sensory perception leads the elderly to make false judgments about the environment, and often arouses feelings of isolation and apathy. See Alfred D. Weiss, "Sensory Functions," and Harry W. Braun, "Perceptual Processes," in J. E. Birren, ed., *Handbook of Aging and the Individual: Psychological and Biological Aspects* (Chicago: University of Chicago Press, 1959), pp. 503-542 and 543-561, respectively.

19. Marcel Bélanger, "J'ai choisi de devenir géographe," *Revue Canadienne de Géographie*, Vol. 13 (1959), pp. 70-72, on p. 70. This version of Heraclitus is in Bertrand Russell, *A History of Western Philosophy* (New York: Simon and Schuster, 1945), p. 45; a somewhat different phrasing appears in Plato's "Cratylus" (*The Dialogues of Plato*, B. Jowett, tr., 2 vols. [New York: Random House, 1937], Vol. 1, p. 191).

20. Loren Eiseley, *The Firmament of Time* (New York: Atheneum, 1960), p. 38. Scientists at the French Academy in the seventeenth century denied evidence for the fall of meteorites, obvious to most observers, because they opposed the prevalent superstition that meteorites came by supernatural means. For this and other instances of how " the most stubborn facts will be set aside if there is no place for them in the established framework of science," see Polanyi, *Personal Knowledge*, pp. 138-158.

"smooth, regular, and uniform; without
Mountains, and without a Sea"; to chastise
man for his sins, at or before the Deluge,
God crumpled this fair landscape into continents and ocean deeps, with unsightly crags
and chasms; modern man thus looked out on
"the Ruins of a broken World." This version
of earth history was overthrown, not by
geological evidence, but principally by a
more sanguine view of God and man, and by
a new esthetic standard: to eighteenth century observers, mountains seemed majestic
and sublime, rather than hideous and
corrupt.[21]

**Anthropocentric Character of the World
View.** Mankind's best conceivable world
view is at most a partial picture of the
world—a picture centered on man. We inevitably see the universe from a human point of
view and communicate in terms shaped by
the exigencies of human life. " 'Significance'
in geography is measured, consciously or
unconsciously," says Hartshorne, "in terms
of significance to man"; but it is not in geography alone that man is the measure. "Our
choice of time scale for climatology,"
according to Hare, "is conditioned more by
the length of our life span than by logic";
the physics of the grasshopper, Köhler
points out, would be a different physics than
ours.[22] "All aspects of the environment," as
Cantril puts it, "exist for us only in so far as

they are related to our purposes. If you leave
out human significance, you leave out all
constancy, all repeatability, all form." [23]

Purpose apart, physical and biological
circumstances restrict human perception.
Our native range of sensation is limited;
other creatures experience other worlds than
ours. The human visual world is richly differentiated, compared with that of most
species, but others see better in the dark,
perceive ultraviolet rays as colors, distinguish finer detail, or see near and distant
scenes together in better focus. To many
creatures the milieu is more audible and
more fragrant than to us. For every sensation, moreover, the human perceptual world
varies within strict limits; how bright the
lightning looks, how loud the thunder
sounds, how wet the rain feels at any given
moment of a storm depends on fixed formu-
lae, whose constants, at least, are unique to
man.[24]

---

21. Marjorie Hope Nicolson, *Mountain Gloom and
Mountain Glory: The Development of the Aesthetics of the Infinite* (Ithaca: Cornell University
Press, 1959); quotations (from Thomas Burnet's
Sacred Theory of the Earth [London, 1684]) on
pp. 198, 206.
22. Hartshorne, *Perspective on the Nature of
Geography*, p. 46; F. Kenneth Hare, "The Wester-
lies," *Geographical Review*, Vol. 50 (1960), p. 367;
Wolfgang Köhler, *The Place of Value in a World of
Facts* ([1938 ed.] New York: Meridian Books,
1959). "There is no ultimate source for the physicist's concepts," adds Köhler, "other than the
phenomenal world" (p. 374).

23. Hadley Cantril, "Concerning the Nature of
Perception," *Proceedings of the American Philosophical Society*, Vol. 104 (1960), pp. 467-473, on
p. 470. "The environment with which we are concerned is not the one which is measured in
microns, nor that which is measured in light years,
but that which is measured in millimeters or
meters . . . [It] is not that of particles, atoms,
molecules, or anything smaller than crystals. Nor is
it that of planets, stars, galaxies, or nebulae. The
world of man . . . consists of matter in the solid,
liquid, or gaseous state, organized as an array of
surfaces or interfaces between matter in these
different states" (James J. Gibson, "Perception as a
Function of Stimulation," in Sigmund Koch, ed.,
*Psychology: a Study of a Science, Study I. Con-
ceptual and Systematic: Vol. I. Sensory, Perceptual, and Physiological Foundations* [New York:
McGraw-Hill, 1959], pp. 456-501, on p. 469).
24. S. S. Stevens, "To Honor Fechner and Repeal
His Law," *Science*, Vol. 133 (1961), pp. 80-86.
For human and animal sensory and perceptual
capacities see Adolf Portmann, "The Seeing Eye,"
Landscape, Vol. 9 (1959), pp. 14-18; Ernest
Baumgardt, "La vision des insectes," *La Nature*,
Vol. 90 (1960), pp. 96-99; Donald R. Griffin,
"Sensory Physiology and the Orientation of

The instruments of science do permit partial knowledge of other milieus, real or hypothetical. Blood ordinarily appears a uniform, homogeneous red to the naked eye; seen through a microscope, it becomes yellow particles in a neutral fluid, while its atomic substructure is mostly empty space. But such insights do not show what it is actually like to see normally at a microscopic scale. "The apparently standardized environment of flour in a bottle," Anderson surmises, "would not seem undifferentiated to any investigator who had once been a flour beetle and who knew at firsthand the complexities of flour-beetle existence."[25] The perceptual powers and central nervous systems of many species are qualitatively, as well as quantitatively, different from man's. We can observe, but never experience, the role of surface tension and molecular forces in the lives of small invertebrates, the ability of the octopus to discriminate tactile

impressions by taste, of the butterfly to sense forms through smell, or of the jellyfish to change its size and shape.

The tempo of all varieties of experience is also specific. Time yields humans on the average eighteen separate impressions, or instants, every second; images presented more rapidly seem to fuse into continuous motion. But there are slow-motion fish that perceive separate impressions up to thirty each second, and snails to which a stick that vibrates more than four times a second appears to be at rest.[26]

As with time, so with space; we perceive one of many possible structures, more hyperbolic than Euclidean.[27] The six cardinal directions are not equivalent for us: up and down, front and back, left and right have particular values because we happen to be a special kind of bilaterally symmetrical, terrestrial animal. "It is one contingent fact about the world that we attach very great importance to things having their tops and bottoms in the right places; it is another contingent fact [about ourselves] that we attach more importance to their having their fronts and backs in the right places than their left and right sides."[28] Up and down

Animals," *American Scientist*, Vol. 41 (1953), pp. 208-44; M. J. Wells, "What the Octopus Makes of It: Our World from Another Point of View," *Advancement of Science*, Vol. 17 (1961), pp. 461-471; J. von Uexküll, *Umwelt und Innenwelt der Tiere* (Berlin: Julius Springer, 1909); Karl von Frisch, *Bees: their Vision, Chemical Senses, and Language* (Ithaca: Cornell University Press, 1950), pp. 8 12, 34 36; Donald R. Griffin, *Listening in the Dark: the Acoustic Orientation of Bats and Men* (New Haven: Yale University Press, 1958); K. von Frisch, "Über den Farbsinn der Insekten," and G. Viaud, "La Vision chromatique chez les animaux (sauf les insectes)," in *Mechanisms of Colour Discrimination* (New York: Pergamon Press, 1960), pp. 19-40 and 41-66, respectively; Conrad G. Mueller, "Visual Sensitivity," Irwin Pollack, "Hearing," and Lloyd M. Beidler, "Chemical Senses," in *Annual Review of Psychology*, Vol. 12 (1961), pp. 311-334, 335-362, and 363-388, respectively.
25. Edgar Anderson, "Man as a Maker of New Plants and New Plant Communities," in William L. Thomas, Jr., ed., *Man's Role in Changing the Face of the Earth* (Chicago: University of Chicago Press, 1956), pp. 763-777, on p. 776.

26. J. von Uexküll, *Theoretical Biology* (London: Kegan Paul, 1926), pp. 66-68; Ludwig von Bertalanffy, "An Essay on the Relativity of Categories," *Philosophy of Science*, Vol. 22 (1955), pp. 243-263, on p. 249.
27. Visual space is Euclidean only locally; for normal observers with binocular vision, space has a constant negative curvature corresponding with the hyperbolic geometry of Lobachevski. See Rudolph K. Luneburg, *Mathematical Analysis of Binocular Vision* (Princeton: Princeton University Press, 1947), and Albert A. Blank, "Axiomatics of Binocular Vision. The Foundations of Metric Geometry in Relation to Space Perception," *Journal of the Optical Society of America*, Vol. 48 (1958), pp. 328-334. But under optimal conditions, Gibson maintains, perceptual space is Euclidean ("Perception as a Function of Stimulation," pp. 479-480).
28. Bernard Mayo, "The Incongruity of Counter-

are everywhere good and evil: heaven and hell, the higher and lower instincts, the heights of sublimity and the depths of degradation, even the higher and the lower latitudes have ethical spatial connotations. And left and right are scarcely less differentiated.

Other species apperceive quite differently. Even the fact that physical space seems to us three-dimensional is partly contingent on our size, on the shape of our bodies (an asymmetrical torus), and, perhaps, on our semicircular canals; the world of certain birds is effectively two-dimensional, and some creatures apprehend only one.[29]

Man's experienced world is, then, only one tree of the forest. The difference between this and the others is that man knows his tree is not the only one; and yet can imagine what the forest as a whole might be

like. Technology and memory extend our images far beyond the bounds of direct sensation; consciousness of self, of time, of relationship, and of causality overcome the separateness of individual experiences.[30] Thanks to what has been likened to "a consummate piece of combinatorial mathematics,"[31] we share the conception of a common world. Whatever the defects of the general consensus, the shared world view is essentially well-founded. "We are quite willing to admit that there may be errors of detail in this knowledge," as Russell wrote, referring to science, "but we believe them to be discoverable and corrigible by the methods which have given rise to our beliefs, and we do not, as practical men, entertain · for a moment the hypothesis that the whole edifice may be built on insecure foundations."[32]

parts," *Philosophy of Science*, Vol. 25 (1958), pp. 109-115, on p. 115; Martti Takala, *Asymmetries of Visual Space [Annales Academie Scientiarum Fennicae*, Ser. B., Vol. 72, No. 2] (Helsinki, 1951). Because gravity, unlike bilateral symmetry, affects everything on earth, people adapt more rapidly to distorting spectacles that invert up and down than to those that reverse left and right (Julian E. Hochberg, "Effects of the Gestalt Revolution: the Cornell Symposium on Perception," *Psychological Review*, Vol. 64 [1957], pp. 74-76).
29. G. J. Whitrow, "Why Physical Space Has Three Dimensions," *British Journal for the Philosophy of Science*, Vol. 6 (1955), pp. 13-31; I. J. Good, "Lattice Structure of Space-Time," *ibid.*, Vol. 9 (1959), pp. 317-319. On righteousness as a function of height, see Geraldine Pederson-Krag, "The Use of Metaphor In Analytic Thinking," *Psychoanalytic Quarterly*, Vol. 25 (1956), p. 70. Of the opposition of right and left, Robert Hertz remarks, "if organic asymmetry had not existed, it would have had to be invented" (*Death and the Right Hand* [Glencoe, Ill.: Free Press, 1960], p. 98), and Rodney Needham concludes that "in every quarter of the world it is the right hand, and not the left, which is predominant" ("The Left Hand of the Mugwe: an Analytic Note on the Structure of Meru Symbolism," *Africa*, Vol. 30 [1960], p. 20).

30. "Il y a une différence fondamentale dans la 'facon d'être-au-monde' de l'homme et de l'animal supérieur: ce fait d'être comme englué dans l'objet, de ne pouvoir le survoler, dû . . . à l'unité que fait l'animal avec le monde. . . . L'animal ne peut transcender le réel immédiat" (Jean-C. Filloux, "La nature de l'univers chez l'animal," *La Nature*, Vol. 85 [1957], pp. 403-407, 438-443, 490-493, on p. 493). Analogous points are made by Boulding, *Image*, p. 29; Géza Révész, "The Problem of Space with Particular Emphasis on Specific Sensory Spaces," *American Journal of Psychology*, Vol. 50 (1937), p. 434n; Ernst Cassirer, *An Essay on Man: Introduction to a Philosophy of Human Culture* (New Haven: Yale University Press, 1944 and New York: Doubleday Anchor Books, n.d.), p. 67.
31. Max Born, *Natural Philosophy of Cause and Chance* (Oxford: Clarendon Press, 1949), p. 125. For a critique on the formation of the common world view, see J. P. McKinney, "The Rational and the Real: Comment on a Paper by E. Topitsch," *Philosophy of Science*, Vol. 24 (1957), pp. 275-280.
32. Bertrand Russell, *Our Knowledge of the External World* (New York: Mentor, 1960), p. 56. The question whether the so-called real world actually exists lies beyond the scope of this paper. As Russell says (p. 57), "universal skepticism,

Personal Geographies

Separate personal worlds of experience, learning, and imagination necessarily underlie any universe of discourse. The whole structure of the shared picture of the world is relevant to the life of every participant; and anyone who adheres to a consensus must personally have acquired some of its constituent elements. As Russell put it, "If I believe that there is such a place as Semipalatinsk, I believe it because of things that have happened to *me*."[33] One need not have been in Semipalatinsk; it is enough to have heard of it in some meaningful connection, or even to have imagined (rightly or wrongly) that it exists, on the basis of linguistic or other evidence. But if the place did not exist in some—and potentially in all—personal geographies, it could scarcely form part of a common world view.

Individual and Consensual Worlds Compared. The personal *terra cognita* is, however, in many ways unlike the shared realm of knowledge. It is far more localized and restricted in space and time: I know nothing about the microgeography of most of the earth's crust, much less than the sum of common knowledge about the world as a whole and larger parts, but a great deal about that tiny fraction of the globe I live in—not merely facts that might be inferred from general knowledge and verified by visitors, but aspects of things that no one, lacking my total experience, could ever grasp as I do. "The entire earth," as Wright says, is thus "an immense patchwork of miniature

terrae incognitae"[34]—parts of private worlds not incorporated into the general image. Territorially, as otherwise, each personal environment is both more and less inclusive than the common realm.

Complex Nature of Personal Milieus. The private milieu is more complex and many aspects of it are less accessible to inquiry and exploration than is the world we all share. "Like the earth of a hundred years ago," writes Aldous Huxley, "our mind still has its darkest Africas, its unmapped Borneos and Amazonian basins. . . . A man consists of . . . an Old World of personal consciousness and, beyond a dividing sea, a series of New Worlds—the not too distant Virginias and Carolinas of the personal subconscious . . . ; the Far West of the collective unconscious, with its flora of symbols, its tribes of aboriginal archetypes; and, across another, vaster ocean, at the antipodes of everyday consciousness, the world of Visionary Experience . . . Some people never consciously discover their antipodes. Others make an occasional landing."[35]

To be sure, the general world view likewise transcends objective reality. The hopes and fears of mankind often animate its commonsense perceptions. The supposed loca-

---

though logically irrefutable, is practically barren." Sanity and survival depend on the "sense of being a solid person surrounded by a solid world" (Money-Kyrle, *op. cit.* [see fn. 13], p. 96).

33. Bertrand Russell, *Human Knowledge: Its Scope and Limits* (New York: Simon and Schuster, 1948), p. xii. But see J. K. Feibleman, "Knowing about Semipalatinsk," *Dialectica*, Vol. 9 (1955), pp. 3-4.

34. Wright, "Terrae Incognitae," pp. 3-4. On the other hand, the consensual universe of discourse comprises elements from an infinite number of private worlds—not only those of existing persons, but also those that might conceivably be held. No square mile of the earth's surface has been seen from every possible perspective, but our view of the world in general is based on assumptions about such perspectives, as analogous with those that have been experienced. The Amazon basin would look different in design and detail from the top of every tree within it, but we know enough of the general character and major variations of that landscape to describe it adequately after climbing—or hovering in a helicopter over—a small fraction of its trees.

35. *Heaven and Hell* (New York: Harper, 1955), pp. 1-3.

tion and features of the Garden of Eden stimulated medieval mapmakers; many useful journeys of exploration have sought elusive El Dorados. Delusion and error are no less firmly held by groups than by individuals. Metaphysical assumptions, from original sin to the perfectibility of man, not only color but shape the shared picture of the world. But fantasy plays a more prominent role in any private milieu than in the general geography. Every aspect of the public image is conscious and communicable, whereas many of our private impressions are inchoate, diffuse, irrational, and can hardly be formulated even to ourselves.

The private milieu thus includes much more varied landscapes and concepts than the shared world, imaginary places and powers as well as aspects of reality with which each individual alone is familiar. Hell and the Garden of Eden may have vanished from most of our mental maps, but imagination, distortion, and ignorance still embroider our private landscapes. The most compelling artifacts are but pale reflections of the lapidary architecture of the mind, attempts to recreate on earth the visionary images ascribed by man to God; and every marvel unattained is a Paradise Lost.[36]

36. "Man's spatialization of his world . . . never appears to be exclusively limited to the pragmatic level of action and perceptual experience. . . . Human beings in all cultures have built up a frame of spatial reference that has included the farther as well as the more proximal, the spiritual as well as the mundane, regions of their universe" (A. Irving Hallowell, *Culture and Experience* [Philadelphia: University of Pennsylvania Press, 1955], pp. 187-188). The genesis of these mental maps is explained in R. E. Money-Kyrle, *Man's Picture of His World: a Psycho-analytic Study* (London: Duckworth, 1960); see p. 171. For instances of theological location, see Erich Isaac, "Religion, Landscape and Space, *Landscape*, Vol. 9 (1959-60), pp. 14-18. The visionary transfiguration of the everyday world by means of gems and precious stones is a central theme in Huxley, *Heaven and Hell*.

In each of our personal worlds, far more than in the shared consensus, characters of fable and fiction reside and move about, some in their own lands, others sharing familiar countries with real people and places. We are all Alices in our own Wonderlands, Gullivers in Lilliput and Brobdingnag. Ghosts, mermaids, men from Mars, and the smiles of Cheshire cats confront us at home and abroad. Utopians not only make mythic men, they rearrange the forces of nature: in some worlds water flows uphill, seasons vanish, time reverses, or one- and two-dimensional creatures converse and move about. Invented worlds may even harbor logical absurdities: scientists swallowed up in the fourth dimension, conjurors imprisoned in Klein bottles, five countries each bordering on all the others.[37] Non-terrestrial geometries, topographical monsters, and abstract models of every kind in turn lend insight to views of reality. If we could not imagine the impossible, both private and public worlds would be the poorer.

Extent to Which Private Worlds Are Congruous with "Reality." Though personal milieus in some respects fall short of and in others transcend the more objective consensual reality, yet they at least partly resemble it. What people perceive always pertains to the shared "real" world; even the landscapes of dreams come from actual scenes recently viewed or recalled from memory, consciously or otherwise, however much they may be distorted or transformed. Sensing can take place without external perception (spots before the eyes; ringing in the ears), but "so expressive a phrase as 'the

37. Edwin A. Abbott, *Flatland, a Romance of Many Dimensions* (New York: Dover, 1952 [London, 1884]), is a classic of two-dimensional life. For samples of the impossible, see Clifton Fadiman, ed., *Fantasia Mathematica* (New York: Simon and Schuster, 1958), notably Martin Gardner, "The Island of Five Colors," pp. 196-210.

mind's eye' " is current, Smythies points out, because there is "something very like seeing about having sensory mental images."[38]

Illusions do not long delude most of us; "we see the world the way we see it because it pays us and has paid us to see it that way."[39] To find our way about, avoid danger, earn a living, and achieve basic human contacts, we usually have to perceive what is there. As the Sprouts express it, "the fact that the human species has survived (so far) suggests that there must be considerable correspondence between the milieu as people conceive it to be, and as it actually is."[40] If the picture of the world in our heads were not fairly consistent with the world outside, we should be unable to survive in any environment other than a mental hospital. And if our private milieus were not recognizably similiar to one another, we could never have constructed a common world view.

Range and Limits of Personal Knowledge of the World. However, a perfect fit between the outside world and our views of it is not possible; indeed, complete fidelity would endanger survival. Whether we stay put or move about, our environment is subject to sudden and often drastic change. In consequence, we must be able to see things not only as they are, but also as they might become. Our private milieus are therefore flexible, plastic, and somewhat amorphous. We are physiologically equipped for a wide range of environments, including some of those that we create. But evolution is slow; at any point in time, some of our sensate and conceptual apparatus is bound to be vestigial, better suited to previous than to present milieus.

As individuals, we learn most rapidly about the world not by paying close attention to a single variable, but by superficially scanning a great variety of things. "Everyday perception tends to be selective, creative, fleeting, inexact, generalized, stereotyped" just because imprecise, partly erroneous impressions about the world in general often convey more than exact details about a small segment of it.[41] The observant are not

38. J. R. Smythies, "The Problems of Perception," *British Journal for the Philosophy of Science*, Vol. 11 (1960), pp. 224-238, on p. 229; see also his *Analysis of Perception* (New York: Humanities Press, 1956), pp. 81-105. "The widespread belief that a mirage is something unreal, a sort of trick played on the eyes, is wrong. The picture a mirage presents is real but never quite accurate" (James H. Gordon, "Mirages," in *Smithsonian Institution, Annual Report for 1959* [Washington, D. C., 1960], pp. 327-346, on p. 328). On the form and content of landscapes in dreams, mirages, and hallucinations, and their relations with "reality," see Charles Fisher, "Dreams, Images and Perception: A Study of Unconscious-Preconscious Relationships," *Journal of the American Psychoanalytic Association*, Vol. 4 (1956), pp. 5-48; Charles Fisher and I. H. Paul, "The Effect of Subliminal Visual Stimulation on Images and Dreams: a Validation Study," *ibid.*, Vol. 7 (1959), pp. 35-83; Peter Hobart Knapp, "Sensory Impressions in Dreams," *Psychoanalytic Quarterly*, Vol. 25 (1956), pp. 325-347; C. T. K. Churi, "On the 'Space' and 'Time' of Hallucinations," *British Journal for the Philosophy of Science*, Vol. 8 (1958), pp. 302-306; Aldous Huxley, *The Doors of Perception* (London: Chatto and Windus, 1954).
39. Boulding, *The Image*, p. 50.
40. Harold Sprout and Margaret Sprout, *Man-Milieu Relationship Hypotheses in the Context of International Politics* (Princeton University Center of International Studies, 1956), p. 61. The essential correspondence between the perceived and the actual milieu is stressed in James J. Gibson, *The Perception of the Visual World* (Boston: Houghton Mifflin, 1950).
41. *Ibid.*, p. 10; see also Miller, "The Magical Number Seven" [see fn. 12], pp. 88-89. We can count only a few of the stars or raindrops we see, beyond which everything becomes blurred; but our vagueness could not be rectified by looking longer or more carefully: "the blur is just as essential a feature of sense perception as other features are. . . . Sense perception is inexact in a very different sense from that in which . . . a map is inexact"

necessarily most accurate; effective observation is never unwaveringly attentive. As Vernon emphasizes, "changing perceptions are necessary to preserve mental alertness and normal powers of thought." Awareness is not always conducive to survival. He who fails to see a tiger and hence does not attract its attention "may escape the destruction which his more knowing fellow invites by the very effects of his knowledge." So, Boulding concludes, "under some circumstances, ignorance is bliss and knowledge leads to disaster." [42]

Essential perception of the world, in short, embraces every way of looking at it: conscious and unconscious, blurred and distinct, objective and subjective, inadvertent and deliberate, literal and schematic.

Perception itself is never unalloyed: sensing, thinking, feeling, and believing are simultaneous, interdependent processes. A purely perceptual view of the world would be as lame and false as one based solely on logic, insight, or ideology. "All fact," as Goethe said, "is in itself theory." The most direct and simple experience of the world is a composite of perception, memory, logic,

and faith. Looking down from a window, like Descartes, we say that we see men and women, when in fact we perceive no more than parts of hats and coats. The recognition of Mt. Monadnock, Chisholm demonstrates, is a conceptual as well as a visual act: [43]

Suppose that you say to me, as we are riding through New Hampshire, "I see that that is Mt. Monadnock behind the trees." If I should ask, "How do you know it's Monadnock?" you may reply by saying, "I've been here many times before and I can *see* that it is." . . . If I still have my doubts about what you claim to see . . . I may ask, "What makes you *think* that's Monadnock that you see?" . . . An appropriate answer would be this: "I can see that the mountain is shaped like a wave and that there is a little cabin near the top. There is no other mountain answering to that description within miles of here." . . . What you now claim to see is, not that the mountain is Monadnock, but merely that it has a shape like a wave and that there is a cabin near the top. And this new "perceptual statement" is coupled with a statement of independent information ("Monadnock is shaped like a wave and there is a cabin near the top; no other mountain like that is within miles of here")—information acquired prior to the present perception.

And each succeeding perceptual statement can similarly be broken down into new perceptual claims and other additional information, until "we reach a point where we find . . . no *perceptual* claim at all."

Uniqueness of Private Milieus

Despite their congruence with each other and with the world as it is, private milieus do diverge markedly among people in different cultures, for individuals within a social group, and for the same person as child and

(Waismann, "Analytic-Synthetic" [see fn. 6], *Analysis*, Vol. 13 [1953], pp. 76-77). Types and ranges of perception and learning are surveyed in M. D. Vernon, *A Further Study of Visual Perception* (Cambridge: The University Press, 1952); R. J. Hirst, *The Problems of Perception* (London: Allen & Unwin, 1959); James Drever, 2d., "Perceptual Learning," in *Annual Review of Psychology*, Vol. 11 (1960), pp. 131-160. For a concise theoretical review, see William Bevan, "Perception: Development of a Concept," *Psychological Review*, Vol. 65 (1958), pp. 34-55.

42. Magdalen D. Vernon, "Perception, Attention and Consciousness," *Advancement of Science*, Vol. 16 (1959), pp. 111-123, on p. 120; Boulding, *The Image*, p. 169. The classic story illustrating the virtues of ignorance of the geographical environment is in Kurt Koffka, *Principles of Gestalt Psychology* (New York: Harcourt-Brace, 1935), pp. 27-28.

43. Chisholm, *Perceiving*, pp. 55-58; for the Descartes argument, from his *Meditations*, see pp. 154-56. See also Joseph R. Royce, "The Search for Meaning," *American Scientist*, Vol. 47 (1959), pp. 515-35; Ernst Cassirer, *The Philosophy of Symbolic Forms; Volume Three: The Phenomonology of Knowledge* (New Haven: Yale University Press, 1957), p. 25.

as adult, at various times and places, and in sundry moods. "The life of each individual," concludes Delagado, "constitutes an original and irreversible perceptive experience."[44]

Each private world view is unique, to begin with, because each person inhabits a different milieu. "The fact that no two human beings can occupy the same point at the same time and that the world is never precisely the same on successive occasions means," as Kluckhohn and Mowrer put it, that "the physical world is idiosyncratic for each individual." Experience is not only unique; more significantly, it is also self-centered; I am part of your milieu, but not of my own, and never see myself as the world does. It is usually one's self to which the world attends; "we will assume that an eye looks at us, or a gun points at us," notes Gombrich, "unless we have good evidence to the contrary."[45]

Each private world view is also unique because everyone chooses from and reacts to the milieu in a different way. We elect to see certain aspects of the world and to avoid others. Morever, because "everything that we know about an object affects the way in which it appears to the eye," no object is apt to seem quite the same to any two percipients.[46] Thus "in some respects," as Clark says, "each man's appraisal of an identical situation is peculiarly his own."[47]

Cultural Differences in Aspects of World Views. Appraisals are, of course, profoundly affected by society and culture. Each social system organizes the world in accordance with its particular structure and requirements; each culture screens perception of the milieu in harmony with its particular style and techniques.[48]

Consider social and cultural differences in habits of location and techniques of orientation. Eskimo maps, Stefansson reports, often show accurately the number and shape of turns in routes and rivers, but neglect lineal distances, noting only how far one can travel in a day. The Saulteaux Indians do not think of circular motion, according to Hallowell; to go counter-clockwise is to move, they say, from east to south to west to north, the birth order of the four winds in their mythology. To find their way about, some peoples utilize concrete and others abstract base points, still others edges in the landscape, or their own locations. The Chukchee of Siberia distinguish twenty-two compass directions, most of them tied to the position of the sun and varying with the seasons. The precise, asymmetrical navigation nets of Micronesian voyagers made use of constellations and islands. Tikopians, never far from the ocean, and unable to conceive of a large land mass, use *inward* and *seaward* to help locate anything: "there is a spot of mud on

44. Delgado, "A Possible Model for Ideas" [see fn. 12], p. 255.
45. Clyde Kluckhohn and O. H. Mowrer, " 'Culture and Personality' : a Conceptual Scheme," *American Anthropologist*, Vol. 46 (1944), pp. 1-29, on p. 13; E. H. Gombrich, *Art and Illusion: A Study in the Psychology of Pictorial Representation* (New York: Pantheon Books, 1960 [Bollingen Series, XXXV, No. 5]), p. 276. See also Sprout, *Man-Milieu Relationship Hypotheses*, p. 18.
46. Vaughan Cornish, *Geographical Essays* (London: Sifton, Praed, [1946]), pp. 78-79.
47. K. G. T. Clark, "Certain Underpinnings of Our Arguments in Human Geography," *Transactions of the Institute of British Geographers*, No. 16 (1950), pp. 15-22, on p. 20.
48. "Only exceptionally do we react in any literal sense to stimuli. . . . Rather, we react to our interpretations of stimuli. These interpretations are derived in considerable part from our culture and from each person's specific experiences in that culture" (Clyde Kluckhohn, "The Scientific Study of Values and Contemporary Civilization," *Proceedings of the American Philosophical Society*, Vol. 102 [1958], pp. 469-476, on p. 469). The classic case study is T. T. Waterman, *Yurok Geography* (Berkeley: University of California Press, 1920); see also Erik H. Erikson, *Childhood and Society* (New York: W. W. Norton, 1950), pp.

your seaward cheek."[49] In the Tuamotus, compass directions refer to winds, but places on the atolls are located by reference to their direction from the principal settlement. Westerners are more spatially egocentric than Chinese or Balinese. The religious significance of cardinal directions controls orientation indoors and out on the North China plain, and the Balinese give all directions in terms of compass points. Where we would say "go to the left," "towards me," or "away from the wall," they say "take the turn to the West," "pull the table southward," or, in case of a wrong note on the piano, "hit the key to the East of the one you are hitting."[50] Disorientation is universally disagreeable; but inability to locate north quite incapacitates the Balinese. The English writer Stephen Potter was amazed to find that most Americans neither knew nor cared what watershed they were in, or which way rivers flowed—facts he maintained were second nature to Englishmen.[51]

Apperception of shape is also culturally conditioned. According to Herskovits, an electrical engineer working in Ghana complained that "When a trench for a conduit must be dug, I run a line between the two points, and tell my workers to follow it. But at the end of the job, I invariably find that the trench has curves in it." In their land "circular forms predominate. . . .They do not live in . . . a carpentered world, so that to follow a straight line marked by a cord is as difficult for them" as drawing a perfect freehand circle is for most of us.[52] Zulus tested with the Ames trapezoidal window actually saw it as a trapezoid more often

141-60. The literature on world views is ably summarized by Clyde Kluckhohn, "Culture and Behavior," in Gardner Lindzey, ed., *Handbook of Social Psychology*, 2 vols. (Cambridge, Mass.: Addison-Wesley, 1954), Vol. 2, pp. 921-976.
49. Raymond Firth, *We, the Tikopia: a Sociological Study of Kinship in Primitive Polynesia* (London: Allen & Unwin, 1936), p. 19. For the previous examples, see the letter from Vilhjalmur Stefannson quoted in Erwin Raisz, *General Cartography* (New York: McGraw-Hill, 1948), p. 4; Hallowell, *Culture and Experience*, p. 201; Waldemar Bogoras, *The Chukchee. II.—Religion.* The Jesup North Pacific Expedition, Vol. VII, Memoir of the American Museum of Natural History (Leiden: Brill; New York: Stechert, 1907), pp. 303-304. The cultural and environmental contexts of orientation are considered at length in Hallowell, *op. cit.*, pp. 184-202, and Kevin Lynch, *The Image of the City* (Cambridge, Mass.: Technology Press and Harvard University Press, 1960), pp. 123-133.
50. Bengt Danielsson, *Work and Life in Raroia: an Acculturation Study from the Tuamotu Group, French Oceania* (London: Allen & Unwin, 1956), pp. 30-31; Derk Bodde, "Types of Chinese Categorical Thinking," *Journal of the American Oriental Society*, Vol. 59 (1939), pp. 200-219, on p. 201n; Jane Belo, "The Balinese Temper," *Character and Personality*, Vol. 4 (1935), pp. 120-146, quote on pp. 126-127. Einar Haugen, "The Semantics of Icelandic Orientation," *Word*, Vol. 13 (1957), pp. 447-459, shows how cardinal orientation can depend on one's location with reference to an ultimate destination; thus an Icelander heading for the southern tip of the island is going "south" even if his coastwise route happens to be southwest or west. For other early or "primitive" methods of pathfinding, see B. F. Adler, *Maps of Primitive Peoples* (St. Petersburg, 1910), abridged by H. de Hutorowicz, *Bulletin of the American Geographical Society*, Vol. 43 (1911), pp. 669-679; Waldemar Bogoras, "Ideas of Space and Time in the Conception of Primitive Religion," *American Anthropologist*, Vol. 27 (1925), pp. 212-215; Pierre Jaccard, *Le Sens de la direction et l'orientation lointaine chez l'homme* (Paris: Payot, 1932); Harold Gatty, *Nature is Your Guide: How to Find Your Way on Land and Sea by Observing Nature* (New York: Dutton, 1958).
51. "I hardly found an American who knew which watershed he was in, which left me, as an Englishman who is uneasy unless he knows which ocean will receive his urination, somewhat scandalized" (*Potter on America* [London: Hart-Davis, 1956] p. 13).
52. Melville J. Herskovits, "Some Further Comments on Cultural Relativism," *American Anthropologist*, Vol. 60 (1958), pp. 266-273, on pp. 267-268.

than Americans, who usually see it as a rectangle; habituated to man-made rectangular forms, we are apt unconsciously to assume that *any* four-sided object is a rectangle.[53]

Territoriality—the ownership, division, and evaluation of space—also differs from group to group. In American offices, workers stake out claims around the walls and readily move to accommodate new employees; but the Japanese gravitate toward the center of the room, and many Europeans are loathe to relinquish space once pre-empted. Eastern Mediterranean Arabs distinguish socially between right and left hand sides of outer offices, and value proximity to doors. In seeing and describing landscapes, Samoans emphasize the total impression, Moroccans the details. The Trukese sharply differentiate various parts of open spaces, but pay little attention to dividing lines or edges—a trait which makes land claims difficult to resolve.[54]

As with shapes, so with colors. Our most accustomed hues, such as blue and green, are not familiar in certain other cultures; whereas gradations scarcely perceptible to us may be part of their common experience. "There is no such thing as a 'natural' division of the spectrum," Ray concludes. "Each culture has taken the spectral continuum and has divided it into units on a quite arbitrary basis. . . . The effects of brightness, luminosity, and saturation are often confused with hue; and the resulting systems are emotional and subjective, not scientific."[55] Among the Hanunóo of Mindoro, Conklin shows, the most basic color terms refer to degrees of wetness (saturation) and brightness; hue is of secondary interest.[56]

As the diverse views of color suggest, it is not merely observed phenomena that vary with culture, but whole categories of experience. A simple percept here may be a complex abstraction there. Groupings of supreme importance in one culture may have no relevance in another. The Aleuts had no generic name for their island chain, since they did not recognize its unity. The Aruntas organize the night sky into separate, overlapping constellations, some out of bright stars, others out of faint ones. To the Trukese, fresh and salt water are unrelated substances. The gauchos of the Argentine are said to have lumped the vegetable world into four named groups: cattle fodder, bedding straw, woody material, and all other plants—including roses, herbs, and cab-

53. Gordon W. Allport and Thomas F. Pettigrew, "Cultural Influence on the Perception of Movement: the Trapezoidal Illusion among Zulus," *Journal of Abnormal and Social Psychology*, Vol. 55 (1957), pp. 104-113. Under "optimal" visual conditions, however, the Zulus mistook the trapezoid for a rectangle almost as often as Americans do, perhaps because most of them recognized it as a model of a Western-type window (Charles W. Slack, "Critique on the Interpretation of Cultural Differences in the Perception of Motion in Ames's Trapezoidal Window," *American Journal of Psychology*, Vol. 72 [1959], pp. 127-131). Another aspect of spatial perception which varies with culture is surveyed in Donald N. Michael, "Cross-Culture Investigations of Closure," in David C. Beardslee and Michale Wertheimer, eds., *Readings in Perception* (New York: Van Nostrand, 1958), pp. 160-170.
54. Edward T. Hall, *The Silent Language* (New York: Doubleday, 1959), pp. 197-200, and "The Language of Space," *Landscape*, Vol. 10 (1960), pp. 41-45; Thomas Gladwin and Seymour B. Sarason, *Truk: Man in Paradise*, Viking Fund Publications in Anthropology No. 20 (New York: Wenner-Gren, 1953), pp. 225-226, 269-270.

55. Verne F. Ray, "Techniques and Problems in the Study of Human Color Perception," *Southwestern Journal of Anthropology*, Vol. 8 (1952), pp. 251-259, quotes on pp. 258-259; see also Ray, "Human Color Perception and Behavioral Response," *Transactions of the New York Academy of Sciences*, Ser. II, Vol. 16 (1953), pp. 98-104.
56. Harold C. Conklin, "Hanunóo Color Categories," *Southwestern Journal of Anthropology*, Vol. 11 (1955), pp. 339-344.

bages.[57] There is no natural or best way to classify anything; all categories are useful rather than true, and the landscape architect rightly prefers a morphological to a genetic taxonomy. The patterns people see in nature also vary with economic, ethical, and esthetic values. Esthetically neutral to Americans, colors have moral connotations to Navahos; an Indian administrator's attempt to use colors as impartial voting symbols came to grief, since the Navahos viewed blue as good and red as bad.[58]

The Significance of Linguistic Differences in Apperception of the Milieu. The very words we use incline us toward a particular view of the universe. In Whorf's now classic phrase, "We dissect nature along lines laid down by our native languages. . . . We cut nature up, organize it into concepts, and ascribe significances as we do, largely because we are parties to an agreement to organize it in this way—an agreement that holds throughout our speech community." [59] To be sure, language also adjusts to the world view, just as environment molds vocabulary: within a single generation the craze for skiing has given us almost as many different words for *snow* as the Eskimos have.

Linguistic patterns do not irrevocably imprison the senses, but rather, Hoijer judges, "direct perception and thinking into certain habitual channels." [60] Things with names are easier to distinguish than those that lack them; the gauchos who used only four floristic terms no doubt saw more than four kinds of plants, but "their perceptual world is impoverished by their linguistic one." [61] Classifications into animate or inanimate, masculine, feminine, or neuter, and mass (sand, flour, grass, snow) or particular nouns (man, dog, thimble, leaf) variously affect the way different speech communities view things. We tend to think of waves, mountains, horizons, and martinis as though they were composed of discrete entities, but conceive surf, soil, scenery, and milk as aggregates, principally because the former terms are plurals, the latter indefinite nouns.[62]

57. The Argentine data are cited in Karl Vossler, "Volkssprachen und Weltsprachen," *Welt und Wort*, Vol. 1 (1946), pp. 97-101, on p. 98, and discussed by Harold Basilius, "Neo-Humboldtian Ethnolinguistics," *Word*, Vol. 8 (1952), pp. 95-105, on p. 101. For the rest, see Gladwin and Sarason, *Truk*, p. 30, and Lynch, *op. cit.*, pp. 131-132.
58. Hall, *Silent Language*, pp. 132-133. Many landscape features exist as separate entities only in our minds. As Gombrich says (*Art and Illusion*, p. 100), "There is a fallacy in the idea that reality contains such features as mountains and that, looking at one mountain after another, we slowly learn to generalize and form the abstract idea of mountaineity." Owing to the 19th-century popularity of Alpine climbing, the English standard of mountains changed dramatically: for Gilbert White the 800-foot Sussex Downs were "majestic mountains"; today anything below 2,000 feet is at best a "hill" [Vaughan Cornish, *Scenery and the Sense of Sight* (Cambridge: University Press, 1935), p. 77].
59. "Science and Linguistics" [1940], in *Language, Thought, and Reality; Selected Writings of Benjamin Lee Whorf*, John B. Carroll, ed. (Cambridge, Mass.: Technology Press; New York: Wiley; London: Chapman and Hall, 1956), p. 213.
60. Harry Hoijer, "The Relation of Language to Culture," in A. L. Kroeber *et al.*, *Anthropology Today: an Encyclopedic Inventory* (Chicago: University of Chicago Press, 1953), pp. 554-573, on p. 560.
61. Garrett Hardin, "The Threat of Clarity," *ETC.: a Review of General Semantics*, Vol. 17 (1960), pp. 269-278, on p. 270. Similarly, people more readily perceive and identify colors that have widely-known specific names (like blue and green) than those that do not (Roger W. Brown and Eric H. Lenneberg, "A Study in Language and Cognition," *Journal of Abnormal and Social Psychology*, Vol. 49 [1954], pp. 454-462).
62. "English terms, like 'sky, hill, swamp,' persuade us to regard some elusive aspect of nature's endless variety as a distinct THING, almost like a table or chair" (Whorf, *Language, Thought, and*

The structural aspects of language influence ways of looking at the world more than do vocabularies. Seldom consciously employed, usually slow to change, syntax pervades basic modes of thought. In Shawnee, La Barre suggests, "I let her have one on the noggin" is grammatically analogous to "The damned thing slipped out of

Reality, p. 240; see also pp. 140-141). But Roger W. Brown (*Words and Things* [Glencoe, Ill.: Free Press, 1958], pp. 248-252) maintains that the distinction between mass and specific nouns makes perceptual sense and corresponds well with perceived reality.

One can easily, as critics of Whorf have pointed out, make too much of such distinctions. The fact that the word for *sun* is masculine in French and feminine in German, whereas that for *moon* is feminine in French and masculine in German, cannot easily be correlated with the habits of thought or *Weltanschauung* of either people. The fact that in Algonquian languages the gender class of "animate" nouns includes such words as *raspberry, stomach,* and *kettle,* while "inanimate" nouns include *strawberry, thigh,* and *bowl* does not imply "that speakers of Algonquian have a shrine to the raspberry and treat it like a spirit, while the strawberry is in the sphere of the profane" (Joseph H. Greenberg, "Concering Inferences from Linguistic to Nonlinguistic Data," in Harry Hoijer, ed., *Language in Culture,* American Anthropological Association, Memoir No. 79 [Chicago, 1954], pp. 3-19, on pp. 15-16). In short, "If grammar itself was once founded on an unconscious metaphysic, this linkage is now so vestigial as to have no appreciable bearing on the structure of philosophic ideas" (Lewis S. Feuer, "Sociological Aspects of the Relation Between Language and Philosophy," *Philosophy of Science,* Vol. 20 [1953], pp. 85-100, on p. 87). This may be true of most aspects of language, and of philosophical ideas in their broadest sense. On the other hand, the fact that English-speaking mid-Victorians clad table and piano legs in ruffs and deplored direct reference to them in mixed company was not a necessary outgrowth of prudery but depended also on the metaphorical extension of the word for humans limbs to furniture—a connection not made by speakers of other languages. In this respect, language certainly altered the English—and still more the American—home landscape.

my hand."[63] Lacking transitive verbs, Greenlanders tend to see things happen without specific cause; "I kill him," in their language, becomes "he dies to me." In European tongues, however, action accompanies perception, and the transitive verb animates every event with purpose and cause. The Hopis have subjectless verbs, but most Indo-European subjects have objects, which give expression a dualistic, animistic stamp. In Piaget's illustration, to say "the wind blows" "perpetrates . . . the triple absurdity of suggesting that the wind can be independent of the action of blowing, that there can be a wind that does not blow, and that the wind exists apart from its outward manifestations."[64] Important differences also occur

63. Weston La Barre, *The Human Animal* (Chicago: University of Chicago Press, 1954), p. 204. See Whorf, *op. cit.,* p. 235.
64. Piaget, *Child's Conception of the World,* p. 249. A book has been written to tell parents how to answer a child who asks such questions as "what does the wind do when it's not blowing?" (Ruth Purcell, "Causality and Language Rigidity," *ETC.,* Vol. 15 [1958], pp. 175-180, on p. 179). Whorf (*Language, Thought, and Reality*) compares Hopi language and thought with that of "Standard Average European" in several papers (*e. g.,* pp. 57-64, 134-159, 207-219).

Unlike most psychologists and anthropologists, geographers have tended to assume, with positivistic philosophers, that we could rid ourselves of animistic and teleological kinds of explanation and ways of looking at the world by substituting other words and phrases in our language. "Ritter's teleological views . . . though they colour every statement he makes, yet do not affect the essence," according to H. J. Mackinder; "it is easy to re-state each proposition in the most modern evolutionary terms" (President's address, Section E, British Association for the Advancement of Science, *Report of the 65th Annual Meeting,* Ipswich, 1895 [London: Murray, 1895], pp. 738-748, on p. 743); that is, Mackinder found it easy to accommodate Ritter's brand of determinism to his own. For other views on the relation between teleological language and habits of thought, see Sprout, *Man-Milieu Relationship Hypotheses,* pp. 27-28; A. J.

within linguistic families. The French distinction between the imperfect tense (used for things and processes) and the perfect (used for man and his actions) contrasts the uniformity of nature with the uniqueness of man in a way that English does not ordinarily express.

That such distinctions can all be conveyed in English shows that language does not fetter thought; with sufficient care and effort, practically everything in any system of speech can be translated. Nevertheless, a concept that comes naturally and easily in one tongue may require awkward and tedious circumlocution in another. The difference between what is customary for some but difficult for others is apt to be crucial in terms of habits of thought and, perhaps, orders of events. European scientists, whose languages lump processes with substances as nouns, took much longer to account for vitamin deficiencies than for germ diseases, partly because "I have a germ" was a more natural locution than "I have a lack of vitamins." In short, as Waismann says, "by growing up in a certain language, by thinking in its semantic and syntactical grooves, we acquire a certain more or less uniform outlook on the world. . . . Language shapes and fashions the frame in which experience is set, and different languages achieve this in different ways."[65]

Personal Variations in Aspects of the World View. Private world views diverge from one another even within the limits set by logical necessity, human physiology, and group standards. In any society, individuals of similar cultural background, who speak the same language, still perceive and understand the world differently. "You cannot see things until you know roughly what they are," comments C. S. Lewis, whose hero on the planet Malacandra at first perceives "nothing but colours—colours that refused to form themselves into things."[66] But what you think you know depends both on what is familiar to you and on your proclivities. When the well-known is viewed from fresh perspectives, upside down or through distorting lenses, form and color are enhanced, as Helmholtz noted; the unexpected has a vivid, pictorial quality. On the other hand, prolonged observation may change red to apparent green, or shrink a figure in proportion to its surroundings.[67]

Bernatowicz, "Teleology in Science Teaching," *Science*, Vol. 128 (1958), pp. 1402-1405; Ernest Nagel, "Teleological Explanation and Teleological Sytems," in Feigl and Brodbeck, *Readings in the Philosophy of Science*, pp. 537-558; Karl A. Sinnhuber, "Karl Ritter 1779-1859," *Scottish Geographical Magazine*, Vol. 75 (1959), p. 160.
65. Waismann, "Analytic-Synthetic" [see fn. 6], *Analysis*, Vol. 13 (1952), p. 2. "The fact that an ethnologist can describe in circumlocution certain distinctions in kin that are *customarily* made by the Hopi does not alter his conclusion that the Hopi name kin and behave toward them differently from us" (Harry Hoijer, review of Roger W. Brown, *Words and Things*, in *Language*, Vol. 35 [1959], pp. 496-503, on p. 501). For a range of views on metalinguistics see Eric H. Lenneberg, "Cognition in Ethnolinguistics," *Language*, Vol. 29 (1953), pp. 463-71; Franklin Fearing, "An Examination of the Conceptions of Benjamin Whorf in the Light of Theories of Perception and Cognition," in Hoijer, ed., *Language and Culture*, pp. 47-81; Anatol Rapoport and Arnold Horowitz, "The Sapir-Whorf-Korzybski Hypothesis: a Report and a Reply," *ETC.*, Vol. 17 (1960), pp. 346-363.
66. *Out of the Silent Planet* (New York: Macmillan, 1952), p. 40.
67. For Helmholtz, see Cassirer, *Philosophy of Symbolic Forms*, Vol. 3, pp. 131-132. On changes in apparent color and size, see T. N. Cornsweet *et al.*, "Changes in the Perceived Color of Very Bright Stimuli," *Science*, Vol. 128 (1958), pp. 898-899; Dorothea Jameson and Leo M. Hurvich, "Perceived Color and Its Dependence on Focal, Surrounding, and Preceding Stimulus Variables," *Journal of the Optical Society of America*, Vol. 49 (1959), pp. 890-898; Wolfgang Köhler, *Dynamics in Psychology* (New York: Grove Press, 1960 [1940]), pp. 84-86.

The purpose and circumstances of observation materially alter what is seen. The stage electrician cares how the lights look, not about the actual colors of the set; the oculist who tests my eyes is not interested in what the letters are, but in how they appear to me. Intent modifies the character of the world.[68]

Outside the laboratory, no two people are likely to see a color as the same unless they similarly identify the thing that is colored. Even then, preconceptions shape appearances, as Cornish points out: "The exquisite colours which light and atmosphere impart to a snowy landscape are only half seen by many people owing to their opinion that 'snow is really white.' "[69] Such stereotypes may outweigh other physiological facts. The United States Navy was advised to switch the color of survival gear and life jackets from yellow to fluorescent red, not so much to increase visibility as to buoy the confidence of the man lost at sea; dressed in red, he imagines, "They can't fail to see me."[70]

The way a landscape looks depends on all the attendant circumstances, for each sense is affected by the others. Velvet looks soft, ice sounds solid, red feels warm because experience has confirmed these impressions. The sight of gold and blond beech trees lit by sunlight made Cornish forget that he was cold; but he could not appreciate a "frosty" blue landscape seen from a cold railway carriage. "Quite often," notes H. M. Tomlinson, "our first impression of a place is also our last, and it depends solely upon the weather and the food."[71]

Circumstance apart, each person is distinctively himself. "The individual carries with him into every perceptual situation . . . his characteristic sensory abilities, intelligence, interests, and temperamental qualities," according to Vernon; and his "responses will be coloured and to some extend determined by these inherent individual qualities."[72] Ability to estimate vertical and horizontal correctly, for example, varies with sex and personality as well as with maturity: strongminded men are better at telling which way is up than are women, neurotics, and children, whose kinesthetic sense reinforces visual perception less adequately.[73] The story of the Astronomer-Royal, Maskelyne, who dismissed a faithful assistant for persistently recording the passage of stars more than half a second later than he did, is often told to illustrate the inevitability of perceptual divergence under the best of circumstances.[74] Each of

68. "Without the conception of the individual and his needs, a distinction between illusion and 'true' cognition cannot be made" (Horace B. English, "Illusion as a Problem in Systematic Psychology," *Psychological Review*, Vol. 58 [1951], pp. 52-53). The size and shape of objects seem appropriately and necessarily constant, but most of us can afford to be "fooled" by the apparent bending of a stick half-submerged in water.
69. Cornish, *Scenery and the Sense of Sight*, p. 22. On the dissimilar impressions of identical shapes and colors, see Karl Duncker, "The Influence of Past Experience upon Perceptual Properties," *American Journal of Psychology*, Vol. 52 (1939), pp. 255-265; Jerome S. Bruner and Leo Postman, "Expectation and the Perception of Color," *American Journal of Psychology*, Vol. 64 (1951), pp. 216-227; Arthur Kapp, "Colour-Image Synthesis with Two Unorthodox Primaries," *Nature*, Vol. 184 (1959), pp. 710-713; Edwin H. Land, "Experiments in Color Vision," *Scientific American*, Vol. 200, No. 5 (May 1959), pp. 84-99.
70. "Navy Research on Color Vision," *Naval Research Reviews* (October, 1959), p. 19.

71. *The Face of the Earth; with Some Hints for Those About to Travel* (Indianapolis: Bobbs-Merrill, 1951), p. 52.
72. Vernon, *A Further Study of Visual Perception*, p. 255.
73. H. A. Witkin *et al.*, *Personality Through Perception: an Experimental and Clinical Study* (New York: Harper, 1954); Herman A. Witkin, "The Perception of the Upright," *Scientific American*, Vol. 200, No. 2 (February 1959), pp. 51-56.
74. Polanyi, *Personal Knowledge*, pp. 19-20, re-

us warps the world in his own way and endows landscapes with his particular mirages.

People at home in the same environments, for example, habitually select different modes of orientation. There is only one published "New Yorker's Map of the United States," but Trowbridge found a great variety of personal imaginary maps. Individual deviations of direction ranged from zero to 180 degrees off course; some were consistent, others more distorted at Times Square than at the Battery, or accurate about Albany but not about Chicago. Still others assumed that streets always point towards cardinal directions, or imagined all distant places as lying due east or west. A few know which direction they face the moment they emerge from subways and theatres, others are uncertain, still others are invariably mistaken. Lynch characterizes structural images of the environment as positional, disjointed, flexible, and rigid, depending on whether people orient themselves principally by distant landmarks, by memories of details in the landscape, by crossings, street turns, or directions, or by maps.[75]

Subjective Elements in Private Geographies. Another reason why private world views are irreducibly unique is that all

information is inspired, edited, and distorted by feeling. Coins look larger to children of the poor,[76] the feast smells more fragrant to the hungry, the mountains loom higher to the lost. "Had our perceptions no connexion with our pleasures," wrote Santayana, "we should soon close our eyes on this world."[77] We seldom differentiate among people, places, or things until we have a personal interest in them. One American town is much like another to me, unless I have a good motive for telling them apart. The most exhaustive study of photographs and ethnological evidence does not enable us to distinguish among individuals of another race with the ease, speed, and certainty generated by strong feeling. All Chinese may look the same to me, but not to the man—however foreign—with a Chinese wife. Only the flea circus owner can tell you which is which among his performing fleas.[78]

---

76. Jerome S. Bruner and Cecile C. Goodman, "Value and Need as Organizing Factors in Perception," *Journal of Abnormal and Social Psychology*, Vol. 42 (1947), pp. 33-44. Further tests yielded significant differences in size estimation principally when coins were judged from memory (Launor F. Carter and Kermit Schooler, "Value, Need, and Other Factors in Perception," *Psychological Review*, Vol. 56 [1949], pp. 200-207), but the initial general hypothesis has been substantially confirmed (J. S. Bruner and George S. Klein, "The Functions of Perceiving: New Look Retrospect," in Bernard Kaplan and Seymour Wapner, eds., *Perspectives in Psychological Theory: Essays in Honor of Heinz Werner* [New York: International Universities Press, 1960], p. 67).

77. George Santayana, *The Sense of Beauty; Being the Outline of Aesthetic Theory* [1896] (New York: Dover Publications, 1955), p. 3. "I cannot," writes Gardner Murphy, "find an area where hedonistic perceptual theory cannot apply" ("Affect and Perceptual Learning," *Psychological Review*, Vol. 63 [1956] p. 7).

78. Anton Ehrenzweig, *The Psycho-Analysis of Artistic Hearing and Vision: an Introduction to a Theory of Unconscious Perception* (New York: Julian Press, 1953), p. 170. See also James J. Gibson and Eleanor J. Gibson, "Perceptual Learn-

---

counts this and similar episodes. H. J. Eysenck, "Personality and the Perception of Time," *Perceptual and Motor Skills*, Vol. 9 (1959), pp. 405-406, shows that introverts and extroverts clock the passage of time at systematically different rates. See also John R. Kirk and George D. Talbot, "The Distortion of Information," *ETC.*, Vol. 17 (1959), pp. 5-27; Melvin Wallace and Albert I. Rubin, "Temporal Experience," *Psychological Bulletin*, Vol. 57 (1960), pp. 221-223.

75. C. C. Trowbridge, "On Fundamental Methods of Orientation and 'Imaginary' Maps," *Science*, Vol. 38 (1913), pp. 891-892; Lynch, *Image of the City*, pp. 88-89, 136-137. See also T. A. Ryan and M. S. Ryan, "Geographical Orientation," *American Journal of Psychology*, Vol. 53 (1940), pp. 204-215.

Stereotypes influence how we learn and what we know about every place in the world. My notions of Australia and Alaska are compounds of more or less objective, veridical data and of the way I happen to feel about deserts, icefields, primitive peoples, pioneers, amateur tennis, and American foreign policy. Similar evanescent images come readily to mind; to Englishmen in the 1930's, according to one writer, Kenya suggested "gentleman farmers, the seedy aristocracy, gossip columns and Lord Castlerosse"; South Africa "Rhodes and British Empire and an ugly building in South Parks Road and Trafalgar Square."[79] Education and the passage of time revise but never wholly displace such stereotypes about foreign lands and people. The present consensus of teen-aged geography students in an English school is that "South Africans break off from the Boer War to eat oranges, make fortunes from gold and diamonds, and oppress natives, under a government as merciless as the ever-present sun."[80] Those who

think of China as an abode of laundrymen, France as a place where people eat snails, and the Spanish as hotblooded are only a trifle more myopic than anyone else; it is easier to deplore such generalizations than to replace them with more adequate and convincing images.

Because all knowledge is necessarily subjective as well as objective, delineations of the world that are purely matter-of-fact ordinarily seem too arid and lifeless to assimilate; only color and feeling convey versimilitude. Besides unvarnished facts, we require fresh firsthand experience, individual opinions and prejudices. "The important thing about truth is not that it should be naked, but what clothes suit it best."[81] The memorable geographies are not compendious texts but interpretative studies embodying a strong personal slant. A master at capturing the essence of a place, Henry James did so by conveying "less of its appearance than of its implications."[82] In Blake's lines,[83]

ing: Differentiation or Enrichment?" *Psychological Review*, Vol. 62 (1955), pp. 32-41. Science is more often apt to be accelerated "by the passionate, and even the egocentric partisan bias of researchers in favour of their own chosen methods or theories" than by disinterested impartiality (W. B. Gallie, "What Makes a Subject Scientific?" *British Journal for the Philosophy of Science*, Vol. 8 [1957], pp. 118-139, on p. 127). Metaphysical doctrines which can neither be proved nor disproved "play regulative roles in scientific thinking" because "they express ways of seeing the world which in turn suggest ways of exploring it" (J. W. N. Watkins, "Confirmable and Influential Metaphysics," *Mind*, Vol. 67 [1958], pp. 344-365, on pp. 360, 356).

79. Graham Green, "The Analysis of a Journey," *Spectator*, Vol. 155 (1935), pp. 459-460. "Even if we remember as many facts about Bolivia as about Sweden, this has little relevance to the relative importance of these two countries in our psychological world" (Robert B. MacLeod, "The Phenomenological Approach to Social Psychology," *Psychological Review*, Vol. 54 [1947], p. 206).

80. John Haddon, "A View of Foreign Lands," *Geography*, Vol. 65 (1960), pp. 286-289, on p.

286. If their view of South Africa is recognizable, the students' impressions of America leave more to be desired: "America is a country of remarkably developed, highly polished young women, and oddly garbed, criminally inclined young men travelling at great speed in monstrous cars along superhighways from one skyscraping city to the next; the very largest cars contain millionaires with crew-cuts; everyone is chewing gum" (p. 286). Such stereotypes die hard, even face to face with contrary realities, as one traveler noted among Americans in Russia (Richard Dettering, "An American Tourist in the Soviet Union: Some Semantic Reflections," *ETC.*, Vol. 17 [1960], pp. 173-201).

81. Russell Brain, *The Nature of Experience* (London: Oxford University Press, 1959), p. 3.

82. A. Alvarez, "Intelligence on Tour," *Kenyon Review*, Vol. 21 (1959), pp. 23-33, on p. 29; see Henry James, *The Art of Travel*, Morton D. Zaubel, editor, (New York: Doubleday, 1958). The virtues of the personal slant on description are discussed by Freya Stark, "Travel Writing: Facts or Interpretation?" *Landscape*, Vol. 9 (1960), p. 34, and Wright, "Terrae Incognitae" [see fn. 2], p. 8.

83. William Blake, "The Everlasting Gospel" [c.

This Life's dim Windows of the Soul
Distorts the Heavens from Pole to Pole
And leads you to Believe a Lie
When you see with, not thro', the Eye.

The ideal traveler, according to one critic, ought to be "aware not only of the immediate visual aspect of the country he visits, its history and customs, its art and people, but also of his own relation to all these, their symbolic and mythic place in his own universal map." [84] We mistrust science as the sole vehicle of truth because we conceive of the remote, the unknown, and the different in terms of what is near, well-known, and self-evident for us, and above all in terms of ourselves. What seems to us real and true depends "on what we know about ourselves and not only on what we know about the external world. Indeed," writes Hutten, "the two kinds of knowledge are inextricably connected." [85]

The Role of the Individual Past in Apperception of the Milieu. Personal as well as geographical knowledge is a form of

sequent occupance. Like a landscape or a living being, each private world has had a career in time, a history of its own. Since personality is formed mainly in the earliest years, "we are determined, simultaneously, both by what we were as children and by what we are experiencing now." In Quine's words, "We imbibe an archaic natural philosophy with our mother's milk. In the fullness of time, what with catching up on current literature and making some supplementary observations of our own, we become clearer on things. But . . . we do not break with the past, nor do we attain to standards of evidence and reality different in kind from the vague standards of children and laymen." [86]

The earlier mode of thought continues throughout life. According to Portmann, we all remain to some extent pre-Copernican: "The decisive early period in our contact with nature is strongly influenced by the Ptolemaic point of view, in which our inherited traits and responses find a congenial outlet. . . . Nor is the Ptolemaic world merely a phase to be outgrown, a kind of animal experience; it is an integral part of our total human quality." [87]

As every personal history results in a particular private milieu, no one can ever duplicate the *terra cognita* of anyone else. An adult who learns a foreign word or custom does not start from *tabula rasa*, but tries to match concepts from his own language and culture—never with complete success.

1818], in *Selected Poetry and Prose*, pp. 317-328, on p. 324.

84. Peter Green, "Novelists and Travelers," *Cornhill Magazine*, Vol. 168 (1955), pp. 39-54, on p. 49. "Man can discover and determine the universe inside him only by thinking it in mythical concepts and viewing it in mythical images" (Cassirer, *Philosophy of Symbolic Forms*, Vol. 2, p. 199; see also pp. 83, 101).

85. Ernest H. Hutten, "[review of] *Sigmund Freud: Life and Work*, Vol. 3, by Ernest Jones," *British Journal for the Philosophy of Science*, Vol. 10 (1959), p. 81. Experience always influences the severest logic: no matter how convinced a man is that heads and tails have exactly equal prospects, he is not likely to bet on tails if heads has come up the previous fifty times (Popper, *Logic of Scientific Discovery*, pp. 408, 415; John Cohen, *Chance, Skill, and Luck: the Psychology of Guessing and Gambling* [Baltimore: Penguin Books, 1960, pp. 29, 191]). See also Ernst Topitsch, "World Interpretation and Self-Interpretation: Some Basic Patterns," *Daedalus*, Vol. 88 (Spring, 1959), p. 312.

86. Hutten, *op. cit.*, p. 79; Quine, "Scope and Language of Science" [see fn. 5], p. 2.

87. Portmann, "The Seeing Eye," *Landscape*, Vol. 9 (1959), p. 18. See also D. O. Hebb, *The Organization of Behavior; a Neuropsychological Theory* (New York: Wiley, 1949), p. 109; Felix Deutsch, "Body, Mind, and Art," in *The Visual Arts Today*, special issue of *Daedalus*, Vol. 89 (Winter, 1960), pp. 34-45, on p. 38; Edward S. Tauber and Maurice R. Green, *Prelogical Experience: an Inquiry into Dreams and Other Creative Processes* (New York: Basic Books, 1959), p. 33.

Among "children, exposed serially to two cultures," notes Mead, " . . . the premises of the earlier may persist as distortions of perception into later experience, so that years later errors in syntax or reasoning may be traced to the earlier and 'forgotten' cultural experience."[88]

We are captives even of our adult histories. The image of the environment, as Boulding says, "is built up as a result of all past experience of the possessor of the image. Part of the image is the history of the image itself." I have touched on this in connection with color perception: "The color in which we have most often seen a thing is imprinted ineffaceably on our memory and becomes a fixed attribute of the remembered image," says Hering. "We see through the glass of remembered colors and hence often differently than we should otherwise see them."[89] The sitter's family invariably complain that the painter has made him look too old, because they view as a composite memory the face the painter confronts only today. "Everyone sees the world as it was in the past, reflected in the retarding mirror of his memory."[90]

Memory need not be conscious to influence images; as Hume pointed out, aspects of our past that we fail to recall also leave their imprint on mental maps. "The unconscious inner world," writes Money-Kyrle, "is peopled by figures and objects from the past, as they are imagined often wrongly to have been." Correct or not, recollections can virtually efface aspects of the actual contemporary landscape. Pratolini's *Il Quartiere* portrays inhabitants of a razed and empty section of Florence who instinctively continued to follow the lines of the former streets, instead of cutting diagonally across the square where buildings had stood.[91]

Memory likewise molds abstract ideas and hypotheses. Everything I know about America today is in part a memory of what I used to think about it. Having once conceived of the frontier as a cradle of democracy, it is quite another thing for me to learn that it was not than it is for someone else to learn the "true" fact without the old error. What we accept as true or real depends not only on what we think we know about the external world but on what we have previously believed.

Shared perspectives of whole cultures similarly incorporate the past. "Meanings may reflect not the contemporary culture but a much older one." The landscape in general, Lynch remarks, "serves as a vast mnemonic system for the retention of group history and ideals."[92]

Every image and idea about the world is compounded, then, of personal experience, learning, imagination, and memory. The places that we live in, those we visit and travel through, the worlds we read about and

88. Magorah Maruyama, "Communicable and Incommunicable Realities," *British Journal for the Philosophy of Science,* Vol. 10 (1959), pp. 50-54; Margaret Mead, "The Implications of Culture Change for Personality Development," *American Journal of Orthopsychiatry,* Vol. 17 (1947), pp. 633-646, on p. 639.

89. Boulding, *The Image,* p. 6; Ewald Hering, *Grundzüge der Lehre vom Lichtsinn* (Berlin: Springer, 1920), pp. 6 ff.; quoted in Cassirer, *Philosophy of Symbolic Forms,* Vol. 3, pp. 132-133. See also J. S. Bruner and Leo Postman, "On the Perception of Incongruity: a Paradigm," in Beardslee and Wertheimer, *Readings in Psychology,* pp. 662-663; Bruner and Klein, "Functions of Perceiving" [see fn. 78], p. 63.

90. Maurice Grosser, *The Painter's Eye* (New York: Rinehart, 1951), p. 232.

91. David Hume, *A Treatise of Human Nature* [1739], Book I, part iv, sec. vi; Money-Kyrle, *Man's Picture of His World,* p. 107; Vasco Pratolini, *The Naked Streets* (New York: A. A. Wyn, 1952), p. 204.

92. Kluckhohn, "Culture and Behavior" [see fn. 48], p. 939; Lynch, *Image of the City,* p. 126.

see in works of art, and the realms of imagination and fantasy each contribute to our images of nature and man. All types of experience, from those most closely linked with our everyday world to those which seem furthest removed, come together to make up our individual picture of reality.[93] The surface of the earth is shaped for each person by refraction through cultural and personal lenses of custom and fancy. We are all artists and landscape architects, creating order and organizing space, time, and causality in accordance with our apperceptions and predilections. The geography of the world is unified only by human logic and optics, by the light and color of artifice, by decorative arrangement, and by ideas of the good, the true, and the beautiful. As agreement on such subjects is never perfect nor permanent, geographers too can expect only partial and evanescent concordance. As Raleigh wrote, "It is not truth but opinion that can travel the world without a passport."[94]

93. As natives of places we acquire and assimilate information differently than we do as travelers; and personal observation, whether sustained or casual, yields impressions different in quality and impact from those we build out of lectures, books, pictures, or wholly imaginary visions. The climates of each of these modes of geographical experience, and the kind of information they tend to yield about the world, will be considered in a series of essays to which this one is meant to be introductory.

94. Quoted in C. V. Wedgwood, *Truth and Opinion: Historical Essays* (London: Collins, 1960), p. 11.

✻✻✻✻✻✻✻✻✻✻✻✻✻✻✻✻✻✻✻✻✻✻✻✻✻✻✻✻✻

GEOGRAPHY, PERCEPTION, AND THE BEHAVIORAL ENVIRONMENT

Joseph Sonnenfeld

Environment is easy to describe but difficult to define, a characteristic which it shares with such terms as culture and behavior. One can enumerate elements of environment, just as one can characterize objects as cultural, and actions as behaviors. These terms are so broad in their implications, and so widely and so generally used, as to be capable of many meanings.

The problem of definition arises only when one attempts to restrict the concept or to quantify it or to otherwise impose bounds; to distinguish between such as higher and lower forms of behavior; or between what is cultural and non-cultural; or between what is natural and artificial in environment. In other words, it is not a lack of awareness of the problem of definition that makes many of us reticent to be more precise in our usage, but rather too clear an awareness of what problems must arise in defining and setting limits; and, perhaps, too, a conviction — or rationalization — that such definition is not really crucial, that the

Mr. Sonnenfeld's paper, previously unpublished, was delivered orally at the American Association for the Advancement of Science meeting, December 27, 1968.

use of the broader term is adequate for comprehension.

Yet there is value in raising the issue of definition, since the environment from the standpoint of the behavioral scientist can be quite different from the environment that most geographers, and natural scientists as well, have been concerned with, or aware of, and assume to be *The Environment*; and, incidentally, assume others are aware of and cognizant of: viz, the natural/physical environment, or, as often called by non-geographers, the geographic environment. It is rather disconcerting, even to one familiar with the behavioral literature, to realize that environment for others in the social and behavioral sciences is usually only minimally the natural environment of topography, climate, and biota; that environment may encompass also the completely artificial environment of a psychiatric ward, at the one extreme, and the completely social environment of an interacting peer group at the other.

Such a range of usage of environment by social and behavioral scientists and the increased recent use of "space" as environment by geographers suggest that requests for definition and perhaps a re-evaluation of the concept of environment are not out of order. I am not convinced that such definition is necessary for viable research in the environmental sciences — natural or social — since I think most researchers are willing to accept the concept of environment at its broadest, or can define it to fit their purposes. But since such definition may help in the evaluation of what environmental research is and, in my own case, since the question of environmental behavior is also at issue, in which the term environment is used in a sense different from that which geographers on the one hand and behavioral scientists on the other normally use and

understand it, the effort may be a worthwhile one.

The Environment of Behavior

Not all of environment is significant for the behaving organism. Not all of that behavior which is directed toward environment has its origins in environmental stimulation. Not all in environment that stimulates one individual or a group or culture is equally stimulating for other individuals or groups or cultures. In its objective dimensions the behavioral environment exists as a complex subset of the broader geographical environment, but in its subjective perceived dimensions it also exists as the individual's psychological environment, a mental projection of a kind which, conditioned as it is by personality and culture, may only in part be congruent with the real world. This dichotomy of location — an environment which exists in the one case in the real world and in the other case in the mind of the individual — provides a dilemma for geographers who require definition of an environment amenable to objective study, an environment which can be studied by multiple observers using their separate techniques of analysis, all of which are capable of being focused on the same elements of landscape or resource, location or distribution, with some certainty that they are dealing with the same environment. But we cannot ignore the fact that the behaving organism — man — is reacting only in part to what could be considered objective elements of the environment, whether these involve landscape, or resource, or spatial arrangement.

Classifying Environment

Traditional definitions of environment emphasize generally the social-nonsocial distinction or simply the human-nonhuman distinction: thus the natural environment of vegetation or landform by contrast with the cultural environment of variably altered surfaces and atmospheres, with cities and houses and roads and field patterns and other compounds of man and nature (not always separable into their original components), which are the result of man's conscious or unconscious impact on the environment.

Yet distinctions such as these are irrelevant within the context of behavior: an organism responds to threat in environment whether these are natural or artificial, in ways not much different one from the other. He attempts to control environment or to alter it aesthetically in ways consistent with his technology and taste, and the fact of the environment being natural or artificial is irrelevant from the standpoint of his manipulative behavior. In other words, if there is a basis for distinguishing between environments which are natural and those which are artificial or cultural or man altered, as the Russians seem interested in proving,[1] there is no equivalent basis for distinguishing between behavior which is directed toward the natural environment and that which is directed toward the artificial.

Two issues are critical: First, what is to be excluded from the behavioral environment, since, if it includes everything, then we have difficulty in distingushing it from the broader geographical environment in the one case and from the non-geographical environment in the other. Second is the boundary problem, concerning the location of this behavioral environment: the extent

to which the internal and external impinge on one another, and the nature of the interaction that results. The one helps to distinguish the geographic study of the behavioral environment from that studied both by other geographers and by behavioral scientists, while the other elaborates on ties between geography and the behavioral sciences: a function of our mutual interest in the mind-environment-behavior interaction. In this paper, I will elaborate on the first issue, distinguishing between the behavioral and geographical environment, and leave for a later paper the tackier issue of the interaction between internal and external environments.

A Behavioral Classification of Environment

The behavioral environment can perhaps be best understood by defining its relation to the broader geographical environment. In the scheme which follows I have attempted to define the behavioral environment as one of a nested set of environments each of which is differently inclusive of elements important for man. (See Fig. 1.) At the

1. See Yu. G. Saushkin, "Concerning a certain controversy," *Soviet Geography* Vol. 7(2), 1966, pp. 9-14; and S. V. Kalesnik, "A few more words about the geographical environment," *Soviet Geography* Vol. 7(10), 1966, pp. 46-52. Also, M. M. Zhirmunskiy, "The interaction between nature and society and economic geography," *Soviet Geography* Vol. 7(7), 1966, pp. 19-27.

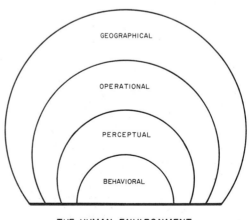

Figure 1. A behavioral classification of environment.

broadest level is the geographical environment, constituting both proximal and distal elements of man's universe. This is reduced in stages to the operating environment, which is that environment impinging on man with which in some way or another he is likely to be directly involved; to the perceptual environment, which is that environment of which man is aware; and finally to the behavioral environment, the environment which elicits a behavioral response from the individual.

The Geographical Environment. At the grossest level is the objective geographical environment. This is in effect the whole environment which is external to the organism: it is an environment which is measurable and quantifiable by some objective standard or scale; equivalent phenomena or energies, separated in space and time, have equivalent values when measured by equivalent instruments or sensors along equivalent scales. It is the most inclusive of environments, being the source of all that is objective of the operational, perceptual, and behavioral environments, but including in addition elements which as far as the individual is concerned do not exist or have no meaning. This does not mean that one can specify elements of the geographic environment to which all man is insensitive, unaware, and must necessarily remain so; only that for groups and especially for individuals there are many elements of the environment which do not "exist," i.e. are not part of the environment required by the individual for him to function normally. For an isolated tribe in the Amazon, unaware of the rest of the world, the rest of the world might as well not exist as far as any influence the rest of the world has on their environmental behaviors, even though what happens in the rest of the world may in fact influence the state of their isolation. One of the earliest references to the Polar Eskimo of Northwest Greenland, describing their discovery in the late 1800's by an Eskimo who crossed over from Baffinland, remarked on how surprised they seemed to be to learn of the existence of other people, especially people to the south of them, who lived in a country which by their own reasoning should have been uninhabitable. Since the icebergs which formed in their part of the world all seemed to flow south, the south was then a land of masses of accumulated icebergs, which made it unsuitable for the kind of existence the Polar Eskimo enjoyed, and therefore obviously uninhabitable for man.

Generally, the more isolated and less developed technologically a population is, the larger the portion of its geographical environment which is neutral or non-functional, though clearly there is no necessary relationship between the visual environment to which a people is sensitive, and the level of its technological sophistication.

The Operational Environment. The functional portion of the geographical environment, that which impinges on man as individual or group,[2] influencing behavior in some way or another, is the operational environment, the environment in which man operates. The exact makeup of the operational environment varies, according to physiology, sensory sensitivity, and behavioral orientation and inclination. Thus a basic distinction between the geographical environment and the operational environment is that while the former is the same for all of man, the operational environment differs as physiological, psychological, and cultural man differs, race from race, culture from culture, and individual from individual. The

2. This usage was suggested by the concept of "operational environment" developed more rigorously by ecologists for an organism-environment relationship in H. L. Mason, and J. H. Langenheim, "Language analysis and the concept environment," *Ecology* Vol 38(2), 1957, pp. 325-40.

biologist, geologist, physicist, chemist, and astronomer may study the geographical environment in the abstract whether or not it impinges on man or is important in his behavior. When the physiologist, anthropologist, historian, economist, and political scientist study environment, they study the operational environment, generally for the purpose of understanding man and his organic, cultural, economic, and political behaviors. The kind of environment that the human geographer studies is also the operational environment.

The Perceptual Environment. Nested within the operational environment is the perceptual environment, that portion of the operational environment of which man is conscious either because of an organic-sensory sensitivity that exists because of a lack of body adaptation — i.e. the elements lie outside the range of conditions to which the body can react "unconsciously" (e.g. temperature, atmospheric pressure, oxygen concentration of the atmosphere) — or instead because of a sensitivity that derives from man's learning and experience. That portion of the operational environment of which man is unaware, or to which he is insensitive, lies outside the perceptual environment.

While the operational and geographical environments are both objective environments, in the sense that the elements of both have objectively measurable or quantifiable elements, this is only in part the case with the perceptual environment; this is because the perceptual environment has both sensory and symbolic dimensions. The sensory portion of the perceptual environment involves a variety of objectively measurable energies capable of stimulating the individual, though awareness of these energies may differ from one to another person or population. Temperature and humidity and sound and brightness all may be variably sensed according to

the sensitivity of sensory mechanisms, and according to the level of sensory adaptation. For the symbolic environment, however, the stimulus may or may not have its origin in environment. The geographic environment provides stimuli for the symbolic environment only in the sense that it provides landscape images to focus on. These images constitute reminders rather than sources of meaning. Unlike the sensory elements of environment (temperature, light, sound, odor) in which meaning is derived from the nature of the stimuli, landscape images as such have no inherent symbolic meaning. Homeland, for example, is made up of environmental elements which, if located elsewhere than in the home country, will not have the same meaning for even the same population, much less for a population differently identifying with place, even if its own place. The basic difference between the sensory environment of universal elements and the symbolic environment of idiosyncratic elements is that while the sensory elements have meaning derived from the nature of their composition or energy, the elements of the symbolic environment require a cultural and personality transformation before they achieve meaning. The special meanings or values attributed to the elements of the symbolic environment subsequently determine the sensitivity of the individual or group to their existence.

The aesthetic environment is part of the symbolic environment; so is the social or political environment; also the habitable environment, any objective measure of which requires a technologically determined value transformation. In none of these environments does the information necessary for meaning come from the environment, as is the case with the sensory environment of temperature, sound, and odor. And while one can measure the temperature, sound, and odor which make up the sensory environment, there is no objective means for measuring the environmental elements whose values are symbolic ones. It may be extremely difficult to isolate the individual elements which make up the symbolic environment since, as suggested, sensitivity to these does not derive from the environment as such but rather from the individual. There may be a variety of environmental cues — energies of stimuli — which, as they occur or intensify or are extinguished, elicit the attention of the sensor-observer. But increasing awareness may as well derive from thought patterns internally stimulated, which cause the individual to become aware of and sensitive to his surroundings, which he then searches for elements prescribed by his culture, personality, and environmental experience.

The Behavioral Environment. Search involves behavior directed toward surrounding, and this requires the distinction of the last of the set of environments proposed. The behavioral environment can be defined as that part of the environment of which the individual is aware which also elicits a behavioral response or toward which a behavior is directed, such as results in a conscious utilization or transformation of environment. Respiration involves an unconscious use and alteration of environment; the effluents of man generally are not conscious products, but rather by-products of human activity, though the polluted environment may subsequently become the focus of a behavioral response. The behavioral response need not involve a use or alteration of environment, but may instead involve a change in the individual's relationship with or exposure to that environment, such as is often the case with behavior in the sensory environment of temperature and light, given the availability of clothing and sunglasses.

The residuum of the perceptual environment that is not subsumed by the behavioral environment is that of which the individual is aware, of which he has knowledge or an attitude, or concerning which he has a bias but toward which no overt or conscious action or behavior (adjustment, manipulation, etc.) is directed. This distinction between the two may seem tenuous, but it is basic to understanding the different responses of subjects to a questionnaire concerning their attitude toward a real or hypothetical environment, their likes, dislikes, and such, and the problem of extrapolating from these responses for predicting environmental behavior. There is no necessary relationship between that which one perceives to exist, that the individual is sensitive to in his environment, and the way in which he behaves toward that environment. One may value clear atmosphere and pure waters and still be guilty of gross negligence toward both; similarly one may be conscious of the need to preserve or conserve our valued landscapes, but vote down legislation on grounds of opposition to central government. In both cases, the environment which the individual perceives and behaves in response to is the same, but there is no necessary consistency between his perception of the environment in a symbolic — value-transformed — sense, and his behavior, such as would sustain or improve the environment which he is obviously aware of, sensitive to, and even concerned about.

The above suggests that the behavioral environment may really involve more than is contained in the perceptual environment, since it seems to include, as a prelude to behavior, a prediction (or a projection) as to what the effect of that behavior will be.

Summary. Here then we have defined a series of man-orientated environments, differing from the gross geographical environment only in the sense that elements can be isolated and specified operationally, perceptually, and behaviorally. We all live in a geographical environment, but not all of this is operational; and only a part of that which is operational are we aware of; and only a part of that which we are aware of do we consciously adjust for or react to, or in some way accommodate for, manipulate, or attempt to control.

There is now the need for thinking in terms of behaviorally significant and behaviorally insignificant elements of our environment; for distinguishing between elements which are neutral and those which are operational; for distinguishing between that which we are aware of in environment which does not elicit a reaction, from that which does. There is also need to re-evaluate population achievement in environment. This will require us to distinguish between populations in terms of the level at which they differ one from the other in their relationship with environment: whether at the operational, perceptual, or behavioral level.

Geographical and Non-geographical Environments

One final issue: the behavioral environment has been defined as part of the geographical environment. But what is one reasonably to include as geographical environment? By reasonable I mean what is the environment that geographers can reasonably be expected to study? In question are the social elements of environment, and whether to include or exclude these as elements of the geographical environment.

Some social elements are not much different from nonsocial elements in terms of the behavior they elicit from the individual. It was suggested earlier that one may not be able to distinguish behaviors which are directed toward the natural environment from those which are directed toward the artificial environment. Similarly, it may be difficult to distinguish between behaviors

that are directed toward a peopleless environment and those which are directed toward one with figures on the landscape, for example, farmers working in a field, or commuters rushing to and from work, and similar "people images," experienced in any of a variety of ways, but all anonymously. Yet other social entities are not quite so anonymous.

For the sociologist or psychologist, one's mother, teacher, minister, or friend may all be parts of a critical learning environment, e.g. such as influences the development and personality of the child. The concern of the sociologist and psychologist is primarily with behavior in a reacting environment. The concern of the geographer, however, is more often with behavior directed toward a *non-reacting environment.* I would distinguish between elements of the geographical and non-geographical social environment according to whether they are reacting or non-reacting elements, and according to whether interaction is involved or not.

The kind of interaction referred to is a social interaction. The individual interacts with other individuals in his environment who react or who are capable of reacting in like manner. The relationship involved in such interaction is a social relationship, and, according to how one wishes to define it, this may also represent an environmental relationship. But if all social interactions involve also the relationship of an individual with environment, not all man-environment relationships involve interaction. As sociologists Parsons and Shills point out,[3] interaction requires "objects" capable of behav-

3. T. Parsons, and E. A. Shills "Categories of the orientation and organization of action," part 2(1) of *Toward a General Theory of Action*, ed. by Talcott Parsons and Edward A. Shills, Harper and Row, New York; (Harper Torchbook Edition) 1962, pp. 53-109.

ing or adapting to each other; but an organism-physical environment interaction does not occur in the same sense. This is not to say that environmental reactions do not occur when man upsets an equilibrium in a physical or ecological system, but the adjustment that occurs is to the disequilibrium rather than to man as the source of disequilibrium. The same would seem to apply also to the anonymous social environment, which I would therefore see no reason for excluding as geographic environment.

So distinguishing between a geographical and a non-geographical social environment, however, I cannot really argue that geographers ought to ignore this social environment, for without question the social interactions we experience may very much influence our behaviors in the geographical environment. I would only caution that

treating the interacting social system as environment raises questions of environmental influences and determinisms that can only confuse the issue of geographical influences and determinisms. As I have tried to suggest, the geographical environment and the interacting social environment are not really equivalent kinds of environment. Therefore the issue of environmental influences and determinisms is not the same for geographers as it is for sociologists and psychologists. The continuing controversy over the role of geographical environment in human development is sufficiently critical for geographers and other behavioral scientists to be aware of the difference between the environments on which their studies focus, and on which their judgments concerning the validity of an environmentalist position are based.

★★★★★★★★★★★★★★★★★★★★★★★★★★★★

SPATIAL INVASION

Robert Sommer

Dear Abby: I have a pet peeve that sounds so petty and stupid that I'm almost ashamed to mention it. It is people who come and sit down beside me on the piano bench while I'm playing. I don't know why this bothers me so much, but it does. Now you know, Abby, you can't tell someone to get up and go sit somewhere else without hurting their feelings. But it would be a big relief to me if I could get them to move in a nice inoffensive way. . .

Lost Chord

Dear Lost: People want to sit beside you while you're playing because they are fascinated. Change your attitude and regard their presence as a compliment, and it might be easier to bear. P.S. You might also change your piano bench for a piano

stool. (*Abigail Van Buren*, San Francisco Chronicle, *May 25, 1965*)

The best way to learn the location of invisible boundaries is to keep walking until somebody complains. Personal space refers to an area with invisible boundaries surrounding a person's body into which intruders may not come. Like the porcupines in Schopenhauer's fable, people like to be close enough to obtain warmth and comradeship but far enough away to avoid pricking one another. Personal space is not necessarily spherical in shape, nor does it extend equally in all directions. (People are able to tolerate closer presence of a stranger at their sides than directly in front.) It has been likened to a snail shell, a soap bubble, an aura, and "breathing room." There are major differences between cultures in the distances that people maintain—Englishmen keep further apart than Frenchmen or South Americans. Reports from Hong Kong where three million people are crowded into 12 square miles indicate that the population has adapted to the crowding reasonably well. The Hong Kong Housing Authority, now in its tenth year of operation, builds and manages low-cost apartments for families that provide approximately 35 square feet per person for living-sleeping accommodations. When the construction supervisor of one Hong Kong project was asked what the effects of doubling the amount of floor area would be upon the living patterns, he replied, "With 60 square feet per person, the tenants would sublet!" [1]

Although some people claim to see a characteristic aura around human bodies and are able to describe its color, luminosity, and dimensions, most observers cannot confirm these reports and must evolve a concept of personal space from interpersonal transactions. There is a considerable similarity between personal space and *individual distance*, or the characteristic spacing of species members. Individual distance exists only when two or more members of the same species are present and is greatly affected by population density and territorial behavior. Individual distance and personal space interact to affect the distribution of persons. The violation of individual distance is the violation of society's expectations; the invasion of personal space is an intrusion into a person's self-boundaries. Individual distance may be outside the area of personal

space—conversation between two chairs across the room exceeds the boundaries of personal space, or individual distance may be less than the boundaries of personal space— sitting next to someone on a piano bench is within the expected distance but also within the bounds of personal space and may cause discomfort to the player. If there is only one individual present, there is infinite individual distance, which is why it is useful to maintain a concept of personal space, which has also been described as a *portable territory*, since the individual carries it with him wherever he goes although it disappears under certain conditions, such as crowding.

There is a formula of obscure origin that a man in a crowd requires at least two square feet. This is an absolute minimum and applies, according to one authority, to a thin man in a subway. A fat man would require twice as much space or more. Journalist Herbert Jacobs became interested in spatial behavior when he was a reporter covering political rallies. Jacobs found that estimates of crowd size varied with the observer's politics. Some estimates by police and politicians were shown to be twenty times larger than the crowd size derived from head count or aerial photographs. Jacobs found a fertile field for his research on the Berkeley campus where outdoor rallies are frequent throughout the year. He concluded that people in dense crowds have six to eight square feet each, while in loose crowds, with people moving in and out, there is an average of ten square feet per person, Jacobs' formula is that crowd size equals length $\times$ width of the crowd divided by the appropriate correction factor depending upon whether the crowd is dense or loose. On the Berkeley campus this produced estimates reasonably close to those obtained from aerial photographs.[2]

---

1. American Institute of Planners Newsletter, January 1967, p. 2.

2. H. Jacobs, "How Big Was the Crowd?" Talk given at California Journalism Conference, Sacramento, February 24-25, 1967.

Hospital patients complain not only that their personal space and their very bodies are continually violated by nurses, interns, and physicians who do not bother to introduce themselves or explain their activities, but that their territories are violated by well-meaning visitors who will ignore "No Visitors" signs. Frequently patients are too sick or too sensitive to repel intruders. Once surgery is finished or the medical treatment has been instituted, the patient is left to his own devices to find peace and privacy. John Lear, the science editor of the *Saturday Review*, noticed an interesting hospital game he called, "Never Close the Door," when he was a surgery patient. Although his physician wanted him protected against outside noises and distractions, the door opened at intervals, people peered in, sometimes entered, but no one ever closed the door. When Lear protested, he was met by hostile looks and indignant remarks such as, "I'm only trying to do my job, Mister." It was never clear to Lear why the job—whatever it was—required the intruder to leave the door ajar afterwards.[3]

Spatial invasions are not uncommon during police interrogations. One police textbook recommends that the interrogator should sit close to the suspect, with no table or desk between them, since "an obstruction of any sort affords the subject a certain degree of relief and confidence not otherwise obtainable."[4] At the beginning of the session, the officer's chair may be two or three feet away, "but after the interrogation is under way the interrogator should move his chair in closer so that ultimately one of

the subject's knees is just about in between the interrogator's two knees."[5]

Lovers pressed together close their eyes when they kiss. On intimate occasions the lights are typically dim to reduce not only the distracting external cues but also to permit two people to remain close together. Personal space is a culturally acquired daylight phenomenon. Strangers are affected differently than friends by a loss of personal space. During rush hour, subway riders lower their eyes and sometimes "freeze" or become rigid as a form of minimizing unwanted social intercourse. Boy-meets-girl on a crowded rush hour train would be a logical plot for an American theater based largely in New York City, but it is rarely used. The idea of meeting someone under conditions where privacy, dignity, and individuality are so reduced is difficult to accept.

A driver can make another exceedingly nervous by tailgating. Highway authorities recommend a "space cushion" of at least one car length for every ten miles per hour of speed. You can buy a bumper sticker or a lapel button with the message "If you can read this, you're too close." A perceptive suburban theater owner noticed the way crowds arranged themselves in his lobby for different pictures. His lobby was designed to hold approximately 200 customers who would wait behind a roped area for the theater to clear.

When we play a [family picture like] *Mary Poppins, Born Free,* or *The Cardinal,* we can line up only about 100 to 125 people. These patrons stand about a foot apart and don't touch the person next to them. But when we play a [sex comedy like] *Tom Jones* or *Irma la Douce,* we can get 300 to 350 in the same space. These people stand so close to each other you'd think they were all going to the same home at the end of the show![6]

3. John Lear, "What's Wrong with American Hospitals?" *Saturday Review* (February 4, 1967), pp. 59-60.

4. F. E. Inbau and J. E. Reid, *Criminal Interrogation and Confessions* (Toronto: Burns and Mac-Eachern, 1963).

5. Inbau and Reid, *op. cit.*

6. Bob Ellison, "If the Movie Is Comic, Sex Is OK, in Suburbia," *Chicago Sun Times,* Jan. 15, 1967, Section 3, p. 4.

Animal studies indicate that individual distance is learned during the early years. At some stage early in his life the individual learns how far he must stay from species members. When he is deprived of contact with his own kind, as in isolation studies, he cannot learn proper spacing, which sets him up as a failure in subsequent social intercourse—he comes too close and evokes threat displays or stays too far away to be considered a member of the group. Newborn of many species can be induced to follow novel stimuli in place of their parents. If a newly hatched chicken is separated from his mother and shown a flashing light instead, on subsequent occasions he will follow the flashing light rather than his mother. The distance he remains behind the object is a function of its size; young chicks will remain further behind a large object than a small one. [7]

Probably the most feasible method for exploring individual distance and personal space with their invisible boundaries is to approach people and observe their reactions. Individual distance is not an absolute figure but varies with the relationship between the individuals, the distance at which others in the situation are placed, and the bodily orientations of the individuals one to another. The most systematic work along these lines has been undertaken by the anthropologist Ray Birdwhistell who records a person's response with zoom lenses and is able to detect even minute eye movements and hand tremors as the invader approaches the emotionally egotistic zone around the victim. [8]

One of the earliest attempts to invade personal space on a systematic basis was undertaken by Williams, who wanted to learn how different people would react to excessive closeness. Classifying students as introverts or extroverts on the basis of their scores on a personality test, he placed each individual in an experiemental room and then walked toward the person, telling him to speak out as soon as he (Williams) came too close. Afterward he used the reverse condition, starting at a point very close and moving away until the person reported that he was too far away for comfortable conversation. His results showed that introverts kept people at a greater conversational distance than extroverts. [9]

The same conclusion was reached by Leipold, who studied the distance at which introverted and extroverted college students placed themselves in relation to an interviewer in either a stress or a non-stress situation. When the student entered the experimental room, he was given either the stress, praise, or neutral instructions. The stress instructions were, "We feel that your course grade is quite poor and that you have not tried your best. Please take a seat in the next room and Mr. Leipold will be in shortly to discuss this with you." The neutral control instructions read, "Mr. Leipold is interested in your feelings about the introductory course. Would you please take a seat in the next room." After the student had entered and seated himself, Mr. Leipold came in, recorded the student's seating position, and conducted the interview. The results showed that students given praise sat closest to Leipold's chair, followed by those in the neutral condition, with students given the stress instructions maintaining the most distance from Leipold's chair behind the desk. It was also found that introverted and

7. Peter H. Klopfer and J. P. Hailman, *An Introduction to Animal Behavior* (Englewood Cliffs, N.J.: Prentice-Hall, Inc., 1967).
8. R. L. Birdwhistell, *Introduction to Kinesics* (Washington: Foreign Service Institute, 1952).

9. John L. Williams, "Personal Space and its Relation to Extroversion-Introversion" (Master's thesis, University of Alberta, 1963).

anxious individuals sat further away from him than did extroverted students with a lower anxiety level.[10]

Glen McBride has done some excellent work on the spatial behaviors of fowl, not only in captivity but in their feral state on islands off the Australian coast. He has recently turned his attention to human spatial behavior using the galvanic skin response (GSR) as an index of emotionality. The GSR picks up changes in skin conductivity that relate to stress and emotional behavior. The same principle underlies what is popularly known as the lie detector test. McBride placed college students in a chair from which they were approached by both male and female experimenters as well as by paper figures and non-human objects. It was found that GSR was greatest (skin resistance was least) when a person was approached frontally, whereas a side approach yielded a greater response than a rear approach. The students reacted more strongly to the approach of someone of the opposite sex than to someone of the same sex. Being touched by an object produced less of a GSR than being touched by a person.[11]

A similar procedure without the GSR apparatus was used by Argyle and Dean, who invited their subjects to participate in a perceptual experiment in which they were to "stand as close as comfortable to see well" to a book, a plaster head, and a cut-out life-size photograph of the senior author with his eyes closed and another photograph with his eyes open. Among other results, it was found that the subjects placed themselves closer to the eyes-closed photograph than the eyes-open photograph.[12] Horowitz, Duff, and Stratton used a similar procedure with schizophrenic and nonschizophrenic mental patients. Each individual was instructed to walk over to a person, or in another condition a hatrack, and the distance between the goal and his stopping place was measured. It was found that most people came closer to the hatrack than they did to another person. Each tended to have a characteristic individual distance that was relatively stable from one situation to another, but was shorter for inanimate objects than for people. Schizophrenics generally kept greater distance between themselves and others than did non-patients.[13] The last finding is based on average distance values, which could be somewhat inflated by a few schizophrenics who maintain a large individual distance. Another study showed that some schizophrenic patients sat "too close" and made other people nervous by doing this. However, it was more often the case that schizophrenics maintained excessive physical distance to reduce the prospects of unwanted social intercourse.[14]

In order to explore personal space using the invasion technique, but to avoid the usual connotations surrounding forced close proximity to strangers, my own method was to undertake the invasion in a place where the usual sanctions of the outside world did not apply. Deliberate invasions of personal space seem more feasible and appropriate inside a mental hospital than outside. Afterward, it became apparent that this method

10. William E. Leipold, "Psychological Distance in a Dyadic Interview" (Ph.D. thesis, University of North Dakota, 1963).

11. Glen McBride, M. G. King, and J. W. James, "Social Proximity Effects on GSR in Adult Humans," *Journal of Psychology*, LXI (1965), pp. 153-57.

12. Michael Argyle and Janet Dean, "Eye Contact, Distance, and Affiliation," *Sociometry*, XXVIII (1965), pp. 289-304.

13. Mardi J. Horowitz, D. F. Duff, and L. O. Stratton, "Body-Buffer Zone," *Archives of General Psychiatry*, XI (1964), pp. 651-56.

14. Robert Sommer, "Studies in Personal Space," *Sociometry*, XXII (1959), pp. 247-60.

could be adapted for use in other settings such as the library in which Nancy Russo spent many hours sitting too close to other girls.

The first study took place at a 1500-bed mental institution situated in parklike surroundings in northern California. Most wards were unlocked, and patients spent considerable time out of doors. In wooded areas it was common to see patients seated under the trees, one to a bench or knoll. The wards within the buildings were relatively empty during the day because of the number of patients outside as well as those who worked in hospital industry. This made it possible for patients to isolate themselves from others by finding a deserted area on the grounds or remaining in an almost empty building. At the outset I spent considerable time observing how patients isolated themselves from one another. One man typically sat at the base of a fire escape so he was protected by the bushes on one side and the railing on the other. Others would lie on benches in remote areas and feign sleep if approached. On the wards a patient might sit in a corner and place magazines or his coat on adjacent seats to protect the space. The use of belongings to indicate possession is very common in bus stations, cafeterias, and waiting rooms, but the mental patient is limited in using this method since he lacks possessions. Were he to own a magazine or book, which is unlikely, and leave it on an empty chair, it would quickly vanish.

Prospective victims had to meet three criteria—male, sitting alone, and not engaged in any definite activity such as reading or playing cards. When a patient fitting these criteria was located, I walked over and sat beside him without saying a word. If the patient moved his chair or slid further down the bench, I moved a like distance to keep the space between us to about six inches. In all sessions I jiggled my key ring a few times

to assert my dominance, the key being a mark of status in a mental hospital. It can be noted that these sessions not only invaded the patient's personal space but also the nurse's territory. It bothered the nurses to see a high status person (jacket, white shirt, tie, and the title "Doctor") entering their wards and sitting among the patients. The dayroom was the patients' territory vis-à-vis the nurses, but it was the nurses' territory vis-à-vis the medical staff. Control subjects were selected from other patients who were seated some distance away but whose actions could be observed.

Within two minutes, all of the control subjects remained but one-third of the invasion victims had been driven away. Within nine minutes, fully half of the victims had departed compared with only 8 per cent of the controls (see Fig. 1). Flight was a gross reaction to the intrusion; there were many more subtle indications of the patient's

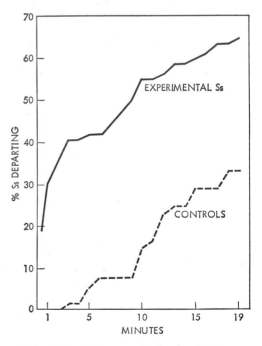

Figure 1. Cumulative percentage of patients departing at each one-minute interval.

discomfort. The typical sequence was for the victim to face away immediately, pull in his shoulders, and place his elbows at his sides. Facing away was an almost universal reaction among the victims, often coupled with hands placed against the chin as a buffer. Records obtained during the note-taking sessions illustrate this defensive pattern.

Example A

10:00. Seat myself next to a patient, about sixty years of age; he is smoking and possibly watching TV.

10:04. Patient rubs his face briefly with the back of his hand.

10:05. Patient breathes heavily, still smoking, and puts his ashes into a tin can. He looks at his watch occasionally.

10:06. He puts out his cigarette, rubs his face with the back of his hand. Still watching TV.

10:12. Patient glances at his watch, flexes his fingers.

10:13. Patient rises, walks over and sits at a seat several chairs over. Observation ended.

Example B

8:46. Seat myself next to a 60-year-old man who looks up as I enter the room. As I sit down, he begins talking to himself, snuffs out his cigarette, rises, and walks across the room. He asks a patient on the other side of the room, "You want me to sit here?" He starts arranging the chairs against the opposite wall and finally sits down.

Ethologist Ewan Grant has made a detailed analysis of the patient's micro behaviors drawing much inspiration from the work of Tinbergen[15] as well as his own previous studies with colonies of monkeys and rats. Among a group of confined mental patients he determined a relatively straight-forward dominance hierarchy based on aggression-flight encounters between individuals. Aggressive acts included threat gestures ("a direct look plus a sharp movement of the head towards the other person"), frowns, and hand-raising. Flight behaviors included retreat, bodily evasions, closed eyes, withdrawing the chin into the chest, hunching, and crouching. These defensive behaviors occurred when a dominant individual sat too close to a subordinate. This could be preceded by some overt sign of tension such as rocking, leg swinging, or tapping. Grant describes one such encounter: "A lower ranking member of the group is sitting in a chair; a dominant approaches and sits near her. The first patient begins to rock and then frequently, on one of the forward movements, she gets up and moves away."[16]

In seventeen British old folks homes Lipman found that most of the patients had favorite chairs that they considered "theirs." Their title to these chairs was supported by the behavior of both patients and staff. A newly admitted inmate had great difficulty in finding a chair that was not owned by anyone. Typically he occupied one seat and then another until he found one that was "unowned." When he sat in someone else's chair, he was told to move away in no uncertain terms.[17] Accidental invasions were an accepted fact of life in these old folks homes. It is possible to view them as a hazing or initiation ceremony for new residents to teach them the informal institutional rules and understandings. Such situations illustrate the importance of knowing not only how people mark out and personalize spaces, but how they respond to intrusions.

We come now to the sessions Nancy Russo conducted in the study hall of a

---

15. N. Tinbergen, *Social Behaviour in Animals* (London: Methuen & Co. Ltd., 1953).

16. Grant, *op. cit.*

17. Alan Lipman, "Building Design and Social Interaction," *The Architects Journal*, CXLVII (1968), pp. 23-30.

college library, a large high-ceilinged room with book-lined walls. Because this is a study area, students typically try to space themselves as far as possible from one another. Systematic observations over a two-year period disclosed that the first occupants of the room generally sat one to a table at end chairs. Her victims were all females sitting alone with at least one book in front of them and empty chairs on either side and across. In other words, the prospective victim was sitting in an area surrounded by empty chairs, which indicated something about her preference for solitude as well as making an invasion relatively easy. The second female to meet these criteria in each session and who was visible to Mrs. Russo served as a control. Each control subject was observed from a distance and no invasion was attempted. There were five different approaches used in the invasions—sometimes Mrs. Russo would sit alongside the subject, other times directly across from her, and so forth. All of these were violations of the typical seating norms in the library, which required a newcomer to sit at a considerable distance from those already seated unless the room was crowded.

Occupying the adjacent chair and moving it closer to the victim, produced the quickest departures, and there was a slight but also significant difference between the other invasion locations and the control condition. There were wide individual differences in the ways the victims reacted—there is no single reaction to someone's sitting too close; there are defensive gestures, shifts in posture, and attempts to move away. If these fail or are ignored by the invader, or he shifts position too, the victim eventually takes to flight. Crook measured spacing of birds in three ways: *arrival distance* or how far from settled birds a newcomer will land, *settled distance* or the resultant distance after adjustments have occurred, and the *distance*

after departure or how far apart birds remain after intermediate birds have left.[18] The methods employed in the mental hospital and portions of the library study when the invader shifted his position if the victim moved, maintained the *arrival distance* and did not permit the victim to achieve a comfortable *settled distance*. It is noteworthy that the preponderance of flight reactions occurred under these conditions. There was a dearth of direct verbal responses to the invasions. Only two of the 69 mental patients and one of the 80 students asked the invader to move over. This provides support for Edward Hall's view that "we treat space somewhat as we treat sex. It is there, but we don't talk about it."[19]

Architecture students on the Berkeley campus now undertake behavioral studies as part of their training. One team noted the reactions of students on outdoor benches when an experimenter joined them on the same bench. The occupant shifted position more frequently in a specified time-frame and left the bench earlier than control subjects who were alone. A second team was interested in individual distance on ten-foot benches. When the experimenter seated himself one foot from the end of the bench, three-quarters of the next occupants sat six to eight feet away, and almost half placed books or coats as barriers between themselves and the experimenter. Another two students studied eyeblinks and shifts in body position as related to whether a stranger sat facing someone or sat facing away. Observations were made by a second experimenter using binoculars from a distance. A male

18. J. H. Crook, "The Basis of Flock Organization in Birds," in *Current Problems in Animal Behavior*, eds. W. H. Thorpe and O. L. Zangwill (London: Cambridge University Press, 1961).
19. Edward T. Hall, *The Silent Language* (Garden City, New York: Doubleday & Company, Inc., 1959).

stranger directly facing a female markedly increased her eyeblink rate as well as body movements but had no discernible effect on male subjects.[20]

The different ways in which victims react to invasions may also be due to variations in the perception of the expected distance or in the ability to concentrate. It has been demonstrated that the individual distance between birds is reduced when one bird's attention is riveted to some activity.[21] The invasions can also be looked at as nonverbal communication with the victims receiving messages ranging from "This girl considers me a nonperson" to "This girl is making a sexual advance." The fact that regressed and "burnt out" patients can be moved from their places by sheer propinquity is of theoretical and practical importance. In view of the difficulty that nurses and others have in obtaining any response at all from these patients, it is noteworthy that an emotion sufficient to generate flight can be produced simply by sitting alongside them. More recently we have been experimenting with visual invasions, or attempts to dislodge someone from his place by staring directly at him. In the library at least, the evil eye seems less effective than a spatial invasion since the victims are able to lose themselves in their books. If they could not escape eye contact so easily, this method might be more effective. Mrs. Russo was sensitive to her own feelings during these sessions and described how she "lost her cool" when a victim looked directly toward her. Eye contact produced a sudden realization that "this is a human being," which subsided when the victim turned away. Civil rights demonstra-

tors attempt to preserve their human dignity by maintaining eye contact with their adversaries.

There are other sorts of invasions— auditory assaults in which strangers press personal narratives on hapless seatmates on airplanes and buses, and olfactory invasions long celebrated in television commercials. Another interesting situation is the two-person invasion. On the basis of animal work, particularly on chickens crowded in coops, it was discovered that when a subordinate encounters a dominant at very close quarters where flight is difficult or impossible, the subordinate is likely to freeze in his tracks until the dominant departs or at least looks away. Two faculty members sitting on either side of a student or two physicians on either side of a patient's bed would probably produce this type of freezing. The victim would be unlikely to move until he had some sign that the dominants had their attention elsewhere.

The library studies made clear that an important consideration in defining a spatial invasion is whether the parties involved perceive one another as persons. A nonperson cannot invade someone's personal space any more than a tree or chair can. It is common under certain conditions for one person to react to another as an object or part of the background. Examples would be the hospital nurses who discuss a patient's condition at his bedside, seemingly oblivious to his presence, the Negro maid in the white home who serves dinner while the husband and wife discuss the race question, and the janitor who enters an office without knocking to empty the wastebaskets while the occupant is making an important phone call. Many subway riders who have adjusted to crowding through psychological withdrawal prefer to treat other riders as nonpersons and keenly resent situations, such as a stop so abrupt that the person alongside pushes

---

20. These were term projects in Architecture 140 taught by Professor Richard Seaton. They are available on microfilm from the Dept. of Architecture, University of California, Berkeley 94704.
21. Crook, *op. cit.*

into them *and then apologizes*, when the other rider becomes a person. There are also riders who dislike the lonely alienated condition of subway travel and look forward to emergency situations in which people become real. When a lost child is looking for his mother, a person has been hurt, or a car is stalled down the tracks, strangers are allowed to talk to one another.

It is paradoxical but perhaps not illogical that the best way to study invasions of privacy is to stage them deliberately.

****

ON MENTAL MAPS

Peter R. Gould

"Can geography be mixed up with psychology... ?"

Luigi Barzini, The Italians

At the start of this limited enquiry into the mental images that men have of geographic space I offer you no theories or even explicit hypotheses. On the contrary, you will find only unstructured, intuitive hunches, and interpretations pushed, in many cases, beyond the limits that the data allow. Of these speculations, for, indeed, this is what they are, many will undoubtedly be wrong. They will have served their purpose, and more, if they stimulate others to replace them with better notions. As usual, what we really need are more penetrating questions, but before these can be asked we must record what we do and do not know. The boundary of ignorance is not very far away, but it seems only sensible to stake it out before we try to cross it. We know so very little about the spatial images, the mental maps, that are in the minds of men. We know even less about how they are formed, the degree to which they are unique or general, and the way they impinge upon, and are reflected in, the decisions that men make. As human geographers reach out across traditional disciplinary boundaries to the other social and behavioral sciences, it is increasingly apparent that the truly satisfying explanation they seek is going to come from emphasizing the *human* as much as the *geography*. We may, perhaps, define our subject as essentially that which tries to understand the spatial aspects of Man's behavior.[1] If we grant that spatial behavior is our concern, then the mental images that men hold of the space around them *may* provide a key to some of the structures, patterns, and processes of Man's work on the face of the earth. The emphasis upon the conditional tense is quite deliberate, and is only partly a result of intellectual cowardice and a general propensity to broadcast *caveats* in lieu of signing academic insurance policies. The other reason is that we really do not know

1. For an interesting and rather similar view in history see: Lee Benson, "Causation and the American Civil War: Two Appraisals," *History and Theory*, Vol. 1, 1961, p. 163.

From *Michigan Inter-University Community of Mathematical Geographers,* Discussion Paper 9, 1966. Reprinted by permission.

whether mental maps are relevant to our problems. But the suspicion that they are is strong, and at the very least it seems worthwhile making some tentative probes along these lines.

Images and Decisions

The human landscape, in reality, or abstracted and modelled as a map, is nothing more, but equally nothing less, than the spatial expression of the decisions of men. As we examine even the most apparently superficial spatial patterns and processes that are a reflection of these decisions, we quickly become aware of the extreme complexity that underlies them, the myriad of variables that compete for attention, and the way in which these form interlocking and convoluted structures that are numbing in their difficulty. Many of the decisions that men make seem to be related, at least in part, to the way in which they perceive the space around them and to the differential evaluations they place upon various portions of it. For the moment this is a bald and unsupported assertion, but it seems reasonable that the manner in which men view their spatial matrix impinges upon and affects their judgements to some degree. For example, men *decide* to migrate, not on a regular surface of equal opportunity or desirability, but in a world often perceived in an extreme, differential manner.[2] Men *decide* to grow crops and raise animals for their sustenance, not in an arbitrary way, but in part according to their particular views of the space around them. Men *decide* to locate their industries and business activities, and with more and more "footloose" industries coming onto the scene we are finding that

traditional location factors are declining in importance. Törnqvist, for example, has indicated the virtual irrelevance of distance for some industries in Sweden,[3] and in this country Harris's classic paper indicated the vast area in the American Manufacturing Belt that lies around the point of minimum transport cost with only slightly higher access costs to the market.[4] Even traditional Weberian analysis discloses a basic characteristic of many extremum problems, with a large area of only slightly higher aggregate cost around the minimum point. What Rufus Isaacs has termed the "principle of flat laxity" seems to be operating extensively in geographic space,[5] and takes on new meaning as we become critically aware of what *satisficing* behavior in a spatial context implies. Thus, in view of the decline in importance of the more traditional location factors, might not the decision to locate be increasingly related to the image an area has in the minds of a few key people?[6] More and more the quaternary industries, the research and development companies, look to the scenic and recreational facilities, cultural assets and intellectual resources of an area. Snow and mountains are not essential

---

2. Julian Wolpert, "Distance and Directional Bias in Interurban Migratory Streams," paper presented to the annual meeting of the Association of American Geographers, Columbus, Ohio, 1965.

3. Gunnar Törnqvist, *Aktiv Lokaliseringspolitik* (Stockholm: Iduns Trycker iaktiebolag Esselte ab, 1963), pp. 215-292. See also his "Transport Costs as a Location Factor for Manufacturing Industry," *Lund Studies in Geography, Series C. General and Mathematical Geography*, No. 2, 1962.
4. Chauncy Harris, "The Market as a Factor in the Localization of Industry in the United States," *Annals of the Association of American Geographers*, Vol. 44, December 1954.
5. Rufus Isaacs, *Differential Games* (New York: John Wiley and Sons, Inc., 1965).
6. Andrew Wilson, "The Impact of Climate on Industrial Growth: Tucson, Arizona: A Case Study," Chapter 17 in W. R. Derrick Sewell (ed.), *Human Dimensions of Weather Modification* (Chicago: University of Chicago Department of Geography Research Series, No. 105, 1966), p. 249.

to certain well-known electronic companies, but New Hampshire and Colorado are undoubtedly grateful for their physiographic and climatological inheritance. Similarly, large universities in pleasant surroundings are the locational loadstones for the research and development consultants. It is not difficult to think of many other examples where the maps that are carried in men's heads might be relevant in quite crucial ways.

What Do We Know About Mental Maps?

Man's view of geographic space is extremely varied, and the views of individual men are always in part unique. Entering into the particular outlook of a particular man are a host of experiences, prejudices and desires, some shared widely with others, some quite specific to the individual. The Northerner is reluctant to be assigned by his company to the South, for he holds to a mental picture that is part of his northern cultural inheritance—an inheritance absorbed in childhood, and reinforced by his daily sources of information. The townsman, comfortable and safe amidst the roar of traffic and bustle of urban life, is reluctant to live in the green peace of the country, which he associates with the stillness of bucolic decay. The New England family, suddenly presented with greater economic opportunity amongst the tall trees of Oregon, decides to stay with the known view and the familiar friends, for "Oregon is such a long way from civilization." Thus, the political, social, cultural and economic values held by a man blend into an overall image about the space around him, an image whose components may be particular to him or held in common by many.

It hardly seems necessary to add that we know very little about these spatial images in the minds of men. While a concern for the mental maps of geographic space is nothing new, the literature is extremely sparse. We only have a very small number of examples where they are discussed at all, usually as interesting, but definitely peripheral points in larger investigations. For example, Tobler explicitly raised the question of the mental images that people have of their environment,[7] but his basic concern was for the mental transformations of distance that people make. Lowenthal and Prince have discussed the attitudes of a people towards the visual landscape,[8] while the former, in a synthesis that has yet to be equalled, has examined the relevance of the psychological literature in this area.[9] A number of other geographers have focussed upon the perception of environmental hazard and the spatial implications that such images have for locational decisions.[10] In political geography, only Herman seems to have moved beyond fuzzy speculation to investigate truly the changing values and attitudes of a people towards the national space.[11] Occasionally maps such as the "New Yorker's View of the United States" appear, but their humorous context actually obscures the fact that such cartograms of mental images can be extremely illuminating if properly used. Getis

7. Waldo Tobler, *Map Transformations of Geographic Space*, Ph.D. thesis, Department of Geography, University of Washington, 1961, pp. 111-113.

8. David Lowenthal and Hugh Prince, "English Landscape Tastes," *The Geographical Review*, Vol. LV, No. 2, April 1965, pp. 186-222.

9. David Lowenthal, "Geography, Experience, and Imagination: Towards a Geographical Epistemology," *Annals of the Association of American Geographers*, Vol. 51, No. 3, September 1961, pp. 241-260.

10. Ian Burton and Robert Kates, "The Perception of Natural Hazards in Resource Management," *Natural Resources Journal*, Vol. 3, No. 3, January 1964, pp. 412-441.

11. Theodore Herman, "Group Values Towards the National Space: The Case of China," *The Geographical Review*, Vol. XLIX, No. 2, April 1959, pp. 164-182.

has shown how shape distortions can focus the eye upon a particular portion of the map,[12] and Mackay had a map in the late fifties showing Canada through French-Canadian eyes. Unfortunately, it was never published.[13] In a related field, only Lynch, as an urban planner truly concerned with the city as the home of man, has systematically investigated the differential images of the urban landscape, and in his most imaginative series of maps we have our only notions of these mental pictures.[14]

The literature in other fields is equally sparse. The psychologists, in their concern for "Perception," have barely touched upon the investigation of mental pictures of geographic space, for many of their efforts have concentrated upon the physics and physiology of the senses, often within highly controlled laboratory conditions. For example, the space with which Sandström was concerned was far removed in scale from geographical space,[15] and his insights on disorientation and loss of criteria for making locational judgements under formal experimental situations is hard to carry over in any meaningful sense to world scales. Even Hull's work, though a source of extremely stimulating analogy, does not deal with the larger space of the earth's surface.[16] Nor did the swing of some psychologists to the *Gestalt* outlook produce a shift in the *focus* of their concern, and the discussions of space by this particular school do not really deal with the larger area of the earth's surface which is the geographer's realm. Though the pioneering work of the child psychologists Piaget and Inhelder is directly concerned with the way in which children learn about space, the world around them, and geometrical and topological concepts,[17] it does not deal with the essentially *geographic* images that children hold or the way they learn about them. Only Trowbridge's paper on imaginary maps, written half a century ago,[18] specifically raises the question of the spatial images people carry around in their heads. Unfortunately, this line of investigation was never followed up, and his paper represents the solitary gold nugget at the bottom of the psychological pan. The rest is a residue of vaguely structured insight that hardly rewards the effort of panning it out from the ground material.

In other areas the prospect is equally bleak. The mythical space of Cassirer, though treated as a mental construct, seems less than useful to the geographer,[19] and the *Weltanschauungen* or world views that have been discussed by other philosophers may be splendid flowers of many hues, but they are difficult to transplant into the hard earth with which the geographer deals.

12. In William Bunge, *Theoretical Geography* (Lund: C. W. K. Gleerup, 1962), Lund Studies in Geography, Series C. General and Mathematical Geography, No. 1, p. 43.
13. Forrest Pitts, private communication.
14. Kevin Lynch, *The Image of the City* (Cambridge: MIT Press, 1961).
15. Carl Sandstrom, *Orientation in the Present Space* (Stockholm: Almqvist and Wiksell, 1951), pp. 138-147.
16. Clark L. Hull, *A Behavior System: An Introduction to Behavior Theory Concerning the Individual Organism* (New York: John Wiley and Sons, Inc., 1964), pp. 215-274.

17. Jean Piaget and Barbel Inhelder, *The Child's Conception of Space* (London: Routledge and Paul, 1956); Jean Piaget, Barbel Inhelder, and Alina Szeminska, *The Child's Conception of Geometry* (New York: Harper Torchbooks, 1964); Jean Piaget, *The Child's Conception of the World* (Paterson, N. J.: Littlefield, Adams and Co., 1963).
18. C. C. Trowbridge, "On Fundamental Methods of Orientation and Imaginary Maps," *Science*, Vol. 38, No. 990, 1913, pp. 888-897.
19. Ernst Cassirer, *The Philosophy of Symbolic Forms: Volume II: Mythical Thought* (New Haven: Yale University Press, 1955), pp. 83-94.

The Question of Uniqueness and Generality of Viewpoint

Because the *total* experiences of individual men are unique it might seem, at first glance, that they perceive the world around them in quite distinct, totally individualistic ways. But, if this were really so, it would be impossible to say anything of general, and, therefore, of scientific worth about their spatial perception. Though this statement may sound almost tautological, it does raise, by jarring our commonsense experience, the notion that the views of men are not, in fact, totally disparate. We may disagree with some about the desirability or undesirability, the beauty or ugliness, of a particular place, but we can be almost certain of finding someone whose "view from the bridge" closely parallels our own. Perhaps, then, this is the key: a portion of our viewpoint is quite particular to ourselves, while another part is shared, or held in common, with many of our fellows.

Given some information about the preferences of a group of people for various portions of an area, we require a way of separating out the general or shared portion of their perception from that which is quite specific to them individually. Putting it another way, we would like to partition the total variation in space preferences for a given sample of people into those portions that indicate general or common viewpoints, and those that represent unique portions that may be assigned to individuals themselves. It is for this reason that the problem has been approached through principal components analysis.[20]

In all the examples that follow, people were asked to provide rank order listings of their preferences for various areas. The question was posed in the context of residential desirability with "all other things being equal." For example, in the United States, students were asked to imagine themselves married and settling down with a family with complete freedom of location according to their own particular views as to what was desirable. Thus the basic data consisted of a matrix whose rows represented the states—while the columns represented people. Each column contained the rank order values that a particular person had assigned to places in the rows, so that in a crude sense each person became a variable upon which the residential desirability of a place was measured.

Clearly, if two people held very similar views that rank order lists would match quite closely. Thus, the whole basic data matrix may be summarized by a smaller matrix of rank correlations (Figure 1). It is upon such matrices that the principal components analyses are performed to break out the underlying structures of space preferences in terms of a smaller number of dimensions or components. By definition, such dimensions are unrelated to one another, because we are *imposing* an orthogonal structure upon the data,[21] and they may be

---

20. Many standard works are now available. A good introduction to basic notions is Raymond Cattell, "Factor Analysis: An Introduction to Essentials, I. The Purpose and Underlying Models," *Biometrics*, March 1965, pp. 190-215, and ". . . II. The Role of Factor Analysis in Research," *Biometrics*, June 1965, pp. 405-435. Full reference works include H. H. Harman, *Modern Factor*

Analysis (Chicago: University of Chicago Press, 1960), and Paul Horst, *Factor Analysis of Data Matrices* (New York: Holt, Rinehart and Winston, Inc., 1965).
21. Rotations can be performed, but the standardized criteria seem a bit simpleminded for this problem. What we really need is a physical structure in a two- or three-dimensional space which is attached, via a computer, to an oscilloscope displaying the map with a contoured "perception surface." Actual rotation of the structure by the investigator would almost instantaneously produce the new surface interpolated from the new scores based on the new loadings. Our "simple structure"

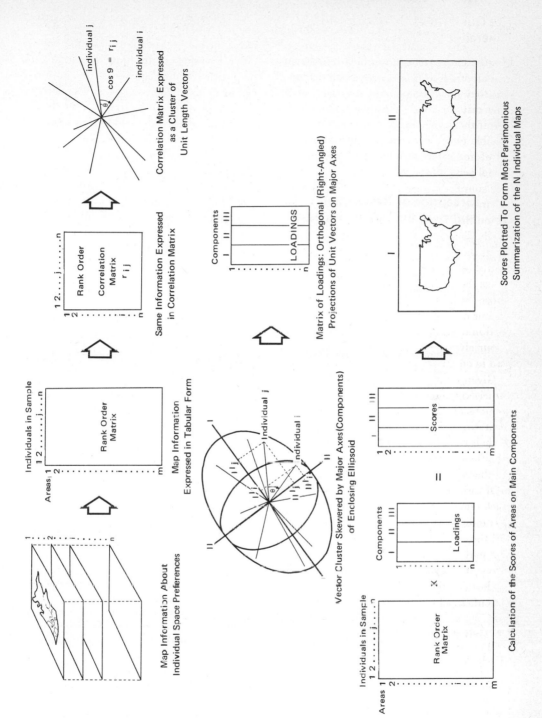

Figure 1. Steps in the construction of the component maps.

thought of as independent scales upon which the areas have particular values or component scores. Thus, to summarize, the maps are constructed from scores on an orthogonal principal components structure, which is merely used descriptively as a statistical summary device, to see if we can break apart and simplify the structure underlying the views and values men hold and place upon geographic space.

The Perception of Residential Desirability in the United States

Apart from turning their attention temporarily on particular places during times of physical or human crisis, perhaps most people in our highly mobile society perceive and think about the geographic space called the United States in terms of residential desirability. At the state universities of California (Berkeley), Minnesota, Pennsylvania and Alabama,[22] students in beginning geography courses were asked to provide rank order lists of the forty-eight contiguous states in terms of their own, quite personal preferences.[23]

Two problems were recognized. First, the state units were quite gross, and any analysis must be made at an extremely general,

macro-level. While it might be better to make the mesh of perception a finer one, either by using county units, or gridding the map with 100 mile squares, such a notion can be quickly dismissed when we realize that people would have to rank literally thousands of areas defined in terms quite unlike those with which they were familiar. At least states, while gross areal units, are familiar objects with quasi-collective images. Secondly, most people faced with the problem of ranking items in order of preference have some immediate, and usually quite strong, likes and dislikes, but there may be a large number of items "in the middle" to which they are more or less indifferent. Thus, instructions were given that where difficulty was experienced in assigning a rank order to a state, that it should be matched against the others in succession with the question in mind "If I *had* to choose, which would I prefer?."[24] It should be recognized, though, that the middle area rankings will be less valid, although there is little reason to suspect any systematic bias and we can probably regard the effect of

criterion would then become truly spatial, which, after all, is what it should be.

22. I would like to thank Professors Alan Pred, University of California, Berkeley, Philip Porter, University of Minnesota, and Eugene Wilson, University of Alabama, for distributing the questionnaires to their students.

23. Sample sizes varied from about twenty-five to fifty. While the lower bound constitutes quite a small sample, repeated samples of this size taken at the Pennsylvania State University have indicated an extremely high degree of consistency in the preferences and in the appearance of the final maps. I would like to thank Messers Marich, Bigelow and Knighton, graduate students in geography at the Pennsylvania State University, for providing me with their seminar exercise results.

24. In later work people were asked to include and rank in their lists Neutral Points. As an individual compiles a list of states, starting with the most desirable, his initial feelings are positive—he would like to live in the areas he most prefers. Further on down the list, however, his feelings become indifferent, at which point he injects the Neutral Point, assigning it the next rank in the list. Thus the Neutral Point provides a base point for any subsequent scales derived from a principal components analysis. See Harold Gulliksen, "Intercultural Studies of Attitudes," in Harold Gulliksen (ed.), *Contributions to Mathematical Psychology* (New York: Holt, Rinehart and Winston, Inc., 1964), pp. 62-108. See too his contribution "The Structure of Individual Differences in Optimality Judgements," and Ledyard Tucker, "Systematic Differences Between Individuals in Perceptual Judgements," both contained in Maynard W. Shelley and Glenn Bryan (eds.), *Human Judgements and Optimality* (New York: John Wiley and Sons, Inc., 1964).

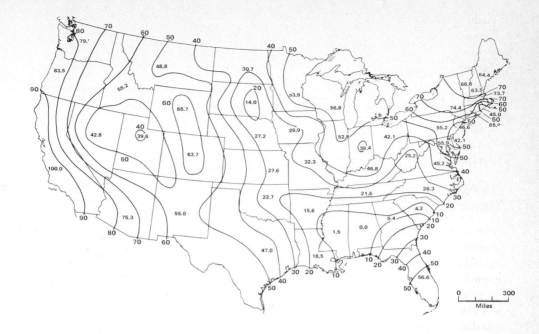

Figure 2. The view from California: the first dimension.

indifference quite legitimately as random noise injected into the data.

The View from California. The surface of perception derived from the first dimension (Figure 2),[25] may be considered a general, overall view of the residential desirability of the United States as seen from California. A ridge of high desirability extends along the entire west coast, with the highest peak of the whole perception surface in California itself. However, the gradient to the east is very steep and there is a clear "Perceptual"

---

25. Factor scores have been transformed to percentage values relative to the highest score to make comparisons easier. These values were plotted at the approximate center of population of each state, and isolines added to form a three-dimensional "surface of perception"—a useful, if somewhat pretentious notion. This is sheer cartographic license, used without apology, to heighten the visual effect and to provide the concept of gradient.

as well as "Great" Basin with a low point in Utah. Overall, as the view moves eastwards, there is a steady decline in desirability to the Great Plains, with the exception of a local peak in Colorado, and a quite definite "sinkhole" in South Dakota. However, upon reaching the ninety-fifth meridian, the general east-west trend of the perception surface changes radically, for the overall orientation shifts by ninety degrees and a very clear discrimination is made in a north-south direction between the Midwest and the Northeast, where the surface begins to rise once more, and the South, which forms the lowest perceptual trough of the entire surface. Alabama, Mississippi, Georgia, and South Carolina, with their images of civil and social unrest, are the last places in the country for California's students. Only Louisiana is perceived as a slightly more desirable place of residence, but even here the gilding is somewhat tarnished and worn. Florida escapes the general Southern trend, and while Californians are not prepared to place this state as high as some other groups, possibly because of an old rivalry for the title of America's premier place in the sun, the gradient is steep from the low point in Alabama. To the north, the surface trends upwards all the way to New England. Noticeable, however, is the way West Virginia distorts the even march of the isopercepts, possibly because of the recent emphasis upon the problems of poverty in Appalachia and the high social awareness usually ascribed to California's students. Thus, much of Kentucky may be in a similar economic plight, but her image and her value on this first, general dimension of perception is bolstered to almost twice that of her well-publicized eastern neighbor. Perhaps white-fenced, bluegrass pastures and sour-mash bourbon with pretensions to spiritous great-

ness, familiar themes in many advertisements, have conveyed an image brighter than the purely economic facts over much of the state would warrant! From Pennsylvania northeast to New England the rise is very rapid, reflecting an image that appears to include more than the bright lights of Megalopolis. The view of the northeastern "cultural hearth" seems to carry visions of the mountains and lakes of Vermont and New Hampshire and the quiet, rock-strewn coasts of Maine.

The View from Minnesota. From Minnesota the view of the United States is almost the same as that from California (Figure 3). True, the highest peak on the perception surface has shifted to the point from which the perception took place, but the high west coast ridge is still very much in evidence, together with the steep gradient to the Utah perceptual basin, the rise to the Colorado high and the fall to the Dakota sinkhole.

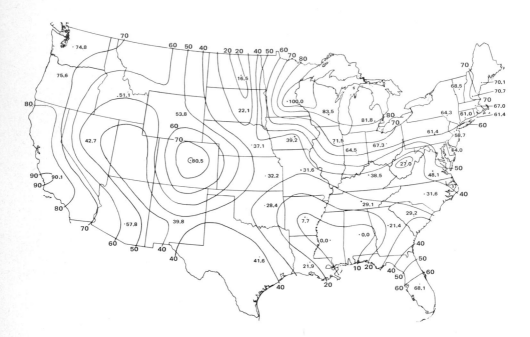

Figure 3. The view from Minnesota: the first dimension.

Indeed, the Minnesotan seems all too aware of his western neighbor, and is most reluctant to trade his "land of sky-blue waters" for the dry flat dreariness a few miles to the west. The steep decline in the surface to the flat country of Iowa reinforces an impression of spatial chauvinism, although to the east Wisconsin appears quite acceptable for residential purposes. Once again, the general west to east trend shifts ninety degrees around the one hundredth meridian, and a low trough, centered in Mississippi and Alabama, blankets the South. Florida is again an exception. Northwards the isopercepts rise, twisted by the West Virginia (Appalachia) distortion, and the Midwestern and New England states bask in residential acceptability with almost uniform values in the sixties.

The View from Pennsylvania. Perhaps more cosmopolitan than the Minnesotans, or set on edge by their rural location at the point of maximum inaccessibility, students at the Pennsylvania State University are seduced by the Californian siren to form the only sample in which the perception point is not the most preferred (Figure 4). Otherwise the surface is almost identical in general form to the Californian and Minnesotan examples. Once again, the perceptual ridges and basins of the West are repeated, and the South is the lowest, or least desired part of the country.

Alabama: Different Values and Different Views. Apart from local peaks of desirability, the three northern and western viewpoints are virtually identical. It is almost as though we had the same perception surface drawn for all three upon a rubber sheet and could reproduce the exact surface by moving a tennis ball beneath it to form, or reinforce, the local point. However, the view of the college student from Alabama, while sharing one or two points of similarity in the West,

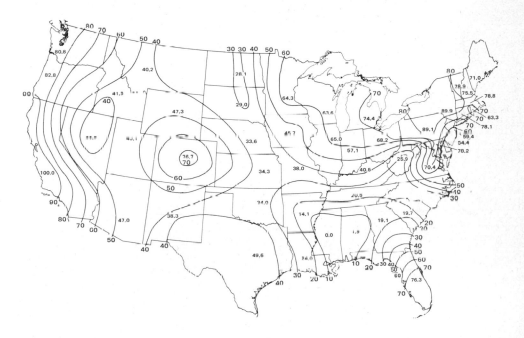

Figure 4. The view from Pennsylvania: the first dimension.

is generally quite different (Figure 5). The high peak of the surface is centered at the point of perception once again, but whereas the previous three samples tended to lump the "South" into a single low trough, Southerners appear to perceive the area with a high degree of spatial discrimination. Most noticeable is the very steep gradient down to Mississippi in the west: there seems to be little love lost between the two states that Northerners tend to place together, possibly because of the *extreme* violence associated with the civil rights movement in that state. A fairly high degree of discrimination is also apparent between South Carolina and North Carolina. While California's politically and socially concerned students did tend to single out the former, generally the difference in desirability perceived by the northern students between these two states was not marked. Southerners, on the other hand, with a more intimate knowledge of this area,

place North Carolina on par with gentlemanly Virginia and Kentucky, while assigning the southern neighbor the next-to-lowest score in the whole South. With the effect of the Civil War still being handed down in the minds of men one hundred years later, the surface falls away rapidly to the northeast, with a very steep gradient along the Mason-Dixon line. North of this historic divide, there is considerable perceptual homogeneity with all the Yankees lumped together in Southern minds, just as the Northern viewpoints blotted out and homogenized possible differences in the South. Such disparagement is shared by the Midwest and the whole set of northern states as far as Washington and Oregon on the Pacific. Northern, remote and blizzard-ridden, with only eye-straining horizons of waving wheat, the Dakotas are the last place in America for the college-bound Alabaman. In the West, only the Californian ridge and

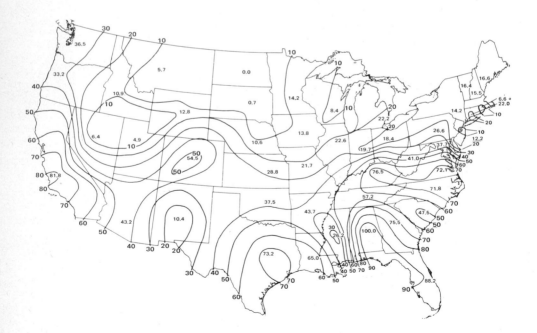

Figure 5. The view from Alabama: the first dimension.

the Colorado peak appear, though less strongly than in the other examples. It is interesting to speculate upon the reason for the sinkhole in New Mexico, compared with the high value of Texas (still in the South), and Arizona (Goldwater country in the election year, shortly after which the sample was taken). What mental image does the word "Mexico" conjure up for the white Southerner that so reduces the desirability of this state far below its neighbors?

Questions and Speculations

The remarkable degree of similarity in the mental maps held by the Californian, Minnesotan and Pennsylvanian samples raises the question of the degree of perceptual homogeneity within the groups themselves. The proportion of the total variation explained in each case by the first component does not vary radically (Table 1), but the differences, if they do not simply arise from sampling fluctuations, are intriguing. Pennsylvania possesses the highest degree of perceptual homogeneity, closely followed by Minnesota, while Californian students appear to agree the least about places of residence. Perhaps this is because the University of California at Berkeley draws upon a more heterogeneous population for its student body, while the state of California itself receives large numbers of migrants from other states in the Union. Surprisingly, the sample with the least homogeneity of outlook is Alabama, and we might postulate a

sort of spatial schizophrenia, for while the most dominant portion clings tightly to Alabama, and shares a mental map that discloses all the century-old clichés about "Yankeeism," the rest are split in their views with little agreement between their mental images.[26]

Other questions also emerge from an examination of the maps based upon the first component scores. One of these is the effect of size on the ordering process. While it has been postulated that in viewing a map our minds act as a high pass filter, so that small-scale features are accentuated,[27] it is worth noting that Rhode Island is consistently lower in overall score than its New England neighbors. Does it really have the image of a less pleasant place to live than nearby Massachusetts and Connecticut? Or is it, in fact, so small that people tend to forget about it, and in partially overlooking it assign a lower rank to it than it might otherwise receive?

Another source of possible bias could result from the propensity for people to group together things that are spatially contiguous.[28] It would be difficult to design a watertight experiment to get at this effect if it existed, but one approach might be as follows. Identical maps of the United States could be given to two groups (one the sample, the other a control), and data obtained on the space preferences. At a later time, the experiment could be repeated with the control group getting the same map as on the first run, while the sample group would receive a "map" showing the outlines

TABLE 1

State	Percentage of Variance Extracted		
	I	II	III
Pennsylvania	46	16	6
Minnesota	41	15	7
California	36	15	9
Alabama	28	13	9

26. Since the sample was confined to white students it would be highly desirable to examine the mental maps of negro students in the same area. The viewpoints might not be identical.
27. J. Keith Holloway, "Smoothing and Filtering of Time Series and Space Fields," *Advances in Geophysics*, Vol. 4, 1958, pp. 386-387.
28. Julian E. Hochberg, *Perception* (Englewood Cliffs: Prentice-Hall, Inc., 1964), p. 86.

of the states located in a random, and non-contiguous fashion. The successive canonical correlations between the control groups' data sets should be very high, while the same correlations between the sample groups' contiguous and non-contiguous sets should be significantly lower if a contiguity effect is operating. The inferential question of the significance of the difference between two successive canonical correlation analyses, even if the usual statistical assumptions are regarded as plausible, seems worth pushing.

Finally, the question of indifference must be raised once again. By requiring each person to insert and rank a Neutral Point in his list of preferences we may obtain at least some notion of the severity of the problem. In the one example presently available for Pennsylvanian students,[29] the overall score of the Neutral Point on the first component places it in the twenty-third rank. Thus nearly one-half of the states are generally perceived as positively desirable to live in; a remarkable comment upon the spatial mobility of the present college population. Indeed, the level at which a Neutral Point appears on the overall scale represented by the first dimension may be considered as a measure of the degree of parochialism of the sample group. A Neutral Point high on the first dimension, indicating that people are positively inclined to only a few states, might measure either a high degree of parochialism or a high level of discrimination, depending upon one's own attitudes towards such value-loaded words. We might hypothesize that the degree of parochialism, as measured by the position of the Neutral Point, would be directly related to the average age of the group, and the degree of social and cultural isolation experienced by the people in it.

The Rise and Fall of a Hypothesis

Our assumption that indifference exists in the rank orders as random noise makes the interpretation of further components somewhat hazardous. Nevertheless, the remarkable consistency (Table 1) in the proportion of the variance explained by these second scales invites interpretation.

Remembering that the dimensions or scales that we impose in a principal components analysis are orthogonal, and, therefore, unrelated to one another, we might expect that successive maps of perception surfaces should illustrate quite independent concepts about the mental images that men have of geographic space. The view from California on the second dimension (Figure 6) immediately suggests that underlying the overall, general surface (Figure 2), there is another surface, quite independent of the first, that is strongly related to distance away from the point of perception. In fact, apart from a rather awkward *contretemps* around Oregon and Washington, and small distorting pockets in the Ohio, Kentucky and West Virginia areas, the correlation of the scores with raw, crow-flying distance from California is remarkably high ($r_s = .90$). Thus, there appears to be some strong evidence that a distance component is present in mental maps, and that mental images of the differential desirability of geographic space cannot be meaningfully represented on a single, general scale.[30]

29. I would like to thank Mr. Bruce Marich, NDEA Fellow in Geography at the Pennsylvania State University, for allowing me to use the results of his paper "Space Speaks: Some Metaphysical Roots of Spatial Decomposition," p. 15. In the West, California, Washington and Texas were above the Neutral Point; in the South only Florida was so perceived; while all the states east of Wisconsin and north of the Ohio River were seen as positively desirable.

30. Implying that the rank of the correlation matrix is greater than one. For readers unfamiliar with the geometry of such a notion, there is an

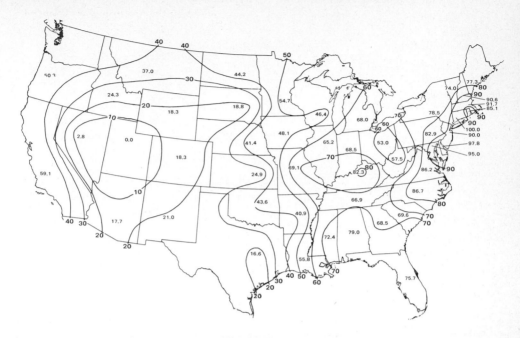

Figure 6. The view from California: the second dimension.

The second perception surface for Pennsylvania (Figure 7) bolsters the idea that a distance component is present. Once again the west coast states prove to be exceptions, destroying the fairly regular march of the isopercepts with distance away from Pennsylvania, but even so the correlation with raw distance is significantly high ($r_s = 64$) New England, too, distorts the distance effect and lowers the overall relationship, but the scores vary with such regularity that one has the feeling that if the map were drawn upon a rubber sheet, mere stretching of the space, rather than tearing or inverting it, could raise the correlation

significantly. In other words, a spatial transformation, with some rather interesting psychological implications, could disclose a much stronger distance effect than the one crudely indicated by the actual association between component scores and straight geographic proximity.[31]

The hypothesis that a distance effect is another dimension to the mental map appears tenable so far. Unfortunately, it is exploded by the next example: Minnesota, true to form, and ever willing to demonstrate geographical inconsistencies, does not fit! If the scores of states on the second component of Minnesota are related to distance (Figure 8), the correlation is virtu-

intriguing physical model in a geographical context in Robert E. Blackith, "Morphometrics," Chapter 9 in Talbot H. Waterman and Harold Morowitz (eds.), *Theoretical and Mathematical Biology* (New York: Blaisdell Publishing Company, 1965), p. 236.

31. Other samples, taken by participants in a seminar at the Pennsylvania State University, confirm the general "east-west" effect of the second component scores.

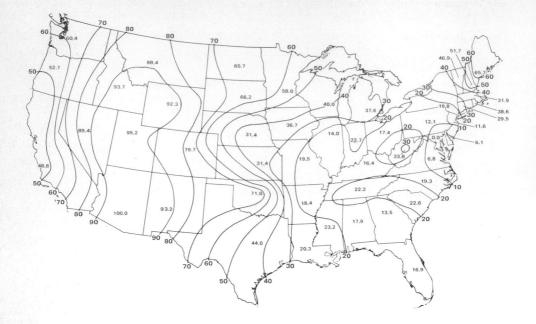

Figure 7. The view from Pennsylvania: the second dimension.

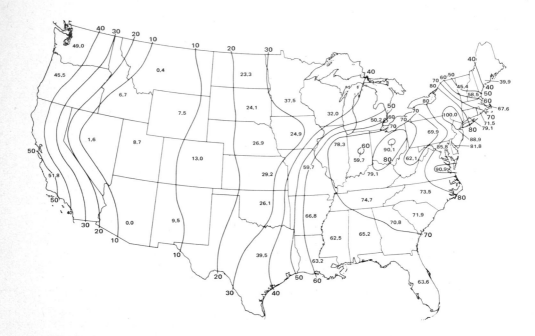

Figure 8. The view from Minnesota: the second dimension.

ally zero, and no amount of stretching of a rubberized surface would appear to make this dimension conform to our distance hypothesis.

But another question now appears worth considering. In all three of the second component maps (Figures 6-8), there appears to be some propensity for the isolines to run generally north and south. In the case of California, the surface is high in the west, dipping to low values over the Great Basin and Mountain states, and rising again slowly at the Great Plains to another high, though convoluted plateau in the east. Similarly, the second perception surface of Minnesota is moderately high in the west, dips to a low trough and rises again with considerable regularity eastwards from the Great Plains only to dip again finally in the New England area. Pennsylvania's second surface also displays the east-west effect to a marked degree, although the shape appears to be the

negative image of California and Minnesota. However, the reversal of the surface raises the question of the mathematical structure of the component model which has been imposed upon the data. If we remember that the loadings of the unit person vectors upon the second component are the elements of the corresponding normalized eigenvector weighted by the square root of the eigenvalue (namely, the length of the second axis of the ellipsoid), then the positive and negative signs may be reversed without changing (1) the variance accounted for by the dimension or (2) the position of the eigenvector in the hyperspace. In other words, the *structure* of the model is quite unchanged by consistently reversing the positive and negative signs of the loadings. When this is done, the Pennsylvanian surface corresponds closely to those of California and Minnesota, with a high western ridge and a low trough over the Basin and Mountain states which

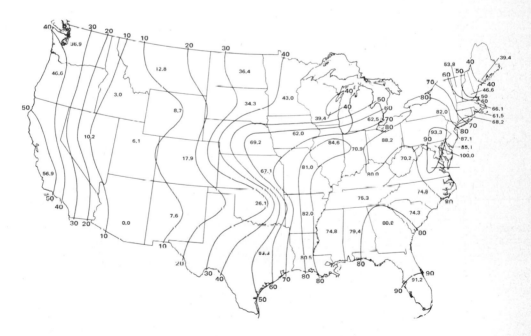

Figure 9. The view from Pennsylvania: the inverted surface on the second dimension.

rises to the eastern plateau to dip, finally, over New England. We might hypothesize, therefore, that there is a second dimension to the mental maps that illustrates a propensity to perceive and evaluate the geographic space of the United States in a fairly consistent east-west direction. Thus, when the point of perception is on the "edge" of the rectangular space, such as in California and to a lesser extent in Pennsylvania, an apparent though spurious distance effect appears reasonably tenable. Only when the perception point moves to the center of the space, as in the case of Minnesota, must the distance hypothesis be discarded to be replaced by an east-west interpretation that is much less intellectually satisfying because it is difficult to relate to any other insights we have. We do know that east-westness in travel produces distinct psychological and physiological effects compared to north-south movement,[32] but this observation provides little confirmation that we are on the right track and the hypothesis awaits much more study with larger and more numerous samples. For example, if one looks at the map of Alabama (Figure 10), through reasonably charitable eyes some confirmation of the east-west hypothesis is obtained. Moving west to east, the high Pacific ridge dips to a north-south trending trough at the 110 meridian followed by a rise in the eastern part of the country. But severe local anomalies, such as Arkansas, occur and the surface appears equivocal in

---

32. G. T. Hauty and T. Adams, *Phase Shifts of the Human Circadian System and Performance Deficit During the Periods of Transition*, Part I. East-West Flight, Part II. West-East Flight, and Part III. North-South Flight (Washington, D.C.: Federal Aviation Agency, Office of Aviation Medicine, 1965).

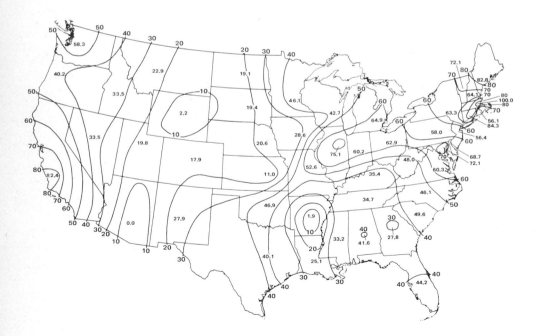

Figure 10. The view from Alabama: the second dimension.

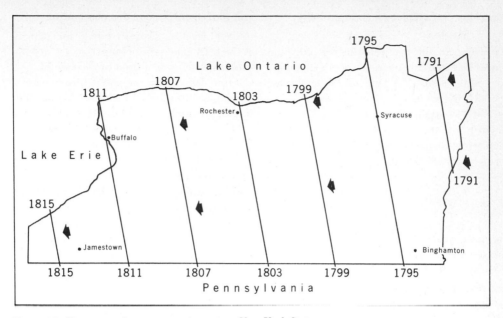

Figure 11. Pioneer settlement waves in western New York State.

its ability to support or deny the rather clear configurations of the other three examples.

On the Reconstruction of Perception Surfaces

On the assumption that people's actions in an area may be partially related to their perception of the space and the differential evaluations they place upon various portions of it, it is possible that by working backwards we can make some rough reconstructions of the mental images held by men long ago. For example, in a recent study of the process of historical settlement in western New York State just after the revolution,[33] trend surface analyses up to the

cubic were carried out in which dates of first settlement in an area (time dimension) were related to the geographical locations (two space dimensions).[34]

We might consider the even march of the isochrones defining the simplest, or linear surface (Figure 11), as indicative of the waves of settlers that might have moved across the country from east to west *if* the area had been perceived as a uniform transport surface completely isotropic in all the opportunities it presented to settlers at that time. However, such an assumption is obviously not tenable. Roads and tracks were beginning to lace the area at this time, making it easier to travel in some directions than others, and the *information* people had about different portions of the space varied and was strengthened by differential feedback processes. While analogies may be

33. I would like to thank Mr. Gary Fuller, NDEA Fellow in Geography, The Pennsylvania State University, for giving me permission to use the maps and information from his seminar paper "Western New York: A Culture Hearth?," June, 1966, to which reference should be made for a much fuller [sic] discussion than is possible here.

34. The idea comes from Peter Haggett and Richard Chorley, "Trend Surface Mapping . . .," *op. cit.*, p. 64.

dangerous, I agree wholeheartedly with Bauer that they ". . . may play two roles: the scientific role of developing generalized knowledge and the practical role of illuminating other events."[35] Thus, in the same way a submarine valley can distort an evenly spaced wave train (Figure 12),[36] so we might think of the underlying surface of perception distorting the even waves of settlement over the land. Fitting the qua-

dratic surface (Figure 13), which represents the next level of accurate description gained at the least expense of complexity,[37] provides us with some notion of the ease of travel in certain directions, the information flowing back to the points of origin, and the way opportunities were perceived by the people at the time. The even settlement waves are pulled along the main route to the west, and the lakes to the north and south of this main corridor are marked. Describing the time and space relationships with the next most complex surface, the cubic (Figure 14) indicates even more strongly the way in which the Lake Ontario plain was per-

35. Quoted by Bruce Mazlish, *The Railway and the Space Program: An Exploration in Historical Analogy* (Cambridge: MIT Press, 1965), p. xiii.
36. Blair Kinsman, *Wind Waves: Their Generation and Propagation on the Ocean Surface* (Englewood Cliffs: Prentice-Hall Inc., 1965), p. 19.

37. Sums of squares increased from 36% to 49%.

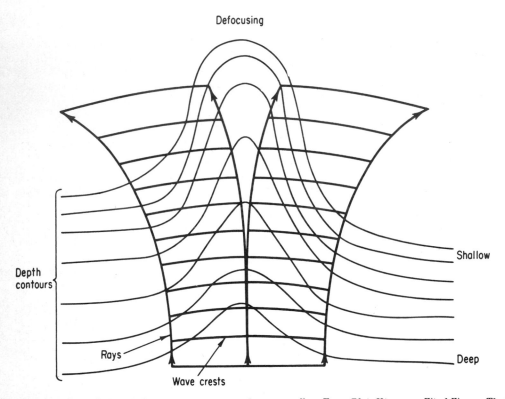

Figure 12. The refraction of a wave train over a submarine valley. From Blair Kinsman, *Wind Waves: Their Generation and Propagation on the Ocean Surface*, (c) 1965. Reprinted by permission of Prentice-Hall, Inc., Englewood Cliffs, New Jersey, and the author.

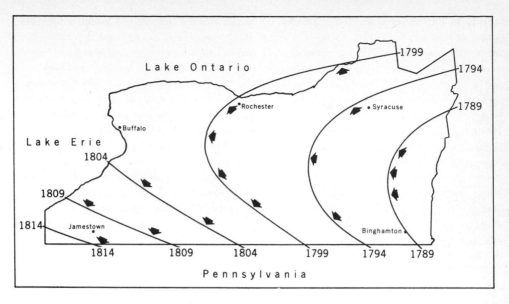

Figure 13. Western New York State: the quadratic surface.

ceived as a less desirable area for settlement, for the time gradient is extremely steep to the north as the settlers by-passed it in their push westwards along the Lake Erie corridor to the new opportunities in Ohio. This was also an area of military activity where towns were frequently raided by the British in the early years of the nineteenth century.[38]

38. Fuller, *op. cit.*, p. 11.

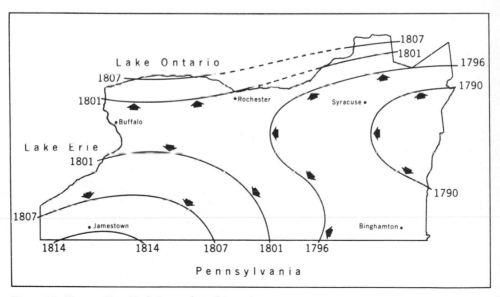

Figure 14. Western New York State: the cubic surface.

Similarly, the southwestern corner forms a pocket of late settlement in an area of rougher terrain that was filled in after the initial waves of settlers had pushed into the new lands of the west.[39]

To separate out the broad regional regularities and trends from the smaller local effects has always been a challenging task for the geographer. Where a dynamic spatial process such as pioneer settlement is going on, the use of trend surface analysis, combining space and time, may not only allow us to achieve such a goal in an efficient and objective manner but to obtain, in addition, some insight into the mental images that men held at the time. If such a notion is valid, we may be able to examine the way in which such mental maps change through time, and so trace the line of inheritance for these images. Perhaps a series of careful content analyses may allow us to observe which areas maintain their brightness in the minds of men, and which are quickly tarnished as new opportunities, new technologies and new values change the very matrix in which they are evaluated and perceived.[40]

Some Implications of Mental Maps

What are some of the implications of these mental maps, and what lines of further in-

vestigation seem worth pursuing? I hope the examples have indicated that there may be an area of inquiry here that is not only geographically intriguing, but one that smears the line between pure and applied research. For perhaps the most obvious implications lie in the broad area of planning, whether this is undertaken by governments or individuals. Many locational decisions in industry are going to be influenced by the mental maps of a few key people. We can see this in the choices of many footloose industries in this country, while in England the image of the southeast is becoming a source of continuing frustration for planners trying to disperse new factories away from the London "magnet" to relieve congestion and to pump-prime other areas that are in need of additional employment opportunities. Even the channel tunnel, which will simply bolster the locational advantage of the southeast, is receiving criticism on the grounds that it will reinforce the pull of the area.[41]

In much of the underdeveloped world, the allocation of social investment is still of critical concern as many countries try to forge the basic infrastructure of transport, education, sanitation, and health facilities. Are the areas that are already "mentally bright" going to receive a large share because they are prominent already in the minds of men? Would an awareness and self-knowledge of this tendency have any beneficial influence? The stricture "Unto them that hath shall be given" seems to describe the basic features of a system of allocation with strong feedback features to produce the agglomerations and clusters of goods and people that are the main feature of the urban revolution.

There are also some implications for administrative planning. In much of the

39. Maps of residuals highlight the areas that were perceived as particularly attractive or repellent. See Fuller, *op. cit.*, p. 14.
40. Useful references include Richard Budd and Robert Thorp, *An Introduction to Content Analysis* (Iowa City: State University of Iowa Press, 1963); Robert North, Ole Holsti, M. George Zaninovich and Dina Zinnes, *Content Analysis* (Evanston: Northwestern University Press, 1963); while imaginative applications include David McClelland, *The Achieving Society* (New York: VanNostrand and Co. Inc., 1961), and Richard Merritt, "Systems and the Disintegration of Empires," *General Systems Yearbook*, Vol. VII, 1962, pp. 91-103.

41. Anon., "Under and Over," *Manchester Guardian Weekly*, July 7, 1966, p. 8.

underdeveloped world particularly, mental maps may closely correspond to the accessible, modernized areas illuminated by the bright lights of the cities and towns. Yet one of the great needs in most of these countries is to get people, particularly teachers of all kinds, into the "bush" areas that are so disparagingly viewed. Are there not some implications here for incentive allowances that might be inversely related to the perceptual scores that various areas receive? Of course, this is not a problem unique to Africa. Salaries for teachers in Alaska are incentively inspired beyond the difference in the cost of living, and the Soviet Union is using very high incentive pay to lure her people into the new and dynamic lands of Siberia.[42]

In the area of migration, too, mental maps may shed some light on the gross and long-term movements of people. Thomlinson, for example,[43] after trying to estimate the effect of many variables on migration in the United States, comments upon the high residual variation of the Pacific states. Interestingly enough, they are all part of a prominent ridge of desirability that is consistent across all the mental maps of the students sampled. Similarly, the areas of marked migrational loss in this country, the Great Plains in particular, are low troughs and sinkholes. The implications for depressed areas are obvious, and in some of the backward pockets of Appalachia it would be useful to know about the mental maps of the young and the old.[44] In

England, work on the mental maps of pupils about to leave school has shed some light on the migrational streams of young people that are causing such concern to regional planners.[45]

At the more academic level, the mental maps raise the question of the geographical implications of the informational flows to which people are subjected. Many writers, across a range of disciplines and concerns, have commented upon the way in which viewpoints are molded by the available information. As Herbert Simon notes in a critique of some common clichés:

> Does a man live for months or years in a particular position in an organization, exposed to some streams of communication, shielded from others, without the most profound effects upon what he knows, believes, attends to, hopes, wishes, emphasizes, fears and proposes?[46]

What are the flows of information that form and mold the surfaces of mental maps? All other things being equal, do they change in content and intensity as one moves up the ladder of central places to the critical nodes of connectivity in an interurban network? St. Paul's migration to Rome may well have been influenced by his mental map of the geographic space that comprised his "world." Surely, by his demonstrated awareness of the relationships between location, information and space, modern geographers can claim him as one of their own? After all, they claim the best of everything else!

---

42. Some investigations are proceeding in New Guinea on the mental maps of district officers for administrative assignments.

43. Ralph Thomlinson, "A Model for Migrational Analysis," *Journal of the American Statistical Association*, Vol. 56, No. 295, September 1961, pp. 675-689.

44. Two thousand questionnaires were recently obtained from high school students by Mr. Robert

Ziegenfus, Department of Geography, The Pennsylvania State University, on this topic.

45. In cooperation with Mr. Peter Haggett, the author is receiving returns from thirty schools widely scattered throughout England, Wales, and Scotland. The results will be used in the 1966 Madingley Lectures at Cambridge University, and will be reported upon at the NSF-sponsored symposium on Advances in Cultural Geography, Columbus, Ohio, November, 1966.

46. Herbert Simon, *Administrative Behavior* (New York: The Free Press, 1965), p. xv.

In Western New York, it was noted that differential flows of information may have had a profound influence upon the rate and direction of pioneer settlement. At a later time, and a little further west, Cochran has described the psychological effect of the railway in altering geographic horizons,[47] and the way the "big city" newspapers raised the information level of the rural population and altered their consciousness of time and space.[48]

Finally, there is the question of the information available to one generation, and the way it is filtered through the minds of the last. To what extent do we inherit our mental maps? It would be interesting to sample the geographic images in successive generations to see what significant changes

existed between them. As Happold notes in a different context:

> One cannot stress too strongly the extent to which our world view has been conditioned by our mental history and development. [49]

Using the notion of the positions of neutral points as indices of parochialism, we may be able to measure, crudely to be sure, but *measure* nevertheless,[50] the changes in mental images from one generation to the next. As Mencius noted more than two millenia ago:

> By weighing, we know what things are light, and what heavy. By measuring, we know what things are long, and what short. The relations of all things may thus be determined, and it is of the greatest importance to measure the motions of the mind. I beg your Majesty to measure it.[51]

47. Thomas C. Cochran, "The Social Impact of the Railway," in Bruce Mazlish (ed.), *The Railroad and the Space Program: An Exploration in Historical Analogy* (Cambridge: MIT Press, 1965), p. 177.

48. *Ibid.,* p. 178.

49. Happold, *op. cit.,* p. 40.
50. Louis Guttman, "The Nonmetric Breakthrough for the Behavioral Sciences," invited address to the Automatic Data Processing Conference of the Information Processing Association of Israel, January 5-6, 1966.
51. Mencius, circa 335 B.C., quoted in Truman Kelley, *Essential Traits of Mental Life* (Cambridge: Harvard University Press, 1935).

✾✾✾✾✾✾✾✾✾✾✾✾✾✾✾✾✾✾✾✾✾✾✾✾✾✾✾✾✾✾✾

THE PERCEPTION OF NATURAL HAZARDS IN RESOURCE MANAGEMENT

Ian Burton and Robert W. Kates

> *"What region of the earth is not full of our calamities?" Virgil*

To the Englishman on his island, earthquakes are disasters that happen to others. It is recognized that "while the ground is liable to open up at any moment beneath the feet

of foreigners, the English are safe because 'it can't happen here.' " [1] Thus is described a not uncommon attitude to natural hazards in England; its parallels are universal.

Notwithstanding this human incapacity

1. Niddrie, *When the Earth Shook* 36 (1962).

From *Natural Resources Journal,* Vol. 3, No. 412 (1964) pp. 412-41. Published by the University of New Mexico School of Law. Reprinted by permission.

to imagine natural disasters in a familiar environment, considerable disruption is frequently caused by hazards. The management of affairs is not only affected by the impact of the calamities themselves, but also by the degree of awareness, or perception of the hazard, that is shared by those subject to its uncertain threat. Where disbelief in the possibility of an earthquake, a tornado, or a flood is strong, the resultant damages from the event are likely to be greater than where awareness of the danger leads to effective precautionary action.

In this article we attempt to set down our imperfect understanding of variations in the perception of natural hazard, and to suggest some ways in which it affects the management of resource use. In so doing we are extending the notion that resources are best regarded for management purposes as culturally defined variables, by consideration of the cultural appraisal of natural hazard.

It may be argued that the uncertainties of natural hazards in resource management are only a special case of the more general problem of risk in any economic activity. Certainly there are many similarities. But it is only when man seeks to wrest from nature that which he perceives as useful to him that he is strongly challenged by the vagaries of natural phenomena acting over and above the usual uncertainties of economic activity. In other words, the management of resource use brings men into a closer contact with nature (be it viewed as friendly, malevolent, or neutral) where the extreme variations of the environment exercise a much more profound effect than in other economic activities.

THE DEFINITION OF NATURAL HAZARDS

For a working definition of "natural hazards" we propose the following: Natural hazards are those elements in the physical environment, harmful to man and caused by forces extraneous to him. According to Zimmerman's view, the physical environment or nature is "neutral stuff," but it is human culture which determines which elements are considered to be "resources" or "resistances." [2] Considerable cultural variation exists in the conception of natural hazards; change occurs both in time and space.

In time, our notion of specific hazards and their causal agents frequently change. Consider, for example, the insurance concept of an "act of God." To judge by the volume of litigation, this concept is under constant challenge and is constantly undergoing redefinition. The "acts of God" of today are often tomorrow's acts of criminal negligence. Such changes usually stem from a greater potential to control the environment, although the potential is frequently not made actual until after God has shown His hand.

In space a varied concept of hazard is that of drought. A recent report adequately describes the variation as follows:

There is a clue from prevailing usage that the term "dought" reflects the relative insecurity of mankind in the face of a natural phenomenon that he does not understand thoroughly and for which, therefore, he has not devised adequate protective measures. A Westerner does not call a rainless month a "drought," and a Californian does not use the term even for an entire growing season that is devoid of rain, because these are usual occurrences and the developed water economy is well bolstered against them. Similarly, a dry period lasting several years, or even several decades, would not qualify as a drought if it caused no hardship among water users.[3]

This may be contrasted with the official

2. Zimmerman, *World Resources and Industries* (1951); see also Zimmermann's diagram, *id.* at 13.
3. Thomas, *The Meterological Phenomenon of Drought in the Southwest, 1942-1956*, at A8 (United States Geological Survey Prof. Paper No. 372-A, 1962).

British definition of an "absolute drought" which is "a period of at least 15 consecutive days to none of which is credited .01 inches of rain or more."[4]

Even such seemingly scientifically defined hazards as infective diseases seem to be subject to changes in interpretation, especially when applied to the assignment of the cause of death. Each decennial revision of the International Lists of Causes of Death has brought important changes to some classes of natural hazards. Thus, the change from the fifth to the sixth revision found a decrease of approximately twenty-five per cent in deaths identified as caused by syphilis and its sequelae as a result of the new definition arising from ostensibly improved medical knowledge.[5]

The definability of hazard is a more sophisticated form of perceiving a hazard. It is more than mere awareness and often requires high scientific knowledge, *i.e.*, we must understand in order to define precisely. But regardless of whether we describe definitions of drought by western water users or the careful restatement of definitions by public health officials, all types of hazard are subject to wide variation in their definition— a function of the changing pace of man's knowledge and technology.

To complicate the problem further, the rise of urban-industrial societies has been coincident with a rapid increase in a type of hazard which may be described as quasi-natural. These hazards are created by man, but their harmful effects are transmitted through natural processes. Thus, man-made

pollutants are carried downstream, radioactive fallout is borne by air currents, and pesticides are absorbed by plants, leaving residues in foods. The intricacies of the man-nature relationship are such that it is frequently not possible to ascribe a hazard exclusively to one class or the other (natural or quasi-natural). A case in point is the question of when fog (a natural hazard) becomes smog (quasi-natural).[6] Presumably some more or less arbitrary standard of smoke content could be developed.

In the discussion that follows, we specifically exclude quasi-natural hazards while recognizing the difficulty of distinguishing them in all cases. Our guide for exclusion is the consideration of principal causal agent.

A CLASSIFICATION OF NATURAL HAZARDS

Table 1 is an attempt to classify common natural hazards by their principal causal agent. It is but one of many ways that natural hazards might be ordered, but it is convenient for our purposes. The variety of academic disciplines that study aspects of these hazards is only matched by the number of governmental basic data collection agencies which amass information on these hazards. The most cohesive group is the climatic and meteorological hazards. The most diverse is the floral group which includes the doctor's concern with a minor fungal infection, the botanist's concern with a variety of plant diseases, and the hydrologist's concern with the effect of phreato-

4. Meteorological Office, United Kingdom Air Ministry, *British Rainfall, 1958*, at 10 (1963). This definition was introduced in British rainfall research in 1887.

5. DHEW, Public Health Service, I Vital Statistics of the United States, 1950, at 31 *(Interpretation of Cause-of-Death Statistics)*, 169 *(Mortality by Cause of Death)* (1954).

6. *Glossary of Meteorology* 516 (Huschke ed. 1959), defines "smog" as follows: "A natural fog contaminated by industrial pollutants; a mixture of smoke and fog. This term coined in 1905 by Des Voeux, has experienced a recent rapid rise in acceptance but so far it has not been given precise definition."

Table 1   Common Natural Hazards by Principal Causal Agent

Geophysical		Biological	
Climatic and Meteorological	Geological and Geomorphic	Floral	Faunal
Blizzards & Snow	Avalanches	Fungal Diseases *For Example:* Athlete's Foot	Bacterial & Viral Diseases *For Example:* Influenza
Droughts	Earthquakes	Dutch Elm Wheat Stem Rust	Malaria
Floods	Erosion (Including Soil Erosion & Shore and Beach Erosion)	Blister Rust	Typhus Bubonic Plague
Fog		Infestations *For Example:*	Veneral Disease
Frost	Landslides	Weeds Phreatophytes	Rabies Hoof & Mouth
Hailstorms	Shifting Sand	Water Hyacinth	Disease Tobacco Mosaic
Heat Waves	Tsunamis	Hay Fever	
Hurricanes	Volcanic Eruptions	Poison Ivy	Infestations *For Example:* Rabbits
Lightning Strokes & Fires			Termites Locusts Grasshoppers
Tornadoes			Venomous Animal Bites

phytes on the flow of water in streams and irrigation channels

In a fundamental way, we sense a distinction between the causal agents of geophysical and biologic hazards. This distinction does not lie in their effects, for both hazards work directly and indirectly on man and are found in both large and small scales. Rather, our distinction lies in the notion of preventability, i.e., the prevention of the occurrence of the natural phenomenon of hazardous potential as opposed to mere control of hazardous effects. A rough rule of thumb is that changes in nature are to be classed as prevention, but changes in man or his works are control.

Given this rule of thumb, it is clear that few hazards are completely preventable. Prevention has been most successful in the area of floral and faunal hazards. Some such hazards (e.g., malaria) have been virtually eliminated in the United States by preventive measures, but they are still common in other parts of the world.

At the present levels of technology, geophysical hazards cannot be prevented, while biological hazards can be prevented in most cases, subject only to economic and budgetary constraints.

We suggest that this is a basic distinction and directly related to the areal dimensions and the character and quantities of energy involved in these natural phenomena. While much encouraging work has been done, we still cannot prevent a hurricane, identify and destroy an incipient tornado, prevent the special concentration of precipitation that often induces floods, or even on a modest scale alter the pattern of winds that shift sand, or prevent the over-steepening and sub-soil saturation that induces landslides. We might again note the distinction between prevention and control: we can and do build landslide barriers to keep rock off highways, and we can and do attempt to stabilize shifting sand dunes.

Despite much loose discussion in popular journals, repeated surveys of progress in weather modification have not changed substantially from the verdict of the American Meteorological Society in 1957, which was that:

Present knowledge of atmospheric processes offers no real basis for the belief that the weather or climate of a large portion of the country can be significantly modified by cloud seeding. It is not intended to rule out the possibility of large-scale modifications of the weather at some future time, but it is believed that, if possible at all, this will require methods that alter the large-scale atmospheric circulations, possibly through changes in the radiation balance. [7]

The non-preventability of the class of geophysical hazards has existed throughout the history of man and will apparently continue to do so for some time to come. Our training, interest, and experience has been confined to this class of hazards. Moreoever, as geographers we are more comfortable when operating in the field of geophysical phenomena than biological. However, we do not know whether the tentative generalizations we propose apply only to geophysical hazards or to the whole spectrum of natural hazards. A priori speculation might suggest the hypothesis that men react to the non-preventable hazard, the true "act of God,"

in a special way, distinct from preventable hazards. Our observations to date incline us toward the belief that there is an orderly or systematic difference in the perception of preventable and non-preventable natural hazards.

This arises from the hiatus between popular perception of hazard and the technical-scientific perception. To many flood-plain users, floods are preventable, *i.e.*, flood control can completely eliminate the hazard. Yet the technical expert knows that except for very small drainage areas no flood control works known can effectively prevent the flood-inducing concentration of precipitation, nor can they effectively control extremely large floods of very rare occurrence. On the other hand, in some parts of the world hoof and mouth disease is not considered preventable, although there is considerable evidence that it is preventable when there is a widespread willingness to suffer large economic losses by massive eradication of diseased cattle combined with vigorous control measures of vaccination.

The hiatus between the popular perception of hazard and the perception of the technician scientist is considered below in greater detail.

THE MAGNITUDE AND FREQUENCY OF HAZARDS

There is a considerable volume of scientific data on the magnitude and frequency of various hazards. The official publications of the agencies of the federal government contain much of it. Examples of frequency data are shown in Figures 1, 2, and 3. In general, these show spatial variations in the degree of hazard in terms of frequency occurrence. The measurement of magnitude is more difficult to portray in graphic form, but in general it is directly related to frequency. For example, areas with higher frequency of hailstorms are also likely to experience the

7. Senate Select Comm. on Nat'l Water Resources, 86th Cong., 2d Sess., *Weather Modification* 3 (Comm. Print No. 22, 1960); see also Batton & Kassander, *Randomized Seeding of Orographic Cumulus* (Univ. Chi. Meteorology Dep't Tech. Bull. No. 12, 1958); Greenfield, *A New Rational Approach to Weather-Control Research* (Rand Corp. Memo. No. RM-3205-NSF, 1962).

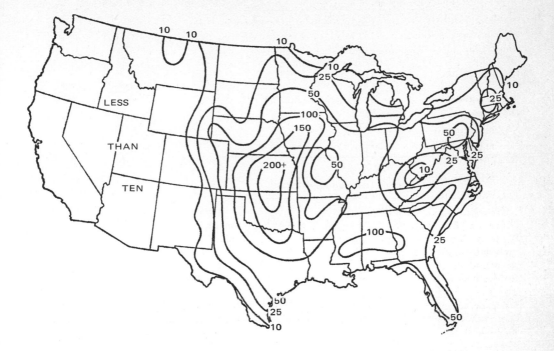

Figure 1. Tornado frequency, 1916-53.

most severe hailstorms. The magnitude of floods is more complex, and attempts to portray variations in magnitude of floods graphically have generally not been successful.[8] We have attempted to show variation in magnitude of floods for New York (Figure 4).

It is our finding that the variations in attitude to natural hazard cannot be explained directly in terms of magnitude and frequency. Differences in perception mean that the same degree of hazard is viewed differently. Part of this variation is due, no doubt, to differences in damage experienced, or in damage potential. In Tables 2 and 3 we

have attempted to set out some examples of damage caused by natural hazards. These tables give some idea of the order of magnitude of damages to life and property. The estimates are in most cases crude. The loss figures given in Table 2 amount to about $12 billion. If we add to this the $25 billion which are spent annually for health care,[9] and the large amounts spent for control and prevention of other natural hazards, then it is clear that our struggle against natural hazards is of the same order of magnitude as the defense budget!

That these estimates are not highly re-

8. See, *e.g.*, the maps prepared by M. Maurice Pardé in Comité National de Géographie, *Atlas de France*, Sheets 20, 22 (1934).

9. Mushkin, *Health as an Investment*, 70 J. Political Economy 129, 137 (1962); see also Merriam, *Social Welfare Expenditures, 1960-1961*, 25 Social Security Bull, 3 (No. 11, 1962).

Table 2   Average Annual Losses from Selected
Natural Hazards

Floods	$350 M (Million) to $1 Billion[10]
Hail	$53 M[11]
Hurricanes	$100 M[12]
Insects	$3,000 M[13]
Lightning Strokes	$100 M[14]
Plant Disease	$3,000 M[15]
Rats and Rodents	$1,000 M to $2,000 M[16]
Tornadoes	$45 M[17]
Weeds	$4,000 M[18]
Total	$11,648 M to $13,268 M

Table 3   Loss of Life from Selected Natural Hazards

Cold Waves	242.[19]	(1959)
Floods	83.4[20]	Average Annual, 1950-1959
Hay Fever	30[21]	(1959)
Heat Waves	207[22]	(1959)
Hurricanes	84.8[23]	Average Annual, 1950-1959
Influenza	2,845[24]	(1959)
Lightning Strokes	600[25]	Average Annual, Years Not Specified
Malaria	7[26]	(1959)
Plague	1[27]	(1959)
Tornadoes	204.3[28]	Average Annual, 1950-1959
Tuberculosis	11,456[29]	(1959)
Venomous Bites & Stings	62[30]	(1959)
Veneral Disease	3,069[31]	(1959)

10. See notes 32-34 *infra*.

11. Flora, *Hailstorms of the United States* 3 (1956).

12. Our estimate.

13. Byerly, *Why We Need Loss Data*, Nat'l Academy of Science, Nat'l Research Council, *Losses Due to Agricultural Pests* 3 (Summary of Conference of the Agricultural Bd. Comm. on Agriculture Pests, Nov. 4-5, 1959).

14. Bureau of Yards & Docks, United States Navy, *Natural Disasters* 24 (Navdocks P-88, 1961).

15. Byerly, *op. cit. supra* note 13.

16. *Ibid.*

17. Flora, *op. cit. supra* note 11.

18. Byerly, *op. cit. supra* note 13.

19. DHEW, Public Health Service, II *Vital Statistics of the United States* 18-36 (1959).

20. Metropolitan Life Ins. Co., *Statistical Bulletin*, vol. 41, at 9 (April, 1960).

21. DHEW, Public Health Service, *op, cit. supra* note 19.

22. *Ibid.*

23. Metropolitan Life Ins. Co., *op. cit. supra* note 20.

24. DHEW, Public Health Service, *op. cit. supra* note 19.

25. Bureau of Yards & Docks, *op. cit. supra* note 14.

26. DHEW, Public Health Service, *op. cit. supra* note 19.

27. *Ibid.*

28. Metropolitan Life Ins. Co., *op. cit. supra* note 20.

29. DHEW, Public Health Service, *op. cit. supra* note 19.

30. *Ibid.*

31. *Ibid.*

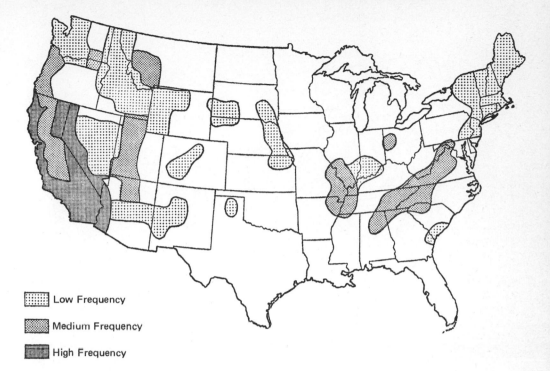

Low Frequency

Medium Frequency

High Frequency

Figure 2. Earthquake areas in the United States.

liable is demonstrated in the wide variation of some of them. Flood damages, for example, are placed at $350 million by the United States Weather Bureau,[32] over $900 million by the United States Army Corps of Engineers,[33] and $1,200 million by the United States Department of Agriculture.[34]

There are partial explanations for the wide discrepancies in these and other similar data. These usually include such questions as definitions used, time period employed, methods of computation, accuracy and

completeness of reporting, changing dollar values, and so on. However, even when all these differences are taken into account the perception of natural hazards still varies greatly. There is variation in the resource manager's perception of hazard. Managers as a group differ in their view as opposed to scientific and technical personnel, and the experts, in turn, differ among themselves. These differences persist even when all the scientific evidence upon which conclusions are based is identical. It is to this complex problem of differing perceptions that we now turn.

VARIATIONS IN PERCEPTION

It is well established that men view differently the challenges and hazards of their

32. Weather Bureau, Dep't of Commerce, Climatological Data, *National Summary*, Annual 1961, at 85 (1962).
33. Senate Select Comm. on Nat'l Water Resources, 86th Cong., 2d Sess., *Floods and Flood Control* 5-7 (Comm. Print No. 15, 1960).
34. Senate Comm. on Banking and Currency, *Federal Disaster Insurance*, S. Rep. No. 1313, 84th Cong., 2d Sess., 69-71 (1956).

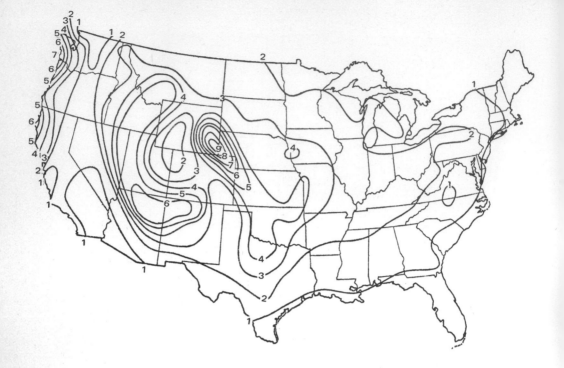

Figure 3. Average number of days with hail. Annual 1904—43.

natural environment. In this section we will consider some of the variations in view of perception of natural hazard. In so doing we will raise more questions than we shall answer; this is a reflection of the immaturity and youth of this line of research.

Our scheme will be to consider the *within group* and *between group* variation in perception of two well-defined groups: resource users, who are the managers of natural resources directly affected by natural hazards (including of course their own persons),[3 5] and technical and scientific personnel—individuals with specialized training and

directly charged with study or control of natural hazards.

Variation in the Perception of Natural Hazard Among Scientific Personnel

The specialized literature is replete with examples of differences in hazard perception among experts. They fail to perceive the actual nature of the hazard, its magnitude, and its location in time and space. Technical personnel differ among each other, and the use of reputable methods often provides estimates of hazards of great variance from one another.

Such variation is due in small part to differences in experience and training, vested organizational interest, and even personality. But in a profound and fundamental way,

---

35. A definition of "resource manager," as we use the term, is found in White, *The Choice of Use in Resource Management*, 1 Natural Resources J. 23, 24 (1961).

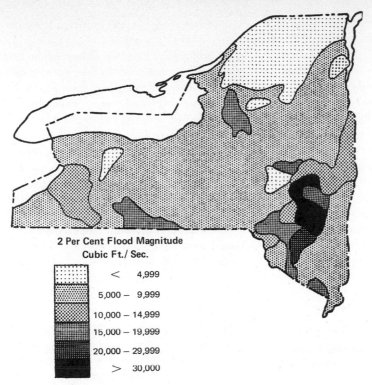

2 Per Cent Flood Magnitude
Cubic Ft./ Sec.

	< 4,999
	5,000 – 9,999
	10,000 – 14,999
	15,000 – 19,999
	20,000 – 29,999
	> 30,000

Figure 4. Regional variations in magnitude of flood with 2 per cent annual chance of occurrence in New York State.

such variation is a product of human ignorance.

The Epistemology of Natural Hazard. We have emphasized the nature of natural hazard as phenomena of nature with varying effects on man, ranging from harmless to catastrophic. To know and to fully understand these natural phenomena is to give to man the opportunity of avoiding or circumventing the hazard. To know fully, in this sense, is to be able to predict the location in time and space and the size or duration of the natural phenomenon potentially harmful to man. Despite the sophistication of modern science or our ability to state the requirements for such a knowledge system, there seems little hope that basic geophysical phenomena will ever be fully predictable. No foreseeable system of data gathering and

sensing equipment seems likely to pinpoint the discharge of a lightning bolt or the precise path of a tornado.

Given this inherent limitation, almost all estimation of hazard is probabilistic in content, and these probabilities may be computed either by counting (relative frequency) or by believing in some underlying descriptive frequency distribution. The probability of most hazardous events is determined by counting the observed occurrence of similar events. In so doing we are manipulating three variables: the magnitude of the event, its occurrence time, and its occurrence in space.

For some hazards the spatial variable might fortunately be fixed. Volcanic eruptions often take place at a fixed point, and rivers in humid areas follow well-defined stream courses. For other hazards there may be broadly defined belts such as storm paths or earthquake regions (see Figure 2). There are no geophysical hazards that are apparently evenly or randomly distributed over the earth's surface, but some, such as lightning, approach being ubiquitous over large regions.

The size or magnitude of the hazard varies, and, given the long-term human adjustment to many hazards, this can be quite important. Blizzards are common on the Great Plains, but a protracted blizzard can bring disaster to a large region.[36] On great alluvial flood plains small hummocks provide dry sites for settlement, but such hummocks are overwhelmed by a flood event of great magnitude.

Magnitude can be thought of as a func-

tion of time based on the apparent truism of extreme events: if one waits long enough, there will always be an event larger than that previously experienced. In the case of geophysical events, waiting may involve several thousand years. Graphically, this is presented for fifty years in Figure 5 for two common hazards.

Most harmful natural phenomena are rare events; if they were not, we humans would probably have been decimated before we became entrenched on this planet. Since the counting of events is the major method of determining probabilities, rare events by their nature are not easily counted. Equally disturbing is the possibility that by climatic change, or improved scientific knowledge, or human interference, the class of natural events may change and create further uncertainties in the process of observing and recording.

Faced with a high degree of uncertainty, but pressed by the requirements of a tech-

---

36. Calef, *The Winter of 1948-49 in the Great Plains*, 40 Ass'n Am. Geographers, Annals 267 (1950).

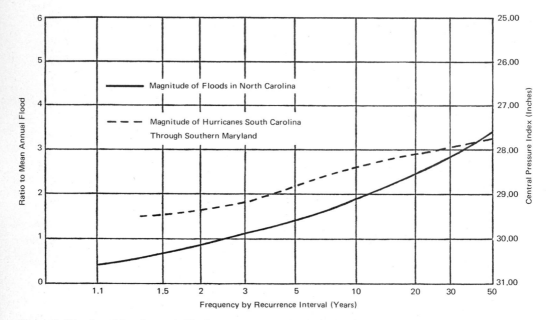

Figure 5. Floods and hurricanes in North Carolina: magnitude and frequency. Source: National hurricane research project report No. 33, *Floods in North Carolina; Magnitude and Frequency.*

nical society for judgments and decisions, scientific and technical personnel make daily estimates of hazard with varying degrees of success.

An example of unsuccessful estimating is seen in the case of the San Carlos Reservoir on the Gila River in Arizona. Completed in 1928, this reservoir has never been filled to more than sixty-eight per cent of its capacity and has been empty on several occasions.[37] The length of stream flow record on which the design of the dam was based was short (approximately thirty years), but it was not necessarily too short. The considerable over-building of this dam, according to Langbein and Hoyt, was due in part to the failure to take into account the increasing variability of annual flows as indicated in the coefficient of variation. In their view, the San Carlos Reservoir is "a victim of a deficiency in research to develop the underlying patterns of fluctuations in river flow."[38] To our knowledge, this deficiency still exists, and we have doubts as to whether such patterns can actually be determined.

Until recent years, that highly reputable practitioner of actuarial precision, the insurance industry, charged rates for hail insurance that were largely a matter of guesswork.[39] Flora notes that

often in widely level areas, where we now know that the hail risk varies but little over a distance of a hundred miles or more, one county might have several damaging hailstorms while adjacent counties might escape entirely. In such instances, the county which had suffered severe damage would be given a much higher insurance rate than others.[40]

With regard to flood insurance, the industry has long apologized for its unwillingness to even enter the fray, using words similar to these:

[The insurance company underwriters believe that] specific flood insurance covering fixed location properties in areas subject to recurrent floods cannot feasibly be written because of the virtual certainty of loss, its catastrophic nature and the reluctance or inability of the public to pay the premium charge required to make the insurance self sustaining.[41]

Some hazards have been only belatedly recognized. Langbein and Hoyt cite the fact that in the *American Civil Engineers Handbook*, published in 1930, there are no instructions about reservoir sedimentation.[42]

Public agencies charged with flood control responsibilities have had to make estimates of the long run recurrence of these phenomena. Despite a great deal of work and ingenuity, results are not overly impressive. Three highly respected methods of flood frequency analysis place the long run average return period of the largest flood of record in the Lehigh Valley as either twenty-seven, forty-five, or seventy-five years.[43]

The disparate views and perceptions of technical and scientific personnel are a reflection of our ignorance of the chance occurrence of events, and more fundamentally of our lack of understanding of the physical forces themselves. There is little hope of eliminating this uncertainty, and the technical-scientific community follows the course of recognizing it, defining it, and finally learning to live with it.

37. Langbein & Hoyt, *Water Facts for the Nation's Future* 229 (1959).
38. *Id.* at 230.
39. Flora, *Hailstorms of the United States* 56 (1956).
40. *Ibid.*

41. American Ins. Ass'n, *Studies of Floods and Flood Damage* 3 (1956).
42. Langbein & Hoyt, *op. cit. supra* note 37, at 232.
43. *Delaware River Basin, New York, New Jersey, Pennsylvania, and Delaware*, H. R. Doc. No. 522, 87th Cong., 2d Sess., VI, Plate 42 (1962).

Variations in the Perception of Natural Hazard Among Resource Managers

Resource users or managers do not display uniformity in their perception of natural hazard any more than do scientific and technical personnel. Not being experts, they have less knowledge or understanding of the various possible interpretations of data and are often amazed at the lack of agreement among the professionals. Their views may be expected to coincide insofar as the lay managers subscribe to the various popular myths of hazard perception (whether "it can't happen here." or "after great droughts come great rains," or "a little rain stills a great wind"). But in this age of enlightenment, perception is not easily limited to such aphorisms. Differences in perception arise both among users of the same resource and between users of different resources.

Perception Among Users of the Same Resource. Urban and rural flood-plain users display differences in the perception of flood hazard. Our own studies of urban [44] and agricultural [45] flood-plain users suggest a great hazard sensitivity in terms of awareness on the part of agricultural land users. However, the frequency of hazard that encourages certain responses on the part of resource users is approximately equal for both urban and agricultural land users.[46]

The limited work on flood plains in variation of perception between users suggests

three explanatory factors: (1) the relation of the hazard to the dominant resource use, including in agriculture the ratio between area subject to flooding and the total size of the management unit, (2) the frequency of occurrence of floods, and (3) variations in degree of personal experience. Interestingly, there seems to be little or no significant effect in hazard perception by the few generalized indicators of level of social class or education that have been tested against hazard perception.

The first factor is essentially a reflection of an ends-means scheme of resource use. We would expect to find a heightened hazard perception in those cases, such as drought in an agricultural region or beach erosion on a waterfront cottage, where the hazard is directly related to the resource use. Where it is incidental, such as lightning or tornadoes, the perception of hazard is variant, vague, and often whimsical.

The second factor suggests that the frequency of natural events is related to the perception of hazard. Where the events in question are frequent, there is little variation among users in their perception. The same holds true where the event is infrequent, for here the failure to perceive a significant hazard is widely shared. It is in the situation of moderate frequency that one expects to find (and does find) considerable variation among resource users.

The third factor is also related to frequency. One would expect that when personally experienced a natural event would be more meaningful and lead to heightened perception. The limited evidence to date does not clearly bear this out. There is a pronounced ability to share in the common experience, and newcomers often take on the shared or dominant perception of the community. Also given a unique or cyclical interpretation of natural events, the experience of an event often tends to allay future

---

44. Kates, *Hazard and Choice Perception in Flood Plain Management* (Univ. Chi. Dep't of Geography Research Paper No. 78, 1962).
45. Burton, *Types of Agricultural Occupance of Flood Plains in the United States* (Univ. Chi. Dep't of Geography Research Paper No. 75, 1962).
46. Kates, *Perceptual Regions and Regional Perception in Flood Plain Management*, Papers of the Regional Science Ass'n (1963). [Ed. note: A volume number has not been assigned to this set of papers.]

anxiety; this is in keeping with the old adage about lighting not striking in the same place twice. Thus the effect of experience as a determinant of hazard perception is considerably blurred.

Perception Between Different Resource Users. Differences in perception are found between coastal and flood-plain land resource users in areas subject to storm damage or erosion. Unfortunately, we cannot say more about hazard perception differences between resource users. To our knowledge, they have never been carefully explored, although such study would undoubtedly throw much light on the problem of comparing the resource management policies of different groups and nations.[47] Some historical comment provides suggestions for the direction that such differences might take.

In a recent article, David Lowenthal notes the changes in our attitude towards wilderness. Once viewed as awesome and tyrannical, nature in the wild is now wonderful and brings us close to the spirit of the Creator. "Our forefathers mastered a continent; today we celebrate the virtues of the vanquished foe."[48] Nature itself has become synonymous with virtue.[49] This subject has been examined in some detail by Hans Huth in his study of the attitudes that led to the establishment of the conservation movement.[50]

The rapid expansion of agriculture in the Great Plains during a relatively humid period by settlers from areas with different environmental experience and background is well known. Unprepared for the climatic hazards they encountered, many settlers "were predisposed to believe that the climate was becoming permanently more humid. In fact, many thought that it was the spread of cultivation that brought about an increase in rainfall."[51]

Study of other hazards suggests that there is considerable difference in the social acceptance of personal injury depending on the kind of hazard that was the causal agent. Edward Suchman notes that "a report of a few cases of polio will empty the beaches, but reports of many more deaths by automobile accidents on the roads to the beaches will have little effect." He suggests that one explanation may lie "in the greater popular acceptance of accidents as inevitable and uncontrollable."[52]

A contrast in awareness of natural hazards is exemplified by a warning sign observed in a coastal location on the island of Hawaii. Affixed to a palm tree in an area subject to *tsunamis* at the front door and the hazard of volcanic eruptions and lava flows at the back door (Mauna Loa volcano), this sign merely advises the reader: "Beware of falling coconuts!"

Variation in Natural Hazard Perception Between Technical-Scientific Personnel and Resource Users

It is our impression that there is considerable divergence between the perception of natural hazard of technical-scientific personnel and resource users. In the case of floods such divergence is widespread.

Although we have emphasized in the previous section the variation in probability

47. For one such attempt see *Comparisons in Resources Management* (Jarrett ed. 1961).
48. Lowenthal, *Not Every Prospect Pleases—What Is Our Criterion for Scenic Beauty?*, 12 Landscape 19 (Winter, 1962-1963).
49. Lowenthal, *Nature and the American Creed of Virtue*, 9 Landscape 24 (Winter, 1959-1960).
50. Huth, *Nature and the American* (1957).

51. Thornthwaite, *Climate and Settlement in the Great Plains, Climate and Man,* USDA Yearbook 177, 184 (1941).
52. Suchman, *A Conceptual Analysis of the Accident Phenomenon*, Ass'n for Aid of Crippled Children, Behavioral Approaches to Accident Research 40 (1961).

that technical people might assign to a given flood event, these are essentially differences in estimation. Over the past several years we have interviewed or spoken with well over one-hundred technical people concerned with floods, and we have never met one who discounted the possibility of a flood occurring again in a valley that had been previously flooded. By contrast, out of 216 flood-plain dwellers interviewed in a variety of small urban places between 1960 and 1962, all of whom had a measurable flood hazard, some 84 categorically did not expect to be flooded in the future.[53]

Another example of the disparity between the technical and resource user perception is found in the occasional experience of the rejection of plans for protective works by at least part of the resource users, even when the cost of such works directly to the users in monetary terms was nominal or non-existent. In Fairfield, Connecticut some users of waterfront property opposed the construction of a protective dike along the shore, principally on the contention that such protection "would seriously interfere with their view and result in loss of breeze." [54] Similarly, dune-levelling which is universally condemned by technical personnel as destructive of nature's main protection against the ravages of the sea, is widely practiced (as at West Dennis, Massachusetts) to improve the scenic view or to make room for more buildings.

Is such behavior adopted out of ignorance of the hazard; is it symptomatic of the irrationality of resource users in hazard situation; or is there some other explanation? While there are resource users who act in total ignorance of natural hazards, their

number is relatively small. Nor can the difference simply be explained away in terms of irrationality. In our view, the difference arises primarily out of the evaluation of the hazard. We offer the following explanation for divergence in hazard evaluation:

1. For some resource users, the differences in perceiving a natural hazard may be a reflection of those existing among scientific and technical personnel themselves. Given the great uncertainty that surrounds the formulation of an "objective" estimate of hazard, the estimate made by a resource user may be no more divergent than that supplied by the use of a different formula or the addition of more data.

2. For some resource users we suspect the divergence in hazard perception may be as fundamental as basic attitudes towards nature. Technical-scientific estimates of hazard assume the neutrality of nature. There are resource users who perceive otherwise, conceiving of nature as malevolent or benevolent. Our language is full of metaphors and descriptions of "Mother nature," "bountiful nature," or, conversely, of "angry storms." Besides attributing motivation to nature, there is also the distinction of man's relation to nature. One recent anthropological study, using a cross-cultural approach, developed a man-nature classification comprising man over nature, man with nature, and man under nature.[55] Each of these three divergent points of view is represented by the following statement:

Man Subject to Nature. "My people have never controlled the rain, wind, and other natural conditions, and probably never will. There have always been good years and bad years. That is the way it is, and if you are wise you will take it as it comes and do the best you can."

Man with Nature. "My people help conditions

---

53. Kates, *op. cit. supra* note 46.
54. *An Interim Hurricane Survey of Fairfield, Connecticut,* H.R. Doc. No. 600, 87th Cong., 2d Sess., 14 (1962).

55. Kluckholm & Strodtbeck, *Variations in Value Orientations* (1961).

and keep things going by working to keep in close touch with all the forces which make the rain, the snow, and other conditions. It is when we do the right things—live in the proper way—and keep all that we have—the land, the stock and the water—in good condition, that all goes along well."

Man over Nature. "My people believe that it is man's job to find ways to overcome weather and other conditions just as they have overcome so many things. They believe they will one day succeed in doing this and may even overcome droughts and floods." [56]

Samples of respondents were selected from five different cultural groups in an area of western New Mexico, and their responses were distributed as shown in Table 4.

The wide divergence of human views of nature, as illustrated in Table 4, is strong testimony to support our contention that variations in perception are significant and are likely to affect management policies. A society in which belief in the dominance of nature is strong, such as among the Spanish-Americans, is less likely to be conscious of the possibilities of environment control than one in which belief in the dominance of man over nature is more pronounced, as among the Texans.

The belief in technical engineering solutions to problems of hazard is widespread in American society. This belief in the efficacy

of man's control over nature is frequently encountered in studies of hazard perception. Thus, it is no longer surprising to find protective powers ascribed to flood control works far beyond their designed capacity. Notable examples are seen in those persons who consider themselves protected by dams downstream from their flood-plain location, or who are satisfied that floods will not occur in the future because a government agency has been established to study the problem.[57]

3. How much of the divergence in hazard perception can be ascribed to fundamental views of nature is speculative. Much more of the divergence is explicable in terms of basic attitudes towards uncertainty.

We are convinced that there is a fundamental difference between the attitudes or values of technical-scientific personnel and resource users towards uncertainty. Increasingly the orientation and formal training of scientific personnel emphasizes an indeterminate and probabilistic view of the

---

56. *Id.* at 86-87.

57. Such a response was given to Burton during recent field work in Belleville, Ontario. There, two respondents considered that the establishment of the Moira Valley Conservation Authority meant that no more floods would occur. Such is, in fact, far from the case. The Authority has not been successful in its attempts to have protective works constructed.

Table 4   Views of Man and Nature by Cultural Groups (in percentages)

Cultural Group	View of Nature			
	Man Subject to Nature	Man with Nature	Man over Nature	Number Interviewed
Spanish-Americans	71.7	10.9	17.4	23
Texans	30.0	22.5	47.5	20
Mormons	25.0	55.0	20.0	20
Zuni Indians	19.0	62.0	19.0	21
Rimrock Navaho Indians	18.2	68.2	13.6	22

Source: *Variations in Value Orientations,* Appendix 4.

world. Common research techniques involve the use of estimates that reflect imperfect knowledge, and stress is placed on extracting the full value of partial knowledge.

We have considerable social science and psychological theory and some evidence that resource users are unwilling or unable to adopt this probabilistic view of the world and are not able to live with uncertainty in such a manner as to extract full value from partial knowledge.

Malinowsky held that every human culture possesses both sound scientific knowledge for coping with the natural environment and a set of magical practices for coping with problems that are beyond rational-empirical control. [58] Festinger describes the role of the concept of "cognitive dissonance" as a motivating force, which may lead to actions or beliefs concerning the state of nature that do not accord with rational or logical expectations.[59] For example, he cites the case of a severe earthquake in India in 1934, in which some people experienced the earthquake but saw no evidence of damage which was quite localized. This situation apparently led to the circulation of rumors which helped to reduce the dissonance created by the fear generated by the earthquake and the absence of signs of damage. People were left in a state of fear but no longer saw reason to be afraid. The rumors that circulated in such a situation have been described by Prasad [60] and include the following:

There will be a severe cyclone at Patna between January 18th and January 19th. [The earthquake occurred on January 15th.]

* * *

There will be a severe earthquake on the lunar eclipse day.

* * *

January 23rd will be a fatal day. Unforeseeable calamities will arise.

In our experience resource users appear to behave in ways that suggest an individual effort to dispel uncertainty. Among floodplain users and in coastal areas, the most common variant is to view floods and storms as a repetitive or even cyclical phenomenon. Thus the essential randomness that characterizes the uncertain pattern of the hazard is replaced by a determinate order in which history is seen as repeating itself at regular intervals. Some experiments in the perception of independent events and probability distributions have been conducted by psychologists. The results of such rigorous tests are interesting but are not yet at the level that affords useful generalizations about the real world.[61] Where the hazard is made repetitive, the past becomes a guide to the approximate timing and magnitude of future hazardous events. An historical example of this is documented by Niddrie.[62] A mild earthquake was recorded in London on February 8, 1750. A somewhat more severe earthquake occurred exactly one lunar month (twenty-eight days) later on March 8th. Predictions were made that a third and

58. Malinowsky, Magic, Science, and Religion in Science, *Religion, and Reality* (Needham ed. 1925).
59. Festinger, The Motivating Effect of Cognitive Dissonance in Assessment of Human Motives (Lindzey ed. 1960); Festinger, *A Theory of Cognitive Dissonance* (1947).
60. Prasad, *A Comparative Study of Rumors and Reports in Earthquakes*, 41 British J. Psychology 129 (1950).

61. Hake & Hyman, *Perception of the Statistical Structure of a Random Series of Binary Symbols*, 45 J. Experimental Psychology 64 (1953); Cohen & Hansel, *The Idea of a Distribution*, 46 British J. Psychology 111 (1955); Cohen & Hansel, *The Idea of Independence*, 46 British J. Psychology 178 (1955); Hyman & Jenkin, *Involvement and Set as Determinants of Behavioral Stereotypy*, 2 Psychological Rep. 131 (1956).
62. Niddrie, *When the Earth Shook* 20-34 (1962).

more terrible earthquake would occur on April 5th. Niddrie describes the events which followed:

A contagious panic spreading through every district of the town required only the slightest indication that those who could afford to leave the town unobtrusively were doing so, for a wholesale evacuation to begin. The gullible who could not leave bought pills "which were very good against the earthquake." As Doomsday came nearer whole families moved to places of safety . . . . By April 3rd it was impossible to obtain lodgings in any neighboring town or village.[63]

When no earthquake occurred on April 5th the prophesies changed to April 8th as though the number eight had some special connotations for earthquakes. Niddrie reports that in fact few of the gentry and well-to-do returned to London until April 9th.

Another view, which is less common, is the act of "wishing it away" by denigrating the quality of the rare natural event to the level of the common-place, or conversely of elevating it to a unique position and ascribing its occurrence to a freak combination of circumstances incapable of repetition. Either variant has the advantage of eliminating the

uncertainty which surrounds hazardous natural phenomenon.

The last alternative view that we can suggest is the completely indeterminate position that denies completely the knowability of natural phenomena. For this group, all is in the hands of God or the gods. Convinced of the utter inscrutability of Divine Providence, the resource users have no need to trouble themselves about the vagaries of an uncertain nature, for it can serve no useful purpose to do so.

These viewpoints are summarized in Table 5.

Divergence of Values. Natural hazards are not perceived in a vacuum. They are seen as having certain effects or consequences, and it is rather the consequences that are feared than the hazard phenomenon per se. Another source of divergence in the perception of natural hazard between technical-scientific personnel and resource users is related to the perceived consequences of the hazard. For very good and sound reasons the set of probabilities related to the occurrence of a natural phenomenon at a given place is not the same as the set of probabilities of hazard for an individual. Given the high level of mobility in our society, the nature of the personal hazard is constantly changing, while

---

63. *Id.* at 29-30.

Table 5 Common Responses to the Uncertainty of Natural Hazards

Eliminate the Hazard		*Eliminate the Uncertainty*	
Deny or Deni-Grate Its Existence	*Deny or Deni-Grate Its Re-currence*	*Make it De-terminate and Knowable*	*Transfer Un-certainty to a Higher Power*
"We have no floods, here, only high water."	"Lightning never strikes twice in the same place."	"Seven years of great plenty. . . . After them seven years of famine."	"It's in the hands of God."
"It can't happen here."	"It's a freak of nature."	"Floods come every five years."	"The government is taking care of it."

the probabilities for a given place remain fixed (although not precisely known).

Thus, the soil erosion that concerns the technicians in Western Iowa, reported in a recent study,[64] is an ongoing continuous long-term hazard. The carefully calculated long-term rates of erosion, however, do not have the same meaning for farmers who averaged only nine years as individual farm managers, or where ownership itself changes hands every fourteen years on the average. Soil losses arise from a series of discrete physical events with intensive rains and high winds acting as the major erosional force. The long-term average of these erosional events may have meaning for the continued occupancy of the agriculture of this area. Hence, the technician's concern for the cumulative soil loss. But given the short average managerial period, the cumulative soil loss seems hardly worth the cost and effort involved in its control for the individual manager.

The Case of the Modern Homesteaders. Evan Vogt's study of the "Modern Homesteader"[65] provides a case study that exemplifies the types of divergence that we have been describing.

Homestead, the site of Vogt's studies during 1951-1952, is in his own words "a small dry-land, bean-farming community" of 200 people in western New Mexico.[66] It was founded in the early 1930's by families from the South Plains Region of western Texas and Oklahoma, but prior to the deep drought of 1934-1936. While spurred by low agricultural prices, Vogt felt they migrated for primarily what they perceived as a good farming opportunity, a chance to receive

640 acres for sixty-eight dollars in fees and residential and improvement investments.[67]

By 1932 eighty-one families had obtained sections under what was objectively governmental encouragement to agricultural settlement in an area with an average rainfall of about twelve inches. By 1935 the official perception of the suitability of the natural environment for agriculture had changed drastically. Under the Taylor Grazing Act,[68] all the land in the area which was still in the public domain was classified for grazing, and no additional homestead applications were accepted. The official estimate had changed, but that of the local citizens had not. To this day they perceive of their submarginal farming area as one quite suitable for dry land farming. In so doing, their perception is at considerable variance with that of the governmental technicians in a variety of ways.

As we suggested before, total ignorance of natural hazards is uncommon. While drought and frost are perennial hazards (two decades have provided seven good years, seven average years, and six crop failures), these were not ignorant city folk lured to the Plains by free land. They came from agricultural families in an area of less than twenty inches average rainfall. They do, however, perceive the marginality of the area in their own fashion. So marked is the divergence of this perception that Vogt reports the following:

But through the critical days of "battle" with the government, which had defined their community as "submarginal" and unsuitable for agriculture, there emerged in the Homesteaders a sense of mission in life: To demonstrate to the experts in the Departments of Agriculture and Interior that the Homestead area is farming country and that they can "make a go of it" in this semi-arid land.

---

64. Held, Blase & Timmons, *Soil Erosion and Some Means for Its Control* (Iowa State Univ. Agri. and Home Econ. Experiment Sta. Special Rep. No. 29, 1962).
65. Vogt, *Modern Homesteaders* (1955).
66. *Id.* at 1.

67. *Id.* at 17-18.
68. 48 Stat. 1269 (1934), as amended, 43 U.S.C. § § 315-315r (1958).

They point to the fact that Pueblo Indians made a living by farming in the area long before the white man arrived. There is a general feeling that somehow the surveys and investigations made by the experts must be wrong. They insist that the Weather Bureau has falsified the rainfall figures that were submitted by the Homestead Weather station in the 1930's, and indeed they stopped maintaining a weather station because they felt that "the figures were being used against us".[69]

Vogt mentions in passing another divergence in hazard perception. Homesteaders appear alert to the high westernly wind hazard that erodes the top soil, and they strip crop and plow across the line of this prevailing wind. In so doing, they look askance at the elaborate terraces constructed by the Soil Conservation Service in the 1930's because these terraces are on the contour, and contour plowing itself inevitably results in some of the rows lying in the direct path of the westerly winds.[70]

Faced with continued drought, sandstorms, and killing frosts, the "Homesteaders" exemplify much of what has been discussed in this paper. Vogt finds the predominant attitude as that of nature being something to be mastered and, arising from this, a heady optimism in the face of continued vicissitudes. He finds the strong need to eliminate uncertainty to the point of not collecting weather data as reported above, or through the widespread resort to agricultural magic, involving signs of the zodiac, planting by the moon, and water witching. It is in this last act, the use of water witching, that we find direct parallels with the behavior of flood-plain users. The geology of the Homestead area as it relates to ground water supply is one of considerable uncertainty. The geological structure generates an uncertainty as to the depth and amount of water available at a particular point. Faced with

such uncertainty, there was a strong-felt need to hire the local water witch to dowse the wells. While the performance ratio of successful wells to dry holes appeared equal whether they were witched or not, Vogt gives a convincing explanation that witching provides a determinate response to uncertainty where the best that the local soil conservation geologists could provide was a generalized description of the ground water situation. Whether, as in Vogt's terms, the motive is to reduce anxiety, or in Festinger's, to reduce cognitive dissonance, or as we would put it, to eliminate uncertainty, there is the apparently strong drive to make the indeterminate determinate. In conclusion, Vogt emphasizes

that despite more secure economic alternatives elsewhere, most "Homesteaders" choose to remain in the community and assume the climatic risks rather than abandon the independence of action they cherish and the leisure they enjoy for the more routinized and subordinate roles they would occupy elsewhere.[71]

Levels of Significance in Hazard Perception. There are men who plow up semiarid steppes, who build villages on the flanks of volcanoes, and who lose one crop in three to floods. Are they irrational? Or, to put it another way, having looked at the variation in hazard perception and speculated on the causes of variation, what can be concluded about the rationality of hazard perception? In general, we find absent from almost every natural phenomena a standard for the objective (i.e., true) probability of an event's occurrence. Even if such existed, we are not sure that man can assimilate such probabilities sufficiently to be motivated to act upon them. If decisions are made in a prohibilistic framework, what level of probability is sufficient for action? In the terms of statistics, what level of significance is appropriate?

---

69. Vogt, *op. cit. supra* note 65, at 68.
70. *Id.* at 70.

71. *Id.* at 176.

What amount of hazard or error is tolerable? Science is of little help here, since levels of statistical significance are chosen at ninety-five per cent or ninety-nine per cent primarily by convention.

Despite the impressive growth of game theory, the growing literature of decision-strategies, and some psychological experimentation with perceived probabilities, the artificiality of the game or laboratory seems to provide at best only limited insights into this complex phenomenon. On the other hand, the derivation of empirical observations, *i.e.*, estimates of the perceived frequency of events or perceived probabilities at which decisions are actually made, provides almost insuperable research difficulties.

In the last analysis, we seem destined to judge the rationality of man's actions vis-à-vis natural hazard out of a mixture of hindsight and prejudice. For the successful gambler in the game against nature there are but a few lonely voices crying that the odds will overtake him. The unsuccessful is clearly judged as foolhardy, ignorant, or irrational. Our prejudice expresses itself in our attitudes towards uncertainty, our preferences for certain types of risk, and how we feel about the objects of resource management.

Conclusion

There is a wide variation in the day-to-day management practices of resource users, even within culturally homogeneous groups. We believe that the variations in hazard perception reported in this article are an important explanatory variable. Unfortunately, careful studies of variation in resource management practices are few and far between. Some of the recent studies of innovation[72] and the study of farm practices in western Iowa, already cited,[73] approach

what we have in mind. To our knowledge there have been no studies which adequately describe variations in management practice and rigorously attempt to assess the role of differing perception.

We can say that there is good reason to believe that variations in perception of hazard among resource managers tends to diminish over time. Those who are unwilling or unable to make the necessary adjustments in a hazardous situation are eliminated, either because disaster overtakes them or because they voluntarily depart. Those who remain tend to share in a uniformity of outlook.

Long-term occupancy of high hazard areas is never really stable, even where it has persisted over time. A catastrophe, a long run of bad years, a rising level of aspiration marked by the unwillingness to pay the high costs of survival—each provides stimulants to change. The "Modern Homesteaders," while determined to stay put and exhibiting a high degree of uniformity in their assessment of the environment and its hazards, may yet yield to a combination of an extended run of drought and frost and the lure of a more affluent society. Long-term occupancy, while potentially unstable, is still marked by a tenacity to persist, reinforced, we think, by the uniformity of hazard perception that develops over time. Thus all of the homesteaders who took jobs elsewhere in the bad drought of 1950 returned to the community. More dramatic is the return of the residents of Tristan da Cunha to their volcanic island home.

We have no evidence of a similar growth in accord between resource users and scientific-technical personnel. Clearly, variations in perception may profoundly affect the chances of success of a new management proposal developed by the experts. Such new programs are constantly being devised, but assessments of past programs are seldom

---

72. See the bibliography in Lionberger, *Adoption of New Ideas and Practices* (1960).
73. Held, Blase & Timmons, *op. cit. supra* note 64.

found. George Macinko's review of the Columbia Basin project is a recent welcome exception.[74] Rarely do such studies review programs in terms of divergence of perception. L. Schuyler Fonaroff's article on differences in view between the Navajo and the Indian Service is another exception which proves the rule.[75]

While lacking many detailed statements of this divergence, we can nevertheless state the implication of our findings to date. The divergence in perception implies limits on the ability of resource managers to absorb certain types of technical advice regardless of how well written or explained. Thus, to expect farmers to maintain conservation practices for long periods of time may be wishful thinking if such practices do not accord with the farmer's view of his resource and the hazards to which it is exposed. Similarly, to expect radical changes in the pattern of human adjustments to floods simply by providing detailed and precise flood hazard information is unduly optimistic. Yet another example is seen in the upper Trinity River area in Texas.[76] To expect farmers to convert flood-plain land from pasture to cotton or other high value cash crops simply because flood frequency is reduced is to assume that he shares the perception of the Soil Conservation Service. Nor is it a strong argument to claim that such changes in land use were indicated as possible by the farmers themselves, if the question was put to them in terms of the technologist's evaluation of the problem. Good predictions of the future choices of resource managers are likely to be based on an understanding of their percep-

tion and the ways in which it differs from that of the technologists.

It seems likely that the hiatus between technical and managerial perception is nowhere greater than in the underdeveloped countries.[77] There is good reason, therefore, for further research into this topic and for attempts to harmonize the discrepancies in technical programs wherever possible.

While the study of natural hazard perception provides clues to the ways in which men manage uncertain natural environments, it also helps to provide a background to understanding our national resource policy. Despite the self-image of the conservation movement as a conscious and rational attempt to develop policies to meet long term needs, more of the major commitments of public policy in the field of resource management have arisen out of crises generated by catastrophic natural hazards (albeit at times aided and abetted by human improvidence) than out of a need to curb man's misuse and abuse of his natural environment. Some years ago this was recognized by White: "National catastrophes have led to insistent demands for national action, and the timing of the legislative process has been set by the tempo of destructive floods." [78] It has also been documented in some detail by Henry Hart.[79] The Soil Erosion Service of the Department of Agriculture was established as an emergency agency in 1933 following the severe drought and subsequent dust bowl early in the

74. Macinko, *The Columbia Basin Project, Expectations, Realizations, Implications*, 53 Geographical Rev. 185 (1963).

75. Fonaroff, *Conservation and Stock Reduction on the Navajo Tribal Range*, 53 Geographical Rev. 200 (1963).

76. Burton, *op. cit. supra* note 45, at 59-73.

77. The results of a recent effort to improve communication between technical experts and resource managers are reported in Central Treaty Organization, *Traveling Seminar for Increased Agricultural Production, Region Tour* (1962).

78. White, *Human Adjustments to Floods* 24 (Univ. Chi. Dep't of Geography Research Paper No. 29, 1945).

79. Hart, *Crises, Community, and Consent in Water Politics*, 22 Law & Contemp. Prob. 510 (1957).

decade. The Service became a permanent agency called the Soil Conservation Service in 1935.[80]

Just as flood control legislation has followed hard upon the heels of major flood disasters, so the present high degree of interest in coastal protection, development, and preservation has been in part stimulated by recent severe storms on the east coast.[81] Such a fundamental public policy as the provision of water supply for urban areas was created partly in response to needs for controlling such natural hazards as typhus and cholera and the danger of fire, as well as for meeting urban water demands.[82] Agricultural and forestry research programs were fostered as much by insect infestations and plant diseases as by the long-range goals of increased production.

Unusual events in nature have long been associated with a state of crisis in human affairs. The decline of such superstitions and the continued growth of the control over nature will not necessarily be accompanied by a reduction of the role of crisis in resource policy. Natural hazards are likely to continue to play a significant role, although their occurrence as well as their effects may be increasingly difficult to separate from man-induced hazards of the quasi-natural variety. The smog of Donora may replace the Johnstown flood in our lexicon of major hazards, and *The Grapes of Wrath* may yield pride of place to *The Silent Spring* in the literature of the effects of environmental hazard, but there will continue to be a pattern of response to crisis in human relations to an uncertain environment. Under these circumstances, understandings of the variations of perception such as we have attempted here are likely to remain significant.

---

80. Buie, *Ill Fared the Land*, USDA Yearbook 155 (1962).
81. Burton & Kates, *The Flood Plain and the Sea Shore: A Comparative Analysis of Hazard Zone Occupance*, 54 *Geographical Rev.* 366 (1964).
82. Blake, *Water for the Cities* (1956).

‡‡‡‡‡‡‡‡‡‡‡‡‡‡‡‡‡‡‡‡‡‡‡‡‡‡‡‡‡‡‡‡

DEPARTURES FROM THE USUAL ENVIRONMENT IN LOCATIONAL ANALYSIS

Julian Wolpert

Confrontations over locational issues may be accompanied by threats and secondary effects via stress responses which are generated in the negotiating process. The outcomes of such crises in locational decisions appear as artifacts of land use and may be recognizable as dysfunctional or maladaptive responses to the needs or demands to which they were meant to serve. A location theory for controversial facilities requires a behavioral framework which is extended to include concepts of threat and its relative impact in an interdependent context.

When urban geographers in A. D. 2000 study the form and structure of American cities, what kinds of conclusions will they arrive at

---

From the *Annals* of the Association of American Geographers, Vol. 60 (1970), pp.220–29. Reprinted by permission.

to explain the distribution of such artifacts as expressways, urban renewal, and public housing projects? Unless our tools for analyzing locational behavior are sharpened, there is a considerable likelihood that we shall then be drawing the same types of inferences from our visual environment as we are doing at present.

The objective in this exploratory paper is to illustrate some of the complexities of these locational decisions, and to suggest a means for extending our framework of study and our methodology in order to avoid some of the pitfalls of observing only the manifestations or artifacts of behavior in space. Sometimes the location finally chosen for a new development, or the site chosen for a relocation of an existing facility, comes out to be the site around which the least protest can be generated by those to be displaced. Rather than being an optimal, a rational, or even a satisfactory locational decision produced by the resolution of conflicting judgments, the decision is perhaps merely the expression of rejection by elements powerful enough to enforce their decision that another location must not be used; alternatively the locational decision may result in a choice against which no strong argument can be raised since such elements either are inarticulate or command too little power to render their argument effective. Past methodologies employed in studying locational decisions have not been able to measure the relative strengths of forces operative in the processes of decision-making.

Too often, these artifacts are merely the end products of policy compromise and they, therefore, do not capture the complex of motivations, responsiveness to events, and situations occurring in metropolitan or other areas. Neither do they reveal the coping strategies which were rejected in favor of the selected alternative which remains as the artifact of that decision—the elements of the visible environment. These artifacts are rarely the "most efficient solutions," and frequently not even satisfactory neither for those responsible for their creation nor for their users. Are we equipped now to analyze the artifacts of the past which may have been neither efficient nor satisfactorily functional at the time of their inception, and are likely to be less so at present? The artifacts are products of decisions, and their forms and structures reflect only the solution to a problem and a decision environment which may remain hidden. This may be very significant because artifacts which may differ considerably in form and structure could very well represent solutions to the same basic problems or the consequences of similar decision environments. Similarly, elements of the visible environment could be almost equivalent in form and structure, but differ significantly in intent or responsiveness to need. What, then, should our study of location focus upon? In the past, we have rarely departed from direct interpretation of the artifacts of our landscape and, therefore, have foregone investigation of the more subtle elements of which the visible phenomena are merely symbolic.

In the urban renewal program which began in the late 1940's and early 1950's, the rationale appeared reasonable and perhaps represented an efficient solution, at least in a limited sense—to rid urban cores of unsightly slums which were judged to have an undesirable impact upon residents' physical and mental health, as well as to augment cities' meager tax bases, and at the same time to rationalize land use. With existing methodology, there would have been little danger in making faulty assumptions in analyzing the distribution of these early renewal projects and asking the questions which geographers typically ask of distribution patterns.

The situation became more complex later, however, as policy-makers continued to search for efficient locations for investment by redevelopment companies, but questions arose as to whose interests were really being served by the proposed projects. The impacted groups which were to be displaced, or their champions, frequently did not share in the belief that renewal was the only rational solution. Once this phase of active opposition had arisen, then subsequent renewal projects of the same form must be looked upon as the consequence of the struggle which the policy-makers had won. Thus, the artifact could very well have remained similar in form but represent a very different phenomenon.

The projects themselves are of relatively trivial import in contrast to the forces responsible for their inception. The decision environments from which the projects had been conceived have now evolved from an early stage of a narrowly efficient solution to a secondary stage which must involve consideration of anticipation, reaction, and response to an opposition which defines rationality and "public interest" in a very different sense. Perhaps we are now moving to a third stage which may result in a good blending of some renewal, some rehabilitation, and some nonintervention. Will an analysis of these forces and adaptations all be included when we observe city structures from a future vantage point, or shall we merely attempt to account for the arrangement of the physical and visible remnants?

The discussion does not imply a rejection of the need for generalization in analyzing distributions and a defense of the unique properties and rationale behind each event or phenomena. Instead, emphasis is given to broadening of our understanding of decision environments and their parameters.

Behavioralism Without Interdependence

In an earlier study an attempt was made to illustrate some of the pitfalls of assuming the presence of economic rationality in decision behavior.[1] The study revealed that the population's goals were multidimensional, and uncertainty and its reduction were prominent factors in its activities. The population differed more in terms of goals and choice behavior than in the form of this expression which could be observed in the landscape. In this case, it was sufficient to apply the concepts of bounded rationality and a negotiated environment to characterize the population's behavior.[2] Only five years ago, we were grateful for the insights into locational analysis provided by the instrusion of "creeping behavioralism." Our interpretive abilities were enhanced without too great a loss of sophistication in methodology. There has been a productive succession from linear programming to its less restrictive elaborations, from simple games against nature to elaborate games of interpersonal interactions and the intensified search for descriptive parameters of behavior through more powerful multivariate tools and more probing simulation studies. We have still, however, penetrated only slightly into the decision structures beyond the zone of "adaptive" rationality. It has taken many years to establish the concepts of adaptively rational behavior and bounded rationality, as defined

1. J. Wolpert, "The Decision Process in Spatial Context," *Annals*, Association of American Geographers, Vol. 54 (1964), pp. 537–58.
2. R. M. Cyert and J. G. March, *A Behavioral Theory of the Firm* (Englewood Cliffs, New Jersey: Prentice-Hall, Inc., 1963); H. A. Simon, "The Role of Expectations in an Adaptive or Behavioristic Model," in M. J. Bowman (Ed.), *Expectations, Uncertainty, and Business Behavior* (New York: Social Science Research Council, 1958).

by Simon and others, into our analyses of locational decisions and the consequent distributions. Adaptive rationality implies adjustment in the direction of rationality subject to the limitations of uncertainty problem-solving ability, and broadly defined utilities. Beyond these bounds, we were once told, lies irrationality or at least arationality, a zone in which theory and generalizations are unproductive. But, a rapidly developing and multidisciplinary literature now enables us to say a good deal about such lapses, which may be termed maladaptive behavior.

Crisis Decision-making

Among the social sciences, the political scientists are closer to the analysis of these extreme situations in their studies of crisis decision-making than are the geographers and sociologists who deal with disaster behavior or the economists who are concerned with paralysis, but there are important linkages between observed behavior in these applications which can yield general statements.[3] It would seem that we owe an important debt to the geomorphologists for their studies of erratics as artifacts of extreme situations. The erratics cannot be the product of observed forces and processes of the "usual" environment, but require the incidence of sporadic events which differ in important respects from those in continuous operation. Our focus here is with the formation of cultural or social erratics which are artifacts of maladaptive behavior under extreme situations.[4] Thus, if we could

properly define adaptively rational behavior and its consequent imprint on the cultural landscape, then we could properly interpret a given artifact as the resulting symbol of a specific adaptively rational decision environment. Similarly, maladaptive decisions give rise to artifacts which may reflect in their characteristics inappropriate, irrelevant, or dysfunctional adjustment.

At this point it is necessary to define more specifically our notion of maladaptive response, which is being used here as a relative and subjective concept. It may, for example, appear quite reasonable and adaptive to construct a thirty foot dike after the most severe flood in two centuries, but its cost of construction may be higher than any potential damage that might arise without a dike. That is, maladaptive refers not to an assessment of an individual's responsiveness to threatening cues but instead to the reasonableness or efficiency or rationality of responsiveness to the original problem. Therefore, it may be quite adaptive for the policy-maker to insist rigidly upon a single prominent alternative when he is faced with a massive overabundance of plans, but his selection may be maladaptive in terms of the suitability of his choice as a solution to the original problem. Furthermore, it is suggested that such solutions can be conveniently placed by the investigator on some continuum of adaptiveness. Our focus is then on the nature of decision environments whose consequences are artifacts in our visual environment classifiable on the proposed adaptive-maladaptive continuum.

The Mutual Exchange of Threat

More recently, another significant dimension of decision environments has been studied in some depth—the degree of threat which the decision-maker perceives and his selection of

---

3. The political studies are well represented by O. R. Holsti, "Perceptions of Time, Perceptions of Alternatives and Pattern Communication as Factors in Crises Decision-Making," *Papers, Peace Research Society*, Vol. 3 (1965), pp. 79–120.
4. N. H. Burns, et al, *Unusual Environments and Human Behavior* (New York: Free Press, 1963).

an appropriate coping strategy. Our focus will be upon the more easily recognizable consequences of decisions made under threat. That is, we shall be assuming no longer the passive decision environment in which alternative choices are carefully and methodically studied until the best choice is made according to some set of defined criteria.

Instead, an excitation is present in the environment which may take the form of time pressure to reach the decision, insufficient information or ambiguity about alternatives or an overabundance of information that cannot be assimilated, or cues from the environment which indicate that one's energy and ability are insufficient to deal with the problem at hand, or other stressors.[5]

Perhaps most critical, however, in the generation of such threats is the interdependent nature of the decision environment in such cases. The location of such facilities as urban expressways, renewal projects, stadiums, and sewage plants are controversial, and the decision environment is more visible than ever before.

The argument then proceeds as follows: Greater involvement and participation in locational decisions by impacted groups, though perhaps essentially a more democratic process, introduces a new dimension of conflict into the decision environment. This escalation of involvement implies, of course, that locational decisions are, more and more, the products of interactions and conflicts and not just the prerogative of policy-makers, firms, or individuals. Moreover, there is less general agreement on what constitutes the "public interest." The participants in such locational issues may have conflicting interests because the incidence of

impact of such projects may be distributed quite unequally within a community.

The confrontation between interest groups, and more specifically between more or less well organized groups who are affected by the decision (the impacted groups), and those people who are legitimately entrusted with the decision (policy-makers), is often (purposefully or inadvertently) accompanied by exchanges of threats which may even be escalated by the confrontation. Threat refers, here, to the possibly harmful effects upon the impacted groups of implementing a proposed project, as well as on the policy-makers through the danger of not being able to implement their decisions.

Threat may be generated by the bargaining process and may affect the bargaining strategy of the participants through its effect upon the degree of organization of the groups and on the way they make decisions. Threat is a crucial variable because, from a rational point of view, the specific outcome of negotiations depends upon the conflict that would arise if no agreement were reached, and the mutual exchange of threats determines what this conflict will be like. But furthermore, from a psychological point of view, the fact that groups are threatening one another with harm that goes beyond purely maintaining the *status quo* affects the perception and decision-making processes of the individuals who are involved.

Thus stated, the problem of interpreting this class of interdependent locational decisions is clearly too complex to be analyzed with a single rigorous model. Instead, attention is focused here on two closely related variables which are relevant to the decision-making process: these variables are threat and stress response. In another paper, the author has discussed the exchange of threats as a basic element in the bargaining process, so that emphasis will be given here only to

---

5. Adapted from Holsti, *op. cit.*, footnote 3.

the escalation of such exchanges of threat to the level of "crisis decision-making." [6] Threats can have secondary effects via stress responses which are generated in the bargaining process. The objective here, then, is to provide some framework linking the communication of threat with a class of impacts of such threats which may be termed stress reactions or responses.

The linkage between threat and stress reaction is not direct, of course, and for this reason a brief review of Lazarus' framework is presented here in order to illustrate the complex processes and their interaction.[7] An attempt is made to parallel this framework with an empirical example which the author has been investigating.

Lazarus posited a two stage appraisal of environmental cues about events which are potentially threatening to decision-makers. There is an initial evaluation of the degree and characteristics (magnitude, imminence, duration, and likelihood of occurrence) of the potential threat. The appraisal of the threat depends upon the attributes of the threat itself but also upon the characteristics of the affected individual or group. Individuals, for example, who have successfully faced similar threats before might be less prone to exaggerate their importance than others without similar experience.

The subsequent appraisal, once the threat has been perceived, according to Lazarus, is of an "appropriate coping strategy," so as to reduce or mitigate the potentially harmful impact, and this may be accompanied by such "dysfunctional" stress reactions as:

1. less adaptive behavior,
2. greater tendency for aggression,
3. fixation on untested hypothesis,
4. increased rate of error,
5. stereotyped responses,
6. disorganized activity,
7. problem-solving rigidity,
8. reduction in focus of attention across time and space,
9. perceived time pressure,
10. less belief in a benign environment,
11. reliance upon *ad hoc* communication channels. [8]

The concepts and framework of Lazarus' model have been outlined in some detail because of the belief that his findings and inferences provide considerable insight into behavior in extreme situations and can serve, therefore, as suitable vehicles for our extensions of adaptive systems to include non-passive decision environments. The approach which is adopted is to allow the process of threat appraisal and coping-strategy evaluation to cycle in the confrontation between the policy-makers and the impacted groups. The strategy adopted by the policy-makers is the environmental cue for the impacted group and in turn its selection of a response provides the environment for the policy-makers' evaluation in the following period. Thus, the basis is established for an adaptive system of the escalating dialogue. This time course of cascading interaction is governed to an extent which must be determined empirically by the parameters and relationships which Lazarus has posited. For example, if the agent of harm cannot be identified easily by impacted groups, then there is a greater likelihood of their adopting a defensive strategy that might involve a very

6. J. Wolpert and R. Ginsberg, "The Transition to Interdependence in Locational Decisions," in K. R. Cox and R. G. Golledge (Eds.), *Behavioral Problems in Geography: A Symposium* (Evanston, Illinois: Northwestern University, Studies in Geography No. 17, 1969).

7. R. S. Lazarus, *Psychological Stress and the Coping Process* (New York: McGraw-Hill Book Company, 1966).

8. Lazarus, *op. cit.*, footnote 7, pp. 349–63; F. E. Horvath, "Psychological Stress," *General Systems Yearbook*, Vol. 4 (1959), pp. 203–30; and Holsti, *op. cit.*, footnote 3.

submissive response of accepting the "inevitable," thereby reducing their potential harm to policy-makers. [9]

The end results of the selected coping strategy may be observed in terms of the adaptability of behavior. Depending upon the degree of threat, the harm potential and the counterharm resources, responses may be adaptive in the sense defined above (*i.e.*, suitable and consistent with the objective situation) or take on the characteristics of a "stress response" perhaps in some of the forms outlined previously (such as rigidity and reduction in the field of alternatives). This formulation then lays the framework for the interpretation of locational decisions which appear to be more the product of stress responses than the end result of a dispassionate and considered selection of alternatives posited by the classical normative approaches or even the Simon scheme of bounded rationality.

Case Study

These processes may be illustrated in the case of a metropolitan university's development plan for expansion into its neighboring community. The actual example is more complex than can be dealt with here fully, so that some simplification and anonymity is introduced to place the context in focus.

The University of X, located in a highly congested zone of blighted housing within a major metropolitan center, more than a decade ago fostered a development plan requiring replacement of some housing with new university facilities. At the time of its inception, the plan appeared clearly in the "public interest," a rational and beneficial

endeavor that would benefit the residents of the entire region. The University of X had almost unilateral discretion to execute the plan, or at least shared this discretion with federal and local urban renewal organizations. The plan, once announced, however, constituted a significant threat to residents who were to be displaced or otherwise to be affected by the construction program. For some of the residents who were to be displaced, removal meant overcrowding into neighboring areas, loss of community, and the prospect of higher housing costs. For some of the shopkeepers, displacement meant a loss in the investment of "good will" and for many, "premature" retirement. The threat was perhaps not so serious for transient residents or for businessmen not strongly dependent upon a "neighborhood market."

The affected population, informed of the impending events, appraised this threat and a variety of responses resulted, mostly interpretable as adaptive, reasonable, and consistent with the actual threat which was posed. Many of the residents who were interviewed seemed to have framed their possible responses as containing options—*i.e.*, a number of possible alternative courses of action were held open, including means of appealing or resisting the decision, and alternative places to which to move when and if that became necessary. Others mentioned fewer options—their previous experience with "officialdom" led them to believe that opposition was costly and fruitless—they evaluated the threat of displacement and chose only to consider alternate places to move. For others, however, responses appeared to be maladaptive, dysfunctional, and in some cases inconsistent with the threat and inappropriate to its severity.

Some excerpts from comments which were made can serve to illustrate the way in

9. J. Wolpert, "A Strategy of Ambiguity in Locational Decisions," paper presented at American Political Science Association Meeting, New York, New York, 1969.

which local residents perceived the threat and had decided to respond:

The University is strong and works with the real estate men—it can put its buildings anywhere, but it just wants to get rid of us—whatever it decides to do, it just does, and we are chased away.

We have no other place to move—the neighborhood is fine—I am afraid to move—there is a lot of crime in those other places and bad gangs—they don't want us there—that other area is unfriendly and costs more than I can afford—the university will change its mind—my friend said that new cheap housing will be built for us.

We are angry—this is the third time I have had to move—the only way to stop them is to make them hurt—they can't get away with it—they are not pushing me out—that leader of ours, he's going to sell us out.

Meetings, meetings, meetings—all they do is talk and argue—I do not trust meetings—I only trust my friends—we do not argue or fight—we'll make our plans and then do something—they don't threaten me.

Every day there is a new story and everybody tells you something different—I can't keep up, it is so confusing—I was speaking to a friend from over there and another guy from work and they know what to do.

Of course, the process of diagnosing responses to threats as stress reactions is highly speculative, but the superficial similarity between observed patterns and the findings in the stress literature strongly suggests that some tentative hypotheses are warranted. Fried has noted, for example, in his study of displacees from a renewal project in Boston, that some experienced grief for their lost home akin to the feeling of loss for a dead friend or relative.[10] The concern here, however, is with responses that affect the negotiation process and that introduce elements of crisis into the bargaining mechanism. If the long-range objective of those to be displaced, in our example, was to be permitted to retain their homes and

community or at least to receive a sufficiently high inducement so as to cushion the relocation process, then reactions which conflict with these alternate goals may be tentatively identified as stress reactions.

Those who fled from the area at the first sign of intimidation missed the opportunity to receive relocation expenses and undervalued their potential effectiveness in opposing the plan. They overestimated the time pressure to move and in many cases moved directly to other areas soon to be cleared of housing. Some were apathetic and others denied that they would be displaced at all. Of course, this form of response was highly beneficial to the policy-makers, effectively reducing the required expenditure for relocation allowance. Another category of response occurred, however, which is much more directly relevant to the subsequent negotiations. Some members of the community threatened that the university would be "burned to the ground" and that individual acts of violence just might occur to the university-connected population, that the construction would be sabotaged, and that university connections with the community would be totally severed. These counter-threats were not the consequence of considered judgment, nor the outcome of a rational selection from among a number of available alternatives but represented much more a striking back in anger.

The policy-makers had then to contend with two types of opposition groups: (1) A coalition of individuals who made use of persuasion, court injunctions, and other similar mechanisms of "rational bargaining," and (2) a confederation of people whose responses were not predictable nor easily countered by compromise or similar inducements. Both forms of opposition were threatening to the policy-makers—their unilateral discretion had been lost and an element of uncertainty had been introduced

---

10. M. Fried, "Grieving for a Lost Home," in L. Duhl (Ed.), *Urban Condition* (New York: Basic Books, 1963).

into the expansion program. There was a chance now that the program could not be implemented, would be delayed, or would be more costly because of the necessity for inducements to reduce the opposition and the fixed investment might be lost if the project had to be abandoned.

The second group of opponents were more directly responsible for the high variance attached to such expected costs for overcoming opposition, as nothing short of abandoning the project would be certain to overcome their opposition. The university policy-makers made counter proposals to the first group of opponents which were consistent with their negotiating power and a successful compromise was worked out. But a direct counter-threat was aimed at the second group of opponents and the interaction froze within a stage of rigidity on both sides and threatened to escalate further. The issue was finally settled when both parties accepted a facesaving agreement imposed from the outside just in time to avert violence. The consequences of the agreement are land use decisions and have implications in terms of the subsequent distribution of the university's facilities and the resettlement of the affected population. These consequences are inseparable from the bargaining process including both the rational adaptive and functional negotiation as well as the secondary stress reactions, were they indeed present.

The two forms of stress reaction hypothesized as being present in the case study (those who fled prematurely and those who threatened or who struck back in anger) represent a parallel to Lazarus' categories of coping strategies as action tendencies as opposed to defense mechanisms. [11] This first category involving action is aimed at eliminating or mitigating the anticipated threatening elements, whereas defense involves maneuvers to alter the appraisal of threat without actions directed at changing the objective situation. Whether one form of coping or the other occurs depends upon the ability to locate those responsible for the potential harm, the magnitude of the threat itself, and the resources which the individual or group has access to, to counter the threat, as well as the pattern of motivation or optimism which determines the "cost or utility" of certain coping alternatives.

Decision-Making in Political Crises

The unfolding of this crisis locational issue has some important parallels with crisis decision-making in other contexts. Holsti, for example, relates the internation escalation leading to World War I to a form of stress response on the part of the political leaders who were involved.[12] The escalation, once begun, intensified until the war was triggered off by a relatively minor incident. Holsti tested his empirical data concerning the communications between the political leaders in terms of the following set of hypotheses and found that within the limits of his validating procedures, the hypotheses appeared to provide some insight:

> As stress increases in a crisis situation:
> 1. Time will be perceived as an increasingly salient factor in decision-making;
> 2. decision-makers will become increasingly concerned with the immediate rather than the distant future.
>
> In a crisis situation, decision-makers will perceive:
> 1. Their own range of alternatives to be more restricted than those of their adversaries;
> 2. their allies' range of alternatives to be more restricted than those of their adversaries.

11. Lazarus, *op. cit.*, footnote 7.

12. Holsti, *op. cit.*, footnote 3.

As stress increases, decision-making will perceive:

1. The range of alternatives open to themselves to become narrower;
2. the range of alternatives open to adversaries to expand.

The higher the stress in a crisis situation:

1. The heavier the overload upon the channels of communication;
2. The more stereotyped will be the information content of messages;
3. the greater the tendency to rely upon extraordinary or improvised channels of communication;
4. the higher the proportion of intra-coalition—as against intercoalition—communication.

This set of hypotheses appears as appropriate to the locational issue that has been discussed here as well as to a number of other confrontations that the author has been investigating. The critical question seems to be: Is the outcome of the confrontation consistent with the objectives of the participants and their negotiations? In those cases when a negative response appears relevant, then the assumption of a stress reaction is more safely rooted. The requirement imposed by findings of this type is that the investigation process must be extended much more deeply. It would not be sufficient to imply that an adaptive, functional locational process was in operation, even if allowances were made for negotiation between contestants. The locational decision must be tied to the high degree of threat present in the decision environment and the consequent dysfunctional reactions.

A Gaming Construct

Many of the properties of a desirable operational model of decisions under stress may be incorporated as elements in gaming formulations. By means of these simplified constructs, choice behavior in simulation or experimental trials may be observed as some function of controlled parameters. Consid-

Table 1   Illustrative Prisoner's Dilemma Payoff Matrices

		Player 2					
		C_2	D_2		C_2	D_2	
Player 1	C_1	1,1	−10,10	C_1	R,R	S,T	
	D_1	10,−10	−1,−1	D_1	T,S	P,P	

Source: developed by author.

erable insight may be gained through the observation of sequential choices represented by a series of plays which can serve to enrich an operational model as well as aid the search for behavioral cues in an empirical study. The behavior of several types of adaptive systems are being investigated using a machine-simulated stochastic model based upon a version of a Bush-Mosteller learning model.[13] Initial experiments have been based upon two-person non-zero sum, non-cooperative games using as an example Prisoner's Dilemma (PD).[14] The PD game admits of no short-term "rational" solution in terms of plays and pay-offs in the sense of game theory, but does offer insight into the mechanisms and time-courses of adaptive or nonadaptive behavioral patterns (Table 1). Each of the two players has the option of either cooperating (C), or defecting (D). The first value in each cell is the pay-off for player *1*, the second value refers to player 2's pay-off. For this pay-off matrix, if both

13. See R. R. Bush and F. Mosteller, *Stochastic Models for Learning* (New York: John Wiley & Sons, 1955); J. Wolpert, J. Herniter, and A. Williams, "Learning to Cooperate," *Papers, Peace Research Society*, Vol. 7 (1967); J. Wolpert and J. Herniter, "Coalition Structures in the Three-Person Non-Zero-Sum Game," *Papers, Peace Research Society*, Vol. 8 (1968).
14. A. Rapoport and A. M. Chammah, *Prisoner's Dilemma* (Ann Arbor: University of Michigan Press, 1965).

players cooperate, each gets a positive pay-off (plus 1). If we view the generalized pay-off matrix, R is the reward for cooperating, S is the penalty for cooperating while the other player defects (the Sucker's pay-off), T is the defector's Temptation, and P the Punishment for double defection. The order of pay-offs is T>R>P>S for each player. In planning a series of plays, in order to analyze sequences as we shall be doing, another rule is needed: 2R>S + T.

The pay-off matrix illustrates the interesting implications of the game. If there is only one play, the "rational" solution for each player is to defect (in the absence of other information). But if each player follows this strategy over a series of plays, the response is harmful to both (a DD trap). The CD and DC positions are normally short-run because of the opportunity for retaliation, and bilateral cooperation is needed, therefore, to extract players from the DD trap.

Rapoport has demonstrated an effective means for defining operationally a number of terms by means of play sequences which are useful in our framework.[15] For example, trustworthiness is the probability of co-operation by the player following a CC outcome, forgiveness following a CD play, repentance following a DC, and trust after a DD play. In addition, other definitions have been developed by Ackoff and Sisson to evaluate the parameters of competitiveness, memory, foresight, and rigidity.[16] The distinction has also been drawn between tactics (choice on the next play) and strategies (plan for a sequence of plays). Measurements may also be applied to the series of plays to measure the degree of cooperation, conflict, and exploitation. Adaptive as well as maladaptive behavior may be defined in accordance with a prescribed criterion.

The very simplified learning model can be expanded to encompass responses to controlled deviations in the "usual environment" of the gaming context. Using as a yardstick the results obtained for adaptively rational play, we are attempting to observe the deviations occurring, for example, under controlled situations of threat, such as with the introduction of ambiguity, unequal distribution of power, underload or overload of cues, and unequal utility of pay-offs, and subsequently by means of various coalition structures.[17] In the normal course of play in the two-person PD game, there are three distinct, stages, as Boulding has pointed out: An initial period of naïve trust, followed by a stage of naïve distrust during which time players occasionally defect without considering the inevitability of retaliation; and finally a period of bilateral lock-in on cooperation termed sophisticated trust because players have learned the value of cooperative stalemate.[18] Variations exist in the duration of these three stages when the pay-off structures are modified, but with the controlled departures with which we have been experimenting other patterns begin to emerge.

The operational technique involves initially simulating via computer an adaptively rational player playing against a controlled dummy whose plays are present to reproduce a variety of threats. On a second level, human players are pitted against the controlled computer dummy without being told that their opponent is a computer. We are attempting, then, to generate patterns of responsiveness of these contrived sources of

---

15. Rapoport and Chammah, *op. cit.*, footnote 14, pp. 71–73.
16. R. Ackoff and R. Sisson, "Toward a Theory of the Dynamics of Conflict," *Papers, Peace Research Society*, Vol. 5 (1965).

17. Wolpert, *op. cit.*, footnote 9.
18. Seminar discussion of PD research, Center for Research on Conflict Resolution, University of Michigan, Ann Arbor. 1965.

stress which may be compared to those in the usual environment in order to observe the differences in the time course of play and the degree of cooperation.

Initial results, though very tentative, indicate that ambiguity and inequality of power distribution reduce significantly the degree of cooperative play in an additive manner and work considerably to the disadvantage of the weaker member who is receiving ambiguous cues from the environment. Our major objective at this point is to build up a fund of case histories involving measures of sensitivity and stability of gaming behavior to control deviations without the expectation that direct parallels to empirical situations can be constructed. The simulation trials are designed rather to identify significant questions with which to confront the real world. Such questions might be:

1. What is the effect of an unequal power distribution between policy-makers and impacted groups?
2. How can policy-makers reduce the flow of information to impacted groups and what would the consequences be?
3. What is the effect of involving participants with a long history or a good memory of previous interactions with opponent groups?
4. What is the relative value of rewards for compliance and opposed to punishments for noncompliance?
5. What are the effects of adding additional participating groups on the stability of interaction?

6. What are the consequences of reducing the number of alternatives, of rigidity, of collusion, or of misclassification of opponents' objectives?

The objective, then, of this phase of the analysis is to initiate an exploration into the extreme situations which are the products of threat in the decision environment. The simulations are designed to make operational the Lazarus stress model so as to locate critical control variables.

Conclusion

The development of behavioral decision models has augmented our ability to describe reality more adequately than the normative models of rationaltiy. Extensions into extreme situations can further expand our predictive abilities. These developments should be made applicable to a wide variety of situations arising from either natural or man-made threats. Psychologists, as well as researchers in all of the social sciences have provided us with experimental and empirical findings which may be integrated within a comprehensive operational model. The technique of gaming via simulation and experimentation may be used to generate at least an abstracted version of the complexities of stress behavior. We are not yet, of course, even close to the point of being able to explain the current artifacts of our visual environment, but perhaps we shall be much better equipped to understand those which are currently being fought over and debated. The environment which we confront is rarely passive—it can be highly beneficial or aggressive. We must know it in all its forms.

✠✠✠✠✠✠✠✠✠✠✠✠✠✠✠✠✠✠✠✠✠✠✠✠✠✠✠✠✠✠✠

BIBLIOGRAPHY

Environmental Perception and Behavior

APPLEYARD, DONALD, KEVIN LYNCH, and JOHN R. MYER, *The View from the Road*, Cambridge: The M.I.T. Press, 1964. This small volume examines the "aesthetics" of metropolitan highways and offers techniques that can measure the artistic content of the urban panorama, as well as suggestions for design.

APPLEYARD, DONALD, KEVIN LYNCH, and JOHN R. MYER, "The View from the Road," in David Lowenthal (ed.), *Environmental Perception and Behavior*, Chicago: University of Chicago, Department of Geography, Research Paper No. 109, 1967, pp. 78-88. The highway experience can be pleasant, exciting, and memorable. The authors urge the adoption of some fundamental artistic techniques to inject continuity and rhythm into the metropolitan expressway pattern.

BARKER, ROGER G., "On the Nature of the Environment," *Journal of Social Issues*, Vol. 19, No. 4 (October 1963), pp. 17-38. Barker attempts to provide a theoretical analysis of the "texture of the environment" and its influence on interpersonal behavior.

BECK, ROBERT, "Spatial Meaning, and the Properties of the Environment," in David Lowenthal (ed.), *Environmental Perception and Behavior*, Chicago: University of Chicago, Department of Geography, Research Paper No. 109, 1967, pp. 18-41. The development of spatial meaning and several types of space ("objective," "ego," and "immanent") are discussed in terms of the interaction of man and his stimulus field, the environment.

BOXER, BARUCH, "Space, Change and Feng-Shui in Tsuen Wan's Urbanization," *Journal of Asian and African Studies*, Vol. 3 (1968), pp. 226-40. The pattern of urban change in Hong Kong is examined in terms of metaphysical and symbolic ideas and values.

BUTTIMER, ANNE, "Social Space in Interdisciplinary Perspective," *Geographical Review*, Vol. 59 (1969), pp. 417-26. A brief historical account of various approaches to social space.

CANTRIL, HADLEY, "Concerning the Nature of Perception," *Proceedings of the American Philosophical Society*, Vol. 104 (1960), pp. 467-73.

After discussing four varieties of human experience, Cantril attempts to explain how man acquires perceptions.

CRAIK, KENNETH H., "The Comprehension of the Everyday Physical Environment," *Ekistics*, Vol. 25 (1968), pp. 413-19. A provocative outline for studying the problem of understanding how people comprehend their everyday physical world.

DEJONGE, DERK, "Images of Urban Areas: Their Structure of Psychological Foundations," *Journal of the American Institute of Planners*, Vol. 28 (1962), pp. 266-76. The principles and techniques developed by Lynch are applied in Holland. DeJonge concludes that the results can be generalized to literate man in Western society.

FONAROFF, L. SCHUYLER, "Conservation and Stock Reduction on the Navajo Tribal Range," *The Geographical Review*, Vol. 53 (1963), pp. 200-223. The continuing failure of federal programs to halt over-grazing of the Navajo range is explained historically in terms of traditional Navajo attitudes toward property ownership and the social value of sheep.

GOULD, PETER R., "Wheat on Kilimanjaro: The Perception of Choice within Game and Learning Model Frameworks," *General Systems*, Vol. 10 (1965), pp. 157-66. A two-person—zero-sum game is constructed to describe and optimize farming decisions, given certain environmental hazards and an increasing level of technological development.

GOULD, PETER R., and R. R. WHITE, "The Mental Maps of British School Leavers," *Regional Studies*, Vol. 2 (1968), pp. 161-82. The authors operationalize the concept of the mental map by examining cartographically the residential preferences of pupils of twenty-three British schools. The resulting patterns suggest that there is an observable orderliness in the perception of residential space.

GULICK, JOHN, "Images of an Arab City," *Journal of the American Institute of Planners*, Vol. 29 (1963), pp. 179-98. Following Lynch, Gulick concludes that urban imageability is a product of the perception of visual form and of the conception of social significance.

GUTMAN, ROBERT, "Site Planning and Social Behavior," in R. W. Kates and J. F. Wohlwill (eds.), "Man's Response to the Physical Environment," *Journal of Social Issues*, Vol. 22 (1966), pp. 103-15. The social effects of site planning are evaluated in terms of previous empirical research.

HALL, EDWARD T., *The Silent Language*, Garden City, New York: Doubleday, 1959. People of different cultures are known to behave differently, and these culturally derived differences affect their attitudes toward each other and toward other cultures. Hall tries to explain the failure of American political and social ventures abroad in terms of conflicting behavioral "languages."

HALL, EDWARD T., "The Language of Space," *Landscape*, Vol. 10 (1960), pp. 41-45. Space communicates and can have significant effects upon its occupants. Hall discusses some cultural variations in uses of and attitudes toward space.

HALL, EDWARD T., *The Hidden Dimension*, Garden City, New York: Doubleday, 1966. This volume examines the biological basis for human interaction and perception and attempts to account for selected cultural variations in the way people communicate by their use of and response to space.

HEATHCOTE, R. L., "Drought in Australia: A Problem of Perception," *The Geographical Review*, Vol. 59 (1969), pp. 175-94. Overt patriotism, as well as undue optimism, has defeated legitimate attempts to recognize, appraise, and prepare for the adverse effects of drought in Australia.

JACKSON, J. B., "A New Kind of Space," *Landscape*, Vol. 18 (1969), pp. 33-35. Jackson presents a concise history of the reorganization of American space.

KATES, ROBERT W., "Perceptual Regions and Regional Perception in Flood Plain Management," *Regional Science Association, Papers and Proceedings*, Vol. 11 (1963), pp. 217-27. Initial evidence from seven study sites indicates that perception of flooding increases with experience, and Kates suggests that it is the regions of infrequent but regular flooding that demand attention from flood plain management agencies. He also questions the viability of the watershed or river basin as the proper unit of regional water development.

KATES, ROBERT W., "Stimulus and Symbol: The View from the Bridge," in R. W. Kates and J. F. Wohlwill (eds.), "Man's Response to the Physical Environment," *Journal of Social Issues*, Vol. 22 (1966), pp. 21-28. The principal task of the social and behavioral sciences in the study of the environ-

ment is to relate the stimulus properties of the environment to their symbolic human manifestations.

KATES, ROBERT W., "The Perception of Storm Hazard on the Shores of the Megalopolis," in David Lowenthal (ed.), *Environmental Perception and Behavior*, Chicago: University of Chicago, Department of Geography, Research Paper No. 109, 1967, pp. 60-74. Residents of the east coast express both an awareness of storm hazard and an optimistically distorted view of the frequency of storms.

KIRK, WILLIAM, "Problems of Geography," *Geography*, Vol. 48 (1963), pp. 357-71. This discussion of the elusive "core" of geography explores the behavioral and phenomenal environments in geographical research.

LOWENTHAL, DAVID, "Daniel Boone Is Dead," *Natural History*, Vol. 77, No. 7 (1968), pp. 8-16ff. Lowenthal takes a gentle swipe at hardy naturalists and advocates a more personal communion with nature in all of its various forms, rural and urban.

LOWENTHAL, DAVID, ed., *Environmental Perception and Behavior*, Chicago: University of Chicago, Department of Geography, Research Paper No. 109, 1967. This brief collection of articles explores the man-environment theme as revealed in literature and art, social attitudes, and behavior.

LYNCH, KEVIN, *The Image of the City*, Cambridge: The Technology Press and Harvard University Press, 1960. Lynch examines aesthetic and visual images of people in Boston, Jersey City, and Los Angeles.

PARR, A. E., "Psychological Aspects of Urbanology," in R. W. Kates and J. F. Wohlwill (eds.), "Man's Response to the Physical Environment," *Journal of Social Issues*, Vol. 22 (1966), pp. 39-45. Some psychological inadequacies of urban design are related to rapidly and radically changing architectural surroundings and increased feelings of insecurity.

PETERSON, GEORGE L., "Measuring Visual Preferences of Residential Neighborhoods," *Ekistics*, Vol. 23 (1967), pp. 169-73. Peterson suggests that visual appearances of the physical environment can be quantitatively classified in terms of perceptions and preferences.

RAPOPORT, AMOS, and ROBERT E. KANTOR, "Complexity and Ambiguity in Environmental Design," *Journal of the American Institute of Planners*, Vol. 33 (1967), pp. 210-21. Humans prefer complex patterns in their visual field, thus building in a complex fashion would be more satisfying psychologically than would the simplicity sought by many designers.

ROONEY, JOHN F., JR., "The Urban Snow Hazard in the United States: An Appraisal of Disruption," *The Geographical Review*, Vol. 57 (1967), pp. 538-59. In this analysis, the snow environment is the independent variable, the urban individual is the dependent variable and man's attitudes and perceptions are the intervening variables.

SAARINEN, THOMAS FREDERICK, *Perception of Environment*, Washington: Association of American Geographers, Commission on College Geography, Resource Paper No. 5, 1969. A survey of the increasing body of literature dealing with man's perception of natural and altered environments.

SAARINEN, THOMAS FREDERICK, *Perception of the Drought Hazard on the Great Plains*, Chicago: University of Chicago, Department of Geography, Research Paper No. 106, 1966. Drought and perception of drought hazard on the Great Plains are discussed.

SOMMER, ROBERT, "Man's Proximate Environment," in R. W. Kates and J. F. Wohlwill (eds.), "Man's Response to the Physical Environment," *Journal of Social Issues*, Vol. 22 (1966), pp. 59-70. Sommer suggests that systematic studies of human spatial needs and agreement on various spatial concepts would benefit the design professions.

SOMMER, ROBERT, *Personal Space: The Behavioral Basis of Design*, Englewood Cliffs, New Jersey: Prentice-Hall, 1969. The author discusses attitudes toward immediate environments. A better understanding of the way in which human manipulation of the environment psychologically effects its users should condition design.

SONNENFELD, JOSEPH, "Variable Values in Space and Landscape: An Inquiry into the Nature of Environmental Necessity," in R. W. Kates and J.F. Wohlwill (eds.), "Man's Response to the Physical Environment," *Journal of Social Issues*, Vol. 22 (1966), pp. 71-82. Sonnenfeld argues that environmental values differ within and between populations. Universally valued spaces and landscapes do not exist, and environmental adaptation levels are quite variable.

SONNENFELD, JOSEPH, "Environmental Perception and Adaptation Level in the Arctic," in David Lowenthal (ed.), *Environmental Perception and Behavior*, Chicago: University of Chicago, Department of Geography, Research Paper No. 109, 1967, pp. 42-59. An attempt to measure and account for variations in man's sensitivity to the environment among cultural groups in northern Alaska.

SONNENFELD, JOSEPH, "Equivalence and Distortion of the Perceptual Environment," *Environment and Behavior*, Vol. 1 (1969), pp. 83-99. A study of native and non-native populations in Alaska reveals significant differences in environmental sensitivity and attitudes between cultural groups. There may be an index of environmental personality types that can account for similarities between populations and differences within populations with respect to environmental behavior.

STEA, DAVID, "Space, Territory and Human Movements," *Landscape*, Vol. 15 (1965), pp. 13-16. The concepts of territory and boundary are related to the office environment to explain worker efficiency, boredom and restlessness.

STRAUSS, ANSELM M., ed., *The American City: A Sourcebook of Urban Imagery*, Chicago: Aldine, 1968. This collection of readings on American cities samples the older and more recent literature relating to persistent themes such as the city as a place of diversity, as a dehumanizing environment, and as a place where complex relationships exist among the social classes.

STRODTBECK, F. L., and L. J. HOOK, "The Social Dimensions of a Twelve-Man Jury Table," *Sociometry*, Vol. 24 (1961), pp. 397-415. The three primary components of social distance in the jury setting were table length, visual accessibility and table width. These components were used to characterize the attributes of different positions.

THOMPSON, KENNETH, "Insalubrious California: Perception and Reality," *Annals, Association of American Geographers*, Vol. 59 (1969), pp. 50-64. Part of the state was once viewed as unhealthy owing to malaria and related diseases. A change in perception of these marshy places has created new possibilities for environmental enhancement.

TINKLER, K. J., "Perception and Prejudice: Student Preferences for Employment and Residence in Uganda," in *Perception and Nodality in Uganda*, Makerere: University College, Department of Geography, Occasional Paper No. 15, 1970, pp. 1-25. The residential preferences for eighteen districts in Uganda were recorded for a group of Uganda students and compared with those of a group of Kenya students in an attempt to measure the effect of prejudiced personal perception on residential desirability.

TUAN, YI-FU, "Attitudes toward Environment: Themes and Approaches," in David Lowenthal, ed., *Environmental Perception and Behavior*, Chicago: University of Chicago, Department of Geography, Research Paper No. 109, 1967, pp. 4-17. Tuan discusses the historical roots of western attitudes towards the desert and the tropical island as a comparative example of the relevance of literature and art to research in geography.

VAN ARSDOL, MAURICE D. JR., GEORGES SABAGH, and FRANCESCA ALEXANDER, "Reality and the Perception of Environmental Hazard," *Journal of Health and Human Behavior*, Vol. 5 (1964), pp. 144-53. The distribution, intensity, and frequency of five environmental hazards—smog, noise, floods, earth slides, and brush fires—are mapped for the Los Angeles SMSA and compared with the indicated hazard awareness of the residents of the area. Discrepancies arise among cultural and ethnic groups.

WAGNER, PHILIP, "America Emerging," *Landscape*, Vol. 13 (1963), pp. 22-26. The American landscape, as a dynamic expression of the dual forces of technology and democracy, has been drastically remade in recent decades. Man-land relationships are undergoing locational and technical, as well as territorial and perceptual, alteration.

WHITE, GILBERT F., "Formation and Role of Public Attitudes," in Jarret (ed.), *Environmental Quality in a Growing Economy*, Baltimore: Johns Hopkins Press, 1966, pp. 105-27. White uses the examples of sewage disposal and water supply in Boulder, Colorado, to establish how final policy decisions were reached and how public attitudes influenced them.

WOHLWILL, J. F., "The Physical Environment: A Problem for a Psychology of Stimulation," in

R. W. Kates and J. F. Wohlwill (eds.), "Man's Response to the Physical Environment," *Journal of Social Issues*, Vol. 22 (1966), pp. 29-38. The relationship between the physical environment and behavior is a topic for experimental psychologists who study motivation, stimulation, and response.

WOLPERT, JULIAN, "The Decision Process in Spatial Context," *Annals, Association of American Geographers*, Vol. 54 (1964), pp. 537-58. A study of Middle Sweden's farming population suggests that "spatial satisficing" is a more useful concept than models based on rational (Economic Man) behavior and that the findings can be generally applied to industrial decision-making as well.

WOLPERT, JULIAN, "Behavioral Aspects of the Decision To Migrate," *Papers and Proceedings, Regional Science Association*, Vol. 15 (1965), pp. 159-69. The concepts of place utility, a field-theory approach to search behavior, and the life-cycle approach to threshold formation are relevant to the study of migration. An operating predictive model is proposed which incorporates behavioral theory into migrational analysis and thus presents a truer representation of the "mover-stayer problem" than have earlier efforts.

WOLPERT, JULIAN, "Migration as an Adjustment to Environmental Stress," in R. W. Kates and J. F. Wohlwill (eds.), "Man's Response to the Physical Environment," *Journal of Social Issues*, Vol. 22 (1966), pp. 92-102. Wolpert relates the decision to move or stay to the compatability of or "harmony" between the individual and his environment and offers a model that incorporates the concept of stress into the decision process.

THE
SPATIAL
STRUCTURE
OF HUMAN
BEHAVIOR

4

SPATIAL
DIFFUSION

Man's thorough examination of the land surface of the earth as potential habitat has permitted a substantial occupation and organization of terrestrial space. If man had an early site-specific origin in Africa, then processes of spatial diffusion are fundamental aspects of human history. The questions regarding his settlement of the earth's more accommodating areas relate to those processes. Was the movement primarily that of a gradual spreading over connected land surfaces? Did early man make major leaps over great distances, to establish new centers of human dispersal? If so, what was the directional orientation, and why? At what points during the long development of his ecosystem would man most probably be involved in simultaneous expansion and relocation? At what levels of spatial complexity would separated ecosystems tend toward independent origin of similar culture traits? What forces generate the diffusion of any phenomenon through human societies? What is the final spatial expression of that diffusion? Is this impact on the ecosystem sufficient to affect the spatial pattern of subsequent diffusion?

Quite clearly, then, the geographer who seeks answers to such questions is confronted with spatially dynamic environments over time, occupied by communities whose varied culture traits serve to obfuscate the generalities of spatial process. It is not surprising that geographers should have attacked such problems with more than one intellectual approach. Although a prominent review of various disciplines in 1962 did not identify geography as having a significant tradition of research in innovation diffusion,[1] Sauer's Agricultural Origins and Dispersals *and Hägerstrand's* Propagation of Innovation Waves *were both published a decade earlier. The authors of these volumes are*

---

1. Everett M. Rogers, *Diffusion of Innovations,* Free Press, New York, 1962.

each singularly identified with a separate scholarly emphasis.

In the tradition sponsored at Berkeley by Sauer, the approach involves treating diffusion as an auxiliary theme within the over-all concern for cultural landscape. There have been two principal interests of the Berkeley school: (1) the *origins* of phenomena, and (2) the identification of *pattern*. In neither case were concerns centered on the processes involved. This led, in turn, to more emphasis on ethnographic records than on field work. The non-contextural nature of these materials made it difficult to examine process. The legitimate concern of the tradition in matters of identification, specification, and typology of culture trait and culture complex did not often lead its students to the rigor available in the contemporary methodology of science. Perhaps it is for this reason that the tradition remained centered largely on the original node, with a dramatic distance-decay function.

From Lund, Hägerstrand provided a different emphasis. The thrust there was on spatial aspects of the communication process, which was theorized as generating diffusion. Attention to theory, and the ways of testing related hypothetical constructs, established methodological precedents that were, belatedly, near independent adoption at Washington and Iowa. Over much of the time since Hägerstrand's work first appeared, a diffusion of quantitative technique has occurred within geography as one aspect of a heightened concern for scientific method. The geographer's effort to achieve methodological rigor has been matched in its noisy desperation by a substantial but relatively quiet measure of success. The diffusion literature of the Hägerstrand tradition has consistently stressed processes related to innovation diffusion, has pointed up analytical procedures of a hopefully general nature, and has finally been extended beyond innovation diffusion to a wide range of problems concerning human spatial behavior.

An outline of the basic aspects of a typical spatial diffusion structure suggests the following six elements: (1) an environmental space; (2) a diffusion-time, in two or more intervals; (3) an innovation or "message" to be diffused; (4) a set of message holders in the initial time interval; (5) a set of message-receivers in the second time interval (minimally); and (6) interaction paths between message holders and message receivers.[2] These represent the formal minima for diffusion model construction, and yet they are only indirectly suggestive of other elements that should be considered in examining spatial diffusion in any culture. Of these, several should be identified explicitly for the particular topic of innovation diffusion. (Because spreading culture traits may be regarded as innovations, and migrants often are message bearers, a variety of other diffusion situations are involved.) Much that has to be said hinges on the third element listed above, the specific "message" to be transmitted. Once a particular innovation has been identified, then the first additional element can also be noted: a sub-set of *specific early receivers*, for element (5) above, defined by the *nature of the innovation* and the *centrality level of the sub-set*. Although it is possible that a set of spatially distributed human beings is sufficient, more often this is only the necessary precondition. An illustration may be drawn easily from an agricultural innovation diffusion in an underdeveloped portion of South Asia, Shimoga District of Mysore State. In 1966 in an effort to modernize rice cultivation throughout the district, a new high-yielding hardy variety, Taichung-65, was suggested through a change-agent system of agricultural extension officers and village level workers that

---

2. Brown (*op. cit.*, pp. 9-38).

reached virtually every village in the district. Yet, after the first major round of district-wide efforts by the change-agents, only eight farmers had agreed to plant Taichung-65. It is the peculiarly cosmopolitan nature of the eight that identifies the sub-set: all affluent in the context of their society; all received newspapers and journals in both Kannada and English in their homes; all owned radios; and all could suggest additional personal interstate and metropolitan contacts for agricultural information.

Second, in a given ecosystem context, *the sub-set acts on the basis of prior diffusions.* This may be simply a pre-diffusion of information, but in most cases, particular diffusions can be specified as that on which the most recent has built. This prior diffusion may be the set of change agents themselves, or it may be a seductively successful practical innovation. In the Shimoga example, the eight innovators were among the first two dozen farmers to adopt successfully slightly higher inputs of nitrate on local (Indicus) varieties of rice, over the preceding five years.

Third, the *perceived fit of the new behavior pattern must be positive.* None of the eight Indian farmers were concerned over how their adoptions might be viewed by their neighbors, but seven of the eight discussed the alleviation of contemporary food shortages in broader India (not Mysore) as a patriotic duty. One, who was supervising the plowing of one portion of a field while a crop of Taichung-65 was being removed from the remaining portions, vowed proudly that he would be the first farmer in Shimoga ever to harvest three successive rice crops in the same field in a year's time. And this, he noted, when Bihar and Uttar Pradesh were suffering famine.

Fourth, as interaction pathways do not assure interaction, *the spatial network of message receivers must be energized.* For example, without the provision of locally adequate supplies of seed, and substantial reserves of nitrate fertilizer, neither repetitive advocacy of Taichung-65 nor field demonstrations of its high yields could facilitate *adoption* of that rice variety in Shimoga. It might be added that this energy must not only be released, but it must be made apparent as well.

A mélange of "messages" brought primarily by mass media were under evaluation by the eight Shimoga farmers, so it is not surprising that all suggested that the prospect of high yields was instrumental in their trying the Taichung-65 rice variety. Interestingly, high yields were not obtained by five of the eight, and the diffusion suddenly faltered. At the heart of this failure lies a fifth principle related to the diffusing message itself, which is of importance to scholar and planner alike: *the full content of the message must be registered.* All eight of the Shimoga farmers were literate, highly motivated innovators. Yet five of the eight "adopted" Taichung-65 in seed only, i.e. they did not also adopt the technology—the agricultural practices—required to produce the desired yields. These tractor-owning farmers who control insects with chemical sprays, who invest heavily in the mechanics and practice of irrigation, did not follow one or the other (or neither) of two critical bits of information given to them repeatedly (transplant very early and fertilize very heavily,). The traditional seed-bed duration of forty to forty-five days had been reduced to twenty-one for Taichung-65, and nitrate inputs were doubled. This had been stated explicitly, both orally and in printed instructions. The change agents did not foresee a folk-knowledge response from more than half the district's leading innovators—a response that resulted in a flowering of the rice in the seed beds, or in pale, inadequate

Table 1   Types of Diffusion Processes

Structural Character	Dispersal Character	
	Expansion	*Relocation*
Contagious	The spread of adoption of "Mexican wheat" seed by Indian villagers in Ludhiana District, Punjab, from only a few trial sites	A wave of seasonal labor migration from southern to northern California
Hierarchical	A popular music hit as a fad moving from New York to successively smaller cities in the United States.	A student's movement from high school to junior college to university, at successive locations.

plants when transplanted as advised but not fertilized adequately.

The tradition of spatial diffusion research in geography is richly diversified, and encompasses much more than the diffusion of innovation. The study of diffusion processes has permitted a variety in both phenomena studied and method employed.[3] The following table suggests examples of major *types* of diffusion processes. All these processes of diffusion may be affected by barriers. The boundary with Mexico, suggesting strong cultural differences, may act as a largely *absorbing* barrier, as it greatly reduces the further spread of much U. S. popular music to the south, and effectively prevents the areal saturation achieved in the United States. But the Canadian boundary is much more *permeable*, permitting a large portion of the hits of the day to establish themselves to the north. Some barriers reflect a

diffusion. Physical barriers such as rough, non-cultivable terrain along the great agricultural valleys of California direct the movement pattern of migrant laborers. In the narrower portions of the valleys, this labor may bunch together, forcing incoming trucks to move their human cargoes much farther up the valley in order to find less competitive employment. It should be added that barriers do not have to be "real," but only perceived as real. For several decades, Terre Haute, Indiana, was plagued in its effort to attract new industry by a lingering reputation as a town with chronic labor problems. The operational success and good labor records of the major manufacturing firms already there were not as widely known as the town's very early involvement with the unionization of nearby coal miners and its reputation as the home of the controversial labor organizer Eugene V. Debs.

It should be noted that the examples of diffusion are suggestive of strong differences in *scale*. There can be substantial variation in both the size of areal units involved and the complexity in level of adoption. The entry of a state into the United Nations may have entailed months or years of political maneuvering at the "macro" international level. An

3. One of the least technical yet conceptually sound reviews of geographic research in diffusion is that provided by Gould, in his resource paper for the Commission on College Geography, published by the Association of American Geographers. Unfortunately, this excellent review could not be included, here. A student making his first venture into the literature on spatial diffusion will be well rewarded by reading Gould's resource paper.

Indian farmer's decision to adopt a new seed type may require as many months before the actual adoption, but such individual behavior is highly localized. His micro-level decision plays a significant part in the processes of *regional* diffusion of an innovation, an intermediate scale level. A city's decision to add fluoride to its water also reflects an intermediate scale of diffusion, but has very often been related to decision-making by other units in the broader urban hierarchy. Although the processes may be the same for the several scales suggested, the level of resolution may influence strongly the analytical approach to be taken. At the level of the individual Indian farmer, the researcher may wish to aggregate that interaction pattern with those of other villagers into a Mean Information Field, for purposes of estimating the overall propensity for human contact at that level. At the national level, one may be most concerned with the step-like breaks in the urban hiearchy, examining the communication linkages or the relative effects of increased distances within the system.

Hägerstrand's study is not only a continuation of his early interest in diffusion processes but is also a review of his basic methodology. He stresses the "spatial properties of the network of social communication," and in doing so drives home the need for spatial data over time to test theory. His use of Festschrift subscriber lists and the records of Rotary International are suggestive of the broad applicability of the information field concept. In a closing passage, he gives a rudimentary description of the process of hicarchical diffusion.

It is Berry's work that provides a lucid illustration of a hierarchical spatial network routing an innovation down the linkages and levels of the network to the nodes of successively lower order, facilitating the spread of that innovation within the interaction fields of the nodes as the innovation reaches them.

Perhaps the most important summary notion provided by his various studies is that related to the probable time that an innovation becomes available to the dispersed household within an urban region. That is, it depends on both the hierarchical order of the center and the relative location of the center with respect to the site-origin of the diffusion.

As noted before, the "macro" approach to diffusion is only one side of the geographer's coin, as others have looked first for micro-measures. Morrill and Pitts examined the spatial behavior of the individual. Noting the complex pattern of spatial mobility for the individual, they move upward toward generality by treating aggregate spatial behavior structures as community mean information fields. In developing the linear distance between partners to marriages as a surrogate measure of the mean information field, data from the Western United States, Sweden, and Japan are utilized. For those wishing to pursue similar investigations, the section treating the relation of distance to movement is one of the more helpful ones in the literature.

In a field study which investigates the spatial pattern of marriage distances in three widely separated rural areas in India (Punjab, Gujerat, and Mysore), Mayfield examines the marriage distances as a mean information field surrogate. The research revealed significant differences in the spatial pattern of the marriage distance between occupational groups and between the regions of the study. For the patrilineal, male centered social system studied, he finds a possible underestimation of the villager's information field when the marriage distance is so used. Visits to blood-related kin and friends of the male household head are suggested as more useful surrogates for the mean information field in the Indian regions examined.

Noting the increased inefficiency over

time of gravity model formulations dealing with human movements over space, Wolpert develops a model based on behavioral theory. Three primary concepts are operationalized: the notion of place utility, the field theory approach to search behavior, and the life-cycle approach to threshold formation. A series of matrices are described as inputs for the proposed model designed to relate aggregate behavior in terms of migration differentials to measures of place utility relevant for individuals.

The historical significance of the relation between diffusion pattern and the structure of human interaction over space is neatly illustrated by Pyle's study of three cholera epidemics in the United States. After identifying the ports of entry as major port cities of the nation, he traces the reported spread

of the disease against the transportation networks and the urban hiearchy of the respective periods. As the network becomes more complex over time, the hierarchical structure matures. Pyle convincingly suggests that the diffusion process shifts accordingly and he separates sets of routes for each epidemic. His article is an excellent example of the broad use one may make of a knowledge of spatial diffusion concepts in contemporary human geography.

The diversity of the authors' contributions to spatial diffusion reflects the complexity of the processes generating movement over space. The complex content of space at any point in time also contributes to this diversity. A tradition of research in spatial diffusion is most particularly alive and well in human geography.

⁂⁂⁂⁂⁂⁂⁂⁂⁂⁂⁂⁂⁂⁂⁂⁂⁂⁂⁂⁂⁂⁂⁂⁂⁂⁂⁂

ASPECTS OF THE SPATIAL STRUCTURE OF SOCIAL COMMUNICATION AND THE DIFFUSION OF INFORMATION

Torsten Hägerstrand

Diffusion of innovation is by definition a function of communication. One cannot adopt an innovation which is not one's own invention unless one has first seen it, heard of it, or read about it. This is not to say that communication tells the whole story. A time-lag between information and adoption is a normal feature, and what is going on during that time is equally important though it may be less easy to grasp because it is largely an unobservable mental process.

The analysis of diffusion of innovation

may, for the sake of convenience, be broken into two parts: the study of links and the study of nodes. The links are the routes along which information and influence flow. The nodes are the individuals in their reactions to information.

The following is a preliminary report on some empirical findings from ongoing research on the function of links. The ultimate goal is to understand—and perhaps predict—the time-space course of diffusion of innovation through society.

From *Papers*, Regional Science Association, Vol. 16, 1965. Reprinted by permission.

The approach chosen springs from the long tradition in European cultural geography and cultural history going back to the work of Ratzel. In that tradition maps showing the distribution of selected cultural elements have been the fundamental instrument for presentation, and such concepts as "centers of innovation," "channels of spread," "cultural boundaries" and "cultural areas" have been invented as organizing means of analysis. In most cases available information has not allowed consideration of the distribution of a particular item at more than one isolated point in time. From this single spatial picture one has had to make guesses about that probable historical process which could be supposed to have led up to the known situation. Among the wealth of maps of cultural distributions produced by students of European folk-culture one very seldom finds instances where it has been possible to go further and actually follow step by step some spreading element from place to place over a period of time. This fact is not surprising, however, bearing in mind that historical sources, interviews, or field-work hardly can supply full information as to place, time, and quantity.

The only way to overcome such difficulties occasioned by limited data is to take up present-day instances of diffusion where written sources exist or the ongoing process can be studied in the field.

For some years I have been trying to trace various written sources which fully substantiate the recent spread of particular innovations as to time, place, and quantity. With such a program it is unavoidable that one cannot decide in advance what spreading elements one would like to investigate. On the contrary it is necessary to make the best possible use of those cases which emerge, even if they sometimes look peculiar.

The fullest sets of data found so far concern agricultural innovations. It has been possible in a number of cases to follow how innovations proceed year by year from farm to farm inside smaller agricultural areas.[1] Also a number of items spreading through a whole country have been found and studied.[2] From these observations certain generalizations may be ventured. The reader is referred to these earlier publications for empirical evidence.

Innovations can be of very different nature and still their spread tends to show a number of recurring traits. Most easily observed from ordinary statistical information is the "curve of cumulative growth." When the number of adopters—individuals, firms, cities, as the case may be—is measured over time an S-shaped curve normally appears. This curve shows a slow take-off stage of varying length, an intermediate stage of more rapid development and a final stage of declining growth which asymptotically seems to approach a ceiling. Different innovations run through this process with very different speed; also various degrees of irregularity are noted.

The three parts of the growth curve seem to have certain counterparts in the spatial distribution of adopters. In the initial stage adopters are usually concentrated in a small cluster or a set of small clusters. Expansion then takes place in a way which indicates that a new adoption is more likely to occur in the vicinity of existing adoptions than further out from them. It is convenient conceptually to talk about this phenomenon as the "neighborhood effect." The saturation stage may be reached in the central area

1. T. Hägerstrand, "A Monte Carlo Approach to Diffusion," *Archives Européenes de Sociologie*, vol. 6, 1965, pp. 43-67.
2. T. Hägerstrand, "Quantitative Techniques for Analysis of the Spread of Information and Technology," in *Education and Economic Development*, C. A. Anderson and M. J. Bowman, eds., Chicago, Aldine, 1965.

of dispersal while the density of adoptions is still low in peripheral areas.

The importance of the neighborhood effect suggests that the links between individuals in circles of acquaintances and friendship play a remarkably important role for directing information and influence. Perhaps it is not too surprising that this is so in a farming population. But the same thing seems also to hold true in population groups which should be fully qualified to react on written information alone. Investigations of a quite different type point in the same direction. For example Coleman, Katz and Menzel showed that the use of new drugs spread through the medical profession largely along the links of a social network, in particular as long as uncertainty existed about the usefulness of the new product.[3] Further, it is important to note that innovations which emanate from the same center but start spreading at different points in time still tend to propagate along similar "roads" and in the same spatial pattern, without of course repetition in details. One gets the impression that information and influences travel in a system of communication with a rather stable spatial configuration. The number of links between areas and places seems to remain very much the same over time even when the acting individuals change.

Given the time-space properties of the diffusion of innovation just summarized it has been tempting to venture the construction of a theoretical model—or rather a family of models—which could give some deeper insights into the mechanisms at work. The type of model chosen was a simulation setup of the so-called Monte Carlo variety. Since this model subsequently has taken on the function of a frame of reference for

further research it will explain why such data have been collected as will be presented later in the report. Therefore a short presentation seems to be in order, beginning with a few words about simulation.

Most— if not all—of the processes which interest a social scientist are of a probabilistic nature. When man is involved we cannot establish such deterministic relationships between causes and effects as the experimenter in classical physics can. On the other hand social events are not entirely unpredictable. Statistical descriptions of society exhibit a rich collection of characteristic distributions which change only gradually over time. While these distributions do not allow prediction of the position or behavior of the single individual, one can often make reliable propositions about collections of people.

If several sets of events interact, each having its own known probability distribution, then the joint outcome is not always easy to calculate by the aid of ordinary analytical methods, in particular if we are not only interested in the final result but also in the way things develop as interaction goes on. This difficulty can partly be overcome by making a game of the process. We may let a die, a table of random numbers, or a computer pick out artificial sets of events in accordance with the given probability distributions and make a record of the joint outcome as it evolves. One advantage is that our guiding distributions need not be expressible as mathematical functions. It is sufficient if they only can be described in tables or graphs. Playing such games has become known as Monte Carlo simulation, or stochastic sampling.

The purpose of the actual diffusion model is to show how society operates as a communication system when a "disturbance" of the innovation type enters at

3. J. S. Coleman, E. Katz, and H. Menzel, "The Diffusion of an Innovation Among Physicians," *Sociometry,* vol. 20, 1957, pp. 253-70.

some point and subsequently is propagated through the network.

In practice it is obviously impossible to create a full picture of the network of social communication for a population of even a moderate size. Instead suitable generalizations and simplifications have to be introduced. At this point the spatial approach turns out to be particularly useful. One might say that society with acting individuals and material equipment is spread out over the Earth's surface like a thin film. Even purely social processes (as the exchange of information between individuals) have, therefore, along with other characteristics, certain spatial properties as well. What is happening is often easier to observe and to generalize about in this dimension than when data have otherwise been ordered.

In the study of the spatial properties of the network of social communication it is convenient first to define a fundamental unit which may later serve as a building block. Suppose that we have been able to observe an individual A during a period of time, $t_n - t_{n+1}$, and noted the spatial distribution of those other individuals with whom A communicated. The resulting configuration is called the "private information field" of A with respect to $t_n - t_{n+1}$.

Repeating our observations for some following period of time, say $t_{n+1} - t_{n+2}$, we will in all probability find that the information field of A is mainly unchanged if he is still living in the same place. Of course the truth of this proposition depends on the length of the period. If it is too short the amount of random differences will be great. If is is very long we introduce life time trends into the picture. How things actually are remains a problem for empirical investigation. The assumed stability is naturally less evident if we go down in detail to the individual level than if we are satisfied with noting the pure spatial relationships.

It is reasonable to believe that the private information fields of individuals can be classified into spatial types, each with its own characteristic pattern of contact probabilities. These types certainly differ between rural and urban populations and between smaller groups within these two major classes. Each type which it will prove possible to distinguish will be called a "mean information field." The hope is that the extremely complicated total fabric of links finally can be described by the aid of a limited set of such mean information fields. The description must then also contain probabilities of connections between the various types including the location of such connections (central, peripheral or spread). The whole procedure is, as it were, of the same nature as when the continuum of sound in spoken language is translated to the small set of letters.

In its simplest form the diffusion model referred to earlier operates in the following way:

Given: 1. A population, distributed with even density over a plane. For convenience of operation the plane is divided into square cells.

2. An innovator living in the center of the plane.

Rules: 1. The innovation is adopted as soon as heard of.

2. Information is spread exclusively through private tellings at pairwise meetings.

3. The tellings take place at constant intervals of time (called generation intervals); then every adopter informs another individual, adopter or nonadopter.

4. The destination of every telling is given by the aid of random numbers according to

probabilities assigned by the aid of empirical estimates.

In practice destinations of tellings are found with the aid of a floating grid (with cells of the same size as the cells on the model plane). The central cell of this floating grid is always located over the cell on the model plane where the observed individual "lives".

$P_1, P_2, P_3,, \ldots$ give the probabilities by which the message is supposed to pass from the center to cells in surrounding areas.

P_1	P_2	P_3	P_4	P_5
P_6	P_7	P_8	P_9	P_{10}
P_{11}	P_{12}	$\underline{P_{13}}$	P_{14}	P_{15}
P_{16}	P_{17}	P_{18}	P_{19}	P_{20}
P_{21}	P_{22}	P_{23}	P_{24}	P_{25}

In the simplest case probabilities decrease symmetrically from the peak P_{13}. This floating grid with its assigned probabilities represents the mean information field of the population under observation.

Investigations of local migration and local telephone traffic have shown the links between individuals in a farming population have a very strong distance bias. For an agricultural area in Sweden the following figures were applicable:

.0096   .0140   .0168
         .0301   .0547   . . .
                  .4431

and so on symmetrically. The sum of these probabilities equals unity.

Assuming a grid-size of 5×5 km. and 30 inhabitants per cell of the model plane, some possible outcomes of one run of the simulation are exemplified in Figure 1.

Since telling over shorter distances is much more common than over longer ones the neighborhood effect comes out very strongly. The diffusion develops as an outward movement in small steps and a simultaneous inner condensation takes place.

Occasional jumps of the innovation over longer distances at the beginning of the process tend to create secondary centers later on.

It is interesting to note that each new generation means multiplication by a factor of two only in the beginning. Soon the growth slows down as it should according to empirical experience. In the model this is because of an inevitable loss of tellings which happens when adopter tells adopter or when two or more adopters tell one and the same non-adopter.

Even this simple version of the model bears some resemblance to reality: for example, it has similarities with small-scale cases of diffusion of innovation among farmers. It is now fairly easy to introduce variations to make the model compare to actual situations even more. Such variations as have been tried are to work on a plane with an uneven distribution of population and with barriers to communications.[4] A more fundamental variation is to introduce resistance to change by requiring that people need to hear about the innovation several times before adoption.

From work at the smallest scale it has been tempting to pass to the other extreme and see if the same set of concepts can be used as one tries to survey diffusion of innovation over a whole continent, and if the simulation approach still seems promising as a predictive device. This will be tried in the following discussion. For the much larger area the same procedure will be followed as before: involving, on the one hand, investigations of information fields in order to find probabilities in the floating grid, and, on the other hand, a search for actual cases of spread.

Just as the farmers in the earlier case,

---

4. Hägerstrand, "A Monte Carlo Approach to Diffusion," *op. cit.*

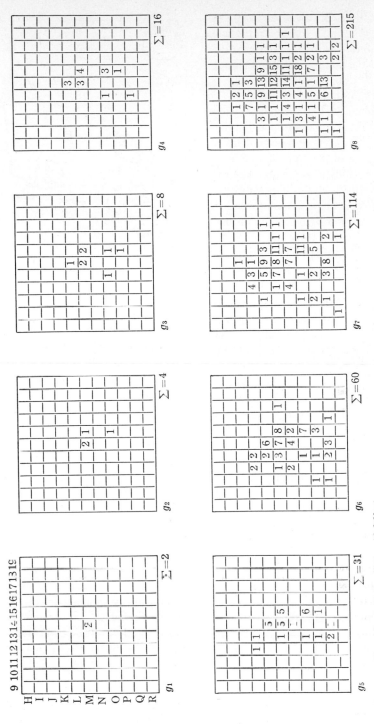

Figure 1. Hypothetical simulation of diffusion.

certain large groups of people can be handled as aggregates at the new scale, and perhaps with more justification. More difficult to investigate is the small but important part of the population which plays a leading role in political, industrial, scientific, and cultural affairs; people who to no small degree act as gate-keepers in relation to innovations. There is not much hope that the behavior of these people can be unveiled successfully in any direct way since actual observation is all but impossible. So one has in the first place to look for indirect means. A small set of such indirect means can be devised. One of these will be presented here. Work has only recently started, so the amount of information is still small.

Since the end of the nineteenth century certain circles in Europe have developed the custom of paying homage to colleagues and friends on birthdays or other occasions by issuing a kind of book which has come to be known as a *Festschrift*. A "tabula gratulatoria," containing names of subscriber-friends behind the enterprise, is in most cases attached to such a publication. Although these lists do not give clues to variations in frequency or intensity of contacts with other individuals, they nevertheless provide an inventory of specified links with the rest of the social network developed by an individual over his life-time. Of course, the lists cannot be entirely unbiased. Family-relations seem to be excluded in most cases. It is more probable that the lists are overcrowded and that many participants have only peripheral and infrequent relations to the congratulated individual. Be that as it may, these lists are too interesting as cross-sections of communication groupings to be left unused in our context.

A very large number of these publications are available in public libraries. Unfortunately, but not unexpectedly, academic people

Map 1. Distribution of "Festschrift" contributors.

dominate the lists; the most complete information available refers to a group which scarcely reflects the situation of individuals who are more politically and economically active. (In the collection of data the most extreme cases of exclusive university affiliation have been avoided.) A purely technical difficulty considerably hampers the use of some of this material: addresses are all too often missing. It is not impossible, but tedious, to fill the gaps with the aid of other sources; sometimes it is out of the question to establish the identity of individuals having common names.

A sample case with complete data is presented on Map 1. The cells of the grid have the size of 100×100 km. Figures in cells give the absolute number of *individuals* contained in the various information fields. Institutions and organizations have been omitted. The case chosen as an example refers to a *Festschrift* dedicated to a Stockholm journalist and politician.[5]

5. Other cases examined include: (1) Politician and leader of the Cooperative Movement, Stockholm; (2) Politician, Stockholm; (3) Novelist, Stockholm; (4) Politician, Copenhagen; (7) Econo-

Two thirds of the total distribution of contributors are concentrated in the Stockholm area. Next in rank, but very far behind, comes the second urban area of Sweden (Goteborg, with sixteen contributors). For the rest, scattered contacts are found almost all over the country. The friction of distance seems to come out strongly, with very few contacts evident in the northern regions. Beyond the national borders we note some connections in surrounding capitals (Oslo 2, Copenhagen 3, Helsinki 2, London 1, Paris 1).

The range of the information fields with respect to this type of data is far greater than was found earlier among the rural population. On the other hand there are strong limiting factors. The national borders practically always appear as such ones exerting strong influences. Contacts abroad—when they exist at all—are mainly confined to capitals or other leading cities, and are largely restricted to neighboring countries.

Close to the home base, the friction of distance is very evident. The purely local area always contains the majority of contacts. Beyond this central peak, however, effects of distance are felt all through the national area. Friction effects of distance seem to be stronger for people living in provincial centers than for people living in capitals.

Better measurements need be made of the professional composition of the various groupings, relations to population density, urban structure, friction of distance, individual and spatial overlap, and so forth. Obviously many more cases are needed and other kinds of data have to be brought into the picture before types of mean information fields can be established. But what has been found appears to be sufficiently regular

mist, Bern; (8) Jurist and economist, Paris; (5) Civil servant, Ostersund.

to make further work promising. The next step will be to follow a recent case of diffusion of innovation through Europe.

It is extremely difficult to find with a limited amount of work good examples of innovations which can be followed over an area comprising several countries. In particular this is the case with innovations which are really important from a technical, economical or cultural point of view. One reason is that statistical accounts so seldom are internationally uniform or broken down into sufficient local detail. Therefore, as a rule one has to build upon primary sources and accept what can be found.

One type of cultural element which is very often documented in complete registers for nations is social organizations and movements. Sometimes one can even find international registers of this kind. The spread of one such movement will be demonstrated here: Rotary International. We are not interested in this movement *per se* but will use it as a trace element for finding out about the function of social communication in diffusion of innovation.

The Rotary movement is too well known to make a closer presentation of purpose and local organization necessary. Some notes on the early history though are in order. The first Rotary club was constituted in Chicago in 1905. Very soon similar clubs were formed in other cities of the United States and Canada. As of 1911 one club existed in Dublin and one in London. The movement spread rapidly in the British Isles, and, after World War 1, pioneering clubs came into being in continental Europe.

A series of maps have been designed to illustrate the subsequent course of diffusion on the Continent and in northern Africa through 1950. The figures shown on the maps are cumulative. They give the sum total of clubs organized from the beginning and up through stated years. Some defi-

Map 2. Diffusion of Rotary clubs, Europe, 1922.

ciencies may exist in the eastern parts of
Europe since it has not so far been possible
to check whether some clubs which have

Map 4. Diffusion of Rotary clubs, Europe, 1924.

now disappeared may have existed in these
areas before World War II.

The innovation was introduced in a set of

Map 3. Diffusion of Rotary clubs, Europe, 1923.

Map 5. Diffusion of Rotary clubs, Europe, 1925.

Map 6. Diffusion of Rotary clubs, Europe, 1927.

Map 8. Diffusion of Rotary clubs, Europe, 1935.

big cities facing Great Britain: Paris, Amsterdam, Copenhagen and Oslo. Very soon the neighborhood effect manifested itself

around Amsterdam at the same time as a somewhat shapeless secondary cluster developed in the region of North Italy—South

Map 7. Diffusion of Rotary clubs, Europe, 1930.

Map 9. Diffusion of Rotary clubs, Europe, 1940.

Map 10. Diffusion of Rotary clubs, Europe, 1945.

France (Genova, Milano, Lyon, Toulouse). From this beginning a spatial pattern was imprinted which is discernible over as long a

Map 11. Diffusion of Rotary clubs, Europe, 1950.

time period as is covered by this series of vaps. Thus in 1927 we observe three separate clusters of adoptions: one generated around the axis Copenhagen-Oslo, a second around Amsterdam and a third along the Alps. Through outward spread step by step and a simultaneous inner condensation, bridges gradually developed between these centers at the same time as they kept their quantitative leadership.

A closer analysis shows that the spread along the initial "frontier" is led through the urban hierarchy. The point of introduction in a new country is its primate city; sometimes some other metropolis. Then centers next in rank follow. Soon, however, this order is broken up and replaced by one where the neighborhood effect dominates over the pure size succession. Illustrative of what then happens is the regular northward procession in the Scandinavian countries.

The more precise relation between time of adoption and size of city (Sweden to 1950) is shown in Table 1. Adoptions are taken in order in groups of ten (columns). All towns in the country have also been ordered according to size of population (1935) and divided into groups of tens (rows). Figures in cells then give the number of adopters. As is seen a strong correlation between city-size and order of adoption comes out only in the beginning of the spread. The relationship of the diffusion process to the urban hierarchy requires further analysis but there is a strong case for the belief that cities of high rank are also in close communication through a multitude of private links which skip over lower order places in between.

Noting only the situation at time t_n in relation to time t_{n+1} and leaving scale out of consideration gives the impression of a pattern of growth which is not fundamentally different from what we could observe in the very small scale when some

Table 1 Adoption of Rotary Clubs, Swedish Towns, by Size, to 1950

		Population, Swedish Towns in Order of Rank (1935)												
		35,000	20,000	15,000	12,000	9,500	8,000	6,000	5,800	4,500	3,500	2,900	2,000	Other Localities
		1–10	11–20	21–30	31–40	41–50	51–60	61–70	71–80	81–90	91–100	101–110	111–120	121–130
1932	1–10	7	2	1										
1935	11–20	2	5	1	1					1				
1936	21–30	1	1	1	2	1	3	1						
1938	31–40			1	3	1	1	1	1	1		1		1
1945	41–50			1	2					2		4		1
1946	51–60		2	1			1	1	1	3			1	
1947	61–70					1		1	1		2	1	2	2
1948	71–80		1				1	1	2	1	2	1		1
1949	81–90				1		1	2	1	1				4
1950	91–96				1			1	2	1				5
	Non-adopter	–	1	2	2	3	2	2	3	2	6	3	7	9

innovation is spreading in the farming community. It does not seem to be entirely out of place to consider the run of the simulation presented in the first graph as still valid, provided modifications are included which take care of (1) the new scale, (2) urban hierarchies, and (3) the barriers which national boundaries sometimes form.

At this preliminary stage we can only consider in a very general way whether the cases of information fields discussed earlier from the European scene and the course of our ease of diffusion are in keeping with each other. Verification has to await a fuller picture of communication probabilities.

It is obvious, however, that there is good correspondence in scale between information fields and the spread. Further against the background of the information fields it is reasonable to find that innovations coming from abroad get their first adopters in capitals or other bigger cities. An innovator in, say, Copenhagen, who has international contacts at all, is likely to have them in such places as Oslo, Bergen, Goteborg, Stockholm and Helsinki.

Also the leading cities within a country should give impulses first of all to towns next in rank. The further spread is then heavily regulated by distance friction; strong ties of the major towns with the capital over a rather long distance occur; then local influence is exerted on lower-order centers closer by.

⁂⁂⁂⁂⁂⁂⁂⁂⁂⁂⁂⁂⁂⁂⁂⁂

HIERARCHICAL DIFFUSION: THE BASIS OF DEVELOPMENTAL FILTERING AND SPREAD IN A SYSTEM OF GROWTH CENTERS

Brian J. L. Berry

"Growth," wrote Perroux in 1955, "does not appear universally at any one time but manifests itself at points or poles of growth . . . and diffuses through the economy in definite channels." Growth cannot, in this view, be separated from the diffusion of innovations, a process involving the "acceptance over time of some specific idea or practice by individuals, groups or other adopting units linked to specific channels of communication, to a social structure, and to a given system of values of culture." [1]

In this paper I try to expand upon Perroux's original notion, arguing that the role played by growth centers in regional development is a particular case of the general process of innovation diffusion, and therefore that the sadly deficient "theory" of growth centers [2] can be enriched by turning to the better-developed general case. In particular, I argue that growth centers' developmental role involves the simultaneous *filtering* down of the innovations that bring growth down through the urban hierarchy and the *spreading* of the benefits accruing from the resulting growth, both nationally

1. Elihu Katz, Martin L. Levin, and Herbert Hamilton, "Traditions of Research in the Diffusion of Innovations," *American Sociological Review*, Vol. 28 (1963), pp. 237-52.

2. Vida Nichols, *Growth Poles: An Investigation of Their Potential as a Tool for Regional Economic Development*. Philadelphia: Regional Science Research Institute Discussion Paper No. 30, 1969.

from core to hinterland regions, and within these regions from their metropolitan centers outwards to the intermetropolitan periphery. Regional inequities arise in this scheme because the income effect of a given innovation is a declining function of time and is also subject to a threshold limitation—a minimum size of region—beyond which diffusion will not proceed. As a consequence, the lowest levels of welfare are found in areas peripheral to small urban centers in outlying hinterland regions.

A MODEL OF THE HIERARCHICAL DIFFUSION PROCESS: DERIVATION AND PROOFS

Previous attempts to model the hierarchical diffusion process have been made by Boon,[3] Hudson,[4] and Pedersen[5] following earlier suggestions by Bowers,[6] McVoy,[7] Hägerstrand,[8] Crain,[9] Friedmann,[10] and

3. Françoise Boon, *A Simple Model for the Diffusion of an Innovation in an Urban System.* Chicago: Center for Urban Studies, University of Chicago, 1967.
4. John C. Hudson, "Diffusion in a Central Place System," *Geographical Analysis,* Vol. 1 (1969), pp. 45-58.
5. Poul Ove Pedersen, "Innovation Diffusion within and Between National Urban Systems," *Geographical Analysis,* Vol. 2 (1970), pp. 203-54.
6. Raymond V. Bowers, "The Direction of Intra-Societal Diffusion," *American Sociological Review,* Vol. 2, (1937), pp. 826-36.
7. Edgar C. McVoy, "Patterns of Diffusion in the United States," *American Sociological Review,* Vol. 5 (1940), pp. 219-27.
8. Torsten Hägerstrand, *Innovation Diffusion as a Spatial Process.* Chicago: University of Chicago Press, 1953, 1967.
9. Robert L. Crain, "Fluoridation: The Diffusion of an Innovation among Cities," *Social Forces,* Vol. 44 (1966), pp. 467-76.
10. John Friedmann, *Regional Development Policy: A Case Study of Venezuela.* Cambridge: The M.I.T. Press, 1966.

Thompson.[11] In this paper we build upon these contributions, drawing together and extending the insights they provide by focusing on models that involve probability maximizing assumptions, and by linking national spread and hierarchical diffusion of growth opportunities from one urban center to another to the spread effects within urban fields that arise from the use households make of these opportunities. Thus, at the broader scale we are concerned with what Pedersen[12] terms "entrepreneurial innovations," i.e. those innovations which, when applied, have direct consequences for people other than the adopter (which may be a person, a business, a city, or some other institutional unit), whereas the spread effects within urban fields involve "household innovations" whose immediate impact is only on the adopting unit (usually the person or the family). Regional growth always involves both types of innovation, in that it depends upon diffusion of the growth opportunity on the one hand and the utilization of the opportunity by potential beneficiaries on the other.

The Urban System

The first step is to characterize the urban system in which the entrepreneurial innovations take place. In what follows we use a rank-size distribution of cities as the most relevant model of the urban system against which to study the innovation diffusion processes, because it is the most probable distribution. When innovations filter downward in the ranks of centers, we will term the process *hierarchical filtering.* However,

11. Wilbur Thompson, "Internal and External Factors in the Deveopment of Urban Economies," in H. S. Perloff and L. Wingo (eds.), *Issues in Urban Economics.* Baltimore: The Johns Hopkins Press, for Resources for the Future, Inc., 1968.
12. Poul Ove Pedersen, *op cit.*

one requirement of using such a model should be noted: the diffusion process should be one which leads to equal expectations of population growth in all centers above some threshold. Hence, any regional inequities can only arise because the income effect imparted by a given innovation decreases in time while the growth of population proceeds steadily.

The Diffusion Process

Several possible reasons for hierarchical filtering can be posited,[13] among them a "market-searching" process in which an expanding industry exploits market opportunities in a larger-to-smaller sequence,[14] a "trickle-down" process in which an activity faced with rising wage rates in larger cities moves to smaller cities in search of cheaper labor,[15] an "imitation" process in which entrepreneurs in smaller centers mimic the actions of those in larger cities,[16] or a simple probability mechanism in which the probability of adoption depends upon the chance that a potential entrepreneur residing in a given town will learn of the innovation, a probability which declines with size of town.[17] Any or all of these reasons would result in a pure model of hierarchical diffusion in which the innovation potential varies directly with city size.

In other words, the innovation potential of a center is a product of its position in the

urban hierarchy, and the force exerted on it by centers that have already adopted the innovation (recall that in physics, energy is $(GM_i M_j)/s_{ij}$ whereas force is $(GM_i M_j)/s^2_{ij}$). Therefore, looking back at an entire diffusion sequence, adoption time should be a function of the product of hierarchical position and population potential.

To rephrase the conclusion, the innovation potential of a center is a function of its own rank in the urban hierarchy, and the force exerted on it by virtue of its location relative to the other centers in the hierarchy that have already adopted the innovation.

Household Innovation. The most probable time that an innovation becomes available to the households within an urban region therefore depends upon the functional location of the urban center within the hierarchy of towns and its geographic location or centrality within the force field of innovative potentials arising from general access to information provided by the early adopters. After the town has adopted, a logistic spatial-temporal trend may be postulated for the utilization of the innovation by households within its field of influence:[18]

$$y(t, s) = 1/[1 + \exp. (a_0 + a_1 s + a_2 s^2 + b_0 t + b_1 st + b_2 s^2 t)]$$

where the a's and b's are parameters, t is time and s is the effective distance that a household resides from the urban center. "Effective distance" may, of course, be expressed in a variety of ways, but whatever the particular expression, a wavelike process of household innovation is therefore envisaged, and at any moment the spatial pattern of relative use of the innovation by people living within an urban region will be a negative exponential function of this effec-

13. Edwin Mansfield, *The Economics of Technological Change.* New York: W. W. Norton and Co., 1968; Mansfield, Edwin, *Industrial Research and Technological Innovation.* New York: W. W. Norton and Co., 1968.
14. Chauncy D. Harris, "The Market as a Factor in the Localization of Industry in the United States," *Annals, Association of American Geographers,* Vol. 44 (1954), pp. 315-48.
15. Wilbur Thompson, *op. cit.*
16. Poul Ove Pedersen, *op. cit.*
17. John C. Hudson, *op. cit.*

18. E. Casetti and R. K. Semple, "Concerning the Testing of Spatial Diffusion Hypotheses," *Geographical Analysis,* Vol. 1 (1969), pp. 254-59.

tive distance from the urban center.[19] Again, it is relatively easy to demonstrate that the negative exponential is a maximally-probable state.[20]

EMPIRICAL VERIFICATION: DIFFUSION OF TELEVISION STATIONS AND MARKET PENETRATION BY THE TELEVISION INDUSTRY IN THE UNITED STATES, 1940-1968.

The concepts outlined above are clearly borne out by the evidence on diffusion of television stations and progressively greater market penetration by the television industry in the United States in the years 1940-68. This joint process of entrepreneurial and household innovation was characterized, quite clearly, by a combination of hierarchical diffusion and spread effects.

Three cities opened TV stations on the eve of the Second World War (New York, Chicago, and Philadelphia), but there was a wartime cessation of activity. Another 58 cities opened stations in the years 1947-50, but again diffusion was ended for two years by an FCC-ordered freeze during the Korean

war. In the two years following Korea, 144 cities opened stations for the first time. By 1958 complete national coverage had been obtained, and thereafter only 10 more cities opened their first TV stations. Allowing for the two periods of war, the time-path of the entrepreneurial innovation was logistic (Figure 1-solid line actual, dotted line a perfect logistic). Moreover, it was essentially hierarchical; the smaller the city, the later the opening of its TV station, as Figure 2 clearly reveals. Figure 2 displays other things too. For example, the greater density of points immediately following the Korean war unmistakably shows that the FCC-imposed wartime freeze simply postponed openings of TV stations that would normally have occurred between 1950 and 1952, and

19. Brian J. L. Berry, *Growth Centers and Their Potentials in the Upper Great Lakes Region.* Washington, D. C.: Upper Great Lakes Regional Commission, 1969; Lawrence A. Brown, *Diffusion Processes and Location.* Philadelphia: Regional Science Research Institute, Bibliography Series No. 4, 1968: Lawrence A. Brown, *Diffusion Dynamics*, Lund Studies in Geography, Series B, Human Geography, No. 29, 1968; Torsten Hägerstrand, *op. cit.*
20. M. J. H. Mogridge, "Some Factors Influencing the Income Distribution of Households within a City Region," in A. J. Scott (ed.), *Studies in Regional Science.* London: Pion Limited, 1969, pp. 117-42.

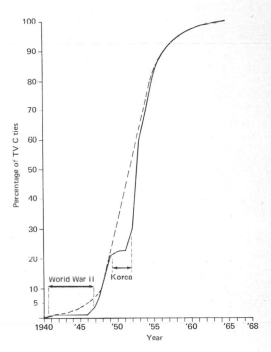

Figure 1. Logistic increase in number of TV cities, 1940-68. Solid line is actual pattern, affected by two periods of war. Dotted line is the imputed smooth logistic trends.

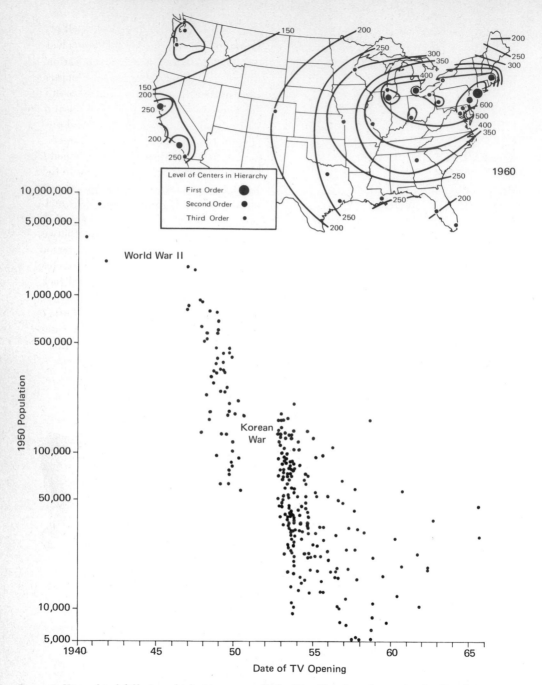

Figure 2. Hierarchical diffusion of television among U. S. cities. Note how the greater density of occurrences immediately following the Korean war reveals the delaying effect of the FCC embargo on new stations during the war. *Inset:* the uppermost three levels of the U.S. urban hierarchy occupy the most central locations in the country, as defined by population potentials.

therefore that in the absence of the war the actual time-sequence of adoptions would have been closer to a perfect logistic trend.

Similarly, market penetration (measured by the percentage of households innovating) progressed in the manner predicted. Satisfactory national data on the spread of TV ownership are unavailable for the first seven years following the Second World War, although we do know that in 1946 only 6,500 television sets were produced, increasing to 178,000 in 1947, 867,000 in 1948, and that production exceeded a million sets annually thereafter. We have to pick up the process in 1953, just as the Korean embargo was lifted, using the industry's estimates of "TV households."[21]

Figure 3 shows the pattern of market

---

21. A. C. Nielsen Co., *T. V.: Households by Regions, States and Counties*, 1953, 1956, 1959.

penetration in 1953. At that time all of the nation's highest-order urban centers had opened TV stations. Market penetration declined with distance from these centers, and was uniformly high in the zones of highest population potentials (Fig. 1—inset map). Large areas of the country remained unserved. Interestingly, all of those larger American cities that have never opened their own television stations are located in these zones of fairly rapid complete initial market penetration of the yet-larger nearby metropoli—Fall River, Lawrence, Bridgeport, New London, Norwalk, Stamford, etc., between Boston and New York; Newark, Paterson, and Trenton in New Jersey; Canton, etc. in Ohio; Ann Arbor, Battle Creek, and Jackson in Michigan; Kenosha and Racine between Chicago and Milwaukee; Council Bluffs on the doorstep of Omaha; and similar cases in other parts of the country. In part, this

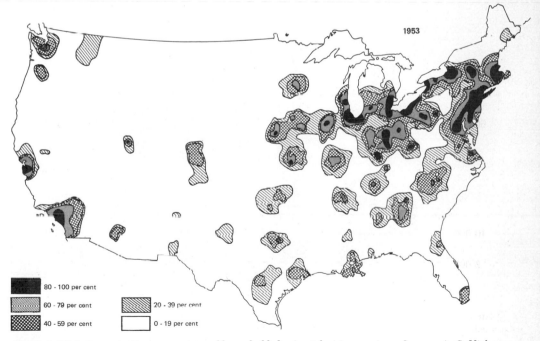

Figure 3. Market penetration: percentage of households having television receivers. Source: A. C. Nielsen, 1953.

reflects federal licensing policies, but these policies in turn simply codify the fact that the higher order neighbors of these non-adopting cities adopted earlier and achieved such a degree of market domination that they forestalled any entrepreneurial innovation by nearby smaller centers.

By 1956 the combination of further station openings and increased market penetration by stations in existing cities (most of which added second, third, and more stations and increased their effective radiated power) had led to coverage of all but the least-populated parts of the country (Fig. 4). Zones of high penetration stood out in the national heartland of the manufacturing belt and in California. The areas with the lowest degrees of household innovation were,

broadly speaking, the zones of lowest national market access (compare with Fig. 2—inset map).

Complete national coverage was achieved in 1958-59 (Fig. 5), and the diffusion dynamics were such that the time necessary for geographic spread to make television available for all households in the country was also sufficient for near-complete market penetration to be achieved throughout the north and in California. Three years later (Fig. 6), market penetration had increased apace, and only the relatively poor and more inaccessible parts of the South, the Rio Grande valley and the mountainous West displayed substantially lower degrees of TV ownership, a pattern remaining, although to a lesser degree, in 1965 (Fig. 7).

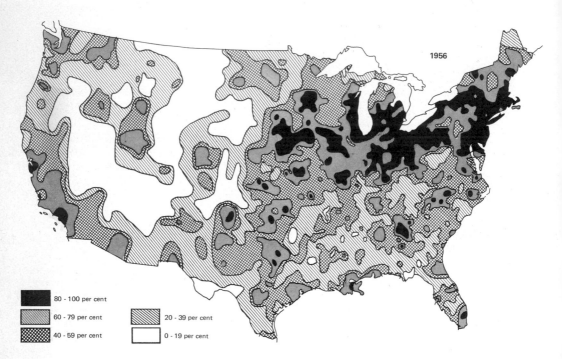

1956

80 - 100 per cent

60 - 79 per cent   20 - 39 per cent

40 - 59 per cent   0 - 19 per cent

Figure 4. Market penetration: percentage of households having television receivers. Source: A. C. Nielsen, 1956.

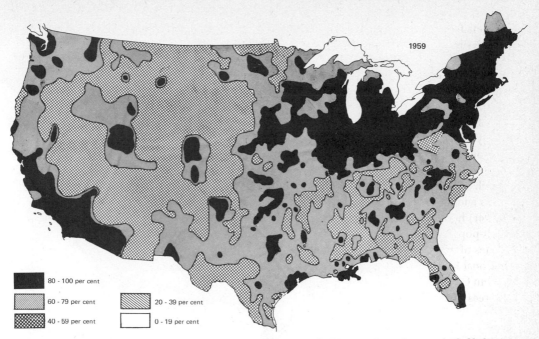

■ 80 - 100 per cent	
▨ 60 - 79 per cent	▧ 20 - 39 per cent
▩ 40 - 59 per cent	□ 0 - 19 per cent

Figure 5. Market penetration: percentage of households having television receivers. Source: A. C. Nielsen, 1959.

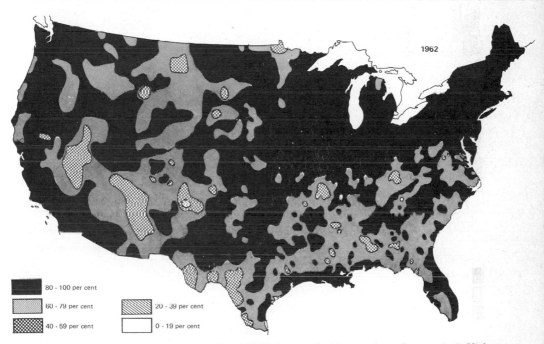

■ 80 - 100 per cent	
▨ 60 - 79 per cent	▧ 20 - 39 per cent
▩ 40 - 59 per cent	□ 0 - 19 per cent

Figure 6. Market penetration: percentage of households having television receivers. Source: A. C. Nielsen, 1962.

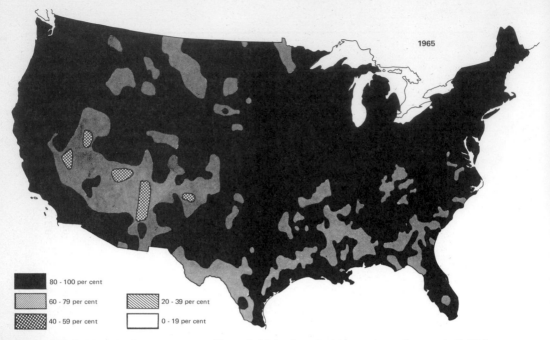

Figure 7. Market penetration: percentage of households having television receivers. Source: A. C. Nielsen, 1965.

80 - 100 per cent

60 - 79 per cent   20 - 39 per cent

40 - 59 per cent   0 - 19 per cent

Models of the Entrepreneurial Innovation

That diffusion of television stations among American cities was largely hierarchical is clearly borne out by statistical analysis. Taking the cities with TV stations (270 in all) as the observations, and the date at which the first TV station in each city began broadcasting as the dependent variable, a variety of regression equations consistent with the models developed earlier were estimated, some of which are reported in Table 1.

Three alternative measures of city size of status of urban centers in the hierarchy were examined: city population in 1950, essentially at the beginning of the process; city population in 1960, toward the end; and a multivariate index of the functional size of urban centers in the hierarchy developed in a study of the latent structure of the American urban system.[22] Additionally, two measures of accessibility were input: population potentials in 1950, as an index of national market access; and the population of the labor market or functional economic area dominated by the urban center,[23] as an index of local access. Experimentation also showed that the diffusion proceeded more rapidly than expected into the oilfield areas of the Southwest (where, presumably, more risk capital was available) and into those "outer rim" sections of the nation where the foreign-born population was greatest, but was retarded in college towns where the size

22. Brian J. L. Berry, "Latent Structure of the American Urban System," in Berry (ed.), *Classification of Cities: New Methods and Evolving Uses.* San Francisco: Chandler Publishing Co., 1970.
23. Brian J. L. Berry, *op. cit.,* 1969.

Table 1 Diffusion of Television Stations Among U.S. Cities

Independent Variable		Dependent Variables							
TV Opening Date		Measures of City Size			Size of Dependent Area	City Characteristics			General Accessibility
$x = 53.548$ $S_x = 3.471$		Functional Size in Urban Hierarchy (Factor 1)[4]	Log. Population 1969	Log. Population 1950	Log. FEA Population	Mining Base (Factor 13)[4]	College Towns (Factor 6)[4]	Foreign Born Population (Factor 7)[4]	Log. Population Potential 1950
Model									
1. $R^2 = .565$	b[1]	−1.752	—	—	—	0.752	0.323	−0.341	—
	S_b[2]	0–113	—	—	—	0.185	0.144	0.186	—
	$r*$[3]	−0.687	—	—	—	0.242	0.136	−0.112	—
2. $R^2 = .619$	b	−1.028	—	—	−2.652	0.459	0.436	−0.324	—
	S_b	0.159	—	—	0.433	0.180	0.136	0.175	—
	$r*$	−0.369	—	—	−0.352	0.155	0.193	−0.113	—
3. $R^2 = 0.559$	b	—	—	—	−4.731	0.420	0.542	−0.384	—
	S_b	—	—	—	0.311	0.193	0.145	0.187	—
	$r*$	—	—	—	−0.682	0.133	0.223	−0.125	—
4. $R^2 = 0.599$	b	—	−2.927	—	−1.795	0.517	0.471	−0.285	—
	S_b	—	0.531	—	0.655	0.186	0.140	0.180	—
	$r*$	—	−0.296	—	−0.167	0.169	0.203	−0.097	—
5. $R^2 = 0.587$	b	—	−4.347	—	—	0.645	0.424	−0.258	—
	S_b	—	0.258	—	—	0.182	0.140	0.182	—
	$r*$	—	−0.706	—	—	0.213	0.182	−0.087	—
6. $R^2 = 0.604$	b	—	—	−3.231	−1.522	0.301	0.476	−0.287	—
	S_b	—	—	0.598	0.663	0.185	0.139	0.179	—
	$r*$	—	—	−0.316	−0.140	0.100	0.207	−0.098	—
7. $R^2 = 0.596$	b	—	—	−4.458	—	0.322	0.441	−0.267	—
	S_b	—	—	0.269	—	0.186	0.139	0.180	—
	$r*$	—	—	−0.714	—	0.106	0.191	−0.091	—

Table 1   Diffusion of Television Stations Among U.S. Cities

Independent Variable	Dependent Variables							
	Size of Dependent Area				City Characteristics			General Accessibility
TV Opening Date	Measures of City Size							
	Functional Size in Urban Hierarchy (Factor 1)[4]	Log. Population 1960	Log. Population 1950	Log. FEA Population	Mining Base (Factor 13)[4]	College Towns (Factor 6)[4]	Foreign Born Population (Factor 7)[4]	Log. Population Potential 1950
x = 53.548								
S_x = 3.471								
8. R^2 = 0.596 b	—	—	− 4.406	—	0.283	0.448	− 0.227	− 0.334
S_b	—	—	0.305	—	0.216	0.140	0.182	0.941
r*	—	—	− 0.663	—	0.081	0.192	− 0.093	− 0.022
9. Log. TV Opening date b	—	—	− 0.036	—	0.002	0.003	− 0.002	− 0.004
S_b	—	—	0.002	—	0.001	0.001	0.001	0.007
R^2 = 0.618 r*	—	—	− 0.675	—	0.086	0.183	− 0.104	− 0.036

1. b = metric regression coefficient.
2. S_b = standard error of b.
3. r* = partial correlation of independent variable with dependent-stepwise model.
4. Berry (1970 b).

of town is greater than the effective television market because of the student population and because in the earlier years of television there was greater resistance to the medium by those of higher educational levels. Therefore, three indices of those factors[24] were retained in the regression models. A variety of other variables showed no significant relationship to the diffusion sequence, among them the growth rate of the cities 1950-60, the socio-economic status and stage in life-cycle of the town's residents, the principal features of the town's economic base, etc.

As Table 1 shows, there are few differences in the power of the alternative models resulting from different combinations of these variables. City population at the beginning of the process in 1950 gives slightly better fits than the data for 1960 on the multivariate index, which is a satisfying verification of the gravity formulation. The measure of local access splits the variance attributable to size alone, and its inclusion improves the regression estimates only slightly, suggesting that city population provides an approximately proportional estimate of market size. Population potentials do not make a significant addition to the power of the model, however, confirming that the diffusion pattern graphed in

Figure 2 is largely hierarchical in nature. But this is not unexpected since, as seen in the inset to Figure 2, the highest order centers occupy and in fact create the zones of highest population potentials and greatest national market access. Thus, if model 8 is solved for a range of population sizes and potentials, assuming that the three other variables take their average values of zero [the indices are orthonormal, [25] so the equation is Opening date = 76.26 - 4.406 (Log. 1950 Population) -0.334 (Log. of 1950 Population Potentials)] the expected innovation dates are as indicated in Table 2. Potentials force at most a nine-month delay on the entrepreneurial innovation process, whereas the expectation is that a center of the lowest level in the hierarchy above the adoption threshold will lag more than thirteen years behind the nation's largest metropoli. This span coincides with the post-World War II years in which all but nine of the nation's TV cities installed their stations.

Models of the Household Innovation

Earlier, we suggested that, given an available entrepreneurial innovation, the individual innovation sequence should be wavelike, increasing in time outwards from cities according to effective distance from these cities. Therefore, in our first attempt to

24. Brian J. L. Berry, op. cit., 1970.

25. Brian J. L. Berry, op. cit., 1970.

Table 2   Expected Innovation Dates for Cities of Different Sizes and Varying Population Potentials

City Size	Population Potentials			
	10,000	100,000	1,000,000	10,000,000
10,000,000	1944.082	1943.748	1943.416	1943.080
1,000,000	1948.488	1948.154	1947.820	1947.486
100,000	1952.894	1952.560	1952.226	1951.892
10,000	1957.300	1956.966	1956.632	1956.298
1,000	1961.706	1961.372	1961.038	1960.704

model household innovations we took as independent variables the percentage of households with TV in 1953, 1956, 1959, 1962, and 1965, computed for each of the 3100+ counties in the United States, and regressed them in turn on the broadcasting start date of the TV cities serving as the centers of the Designated Television Market Areas to which the counties belonged [26] and two measures of local access. The first of these local access measures was the percentage of workers resident in the country who commuted to the TV city to work each day, selected as a nationally meaningful standard for comparing locally variable accessibility conditions, because the intensity of commuting tends to drop off negative exponentially with effective distance (refer back to equation 39). The second measure used was population potentials, because it was noted that in zones of high potentials local communications access is high even where local commuting may be limited. Thus, the commuting area of Newark, N. J., for example, remains tied closely via the mass media to New York City.

The five resulting three-variable regressions are called Model 1 in Table 3. They are augmented by the rate of population change 1950-60 to form the five Model 2 equations, since it was thought that household diffusion might proceed more rapidly in areas of growth than in relatively stagnant or declining areas. Of course, a variety of other considerations might be introduced, and therefore Table 3 also contains more elaborate equations designated Model 3 (actually selected from a large set of more extensive regression estimates). These Model 3 equations are extended to include income and family size data because, looking at the U.S. Census

data on TV ownership in 1950, Dernberg, Rosetti, and Watts,[27] in an earlier statistical study of market penetration, concluded that the ownership of TV sets was directly related in 1950 to the length of time TV had been available and the extent of TV station coverage of the country. They found ownership to be directly related to income up to a 1950 figure of $7,000.00, and inversely thereafter; holding average income constant it was inversely related to the dispersion of income except in very low income areas. Finally, they found ownership to be highest where educational levels were, on the average, 10-12 years, and to be lower for higher and lower levels of education. To extend the Dernberg findings, we decided to add variables measuring the median and tails of the income distribution to our model, as well as median age (the tails of the age distribution were not statistically significant), race, and whether or not the TV city was identified by Nielsen as a smaller satellite in a Designated Market Area that had a larger TV city located within it. Other variables initially included but later dropped for lack of statistical significance were educational levels (the effect is already included in the TV start date), occupational characteristics, and a variety of other summary dimensions of county characteristics.[28]

As is to be seen in Table 3, Model 3 is more powerful than Model 2, and this is in turn more powerful than Model 1, in every year studied, but the power of each model declines year by year from 1953 to 1965, as market penetration proceeds and the county-to-county variance expressed in the dependent variable is progressively reduced, the range being 100 per cent in 1953 but only 25 per cent in 1965.

26. A. C. Nielsen Co., *Designated Market Areas 1967-68*, 1967-68.

27. T. Dernberg, R. Rosetti, and H. Watts, *Studies in Household Consumer Behavior*. New Haven, Conn.: Yale University Press, 1958.
28. Brian J. L. Berry, *op. cit.*, 1970.

Table 3 Diffusion of Television Sets Among U.S. Households

Independent Variable		TV Start Date	Log. Pct. Workers Population Potential	Population Commuting to City	Change 1960/1950	Median Income	Pct. with >$9999	Pct. with <$3000	Median Age	Log. Pct. Nonwhite	Satellite TV City
A. Market Penetration, 1953											
Model											
1. $R^2 = 0.586$	b^1	−2.66	0.00003	6.423							
	S_b^2	0.094	0.000003	0.556							
	r^{*3}	−0.564	0.448	0.203							
2. $R^2 = 0.601$	b	−3.489	0.0008	4.825	11.092						
	S_b	0.095	0.000003	0.565	1.026						
	r^*	−0.547	0.465	0.151	0.191						
3. $R^2 = 0.633$	b	−3.15	0.000085	3.265	2.704	Deleted by Regression	0.546	−0.156	0.342	1.352	Deleted by Regression
	S_b	0.094	0.000003	0.560	1.153		0.071	0.034	0.080	0.525	
	r^*	−0.513	0.482	0.104	0.042		0.138	−0.121	0.077	0.046	
B. Market Penetration, 1956											
Model											
1. $R^2 = 0.430$	b	−2.033	0.000064	9.800							
	S_b	0.096	0.000003	0.557							
	r^*	−0.354	0.367	0.301							
2. $R^2 = 0.446$	b	−1.881	0.000067	8.383	9.833						
	S_b	0.096	0.000003	0.569	1.033						
	r^*	−0.330	0.382	0.256	0.169						
3. $R^2 = 0.549$	b	−1.381	0.000065	7.358	3.706	Deleted by Regression	Deleted by Regression	−0.229	0.834	−18.039	
	S_b	0.090	0.000003	0.525	1.051			0.019	0.075	1.285	
	r^*	−0.265	0.406	0.244	0.063			−0.202	0.194	−0.245	

Dependent Variables[4]

Table 3 Diffusion of Television Sets Among U.S. Households

Independent Variable		TV Start Date	Log. Pct. Workers Population Potential	Population Commuting to City	Change 1960/1950	Median Income	Pct. with >$9999	Pct. with <$3000	Median Age	Log. Pct. Nonwhite	Satellite TV City
C. Market Penetration, 1959											
Model											
1. R² = 0.311	b	-1.292	0.000034	7.215							
	Sb	0.079	0.000002	0.463							
	r*	-0.280	0.274	0.270							
2. R² = 0.327	b	-1.186	0.000035	6.173	7.413						
	Sb	0.079	0.000002	0.473	0.856						
	r*	-0.258	0.284	0.228	0.154						
3. R² = 0.505	b	-0.653	0.000036	5.282	2.127	Deleted	Deleted	-0.215	0.659	-1.897	-23.059
	Sb	0.071	0.000002	0.414	0.830	by	by	0.015	0.059	0.393	1.015
	r*	-0.162	0.302	0.223	0.046	Regression	Regression	-0.239	0.194	-0.086	-0.378
D. Market Penetration, 1962											
Model											
1. R² = 0.040	b	-0.445	0.00001	5.495							
	Sb	0.121	0.000003	0.705							
	r*	-0.066	0.056	0.138							
2. R² = 0.058	b	-0.298	0.000012	4.058	10.233						
	Sb	0.121	0.000003	0.722	1.308						
	r*	-0.044	0.064	0.100	0.139						
3. R² = 0.167	b	-0.249	0.00001	3.023	Deleted	Deleted	0.399	-0.215	0.463	-2.484	-20.428
	Sb	0.121	0.000003	0.697	by	by	0.085	0.027	1.100	0.646	1.700
	r*	0.037	0.054	0.078	Regression	Regression	0.084	-0.138	0.083	-0.069	-0.211

Dependent Variables[4]

E. *Market Penetration, 1965*

Model

1. R² = 0.066	b	−0.174	0.000012	3.532						
	Sb	0.067	0.000002	0.392						
	r*	−0.046	0.160	0.122						
2. R² = 0.332	b	−0.338	0.000013	2.236	Deleted by Regression	Deleted by Regression	−0.193	0.324	−2.493	−21.302
	Sb	0.060	0.000002	0.345			0.011	0.050	0.325	0.857
	r*	−0.101	0.133	0.115			−0.282	−0.136	−0.136	−0.408

1. b = metric regression coefficient.
2. Sb = standard error of b.
3. r* = partial correlation of independent variable with dependent-stepwise model.
4. 1950 census data for 1953 and 1956 analyses, 1960 data for 1959; 1962 and 1965.

In 1953, TV start date is clearly of the greatest importance, along with potentials (confirming the value of the gravity formulation in looking at household innovations also). Household adoption declines with distance from the TV city, is greater in growing high-income areas, and is retarded in low-income communities and where age levels are lower.

The findings are similar in 1956, although start date and potentials have declined in importance, local access has increased, the high-income variable is no longer statistically significant (presumably, because penetration in such areas is relatively complete), but lower penetration in low-income areas and in counties with substantial non-white populations is more marked. In addition, a significantly lower degree of market penetration by the outlying satellite TV cities is revealed.

The same findings apply in all succeeding years, and by the mid-sixties the effects of the variables originally most significant in moulding the household diffusion process (TV start date, potentials, local access) though still statistically significant, have been surpassed in importance because of the universally high levels of market penetration in the nation by those variables which identify the "hold-out" zones of lowest market penetration. These are areas in which the proportion of the population with incomes less than $3,000 is greatest, where a greater part of the population is non-white, where more of the population is youthful, and where satellite TV cities are least effective in penetrating the market. In effect, Figures 6 and 7 pick out the regions of greatest rural poverty in the United States.

The changing nature of the pattern can be shown in other ways. Tables 4-7 record the transitions made by counties from one penetration category to another in each of the four-year time-spans. Clearly, the transition probabilities are not stable. Table 8

Table 4   Matrix of Transition Numbers from TV Diffusion Data, 1953–56

Per Cent of Families with TV in 1956	Per Cent of Families with TV in 1956									
	0–10	11–20	21–30	31–40	41–50	51–60	61–70	71–80	81–90	91–100
0–10	63	152	255	405	292	239	121	60	32	0
11–20	0	0	22	68	103	74	38	32	10	0
21–30	0	0	4	25	63	66	70	29	15	0
31–40	0	0	2	6	16	55	80	47	17	0
41–50	0	0	0	3	8	29	52	63	47	0
51–60	0	0	0	1	0	10	16	35	73	0
61–70	0	0	0	0	0	3	2	23	82	0
71–80	0	0	0	0	0	1	2	12	73	0
81–90	0	0	0	0	0	0	0	5	68	10
91–100	0	0	0	0	0	0	0	0	21	2

records the regression relationships among each successive pair of maps. Basically, one set of relationships holds until complete geographic coverage of the national market had been achieved, and a distinct shift in pattern develops thereafter. *This is consistent with the notion that an orderly wave-like process of household innovation follows from a hierarchical pattern of entrepreneurial innovation. Hierarchical diffusion extends down to some threshold, and then entrepreneurial innovation ceases. House-hold innovations continue until some saturation level is reached within all areas accessible to the hierarchy of places that have experienced entrepreneurial innovation. Remaining unserved are these areas peripheral to the adopting hierarchy.*

INCOME CHANGES ACCRUING FROM THE DIFFUSION SEQUENCE

It is not unreasonable to expect that adoption of an innovation will provide a

Table 5   Matrix of Transition Numbers from TV Diffusion Data, 1956–59

Per Cent of Families with TV in 1956	Per Cent of Families with TV in 1959									
	0–10	11–20	21–30	31–40	41–50	51–60	61–70	71–80	81–90	91–100
0–10	34	0	0	0	29	0	0	0	0	0
11–20	0	0	0	7	117	26	1	1	0	0
21–30	0	0	0	0	77	191	15	0	0	0
31–40	0	0	0	0	2	299	190	17	0	0
41–50	0	0	0	0	0	20	369	91	2	0
51–60	0	0	0	0	0	1	44	364	67	1
61–70	0	0	0	0	0	0	0	165	214	2
71–80	0	0	0	0	0	0	0	7	275	24
81–90	0	0	0	0	0	0	0	0	93	345
91–100	0	0	0	0	0	0	0	0	0	12

Table 6   Matrix of Transition Numbers from TV Diffusion Data, 1959–62

Per Cent of Families with TV in 1959	Per Cent of Families with TV in 1962									
	0–10	11–20	21–30	31–40	41–50	51–60	61–70	71–80	81–90	91–100
0–10	34	0	0	0	0	0	0	0	0	0
11–20	0	0	0	0	0	0	0	0	0	0
21–30	0	0	0	0	0	0	0	0	0	0
31–40	0	0	0	0	0	1	1	3	2	0
41–50	0	0	0	1	13	23	48	67	65	8
51–60	0	0	0	1	7	30	118	225	142	14
61–70	0	0	0	0	1	7	44	217	307	43
71–80	0	0	0	0	0	0	11	99	440	95
81–90	0	0	0	0	0	0	1	9	314	327
91–100	0	0	0	0	0	0	0	1	18	365

given employment and therefore population growth impetus to the adopting region,[29] and that if a succession of innovations diffuses down the urban hierarchy all regions benefitting will experience the same population growth rate, thus satisfying Gibrat's law, all regions below the smallest threshold will stagnate, and those regions lying in the range of sizes between the smallest and the greatest innovation thresholds will have

growth rates directly related to size. If, on the other hand, the income effect of an innovation declines in time so that later adopters receive a lesser income increment than earlier adopters a sequence of cases will arise:

a. Large cities which adopt early and have rapidly rising incomes.

b. Medium and smaller-sized cities above all thresholds, experiencing the same population growth rates as those of class a, but rates of real income growth more nearly

29. Edwin Mansfield, *op. cit.*

Table 7   Matrix of Transition Numbers from TV Diffusion Data, 1962–65

Per Cent of Families with TV in 1962	Per Cent of Families with TV in 1965									
	0–10	11–20	21–30	31–40	41–50	51–60	61–70	71–80	81–90	91–100
0–10	34	0	0	0	0	0	0	0	0	0
11–20	0	0	0	0	0	0	0	0	0	0
21–30	0	0	0	0	0	0	0	0	0	0
31–40	0	0	0	0	0	2	0	0	0	0
41–50	0	0	0	0	1	5	15	0	0	0
51–60	0	0	0	0	0	1	49	11	0	0
61–70	0	0	0	0	0	0	12	198	13	0
70–80	0	0	0	0	0	0	0	115	504	2
81–90	0	0	0	0	0	0	1	0	585	702
91–100	0	0	0	0	0	0	0	0	4	848

Table 8   Relationships Among Successive Diffusion Patterns: TV Market Penetration, 1953-1965

Dependent* Variable	Independent Variable	Multiple R	Intercept	Regression Coefficient	
				Metric	Standarized
Pct. with TV, 1956	Pct. with TV, 1953	0.713	40.29	0.609	0.713
Pct. with TV, 1959	Pct. with TV, 1956	0.945	34.14	0.712	0.945
Pct. with TV, 1962	Pct. with TV, 1959	0.498	37.27	0.643	0.498
Pct. with TV, 1965	Pct. with TV, 1962	0.615	58.87	0.346	0.615

* Data for 3101 counties.

those of the nation. In general, the larger and/or more central cities will gain more than the smaller and more peripheral.

c. Small places satisfying some thresholds but not others. The population growth rate and the rate of change of incomes will be positively related to size, because the larger and/or more accessible of these places will satisfy more thresholds than the smaller and more peripheral.

d. Declining small towns in inaccessible intermetropolitan peripheries, with lagging relative income levels, and declining populations because the more energetic and able residents emigrate, largely to places in class a, creating in turn the central city ghettoes of these large metropolitan areas.
In each case, of course, the degree to which surrounding populations benefit is indexed by the extent of their participation in the opportunities provided by the central city— in general, measurable by relative location in the city's commuting field.[30]

Some statistics again bear this out. Between 1950 and 1960, the cities with TV stations grew as follows:

$$\text{Log } P_{1960} = 0.32 + 0.98 \text{ Log } P_{1950}$$
$$R^2 = 0.95$$
$$S_e = 0.13$$

30. Brian J. L. Berry, *op. cit.* 1970.

whereas the comparable expression for all 3101 counties in the country was:

$$\text{Log } P_{1960} = -0.20 + 1.05 \text{ Log } P_{1950}$$
$$R^2 = 0.95$$
$$S_e = 0.12$$

Clearly, small counties were declining, in those of intermediate size growth rates were a positive function of size, whereas for TV cities the growth rate was approximately independent of size. On the other hand, median family income of the 3101 counties in 1960 could be expressed as follows:

Med. family income$_{1960}$ = -3112
+ 736 Log. population$_{1960}$
+ 164 Log. pct. commuting
-0.00168 Pop. potential$_{1960}$
-21 Pct. nonwhite$_{1960}$
+ 1716 [Income$_{1960}$/ Income$_{1950}$]
+ 1525 [Population$_{1960}$/ Population$_{1950}$]
$R^2 = 0.612$

Since the regression model used was stepwise, the only surprising term, that for population potentials, can easily be interpreted as expressing the relative wealth of the southern and western rims of the nation. Otherwise, all of the postulates hold: incomes are higher the higher the level in the urban hierarchy and the greater the degree of participation in the employment opportunities of the central city, and in a circular fashion, these same areas are the zones of most rapid growth of incomes. *This suggests that hierarchical diffusion and attendant geographic spread effects characterize the entire range of innovations that bring growth and incomes to cities and regions.*

HIERARCHICAL DIFFUSION AND GROWTH CENTER THEORY

In consequence, diffusion theory provides a sound conceptual base for the growth center idea. Growth occurs as a consequence of the filtering of innovations downwards through the urban hierarchy, and the spread of use of the innovations among consumers residing within the urban fields of the adopting centers. The operation of the growth center mechanism in a country like the United States is spontaneous, and it is subject to minimum threshold conditions that leave abandoned broad peripheral zones of low and declining incomes, substantial emigration, and, where natural rates of increase are not exceptionally high, of population decline.

Can growth centers be used to induce development in these lagging poverty regions?[31] If by "development" is meant bringing population growth to approximately that of the nation with steadily rising real incomes, the models presented earlier suggest several variables to be influenced in achieving such goals:

1. *Threshold limitations.* Any policy that reduces thresholds will induce development to penetrate further down the hierarchy and out into the intermetropolitan periphery.
2. *Diffusion times.* Since the income effect is a declining function of time, any hastening of the diffusion process will bring a greater income effect to smaller and more distant areas.
3. *Accessibility.* Particularly in the case of household innovations, the extent to which families make use of new innovations in urban centers that have adopted them is a function of their access to these centers. Any decrease in effective distance will have a multiplicative effect on use of innovations, because the distance-decay effect is negative exponential.

---

31. A. O. Hirschman, *The Strategy of Economic Development.* New Haven, Conn.: Yale University Press, 1958; J. B. Parr, *The Nature and Function of Growth Poles in Economic Development.* Seattle: University of Washington Press, 1965.

⚓⚓⚓⚓⚓⚓⚓⚓⚓⚓⚓⚓⚓⚓⚓⚓⚓⚓⚓⚓⚓⚓⚓⚓⚓⚓⚓

MARRIAGE, MIGRATION, AND THE MEAN INFORMATION FIELD: A STUDY IN UNIQUENESS AND GENERALITY

Richard L. Morrill and Forrest R. Pitts

From an early emphasis on the physical environment down to the study of geographical aspects of the economy, recent scholarly attention has turned more and more toward the social: to the spatial processes of migration, patterns of social contact,

---

From the *Annals* of the Association of American Geographers, Vol. 57, 1967. Reprinted by permission.

the spread of ideas, marriage, vacation travel, and other forms of movement.[1] Perhaps these have been neglected because they are not so obviously physical or because it was considered impossible or improper to study such direct human behavior. Any hesitation has now been erased, and many recent studies in many parts of the world have made valuable contributions toward increasing our knowledge of these subjects.[2]

In studies of large numbers of people, for example migrants, a striking geographic fact was observed: that there was a relationship between distance and frequency of moves.[3] This empirical regularity was soon formulated into demographic laws of spatial interaction. These inverse-distance or distance-decay relations have been widely developed by Zipf, Stewart, Warntz, and others, and have been found applicable to many kinds of movements.[4] Thus, for example, given a large population, the frequency of migrants away from some origin will tend to be some inverse function of distance. This result was of theoretical significance to geography, since it was one of the first cases of a fairly direct relation between distance or area and human behavior, and served to provide a basis for successful prediction. Very important, too, was the revelation that the generality of the principle extended over many kinds of data.

Development of a predictable macro-geography, however, was not completely satisfying. It is sometimes a little hard to see that distance, as such, is really the cause of, or explanation of, how far people move. The macro-behavior model may beg the basic question. More important, since the spatial behavior of many people must be the composite of what individuals do, how may we understand individual and small group behavior? This is both a difficult and fascinating problem. What underlying forces derived from a study of individuals produce the empirical regularities which we observe on a large scale? What really influences how far and in what direction individuals will move or have contact?

It is fashionable to speak of the possibility of explanation for the behavior of large numbers, but to conceive of individual behavior as unique and unpredictable.[5] Thanks to the pioneering work of Hägerstrand and others in the fields of migration and the diffusion of information and innovations, we can now focus meaningfully on the level of the individual.[6] Their work

1. E. A. Ackerman, "Geography as a Fundamental Research Discipline" (Chicago: University of Chicago, Department of Geography, *Research Paper*, No. 53, 1958), pp. 24 ff.

2. For example, the expansion of population studies. See W. Zelinsky, "A Bibliographic Guide to Population Geography" (Chicago: University of Chicago, Department of Geography, *Research Paper*, No. 80, 1962). See also the groundbreaking series, *Lund Studies in Geography*, Series B, Human Geography, David Hannerberg, Torsten Hägerstrand, and Bruno Odevink (Eds.), "Migration in Sweden." There are also important symposia, such as Jean Sutter (Ed.), "Entretiens de Monaco en Sciences Humaines: May 1962: Human Displacements" (Monaco, 1963).

3. E. G. Ravenstein, "The Laws of Migration," *Journal of the Royal Statistical Society*, Vol. 48 (1885) and Vol. 52 (1889).

4. G. K. Zipf, *Human Behavior and the Principle of Least Effort* (Reading, Massachusetts: Addison-Wesley Press, 1949); J. Q. Stewart, "Empirical Mathematical Rules Concerning the Distribution and Equilibrium of Population," *Geographical Review*, Vol. 37 (1947), pp. 467-85; J. Q. Stewart and W. Warntz, "Physics of Population Distribution," *Journal of Regional Science*, Vol. 1 (1958), pp. 99-123.

5. E. Jones, "Cause and Effect in Human Geography," *Annals*, Association of American Geographers, Vol. 46 (1956), pp. 369-77. In particular note his statement (p. 373): "At best a geographer is dealing with a large micrososm whenever human behavior has to be taken into consideration."

6. T. Hägerstrand, *Innovationsforloppet ur korologisk synpunkt* (Lund: Gleerup, 1953).

demonstrates the falseness of the supposed dichotomy according to which one can make general statements concerning the behavior of the mass, but cannot hope to understand the individual. One difference is that the individual decision cannot be so determined or predicted, but the probability of making a range of decisions can be found. It is also possible to speak of the expected behavior of a typical individual, without reference to a particular one.

PURPOSE

Our purpose, then, is to examine many individual cases in order to discover the general principles underlying geographic movements. This permits, in turn, recognition that individual behavior may be viewed both as a unique phenomenon and as a variant of a general theme; and finally such study allows us to develop models of expected individual behavior.

Many patterns of movements of individuals or small groups are found to be possible products of a spatial diffusion process, which, when applied to large numbers over a long period, produces the empirical regularities we observe. The precise nature of the distribution of an individual's movements remains unique, but it may be fruitfully viewed also as a special illustration of a general principle of reaction to space.

This work is corollary and very indebted to the excellent study of Marble and Nystuen on the measurement and derivation of mean information fields.[7] Much of the same data are used, and our hope is to extend and generalize upon their findings, as well as to present some geographic implications.

7. D. F. Marble and J. D. Nystuen, "An Approach to the Direct Measurement of Community Mean Information Fields," *Papers and Proceedings*, Regional Science Association, Vol. 11 (1962), pp. 99-109.

SPATIAL DIFFUSION

If we examine an individual's trips for a period of time, we know that only one trip is possible at any one time. At that moment, the individual is confronted with an enormous number of possible destinations, at any distance or direction. He can only choose one or none. He may be more likely to choose some distance or directions than others, and in a series of such location decisions, a pattern of moves gradually evolves. Such a pattern is then one of isolated events (single moves) in time and space, in which the decisions are made probabilistically (under uncertainty).[8] How does such a process operate? If the decision is made under uncertainty, the reader may ask whether we have really gained anything in our understanding of individual behavior. Will not the results of such a process be chaotic? The vital tie to generality is provided by the fact that, whereas moves cannot be precisely determined, the destinations chosen are strongly influenced by systematic forces. From the overall statistics of the behavior of large numbers we know for an area and period of time how many people move how far and in what directions. Since we can rarely, if ever, have the statistics for everybody, it is simple and proper to look at these frequencies as probabilities. Given a large number of people, we expect certain proportions are likely to move various distances and directions. Since individual trips taken together make up the overall statistics, the typical individual may also act according to these same probabilities. He must be more likely to go one mile than five, and five miles than ten, or the overall pattern would not be as it is.

To illustrate, imagine that from a study

8. T. Hägerstrand, "A Monte Carlo Approach to Diffusion," *Archives Européennes de Sociologie*, Vol. 6 (1965), pp. 43-67.

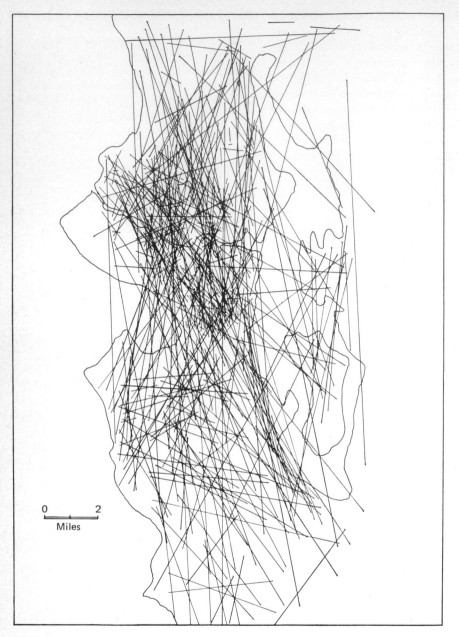

Figure 1. Spatial influence on marital selection in Seattle, 1962. Lines extend between addresses of bride and groom.

of a large number of persons and their trips we can construct a map similar to the patterns shown in Figures 1, 2, or 3. To bring order out of the chaos, we can ask how many or what proportions of these trips were to various distances and in various

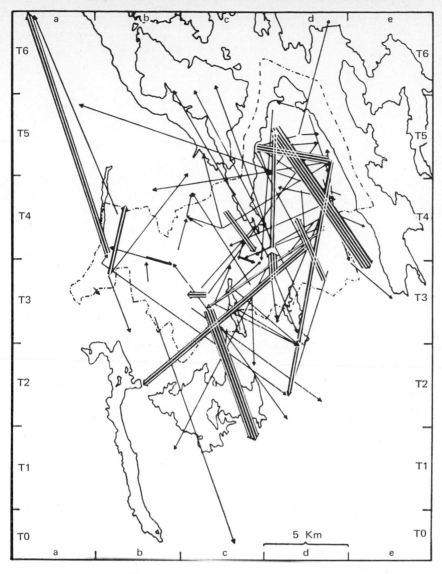

Figure 2. Local migration in the Asby area, Sweden, 1935.

directions. Results may be diagrammed simply by bringing all the respective origins to a common point. Figure 4 shows absolute flows and Figure 5 shows flows expressed as proportions of the total. In cases of a common origin, for example long-distance calls from a central switchboard, this device is not necessary. To simplify presentation, lines in Figure 4 were combined into single lines proportional in width to frequency in that direction and distance. Figure 5 summarizes the fact, then, that twenty percent of people, making trips, remain in the same square mile, eight percent move to the

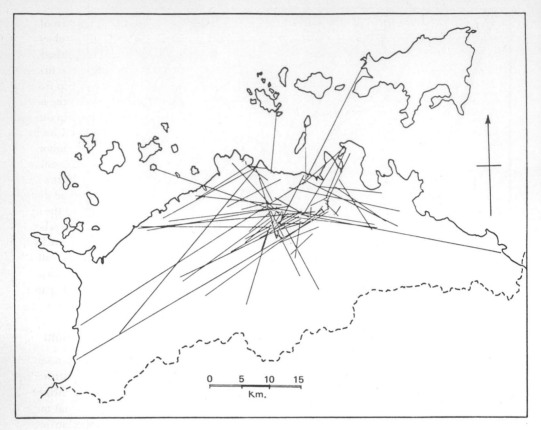

Figure 3. Marriage moves in Kagawa, Japan, 1951.

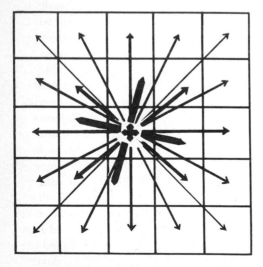

Figure 4. Observed flows from a common origin.

1	2	3	2	1
2	4	8	4	2
3	8	20	8	3
2	4	8	4	2
1	2	3	2	1

Figure 5. Observed flows as an informational field (per cent moving to cells from origins).

square mile north of them, and so forth. In accordance with the previous discussion we may consider these proportions as also giving the probability for future or any typical trips for any individual from his origin.

In one thousand hypothetical trips, we expect that 200 will remain (take very short trips) within the cell or close to the origin of the trip, eighty will travel one cell north of the present cell, and so on. But if we have the information that a small group of persons will make twenty-five individual trips, how can we allocate them? Deterministically, the corner cells should get one-quarter of a trip! For small groups, we may better treat the proportions as probabilities rather than clear expectations. The dilemma of the quarter-trip is resolved by a simple random number allocation model which selects particular destinations within the overall framework of probabilities. The probabilities are first expressed accumulatively in whole numbers, as illustrated in Figure 6. This provides a basis for unique selection when a set of twenty-five random numbers between 0 (100) and 99 are matched against these

1	2-3	4-6	7-8	9
10-11	12-15	16-23	24-27	28-29
30-32	33-40	41-60	61-68	69-71
72-73	74-77	78-85	86-89	90-91
92	93-94	95-97	98-99	100

Figure 6. Information field (in accumulated probabilities).

accumulated probabilities. A pattern of random spatial diffusion of trips, subject to the given probabilities, is accomplished (Figures 7 and 8). For example, the first random number, 23, indicates a trip from origin a to the cell north of itself; the next random number, 36, indicates a trip one cell to the left of b's origin. In Figure 8 we have again depicted the trips from a common origin in order to illustrate that a seeming chaos of individual trips does exhibit a systematic distribution of distances and directions traveled. Because the trips of the small group are such a minute part of the whole, they seem quite peculiar, yet they are by definition a product of the same overall regular probabilities. We say that such a pattern is produced by a process of spatial diffusion.

The Individual Information Field

At this point all we have done is to assert that we can apply large scale regularities to individual behavior via the spatial diffusion process. We have still to answer what underlying forces give rise to these regularities. An individual lives in a small cluster (family) of individuals at a point in space. Normally he must leave the point temporarily for work, education, shopping, or social intercourse, and occasionally he is induced by some combination of attractions and repulsions to change his locus of operations. The destination of most moves seems to be governed by the interplay of distance and information. Information consists of the knowledge an individual has of the world, and his information field is the spatial distribution of that knowledge. The quantity and quality of information available is a function both of distance from usual centers of operation and of the varying information content of areas; that is, it reflects economic, social, and other differences. Distance can be both a direct hindrance to moves, even given information

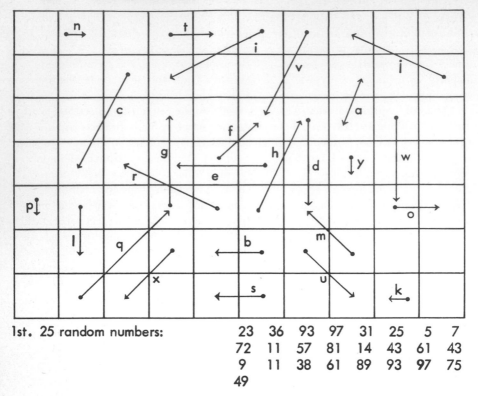

1st. 25 random numbers:

23	36	93	97	31	25	5	7
72	11	57	81	14	43	61	43
9	11	38	61	89	93	97	75
49							

Figure 7. Simulated moves (actual map).

that attracts, and as well partly governs the kind of information we obtain. Yet superior information can overcome great distances.

To some extent individuals measure distance as a direct cost: in time, money, miles, or driving effort. Thus many of our recreational, shopping, and other trips are partly governed by goals of distance minimization. However, the individual may not think of distance as a direct barrier. Still, we appreciate the geometrically increasing capacity of space for new possible contacts or destinations as the individual moves from his home base, and we know at the same time the very real limitations upon the individual as to time[9] (to get to work or to school, for

shopping or visiting) and energy (to maintain or increase relationships, to travel farther). The number of opportunities increases vastly with greater distance, just as the capacity of the individual to react to these declines. Thus the sheer geometry of the setting encourages us to concentrate our contacts and trips or moves at shorter distances.

The effect of distance is not smooth, because all segments of space at a given distance are not in fact of equal importance to an individual.[10] The real world exhibits extreme inequality in population, development, social status, and in communication, and the individual's awareness of these differences. The easier and cheaper transpor-

9. R. Porter, "Approach to Migration through its Mechanism," *Geografiska Annaler*, Vol. 38 (1956), pp. 317-343.

10. P. Nelson, "Migration, Real Income and Information," *Journal of Regional Science*, Vol. 1 (1959), pp. 43-74.

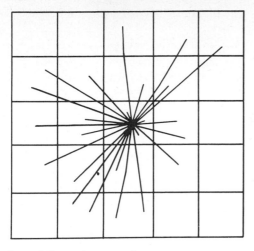

1st. 25 random numbers:

23	36	93	97	31	25	5	7
72	11	57	81	14	43	61	43
9	11	38	61	89	93	97	75
49							

Figure 8. Simulated pattern of moves (from a common origin).

tation becomes, and the greater specialized differentiation of space becomes, the more the individual's pattern of contacts will deviate from a smooth attenuation with distance. Thus we maintain close ties with a distant friend or relative, and we avoid a neighbor whom we distrust. We are simply unaware of most opportunities for contact, but certain places are more known to us through advertising, travel, and in other ways. In the economy of living we can maintain only a limited number of relationships, and these become localized and reinforced. Bias or concentration in certain areas is established. Our evaluation of places, based upon what we know about them, has then a powerful modifying effect on the purely distance aspect.

Around the individual are contact fields, for example, Figure 9, or the patterns of locations of family, friends, and associates at places of work, frequented businesses, favor-

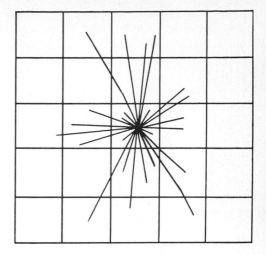

Figure 9. Individual contact field.

ite recreation spots, and so on, and which in turn reflect the facts of information and space. His present and past pattern of contacts constitutes the expectations and probabilities for near future behavior. Different, but overlapping sets of these contacts may be important to the individual in decisions of different kinds. If we take the individual's contact field for some purpose, for example, social and recreational trips from the home, we can express it as an actual individual information field,[11] which gives the probability of contacts in the various directions and distances simply by indicating the proportion of total contacts accounted for by cells on a superimposed grid (for example, the smaller numbers in Figure 9).

The Mean Information Field: Generality and Uniqueness

Every field of contacts, whether of the same individual or of different individuals, is unique, since everyone differs from everyone

11. The only mapped individual information field known to us occurs in: P. H. Chombart de Lauwe, et al., "Paris et l'agglomeration Parisienne," *Bibliotheque de Sociologie contemporaine*, Series B, (1952).

else and himself a different person in varying circumstances. Each field must vary in spatial detail, and yet almost all are at the same time of a general form. The fields can be seen as chance variants of the general theme. The essential characteristics of these personal information fields and that which permits us to make predictions, no matter how hedged, about individual behavior, is that each unique field makes at the same time a contribution to a mean information field. Individuals of an area, or within a meaningful unit, as a social group, define together by their contacts a composite information field: that pattern of relations among themselves that constitutes a social space. That is, although the individual patterns are unique, they are so similar that we can look at them as products of the same parameters of willingness to make trips, kinds of contacts desired, interpretation of distance and so on. Neighboring families' trips might look very different for a given week, but aside from the main work trip, might be of very like form over the period of a year. From one point of view the sum of many individual fields, peculiar as they may be, yields the average pattern or empirical regularity which is obtained from the study of a large number of people. Why not, then, from the opposite point of view, treat the mean information field, that average field defined by many individuals' trips, as giving the expected probability for individual behavior? If we then generate patterns of individual contact, these will be of the same nature as the actual fields. These may differ greatly from one another at quick glance, but they differ predictably, since they were products of the same probabilities. The mean field may be defined by thousands of contacts which tend to produce a smooth decrease of intensity of contact away from an origin. In the field of the individual, relatively few contacts are made amid an overwhelming number of possibilities.

Let us illustrate this fundamental point. Fields of actual contacts, centered on the home, for example, are illustrated in Figure 9. (In this example each line represents a single contact of equal strength, and does not weight repeated trips, such as to work, although for other purposes, the lines might well be weighted by frequency of contacts.) Imagine hundreds of these, each somewhat different. Summing these all together around a common origin, we might obtain the very results already shown in Figures 4 and 5. This mean information field is an empirical regularity obtained from the summing of many individual patterns. Thus we can reverse the procedure and consider these proportions as probabilities for a typical individual to travel various distances and directions. Figures 7 and 8 are such a prediction. These predicted fields will not correspond exactly to the unique fields (Figure 9) of particular individuals. The point is that they are of the same general form and could have been produced by the same forces. It is not a question of unique or general kinds of phenomena: we can see the same fact both as a unique pattern and as a typical form, product of a general principle.

Analysis of Information Fields

A typical individual travel pattern over a period of time is seen as a result of a spatial diffusion process in which uncertainty is present, though habits associated with finite distance act as strong guides. This conclusion may only be accepted through the appropriate analysis. Does the example of actual cases corroborate the notion of generality extending to individuals and to a diversity of movements? Are there forms of contact or movements other than marriage, migration, and direct contact which may have similar behavior? Of what use are the mean information fields if they are valid? May we develop models of expected individual behavior in space? In this paper we analyze diverse sets of data concerning migration, distance between pre-marriage residences of bride and groom, and patterns of direct contact from the United States, Sweden, and Japan for both rural and urban environments. From these data we summarize the frequencies of moves of varying distances (Tables 1-5), setting aside known or unknown information variability, and attempt to find the best mathematical expression to describe the relations of distance and movement. The fitted equations are used to define the mean information fields.

One component of information, directional bias, or prevalence of greater contact in certain directions, has been studied, but only the Seattle results are used here to modify and construct information fields (Figures 1, 16, 18). All the diverse data are found to describe remarkably similar behavior. Both the mean and individual fields are essentially alike in different cultures and for different purposes of movement. The fields do vary of course in extent; for example, the pattern of migrants who invest a major cost in movement is more widespread

Table 1   Migration in the Cleveland Area, 1933-36

| | | | Predicted frequencies | | | | | |
| Ring center distance in miles | Number of migrating households | Migrating households per square mile | Pareto: number of migrating households | Pareto-exponential: households per sq. mi. | Migrating households (Pareto) | | Households per square mile | |
					Actual	Predicted	Actual	Predicted
0.29	5,585	5,475	4,630[a]	4,900	0.459	0.444	0.805	0.830
0.86	2,471	808	2,220	577	0.662	0.657	0.924	0.927
1.43	1,313	263	950	195	0.770	0.749	0.963	0.961
2.00	737	104	582	91	0.831	0.805	0.978	0.976
2.57	431	47	401	50	0.866	0.842	0.985	0.984
3.14	320	29	294	30	0.886	0.870	0.989	0.989
3.71	217	16	245	19.2	0.902	0.895	0.991	0.991
4.28	178	12	183	13.0	0.917	0.912	0.993	0.993
4.85	172	10	155	8.9	0.931	0.927	0.995	0.994
5.42	125	6.5	132	6.35	0.941	0.937	0.996	0.996
5.99	137	6.4	114	4.57	0.952	0.950	0.997	0.997
6.56	106	4.5	99	3.42	0.961	0.960	0.998	0.998
7.13	85	3.3	87	2.52	0.968	0.968		
7.70	102	3.8	77	1.90	0.976	0.974	0.999	0.999
8.27	102	3.5	70	1.49	0.984	0.981		
8.84	57	1.8	64	1.14	0.992	0.988		
9.41	30	0.9	58	0.89	0.995	0.995		
9.98	39	1.1	53	0.70	1.000	1.000	1.000	1.000

	Max. Diff.	0.026	Max. Diff. 0.025
	Critical D	0.02	Critical D 0.027

* Possible significant difference (Kolmogorov-Smirnov test).

[a] We consider more accurate for calculation the distance 0.40 which divides the band area in half.

Source: Adapted from material in S. Stouffer, "Intervening Opportunities: A Theory Relating Mobility and Distance," *American Sociological Review*, Vol. 5 (1940), pp. 845–67.

Table 2   Cedar Rapids Direct Contact Data, 1949

| Distance in miles | Number of Contacts | Contacts per Square Mile | Predicted member of contacts (Pareto-Exponential) | Predicted contacts per square mile | |
				(Pareto)	(Pareto-Exponential)
0–0.5	546	695.5	444	725[a]	565
0.5–1.0	160	67.9	334	83.7	142
1.0–1.5	235	60.2	207	22.2	53
1.5–2.0	85	15.5	132	8.85	24
2.0–2.5	68	9.6	86	4.45	12.2
2.5–3.0	94	10.9	58	2.57	6.7
3.0–3.5	50	4.9	39.6	1.61	3.88
3.5–4.0	2	0.17	28.1	1.10	2.39
4.0–4.5	9	0.67	19.0	0.80	1.41
4.5–5.0	4	0.27	12.7	0.57	0.86
5.0–5.5	3	0.18	9.0	0.435	0.54
5.5–6.0	10	0.55	6.25	0.34	0.344
6.0–6.5	4	0.20	4.48	0.27	0.224
6.5–7.0	4	0.19	3.06	0.22	0.145

[a] Mean distance for innermost band, Pareto derivation, was 0.35, for the next, 0.77. See Table 1.
Source: Marble and Nystuen, cited in footnote 7.

Table 3   Seattle Marriage Distances, 1962

| Distance in Miles | Number of Marriages | Marriages per Square Mile | Predicted no. of marriages | | Predicted marriages per Square mile | |
			Pareto	Exponential	Pareto	Exponential
0– 1	47	15.00	55.4	45.6	17.62	14.52
1– 2	41	4.36	36.8	39.1	3.92	4.17
2– 3	30	1.91	29.0	33.5	1.84	2.13
3– 4	28	1.27	24.5	28.7	1.11	1.30
4– 5	20	0.71	21.5	24.6	0.76	0.97
5– 6	22	0.61	19.3	21.1	0.535	0.585
6– 7	22	0.54	17.6	18.0	0.43	0.44
7– 8	17	0.36	16.3	15.4	0.345	0.326
8– 9	14	0.26	15.2	13.2	0.28	0.245
9–10	10	0.17	14.4	11.3	0.244	0.192

Directional bias: of 312 marriage pairs, 235 were north-south oriented, 77 east-west.

Source: James Henderson, "Distance and Marital Selection," Department of Geography, University of Washington, Seattle, 1962. Note: the distance variable was defined as the outer limit of the band.

Table 4   Asby, Sweden: Marriage and Migration Data, 1930–39

Distance Band (Kilometers)	Moving Units	Units per Square Kilometer	Predicted moving units			Predicted units per square kilometers[2]		
			Pareto	Exponential	Par-expon.	Pareto	Exponential	Par-expon.
0.0– 0.5	9	11.39	28.5[1]	4.87	14.9	36.4	6.20	19.0
0.5– 1.5	45	7.17	39.4	29.6	34.4	6.26	4.71	5.46
1.5– 2.5	45	3.58	26.3	41.0	33.2	2.09	3.26	2.64
2.5– 3.5	26	1.38	20.7	42.8	30.0	1.10	2.27	1.59
3.5– 4.5	28	1.11	17.6	39.4	26.4	0.70	1.57	1.05
4.5– 5.5	25	0.80	15.3	34.2	23.0	0.487	1.09	0.73
5.5– 6.5	20	0.53	13.8	28.6	20.0	0.366	0.76	0.53
6.5– 7.5	23	0.52	12.6	23.4	17.2	0.286	0.53	0.392
7.5– 8.5	18	0.36	11.7	18.4	14.8	0.234	0.366	0.294
8.5– 9.5	10	0.18	10.9	14.3	12.65	0.193	0.254	0.224
9.5–10.5	17	0.27	10.3	11.1	10.8	0.164	0.177	0.172
10.5–11.5	7	0.10	9.6	8.5	9.2	0.139	0.123	0.133
11.5–12.5	11	0.15	9.2	6.4	7.8	0.123	0.085	0.1035
12.5–13.5	6	0.07	8.8	4.9	6.6	0.108	0.06	0.081
13.5–14.5	2	0.02	8.4	3.6	5.65	0.095	0.041	0.064
14.5–15.5	5	0.05	8.1	2.7	4.8	0.086	0.029	0.051

See Table 6 for significance of results.

[1] See Table 1.

[2] See also G. Kulldorff, "Migration Probabilities," *Lund Studies in Geography*, Ser. B., Human Geography, No. 14 (1955) for somewhat closer results, using more complex expressions.

Source: Hagerstrand, *op. cit.*, footnote 6.

than that of daily contacts. The form, however, does not much alter.

The data for calculation of mean information fields include:

1	Cleveland	Migration
2	Cedar Rapids[1,2]	Direct day-to-day contact
3	Seattle	Marriage distances
4	Asby	Migration and marriage distances
5	Kagawa (Japan)[1,2]	Marriage distances
6	Oregon	Marriage distances
7	Okinawa	Bus Trip distances

12. For Cedar Rapids, see Marble and Nystuen, *op. cit.*, footnote 7. The data for Kagawa were gathered by Pitts in February, 1962, as part of

Maps of actual movement patterns are given for Seattle (Figure 1), Asby (Figure 2), and Kagawa (Figure 3).

Data for Oregon and Okinawa are still in the process of study. Additional breakdowns of frequencies by contact types (trip purposes) will become available when the Cedar Rapids data are fully analyzed. Tables 1-5 present the first five sets of data, both in terms of frequency of contacts (or migration or marriages) within a band of area between specific distances and also in terms of unit-area frequencies. The tables present actual frequency and predicted frequencies, utilizing the functions which better fit the data. The actual functions and their adequacy are tested by appropriate statistics (Table 6).

research supported by the Social Science Research Council.

Table 5   Kagawa (Japan) Marriage Distances, 1951

Distance Band (Kilometers)	Marriages Within Band	Marriages per Square Kilometer	Predicted Marriages per Square Kilometer		Predicted Marriages in Bands	
			Pa-reto[1]	Pareto-Exponential	Pa-reto	Pareto-Exponential
0.0– 0.5	43	78.48	76.5	69.0	58	54
0.5– 1.5	65	10.35	14.0	15.2	88	95
1.5– 2.5	63	5.01	4.85	6.4	61	80.5
2.5– 3.5	56	2.97	2.59	3.6	49	68
3.5– 4.5	60	2.39	1.67	2.26	43	57
4.5– 5.5	83	2.64	1.19	1.54	37.4	58.5
5.5– 6.5	56	1.49	0.90	1.08	33.9	41
6.5– 7.5	46	1.05	0.71	0.78	31.3	34
7.5– 8.5	34	0.68	0.58	0.58	29.2	29
8.5– 9.5	35	0.62	0.48	0.43	27.4	24.3
9.5–10.5	29	0.46	0.41	0.33	25.9	20.7
10.5–11.5	21	0.30	0.35	0.25	24.8	17.3
11.5–12.5	17	0.23	0.312	0.20	23.7	14.9
12.5–13.5	16	0.20	0.277	0.153	22.6	12.6
13.5–14.5	10	0.11	0.246	0.12	21.7	10.6
14.5–15.5	13	0.14	0.219	0.094	20.7	9.0

[1] Mean position of first band for calculations was 0.33. See Table 1.

Source: Data provided thorugh the courtesy of the Shikoku District Court and the Takamatsu City Government, 1962.

The Relation of Distance and Movements[13]

What is the spatial form of these fields? Setting aside information variability, this is to ask what is the relation between distance and the frequency of contact or movement. The question here is not whether the effect of distance is identical in all cases, but whether the role is consistent in form. The fitting of an ideal curve to observed data is

13. See R. Morrill, "The Distribution of Migration Distances," *Papers and Proceedings*, Regional Science Association, Vol. 11 (1963), pp. 75-84. These fitted functions are simply descriptive approximations to observed frequencies. They are meaningfully restricted to the range of observed values only and are not intended to be probability density functions. Some band-frequency functions may be constituted as probability functions; unit-area frequencies must first be converted to band expectations.

to be sure a practical matter, employed to derive the mean information field. But the possible functions which might be used are not without their own meanings in terms of assumptions about the underlying populations and processes. It is logical, for example, to find out whether the patterns of contact are a product of normal diffusion, as if people randomly walked in various directions to different distances, and each walk was unrelated to any other. Here the mean information field would best be fit by a normal spatial distribution.[14] In fact, such a pattern of contact is extremely rare. Rather, there is greater contact at very close and at rather great distances. Limitations of time, as the length of the day and the strong ten-

14. R. Bachi, "Statistical Analysis of Geographical Series," *Bulletin de l'Institut International de Statistique*, Vol. 36, part 2 (Stockholm, 1958).

dency to repeat the easier contacts already made, strongly reinforce the short distances. At the same time, the widespread nature of our communication system and the fact of great concentrations of people, influence, and information at large, rather distant centers help lengthen the information fields of individuals. For this kind of world, various expressions have been proposed: the most common are the Pareto or gravity formulation, the lognormal distribution, exponential functions, combinations of these (for example what we may term the Pareto-exponential function), chi-square distributions, and more general gamma and beta functions.

Behind the Pareto function of the form:

$$y = aD^{-b} \quad (D = \text{distance}) \qquad (1)$$

is the gravitational concept, the relation of the attractiveness of destinations at various distances to be overcome. The mood is one of purposeful moves. A difficulty with this function is that it is not basically a probability function, and tends seriously to exaggerate close-in frequencies.

The lognormal function of the form:

$$y = ae^{-(b \log D)^2} \qquad (2)$$

is well suited to data with a multiplicative element, such as repeated trips over the same path and the fact that we deal with a process through time.[15]

The exponential function of the form:

$$y = ae^{-bD} \qquad (3)$$

is suited to data in which successive moves or contacts are in fact correlated in length and direction. Here there is a feeling that moves are more accidental than purposeful.[16] Such are very often the conditions underlying individual moves. The exponential distribution often produces frequencies very close to those of the lognormal. Both of these tend to underestimate the close-in contacts. Therefore these may be combined with the "gravitational" concept into a Pareto-exponential function[17] of the form:

$$Y = aD^{-b}e^{-cD}. \qquad (4)$$

If this were to fit best, the movements under study would seem to combine notions of purposeful and accidental behavior.

Chi-square functions, more difficult to work with, have been fit to some data. All of these are special cases of the more general gamma functions,[18] which permit greater flexibility in fitting diverse data. Fortunately, the simpler functions usually prove adequate, as far as describing the role of distance is concerned.

Most of the above functions may be expressed in linear form. Thus the relation between distance and frequency may be found by standard least-squares regression:

(1) $\log y = \log a - b \log D$

(2) $\log y = \log a - b[(\log D^2)(\log e)]$

---

15. G. Kulldorff, "Migration Probabilities," *Lund Studies in Geography*, Series B, Human Geography, No. 14 (1955), 46 pp.

16. A. J. Bateman, "Is Gene Dispersal Normal?," *Heredity*, Vol. 4 (1950), pp. 353-63.

---

17. The Pareto-exponential function describes, for example, the absorption of a flow emanating from a center by a medium; see O. H. Johnson, "En Tadsflyttning och Födelseortsfälts," *Svensk Geografisk Arsbok*, 1952.

18. See L. Cavalli-Sforza, "The Distribution of Migration Distances: Models and Applications to Genetics," in Sutter, *op. cit.*, footnote 2, pp. 135-58; Dacey prefers a truncated incomplete gamma curve as the best fit for the Asby data: M. F. Dacey, "An Observation on Migration in the Asby Area" (Philadelphia: Wharton School of Finance and Commerce, University of Pennsylvania, June 20, 1963), 5 pp. mimeographed. In general, a gamma distribution is: $\frac{x^{n-1} \, b^n e^{-bx}}{n}$. The Pareto-exponential function (4), when converted to band frequencies, can with appropriate parameters yield a gamma distribution. If not, an exponential results.

(3) $\log y = \log a - b[D \log e]$

(4) $\log y = \log a - b \log D - c[D \log e]$.

The preceding equations treat the relation of distance and movement only. Far more complex expressions, taking into account social, economic, and other phenomena are of course possible. For example, we recognize that real data often exhibit a J shape, an increase in frequency of moves associated with very attractive distant destinations. Presumably this shape reflects the great unevenness of population and activity, or the possibility that two kinds of migrants, one being more sensitive to distance, are represented in the data.[19]

Tests of "Goodness of Fit"

In fitting these theoretical functions to observed data of this sort, we do not expect to find close correspondence, inasmuch as we have not attempted to separate out non-distance factors, such as variations in underlying population density, topography, social differences, and many more. In spite of this, the sample distributions proved to be surprisingly regular. Some were judged to be not significantly different from theoretical expectations (Table 6).[20] The summary table contains values from Kolmogorov-Smirnov tests. Goodness of fit tests are made by comparing actual frequencies by bands or unit areas with the frequencies that would be expected if the data corresponded exactly to the fitted function. The reader may observe that the use of unit-area frequencies

19. J. Wolpert, "Directional and Distance Bias in Inter-urban Migratory Streams" (unpublished manuscript, 1965).

20. S. Siegel, *Nonparametric Statistics for the Behavioral Sciences* (New York: McGraw-Hill Book Co., 1956), chapters 5-6. Measures of goodness of fit are cross-referenced in I. R. Savage, *Bibliography of Nonparametric Statistics* (Cambridge: Harvard University Press, 1962).

involves a sort of built-into-the-function diminution with distance. The band frequencies therefore provide the better or more powerful test. Typical chi-square tests of goodness of fit are not appropriate here, since our data units are modifiable areas. In the Kolmogorov-Smirnov test, two distributions will be judged significantly divergent if the maximum difference between the accumulated proportions is greater than a critical value (dependent upon size of sample). The use of the test is illustrated on Tables 1 and 4. This test does not prove that the distributions are from the same population; it shows only that we cannot be sure that they are different!

The data studied here were sufficiently diverse to demonstrate that no one function is likely to be always superior. From the point of view of the Smirnov test, the Pareto-exponential function tended to be superior to either of the functions separately, but this was not always the case. What is appropriate for a given problem seems to depend upon the kinds of movements studied. In general, we believe a Pareto formulation may work better for moves or contacts which do not involve permanent or costly moves, and the other functions may be better for migration and marriage distances.

The Effect of Information on Movements

A thorough analysis of the directional and other biases introduced by information distances will not be attempted here, since most sets of data are not sufficiently detailed. Provisional analysis of the Cedar Rapids direct contact data suggests a strong directional bias towards the Central Business District. An extremely strong north-south bias in the Seattle marriage data is evident (Figure 1 and Table 3), but this certainly reflects the dominant topography and popu-

Table 6   Summary of Fitted Equations and Tests of Goodness of Fit

| Data Set and Functions | Fitted Equations | D value for Kolmogorov-Smirnov test* | |
		Unit Areas	Bands
Cleveland:			
Pareto	$y = 459\, D^{-2.49}$	0.089	0.026
Exponential	$y = 631\, e^{-0.716D}$	poor	poor
Pareto-Exponential	$y = 530\, D^{-1.85} e^{-0.24D}$	0.025	0.035
Cedar Rapids (original sample)			
Pareto	$y = 40.9\, D^{-2.74}$	0.057*	0.19
Exponential	$y = 221\, e^{-1.87D}$	poor	poor
Pareto-Exponential	$y = 162\, D^{-1.4} e^{-0.643D}$	0.081*	0.059*
Seattle[a]			
Pareto	$y = 55.4\, D^{-0.589}$	0.05*	0.024*
Exponential	$y = 53.3\, e^{-0.155D}$	0.023*	0.026*
Asby (Sweden)			
Pareto	$y = 6.26\, D^{-1.585}$	0.33*	0.087*
Exponential	$y = 6.8\, e^{-0.365D}$	0.122	0.091*
Pareto-Exponential	$y = 6.55\, D^{-0.8} e^{-0.18D}$	0.174*	0.044*
Kagawa (Japan)			
Pareto	$y = 14\, D^{-1.532}$	0.026*	0.084*
Exponential	$y = 20\, e^{-0.352D}$	poor	poor
Pareto-Exponential	$y = 18\, D^{-1.0} e^{-0.17D}$	0.055*	0.130

[a] The two Seattle equations are for band frequencies. All others are for unit areas, since the point of view if the probability of an individual moving between two places. The equations and frequencies are converted from one to the other by adjusting for changes in the areas of the bands.

* Indicates that it is possible that there is no difference between the observed frequencies and the fitted functions. See Table 1 for example.

Source: Calculated by authors.

lation distribution in the city, and not orientation to any particular part of the city.

The Seattle data illustrate as well the effect of geographic or social variability, or breaks in information. Thus, there is low contact across Lake Washington to the east, reduced contact across the downtown business and manufacturing area, and strong local orientation within the Negro community. There is also a sharply defined break at the limits of the urbanized area (9—10 miles). The barrier effect between rural and urban social circles produces a drop in contact greater than that expected from density changes. Yet these breaks are not extreme.

The data show great mobility between sectors of the city; for example, there is no strong tendency for marrying someone within the neighborhood or even within a similar income area. Presumably, this results from the tremendous mixing at points of social contact and employment.

Construction of the Mean Information Fields

The appropriate fitted equations for unit areas are used to estimate expected migration or trip frequencies. We may graph the resultant equations. Figures 10 and 11 illustrate the manner in which frequencies de-

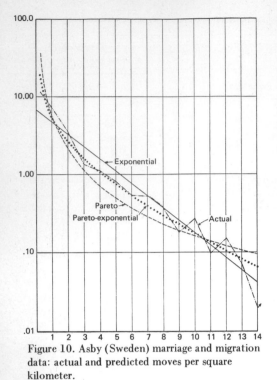

Figure 10. Asby (Sweden) marriage and migration data: actual and predicted moves per square kilometer.

with rectilinear, hexagonal, or equal area units of concentric bands.

As an example, for the Cleveland data, the Pareto equation is $y = 495 D^{-2.5}$. We may approximate the expected frequency for a square mile cell centered at two miles from the origin by: $y = 459/2^{2.5}$, or 81.3. Figure 12 illustrates a more complicated construction, since it involves grid areas of more than a square mile and conversion to kilometers as well. Since each grid square is 5 kilometers, or 3.1 miles, on a side, the expected frequencies will be $(3.1)^2$ times the frequencies for a square mile centered in the cell. Thus, for the cell above the central one, we have:

$$y = \frac{459(3.1)^2}{(3.1)^{2.5}} \text{ or } 263.7.$$

The other figures are similarly constructed.

Expected frequencies in the form of proportions of the total constitute probabilities for the mean information fields. Examples are given in Figures 12, 13, 14, 15, 17, 19, 20, and 21 for Cleveland, Cedar Rapids, Seattle, Asby, and Kagawa; they illustrate Pareto, exponential, and Pareto-exponential derivations. For example on the average thirty-nine percent of Seattle mar-

cline with distance for the actual data and for three fitted equations for the Asby data, and two fitted equations for the Seattle data. Or we may construct the more generally useful gridded mean information field

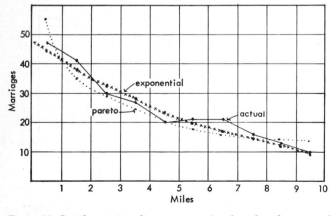

Figure 11. Seattle marriage distances: actual and predicted contacts for distance bands.

19.98	35.72	47.28	35.72	19.98
35.72	111.88	263.7	111.88	35.72
47.28	263.7	9440.	263.7	47.28
36.72	111.88	263.7	111.88	35.72
19.98	35.72	47.28	35.72	19.98

3 miles

Figure 12. Expected migration grid for the Cleveland area.

.0009	.0017	.0024	.0017	.0009
.0017	.0061	.0157	.0061	.0017
.0024	.0157	.8858	.0157	.0024
.0017	.0061	.0157	.0061	.0017
.0009	.0017	.0024	.0017	.0009

3 miles

Figure 14. Mean information field for Cedar Rapids.

.0017	.0031	.0041	.0031	.0017
.0031	.0097	.0229	.0097	.0031
.0041	.0229	.8211	.0229	.0041
.0031	.0097	.0229	.0097	.0031
.0017	.0031	.0041	.0031	.0017

3 miles

Figure 13. Mean information field for the Cleveland area.

.0105	.0148	.0180	.0148	.0105
.0148	.0352	.0585	.0352	.0148
.0180	.0585	.3920	.0585	.0180
.0148	.0352	.0585	.0352	.0148
.0105	.0148	.0180	.0148	.0105

4 miles

Figure 15. Mean information field for Seattle (pareto derivation).

.0105	.0198	.0270	.0198	.0105
.0099	.0352	.0877	.0352	.0099
.0090	.0292	.3920	.0292	.0090
.0099	.0352	.0877	.0352	.0099
.0105	.0198	.0270	.0198	.0105

4 miles

Figure 16. Mean information field for Seattle (corrected for directional bias).

.0094	.0133	.0164	.0133	.0094
.0133	.0411	.0673	.0411	.0133
.0164	.0673	.3690	.0673	.0164
.0133	.0411	.0673	.0411	.0133
.0094	.0133	.0164	.0133	.0094

4 miles

Figure 17. Mean information field for Seattle (exponential derivation).

riage partners lived within the same square mile (Figure 15).

These pure symmetric mean information fields may seem oversimplified, particularly if we know the nature of directional bias in a given area, or obvious social breaks (as in the Seattle study). The information fields may be corrected fairly easily for such bias (Figures 16 and 18), reflecting the greater likelihood in this case of north-south contact. When information fields are used in empirical predictive studies, even topographic features and other barriers may be directly taken into account. These adaptations have been illustrated in studies of the spread of innovations.[21] Or in order to predict Seattle marriages (Figure 1) different probabilities (information fields) would pertain to residents in the center and at the eastern periphery.

Obviously the 'mean information field' works best where similar patterns of move-

.0094	.0178	.0246	.0178	.0094
.0089	.0411	.1010	.0411	.0089
.0082	.0337	.3690	.0337	.0082
.0089	.0411	.1010	.0411	.0089
.0094	.0178	.0246	.0178	.0094

4 miles

Figure 18. Mean information field for Seattle (exponential derivation) corrected for directional bias.

---

21. Hägerstrand, *op. cit.*, footnote 8.

.0096	.0140	.0168	.0140	.0096
.0140	.0301	.0547	.0301	.0140
.0168	.0547	.4431	.0547	.0168
.0140	.0301	.0547	.0301	.0140
.0096	.0140	.0168	.0140	.0096

5 km

Figure 19. Mean information field for Asby, Sweden (pareto derivation).

.0103	.0150	.0181	.0150	.0103
.0150	.0279	.0557	.0279	.0150
.0181	.0557	.4319	.0557	.0181
.0150	.0279	.0557	.0279	.0150
.0103	.0150	.0181	.0150	.0103

5 km

Figure 21. Mean information field for Kagawa, Japan (pareto derivation).

.0054	.0118	.0153	.0118	.0054
.0118	.0402	.0798	.0402	.0118
.0153	.0798	.3360	.0798	.0153
.0118	.0402	.0798	.0402	.0118
.0054	.0118	.0153	.0118	.0054

5 km

Figure 20. Mean information field for Asby, Sweden (pareto-exponential derivation).

ments are fairly continuous over space (Figure 2, Asby) or where movements are into and out of a concentrated center. In the latter, sophisticated modifications of the fields are possible and justified. But in problems where there is no center, or where patterns exhibit sharp breaks at social or physical barriers, or breaks owing to very uneven attractiveness, we cannot justify use of a stable information field for more than a small part of a study area. Rather we may express the probabilities of moving from each sub-area to all other areas in a function relating both distance and characteristics of all possible destinations. This means finding a different information field around every possible origin, rather than trying to adopt a general field to each particular situation. This is most practicably done by computer.[22]

22. F. R. Pitts, "HAGER III and HAGER IV: Two Monte Carlo Computer Programs for the Study of Spatial Diffusion Problems," *Technical Report*

MEAN INFORMATION FIELDS AND OTHER KINDS OF MOVEMENT OR CONTACT

Marriage, migration, and direct social contact are perhaps the most pervasive and important of a class of movements, but it is appropriate to consider briefly other possible movements or contacts which may have a similar basis. We may also study them as possible surrogates when we wish to study marriages or migrations, but have no direct data available. It will be useful to treat these at three levels: local, regional, and metropolitan.

Measures of Local Information Fields

Half a dozen measures of local information fields have been considered. In Sweden, where each farm has a distinctive name, Hägerstrand has suggested asking farmers, "How many farms can you name, starting from your own and working out?"[23] The distances mentioned by perhaps one hundred farmers are recorded to form the data for calculation of a local field. A variant of this method was given a provisional test in Japan when Pitts asked several farmers to identify the *aza* in which they lived, and the names for all other *aza* that they could recall. (Aza are ancient village area names, and survive as cadastral units).[24]

In any country, people may be persuaded to recall the place where they last visited a

relative, or conversely, the place from which a relative visited them. A sample of several hundred such visits would provide an acceptable information field. In the United States, it might be illuminating to study for draftees the distance between address recorded at draft boards and the address of actual residence when called into service. The distribution of ambulance calls, newspaper circulation, and births at a hospital, where distances between residences and places of service are the raw data for contacts, defines service areas, which are a kind of information field.[25]

Regional Information Fields

These are somewhat easier to come by. Nine sources may be listed from a wealth of possibilities:

1) Places of birth and of present residence of respondents[26] to questionnaires sent out by a friendly local sociologist.
2) Birthplaces of marriage partners; in industrialized countries, the distances are likely to be longer than those gained from address-before-marriage data.
3) Addresses of the two owners of automobiles in two-car collisions.
4) Places of auto purchase (many cars are not purchased locally).
5) The home town addresses of the last three coeds dated by unmarried graduate students in one's university.
6) Places visited during the last vacation trip of a sample of families
10 Places of birth and death of persons noted in newspaper obituaries.

Number 4, Spatial Diffusion Study, Department of Geography, Northwestern University, 1965. Sponsored by the Geography Branch, Office of Naval Research, Task No. 389-140, Contract Nonr 1228(33).

23. In conversation with Pitts, January, 1962.
24. Lack of time prevented a full survey. However, a Summer, 1966, test of the *aza*-naming technique was conducted in the Kagawa area.

25. Density distance functions for legal addresses of hospital born babies now being calculated by Pitts formally combines aspects of central place theory and information theory.
26. Birthplace fields for southern Sweden are considered fully in K. E. Bergsten, *Sydsvenska Födelseortsfält* (Lund: Gleerup, 1951), 102 pp.

8) Bus travel between cities.[27]
9) Homes of noncity students at a city university.

Metropolitan or Long-Distance Information Fields

Long-distance fields might be compiled from letters to a Chamber of Commerce from persons seeking information, from data on intercity long-distance phone calls, and from the addresses of Christmas cards people receive. Home addresses of nonlocal persons buying fishing licenses, and vacation-spot logbook addresses would measure the attractive forces of recreation areas, and might conceivably be used in studying the spread of conservation ideas. Mean information fields based upon use of specific kinds of recreational facilities could be used to simulate use levels for new recreational areas planned as part of the Appalachia economic development effort. One might sample individual acquaintance fields. Morrill's attempt to do this yielded approximately $D^{-1.8}$ (Pareto) for the role of distance.

Finally, the relation between pure social information fields and economic activity fields such as trade areas, is a subject for investigation. Density functions for trade areas may have significant relation to mean information fields, either directly or by transform. Economic activity fields may be viewed as composite cross sections of individual information fields; that is, the pattern of shoppers around a shop is the accumulation of just one purpose from many individuals. From the individual's point of view, trips to stores may be an important part of

his total information field.[28] Thus, we do not expect the shape to be too different. The economic or trade area field is certainly more closely dependent on cost or time considerations—an attempt at least cost or optimal movement—whereas personal information fields are less regular and involve more noneconomic values less obviously related to distance, or even more related to information than to distance.

Historical Mean Information Fields

After we finish investigating the graduate students' love lives and our neighbors' Christmas cards, it may be wiser to look to the past while things calm down. Is it theoretically possible to reconstruct information fields for former periods as a first step toward studying the processes in information and innovation spread, the spread of settlement, the extension of the frontier, migration and urban development, the spread of industrialization? The answer is affirmative. Some early data exist or can be inferred from maps or records concerning the establishment of churches or factories or villages, the adoption of different religions or political forms, or eating habits, early moves from farm to town, and pioneers into new territory. With some idea of the median or typical distance of travel or contact, and the extreme range of greatest and least contact, the historical field may be reconstructed. For example, Edmonson has postulated for the Neolithic period a mean diffusion rate of 1.2 to 2 kilometers per year.[29]

---

27. Pitts is currently processing information on some 15,000 intercity bus trips taken in Okinawa on 15 January 1954. Traffic density data useful in graph theory and mean information field data valuable in simulation will result from this study.

28. J. D. Nystuen, *Geographical Analysis of Customer Movements and Retail Business Locations: (1) Theories, (2) Empirical Patterns in Cedar Rapids, Iowa,* and *(3) A Simulation Model of Movement.* (Unpublished doctoral dissertation, University of Washington, 1959).
29. M. S. Edmonson, "Neolithic Diffusion Rates," *Current Anthropology,* Vol. 2, (1961), pp. 71-102.

'The distances which are critical for reconstruction of an information field must be found by working patiently with data, adjusted to local conditions of population density and physical conditions. Once the land use characteristics of critical distances are isolated, the stage will be set for going back into the literature and mining detailed land use maps for their newly valuable intellectual ore.[30]

Should such an approach prove successful, it would open the way to further reconstruction of information fields based on quite different criteria. We are thinking, for example, of the diminution of yield on farms, owing to increasing distance to parcels. Chisholm gives data[31] (Table 7) which are very instructive:

---

30. We have in mind maps of the sort presented by de Schlippe and Prothero. P. de Schlippe, *Shifting Cultivation in Africa: the Zande System of Agriculture* (London: Routledge and Paul, 1956); and R. M. Prothero, "Land Use at Soba, Zaria, Northern Nigeria," *Economic Geography*, Vol. 33 (1957), pp. 72-86.

31. M. Chisholm, *Rural Settlement and Land Use* (London: Hutchinson's University Library, 1962), p. 125.

Table 7   Estimated Effect of Distance Between Settlements upon the Average Net Product per Hectare

Distance Between Settlements in Kms.	Average Distance to Cultivated Land in Kms.	Average net product per Hectare, zero Distance to land Equals 100
0.5	0.18	94
1.0	0.35	90
1.5	0.53	85
2.0	0.70	80
2.0	1.10	72
4.0	1.40	66
6.0	2.11	55
8.0	2.81	47

Source: Chisholm, cited in footnote 31.

USES OF MEAN INFORMATION FIELDS

Information fields are valuable as a generalization of the form and extent of existing patterns of contact, but have greater purpose as measures of tendency to communicate or move over distance. Thus, they constitute a fundamental part of any model of expected behavior in space.

The above analysis illustrates the use of information fields as a descriptive or summarizing device. Any geographic pattern of the distance-decay sort can be approximated by the information field under which the location decisions are presumably made.

For purposes of fuller explanation and possible prediction, models of travel behavior may be proposed. For large numbers of people and/or trips, information fields may be incorporated into deterministic models (as interaction models). The advantage of the fact that individual information fields may be seen as a typical product of a mean information field is that we may construct *simulation* models of expected individual or small group behavior. Such a model simulates, or generates, patterns *like* real ones by allowing individual choice within the general probabilities of the mean information field. Figures 4–8 provided a simple example of such a model. Obviously, the greater the number of trips and the greater the concentration of probabilities in a few destinations, the smaller the uncertainty and variability of pattern (the more deterministic the solution becomes). Simulation models have been developed or proposed for migration by Price and by Morrill, the spread of a settlement frontier by Bylund, the spread of a minority ghetto by Morrill, urban growth in general by Garrison and by Pitts, the growth of the urban fringe by Morrill, the spread of innovations by Rogers, the spread of hybrid seed corn in Iowa by Tiedemann, the spread of irrigation wells in eastern Colorado by

Bowden, the study of physical barrier effects by Yuill, prediction of the disappearance of horses as rural mechanization progresses by Pitts, and for reconstruction of past distributions by Pitts and Marble.[32] All these

32. D. Price, "A Mathematical Model of Migration Suitable for Simulation on an Electric Computer," *Proceedings*, International Population Conference (Wien: 1959), pp. 665-73; and R. L. Morrill, "The Development of Spatial Distributions of Towns in Sweden: An Historical-Predictive Approach," *Annals*, Association of American Geographers, Vol. 53 (1963), pp. 1-14, and his monograph, "Migration and the Spread and Growth of Urban Settlement," *Lund Studies in Geography*, Series B. Human Geography No. 26, 1965; E. Bylund, "Theoretical Considerations Regarding the Distribution of Settlement in Inner Northern Sweden," *Geografiska Annaler*, Vol. 42 (1960), pp. 225-31; R. L. Morrill, "The Negro Ghetto: Problems and Alternatives," *The Geographical Review*, Vol. 55, no. 3 (1965), pp. 339-61; W. L. Garrison, "Toward a Simulation Model of Urban Growth and Development," in K. Norborg (Ed.), *The IGU Symposium in Urban Geography* (Lund, 1960), pp. 91-108; F. R. Pitts, "Scale and Purpose in Urban Simulation Models," in W. Maki and B. J. L. Berry (Eds.), *Research and Education for Regional and Area Development* (Ames: Iowa State University Press, 1965); R. L. Morrill, "Expansion of the Urban Fringe: A Simulation Experiment," *Papers and Proceedings*, Regional Science Association, 1964, Vol. 15 (1965), pp. 135-99; E. M. Rogers, *Diffusion of Innovations* (New York: The Free Press of Glencoe, 1962); C. E. Tiedemann and C. S. Van Doren, "The Diffusion of Hybrid Seed Corn in Iowa: A Spatial Simulation Model," *Technical Bulletin* T-44, Institute for Community Development and Services, Michigan State University, December, 1964, 12 pp. (mimeographed); L. W. Bowden, "Simulation and Diffusion of Irrigation Wells in the Colorado Northern High Plains," Paper of Merit, Plenary Session, AAG meeting, Syracuse, N. Y. (March 31, 1964). An expanded version of this has appeared as *Research Paper* No. 97, University of Chicago, Department of Geography; R. S. Yuill, "A Simulation Study of Barrier Effects in Spatial Diffusion Problems," *Technical Report* Number 1, Spatial Diffusion Study. Geography Branch, Office of Naval Research, Task No. 389-140, Contract Nonr 1228(33). November, 1964, 47 pp.; F. R. Pitts, "Chorology Revisited—

make use of distance-decay or information fields around the areas of origin. Also, since settlement distributions exist under specific social information fields,[33] it may be possible to reconstruct both the character of such fields and changes in them from such data as the mapped distribution of parish churches in the preindustrial period, the distribution of stations on the new railways, and the pattern of decline and growth of settlements.

Computational Problems

A serious problem in simulation models, and one reason for their rather recent development, is the very great computational work. Dealing with hundreds of individual decisions, each of which involves in turn the acceptance or rejections of many possibilities, can be a long and tedious process. Fortunately, models have been programmed for computer in several variations, and it is now possible to undertake more complex and interesting problems.[34] Computer simulation programs can easily be written to call upon any of the suggested functions for contact probabilities, as needed and as appropriate.

Mean information fields in simulation are most efficiently usable in computers owing to the great amount of time required for

Computerwise," *The Professional Geographer*, Vol. 14, No. 6 (November, 1962), pp. 8-12; F. R. Pitts and D. F. Marble, "Some Applications of the Hägerstrand Diffusion Model to Problems in Historical and Human Geography," forthcoming as a *Technical Report*, Spatial Diffusion Study, as a part of the contract cited in footnote 40.

33. G. Boalt and C.-G. Janson, "Distance and Social Relations," *Acta Sociologica*, Vol. 2 (1957), pp. 73-97.

34. Alternative simulation programs for Hägerstrand type models are discussed in F. R. Pitts, "Problems in Computer Simulation of Diffusion," *Papers and Proceedings*, Regional Science Association, Vol. 11 (1963), pp. 111-19.

hand simulations. To date, problems of storage, of running speed of simulation programs, and of the relative lack of flexible simulation languages have generally faced the geographer who desires to use this tool for research. Within the very near future many of these problems will be solved or materially reduced. Storage may be increased to adequate amounts by random access disk packs; computer speeds are faster with the new technologies; and more flexible ways of writing simulation programs are being developed. Two general languages developed for nonspatial simulation, SIMSCRIPT, and Information Programming Language-V may be used for spatial allocation if a geographer supervises the writing of programs tailored to his needs.[35] A more newly developed list-processing language, SLIP,[36] shows promise of having the

---

35. H. M. Markowitz, B. Hausner, and H. W. Karr, *SIMSCRIPT: A Simulation Programming Language,* (Santa Monica: The RAND Corporation, 1962); A. Newell; F. M. Tonge; E. A. Feigenbaum; B. F. Green, Jr.; G. H. Mealy, *Information Processing Language-V Manual,* 2nd ed. (Englewood Cliffs: Prentice-Hall, 1964), 267 pp.

36. The SLIP language was developed by Joseph Weizenbaum of M.I.T. It is operative at several

simplicity of the widely used FORTRAN and the flexible power of IPL-V.

SUMMARY

1. Information fields, defined as measures of tendency to communicate over distance, have proven valuable as means of description and as tools in simulating the spread or movement of people or ideas.

2. The distance-frequency aspect of fields may be described by curves of close fit, the appropriate function depending on the kind of data.

3. The information component of the fields is great, and needs to be incorporated into any model of movement.

4. Many additional kinds of movements or contacts may be used to derive mean information fields in addition to marriage, migration, and direct contact. Historically valid information fields can be devised.

5. The paradox of simultaneous uniqueness and generality of individual behavior is hopefully explained through the analysis of how individual patterns are possible examples of general patterns.

University computation centers, though no manual has yet been published.

✝✝✝✝✝✝✝✝✝✝✝✝✝✝✝✝✝✝✝✝✝✝✝✝✝✝✝✝✝✝

THE SPATIAL STRUCTURE OF A SELECTED INTERPERSONAL CONTACT: A REGIONAL COMPARISON OF MARRIAGE DISTANCES IN INDIA

Robert C. Mayfield

The geographer's concern for problems of spatial structure dates to the founding of the discipline. Very early he attempted classification of segments of the earth's surface into regional divisions; more recently, he has begun to develop mathematical models of spatial pattern. A directed interest in the parameters of spatial interaction has elicited a wide range of studies over the past fifteen years. Pioneering works, such as those of Garrison and Hägerstrand, have been amplified and extended, developing a body of substantive literature which complements work in other disciplines. The present report has been prepared in the hope that it will prove of interest to those researchers concerned with the broad problem of human behaviour in spatial context.

Generally, the research reported here deals with the distances and directions moved by Indian villagers in completing interpersonal contacts. A principal contribution of the study of selected movement pattern by individuals has been suggested by Morrill and Pitts: "The essential characteristic of these personal information fields and that which permits us to make predictions, no matter how hedged, about personal behavior, is that each unique field makes at the same time a contribution to the mean information field."[1]

As a contribution to a larger investigation of innovation diffusion in Indian agriculture, an investigation which will utilize the notion of mean information fields, the present study deals specifically with the spatial separation of husband's village and wife's village—the marriage distance. Marble and Nystuen, Henderson, and others have investigated the utility of this distance in defining the information field of the individual in Western society.[2] Pitts has also found the distance to be of value in the simulation of innovation diffusion in Japanese agriculture.[3] In 1965, the author's field research

1. Richard L. Morrill and Forrest R. Pitts, "Marriage, Migration and the Mean Information Field: A Study in Uniqueness and Generality," forthcoming, *Annals*, Association of American Geographers, 1967.
2. Duane F. Marble and John D. Nystuen, "An Approach to the Direct Measurement of Community Mean Information Fields," *Papers*, Regional Science Association, Vol. XI (1962). James Henderson, "Distance and Marital Selection," unpublished seminar paper, Department of Geography, University of Washington, Seattle, 1962.
3. Forrest R. Pitts, "Computer Simulation of

Technical Report No. 6, Spatial Diffusion Study, Department of Geography, Northwestern University under contract with Office of Naval Research, Geography Branch, ONR Task No. 389-140, Contract Nonr 1228 (33). Reprinted by permission.

in India offered an opportunity for observing patterns of this interpersonal contact distance in another non-Western area. Support for the study of Indian marriage distances as a possible information field surrogate has been provided by W. L. Rowe, from a study of a village in Uttar Pradesh. After noting a tendency for a change in social structure from the traditional vertical intra-village caste orientation to one of horizontal interaction with other villages within the marriage network, he writes: "The network increases its structural importance in the total social organization and raises the question of its possible function as a channel of further change".[4]

Data collection was undertaken in 1965 in three rather widely dispersed states within India: the undivided Punjab, Gujarat, and Mysore.[5] (See Fig. 1.) The regional design is an important aspect of the research. Although several studies of Indian villages have included distances moved by the inhabitants,

none known to this writer has studied the topic for a large area, systematically, or have introduced strict regional comparisons. One of the purposes of this study is to suggest whether the regional disparities in interpersonal contact distances are sufficient to warrant separate probability statements for the distance-decay function by region, by size of village, by quality of local surface communications, and by a simple stratification of occupation types—that of farmer and non-farm service personnel. Another objective of the study is an examination of directional bias in the pattern of movement. An investigation of the ability of the villagers to estimate distances and directions was also undertaken. Little had been reported by 1965 as to whether the resident of the small, dispersed Indian settlement had a relatively accurate mental map of the area over which he interacted. The data collected provided a preliminary examination of this topic.[6] Comparisons of marriage distances with distances to frequently visited friends and relatives of the husband are also made, examining each briefly as to its usefulness as a surrogate for the mean information field.

THE STUDY AREAS AND SELECTION CRITERIA

District sites for study were selected in the three states as follows: Ambala in the Punjab, Surat in Gujarat, and Kolar in Mysore State. A brief introduction to these may be of interest to the reader.

All the districts have certain characteristics in common. Each has a principal city bearing the same name as the district. Each has a relatively well developed hard surfaced road network with bus services that compete heavily with the railroad of the district as

Diffusion in the Japanese Rural Economy." Paper read at the Northwest Anthropological Conference, University of Oregon, Eugene, 1962, 8 pp.

4. William L. Rowe, "The Marriage Network and Structural Change in a North Indian Community," *Southwest Journal of Anthropology*, Vol. 16 (1960). For an earlier reference to the same area, see Morris Opler, "The Extensions of an Indian Village," *Journal of Asian Studies*," Vol. 16 (1956). Rowe reports also, in a footnote, on a pertinent paper by James M. Mahar, "Extra-village Visits and Delineation of Unit Boundaries," presented at the annual meeting of the American Anthropological Association, 1959. Mahar reported that 87 per cent of all visits by the Chamars of his village were of a kinship nature; Rowe suggests 86 per cent of 123 intervillage visits were to or from households with marital relationships. Most of the "village India" volumes (Lewis, Marriott, Srinivas, etc.) have scattered, relevant materials.

5. Data collection in a fourth study area, coastal Andhra Pradesh, was interrupted and left incomplete by complications arising from the coinciding "summer war" between India and Pakistan.

6. Peter R. Gould, "On Mental Maps," Discussion Paper No. 9, Michigan Inter-University Community of Mathematical Geographers, September 1966.

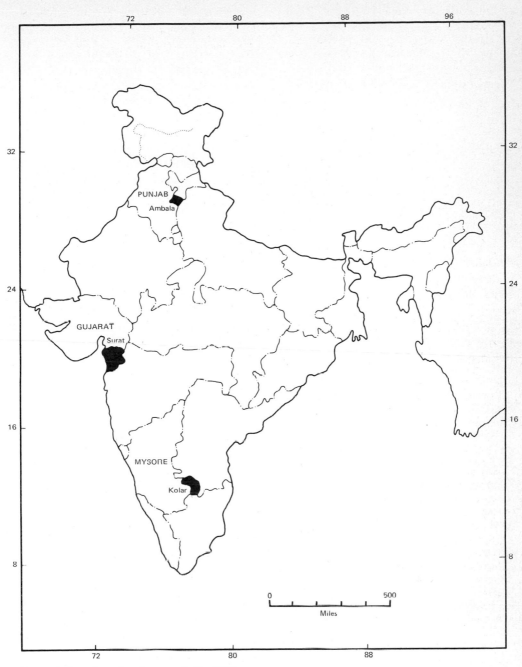

Figure 1. Location of study areas. India, 1965.

carriers of passengers. Although a variety of agricultural products is produced in each, all the districts are producers of primary food-grains: wheat and maize in Ambala, rice and sorghum in Surat, and millet and rice in Kolar. Within each district, a political sub-division was selected according to the following criteria:

1. The area must be predominantly agri-cultural (one part of Kolar District is impor-tant for gold mining).

2. Villages within the subdivision must be at least 12 to 15 miles from the district capital; i.e. slightly more than a day's round trip walking distance, according to local practices.

3. The subdivision must contain a hard-surfaced road network with an active daily bus service.

4. A sufficient number of villages both on and off the road network must be present in the subdivision in order to provide inter-action opportunities in all directions.

5. Certain size and road class restrictions should be met by the villages selected within the subdivision.

Four strata of village population size (1 = 500; 501 = 1000; 1001 = 1500; and 1501 = 2000) were selected as basically adaptable to any area. As this size-class strat-ification had been found to be statistically significant in an earlier study of the range of consumer goods in the Punjab, it was intro-duced again.[7] A communication classifica-tion was quite arbitrarily defined as "good" or "poor." A village with a rating of "good" was served by a road with either a "metalled" (hard) surface or a compact gravel surface supporting bus traffic, pre-sumably without undue discomfort to the passengers of the bus. There were very few

villages on hard surfaced roads without bus service in the subdivisions studied. A "poor" classification ranged from the near absence of a connecting route, to the presence of a dirt-surfaced track of considerable uneven-ness. The reader is spared any attempt at evaluation of user discomfort, but the prime characteristic was that bus service had *not* developed regardless of surface condition of the route. (There were some villages on extremely bad roads that had bus service, but these were not included in this study.)

The subdivision and villages, identified in Table 1, were selected according to the size and communication restraints given pre-viously.

Within each village, informants were selected from two broad groups based on actual occupation, rather than specified caste. The primary interest of the broader study is in the diffusion of farm practices. For the three study areas, interviews were held with farmers reporting twenty-three "castes" (including some who reported their religion as Christian, their caste as Protes-tant). Fifty-seven "castes" were suggested by the non-farming villagers. A consideration more pertinent than caste differential was whether significant differences existed be-tween the farming and non-farming groups. The farmers were specified as owner-culti-vators of their lands. This restriction was placed in order to ensure that the respon-dents would be members of the primary target group for technological change in Indian agriculture. The second group selected was less restrictive in membership—those who perform non-farm services in the village. The largest number of service respon-dents from a single occupational category were shopkeepers, but carpenters, barbers, smiths, weavers, tailors, washermen, cob-blers, and brick-makers were among those interviewed. The requirement that these be full-time service personnel reduced the num-

7. Robert C. Mayfield, "The Range of a Central Good," *Annals*, Association of American Geog-raphers, Vol. 53 (1963).

Table 1   Villages Contained in the Stratified Sample

District	State	Communication Class	Size Class (0–500)	(501–1000)	(1001–1500)	(1501–2000)
Ambala	Punjab	Good	Siswan	Chanalon	Khanpur	Sahawran
		Poor	Akalgarh	Mundhon-Sangtia	Mattor	Kumbhra
Surat	Gujarat	Good	Bamroli	Kharwasa	Menekpur	Umra
		Poor	Chhitra	Goji	Uva	Jervavla
Kolar	Mysore	Good	Varadanaik-anahalli	Abladu	Malamachana-halli	Melur
		Poor	Gudihalli	Muthoor	Sugatur	Bhakhthar-ahalli

ber of respondents available, particularly in very small villages. In such communities, services are often provided by "part-time" farmers.

THE CONTACT DISTANCES

Contributions to the literature on inter-personal contacts over space in India include a wide range of studies concerning such topics as marriage, religion, caste, kinships, interlocal fairs, etc.[8] Many of these have been authored by anthropologists with special interests in a single village. For several of these studies, the villages selected are within walking distance of a town or city many times the size of the village—in one case, the distance is only two miles.[9] A

number of pertinent publications have come from the study of a community of some 5,000 inhabitants.[10] However, it should be noted that most Indian villagers live in much smaller places. It cannot be questioned that such studies yield fruitful insights, meriting a somewhat wider application of findings. Geographers familiar with India's regional variation, the differences in tertiary economic activity, and range of communication level between the village of 500 and that of 5,000; as well as the forces operating on communities in urban peripheral sites, would be unwilling to overlook the dangers of suggesting spatially broad generalizations from these studies.

    The study of interpersonal contact distances presented here is limited in both spatial and temporal extent. It includes preliminary data from twenty-four villages, eight in each of a single district in the three

8. The literature related to interpersonal communication in India is extensive and prohibits a detailed listing, but interested readers might begin with Y. B. Damle, *Communication of Modern Ideas and Knowledge in Indian Villages* Cambridge: M.I.T., (1955) and D. N. Majumdar, *Caste and Communication in an Indian Village* (Bombay: Asia Publishing House, 1958) See Footnote 4 also.

9. K. Ishwaran's "Kinship and Distance in Rural India," *The International Journal of Comparative*

Sociology, Vol. II, No. 1, (1965), is pertinent, but limited empirically.

10. Kholapur, some eighty miles north of New Delhi, is one of the most closely studied communities in the sub-continent, having been the subject of investigation for a team of Indian and American anthropologists.

states, for a time period of only a few months. It does not attempt to explore the daily interpersonal contact structure within the village which encompasses the bulk of these contacts. What it does consider are certain recurring contacts which take the villager outside his residential community. The 570 individuals who create the patterns studied here are distributed by districts as follows: Ambala, 191; Surat, 194; Kolar, 185. For all the regions, more viable interviews were obtained from farmers than from service personnel.

As a convenient method of arraying the data, the auxiliary plotter of a computer was utilized to prepare a map showing the correct distance and direction of the wife's village from that of the husband. Figures 2, 3, and 4, redrawn from the computer plots, give this data for Ambala, Surat, and Kolar districts. Locations falling outside the plot

boundary were shown correctly by direction, with arrows. For each of these figures, the eight villages of each district for which data were obtained are shown by shaded rectangles. The high density for farmers in Kolar is apparent; the comparable density for the Gujarati farmers is less readily seen. The wider separation of villages selected would seem to account for the visual disparity. There is ample visual evidence of the more widely dispersed marital selections of the Ambala villagers.

Frequency of Contact

As stated earlier, interest in the marriage distance stems from its use as a mean information field surrogate in previous studies. The data collected for this study do not offer evidence of the *adequacy* of the marriage distance as a surrogate for the mean of an Indian villager's interpersonal contacts

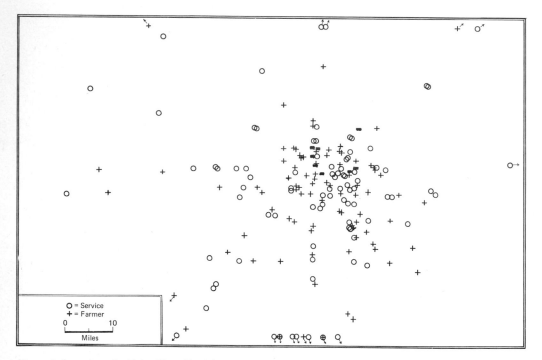

Figure 2. Location of wife's village, Punjab.

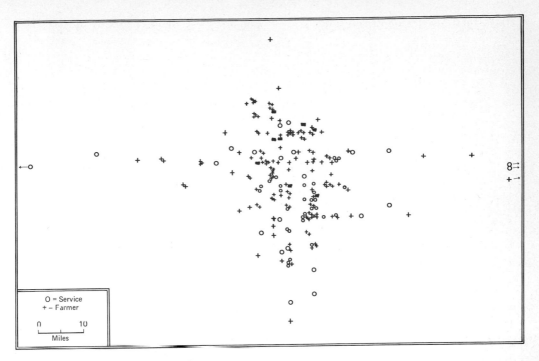

Figure 3. Location of wife's village, Gujarat.

over space. There is some indication of whether the marriage distance is a recurring component of that spatial pattern. The relative significance of *trips* to the wife's village, in terms of information transfer, was somewhat an open question in spite of pertinent, positive comments by Rowe[11] and H. A. Gould.[12] (Both reported on single villages in Uttar Pradesh.) It may be noted that all but a half-dozen of the 570 villagers interviewed

for the study presented here gave evidence of being patrilocal (the exceptions were all Mysoreans). Information was sought as to the relative frequency of visits to the wife's village over the past year, dating from the interview.

In each district, a few who were interviewed were not married, yet were considered head of the household with respect to decision-making. These could not be included in this calculation. In the south, particularly, there were wives taken from the same village as the husband. These were omitted from the count. (All but one of Kolar's 19 such cases reported daily contact with the wife's family, and the exception suggested contacts of "at least every other day.") In a more pertinent vein, there were those who were married, but had not visited the village and family of the wife in the past year. (Two volunteered that they had *never*

11. Rowe, *op. cit.*
12. Harold A. Gould, "The Micro-Demography of Marriage in a North Indian Area," *Southwest Journal of Anthropology*, Vol. 14 (1960). An extract of a thesis by B. Banerji, reported in Karve's *Kinship Organization in India* (Bombay: Asia Publishing House, 1965) p. 310, indicates that over 67 per cent of the marriages in two southern Mysore Vokkaliga villages had been arranged within five miles of the villages. Of these, some 27 per cent of the marriage pairs were "local," arranged within the villages studied.

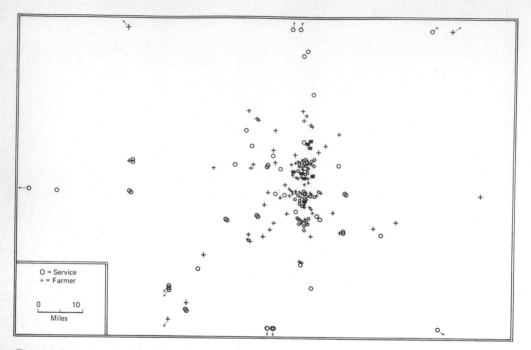

Figure 4. Location of wife's village, Mysore.

visited.) These were greatest in the north, with Ambala reporting 31 non-visiting husbands, Surat only 8, and Kolar 13. If these are included in the averaging, the trip frequency mean for the Ambala villagers is 4.2 trips per year, for Surat 3.6, and for Kolar 9.6. If the non-visiting husbands are omitted from the averaging, mean frequencies of visit rise to 5.1 for Ambala, 3.7 for Surat, and 10.6 for Kolar.

Approximately 90 per cent of those completing trips in Ambala made ten or fewer visits. Modal frequency was two trips per year, with 35 persons reporting that number. Certain of the Ambala cultivators suggested that too many trips to the wife's village could be "unpleasant." Some informants stated that it is not wise, economically to be "too close" to the wife's family. Others offered that they had very cordial relations with the family of the wife, but saw no

reason to visit "frequently." For Surat, modal frequency speaks even more clearly: 81 villagers reported two trips and (74 reported three). "Explanations" similar to those given in Ambala were made, but no single cultural factor can be identified as accountable for the low frequencies in Surat. Costs of movement tend to be relatively high, due to the less well-developed communications. Kolar's high mean frequency, and its mode of 10 trips, reflects the accepted local practice of first-cousin marriage, with little or no social separation of the marriage pair families.[13]

There were slight, statistically non-significant differences in trip frequency (checked at the 5 per cent level) for farmers vs. service personnel.

---

13. The Kolar survey exhibited six cases of uncle-niece marriage.

The Marriage Distance

The mean distances to wife's village, by district, give figures of 20.6 miles for Ambala villagers, 12.0 for those of Surat's talukas, and 16.5 for Kolar. (For their villages in Uttar Pradesh, Rowe[14] and Gould[15] have suggested marriage distance means of 12 and 10.5 miles, respectively.) This observer made an intuitive evaluation, in the field, of overall level of communications within the district subdivisions. Ambala was placed well to the top, followed by Kolar, then Surat. To a geographer who strongly mistrusts his abilities to conduct "visual" regional analysis, the distance means by district were only partly encouraging.

It was noticed from the first villages surveyed in the Punjab that service personnel were reporting greater distances to their wives' villages than were farmers. Inquiry in all regions revealed the same probable demographic clue. There are fewer families performing services. They (or more accurately, their match-makers) must travel farther to arrange a suitable marriage, whatever the endogamy—exogamy restraints regarding caste, lineage, or family. Table 2 gives the mean distances by district and occupation.

This table provides a somewhat closer look at the data than that provided by the distance means reported earlier, but it may

14. Rowe, *op. cit.*
15. Gould, *op. cit.*

Table 2 Mean Distance in Miles to Wife's Village by District and Occupation

District	Occupation	
	Farmer	Service
Ambala	15.1	26.1
Surat	9.7	14.4
Kilar	9.1	23.8

Table 3 Mean Distance in Miles to Wife's Village by District and Village Communication Level

District	Communication Level	
	Good	Poor
Ambala	25.9	15.3
Surat	12.3	11.7
Kolar	19.8	13.1

lead to an inadequate generalization. Of all the district groups, the farmers of Kolar have the smallest trip distance mean. It is this group who most frequently complete trips to wife's village, averaging almost twelve trips annually. One might make the assumption that it is a distance factor only which governs frequency. However, with a further breakdown of the data, a more complex structure is suggested. Table 3 gives the distance means for the districts by communication level: Tables 4 and 5 introduce that factor by occupation, for each district, for distance and frequency. Note that the occupational differences in mean distance remain evident, but those of communication level, as suggested so strongly by Table 3, are no longer clear cut. Correlations of mean distance and frequency are weakened, and for some classifications, reversed.

There are entries in the tables which make for interesting speculation. If there

Table 4 Mean Distance in Miles to Wife's Village by District, Occupation, and Communication Level

District	Occupation	Communication Level	
		Good	Poor
Ambala	Farmer	16.9	13.3
	Service	34.8	17.3
Surat	Farmer	8.0	11.3
	Service	16.7	12.0
Kolar	Farmer	10.2	8.1
	Service	29.4	18.1

Table 5   Trip Frequency Means to Wife's Village by District, Occupation, and Communication Level, 1964-65

| District | Occupation | Communication Level | |
		Good	Poor
Ambala	Farmer	5.1	5.2
	Service	2.9	2.5
Surat	Farmer	4.7	2.2
	Service	2.5	2.6
Kolar	Farmer	13.2	7.9
	Service	9.4	5.6

exists some overriding cultural bar to a high frequency of contact, the upper range for any of the Ambala villagers may be rather easily met in this district of generally widespread bus services and comparatively high agricultural income. It should be remembered that almost one in six of the Punjabis interviewed had not visited the wife's home in the twelve months preceding the survey. For some of these, the distances separating the villages were as short as two miles. (In such cases, the wife makes frequent visits, unaccompanied by her husband).

In Surat, farmers in the less accessible villages secured wives at distances greater than those in better connected communities. A possible factor is that the more isolated villages are regarded as less acceptable sites to which a daughter might be given. Thus a resident's sponsors might have to search a wider band of area to find a willing bride. (Why this should be the case in Surat and not in other districts is a topic that might well be pursued by those concerned with the details of regional classification.) It is worth noting that this group, pressed into an extension of effort to secure marriage partners, exhibited the lowest frequency of contact with the wife's family.

It is Surat's service personnel, quantitatively the smallest of the broad occupational groups surveyed (and most predominantly shopkeepers by profession), who show the greatest disparity in trip frequency means between communication levels. Although farming technology appeared to differ only slightly between villages of good and poor communication level, the provisions of services were notably less for the latter. This may be related to the relatively high cost of recurring trips to stock provisions (for shopkeepers) compared with the relatively few sales trips of farmers. Too, there may be reduced demands by the cultivators in less well-connected communities for the order of central goods indicated by village population size alone.

At best, the tables presented above are a beginning inquiry. An analysis of variance was conducted after a logarithmic transformation of all data pertaining to distance to wife's village. For the analysis of variance tables, let A signify region; B, size class of village, C, communication levels, and D, occupational category. Table 6 presents the results of the "distance to wife's village" analysis.

The analysis indicates that there are statistically significant differences between *regions* and between *occupation* types. The significant interaction between *region* and *occupation* suggests that the effect of the latter does not hold uniformly for all regions. To state the matter somewhat differently, one might suggest that the need for *regional* studies of diffusion, as called for by Coughenour, has been supported.[16] Too, the suggestion that the agricultural and service components of a village should be treated as discrete units lends support to the notion that technological systems may be

16. C. Milton Coughenour, "Technology, Diffusion and the Theory of Action," paper, preliminary session, First World Congress of Rural Sociology, Dijon, 1964.

Table 6   Analysis of Variance: Distance to
Wife's Village

Source	Mean Square	Degrees of Freedom	F-Ratio	Level of Significance (per cent)
Total	2.68	539		
Between	6.01	47		
A	41.98	2	17.78	1
B	4.6	3	1.96	
C	.01	1	.003	
D	48.07	1	20.36	1
AB	4.65	6	1.97	
AC	4.96	2	2.10	
AD	8.74	2	3.70	5
BC	.79	3	.34	
BC	1.04	3	.44	
CD	.08	1	.03	
ABC	2.66	6	1.13	
ABD	4.38	6	1.86	
ACD	.86	2	.36	
BCD	4.34	3	1.84	
ABCD	.52	6	.22	
Within	2.36	492		

Note: Natural logarithmic transformation of distance.

viewed as elements of the individual's environment.[17]

The fact that *size class of village* gave no indication of statistical significance may give some indication of the strength and persistence of cultural factors underlying the system of marriage selections within a region. This is to say that the societal norms regarding marriage are not much affected by changes in the size of villages with a population of less than 2,000, for selected villages in the three widely separated districts. The untransformed variance between size class of village was less than half that of the variance within classes. Perhaps, for India, the distance to wife's village might be a useful surrogate for the mean information field if

interest centers on farmers in smaller communities within a single region. The need for comparing these findings with those for larger villages is apparent. A related need may be the determination of boundaries for the cultural region within which a given surrogate is applicable.

The remaining variable, *level of communication*, merits a brief comment. Without transformation, the variable is statistically significant (at the 5 per cent level). With log transformation, it most certainly is not. The transformation, increasing the symmetry of the distribution and the linearity of relationships, seems appropriate due to the variable's inexact classification. An improved measure of communication level is needed, if that concept is to be evaluated properly for these regions. From the standpoint of spatial preference, the options open to the villager are of interest. A weighted index considering the

17. W. F. Ogburn, "The Meaning of Technology," in F. R. Allen et al., *Technology and Social Change*, Appleton-Century-Crofts, 1957.

number and quality of connections for a village could be developed. A graph theoretic connectivity index derived from the network of road and rail linkages might serve appropriately as a gauge of the level of communication for the Indian village.

Direction

The hypothesis that the marriage pair distances would exhibit directional bias stems from a number of sources. The road network, affecting both the morphology of settlement and the relative accessibility of places, provides an element of bias in the pattern. Indian district and state planners tend to connect one relatively large center to another, and those places along existing transport routes tend to grow at a faster rate than those lying off the network. Thus a gravitational or density bias may emphasize other influences on the movement pattern, particularly along the qualitatively better portions of the network. There are two pertinent suggestions from sociology: that of norm-segregation and interaction-time-cost. [18]

The first implies that normative considerations limit the location of marriage-pair eligibles to residentially isolated or segregated zones. Thus movement involved in a particular bride selection would be confined to a few directions. For an entire village of several caste groups, it would be anticipated that movement would not occur in all directions, but would be along sector or zonal paths, since very few villages have a full complement of all the regional caste groups.

What has been characterized as the "interaction-time-cost theory" is an assemblage of behavioral assumptions which suggest, not surprisingly, that the greater the cost of interaction, the less potential for such interaction. This, of course, has long been a familiar notion in geography. Since the time-cost function is stated as "directly related to distance," [19] we assume that lower costs would extend the range of marital selections. If the Indian villager values a wide range of selection within the restraints of his society, the lower costs (in time, effort, and cash) of moving out along the better road nets could lead to a directed linear extension and corresponding directional bias.

As a means of observing the direction of pairing, Figure 5 was prepared. [20] The base point, the site of the male household-head's village, is for all plots the origin (intersection of abscissa and ordinate). In this preliminary effort, sector rotations were made for Ambala and Surat, so that the ordinate for each district might more closely approximate the alignment of the major transportation route through that district. For Ambala and Surat, a 270° rotation was introduced, as the principal arterials, road and rail, are oriented generally east-west. The Kolar main road is basically a north-south route, turning toward Bangalore (to the southwest) in the southern portion of the study area. Figure 6 gives the generalized alignments for the first and second most important routes traversing

18. For an early statement of norm-segregation, see M. R. Davie and R. J. Reeves, "Propinquity of Residence before Marriage," *American Journal of Sociology*, Vol. 44 (January 1939). For a review of interaction-time-cost and norm-segregation concepts, see Alvin M. Katz and Reuben Hill, "Residential Propinquity and Marital Selection": A Review of Theory, Method, and Fact, *Marriage and Family Living*, Vol. 20 (February 1958).

19. Katz and Hill, *op. cit.*
20. The villager had been asked to indicate the direction to the wife's village as best he could, by pointing. Interviews were conducted with the interviewer facing north as indicated by village consensus, not by compass, as magnetic declinations were not known. A difficulty not fully resolved by experience is that of accurately recording the directions on the printed compass face of the questionnaire.

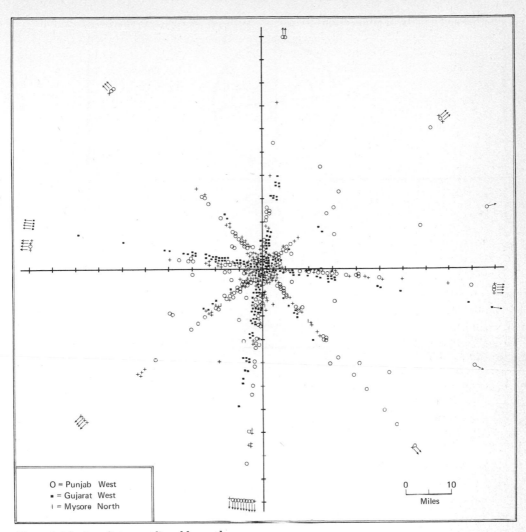

Figure 5. Marriage distances aligned by road.

the study area. Other than the strong distance-decay phenomenon exhibited, the most prominent factor reflected in Figure 5 is that alignment of major roads.

The question arises as to the accuracy with which the villager could indicate direction. Checks of villager accuracy in estimating directions revealed errors that partially account for the strength of the orientation. The first was a tendency to suggest for the direction to wife's village a direction parallel

to the main road, when the true direction was slightly oblique. The second is a tendency to generalize the more oblique directions into secondary, less dense sectors that appear at the quadrantal points approximately 45° from the principal concentrations. Thus a somewhat limited ability was demonstrated for estimating directions to places not on the network of main roads.

One additional note on direction: William McCormack, reporting for a Mysore village,

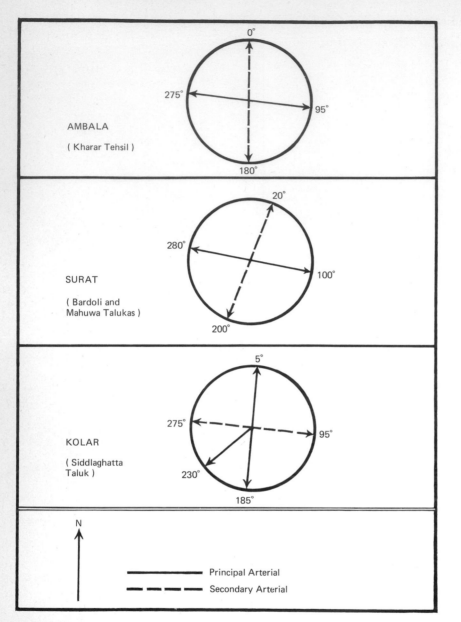

Figure 6. Alignment of main roads.

suggested the active influence of a "ritual custom of *agni muli* which prohibits the taking of a wife from the southeast or northwest of one's own village."[21] There is no

plotted evidence that this custom prevails in the Kolar study area, and inquiries did not reveal villager practice of it.

21. William McCormack, "Sister's Daughter Marriage in a Mysore Village," *Man in India*, Vol. 38, No. 1 (1958).

Distance Estimation

On a random check of 133 interview schedules for accuracy of estimation of distance to wife's village by road (to the nearest mile) 29 misjudged by one mile, but only fourteen more than one mile. Most of the larger errors were for distances exceeding ten miles. It is not surprising that shorter distances were more accurately estimated, but the high level of agreement among members of a village as to the distance to the more important neighboring centers was not anticipated. As an example, the location of centers which the Kolar district villagers had visited for any form of "official" information within the past two years were recorded. (The number who responded comprised approximately 35 per cent of the Kolar interviews.) Figure 7 presents a plot of these trip ends. All trip ends with coinciding coordinates for distance and direction were plotted in a rectan-

gular pattern proceeding counter-clockwise from the first plot of these coordinates. A trip end with a non-coinciding coordinate reading, but falling within a previously plotted rectangle of trip ends, was permitted to overprint. There is a relatively high degree of agreement. It might be mentioned here that few villagers hesitated in suggesting a given distance, and most gave prompt responses to questions of direction. The questions asked were well within the limits of spatial awareness for the Indian villager.

SELECTION OF A MEAN INFORMATION FIELD SURROGATE

It may be that marriage distances can serve as substitute measures for local mean information fields in India, although no proof of that has been attempted here. If

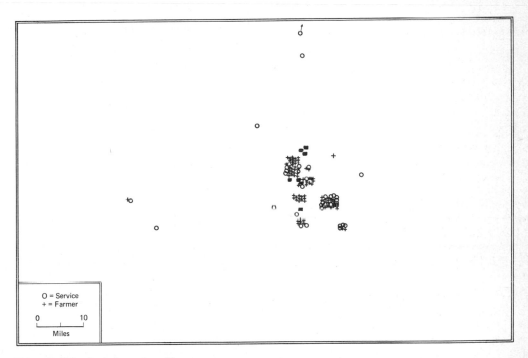

Figure 7. Trips for information, Mysore.

Table 7 Analysis of Variance: Distance to Friends Most Often
Visited Outside the Village

Source	Mean Square	Degrees of Freedom	F-Ratio	Level of Significance
Total	4.49	567		
Between	11.90	47		
A (Region)	22.86	2	5.97	1 per cent
B (Size Class)	7.35	3	1.92	
C (Communication Level)	4.94	1	1.29	
D (Occupation Category)	0.69	1	0.18	

Note: Natural logarithmic transformation.

these should be found to be useful surrogates, the researcher does not have excessive
difficulty in obtaining data. Most of India's
villages are inhabited by patrilocal groups,
and relevant information can be secured
from the male household heads. As Rowe
notes: "In a male-centered society, it is
perhaps not unusual that it is the men who
mostly make visits, that they interact with
men in the villages they visit, and therefore
tend to stress the affinal aspect." [22] In
Indian agriculture, however, there is the
suggestion that the most important contacts
are visits to agnatic, not cognatic, relatives

and to the personal friends of the
cultivator. [23]

Again utilizing the previously adopted
structure regarding region, village size, communication and occupation, analyses of
variance with logarithmic transformations
were conducted regarding the 570 respon-

22. Rowe, *op. cit.*

23. The literature is extensive, but the following
are good examples of work done: S. P. Bose, "The
Diffusion of a Farm Practice in Indian Villages,"
Rural Sociology, Vol. 29 (1964); S. Das Gupta,
"Communication and Innovation in Indian Vil-
lages," *Social Forces,* Vol. 43 (1965); W. B.
Rahudkar, "Communication of Farm Innovation in
an Indian Community," *Journal of Social Work,*
Vol. 23 (1963).

Table 8 Analysis of Variance: Distance to Relatives of Household Head
Most Often Visited Outside the Village

Source	Mean Square	Degrees of Freedom	F-Ratio	Level of Significance
Total	1.50	565		
Between	2.66	47		
A (Region)	3.37	2	2.41	—
B (Size Class)	0.51	3	0.37	—
C (Communication Level)	1.81	1	1.30	—
D (Occupation Category)	2.88	1	2.07	—

Note: Natural logarithmic transformation.

Table 9   Mean Distances in Miles by District and Distance Types

Distance Types	District		
	Ambala	Surat	Kolar
Wife's Village	20.6	12.0	16.5
Household Head's Friends	18.7	15.1	15.5
Household Head's Relatives	23.1	17.0	17.8

dents' trips to friends and relatives of these male household heads. (See Tables 7 and 8.)

For trips to friends, the one statistically significant difference demonstrated was between regions, and this was significant at the 1 per cent level. For trips to the most frequently visited agnatic relatives, none of the four factors introduced account for a significant variation in trip distance. If this holds for the villages selected from three widely separated districts, perhaps this is the intervillage link that might best serve as mean information field surrogate for Indian regions with a variety of distinguishing cultural characteristics. The distance means for visits to agnatic relatives were some two miles greater than for those to cognatic ones;

the standard deviations were smaller. For India, the marriage distance may underestimate the spatial extent of intervillage communication. (See Table 9).

Interesting topics of investigation may be the process of agnatic kin dispersal over space compared with that by which cognatic relatives are diffused, and the particular structure of agnatic relationships involved in the interactions over space.

The value of a rather readily determined surrogate, broadly applicable in a large and complex developing nation, is easily appreciated. Innovation diffusion research and planning for all levels of development could benefit. The need for a continuing investigation is recognized.

⚜⚜⚜⚜⚜⚜⚜⚜⚜⚜⚜⚜⚜⚜⚜⚜⚜⚜⚜⚜⚜⚜⚜⚜⚜⚜

BEHAVIORAL ASPECTS OF THE DECISION TO MIGRATE

Julian Wolpert

During the decade 1950-60, there were sufficient changes from previous patterns of migration streams in the United States to warrant some reexamination and reevaluation of model building attempts in migration analysis. It must be admitted that the gravity

model and its elaborations appear to lose explanatory power with each successive census. When flows are disaggregated, the need becomes greater selectively to determine unique weights for areas and unique distance functions for subgroups of in- and

From *Papers*, Regional Science Association, Vol. 15, 1965. Reprinted by permission.

out-migrants. The Stouffer model of "competing migrants"[1] provided a rather poor prediction of migration streams for the 1955-60 period. Perhaps the most successful of spatial interaction models, which does take into consideration the spatial arrangement of places of origin and destination, is sufficiently rooted in the 1935-40 depression-period movements so as to present serious deficiencies when applied to recent streams. Plots of migration distances defy the persistence of the most tenacious of curve fitters.

The defenders of the wage theory of economic determinism find some validity for their constructs, so long as net, and not gross, migration figures are used and regional disaggregation does not proceed below the state level, thereby neglecting much of the intrastate heterogeneity.[2]

The extremely scanty empirical evidence of the "friends and relatives effect" in directing migration has given birth to a generation of models which, although offering the solace of a behavioral approach, provide little explanation of the actual process involved.[3] Perhaps the most serious gap occurs in the transition from micro- to macro-model and in the selection of appropriate surrogates for testing. Here, the inadequacy of published data in the United States appears to have its most telling effect. Though almost every conceivable method of combining existing data into useful indicators has been tried, explanation through surrogates hardly provides an analysis which is independent of the bias which is introduced.

A good deal of useful information has come from the analysis of migration differentials by categories of occupation, income, race, and, especially, age.[4] However, predictive models have not been designed to include these findings and to consider the interdependence of these characteristics in migration behavior. Demonstrating the potential usefulness of the migration differential approach is one of the objectives of this paper.

A composite of interesting ideas about migration behavior has been incorporated within Price's ambitious proposed simulation model.[5] On the basis of selected character-

1. Samuel A. Stouffer, "Intervening Opportunities and Competing Migrants," *Journal of Regional Science*, 2 (1960), pp. 1-26.

2. Cicely Blanco, "Prospective Unemployment and Interstate Population Movements," *Review of Economics and Statistics*, XVLI (1964), pp. 221–22; Donald J. Bogue, Henry S. Shryock, Siegfried Hoermann, "Streams of Migration Between Subregions," Scripps Foundation Studies in Population Distribution, 5 (1957), Oxford, Ohio; Robert L. Bunting, "A Test of the Theory of Geographic Mobility," *Industrial and Labor Relations Review*, 15 (1961), pp. 76–82; Robert L. Raimon, "Interstate Migration and Wage Theory," *Review of Economics and Statistics*, XLIV (1962), pp. 428–38; Larry A. Sjaastad, "The Relationship Between Migration and Income in the United States," *Papers and Proceedings, Regional Science Association*, VI (1960), pp. 37–64.

3. Clark Kerr, "Migration to the Seattle Labor Market Area, 1940–42," *University of Washington Publications in the Social Sciences*, 11 (1942), pp. 129–88; Phillip Nelson, "Migration, Real Income and Information," *Journal of Regional Science*, 1 (1959), pp. 43–74.

4. Donald J. Bogue, Henry S. Shryock, and Siegfried Hoermann, *op. cit.;* Hope T. Eldridge and Dorothy Swaine Thomas, *Population Redistribution and Economic Growth, United States, 1870–1950.* Philadelphia: American Philosophical Society, 1964; Dorothy S. Thomas, "Age and Economic Differentials in Internal Migration in the United States: Structure and Distance," *Proceedings, International Population Conference*, Vienna, 1959, pp. 714–21; George L. Wilber, "Migration Expectancy in the United States," *Journal of the American Statistical Association*, 58 (1963), pp. 444–53.

5. D. O. Price, "A Mathematical Model of Migration Suitable for Simulation on an Electronic Com-

istics of individuals and of places of origin and destination, migration probabilities are generated reflecting empirically observed regularities. As far as it is known, the model has not become operational—the task for simulating United States migration would overtax the most modern computer. The only successful attempt in this direction has been Morrill's study of the emerging town development in south central Sweden.[6]

The use of Monte Carlo simulation models in migration analysis does offer a viable and promising approach, especially considering the rather persistent tendencies for critical elements or parameters to remain stable over time. Thus, although the streams show considerable variation over time, and the characteristics of the population and of places continuously change, stability persists in migration behavior.

To illustrate this observation it may be noted that Bogue, Shryock, and Hoermann,[7] in their analysis of the 1935-40 migration streams, summarize with the following statements that could as well be applied to the 1955-60 streams:

1. Basic shifts in the regional and territorial balance of the economy guided the direction and flow of migration streams.

2. The two factors that seem to contribute most to the mobility of the population are above average educational training and employment in white collar occupations.

3. Any theory of economic determinism in migration is inclined to be incomplete.

It appears, therefore, that understanding and prediction of migration streams require determining of the constants in migration

behavior and distinguishing these from the variables with respect to population composition and place characteristics which evolve differentially over time.

As indicated, attempts at model building in migration research have largely focused on variables and surrogates such as distance and ecological characteristics of places exerting "push and pull" forces[8] to the exclusion of behavioral parameters of the migrants. The model suggested here is of doubtful usefulness as an exact predictive tool. It borrows much of its concepts and terminology from the behavioral theorists, because of the intuitive relevance of their findings to the analysis of mobility. Verification will be only partial because of the general absence in this country of migrational histories. Instead, greater reliance will be placed upon evidence from a variety of sources and special studies. The framework of the analysis must be classified as descriptive or behavioral and partially dynamic.

Clearly, the focus must remain with the process of internal migration, i.e., a change of residence which extends beyond a territorial boundary. Some attempt will be made, however, to relate this process of "long distance" movement to the more general topic of mobility which encompasses not only shifts within areal divisions but also movement between jobs and social categories. This larger zone of investigation is referred to as the "mover-stayer" problem.[9]

The central concepts of migration behavior with which we shall be concerned are: 1. the notion of place utility, 2. the field theory approach to search behavior, and 3.

puter," *Proceedings, International Population Conference*, Vienna, 1959, pp. 665–73.
6. Richard L. Morrill, "The Development of Models of Migration," *Entretiens de Monaco en Sciences Humaines*, 1962.
7. Donald J. Bogue, Henry S. Shryock and Siegfried Hoermann, *op. cit.*

8. *Ibid.*; Roger L. Burford "An Index of Distance as Related to Internal Migration," *Southern Economic Journal*, XXIX (1962), pp. 77–81.
9. Leo Goodman, "Statistical Methods for the Mover-Stayer Model," *Journal of the American Statistical Association*, 56 (1961), pp. 841–68.

the life-cycle approach to threshold formation.

Before translating these concepts into an operational format within a proposed model, some attempt will be made to trace their relevance to migrational decisions.

Place Utility

Population migration is an expression of interaction over space but differs in certain essential characteristics from other channels of interaction, mainly in terms of the commodity which is being transported. Other flows, such as those of mail, goods, telephone calls, and capital also reflect connectivity between places, but, in migration, the agent which is being transported is itself active and generates its own flow. The origin and destination points take on significance only in the framework in which they are perceived by the active agents.

A degree of disengagement and upheaval is associated with population movements; thus, households are not as readily mobile as other phenomena subject to flow behavior. Yet, it would be unrealistic to assume that sedentariness reflects an equilibrium position for a population. Migrational flows are always present, but normally the reaction is lagged and the decision to migrate is nonprogrammed. Thus, migration is viewed as a form of individual or group adaptation to perceived changes in environment, a recognition of marginality with respect to a stationary position, and a flow reflecting an appraisal by a potential migrant of his present site as opposed to a number of other potential sites. Other forms of adaptation are perhaps more common than change of residence and job. The individual may adjust to the changing conditions at his site and postpone, perhaps permanently, the decision to migrate. Migration is not, therefore, merely a direct response or reaction to the objective economic circumstances which might be incorporated, for example, within a normative transportation model.

In designing the framework for a model of the migration decision, it would be useful at the outset to enumerate certain basic descriptive principles which have been observed to have some general applicability and regularity in decision behavior. To a significant degree these principles have their origin in the studies of organizational theorists.

We begin with the concept of "intendedly rational" man[10] who, although limited to finite ability to perceive, calculate, and predict and to an otherwise imperfect knowledge of environment, still differentiates between alternative courses of action according to their relative utility or expected utility. Man responds to the perception of unequal utility, i. e., if utility is measured broadly enough to encompass the friction of adaptation and change.

The individual has a threshold of net utility or an aspiration level that adjusts itself on the basis of experience.[11] This subjectively determined threshold is a weighted composite of a set of yardsticks for achievement in the specific realms in which he participates. His contributions, or inputs, into the economic and social systems in terms of effort, time, and concern are rewarded by actual and expected attainments.

10. Herbert A. Simon, "Economics and Psychology," in Sigmund Koch, ed., *Psychology: A Study of a Science*, 6, New York: McGraw-Hill, 1963.
11. R. M. Cyert and J. G. Marsh, *A Behavioral Theory of the Firm*. Englewood Cliffs, N. J.: Prentice-Hall, 1963; Kurt Lewin, *Field Theory in Social Science*. New York: Harper and Row, 1951; Joseph W. McGuire, *Theories of Business Behavior*, Englewood Cliffs, N. J.: Prentice-Hall, 1964; S. Siegal, "Level of Aspiration and Decision Making," *Psychological Review*, 64 (1957), pp. 253–63; Herbert Simon, *op. cit.*, 1963; William H. Starbuck, "Level of Aspiration Theory and Economic Behavior," *Behavioral Science*, 8 (1963), pp. 128–36.

The threshold functions as an evaluative mechanism for distinguishing, in a binary sense, between success or failure, or between positive or negative net utilities. The process is self-adjusting because aspirations tend to adjust to the attainable. Satisfaction leads to slack which may induce a lower level of attainment.[12] Dissatisfaction acts as a stimulus to search behavior.

Without too great a degree of artificiality, these concepts of "bounded rationality"[13] may be transferred to the mover-stayer decision environment and a spatial context. It is necessary, only, to introduce a place subscript for the measures of utility. *Place utility*, then, refers to the net composite of utilities which are derived from the individual's integration at some position in space. The threshold reference point is also a relevant criterion for evaluating the individual's place utility. According to the model, the threshold will be some function of his experience or attainments at a particular place and the attainments of his peers. Thus, place utility may be expressed as a positive or negative quantity, expressing respectively the individual's satisfaction or dissatisfaction with respect to that place. He derives a measure of utility from the past or expected future rewards at his stationary position.

Quite different is the utility associated with the other points which are considered as potential destinations. The utility with respect to these alternative sites consists largely of anticipated utility and optimism which lacks the reenforcement of past rewards. This is precisely why the stream of information is so important in long-distance migration—information about prospects must somehow compensate for the absence of personal experience.

All moves are purposeful, for an evaluation process has preceded them, but some are more beneficial, in an *ex post* sense, because of the objective quality of search behavior, the completeness of the information stream and the mating of anticipated with realized utility. If migrations may be classified as either successes or failures in a relative sense, then clearly the efficiency of the search process and the ability to forecast accurately the consequences of the move are essential elements.

Assuming intendedly rational behavior, then the generation of population migration may be considered to be the result of a decision process which aims at altering the future in some way and which recognizes differences in utility associated with different places. The individual will tend to locate himself at a place whose characteristics possess or promise a relatively higher level of utility than in other places which are conspicuous to him. Thus, the flow of population reflects a subjective place-utility evaluation by individuals. Streams of migration may not be expected to be optimal because of incomplete knowledge and relocation lag but neither may we expect that individuals purposefully move in response to the prospect of lower expected utility.

The process of migration is conceived in the model as: 1. proceeding from sets of stimuli perceived with varying degrees of imperfection, and 2. involving responses in a stayer-mover framework.

The stayers are considered lagged movers postponing the decision to migrate for periods of time extending up to an entire lifetime. Thus, the mover-stayer dichotomy may be reduced to the single dimension of time—when to move.

Distinction must clearly be made between the objective stimuli which are relevant for the mover-stayer decision and the stimuli which are perceived by individuals and to which there is some reaction. The

12. R. M. Cyert and J. G. Marsh, *op. cit.*
13. Herbert Simon, *op. cit.*, 1963.

stimuli which are instrumental in generating response originate in the individual's action space which is that part of the limited environment with which the individual has contact.[14] Thus, the perceived state of the environment is the action space within which individuals select to remain or, on the other hand, from which to withdraw in exchange for a modified enviroment.

Field Theory Approach to Search Behavior

Though the individual theoretically has access to a very broad environmental range of local, regional, national, and international information coverage, typically only some rather limited portion of the environment is relevant and applicable for his decision behavior. This immediate subjective environment or action space is the set of place utilities which the individual perceives and to which he responds. This notion of the action space is similar to Lewin's concept of life space—the universe of space and time in which the person conceives that he can or might move about.[15] Some correspondence may exist with the actual external environment, but there may also be a radical degree of deviation. The life space is a surface over which the organism can locomote and is dependent upon the needs, drives, or goals of the organism and upon its perceptual apparatus.[16] Our concern is with man in terms of his efficiency or effectiveness as an information collecting and assimilating organism and thus with his ability to produce an efficient and unbiased estimation or evaluation of the objective environment. It is suggested that the subjective action space

is perceived by the individual through a sampling process whose parameters are determined by the individual's needs, drives, and abilities. There may not be a conscious and formal sampling design in operation, but, nevertheless, a sampling process is inherently involved in man's acquisition of knowledge about his enviroment.

Both sampling and nonsampling errors may be expected in the individual's perceived action space—a spatial bias induced by man's greater degree of expected contact and interaction in his more immediate environment, as well as sampling errors introduced because of man's finite ability to perceive and his limited exposure and observation. The simple organism which Simon describes has vision which permits it to see, at any moment, a circular portion of the surface about the point in which it is standing and to distinguish merely between the presence or absence of food within the circle.[17]

The degree to which the individual's action-space accurately represents the physically objective world in its totality is a variable function of characteristics of both man and the variability of the environment. Of primary emphasis here are the consequences of man's fixity to a specific location—the spatial particularism of the action space to which he responds.

What is conspicuous to the individual at any given time includes primarily information about elements in his close proximity. Representing the information bits as points, the resulting sampling design most closely resembles a cluster in the immediate vicinity of the stationary position. The individual may be considered at the stationary position within the cluster of alternative places, each of which may be represented by a point on a plane. The consequences of this clustered

14. Kurt Lewin, *op. cit.*

15. Kurt Lewin, *op. cit.*

16. Herbert A. Simon, "Rational Choice and the Structure of the Environment," *Psychological Review*, 63 (1956), pp. 129–38.

17 *Ibid.*

distribution of alternatives within the immediate vicinity of the individual is a spatially biased information set, or a mover-stayer decision based upon knowledge of only a small portion of the plane.

Cluster sampling may be expected to exhibit significantly greater sampling bias for a given number of observations than random sampling; its most important advantage is in the reduction of the effort or cost in the collection of information. In the absence of a homogeneous surface, however, the difference in cost may be more than outweighed by the loss in representativeness of a given cluster.

The local environment of the individual may not, of course, be confined purely to his immediate surroundings. The action space may vary in terms of number and intensity of contacts from the limited environmental realm of the infant to the extensive action space within which diplomats, for example, operate. The degree of contact may perhaps be measured by the rate of receipt or perception of information bits.[18] Mass communications and travel, communication with friends and relatives, for example, integrate the individual into a more comprehensive spatial setting but one which is, nevertheless, still biased spatially. Mass communications media typically have coverage which is limited to the service area of the media's transmission center. Here a hierarchy of nodal centers exists in terms of the extent of service area and range of coverage. Thus the amount of transmission and expected perception of information by individuals is some function of the relative position of places within the network of communication channels. The resident in the area of a primary node has an additional advantage

resulting from his greater exposure to information covering a relatively more extensive area of choice. His range of contact and interaction is broader, and the likelihood of an unbiased and representative action space is greater.

The Life Cycle Approach to Threshold Formation

Another significant determinant of the nature and extent of the individual's action space (i.e., the number and arrangement of points in the cluster) consists of a set of factors which may be grouped under the heading of the "life cycle." Illustrative of this approach is Hägerstrand's analysis of population as a flow through a system of stations.[19] Lifelines represent individuals moving between stations. The cycle of life almost inevitably gives rise to distinct movement behavior from birth, education, and search for a niche involving prime or replacement movements. Richard Meier also has examined this notion of the expanding action space of the individual from birth through maturity.[20] The action space expands as a function of information input and growth depends on organization of the environment so that exploration becomes more efficient. Associated with the evolution of the individual's action space through time is a complex of other institutional and social forces which introduce early differentiation. Differences in sex, race, formal education, family income, and status are likely to find their expression early in shaping the area of movement and choice. Although the

18. Richard L. Meier, *A Communications Theory of Urban Growth.* Cambridge: Massachusetts Institute of Technology Press, 1962.

19. Torsten Hägerstrand, "Geographical Measurements of Migration," *Entretiens de Monaco en Sciences Humaines,* 1962.
20. Richard L. Meier, "Measuring Social and Cultural Change in Urban Regions," *Journal of the American Institute of Planners,* XXV (1959), pp. 180–90; Richard L. Meier, *op. cit.,* 1962.

action space is unique for each individual, still there is likely to be a good deal of convergence into a limited number of broad classes. The congruity and interdependence of the effects of race, family income, education, and occupation are likely to result in subgroups of individuals with rather homogeneous action space.

In Lewin's concept, behavior is a function of the life space, which in turn is a function of the person and the environment.[21] The behavior-influencing aspects of the external (physical and social) environment are represented through the life space. Similarly, but in a more limited fashion, the action space may be considered to include the range of choice or the individual's area of movement which is defined by both is personal attributes and environment. Most prominent among the determinants of the alternatives in this action space which are conspicuous to the individual is his position on one of divergent life cycles and location in terms of the communication networks linking his position to other places. His accumulated needs, drives, and abilities define his aspirations—the communication channels carry information about the alternative ways of satisfying these aspirations. To illustrate this structure in terms of the simple organism, we may turn to Simon's model of adaptive behavior.[22] The organism he describes has only the simple needs of food getting and resting. the third kind of activity of which it is capable is exploration for food by locomotion within the life space where heaps of food are located at scattered points. In the schema, exploration and adaptive response to clues are necessary for survival; random behavior leads to extinction. The chances of survival, i.e., the ability to satisfy needs, are dependent upon two parameters describing

the organism (its storage capacity and its range of vision) and two parameters describing the environment (its richness in food and in paths). Of course, with respect to the human organism, aspirations require the fulfillment of many needs, and thresholds are higher. Exploratory search is aided by clues provided by the external environment through communication channels which extend the range of vision.

Other Behavioral Parameters

The discussion was intended to develop the concept of action space as a spatial parameter in the mover-stayer decision. Thus the action space of the individual includes not only his present position but a finite number of alternative sites which are made conspicuous to him through a combination of his search effort and the transmission of communications. The action space refers, in our mover-stayer framework, to a set of places for which expected utilities have been defined by the individual. A utility is attached to his site. The sites may consist of alterna-lower utility has been assigned to the alternative sites. The variables here are the absolute number of alternative sites and their spatial pattern or arrangement with respect to his site. The sites may consist of alternative dwellings within a single block, alternative suburbs in a metropolitan area, or alternative metropolitan areas. The alternatives may not all present themselves simultaneously but may appear sequentially over time.

There are other components of behavioral theories which are relevant in the analysis of migration, especially with respect to the problem of uncertainty avoidance. We have already mentioned the sequential attention to goals and the sequential consideration of alternatives. The order in which the environment is searched determines to a substantial extent the decisions that will be made. In

---

21. Kurt Lewin, *op. cit.*
22. Herbert Simon, *op. cit.*, 1956.

addition, observations appear to confirm that alternatives which *minimize uncertainty* are preferred and that the decision maker *negotiates for an environment of relative certainty*. Evidence shows also that there is a tendency to *postpone decisions* and to rely upon the *feedback of information*, i.e., policies are reactive rather than anticipatory. Uncertainty is also reduced by imitating the successful procedures followed by others.[23]

The composite of these attempts to reduce uncertainty may be reflected in a lagged response. A lapse of time intervenes in a cause and effect relationship—an instantaneous human response may not be expected. As with other stimulus-response models, events are paired sequentially through a process of observation and inference into actions and reactions, e.g., unemployment and outmigration. As developed in economics, a lag implies a delayed, but rational, human response to an external event. Similarly, with respect to migration, responses may be measured in terms of elasticity which is in turn conditional upon factors such as complementarity and substitutability. A time dimension may be added to measures of elasticity, and the result is a specific or a distributed lag—a response surface reflecting the need for reenforcement of the perception of the permanence of change.

Framework of a Proposed Operating Model

The model which is proposed attempts to translate into an operational framework the central concepts with which we have been concerned: the notion of place utility, the field theory approach to search behavior, and the life cycle approach to threshold formation.

The model is designed to relate aggregate behavior in terms of migration differentials

into measures of place utility relevant for individuals. The objective is a prediction of the composition of in- and out-migrants and their choice of destination, i.e., by incorporating the stable elements which are involved in the changes in composition of population of places.

Inputs into the system are the following set of matrices:

1. Matrix A, defining the migration differentials associated with the division of the population by life cycles and by age, represented respectively by the rows and columns.

2. Matrix B, representing the distribution of a place's population within the life cycle and age categories.

3. Matrices C, D, E, and F, representing respectively the gross in-, out-, and net-migration and "migration efficiency"[24] for each of the cell categories corresponding to Matrix B.

The rates for the A matrix are determined on an aggregate basis for the United States population by means of the "one in a thousand" 1960 census sample. These rates are then applied to the B matrix entries for specific places to predict the expected outmigration rates of profile groups at these places. The differences between the expected rates and those observed in the C, D, E, and F matrix tabulations are then used to provide a measure of the relative utility of specific places for the given profile groups which may be specified as a place utility matrix. The net migrations, whether positive or negative for the given cell, represent the consensus of cell members of the utility which the place offers relative to other places which they perceive. The migration

---

23. R. M. Cyert and J. G. Marsh, *op. cit.*

24. Migrational efficiency refers to the ratio of net migration to total gross migration. See H. S. Shyrock, "The Efficiency of Internal Migration in the United States," *Proceedings, International Population Conference*, Vienna, 1959, pp. 685–94.

efficiency measures not only the relative transitoriness of specific subgroups of the population but also the role of the specific place as a transitional stepping stone or station for certain groups.

There is an additional matrix, Matrix G, representing the parameters of search behavior which are characteristic of the subgroup populations. These are specified in terms of the number of alternatives which are perceived and the degree of clustering of these alternatives in space. The destination of the out-migrants predicted by means of the G matrix entries are tested against the observed migration flows in order to derive measures of distance and directional bias.

The concepts of place utility, life cycle, and search behavior are integrated, therefore, within the classification of the population into subgroups. Preliminary testing has revealed a significant degree of homogeneity of migrational behavior by subgroup popula-

tions in terms of differential rate of migration, distance, and direction of movement. The classification procedure, involving the use of multivariate analysis, is designed to provide a set of profile or core groups whose attributes may be represented by prototype individuals. The differential migration rates of Matrix A are assumed, therefore, to be parameters in the migration system, at least for the purposes of short-term forecasting. Individuals move along each row as they grow older and, to some extent, move in either direction along age columns as socioeconomic status changes over time, but the migration rates for the cells remain relatively constant.

Similarly, the utility to the population subgroups of the specific places of origin and destination shift over the long-term but remain relatively constant in the short-run. For long-term forecasting, exogenous measures of economic trends in specific places would be necessary inputs.

⚔⚔⚔⚔⚔⚔⚔⚔⚔⚔⚔⚔⚔⚔⚔⚔⚔⚔⚔⚔⚔⚔⚔⚔⚔⚔⚔⚔

THE DIFFUSION OF CHOLERA IN THE UNITED STATES IN THE NINETEENTH CENTURY

Gerald F. Pyle

Two diffusion processes have been discussed in the literature. The first, which has received substantial attention, focuses on the frictional effects of distance, and emphasizes diffusion sequences operating over space. The second has been studied less, and is concerned with processes moving downward from larger to smaller centers in an urban system; this kind of sequence can be termed hierarchical diffusion.

The example presented in this paper shows that during the early years of the nineteenth century, when access was difficult and the urban system was only embryonic, cholera spread largely through spatial diffusion.[1] By 1866 a rational urban

1. Gerald F. Pyle, *Some Examples of Urban Medical Geography*. Unpublished Master's thesis, University of Chicago, Department of Geography, 1968.

hierarchy had emerged, however, and railroads already provided a modicum of rapid national integration. The cholera epidemic of that year diffused hierarchically.

CHOLERA

The occurrence of cholera is rooted in sub-Asian antiquity. Three major cholera pandemics lashed out at the United States in the nineteenth century. The pestilential movement of the disease through the urban system was rapid, and frequently masses of people fled the possibility of death to no avail. Others never knew what killed them. The recognized epidemic years of national proportions were 1832, 1849, and 1866. This study relates differences in the diffusion of cholera in the United States to the country's evolving urban and transportation environments.

Rosenberg[2] offers a vivid presentation of the three successive waves of the disease in New York City. New York was an international port capable of receiving cholera from dozens of maritime sources, and some of the filthiest slums in the city were adjacent to the port facilities. It was only natural for New York City to be the first to feel the impact of an epidemic, and in most instances this is apparently what happened.

Although accounts for some cities are scanty, the shock of cholera was such that enough has been published to track the spread of each of the three epidemics from one urban center to another. Thus, an attempt can be made to isolate similarities in epidemic movements over time.

Cholera is a serious intestinal disease. Medical writers have often, conventionally, segmented cholera into several stages. As explained by De,[3] the stages are charac-

terized by (1) premonitory diarrhea, (2) copious evacuations, (3) collapse, (4) reaction, and (5) uremia. It is possible in acute circumstances for cholera to start with one of the latter stages, especially after an epidemic is fully developed. Conversely, a mild case may be manifested only by diarrhea.

Man is a prime reservoir for cholera. The several cholera vibrios which spread from one person to another are carried initially by human feces which contaminates water. Geographic conditions favoring the spread of the disease include warm temperatures and prolonged dry spells. The vibrios have a chance to flourish in warm alkaline mediums, and as epidemics spread, sources such as food and flies can carry the disease in addition to contaminated water.[4]

May[5] suggests several possible forms of immunity, but it is clear much is still unknown. The possible immunities, according to May, are (1) natural, (2) excessive hydrochloric acid in the stomach, (3) inoculation, and (4) recent past history of the disease.

During the first part of the nineteenth century, Europeans in Asia received an exposure to a cholera pandemic from 1816 to 1823. This first in a series of pandemics receded only to penetrate all of Europe and, eventually, North America, starting in 1826.

THE EPIDEMIC OF 1832 AND ITS PATH THROUGH THE URBAN SYSTEM

In 1832, the United States was barely more than a frontier country. Most major cities of the time were periodically drowned in mud. Pigs roamed the streets of New York. Sanitation as it is now known was virtually un-

---

2. Charles E. Rosenberg, *The Cholera Years.* Chicago: University of Chicago Press, 1962.
3. S. N. De, *Cholera, Its Pathology and Pathogenesis.* Edinburgh: Oliver and Boyd, 1961. Pp. 1-72.

4. John E. Gordon, (ed.). *Control of Communicable Diseases in Man.* New York: American Public Health Association, 1965. P. 66,
5. Jacques May, *The Ecology of Human Disease.* New York: M.D. Publications, 1958. Pp. 35-56.

heard of. However, the nucleus of the present urban system already existed, and according to Borchert [6] the system was evolving.

The early 1830's were within the great water transportation era of the United States. Traffic was steady on the Ohio-Mississippi system, and the Hudson River and Erie Canal in New York carried heavy flows. The Great Lakes and Atlantic seaboard also were heavily utilized waterways. Poor sanitation coupled with a riverine orientation to produce conditions ripe for a cholera epidemic.

From available accounts,[7] the path of cholera from one city to another in 1832 can be traced. The reconstruction of the epidemic is initially shown in Table 1. The "officially recognized entry dates" on the table are the first possible accounts of an epidemic which could be found for the cities listed. The very violent nature of a major epidemic suggests that early accounts are reasonably reliable in terms of when cholera first struck a city.

Population figures have been added to the table to demonstrate particular urban relationships amongst the 1832 cholera cities. One relationship is obvious from examination of the population clusters: cholera struck larger cities and subsequently showed up in small cities immediately adjacent to the larger cities. The result is a general hierarchy of "cholera fields" throughout the country. For a theoretical analogy within the urban literature, reference is made to Berry. [8]

There are, however, more noteworthy spatial relationships reflected in Table 1. When the cities shown on the table are plotted on a map of the United States, as has been done with Figure 1, it is possible to show patterns of movement from one city to the next. The dates in Table 1 indicate several separate movements.

Canadian Origin

Montreal and Quebec shared the port facilities at Grosse Ile on the St. Lawrence River in 1832, and it was from Grosse Ile the epidemic probably entered North America. It spread rapidly down the St. Lawrence River and continued until it reached Lake Champlain in the United States. By the time the epidemic entered Albany, it had traveled both from the north and from New York to the south. Meanwhile, the pestilence of Canadian origin moved across Lakes Ontario and Erie to Buffalo, Erie, and Pittsburgh. The time of the year during which Detroit, Chicago, and Rock Island reported outbreaks suggests Canadian origins (see Table 1). However, in many instances the original point of departure may have been New York City.

New York Origin: Inland Waterways

There is some confusion within the literature as to whether cholera did or did not first appear in New York City in April, 1832. It may simply have traveled down the Hudson River from Canadian sources in the early summer of that year. Official records [9] indicate that cities in the Lake Champlain-Northern Hudson River area had outbreaks two weeks before New York City. However, the disease was firmly established in New York by late June, and it apparently moved

6. John R. Borchert, "American Metropolitan Evolution," *Geographical Review*, 57 (1967), 301-32.
7. U. S. Surgeon-General's Office. "The Cholera Epidemic of 1873 in the United States," *Executive Document No. 95.* Washington: Government Printing Office, 1875.
8. Brian J. L. Berry, "Cities as Systems Within Systems of Cities," *Papers of the Regional Science Association,* 13 (1964), 147-64.
9. U.S. Surgeon-General's Office, *op. cit.*

Table 1   Officially Recognized Entry Dates for Cholera: 1832 Epidemic

City	Date	City Size
Plattsburg, N. Y.	June 11	4,913
Burlington, Vt.	June 13	3,526
White Hall, N. Y.	June 14	2,888
Niagara, N. Y.	June 22	1,401
Erie, Pa.	June 26	1,329
New York City	June 26	202,589
Pittsburgh, Pa.	July 2	12,542
Albany, N. Y.	July 3	24,238
Philadephia, Pa.	July 5	161.410
Richmond, Va.	July 6	16,060
Detroit, Mich.	July 6	2,222
Newark, N. J.	July 7	10,953
Cleveland, Ohio	July 10	1,076
Schenectady, N. Y.	July 12	11,405
Rochester, N. Y.	July 12	9,269
Chicago, Ill.	July 12	4,470[a]
New Haven, Conn.	July 14	10,180
New Brunswick, N. J.	July 14	7,830
Buffalo, N. Y.	July 15	8,653
Lockport, N. Y.	July 19	2,121
Hartford, Conn.	July 19	7,074
Frankfort, N. Y.	July 22	2,620
Newport, R. I.	July 24	8,010
Norfolk, Va.	July 24	14,998
Jersey City, N. J.	July 26	12,568
Annapolis, Md.	July 30	2,623
Providence, R. I.	July 31	16,836
Baltimore, Md.	August 4	80,625
Boston, Mass.	August 5	61,393
New Castle, Del.	August 6	2,463
Washington, D. C.	August 8	18,827
Andover, Mass.	August 18	4,540
Haverhill, Mass.	August 25	3,912
Rock Island, Ill.	August 26	. . .
Cincinnati, Ohio	September 30	24,831
Covington, Ky.	October 4	743
Charleston, S. C.	Late October	30,286
Lexington, Ky.	November 6	6,104
Frankfort, Ky.	November 6	1,680
Baton Rouge, La.	November 8	9,809
New Orleans, La.	November 18	46,310
Bangor, Me.	December 26	2,863

[a] 1840.

Sources: U.S., Surgeon-General's Office, *The Cholera Epidemic of 1873 in the United States* (Executive Document No. 95; Washington: Government Printing Office, 1875). U.S., Secretary of State, *Census of Population, 1830* (Washington: U.S. Census Office, 1831).

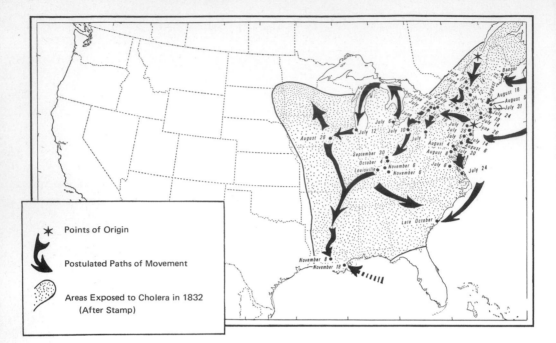

Figure 1. The movement of cholera in 1832.

up the Hudson Valley from that city. It then followed the Erie Canal to western New York State in the wake of the Canadian wave. The movement continued with traffic down the Ohio Canal to the Ohio and Mississippi Rivers, eventually to strike Baton Rouge and New Orleans in November. Meanwhile, the Atlantic seaboard was experiencing similar problems.

New York Origin: Eastern Seaboard

The third path of cholera movement was outward from New York along the Atlantic Coast. The epidemic apparently spread from New York through New Jersey to Philadelphia and on to Baltimore, Virginia, and eventually Charleston. It also spread north to Boston and New England. There were, however, many other possible methods of entry in addition to the sequential movement of the disease from one city in a line to the next. One extreme example of other

modes of cholera spread *and* the strength of the vibrios is given by an account from Bangor, Maine:[10]

During December 1832, a chest of clothing that had belonged to a sailor, who had died of cholera at a Baltic port, arrived at his home in a small village near Bangor, Me. The chest was opened, the clothing was distributed to his friends, and all who received the garments were taken with cholera and died.

The severity of the epidemic is illustrated in contemporary accounts from Philadelphia, hard hit by the epidemic. A report by the College of Physicians in 1832 shows that there were sporadic outbreaks of cholera prior to the 1832 epidemic. For the ten-year period ending in 1831, 2,437 deaths were attributed to cholera. [11] Three general classes of sanitary regulation improve-

10. U.S. Surgeon-General's Office, *op. cit.*
11. John Bell and D. Francis Condie. *Epidemic Cholera.* Report of the College of Physicians to the

ment—those related to place, those to habitation, and those to person—were suggested by the physicians because of the epidemic.

As indicated by Rosenberg,[12] New York was drastically in need of sanitary improvements, and for years responsible citizens had agitated for a new water supply. When the epidemic hit the city, the slum areas were affected first, and it was felt the epidemic would stop in these areas. However, it occasionally crept into the homes of some finer folk through their servants' quarters.[13]

The epidemic eventually hit people of most levels of the New York social hierarchy, just as it hit the various levels of society in many cities. The arrows in Figure 1 give an indication of movement. Of equal importance is the shaded area. Taken from a rendition by Stamp,[14] the shaded portion of the map shows areas of the United States eventually exposed to the epidemic. In the long run, status meant little.

The cholera data for 1832 can be examined in other ways in an attempt to better understand spatial movements. The time sequence from Table 1 was utilized to postulate paths of movement and points of origin. If the populations of these cities, classed into three groups in accordance with point of origin, are plotted against time of exposure, no definite relationship appears to exist. The points are widely scattered.

However, if distance from point of origin is plotted against time of epidemic recognition (Figure 1a), the three paths of movement show up once again. Clearly, in 1832 distance was more important than city size.

Board of Health. Philadelphia: Thomas Desilver, 1832.

12. Charles E. Rosenberg, *op. cit.*

13. Martyn Paine, *Letters on the Cholera Asphyxia as It Appeared in New York.* New York: Collins and Hanny, 1832.

14. Dudley L. Stamp, *The Geography of Life and Death.* London: Collins, 1964. Ch. iii.

There are many possible reasons for the above relationship. Two seem to stand out. The transportation system in 1832 was immature, that is, it was not comprehensive by modern standards, and the urban system, as noted by Borchert,[15] was still evolving.

The importance of the time lag is further explained by the fact that the epidemic wintered over in the Kentucky Bluegrass area, and cholera ravaged that region through most of 1833.

THE EPIDEMIC OF 1849

The next epidemic diffused through the better-structured United States urban system of 1849. In the late 1840's water transportation was still very important in the United States. Railroads were spreading, but many parts of the country now considered as the Midwest were not yet connected to the East by rail.

From 1842 to 1862 cholera once more raked the world as a pandemic originating in South Asia latched onto pilgrimages, commercial vessels, warships, and related transportation movements. There is clear evidence that the disease entered the United States at two points within a nine day period of time. New York was attacked on December 2, 1848, and New Orleans felt the first effects on December 11.

Table 2 has been constructed to show the spatial relationships reflected in the 1849 cholera epidemic in this country. Two things immediately show up: (1) smaller cities immediately adjacent to large cities contacted the disease after the primary centers, and (2) the disease filtered down the U.S. urban hierarchy. Closer examination reveals *two* paths of filtration: one through the interior waterways system, and a second one along the Atlantic seaboard.

15. John R. Borchert, *op. cit.*

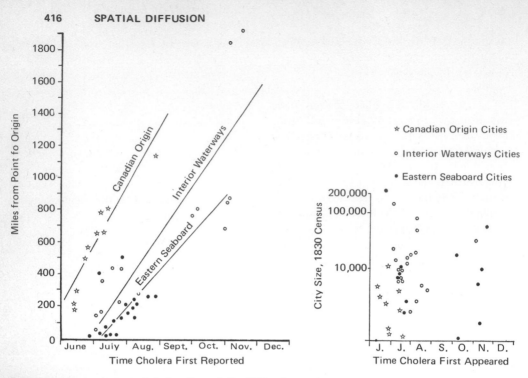

Figure 1a. The movement of cholera through the 1832 urban system.

Interior Waterways

Figure 2 demonstrates the extent of this path of movement. Although the wave of New Orleans origin entered nine days after the eastern epidemic, it traveled farther and lasted longer. Cholera moved rapidly up the Mississippi and Ohio Rivers. By January, 1849, it had reached Cincinnati. It traveled from there through the interior of Ohio. It moved eventually up the Illinois River to Chicago and from there it spread to the east, probably via Great Lakes steamboats which were abundant at that time. It did not arrive in Detroit until August.

In addition, it followed the pioneers west. Chambers[16] renders an accounting of cholera along the California Trail. The disease finally moved into Sacramento in

October, 1850, and from there it quickly moved to San Francisco. Meanwhile, the Eastern United States had already suffered greatly.

Little was still known about the disease. In a report prepared by the City Physician of Boston[17] it was stated that cholera was not contagious. Most of the people who died of cholera were from the class with a high proportion of "foreigners" paying little attention to public facts. To no one's surprise, most of the persons who died of cholera were classed as "Intemperate."

The Eastern Seaboard Movements

After a lag of almost six months, the epidemic spread rapidly up and down the Atlantic seaboard. The dates for entry into

16. J. S. Chambers, *The Conquest of Cholera*. New York: Macmillan Company, 1938.

17. *Asiatic Cholera*. Committee of Internal Health and City Physician, City of Boston. Boston, Mass.: 1849.

Table 2   Officially Recognized Entry Dates for Cholera: 1849 Epidemic

City	Date	City Size
New York City	December 1, 1848	515,547
New Orleans, La.	December 11, 1848	116,375
Louisville, Ky.	December 22, 1848	43,194
Cincinnati, Ohio	December 25, 1848	115,436
St. Louis, Mo.	December 27, 1848	77,860
Nashville, Tenn.	January 20, 1849	10,165
Mobile, Ala.	January, 1849	20,515
Quincy, Ill.	March, 1849	6,902
Cairo, Ill.	April 14, 1849	242
Chicago, Ill.	April 29, 1849	29,963
Philadelphia, Pa.	May 22, 1849	340,045
Baltimore, Md.	May 22, 1849	169,054
Buffalo, N.Y.	May 30, 1849	42,261
Richmond, Va.	May 30, 1849	27,570
Norfolk, Va.	May 30, 1849	14,326
Boston, Mass.	June 4, 1849	136,881
Newark, N. J.	June 4, 1849	38,894
Sandusky, Ohio	July 8, 1849	1,040
Frankfort, Ky.	July 14, 1849	3,308
Detroit, Mich.	August 14, 1849	21,019
Casper, Who.	Spring, 1850	. . .
Sacramento, Calif.	October, 1850	6,820
San Francisco, Calif.	Late 1850	34,776

Sources: U.S., Bureau of Census, *Population Census of 1850* (Washington: U.S. Census Office, 1851). U.S., Surgeon-General's Office, *The Cholera Epidemic of 1873 in the United States* (Executive Document No. 95; Washington: Government Printing Office, 1875). J. S. Chambers, *The Conquest of Cholera* (New York: Macmillan Company, 1938).

specific eastern cities form a definite cluster within Table 2, and the time lag shows up most clearly on Figure 2a. Why the long lag? The temperature could have been low enough to control spread, perhaps combined with bad reporting. One thing was clear: once the epidemic started to spread, there was no stopping it.

Within New York, the epidemic was apparently more widespread. In May, 1849, the New York Board of Health appointed a Sanatory (sic) Committee to investigate the epidemic.[18] The ensuing report shows the

18. *Report of Proceedings of the Sanatory (sic) Committee of the Board of Health in Relation to the Cholera.* New York Board of Health. City of New York: 1849.

first major concentration of the disease was noted in the "Five Points" slum area. From there it diffused outward. There were 15,219 deaths traced either directly to some form of cholera or to symptomatically related maladies in 1849. The chief cause of cholera was thought to exist in the atmosphere.

Even by the end of this second major pandemic, the miasmatic approach prevailed. And if cholera was not caused by bad air (malaria), then it was thought to be due to one's lack of piety. However, shortly after the 1849 epidemic, John Snow in London worked out a plausible scheme for understanding cholera. Snow's approach is a well-known study in urban medical geography.

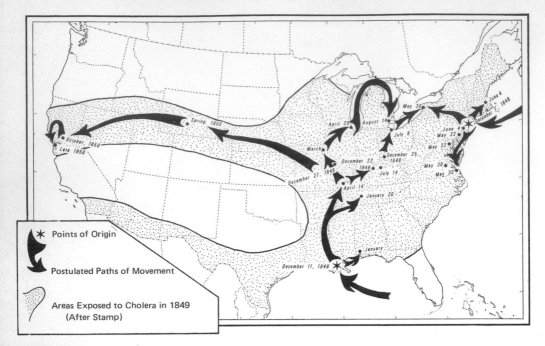

Figure 2. The movement of cholera in 1849.

Snow recognized the spatial variability of cholera cases as they related to location of water pumps. He noticed the area around the Broad Street pump was especially bad and had the pump handle removed. The number of cases immediately went down. Although Snow entertained no serious notions of vibrios, he started a successful sanitation campaign, having discovered one method of arresting the spread of cholera.

Once again, time of entry and population have been compared. The urban-system interrelationships are much clearer than in 1832. Figure 2a shows the two paths of movement and how they reflect the growing urban hierarchy. This suggests that city size by 1849 was as important as distance from point of origin in the spread of cholera along both paths of movement.

THE EPIDEMIC OF 1866

By 1866, the railroad net connecting the eastern part of the United States was essen-

tially completed. The Mississippi River had been bridged. It was possible to move from one part of the country to another by land at a relatively rapid rate compared to 1832 and 1849. An integrated national urban system had now formed.

On May 2, 1866, cholera again entered New York City.[19] During the national epidemic which followed, New York could easily have been the point of origin and dispersal. The dates recorded in Table 3 demonstrate a definite tendency outward from New York toward smaller cities. The familiar hierarchical pattern is also reflected by the "cholera fields" showing up in Table 3. In addition, Figure 3 shows an even more striking movement with time down the urban hierarchy. Postulated paths of movement and the affected area are also shown on Figure 3a.

One path of movement outward from

---

19. *Ibid.*

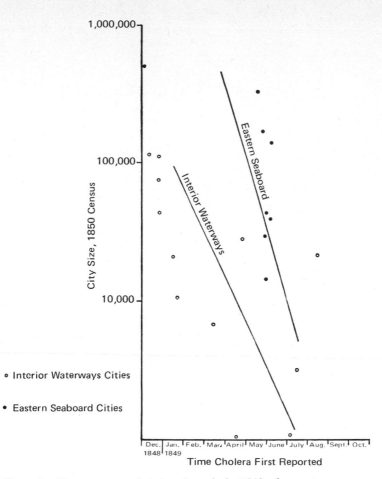

Figure 2a. The movement of cholera through the 1849 urban system.

New York to Detroit, Cincinnati, and Chicago is suggested. It also probably traveled down the Ohio and Mississippi Rivers to Vicksburg. It moved from Chicago to St. Louis and the West. Many Texas cities felt severe epidemics for the first time. Not only were many of them raw frontier towns with inadequate sanitation, but they also supported large army populations. In previous epidemics, cholera followed troops through the Blackhawk and Mexican Wars. The Civil War and later movements against the Indians were certainly no exception.

The epidemic also arrived from New Orleans and along the Gulf Coast area to Galveston and Brownsville. Texas, then, could have received the epidemic from two directions. The disease also moved up the Mississippi to Vicksburg, placing that town in a position similar to that of Albany and Buffalo in 1832.

The disease had previously moved down the Atlantic piedmont to Atlanta and on into the shattered South.

In 1865, miasmatic theories continued to be accepted. However, experience with previous epidemics served to control somewhat the spread of cholera within New York in 1866. In a report published in that city certain "cholera fields" (this is a reference to

Table 3   Officially Recognized Entry Dates for Cholera: 1866 Epidemic

City	Date	City Size
New York City	May 2	942,292
Detroit, Mich.	May 29	79,577
Baltimore, Md.	June 16	267,354
Cincinnati, Ohio	July 11	216,239
New Orleans, La.	July 12	191,418
Savannah, Ga.	July 18	28,235
Chicago, Ill.	July 21	298,977
Galveston, Tex.	July 22	13,818
Little Rock, Ark.	July 28	12,380
Louisville, Ky.	July 29	100,753
Philadelphia, Pa.	Late July	674,022
Richmond, Va.	August 12	51,038
Baton Rouge, La.	August 17	6,498
Brownsville, Tex.	August 20	4,905
Vicksburg, Miss.	August 22	12,443
St. Louis, Mo.	August	310,864
Nashville, Tenn.	September 2	25,865
Memphis, Tenn.	September 6	40,226
Augusta, Ga.	September 9	15,389
Atlanta, Ga.	September 9	21,789
San Antonio, Tex.	September	12,256
Austin, Tex.	September	4,428
Washington, D.C.	October	109,199
Albuquerque, N.M.	October	1,307
San Francisco, Calif.	December	149,473

Sources: U.S. Bureau of Census, *Census of Population, 1870* (Washington: U.S. Census Office, 1871). U.S. Surgeon-General's Office, *The Cholera Epidemic of 1873* in the United States. Chambers, *The Conquest of Cholera.*

parts of the city) were recognized.[20] Strong measures were taken to improve sanitation, and as a result the epidemic was not so severe as it had been in previous years. This was in spite of the fact that New York had almost reached the million population mark.

The United States was visited again by cholera in 1873, but it was not so widespread. Sporadic outbreaks and isolated cases appeared until shortly after the turn of the century when the disease disappeared from this country.

Although accounts of when cholera struck various cities are reasonably clear, there is considerable room for speculation about methods of arrival. Movements up and down the inland waterway systems appear to be easier to trace than those along the eastern seaboard.

Four possible methods of Atlantic coastal attack are suggested: (1) The disease could have spread directly into the eastern urban system from New York by land. (2) It could have entered ports directly from Europe—

20. *Report on Cholera Epidemic.* Council of Hygiene and Public Health: Citizens' Association of New York. New York: Sanford, Hamoun and Co., 1865.

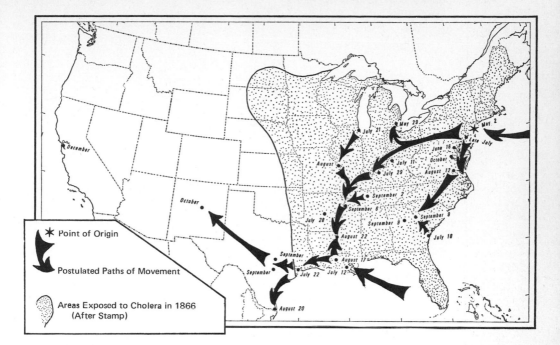

Figure 3. The movement of cholera through the 1866 urban system.

the probability of cholera contact being a function of the amount of overseas maritime contact. (3) Cholera could have slowly moved down the coast with local shipping. (4) The spread could have been a condition of any or all of the first three suggested methods.

Whatever the method of movement, several relationships about cholera diffusion and urbanization stand out. As the disease spread in a different way during each epidemic, contact with the environment was also changing. In 1832, contact with the natural environment was close, transportation was crude, and the urban hierarchy had not yet evolved. In 1849, the disease moved down the evolving hierarchy in two ways, thus reflecting more control over the environment and some integration of the urban system since 1832. The 1866 epidemic shows a completed hierarchy. City size was a prime factor in the spread of cholera over space and through time. Differences in spread of the epidemic were thus related to a changing transportation and urban environment.

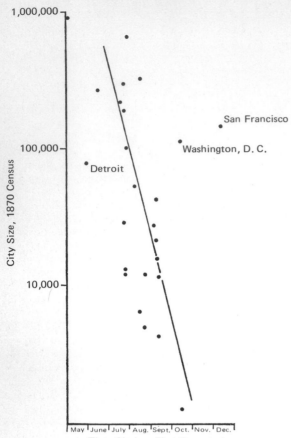

Figure 3a. The movement of cholera in 1866.

✿✿✿✿✿✿✿✿✿✿✿✿✿✿✿✿✿✿✿✿✿✿✿✿✿✿✿✿✿✿

BIBLIOGRAPHY

Spatial Diffusion

BOWDEN, LEONARD, Department of Geography Research Paper No. 97, University of Chicago, 1965. Bowden describes his Monte Carlo simulation of the spread of irrigation wells in northeastern Colorado and its close approximation to the observed spread.

BROWN, LAWRENCE A. and ERIC MOORE, *Diffusion Research in Geography: A Perspective,* Discussion Paper No. 9, University of Iowa, Iowa City, 1968. Brown and Moore discuss "landscapes"

and "process" - oriented approaches to diffusion, emphasizing process-oriented research.

BROWN, L. A., JOHN ODLAND, and REGINALD GOLLEDGE, "Migration, Functional Distance, and the Urban Hierarchy," *Economic Geography*, Vol. 46, No. 3 (July 1970), pp. 472-85. Hierarchical migration fields for SMSA's are developed, in the context of functional distance.

CASETTI, EMILIO, and GEORGE DEMKO, *A Diffusion Model of Fertility Decline: An Applica-*

tion to Selected Soviet Data: 1940-1965, Department of Geography Discussion Paper No. 5, Ohio State University, Columbus 1969. The authors propose a two-phase model of the slowing birth rate as a country modernizes.

CASETTI, EMILIO, and GABRIELLA CASETTI, Spatial Diffusion of Revolutions: A Simple Analytical Model, Department of Geography Discussion Paper No. 8, Ohio State University, Columbus, 1969. The authers use a series of simple differential equations to describe the growth and spread of a revolutionary movement.

DEMKO, GEORGE J., and EMILIO CASETTI, "A Diffusion Model for Selected Demographic Variables: An Application of Soviet Data," Annals, American Association of Geographers, Vol. 60 (1970), pp. 533-39. The authors develop and tests a model of diffusion for rates of birth, death, and divorce for areas around major Soviet cities.

FLORIN, J., The Advance of Frontier Settlement in Pennsylvania 1638-1850, M. A. thesis, Penn State University, 1965. Settlement waves across the state are identified, by reference to a space-time surface.

GOULD, PETER, Spatial Diffusion, Commission on College Geography of the A. A. G., Resource Paper No. 4, 1969. Gould surveys the subject of spatial diffusion, discussing the major approaches to its study as to type and scale.

HÄGERSTRAND, TORSTEN, The Propagation of Innovation Waves, Lund Studies in Human Geography, #4, Lund, 1952. Hägerstrand examines the relation of innovation centers to subsequent diffusion progress.

HÄGERSTRAND, TORSTEN, Innovation Diffusion as a Spatial Process, University of Chicago Press, Chicago, 1967. Hägerstrand's 1953 classic as translated by Allan Pred.

HUDSON, JOHN C., "Diffusion in a Central Place System," Geographical Analysis, Vol. 1, 1969, pp. 45-58. A stochastic model is developed for a hierarchical central place system, yielding cumulatively, an S-shaped curve of adoptions.

KNIFFEN, FRED, "The Covered Bridge," Geographical Review, Vol. 41, 1951, pp. 114-23. Kniffen concludes that the profit motive (tolls) probably led to the fairly rapid diffusion of covered bridges across the United States.

MISRA, R. P., Diffusion of Agricultural Innovations, Mysore, Prasaranga, University of Mysore, 1968. Misra summarizes the subject of innovation diffusion and makes a general application to Indian problems.

MORRILL, RICHARD C., "Expansion of the Urban Fringe: A Simulation Experiment," Regional Science Association Papers, Vol. 15 (1965), pp. 185-99. Expansion of the urban fringe is presented as a spatial diffusion process, in a model incorporating elements of randomness and specific probabilities.

MORRILL, RICHARD L., "The Shape of Diffusion in Space and Time," Economic Geography, Vol. 46 (Supplement, June 1970), pp. 259-68. The influence of distance and time on spatial diffusion is examined, lending general support to the notion of innovation waves.

RAMACHANDRAN, RANGANATHAN. Spatial Diffusion of Innovation in Rural India: A Case Study of the Spread of Irrigation Pumps in the Coimbatore Plateau, Ph. D. Dissertation, Clark University, Worcester, Mass. (1968). A study of the diffusion of electric irrigation pumps among 190 villages within a twenty-mile radius of Coimbatore City in South India.

STANISLAWSKI, DAN, "The Origin and Spread of the Grid-Pattern Town," Geographical Review, Vol. 36 (1946), pp. 105-20. Stanislawski traces the spread of the grid-pattern town, and suggests the conditions required for adoption.

WENDEL, BERTIL, "Regional Aspects of Internal Migration and Mobility in Sweden, 1946-1950," from David Hannerberg, Torsten Hägerstrand, and Bruno Odeving (eds.), Migration in Sweden: A Symposium, Lund Studies in Geography, No. 13, Lund, 1957, pp. 7-26. Wendel examines the relationship of areas of net population loss and areas of net population gain with the spatial mobility of the respective populations.

WEST, ROBERT C., "The Term 'Bayou' in the United States: A Study in the Geography of Place Names," Annals, Association of American Geographers, Vol. 44, No. 1 (1954), pp. 63-74. West examines cartographically the present extent of the term "bayou" and its diffusion from its place of origin.

WOLPERT, JULIAN, A Regional Simulation Model of Information Diffusion, mimeographed paper, Regional Science Dept., University of Penn., 1964. Wolpert discusses his adaptation of Hägerstrand's diffusion model to a regional situation.

WOLPERT, JULIAN, "Directional and Distance Bias in Inter-Urban Migratory Streams," Annals, Association of American Geographers, Vol. 57, No. 3 (1967), pp. 605-16. Wolpert describes migration streams, using measures of central tendency and distance.

WOLPERT, JULIAN, "Migration as an Adjustment to Environmental Stress," *Journal of Social Issues,* Vol. 22, No. 4, pp. 92-102 (1966). A simplified ecological model is developed, suggesting the behavioral consequences of stress and strain evoked by a mismatch of the individual and his environment.

5
THE
REGION

If Geography is concerned with space, *then it is also concerned with* region. *We could not survive as a contemporary discipline if we were intellectually unable to delimit the systems we study. Virtually all that geographers have learned over a very long history of involvement with the regional concept suggests that the region is a spatial definition by the mind, not an objective reality. It is true that there are geographers who make claims for the "concrete" or "objective" region. That they do suggests that some of us are relatively slow learners.*

It is perhaps ironic that the concept of region has served over time to provide a semblance of structural unity to geography, while at the same time has provided our discipline's foremost bonepile of contention. Terminology and definition, concept and method, have all contributed to a disparate parade of viewpoints through the literature. Regions have been suggested to be natural *(but not unnatural),* unit objects, complex organisms, ecological units, *and unfortunately, geographical. Contrasts have been made between the homogeneous and the heterogeneous (read uniform vs. nodal, identity vs. connectivity) in coming belatedly to distinctions between surficial similarity and functional organization over space. It is quite clear that this lengthy involvement with the notion of region is a product of our concern for ordering the information we gather over space. In that context, one can note that from the beginning (1) spatial classification has been a need of the geographer if not his goal; (2) aspects of spatial uniformity have been more readily perceived by him than have elements of spatial organization; (3) the effectiveness of any single set of fixed criteria for ordering spatial data is drastically altered by a change in the scale of regionalization; (4) the order achieved is meaningful only in terms of the purpose of the approach; and (5) the criteria for regionalization can be purposive only with respect to the character of the space examined. Some scholars began with perceived*

425

"pieces" of earth space as individuals to be grouped according to their characteristics, aggregating until the totality of earth-space (often terrestrial only) was reached. This synthesizing procedure, then, has been a part of the geographer's inductive approach to the problem of spatial order. Conversely, the approach which moved analytically from the whole earth to its apparent regional components has been a part of the deductive reasoning of the geographer. In this more common process of "logical" division, the geographer often was trapped by his own success. As it was always possible to continue the process of dividing, it was always likely that he would cover the earth with a detailed, fragmented scheme. The resulting reenforcement of bias led to claims that produced strongly negative reactions both within and outside the descipline.

The early recorded notions as to the character of earth-space seem to suggest that some notion of local identity or perceived uniformity at varying microlevels is a prerequisite to the discovery of areal differences. Too, the nature of the distance-decay phenomenon is such that localized interactions could lead one to miss much of the heterogeneity implicit in broader functional organization. At any rate, it has been difficult, apparently, for the geographer to reach the third stage of eventual development (the first is local homogeneity and the second, areal differentiation): the underlying conformity of spatial process common to all inhabited places. He has been moving slowly into a fourth level of conceptual endeavor: the interface between spatial process and structural form. A higher plane of development, this fourth stage permits a sophisticated treatment of complex regional systems. No other approach will be able to integrate properly those elements which provide a traditional cultural region with its unique character.

The question of scale is linked rather broadly to the problem of classification. In a special way, however, it relates to the problem faced by a practitioner of human geography who wishes to delimit a segment of space for purposes of stud ing a particular culture there. This is a case of dichotomous division creating a two-region system—within and without the culture spa .. The original delimiting criteria which initially fix the scale may determine also whether viable sub-regions can be established within the cultural region. This is an especially important consideration for the geographer, as it bears on the problem of *location*, an aspect of classification peculiar to geographic science. At the initial level of the dichotomous division, location is determined by the delimiting criteria. Areas and points within areas are in or out of the culture space, on the boundary or within a boundary zone. For sub-regions developed within the culture space, location becomes a variable which commands careful attention. It is not a variable in the sense that positions change, but in the fact that different spatial sub-orders will suggest different interrelationships over space. The particular selection of sub-regional criteria thus may determine whether the interactions involved in creating the cultural complex will be identified or made sufficiently apparent to become the subject of hypothetical conjecture. Quite obviously, theory as to the cultural involvement with space is required in order to establish the criteria of spatial definition. These criteria will in turn establish scales in ways that are intellectually valid, operationally sound, and locationally revealing.

Given the state of the geographer's discipline, it is not surprising that we stress the need for theories, and for models which support theory by the challenge of performance. We order our spatial data in a variety of ways, however, so that we might achieve a variety of purposes. We can note the extensive applied use of the regional concept, particularly in planning. We have been rather self-conscious, however, with respect to our own uses of regionalization. In part this is due to our diverse and often contradictory notions, in part to a traditional scarcity of stimulating classification schemes, in part to the inelegant methodology of the past, and in part to the serious challenge posed by regional science in the late 1950's as to our capacity for rigor and competitive conceptual output. One of the outcomes of this self-consciousness is that we are quite reluctant to introduce, or reintroduce, notions of the region as an art form. We should have much to learn from both representational and abstract art in the management of space value. Perhaps if one of our purposes is permitted to be that of aesthetic appreciation, we can suffer the Philistine arrow in order to enjoy the art of regionalization in human geography. A shield may be required first, and that can only be sound theory.

It must be noted that the past decade and a half have been a time of blossoming in the methodological garden of the geographer (and with it an expected fair crop of thorns). What has been lacking in proper proportion is adequate corollary investigation of the content of space as occupied by the variety of cultures we recognize. The fully contributing human geographer of the future will not only be well equipped with the analytical tools and broad conceptual frameworks of his discipline, he will also be more fully aware of the *possibilities* for investigation than ever before. The range of purposive regionalization can widen only to the extent that we realize those possibilities.

The Selections

Étienne Juillard offers a smooth definitional transition from notions of the region based on spatial uniformity and extended as landscape, to that of the region as defined by functional organization. He cites the "need for efficiency" as that which demands a definition of *region*. It is in the domain of networks and nodal fields that he finds what is for him a satisfactory definition. His examples and illustrations are best and most accurate when drawn from the French, and they assist in a careful articulation of functional space. Although he repeats an earlier error by Isard in suggesting that the Lösch spatial formulations preceded those of Christallar, Juillard utilizes notions of centrality and urban hierarchy in developing his theme. The significance of this innovative perspective with respect to French regions should not be overlooked. Not only does he reject the traditional, disfunctional regional propositions of the past, he goes beyond French borders to dwell on supranational regionalization. He comments also on the needs of underdeveloped nations for a voluntary joint management of their spaces, and notes pointedly that the bothersome gap between city and village is one of effective regional organization. He ends with the suggestion that the notion of region is governed by the principle of spontaneous territorial management.

In his study of South Indian plantations, Steene Folke views the concept of region as an analytical tool. He develops a regional hierarchy, specifying alternate levels of generalization which shift from "uniformity criteria" to "organizational" criteria. He views these levels as different aspects of the same areal complex. Folke builds on the ideas of Philbrick in developing what was, for him, a useful ordering of his data. He has described the work as a continued interaction between theoretical ideas and factual material collected in the field.

David Grigg examines the problem of applying formal principles of classification to the development of regional systems. In a review, the procedures of classification are contrasted with those of logical division. Although either taxonomic process yields hierarchical orders, Grigg notes that both are commonly applied by a scientist in deriving a single system. Classification is necessary to eliminate the nuances of nomenclature and facilitate the transmission of knowledge; but its highest purpose is to make possible inductive generalization. In suggesting common misconceptions about classification, Grigg forcefully shatters the notion of the region as concrete reality. Too, he points up the practice of regionalization for the sake of regionalization as a traditional weakness of the discipline. The most thought-provoking section is the examination of the problem of the geographical individual, which provokes an honest questioning of the applicability of classification procedures in regionalization. For those who would attempt to establish a taxonomic system of regions, Grigg concludes with a survey of the principles of classification and logical division, primarily as a guide to the pitfalls of the task. If his article is directed toward methodology, it also plays the important role of questioning not only what has been done but also what we may yet do with the concept of region.

C. S. Davies offers an interesting example of the uses of contemporary methods in regionalization. He tests an earlier, subjective division of Wales by E. C. Bowen with more precise criteria. He makes a rigorous application of a linear discriminant function utilizing factor scores for thirteen counties in Wales. As a scholar and scientist, Davies was well prepared either to accept or reject Bowen's hypotheses of regional delimitation. As a Welshman, he exhibits a bit of pride in accepting the notion that Wales has spatial character other than that of political

entity only. If the careful methodology presented confounds the uninitiated, then perhaps they might like to ease past portions of the study now, to study them fruitfully, later.

The Detroit Geographical Expedition, under the research direction of William Bunge, offers an excellent example of purposive regionalization. In its examination of the problem of school decentralization in Detroit, the guiding principle is not that of practical application, but that of a philosophical application of the method of regionalization. Perhaps no single fact is more instructive in this intriguing document than the notion that given a complex set of restraints involving the number of sub-regions permitted, the size of student population within the sub-region, and the additional philosophical restraint regarding sympathetic authority for black children, 194 plans met the restraints. Only electronic computation could permit an evaluation of these in time to present the particular viewpoint of the researchers. This is a striking example of an effort by scientists to affect policy. The postscript records the game effort of the Expedition to adjust to the realities of the shifting political scene.

In an artistic effort which advocates literary artistry in geography, Yi-Fu Tuan demonstrates beautifully an aesthetic approach to the examination of space. The crux of his art is an awareness that regionalization stems from an intuitive appreciation of landscape.

The concept of region remains a part of the intellectual underpinnings of our discipline. It can be used to order our data, but more importantly, it can assist in the evaluation of hypotheses generated from virtually every approach taken in contemporary geography.

✦✦✦✦✦✦✦✦✦✦✦✦✦✦✦✦✦✦✦✦✦✦✦✦✦✦✦✦✦✦

THE REGION: AN ESSAY OF DEFINITION

Étienne Juillard

Regional synthesis, as Vidal de la Blache said, is the ultimate task of the geographer, the only terrain on which he is fully himself. In explaining and in understanding the internal logic of a fragment of the earth's crust, the geographer expresses an individuality not found anywhere else. Is it not possible, then, to relate to this subject the constant and fruitful dialogue which has developed between regional geography and systematic geography? [1] Despite the fact that France has been noted for its regional studies, the concept of region was not, until recently, an object of systematic generalization. A theoretical structure would free us from unsatisfactory comparisons of monographs. Eliminating those monographs which are little more than enumerated episodes, regional syntheses are ordinarily presented in frameworks, disparate both in composition and scale. Sometimes defined as territory marked by inherent uniformity, ethnic or economic, sometimes as an historical unit that has no actual reality, the region is most often conceived of as a kind of "given," the limits of which one forces oneself to justify at the threshold of the study. Should one be astonished that this conception of geography has no following in countries such as the United States, where the framework of nature and history is larger and less subtle? [2]

In systematic geopgraphy, one precisely defines such words as *pediment, galleria, open field,* and *suburb.* One cannot say the same about a term like "region."

Today, the region is no longer the exclusive domain of geographical research, nor the folkloric framework in which traditional approaches linger. More and more, in the study of economic and social change, development is defined in terms of territorial arrangement, or regionalization. This is true not only in the fragmented countries of Europe, but also in the U.S.S.R., the U.S., and the new African states. In France, planning committees are based on regional economic planning. What kind of regions are used? Initially, for efficiency and administrative convenience, the regional committee were traced on *arrondissements,* departments, and groups of departments; the regional programs are part of a general plan which encompasses all departments. But these frameworks are rarely satisfactory, and J. Labasse has criticized them. [3] The need for efficiency poses the problem of defining the region.

Geographers were not prepared to provide a definition. They commanded, to be sure, intimate knowledge of those regions on

---

1. On this subject, see the penetrating remarks of H. Baulig, *Géographie générale et géographie régionale,* Quebec, 1959, pp. 47-52.
2. See *American Geography: Inventory and Prospect,* 1954, chap. 2, pp. 2 ff.: the region is presented there as *an intellectual concept, an invention of the moment to solve a problem.*
3. J. Labasse, La portée géographique des programmes d'action régionale français, *Annales de Géographie* (1960), pp. 371-393. "The Geographical Basis of the Problems of French Regional Action.)

From *Annales de Geographie,* Vol. 71, 1962. Reprinted by permission of Librairie Armand, Colin, Paris.

which they had written monographs. But regional geography was unprepared to face the broader problems: criteria of delimitation, optimum size, *etc.* Assistance was sought from the economists, who had, in fact, just discovered the region. Having already dealt with theoretical problems and preindustrial spatial hypotheses (von Thunen), they had begun to develop systems of regionalization. The great initiator seems to have been the German, Lösch.[4] It was in the U.S. that *regional science* was most fully developed. From there it was returned to Europe by Léontieff and Walter Isard, who found several enthusiastic and capable followers among the French economists.[5] They applied their specific aptitudes to the generalization of regional reality and quickly developed a technical vocabulary upon which they built structures and precise mechanisms.

But space, as viewed by economists, is not the same as that viewed by geographers, and in this new and fascinating realm of applied research, economics cannot be simply substituted for geography. François Perroux has demonstrated that the economist is concerned with the "dislocation" of men, materials, and activities in expressing physical distance in terms of price and time, while the geographer studies the organization of differentiated space, *per se.*[6] Starting from the simplest and most abstract model possible, the economist complicates it as he

goes along; he proceeds from the general to the particular and finally approaches, with some difficulty, the concrete case. The geographer, on the other hand, starts with specific cases, specific locations, and specific complexes and later extends his observations and comparisons in order to develop a planetary organization of space. In doing so, he is forced to generalize, to become abstract; at this point, he feels uncomfortable in the new role. At the level of the region, one can visualize a fruitful conjunction of the two disciplines, a convergence of their particular viewpoints. But the differences in outlook and vocabulary have made the dialogue difficult. After World War II, this process began in Germany, Poland, and the U.S.S.R., where geographers systematically sought to generalize the concept of region. The French contribution came later.[7]

Uniform Space and Functional Space

The terms in which the regional problem is framed have changed through time; more precisely, attention has been given to a type of spatial organization which, until now, has been ignored.

For a long time, one of the most fertile notions in geography has been that of *landscape*, a complex of physical and human characteristics which give individuality to a territory. If landscape is not uniform it is at least characterized by habitual repetition of certain elements.[8] What we have called the

---

4. On Lösch, see the excellent review by J. P. Rousselot. *La Théorie de l'espace chez August Lösch.* Mimeographed, Fac. Droit, Lille, 1960, 278 pp. See also Ponsard, *Histoire des théories économiques spatiales,* 1958.
5. See in particular the series "Economies régionales," *Cahiers de l'Institute de Science économique appliquée,* directed by J. R. Boudeville.
6. François Perroux, *L'Europe sans rivages,* 1954, pp. 339 ff. The author borrows his ideas on geographical space from J. Gottmann, *La Politique des états et leur géographie,* 1952.

7. Among the most stimulating "regional" theses are those of J. Labasse, *Les Capitaux et la région,* 1955, and Michel Rochefort, *L'Organization urbanine de l'Alsace,* 1960. It is significant that in each subsequent edition, these two great French geographers have allotted a larger place to the concept of region than in their earlier work.
8. The most penetrating analysis of the landscape concept is probably the one by C. Troll, *Die geographische Landschaft un ihre Erforschung* (Studium Generale, 1950, pp. 163-81).

"natural region" is one of these homogeneous entities. But man has placed his mark almost everywhere, sometimes for millennia, so that the major part of the landscape is humanized—what the Germans call *Kulturlandschaft*. Even if one is able to reconstruct what was the natural landscape and define the characteristics of the physical environment, the relationships between natural region and humanized landscape are far from simple. Two similar and even adjoining natural units can give birth to two different landscapes, as for example, the agrarian, demographic, and industrial contrasts between the Vosges and the Black Forest. *A fortiori*, several landscapes can succeed one another over time within the same space. The mutation of agricultural landscapes in the Mediterranean area and the urbanization of the mining basin are examples. Finally, human impact can completely alter the character of natural environment, as did the impact of the Danes in developing for cultivation the most inhospitable portions of their nation.

The landscape therefore reflects a momentary state of interrelationships, an unstable equilibrium between natural conditions, human technology, economic systems, and demographic social structures. In addition, each landscape incorporates a variety of inherited arrangements from the past. The inertia of spatial organization tends to confer a relative permanence to landscape. Although visibly real, the landscape cannot be explained without referring to invisible factors as diverse as underground hydrology, birth rates, land tenure, circulation of capital, and religious practice. Through considerable expenditure of effort on the analysis and synthesis of landscape, geographers have been able to explain the formation of landscapes with increasing precision and have made landscape a specialized domain which no other discipline questions.

Is the notion of region to be confused with the notion of landscape? There is here, undoubtedly, a kind of "regionalization," and landscape research allows us to identify and delimit local territories: for example, agricultural regions, each characterized by a homogeneous arrangement of rural space; urban agglomerations, which as landscapes are themselves subdivided into more or less homogeneous zones, neighborhoods, and suburbs; industrial complexes, individualized by the habitual repetition of certain forms; hilly valleys with dispersed industries; mining zones with heavy industries; complexes of seaports, and so on. The Germans differentiate between *Land* and *Landschaft*. The first term identifies the "individual," regardless of scale; in its total complexity, this unit will never be more than a unique example. The second, "landscape," is susceptible of classification in terms of the distribution of individual characteristics and residuals.[9] For M. Sorre, in 1957, the region was "the product of a geographical landscape."[10] This is more or less what he repeats when, in 1961, he masterfully paints a grand "series" of human landscapes of the developing world. However, he has difficulty in delimiting landscapes in the more developed areas. One finds there, he says, combinations of landscape types; hence the Franco-Belgian Basin "where highly intensive agriculture and prosperous industrial life are closely associated." Developing this idea further in the last chapter, M. Sorre states that economic and social developments determine the hierarchy of organized spaces, that "each region has its proper function, or rather, functions." He suggests that one must identify

9. H. Bobek and J. Schmithusen, *Die Landschaft im logischen System der Geographie* (*Erdkunde*, 1949, pp. 112-20).
10. Max Sorre, *Réncontres de la geographie et del la sociologie*, 1957, p. 33.

centers of gravity, corridors, and focal points of men and materials.

Pursuing this idea further, subdividing territory into a mosaic of uniform areas is not the only way to attack the problem of spatial organization. The landscape is not always (in fact rarely in the highly developed countries) the framework within which group activities occur. In the highly advanced economies, for example, socio-professional complexes and resultant life-styles are superimposed on the same location. The mosaic of landscapes, of humanized spaces, once beyond subsistence level, is altered by currents of exchange and various ways of life which ultimately rest on a network of organizing centers—towns—which structures space into new sets. Uniformity rarely characterizes these sets; complementarity of the various elements is contrary to the rule. Human migrations, the flow of trade, the flux of capital, and administrative decisions which maintain unity are less visible and durable than the elements of landscape. But does this mean that there is any reason to declare these factors non-geographic? To ignore them would be to reduce regional analysis to the decomposition of landscape into elements, to neglect what connects them to one another (that is, the complementary activities of human groups).

Thus there exist two principles of regional unity. One, landscape, rests on a criterion of *uniformity*;[11] the other, on a criterion of cohesion, on the organizational activities of a center. The individual territories, in the latter case, are characterized less by their form than by their functions. We can now speak of *functional* space.

11. We prefer the term "uniform" region rather than "homogeneous" region. The latter could lead to confusion, because Americans frequently use "homogeneous" to characterize complementary combinations of activities.

The Genesis of Functional Space

Once we no longer conceive of space as a juxtaposition of more or less understood areas, but as a field of action, a number of possible "structures" come to mind. One can take into consideration the most diverse forces: polarization created by a leading industry around which revolve satellites (sub-contractors, similar industries, derived industries); the migratory power of attraction of an urban center which one can measure in area of recruitment and in its force; the linkages created by commercial relationships, which are expressed in terms of the market for a product, the hinterland of a harbor, the area covered by a wholesaler; forces of political, social, and spiritual cohesion; relationships of financial dependence, not to mention forces of inertia such as illiteracy, gerontocracy, and other restraints like real estate speculation, demographic or economic Malthusianism, and so on.

These forces interest the geographer in so far as they combine and are translated into a particular organization of space. However, the analysis shows that these forces converge at certain *centers* which reflect a dynamic spatial structure, unperceivable at any given moment. In 1910, Vidal de la Blache, who is definitely the founder of modern geography up to its most recent development, showed that France had started to acquire new regional structures which were organized into a network. "Cities and roads," he wrote, "are the great initiators of unity."[12] He borrowed the word *nodality* from the British geographer Mackinder to indicate the major crossroads which generate change of all kinds and which, as a result, have the greatest power of organization.

This does not operate only in large cities. The same principle of cohesion or "cen-

12. Vidal de la Blache, "Régions françaises," *Revue de Paris* (1910), pp. 821-42.

trality" can be applied to all spatial scales. The agglomerated village surrounded by its lands is already a center, and the star-like network of its rural routes expresses this on the landscape. The small market town in the heart of its agricultural "country," the medium-size town, and the large city constitute a hierarchy of centers which distribute more and more specialized services. On the basis of this hierarchical structure, the economists have developed a theory which demonstrates that hierarchical structure is the product of two factors, *market* and *accessibility*. To the degree that the proffered service is more expensive and less-often needed, the service must have a larger clientele and therefore a dense population or a more extended zone of distribution. Conversely, the factor of transportation density and cost (accessibility) tends to limit this zone to a certain maximum distance. For each service, a system of zones of distribution is created. A third factor, the interdependence of these services, often causes the resultant centers of distribution to coincide with one another at each level of the hierarchy. Thus space is structured spontaneously into zones whose dimensions are functions of transportation techniques, the population density, the needs of the population, and the capacity of this space to fill those needs. August Lösch has developed a model assuming a homogeneous plain with no differences in population density, buying power, productivity of enterprises, or elasticity of markets. He shows that resultant areas assume a hexagonal shape, with each center being surrounded by six centers of the immediately inferior level and located with five other centers of the same level around a higher-order center.[13]

Most certainly, reality is more complex, since it incorporates the diversity of natural conditions, the inheritances of the past, all the inequalities of demographic pressure, and economic and social development. Nevertheless, as soon as these relationships appear, the principle of spatial organization is found in what German geographers have called *Zentralitat*, i.e. an urban network, or as G. Chabot has said, an *urban frame*.[14] In its relationship with its hinterland, the city plays a triple role: distributor, co-ordinator, and driving force. In the domain of education, health, postal- and tele-communications the city is, above all, a convenient mechanism for the diffusion of services; it is the same for wholesaling, warehousing, and so on. As a communications and administrative center, it co-ordinates the activities of a rather extensive area. Most of all the city provides stimulus to its region by focusing a variety of dominating forces: by appropriation of agricultural land, by factories which daily drain a part of the rural labor force, by financial means which concentrate there, and by action on public opinion through the press. Through this system of co-ordinated activities, the zone of urban influence affects behavior, lasting relations are established, and in-group feelings finally develop among its inhabitants, all of which contribute to its personality.

Thus based on a complex of relationships, functional space is expressed less by its boundaries than by its core and the networks it generates. Regional analysis no longer is based on the discovery of uniform spaces, but on the study of the hierarchy of centers, the density and the intensity of change. By testing the "centrality" of cities in southwestern Germany, Christaller rediscovered, in this relatively homogeneous

13. On August Lösch, see the work of J. Rousselot. The American economists and "ecologists" have since then done much work on this question. See in particular Hawley, *Human Ecology*, 1950,

pp. 236ff., and Duncan, *Metropolis and Region*, 1960.
14. G. Chabot, *L'Armature urbaine*.

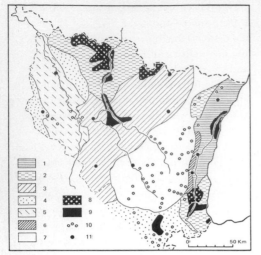

Figure 1. The landscape of eastern France. (1) intensive polyculture, (2) polyculture of medium intensity, (3) cereals and dairying herbages, (4) dairying herbages, (5) dominant wasteland, (6) vineyard, (7) dominant forest, (8) heavy industries (mining, metallurgy), (9) large urban and industrial agglomerations, (10) textile industries or dispersed mechanical industries, (11) medium cities.

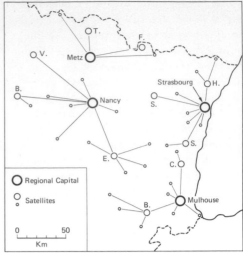

Figure 2. The urban network of the east of France.

area, the five-ordered hierarchy and the hexagonal zones of influence of Lösch's schemata.[15] Relying primarily on an exceptional knowledge of the circulation of capital, Jean Labasse has revealed the diverse polarizations which make the structure of the region around Lyon understandable. In defining the hierarchy of Alsace's urban centers and in establishing their zones of influence, Michel Rochefort has provided the key to the regional organization of this province.

The two maps here (Figs. 1 and 2) show what very different results obtain from the application of these two principles of regionalization.

It is evident that regional research stays closer to human reality by analyzing the organization of activities rather than by uniformity in the physical landscape. This does not diminish interest in the concept of landscape. Plainly, the objective of each of these types of research is different. Intimate knowledge of the spatial combinations which form the landscape is indispensible for one who wants to evaluate the potential of a territory, to measure its value, and to understand the risks of disturbing the delicate equilibrium between the natural milieu and human groups. Conversely, even a highly individualized landscape cannot be separated from neighboring landscapes with which it has complementary relationships; one cannot understand the countryside apart from the city which animates it, nor the city without the support of its *Umland*. That is, indubitably, the view of regional reality. But what do we call *the* region?

The Region—Changing Structure

If one attempts to identify the region among functional spaces, one must specify the echelon where placed so that its content corresponds to its boundaries. In current

15. W. Christaller, *Die zentralen Orte Suddeutschlands,* Iena, 1933; and International Congress of Geography, Amsterdam, 1938, II, pp. 123-28.

usage, the region is a territorial subdivision commonly placed immediately after the state in the hierarchy. This is how it is interpreted in our "regional" plans and the same level is indicated by the Italian "province," the German "land," and the soviet *supersovnarkhoze*. No precise *dimensional* criteria are suitable, because too many variables, as noted above, condition the size of the zones of influence. Therefore, it would be wise to define region in terms of *functional* content. We propose that the region is not generally a state, but it is endowed with a certain self-sufficiency, not in the sense of economic independence, but in the sense that most of the functions and services of primary importance are represented there in such a way that the region is capable of satisfying most of the needs of its inhabitants. The region's metropolis has the power of influence and decision and has recourse to a higher echelon only in exceptional or highly specialized domains. Thus in France itself, Paris makes its influence felt on the entire country, but only from a certain point of view, perhaps because the central government and administration are found there or because Paris is the only international city in France and entirely dominates the country in certain sectors such as finance, information, artistic and literary creativity, and migratory attraction. But several large cities offer almost the complete gamut of requisite functions and superior services, for example: head offices of industrial and commercial enterprises; a stock exchange; a variety of wholesale activities; a large university provided with research laboratories; a large hospital center; facilities such as an international airport, a convention hall, theaters offering international entertainment tours, and so on. The metropolis is surrounded by a network of relay centers by which services are provided over a vast territory. The region, as we understand

it, disappears within the organized space of the metropolis and its satellites. It is obvious that, if all the criteria used are linked to the "tertiary" sector of the economy, the presence of a powerful industrial base is indispensable. Only it could sustain urbanization and buying power sufficient to ensure a reasonable profit for this system. Again, quoting a report of a European organization, we note that the region is "the last level at which the different intervening forces structure and co-ordinate themselves in the economic and social life prior to the national level." Further, one must add, certain states are too small, too underpopulated, or too underdeveloped to include several regions.

In these terms, the regional articulation of a territory is identical to its urban framework, and regionalization keeps pace with economic and social development.

This definition is related to the *nature* of regional functions. It is quite obvious, however, that their *content* varies considerably according to its stage of development, so that the dimensions of the regions vary, in space and time, with the degree of industrialization and urbanization, population densities, levels of living, and the state of communication techniques.

Again, let us use France as an example. The regional centers which we identify today asserted themselves little by little. It is incorrect to assume that "departmentalization" restructured a previous organization into larger regions. France in the eighteenth century was composed of "regional" cells that might be expected in an agricultural economy before the advent of rail transportation. They often were composed of relatively homogeneous areas grouped around markets. The seigneurial administration, then absolute, was frequently organized around these functional spaces, and many of these "areas," bailiwicks and seneschalships, were the ancestors of most of our *arrondisse-*

ments.[16] In the 300 to 400 towns of 2,000 to 10,000 inhabitants (the major centers grouped without great hierarchization) rather elementary services were required for a life of limited horizons that only encompassed a part of the population. Out of these emerged, to be sure, some provincial capitals of 30,000 to 50,000 inhabitants. But their jurisdiction was too vast for a truly regional pattern of life to develop, because the time and expense of travel were too high for them to be able to organize the entire province, except in the administrative and judicial sectors. Only a few high officials and a few great personalities recognized horizons extending beyond the limits of these bailiwicks.

The creation of the departments in 1790 enlarged, in a fairly artificial way, the basic administration framework and suppressed the provinces for well-known political reasons. Certain departments, moreover, among them the least justified in appearance, were created as functional spaces. Thus, René Musset shows that the Bas-Maine had not included any well-characterized "area," but in transforming it into the department of Mayenne, the commissioners took care to include in it all the neighborhoods where flax was cultivated, spun, and woven; as a result, "its surface really was composed of a vast industry whose major center was Laval, the chief town of the department, and whose secondary centers were Mayenne and Chateau-Gontier, the chief towns of the two other *arrondissements.*"[17] But it is only with the construction of the railroads that the prefectures, now railway nodes because of their administrative pre-eminence, advanced beyond the other chief towns of the *arrondissement* and were able to organize a space the size of a department. This is also the time when cities ceased to be simply a product of the needs of coordinating their countrysides (or simply being a market for the produce of the soil) and began to develop a specialized economy to drain an increasing part of the rural population and to play the driving role.[18]

The movement of industrial concentration, itself ordered by the networks of transportation and by the larger cities, further articulated the hierarchical structure. However, the increasing mobility of men, merchandise, capital, and ideas allowed certain large cities to influence territories larger than the departments, with greater speed and efficiency than the chief towns of the *arrondissement* had done over their more modest zones of influence. Higher-order services simultaneously became more and more diversified and concentrated by the combined interplay of market and accessibility factors. Given the reality of technology, certain very expensive services cannot exist with a profit unless they command hinterlands populated by several millions of inhabitants. This is the case for computers used by administrations, for airports, large laboratories of applied re-

16. Bernard Guenée, *La Géographie administrative de la France A la fin du moyen-age: elections et bailliages.* Le Moyen-age, 1961, pp. 293-323, has shown, in respect ot the bailiwick of Senlis, that as early as the end of the Middle Ages, the administrative boundaries were, if not simple, at least stable. He argues effectively the *technical* impossibility of an administrator of that period being able to perceive in its details a horizon larger than the castellany or the provostship. In the eighteenth century, increased road circulation broadened this framework to the dimensions of a bailiwick.

17. René Musset, *Le Bas-Maine, étude géographique,* 1917, p. 20.
18. Thus the population of Reims has represented 30 per cent of those in its *arrondissement* between 1600 and 1850. Only at that moment, did its hinterland stop growing, only to diminish in 1900; in 1950 the Reims agglomeration accounts for 63 per cent, according to a note in the review *Population,* 1961, pp. 722-30.

search, and international entertainment
tours. To be sure, since the middle of the
nineteenth century, the evolution of the
French regional structure has been distorted
by the rigidity of its administrative infrastructure and by the presence of an extremely large capital city in which the
modern transportation network is centered.
Pierre George notes, in his report to the
recent colloquoy at Lyon on *The Region*,
that "during the last quarter of the nineteenth century and the first quarter of the
twentieth century, overseas speculation stole
the march on regional economic development," so that "Paris and the large seaside
ports have drained capital and initiative. Few
provincial centers have been able to resist
this competition, and their capacity to
organize regional space found itself diminished." But in neighboring industrial countries which, it must be noted, hold much
better demographic positions, metropolises
of 500,000 to one million inhabitants
have organized territories around
them of 50 to 100 kilometers in radius,
populated by 3 to 8 million inhabitants—the
equivalent of three to eight of our departments. These represent the actual measure of
the region in Western Europe.[19]

This evolution is not yet finished. The
progress of European integration prohibits a
conception of regional organization in the
context of each separate state. A zone of
capitals and large seaports is concentrated
around the North Sea from Paris to Ham-
burg, the essential organs of decision for
northwestern Europe. This is reminiscent of
what is already built in the U.S., that Megalopolis which Jean Gottmann has analyzed
so well. The Rhine axis is surrounded, from
Switzerland to the Benelux, by the most

industrialized regions, among which linkages
at all levels are self-reinforced. The advance
of this area at the expense of the Atlantic
regions seems to indicate this. It would not
be unreasonable, however, to seek to develop on these margins, regions which are
less populated, less industrialized, but more
strictly specialized, and which could assure
to their inhabitants the same well-being as
the others. In any case, the old Europe of
the *pays*, which gave way to the Europe of
nations, now gives way to supranational
space. This means that a spatial reorganization is in process which ignores national
boundaries, but this does not indicate that
expansion of regional dimensions can continue indefinitely. Increasing population
densities, progressive urbanization, and rising
levels of living create at the same time a
perpetually increasing market for goods and
services which justify the maintenance of
nearby metropolises reinforced by a network
of satellites. After all, the minimum and
maximum size of regions is determined by
human numbers and buying power rather
than by squared kilometers. When one
speaks of European "large space," the question is, in fact, of the increasing specialization of its regions, specialization that reinforces interdependence without forcibly
modifying size.

The Region—Universal Space

The flexibility of our definition allows us to
make a comparison of the actual state of
regional structure in various countries of the
world. Its degree of sophistication correlates
rather exactly with the degree of economic
and social development.

We have just examined the case of Western Europe. France is a unique case, because
the great attractive power of Paris distorts
the normal processes of regional integration.
It is nevertheless possible to ascertain that

---

19. We refer to our theoretical essay delivered at a
colloquoy in Liège in 1960, which has appeared
under the title of: *Théorie et politique de l'expansion régionale*, Brussels, 1961, pp. 203-7.

France is very unequally developed in regard to the degree of urbanization and industrialization. A convenient index of the hinterland of a city is provided by the increasing volume of road traffic in proportion to increasing proximity to the city. When on a trip one notices that the average daily traffic diminishes and later grows, he may say that he has crossed the boundary between the zones of influence of two neighboring centers. If, on the other hand traffic increases from center A to center B, one can assume that A is integrated into the hinterland of B. It is thus possible to subdivide space into "areas of attraction by traffic flows" which reflect functional spaces.[20] The result obtained for France in 1955 is very significant (Fig. 3): some large integrated structures appear around Paris, Lyon, and Marseilles; others barely exceed the size of a department; still others are confined to the dimensions of an *arrondissement,* that is, the influence of the city, the center of the *arrondissement,* has not succeeded in integrating neighboring areas. In a good part of western and central France the hierarchy of urban centers is still weak. The essentially agricultural character of the economy and the weak urbanization of the countryside ensures that, in many areas, the normal framework of human interactions is confined to a space the size of an *arrondissement* that often is mistakenly interpreted as the inherited circumscription of a distant past. Modern France therefore presents examples of diverse stages of the spatial evolution noted above; only its most developed parts have seen the birth of metropolises sufficiently powerful to organize integrated regions. That is why we often label such a regional complex *historical.* Sometimes it is a question of a reversion to the functional framework of the past; sometimes a territory which had kept its name, a little of its physiognomy or a few more or less living traditions is being considered, but whose functional reality has dissolved into a larger whole.

More simple, because more recent, has been the genesis of regional structures in countries which we call "modern," that is, those without a traditional agrarian base. Whereas in the countries of old civilization the first urban centers appeared as the products of the development of the countries themselves, here the city (at least in its pioneer form) pre-dated the country. The human landscapes were born of human interactions. "Their growth is tied to alignments of railroads . . . their existence itself is tied to the possibilities of commercialization."[21] From the beginning, areas such as the American Middle West, Siberia, and Australia have been sparsely populated and outward-looking, practicing a speculative agriculture and dependent on a network of centers. Instead of organizing along the traditional lines of rural society, regional organization began with areas that were too large, and often already exploited by a predatory economy. On this base the areas developed a more complex urban structure. In Europe, the actual satellite cities began by being the equals of the future metropolises, before being bypassed by a more forward-moving center. In these new countries, the first large seaports, such crossroads as Montreal, Chicago, Saint Louis, have a decisive advantage. The medium-sized cities are their modern satellites, born of the need for a more sophisticated structuring. Since there was no pre-existing base, each sector of the economy created its own network. Pierre

20. J. R. Boudeville has applied this method to the delimitation of the Lyon region. See: *L'Economie régionale, espace opérationnel,* cahiers de l'I.S.E.A., No. 69, 1958.

21. Max Sorre, *L'Homme sur la terre,* 1961, p. 321.

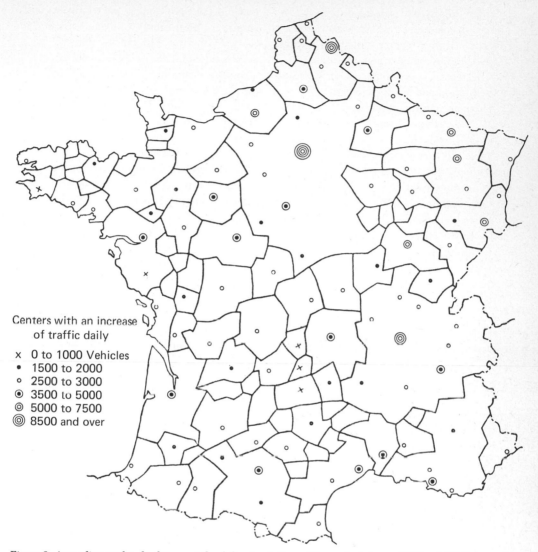

Centers with an increase
     of traffic daily

x   0 to 1000 Vehicles
•   1500 to 2000
o   2500 to 3000
◉   3500 to 5000
◎   5000 to 7500
◎   8500 and over

Figure 3. According to the absolute growth of the circulation of the roads between 1950 and 1955 (counting taken at bridges and causeways on the national roads).

George noted the distortions (the existing overlaps in the U.S., for example) between the zones of influence of railways, banking networks, and so on.[22] Recently, the American administration has attempted to ration-

alize these structures with a view toward constituting real regions, molded by actual conditions. In Europe, the planner who approaches this preliminary and delicate task—which he entrusts to the geographer—must sort out the residue of centuries, from which many of the pieces are missing. In America, on the other hand, he must create

22. Pierre George, *Questions de géographie de la population*, 1959, pp. 193-498.

a coherent network from the dispersed pieces, inverse processes, but with a similar objective. If the "regions" finally delineated in the U.S. have greater area than those of Europe, their size is comparable if expressed in population and levels of living.

There are, on the other hand, huge areas of the globe, those classified as "underdeveloped," which are still far from being organized like large modern regions. Their traditional activities allow only rudimentary forms of human interaction. The only possible subdivisions of space correspond either to natural conditions—mountain ranges, plateaus, fluvial basins—or to areas defined by a way of life, or the territory of an ethnic group. In other words, the subdivisions of space correspond to the natural and human landscapes. Paul Pelissier notes that in Senegal the absence of an urban network and the homogeneity of natural conditions over large areas lead to research on a principle of regionalization among different ethnic groups. Their respective territories constitute uniform zones, inside of which "the exploitation of the environment was pursued with identical techniques, assuring uniform exploitation." These zones have neither "capital cities, nor centers of economic importance." He adds that "economic development and the exigencies of modern administration demand the elaboration of 'regions' centered on cities." These recent creations, born on the margins of homogeneous zones, grow by influencing the complementary fragments of several of these zones.[23]

This absence of structuring does not preclude the presence of higher political organization, but in this case it is an authoritarian type (monarchies of the Middle East) or colonial or para-colonial domination (such as Rome in Gaul, France in its ancient empire, or the United Fruit Company in Central America). Most of the underdeveloped countries today have a dual economy, with only a small part of their territory and their population engaged in an exchange economy.[24] Barring intervention, the gap between the two economies will increase in size, with the congestion of a few large littoral cities as true "islands" enclosed in their territory serving as provincial branches of the great industrial powers. Subject to the increasing cost of provisioning these cities, the rest of the country remains miserable, technically retarded, prey to exodus and political agitation. Between these large cities and the humble peasant communities, there is a complete hiatus in regional organization.

Spontaneous and progressive in old Europe, also spontaneous in the new countries but in other ways, the processes of regionalization do not die when the relations between cities and countries are not the free relations of complementarity, as when the usual human interactions are severed. It could be caused by a political boundary or the presence of real authority, such as large wealthy landowners, or colonial or financial domination. An intervention is thus necessary in the form of a spontaneous organization of space. This is what all of the new, recently emancipated African States must consider. This is also the means by which industrial countries may compensate for certain inconvenient reversions resulting from imbalances born of anarchical evolution. Regional organization is a product of development. It translates, in fact, over space. This is the organizing principle, spontaneous or voluntary, of territory.

---

23. Paul Pelissier, Remarks at *Colloque de géographie appliquée*, Strasbourg, 1961, p. 128, of the *Actes*.

24. See John Friedmann in the *Proceedings and Papers of the Regional Science Association*, 1959, pp. 167 ff.

Thus conceived, the concept of region opens up a tremendous field, barely touched, for geographical research. Some new methods have already been tried; others must be brought to bear. Even more than in the study of landscapes, close collaboration with the other human sciences is necessary in order to clarify policy alternatives.

⁕⁕⁕⁕⁕⁕⁕⁕⁕⁕⁕⁕⁕⁕⁕⁕⁕⁕⁕⁕⁕⁕⁕⁕⁕⁕⁕⁕

AN ANALYTIC HIERARCHY IN COMPARATIVE REGIONAL STUDY

Steen Folke

The conventional approach to regional analysis and description is systematic rather than "truly" regional. The geographic content of a region is analysed itemwise, beginning with the geological structure and ending with the system of communication and trade. Obviously the great advantage of this approach is its ability to provide a systematic account of the chaotic geographic reality. A serious weakness, however, is inherent in this very advantage, namely a tendency to disrupt the complex and delicate geographic fabric of interrelations and linkages. Each systematic item is treated under a separate heading, and hence the total region is viewed more or less as a sum of mutually independent elements.

To solve this problem we need an approach which is radically different. An important contribution has recently been brought forward by Berry,[1] whose three-dimensional "Geographic Matrix" provides a sound basis for regional analysis. The outline of an alternative approach, which in my opinion is "truly" regional, is offered below. Its most conspicious advantage is its simplicity. Neither mathematical models nor electronic computers are involved in its use. Its language is that of everyday geography, and thus it is suggested that the method may have applications in the popular as well as the scientific branch of regional geography.

Essentially the method consists in the application of a pre-determined "analytic hierarchy" to the areas in question. The concept of "regional hierarchy" is certainly not new to geography, and it is not claimed that there is any significant difference in principle between the concepts of "regional hierarchy" and "analytic hierarchy." The difference is rather one of applicability. Thus the "analytic hierarchy" approach should be viewed as an attempt to add to the usefulness of the "regional hierarchy" concept in regional analysis.

The Regional Hierarchy

The need for analysis at different levels in the regional hierarchy was stated in very

1. Brian J. L. Berry, "Approaches to Regional Analysis: A Synthesis," *Annals, Association of American Geographers*, Vol. 54 (1964), pp. 2-11.

From *Geografisk Tidsskrift*, Vol. 64, 1965. Reprinted by permission of the Royal Danish Geographical Society.

general terms by Ackerman[2] and Isard.[3] James[4] proposed the terms "chorographic" and "topographic" for highly generalized small-scale studies and less generalized large-scale studies respectively. Whittlesey[5] examined the concept of "regional hierarchy" in retrospect and suggested the existence of a four-step hierarchy of "compages" with universal validity: Locality—District—Province—Realm. A significant advance in regional theory was brought about by Philbrick,[6] who acknowledged his debt to Robert S. Platt in his treatment of "Principles of Areal Functional Organization in Regional Human Geography." In this important work Philbrick advocates a hierarchy concept which is substantially different from that of Whittlesey. In his own words:

"Stated as a principle, the areal structure of occupance is composed of a number of nested orders of areal functional organization arranged in a functional hierarchy. This nested functional hierarchy is characterized by alternate shifts from parallel relationship to nodal organization as the size and complexity of the units of occupance progresses from parcel to establishment, from groups of parallel establishments to the community,

2. E. A. Ackerman, "Regional Research—Emerging Concepts and Techniques in the Field of Geography," *Economic Geography*, Vol. 29 (1953), pp. 189-197.
3. Walter Isard, "Regional Science, the Concept of Region, and Regional Structure," *Papers and Proceedings, Regional Science Association*, Vol. 2 (1956), pp. 13-26.
4. Preston E. James, "Toward a Further Understanding of the Regional Concept," *Annals, Association of American Geographers*, Vol. 42 (1952), pp. 195-222.
5. D. Whittlesey, "The Regional Concept and the Regional Method," in P. E. James and C. F. Jones, (eds.), *American Geography: Inventory and Prospect*. Syracuse: 1954, pp. 19-68.
6. Allen K. Philbrick, "Principles of Areal Functional Organization in Regional Human Geography," *Economic Geography*, Vol. 33 (1957), pp. 299-336.

etc., in a progression from large to smaller scale."

It will be seen that the theory expounded by Philbrick has its own complicated terminology, partly inherited from Platt and others. As all terms are carefully discussed and defined, the result is a very concise and coherent theory. In my opinion, however, the rather cumbersome terminology limits its usefulness. The following is an attempt to "translate" and modify the theory so as to make it more *operational* in analytic and descriptive regional geography.

A very conspicuous feature in Philbrick's terminology is his effort to avoid as far as possible using the term "region," and consequently he talks of a "functional hierarchy" of "nested orders of areal functional organization" instead of simply a regional hierarchy. An important motive for employing the complicated terminology may be a desire to emphasize the functional/organizational character of the hierarchy. Nevertheless, the substitution of various compound terms for the word "region" hints that dissatisfaction with the inaccuracy of conventional regional terminology is the fundamental reason for inventing a new one. Thus a modified version of the theory—with a somewhat different aim and scope—requires definitions of the basic terms.

Basic Definitions

A recent publication, containing a review of the various concepts of "region" and its main categories, structural (or uniform or formal or homogeneous) and functional (or nodal or organizational), is "Methods of Economic Regionalization."[7] Whereas there is wide agreement on the use of the term "functional" rather than the various alternatives, there is no similar accord on the proper name for the other category of

7. *Geographia Polonica*, Vol. 4 (1964).

regions. The term "structural" is perferred here, because it is felt to be *complementary* to "functional" in the same sense that anatomy and physiology are complementary. In the present study the concept of "region" is viewed purely as an analytical tool, and hence structural and functional regions emerge as results of the application of different types of criteria. Thus:

A *region* is an area with a distinctive character identified by one or more spatially differentiating features.

A *structural* region is a region which is uniform with respect to one or more features.

A *functional* region is a region composed of areas and points which are interconnected.

While these brief definitions do not take into account a number of familiar regional problems concerning cores and boundaries, continuities and discontinuities etc., they are sufficient as a basis for analysis within the framework of an analytic hierarchy. As regards the delimitation of a region the aim throughout is to maximize at the same time the unity or cohesion within the region and the difference or disjunction from the surrounding areas.

Using the terms which are defined above, a regional hierarchy comprises structural and functional regions of different order. In principle a region may be of any size from the humblest rice field to the all-embracing sphere of influence of a primate city. *The regional hierarchy consists of a specific number of levels, each level in turn consisting of a number of regions of the same order. The hierarchy is characterized by alternate shifts between levels of structural and functional regions. The number of levels in the hierarchy depends upon the criteria which form the basis of the analysis.*

The Analytic Hierarchy

The choice of a frame of reference must be one of the first steps in a regional study. A delimitation—at least tentative—of the areas to be studied is a necessary condition for the compilation of the relevant material. Guided by the "regional hierarchy" concept it is suggested that a pre-determined analytic hierarchy be applied to the areas in question.

The analytic hierarchy may be described as consisting of a number of "niveaux," representing different levels of generalization. Each niveau is analysed either from a structural or functional point of view, and the analytic hierarchy is characterized by alternate shifts from structural to functional niveaux (fig. 1).

While the object of the "regional hierarchy" approach is to establish a hierarchy of *meaningful regions,* the object of the "analytic hierarchy" approach is to analyse *spatial patterns*—alternately in a structural and functional sense—at different levels of generalization. *The structural and functional spatial patterns are viewed as different aspects of the same areal complex.*

The analytic hierarchy should be regarded as an approximation to the theoretic regional hierarchy, and the shift between structural and functional niveaux reflects the

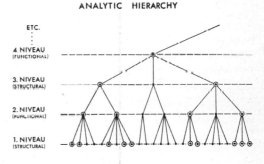

Figure 1. An analytic hierarchy consisting of four (etc.) niveaux comprising 25, 7, 3, and 1 areal units respectively. An arbitrary sample of 10, 4, 2, and 1 areal units is indicated by rings.

alternation of structural and functional
regions in the regional hierarchy. However,
the structural niveaux might also be analysed
from a functional viewpoint and vice versa,
but with less results because of the changing
structural uniformity and functional unity
of the regional hierarchy model. Thus it will
be seen that the difference between the two
concepts is only slight, but important
enough in terms of their application.

The Analytic Hierarchy in Comparative Regional Analysis

The "analytic hierarchy" approach acquires
special significance in the field of comparative regional studies. Comparative studies
will be more penetrating if carried out simultaneously at different levels of generalization. For instance a comparative study of
two 1:100,000 topographic sheets will be
furthered by subsequent comparative studies
of sub-areas and sub-sub-areas by means of
larger-scale topographic sheets 1:50,000,
1:25,000, and 1:10,000. In human geography it will be more appropriate to take
into account the (hierarchical) spatial organization of the areas in question and select the
niveaux in the analytic hierarchy accordingly.

In a comparative study of two areas the
highest niveau of analysis comprises the two
areas in toto. At the next lower niveau the
number of areal units is greater, and some of
them may be selected for comparison while
others are omitted. Descending from niveau
to niveau the number increases continuously, and to cope with this a *sampling procedure* may be adopted (fig. 1), either purposive, random or random stratified. When
suitable niveaux have been established and
the sampling is completed, the analysis
should commence from the bottom of the
analytic hierarchy, i.e. at the lowest level of
generalization.

The areal units thus selected may or may

not be regions in the structural or functional
sense, according to specified criteria. In
drawing up appropriate niveaux the investigator's assumptions about the character of
the regional hierarchy in the area in question
are utilized. But since selection precedes
analysis it is neither certain nor, indeed,
necessary that the areal units emerge as
regions. Here lies one great advantage of the
method. To some extent the areal units are
arbitrary, and their boundaries will often cut
through important continuities or interconnections. This, however, is compensated
at a higher niveau, where the area under
study is larger and where consequently the
same continuities or interconnections are
not interrupted.

An Application of the Analytic Hierarchy

The author has carried out a comparative
study of two South Indian areas, the plantation districts of Nilgiris and Coorg, within
the framework of an analytic hierarchy. To
give an illustration of the "analytic hierarchy" concept the approach followed will
be outlined.

Preliminary studies showed that an
analytic hierarchy consisting of four niveaux
would be feasible. The corresponding areal
units were: 1. The block (of a certain plantation crop). 2. The plantation. 3. The village
(as an administrative area containing a number of plantations). 4. The district. The
block was analysed from a structural, the
plantation from a functional viewpoint.
Again the village was analysed from a structural and the district from a functional point
of view. The number of districts studied was
two, the number of villages four, the number
of plantations twenty-one, and the number
of blocks large. The areal units to be studied
were selected by means of purposive
sampling. An element of subjectivity is a
great weakness in this method, but since the

entire study had to be completed within nine months, and since the samples had to cover a certain range of variation regarding a number of factors, the author was left without choice.

The analytic sequence is brought out by figures, 2, 3, 4, and 5, each depicting an areal unit at one of the four niveaux in the analytic hierarchy. *Proceeding from the lowest (first) to the highest (fourth) niveau the degree of generalization is steadily increased and thus analysis at one niveau serves as an elaboration and corrective to the more generalized analysis at the following higher niveaux. This gives the procedure the character of a synthesis.*

First Niveau (Structural): The Block

Figure 2 shows a tea block, exemplifying the analysis at the first (structural) niveau. The tea plants *(Camellia sinensis)* and the shade trees *(Erythrina lithosperma)* are planted in a regular system, and the entire block may be perceived as a structural region consisting

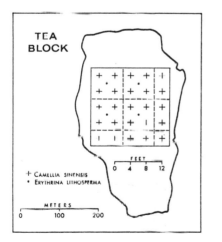

Figure 2. First niveau (structural): a block. The external boundary of the block is shown and the enlarged inset depicts the regular planting system of tea bushes and shade trees which covers the entire block.

of a vast number of uniformly distributed elements, each comprising four tea plants and one shade tree. Planting systems vary considerably from block to block and from plantation to plantation, and as a corollary the cultural landscape will change in appearance.

Plant density and pattern have a significant bearing on soil erosion, which ceteris paribus will be less in a densely planted area. Contour planting is an efficient soil conservation measure on steep slopes. In determining the optimal plant density a cost-benefit type of analysis may be employed. The yield will reach its maximum at an intermediate density; if density is lower the yield will be less due to the smaller number of plants, if density is higher the yield will be less, as well, due to the competition between plants. On the other hand the cost of planting and maintenance increases steadily with increasing plant density. The degree of complication of the planting system also influences the cost factor, and this may be the reason why all conventional planting systems are square or rectangular and not for instance hexagonal.

Second Niveau (Functional): The Plantation

The plantation shown in figure 3 exemplifies the analysis at the second (functional) niveau. To make it clearer the figure has been somewhat simplified; some buildings have been omitted, and a number of blocks have been merged. The plantation is rather peculiar in combining the cultivation and production of tea and coffee. This, however, is not uncommon in the plantation district under study where altitude permits the growth of both coffee *(Coffea arabica* or *Coffea canephora)* and tea. Nevertheless, it often leads to relative neglect of one of the crops; the problems of management, organi-

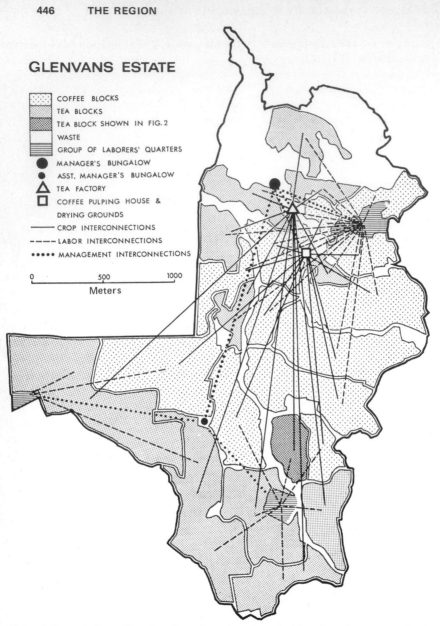

GLENVANS ESTATE

- [ ] COFFEE BLOCKS
- TEA BLOCKS
- TEA BLOCK SHOWN IN FIG. 2
- WASTE
- GROUP OF LABORERS' QUARTERS
- ● MANAGER'S BUNGALOW
- • ASST. MANAGER'S BUNGALOW
- △ TEA FACTORY
- □ COFFEE PULPING HOUSE & DRYING GROUNDS
- —— CROP INTERCONNECTIONS
- ----- LABOR INTERCONNECTIONS
- ••••• MANAGEMENT INTERCONNECTIONS

0   500   1000
Meters

Figure 3. Second niveau (functional): a plantation. Some buildings have been omitted and a number of blocks have been merged to ensure sufficient clearness.

zation, and division of labour in a two-crop system seem to be almost insurmountable.

Operation of the plantation involves various forms of spatial interaction. The main physical elements in this process are the blocks of coffee and tea on one hand and on the other the different types of buildings, the labourers's quarter, the management's houses and the crop-processing establishments. The blocks and buildings are connected by roads and foot paths (not shown in the figure), and it is along these the functional interconnections take place. In the daily routine the labourers walk to and from the factories and blocks carrying tools and other equipment as well as raw materials (manure, pesticides etc.). As a result of their work the daily or seasonally harvested crop (tea resp. coffee) flows towards the processing establishments. All this is directed and supervised by the management. In principle one may distinguish between three types of spatial links: crop interconnections, labour interconnections and management interconnections (raw material interconnections might be regarded as a fourth). These define the plantation as a functional region.

At this point it may be stressed that the analysis need not be confined to the internal functional relations of the areal unit, e. g.

the plantation. The plantation has important external functional links, for instance with wholesale dealers in plantation equipment, with managing agents, and with tea brokers, and these links may be analyzed at the relevant niveau.

Third Niveau (Structural): The Village

Figure 4 is an illustration of the analysis at the third (structural) niveau. At this niveau the analysis is concentrated on the cultural landscape, first of all the pattern of land use. The figure shows a large village (in the administrative sense), Ouchterlony Valley, covering an area of 103 km². The village is peculiar in that it has been developed entirely as a plantation area—since the arrival of the first European pioneers in 1845.

In outline the land use pattern is very simple. The village contains two broad categories, plantations and forests, and only

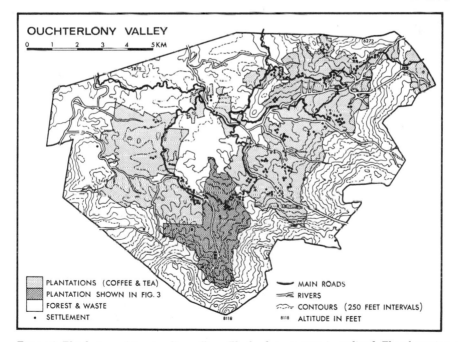

Figure 4. Third niveau (structural): a village. The land use pattern is outlined. The plantation area is divided between a number of large and small estates, but except in one case individual plantations are not shown.

these are shown on the map. However, the forests include some swampy areas in the lower portions and bare rocks in the upper. On the other hand the plantation areas might be subdivided into narrower land use categories. Coffee and tea are the only crops cultivated, but they are planted in a rather intricate pattern (compare fig. 3). Further, a number of recent illegal encroachments by small peasants have not been shown on the map.

With these reservations (at this level of generalization) there is an obvious relationship between relief and land use. The plantations cover the area which is transitional between the steep precipice in E, S and W and the gently undulating plateau in the centre and N. The upper areas have not been cultivated because of their shallow soil, severe erosion, and difficulty of access, while the lower areas have been left out due to their poor drainage. But the intermediate areas with their moderate slope, fairly rich forest soil, excellent drainage, and easy accessibility were considered ideal for the planting of tea and coffee. Consequently they were developed as plantations over more than a century, and now the forest covers as a residual only the areas less suitable for plantation crops (rather: areas considered less suitable by the entrepreneurs).

It may be inferred from figure 4 that the pattern of settlement is largely a corollary of the land-use pattern. The great majority of buildings are within or close to the plantations. Again the road pattern is to a great extent determined by land use and settlement. The main roads give access to all plantations in a circular fashion and relate the village to the outer world in NW, N and NE. On the other hand the influence of relief on the road system is in great evidence. Thus analysis at the third (structural) niveau reveals a whole sequence of areal relationships.

Fourth Niveau (Functional): The District

Nilgiris District, shown in figure 5, exemplifies the analysis at the fourth (functional) niveau. The district is mountainous, comprising ridges, valleys, and plateaus and covering a total area of 2543 km^2. Apart from the important plantation sector it has some indigenous agriculture, a number of hydro-electric projects (some in the construction phase, some completed), a few specialized industries, and tourism as a developing asset. The district is served by a system of central places, which is shown in the figure (and which will be explained in detail in a later paper). Ootacamund, the district centre, and Coonoor, the runner-up, take care of the more specialized functions for the whole district. Gudalur and Kotagiri serve as second order central places for the western and eastern portions respectively. Thirteen central places of first order are scattered over the district, but with a marked concentration in the economically most active Ootacamund–Coonoor area.

The central-place hierarchy shown in figure 5 must not be mixed up with the regional hierarchy or the analytic hierarchy. Plantations are such large undertakings as to have frequent, intimate, and direct contact with central places of several orders. Thus a fourth niveau in the analytic hierarchy comprising a whole district with its system of central places was found to be more suitable than any delimitation involving smaller areal units.

The functional links of Ouchterlony Valley (or rather of the plantations in Ouchterlony Valley, compare fig. 4) are indicated by arrows. Gudalur with its weekly market and bazaar, post office, petrol filling stations etc. caters to daily needs, while Coonoor has among other things a number of establishments related to the plantation sector (tea

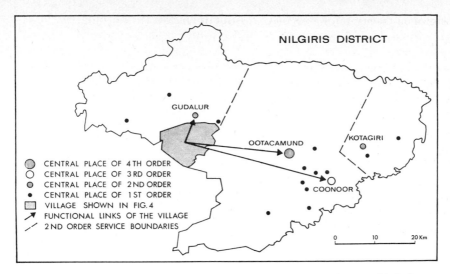

Figure 5. Fourth niveau (functional): a district. The most important functional links between the village of plantations and the system of central places are indicated by arrows. Second order service boundaries are only approximate.

auction, labour union offices, and planters' association), and Ootacamund has district offices, head banks etc. However, the plantation system is such that it involves strong functional connections with the world outside the district, e.g. with a number of sea ports. These ports are the destinations for most of the produce, and the majority of large plantation companies and managing agents have their main offices here.

This leads to an important observation. The present study has been carried out within the framework of an analytic hierarchy comprising four niveaux, but it must be regarded as entirely arbitrary that the analysis has not been carried further. It would certainly be interesting and rewarding to establish and examine higher niveaux in the analytic hierarchy, covering still larger areas of the earth's surface. In principle this might continue to the n'th niveau covering the whole world, but in practice, of course, it will rarely be profitable to proceed thus far.

It is suggested that the "analytic hier-

archy" approach, which has been briefly outlined, may be fruitfully employed in a number of regional studies. In comparison with the conventional "systematic" approach in regional geography it has three great advantages: *1) the subjects of analysis are structural and functional aspects of the areal complex instead of systematic items; 2) the approach takes into account the hierarchical character of the areal complex; 3) the analysis is carried out simultaneously at different levels of generalization.* The approach acquires special significance in comparative regional studies. A sampling procedure may be adopted in the selection of areal units to be compared at different niveaux in the analytic hierarchy, and the subsequent analysis will provide a comprehensive picture of the spatial composition of the areas in question.

An application of the "analytic hierarchy" approach to the study of two South Indian plantation districts has shown the type of analysis that might be carried out at different structural and functional niveaux.

The analytic content, however, has been considerably influenced by the character and aim of this particular study. Economic aspects of human occupance have been heavily dominant while social and political aspects are left vitually untouched. Under other circumstances the analytic content will be entirely different, while the general framework of the analytic hierarchy may be retained. Although the time dimension may be contained in the investigation, the approach outlined here is essentially static, and a transformation in the dynamic direction would constitute a highly significant advance. The present study has dealt with spatial aspects of the plantation system in a tropical country, and application of the "analytic hierarchy" approach to other areas and other problems may require some modifications of the conceptual framework.

✚✚✚✚✚✚✚✚✚✚✚✚✚✚✚✚✚✚✚✚✚✚✚✚✚✚✚✚✚✚✚

THE LOGIC OF REGIONAL SYSTEMS[1]

David Grigg

It has often been noticed that whereas many regional systems have been devised by geographers there have been relatively few attempts to suggest any principles of regional division.[2] By principles we mean procedures which should be followed in constructing any system of regions, and which would be as applicable to a division of the whole world as for a county, and for agricultural regions or climatic regions as much as, say, religious regions. Presumably one person could, if sufficiently industrious, patient, and perceptive infer from existing systems a number of common principles. Yet this would assume that regionalization is a procedure which has no counterpart in any other science. The argument here, which has been implicit in the work of many other geographers,[3] is that regionalization is similar to classification.

If this is so then the principles of classification can be applied to the construction of

---

1. It will be apparent that I owe a great deal to reading the work of J. S. L. Gilmour, M. G. Cline, G. G. Simpson, R. Hartshorne, and W. Bunge. I hope that I have properly understood and correctly interpreted their views. I have also received a great deal of helpful criticism on earlier drafts of this paper from many colleagues and I would like to thank D. W. Harvey, P. Hagget, R. J. Chorley, B. Garner, C. Board, B. H. Farmer, D. Anderson, R. L. Wright, and R. A. G. Savigear, and in particular G. M. Lewis and R. Hartshorne. Needless to say they do not necessarily share the opinions expressed here.

2. Noted, for example, by R. Hartshorne, *The Nature of Geography* (Lancaster, Pennsylvania: Association of American Geographers, 1939), p. 362. Hartshorne surveys some of the previous attempts, particularly those by A. Hettner (pp. 288, 290, 291, 294, 298, 306); later work is reviewed by Hartshorne in *Perspective on the Nature of Geography* (Chicago: Rand McNally, 1959), p. 128 and references.

3. That regionalization is a form of classification appears to have been implied by Hettner, as reported in Hartshorne, *op. cit.*, 1939, footnote 2; the idea has recently been put forward by W. Bunge, *Theoretical Geography* (Lund: Lund Studies in Geography. Series C. General and Mathematical Geography, No. 1, 1962), pp. 14-23.

From the *Annals* of the Association of American Geographers, Vol. 55, 1965. Reprinted by permission.

regional systems. The principles of classification which are discussed later in this work are derived from two sources. First, since the time of Aristotle philosophers have discussed the logical procedures which should be observed when grouping objects into classes. Such rules of formal logic are designed to prevent internal inconsistencies arising within a classification scheme.[4] Second, the theory of classification and division has its most obvious application in taxonomy. In the last quarter of a century the established classifications in botany, zoology, pedology, and other sciences have been subject to increasing criticism, as advances in knowledge have undermined the basis of classifications established in the nineteenth century. Three trends have particular relevance to the problems of regionalization: First, the attempts to apply logical principles to existing botanical and zoological classifications;[5] second, the rise in zoology of numerical taxonomy, which is an attempt to quantify the description and classification of animals;[6] and third, the continuing reappraisal by pedologists of the purpose and methods of soil classification.[7]

Although it must be admitted that there are important differences between the classification of objects and the classification of areas, we believe that the application of the principles of classification to the construction of regional systems is a worthwhile approach to the problems of regionalization. The purpose of this paper is, first, to outline the procedures of classification; second, to examine the extent to which regionalization and classification are analogous procedures; and third, to consider the construction of regional systems in the light of the principles of classification. We hope that this paper will illustrate how similar many of the problems and confusions of classification and regionalization have been over the last 150 years.

THE PROCEDURES OF CLASSIFICATION

Classification is the grouping of objects into classes on the basis of properties or relationships they have in common. Such a grouping can be reached by two distinct methods, classification and division.

In classification objects are grouped on the basis of *properties* they have in common.

---

4. Most textbooks of logic discuss the principles of classification and division. Among the most useful are: W. S. Jevons, *The Principles of Science*, (London: Macmillan, 1887), Chapter XXX; J. S. Mill, *A System of Logic* (London: Longmans, 1959), pp. 465-74. H. W. B. Joseph, *An Introduction to Logic* (Oxford: Clarendon Press, 1946); L. S. Stebbing, *A Modern Elementary Logic* (London: Methuen, 1963).
5. J. S. L. Gilmour: "Taxonomy and Philosophy," *The New Systematics*, Julian Huxley (Ed.) (London: Oxford University Press, 1952), pp. 461-74; "The Development of Taxonomic Theory since 1851," *Nature*, Vol. 168, (1951), pp. 400-02; J. S. L. Gilmour and S. M. Walters, "Philosophy and Classification," *Vistas in Botany*, W. B. Turril (Ed.), Vol. IV (London: Pergamon Press, 1964), pp. 1-22; J. S. L. Gilmour, "Taxonomy," in *Contemporary Biological Thought*, A. M. McLeod and L. S. Cobley (Eds.) (Edinburgh: Oliver and Boyd, 1961); G. G. Simpson, *Principles of Animal Taxonomy* (New York: Columbia University Press, 1961).

6. R. R. Sokal and P. H. A. Sneath, *Principles of Numerical Taxonomy* (San Francisco: Freeman, 1963); P. Sneath and R. R. Sokal, "Numerical Taxonomy," *Nature*, Vol. 193 (1962), pp. 855-60.
7. M. G. Cline, "Basic Principles of Soil Classification," *Soil Science*, Vol. 67 (1949), pp. 81-91; G. Manil, "General Considerations on the Problem of Soil Classification," *The Journal of Soil Science*, Vol. 10 (1959), pp. 5-13; O. W. Bidwell and F. D. Hole, "Numerical Taxonomy and Soil Classification," *Soil Science*, Vol. 97 (1964), pp. 58-62; G. W. Leeper, "The Classification of Soils," *The Journal of Soil Science*, Vol. 9 (1958), pp. 9-19; T. A. Jones, "Soil Classification—a Destructive Criticism," *Journal of Soil Science*, Vol. 10 (1959), pp. 196-200.

The objects which are to be classed are called *individuals* and the total number of individuals considered in any given classification system, the *universe* or *population*. Thus, for example, if the individuals being considered are human beings then they have properties such as skin color, height, weight, nationality, and religious affiliation. In the first stage of classification one property which is possessed in some degree by all the individuals is selected as the basis of grouping: the *differentiating characteristic*. Thus, for example, human beings could be grouped, on the basis of skin color, into three groups: those with yellow skins, those with black, and those with white skins. Now if the differentiating characteristic is carefully chosen, then other properties of the individuals will be found to change as the differentiating characteristic changes. Such a property is called an *accessory characteristic*. Thus in the example chosen, type of hair may be found to change as skin color changes. Or, to take another example, if soils are classified on the basis of soil texture, then as texture changes, so soil moisture content will change. When two properties change in such a manner they are often said to display *covariance*.

The nineteenth century taxonomists were concerned primarily with properties which were inherent in the objects classified. Modern biologists have, however, found a need to classify plants and animals on the basis of *relationships*. Simpson has made a useful distinction between these two approaches.

Following the terminology of a school of psychologists Simpson recognized that grouping into classes can be made either on the basis of similarity between objects or on the basis of a relationship between connected and different objects. The former case he called *association by similarity*; this is the usual procedure in classification. The latter he called *association by contiguity*, and he illustrated his meaning as follows:[8]

> Association by contiguity (for our purposes) is a structural and functional relationship amongst things that, in a different psychological terminology, enter into a single *Gestalt*. The things involved may be quite dissimilar, or in any event their similarity is irrelevant. Such, for instance, is the relationship between a plant and the soil in which it grows, between a rabbit and the fox that pursues it, between the separate organs that compose an organism, amongst all the trees of a forest. . . . Things in this relationship to each other belong both structurally and functionally to what may be defined in a broad but technical sense as a single system.

Individuals may then be grouped into classes on the basis of either similarity or relationship. The first stage in classification is to select a differentiating characteristic and group all the individuals in the universe into classes. This first set of classes is sometimes called a category. But the selection of one property and the formation of only one category of classes may give insufficient insight into the things being classified. The classes of the first category may then be grouped on the basis of a second differentiating characteristic into a second category. The classes of the first category then are included within any subclasses of the classes of the second category. Clearly this procedure can be carried further until all the classes are included within one superclass or class of all classes. This is illustrated in Figure 1. A hierarchy of classes is thus established; the sets of classes or categories are sometimes referred to as classes of the first order, classes of the second order, and so forth. Perhaps the most celebrated example of a hierarchy is the orders of the Linnean system. It is perhaps significant to remember that Linné, when illustrating his hierarchy, took as an analogy the political map;[9]

---

8. Simpson, *op. cit.*, footnote 5, p. 3.
9. J. Lorch, "The Natural System in Biology," *Philosophy of Science*, Vol. 28 (1961), p. 283.

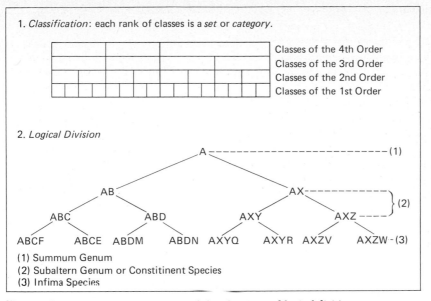

Figure 1. Diagrammatic representation of classification and logical division.

certainly this illustrates the hierarchial system extremely well. Thus, for example, in the United Kingdom the classes of the first order are parishes; every twenty or so parishes are grouped into hundreds. A number of hundreds grouped together constitutes a county whereas counties are themselves grouped together to make four countries, England, Ireland, Wales, and Scotland, which are all subordinate to the highest class, the United Kingdom.

A procedure closely allied to classification is that of *logical division*.[10] But whereas in classification individuals are grouped into classes and classes then included within superclasses, in division an initial class is taken as the universe and this class divided into subclasses on the basis of some principle. This is illustrated in Figures 1 and 2. The class to be divided is called the *genus*. In Figure 2 the genus is Land, and the principle

upon which it is divided is the use of land. The genus is divided into its *constituent species*, and each species can be further subdivided on the same principle, or as it is sometimes called, *fundamentis divisionis*. In Figure 2 only farmland is further subdivided although clearly each species could be further subdivided as they have been in Figure 1.

Logical division and classification are distinct but allied processes and they produce the same result, a classification system with a hierarchy of orders. Although logicians commonly separate the two processes for discussion, as has been done here, many point out that in practical classification the scientist will use both procedures to establish his system.[11] Further, the principles of division, which are discussed later, apply equally well to classification. However, there is one form of division which is quite differ-

10. This section follows Joseph, *op. cit.*, footnote 4, pp. 115-21.

11. This section follows L. S. Stebbing, *A Modern Introduction to Logic* (London: Methuen, 1930), pp. 435-36.

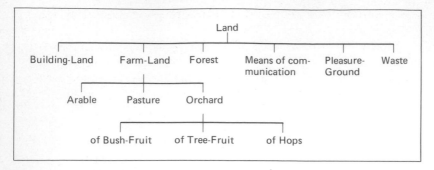

Figure 2. Logical division (after Joseph).

ent from classification and that is *dichoto-mous divison*. The purpose of dichotomous division, is not as in logical division, to distinguish all the species within a genus, but simply to isolate a single species. The genus is divided upon the principle that a class must either possess a given characteristic or not possess it. An example is given in Figure 3. Such a procedure normally is of little value in the sciences because it does not allow the formation of categories and there is no possibility of comparison and thus of useful generalizations. However, as will be seen later, there appears to be a closely analogous procedure in regionalization.

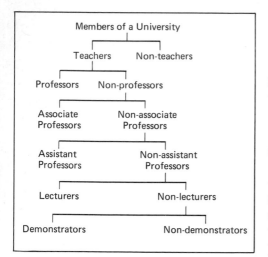

Figure 3. An example of dichotomous division.

The Need for Classification

As Simpson put it:[12]

If each of the many things in the world were taken as distinct, unique, a thing in itself unrelated to any other thing, perception of the world would disintegrate into complete meaninglessness.

The purpose of classification, then, is to give order to the objects studied. Without classification it would be impossible to:

1. Give names to things,
2. To transmit information,
3. To make inductive generalizations.

Classification is a necessary preliminary in most sciences; it is often argued that the state of classification is a measure of the maturity of a science. Thus Stebbing writes:[13]

The earliest stage of a science is the classificatory stage: it is not long since botany passed beyond this stage and sociology has hardly done so yet.

Let us briefly consider the relevance of these three aims to the purposes of regionalization.

1. Names are given to parts of the earth's surface in a number of ways. The inhabitants of a particular area may themselves give it a name; alternatively an influential visitor to an area may give it a name

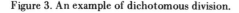

12. Simpson, *op. cit.*, footnote 5, p. 2
13. Stebbing, *op. cit.*, footnote 4, p. 108.

which passes into common usage. Such names may have wide acceptance but rarely define the limits of an area with any precision. Thus, for example, names such as the Weald, the Lake District, or the Fens are used in every-day speech in England but have no precise connotation. A more rigorous areal classification is the administrative division which most countries possess. Such an areal classification is an essential prerequisite for effective government, for without it taxes cannot be raised, mail delivered, nor any of the every-day matters of organized living be pursued. It was dissatisfaction with this form of areal classification which led in the eighteenth century to the rise of the idea of the region. But no regional system devised by geographers has ever had such widespread acceptance that administrative and political classifications have received. Indeed, confusion has arisen in geography because of the use of the same name for different areas in different regional systems. Hence the varying usage of names such as "the Middle East," "the Far East," or "the Midwest." One might here draw an analogy with nomenclature in botany. Most common plants receive local names; but the same plant will have different names in different areas. Thus the necessity for a uniform classification system.

Whereas the exact naming of parts of the earth's surface is important, classification is the basis of a more important form of geographical nomenclature. Geographers require names or terms for similar features of the earth's surface which occur repeatedly. Again every-day language provides much of this terminology; e.g., mountains, plains, and valleys. But if understanding of the earth's surface is to advance, a more precise terminology is needed, and a necessary preliminary is a widely accepted areal classification of these features. Much of the terminology used by geographers is in fact derived from allied systematic sciences; but

within the subject areal classification has produced a terminology. Thus, for example, although many geomorphologists are now skeptical of much of W. M. Davis's work, at the time when he wrote, his terminology, based on a genetic classification of landforms, was invaluable.

2. If a science is to progress, knowledge must be easily exchanged and easily passed on to new students of the subject. Now obviously no one person can know all facts about the character of all parts of the earth's surface; but if similar parts of the earth's surface are grouped together, then statements can be made about that areal class which are applicable to all the smaller parts of the class. This form of generalization is a form of intellectual shorthand which facilitates the transmission of knowledge. Thus, for example, no one person can know all the climatic characteristics of all the world's weather stations. But if the similar stations are grouped into climatic regions then the student can obtain an understanding of climatic differences.

3. But perhaps the most important purpose of classification systems is to permit inductive generalizations to be made about the objects studied. Areal classification, or regionalization, serves a similar purpose. Many generalizations in geography arise from the comparison of two different regional systems; thus, for example, if in any one country an areal classification on the basis of soil type is compared with a classification according to land use, then a number of generalizations about the relationships between the two may be inferred.

Some Misconceptions About Classification

It is generally agreed by logicians that there can be many valid classifications of a given universe of individuals.[14] Thus human beings could be classified according to their religion, their weight, or the color of their skin. The property chosen as the differentiating characteristic depends primarily upon the purpose of the classifications. Such would be a modern view: but the history of classification has been bedeviled by the distinction made by some logicians between *natural* classifications and *artificial* classifications. The definition of a natural classification varies. According to Jones it is that classification which correlates the greatest amount of knowledge about the objects under study.[15] To put it another way, a natural classification is one where the differentiating characteristic has the maximum number of accessory characteristics. An artificial classification is one which is designed for much more limited purposes and the differentiating characteristic has few if any accessory characteristics. Unfortunately, the interpretation put upon this distinction has led to confusion. Latta and Macbeath,[16] for example, defined a natural classification as one which attempts to express the actual order or system of things classified. Some taxonomists assume that if a differentiating characteristic with a large number of accessory characteristics is found then such a natural classification will be the correct classification and will serve all purposes equally well. Hence the art of the classifier is to find the one correct classification.

Indeed so much confusion has arisen from the use of the term "natural classifica-tion" that it would seem wise to follow the suggestion of Gilmour and Walters[17] and use instead general-purpose and special-purpose classifications instead of natural and artificial.

Modern logicians and taxonomists would agree that there can be no natural classification in the sense that there is one and only one classification which will serve all purposes. Geographers will see an obvious echo of this controversy in the history of ideas about regions. Hartshorne[18] noted that at the beginning of the nineteenth century and again in this century, there have been attempts to establish regions as real entities existing in nature. If regions were real entities then there could be a correct regional system. Although this view has been examined and rejected by geographers since Bucher,[19] it is a belief that still persists among some Western geographers; in the Soviet Union the majority believe that there can be a correct system of regions.[20]

It could be added here that even among those who recognize that regional systems are not a classification of entities that exist in nature there is still a tendency to forget that lines on a map are rarely real and that any given classification or regional system is but one way of looking at the world. Well-established regional systems tend to become, in the mind of some readers, the reality rather than simply a device for representing sections of reality. Such attitudes lead to curious consequences. It was, for example,

14. F. M. Chapman and P. Henle, *The Fundamentals of Logic* (New York: Charles Scribner, 1933), p. 283; A. L. Jones, *Logic Deductive and Inductive* (New York: Henry Holt, 1909), p. 32; Gilmour and Walters, *op. cit.*, footnote 5, p. 3; Jevons, *op. cit.*, footnote 4, p. 677.
15. Jones, *op. cit.*, footnote 14, p. 34.
16. R. Latta and A. Macbeath, *The Elements of Logic* (London: Macmillan, 1929), p. 54.

17. Gilmour and Walters, *op. cit.*, footnote 5, p. 5.
18. Hartshorne, *op. cit.*, 1939, footnote 2, p. 250; *op. cit.*, 1959, footnote 2, p. 31.
19. Hartshorne, *op. cit.*, 1939, footnote 2, p. 46.
20. P. M. Alampiyev, "The Objective Basis of Economic Regionalization and its Long-Range Prospects," *Soviet Geography*, Vol. 11, No. 8 (1961), pp. 64-74; Y. G. Saushkin, "On the Objective and Subjective Character of Economic Regionalization," *Soviet Geography*, Vol. 11, No. 8 (1961), pp. 75-81.

once suggested that Köppen's classification of climate should be made the standard climatic classification.[21] In England Herbertson's system of natural regions has received similar veneration. It seems certain that neither Köppen nor Herbertson hoped that their classifications would be viewed so uncritically by later generations.

Although the belief that there can be a "correct" classification has had unfortunate consequences in both the biological sciences and in geography, the misinterpretation of the word natural has led to particular difficulties in the study of regions. The use of this word has been admirably surveyed by Hartshorne.[22] In England the term "natural regions" was introduced by Herbertson,[23] who clearly intially confined its use to regions based solely on features of the physical environment, although in his later work he apparently hoped to extend the term to include human activity.[24] Unstead[25] used the term geographical region to describe

regions where there was a high degree of homogeneity in both physical environment and human activity. The belief that an area can be logically divided into a system of such geographical regions is one that had some currency in England until recently. It is analogous to the belief in the biological sciences that all aspects of the objects studied can be incorporated into one natural classification.

Given the belief that there can be one "correct" natural classification it is not difficult to envisage a situation where the construction of classifications becomes an end in itself. But a prime aim of classification is to enable inductive generalizations to be made about the objects studied,[26] not simply to arrange objects in classes. As Jevons pointed out:[27]

There can be no use in placing an object in a class unless something more than the fact of being in the class is implied.

Some taxonomists have fallen into this trap. Classification becomes no more than a game of identification; once the object has been satisfactorily classed it is forgotten; in soil science some workers have been misled to the point that one recent critic of existing soil classifications could write that few workers are clear "about what they are doing or why they are doing it."[28]

A similar situation has arisen in geography. Many regional systems seem to be devised as an end in themselves; the definition of a region or regions becomes important in itself rather than as a means to understanding the area in question. Here we may profitably return to the distinction between general-purpose classifications and special-

21. Noted by C. W. Thornthwaite, "Problems in the Classification of Climates," *Geographical Review*, Vol. XXXIII (1943), p. 253.
22. Hartshorne, *op. cit.*, 1939, footnote 2, pp. 296-300.
23. A. J. Herbertson, "The Major Natural Regions: an Essay in Systematic Geography," *Geographical Journal*, Vol. XXV, 1905, p. 300-10; *Natural Regions: Abstract of Remarks Opening a Discussion* (British Association for the Advancement of Science, Birmingham, 1913); "The Higher Units," *Scientia*, Vol. XIV, 1913, pp. 199-212.
24. A. J. Herbertson, "Regional Environment, Heredity and Consciousness," *The Geographical Teacher*, Vol. 8, 1915-1916, pp. 147-53.
25. J. F. Unstead, "A Synthetic Method of Determining Geographical Regions," *Geographical Journal*, Vol. XLVIII, 1916, pp. 230-49; "Geographical Regions Illustrated by Reference to the Iberian Peninsula," *Scottish Geographical Magazine*, Vol. XLII, No. 111 (1926), pp. 159-70; "The Lötschental: A Regional Study," *Geographical Journal*, Vol. LXXIX (1938), pp. 298-317; "A System of Regional Geography," *Geography*, Vol. XVIII, Part 3 (1933), pp. 175-87.

26. R. Brown, *Explanations in the Social Sciences* (London: Routledge, Kegan and Paul, 1963), p. 171; Jevons, *op. cit.*, footnote 4, p. 675.
27. Jevons, *op. cit.*, footnote 4, p. 675.
28. Leeper, *op. cit.*, footnote 7, p. 59.

purpose classifications. The natural system of the zoologist has, since Darwin, been based on the assumption that the classification explained the differences between the objects as well as arranging them in classes. In the last two decades some zoologists have pointed out that the properties chosen to classify animals have been weighted, for taxonomists have selected those properties which appear to demonstrate phylogenetic relationships.[29] It has been questioned whether in fact such a relationship is a sufficient explanation of differences. Further it has been pointed out that if differentiating characteristics are sought with such a purpose in mind, then the classification will not serve the purposes of many modern zoologists. One consequence of this criticism has been the rise of numerical taxonomy. This is an attempt to replace the genetic natural classification of animals by purely descriptive classification. Instead of those properties which are presumed to indicate phylogenetic relationships being selected, an attempt is made to use a much wider range of properties as the basis of classification, and further, to quantify the properties.[30]

A similar development may be seen in the history of ideas about regions. Systems of geographical regions were an attempt to embrace the totality of an area within a single classification: they are thus natural classifications in the technical sense. Further, they also tried to explain regional variations in the totality of things seen on the earth's surface. It was assumed that the physical environment and human activity covaried spatially because human activity was con-

trolled primarily by the physical environment. Just as the concept of phylogenetic relationships has seemed to many biologists to be an unsatisfactory basis for classification, so geographical determinism has lost currency and validity among geographers as a satisfactory basis for classification.[31]

Thus it can be seen that classifications based upon such an assumption are unlikely to produce any fruitful generalizations about the objects under study. But this does not mean that general-purpose classifications have no value; they may still be used to transmit information although they may not offer any explanations about the objects classified. One might add that some would claim that a natural classification of areas that was also a satisfactory explanation of differences between those areas is still theoretically possible. But this seems a chimera upon whose pursuit geographers have already spent too much time.

Are Regions Areal Classes?

Many geographers have used the terminology of classification theory in discussing regional systems and some have recognized that many of the principles of classification are applicable to regionalization.[32] But the closest comparison between the two modes of thought has been made but recently by William Bunge.[33] Bunge argued that the

---

29. Sneath and Sokal, *op. cit.*, 1962, footnote 6, pp. 855-60; Bidwell and Hole, *op. cit.*, footnote 7, pp. 58-62; P. R. Ehrlich, "Problems of Higher Classification," *Systematic Zoology*, Vol. 7 (1958), pp. 180-84.
30. Sokal and Sneath, *op. cit.*, 1963, footnote 6, pp. 20-30.

31. E. A. Wrigley, *The Dilemma of Vidal de la Blache*, unpublished mimeographed manuscript, 1964.
32. The work of Unstead and Herbertson shows an awareness of the terminology of classification but perhaps not always of the logical procedures. On the other hand, Hettner's work shows a close understanding of the principles of formal logic and their application to the problems of regionalization. For examples see discussions of Hettner's views in Hartshorne, *op. cit.*, 1939, footnote 2, pp. 290, 294, 298, 306.
33. Bunge, *op. cit.*, footnote 3, pp. 14-22; Bunge follows the terminology of regions used by D.

individual is represented in regionalization by "place"; the properties of places are commonly called elements, whereas differentiating characteristics are usually termed criteria. Places can be grouped into regions or areal classes. Bunge found the similarity between the two procedures to be remarkably close; indeed he went so far as to state that[34]

. . . geographers have independently rediscovered the entire logic of classification systems. . . .

Bunge's argument seems well founded, and it can be further extended. We must begin by considering the types of regions commonly recognized by geographers. Berry and Hankin, following Hartshorne, recognized three types of regions:[35]

1. The "region" in the general sense in which the region is given *a priori*.
2. A homogeneous or uniform region; this is defined as an area
   . . . within which the variations and co-variations of one or more selected characteristics fall within some specified range of variability around a norm, in contrast with areas that fall outside the range.
   Such a region, unlike that previously described, but like the functional region, is a result of the process of regionalization and is not given *a priori*.
3. A region of "coherent organization" or a "functional" region. This region is defined as one in which one or more selected phenomena of movement connect the localities within it into a functionally organized whole.

Although this latter definition could perhaps have been more happily expressed,

the distinction between functional and formal regions is one which most geographers would agree is valid and valuable; yet before the 1930's most regional systems were made up of uniform regions. But as Hempel[36] has pointed out, modern science deals increasingly not with the properties of objects but with their function and with the relationships between such objects. The rise of the idea of the functional region which deals essentially with interconnections between objects rather than with the similarities between those objects, seems to have stemmed from studies of the influence of urban centers over the surrounding areas, although the concept has since become much more sophisticated.[37] But it is of course not only geographers who have felt a need to classify objects on the basis of relationship between objects rather than simply on the basis of the properties of those objects. It was noticed earlier that Simpson[38] has distinguished between association by similarity and association by contiguity, a distinction which he himself took from the terminology of psychology and applied to zoology. Hence it seems that the development of functional and formal regions parallels a development in taxonomy, but it is not apparently a distinction commonly made in logic.

A perhaps more fundamental distinction between methods of arriving at regional systems is between the *synthetic* and *analytical* approach. Synthetic regionalization is a procedure frequently used by geographers, but the term was coined and is rightly asso-

Whittlesey, "The Regional Concept and the Regional Method," in *American Geography: Inventory and Prospect*, P. E. James and C. F. Jones (Eds.) (Syracuse, New York: Syracuse University Press, 1954), pp. 19-69.
34. Bunge, *op. cit.*, footnote 3, p. 23.
35. B. J. L. Berry and T. D. Hankins, *A Bibliographic Guide to the Economic Regions of the United States* (Chicago: University of Chicago Press, Department of Geography Research Paper, No. 87, 1963), p. X.

36. C. G. Hempel, "Fundamentals of Concept Formation in Empirical Science," *International Encyclopedia of United Science*, Vol. II, No. 7 (Chicago: University of Chicago Press, 1952), pp. 5-6.
37. G. W. S. Robinson, "The Geographical Region; Form and Function," *Scottish Geographical Magazine*, Vol. 69 (1953), pp. 49-58.
38. Simpson, *op. cit.*, footnote 5, p. 3.

ciated with Unstead.[39] Unstead argued that the smallest unit area of the earth's surface is the *feature*, and that features (or individuals) can be grouped on resemblance to give first order regions called *stows*; such classes can be successively grouped into higher order categories called *tracts*, *subregions*, *minor regions*, and *major regions* in a hierarchy with five orders or categories. This would seem to be a process very similar to that of classification.

In contrast to this procedure, Herbertson's regional system was obtained by beginning with the world and dividing it into subclasses on the basis of a number of principles.[40] This is a quite different process from synthetic regionalization and has been called analytical regionalization.

This fundamental distinction between methods of arriving at regional systems has been recognized by Hartshorne and Whittlesey.[41] Hartshorne concluded that the two processes are complementary and not mutually exclusive. This is, of course, a statement that most formal logicians would agree with, for the two methods of regionalization appear to correspond to the two methods of grouping objects, classification (synthetic regionalization) and logical division (analytical regionalization). A similar divergence of approach characterizes other sciences, particularly plant ecology and pedology. Whittaker in an excellent review of the problems of classifying plant communities, distinguished between the methods of Braun-Blanquet in Europe and Clements in the United States. The Braun-Blanquet school has emphasized the importance of

floristic composition, detailed analysis, and careful sampling:[42]

Classification might naturally proceed upward from small-scale units derived from local study to higher vegetation units, forming a hierarchy based on floristic relations.

In Clements' work on the other hand,

. . . regional vegetation types defined by physiognomy and dominance provided an initial general picture of major community types of a continent. More detailed classification proceeded downward from these geographic units.

As Whittaker points out these two approaches reflect the different ecology of the two areas studied and the number of botanists available to undertake the work. Nonetheless they also represent the two main methods of grouping objects, either by classification or division. A similar divergence of approach has been noticed by G. Manil[43] in his review of methods of classifying soils. He distinguished between the analytical and descending method, which starts from general facts and principles and goes down to detailed categories, and the synthetic and ascending method, which begins with detailed categories (individuals) and works upward to higher categories.

Thus the distinction between classification and division is reflected not only in geography but also in plant ecology and in soil science. To some extent the distinction is a function of the scale of the classification. Any area may be divided; but to establish a classification for the world, when we need to know the measurable properties of very small unit areas, is extremely difficult. And although it may be theoretically possible to obtain a consistent hierarchy of coordinate classes, we may share Manil's

39. Unstead, *op. cit.*, 1916, footnote 25, pp. 232, 235; *op. cit.*, 1926, footnote 25, p. 159.
40. Herbertson, *op. cit.*, 1905, 1913, footnote 23.
41. Hartshorne, *op. cit.*, 1939, footnote 2, pp. 291-92; Whittlesey, *op. cit.*, footnote 33, 1954, p. 35.

42. R. A. Whittaker, "The Classification of Natural Communities," *The Botanical Review*, Vol. XXVIII, 1962, pp. 1-160; quotations from pp. 77-78, for both items from the two authors.
43. Manil, *op. cit.*, footnote 7, pp. 8-9.

skepticism about the practical possibilities when the individual we begin with is as small as a soil profile.

But there are perhaps more fundamental implications of the distinction between classification and division. In classification individuals are grouped together on the basis of some observable and measurable properties. No assumptions are made, or need to be made, about the cause of the differences and similarities between the individuals grouped in the same class. But in division the *genus* is divided on some principle and thus a division presupposes that there is some understanding of the system being constructed.[44] Analytical regionalization then often implies knowledge of the causes of similarities and differences between the objects studied. Hence it can be argued that a genetic classification is only valid if our understanding of the causes of these differences is full and complete.[45]

It is this point which has led to considerable controversy in the biological sciences. It is argued by many taxonomists[46] that a genetic classification of animals is misleading, partly because a classification, even if its causality is fully understood, does not serve all the purposes of modern zoology; and partly because they consider the traditional understanding of phylogenetic relationships to be incomplete. A similar situation has arisen in pedology. The Russian school of soil classification was based on the assumption that climate is the major determinant of soil differences. This view is now held to be

only partially true and thus genetic classifications based on this assumption are of limited value.[47] In geography similar instances may be cited. The belief, for example, that agriculture is mainly differentiated because of differences in climate has given rise to systems of agricultural regions which are based in the first place upon a climatic division of the earth's surface.[48]

Dichotomous Division and the Region

So far we have examined the similarities between regional systems and classification systems. Yet geographers have often delimited and discussed the content of a single area or region. To what extent is there a parallel between the methods of delimiting such a region and the procedures of classification?

Consider the procedure by which a geographer arrives at such a region, which for the purposes of this argument we will assume to be a uniform or formal region called the English Fenland. We have visited this area, examined it, read about it, and are sensibly persuaded that it is markedly distinct from adjacent areas. The properties which are considered to distinguish the area are then mapped and an approximate accordance found (Fig. 4). We may then feel justified in describing this area as "a region" and then may proceed to analyze it in greater detail.

Now there seems to be no parallel in either classification or logical division for such a procedure, for only one class is formed. But the procedure seems to be very similar to that of dichotomous division. The

44. Latta and Macbeath, *op. cit.*, footnote 16, p. 151

45. Hettner's views of genetic classifications were discussed by Hartshorne, *op. cit.*, footnote 2, pp. 307-11. He believed that classifications should be genetic, a view that reflected the beliefs of the majority of both the logicians and taxonomists of his day.

46. Sokal and Sneath, *op. cit.*, 1963, footnote 6, pp. 5-30.

47. J. Basinski, "The Russian Approach to Soil Classification," *Journal of Soil Science*, Vol. 10 (1959), pp. 14-26.

48. Such systems are critically examined by D. Whittlesey, "Major Agricultural Regions of the Earth," *Annals*, Association of American Geographers, Vol. 26 (1936), pp. 199-213.

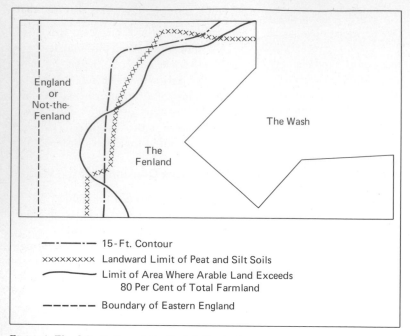

Figure 4. The delimitation of the English Fenland.

purpose of dichotomous division is to isolate a single species within a genus, not to create coordinate classes or species.[49] The procedure is described by Stebbing:[50]

> Any given class can be subdivided into two mutually exclusive and collectively exhaustive subclasses on the basis of a given characteristic which is possessed by every member of one class and is not possessed by any member of the other class.

Figure 5 illustrates how such a procedure is applied to the example of the English Fenland. The class which is subdivided is England; it is initially divided into Eastern England and not-Eastern England, and the successive principles of subdivision are similarly applied. We end by isolating two classes or regions, the Fenland and not-the-Fenland. Such a procedure seems to parallel the process of dichotomous division, and

furthermore, is equivalent to the first type of region recognized by Berry and Hankin, those regions arrived at *a priori*.

The Problem of the Geographical Individual

So far the reader may agree that there is a considerable similarity between the procedures of classification and regionalization. But a number of objections can be raised; they all relate to the difficulty of finding a logical equivalent in regionalization to the *individual* of classification theory.

1. It can be argued that all parts of the earth's surface are unique; classification and regionalization obscure this fundamental fact.

2. Even if this objection is overcome it can be argued that parts of the earth's surface all have the property of location; all locations are unique by definition, hence this is a property that cannot be used as a differentiating characteristic. But a geo-

---

49. Joseph, *op. cit.*, footnote 4, pp. 121-35.
50. Stebbing, *op. cit.*, 1963, footnote 4, p. 109.

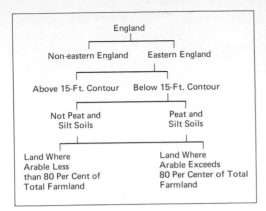

Figure 5. The English Fenland by dichotomous division.

graphical classification which neglects location is of limited value.

3.   In both taxonomy and logic individuals are assumed to be discrete and separate entities; but the earth's surface, considered in its totality, or even in more limited terms, does not consist of a mosaic of entities. It is a continuum.

4.   Lastly, even supposing that we can define a geographical individual, a problem arises. In classification location is ignored in grouping similar individuals into classes; but in regionalization, when we group individuals into regions, it is assumed that all the individuals which are similar are also contiguous. If they are not, then a region is not formed.

There have been a number of discussions of "uniqueness" but generally in a wider context than is necessary here.[51] Although it is certainly true that all parts of the earth's surface are unique, this does not seem an insuperable obstacle. First, it is also true that the objects grouped in taxonomy are unique. The uniqueness of parts of the earth's surface is neither more nor less unique than the objects studied in taxonomy. Second, experience shows that some properties and some combinations of properties repeat themselves over the earth's surface. Such spatial repetition invites explanation, and classification is a preliminary to explanation.

But if we consider location to be an essential property of places, which are our individuals, we are presented with a considerable dilemma. All locations are unique by definition; hence, whereas location can be a property, it cannot be a differentiating characteristic, for a differentiating characteristic must be a property possessed in some degree by all members of the universe. Both Bunge and Hartshorne recognized this problem and pointed out that the map is essential to areal classification and is indeed the only way of adequately expressing location in a classification system.[52]

At a higher level of abstraction geographers have traditionally distinguished between *generic* and *specific* regional systems. Generic regions are[53]

... those which fall into types and may therefore be said to be of a generic character, all the representatives of a particular type resembling each other in certain essential respects, according to the criteria selected—e.g., climate, character of vegetation, or human use.

Such regions may occur in different parts of the world but location is not a property used in their classification. A specific region is however, a region

... whose character is determined not only by the intrinsic conditions of the area in question but by its location and geographic orientation.

51.   Hartshorne, *op. cit.*, 1939, footnote 2, pp. 379-84; *op. cit.*, 1959, footnote 2, pp. 146-53; Bunge, *op. cit.*, footnote 3, pp. 8-13; F. K. Schaefer, "Exceptionalism in Geography: a Methodological Examination," *Annals*, Association of American Geographers, Vol. 43 (1953), pp. 226-49.

52.   Bunge, *op. cit.*, footnote 3, p. 16; Hartshorne, *op. cit.*, 1939, footnote 2, pp. 304-05.
53.   "Classification of Regions of the World," *Geography*, Vol. 22 (1937), pp. 253-82; see also Hartshorne, *op. cit.*, 1939, footnote 2, p. 305.

This distinction seems justified. In generic regional systems we consider an area independent of its relationship to adjacent areas. Clearly much that is discussed in geography deals with the relationship of areas to other areas, and a system of regions which excludes such relationships may be thought to be of limited value. But we have already noted the difficulty of incorporating the property of location into a classification system. If this is so then systems of specific regions cannot be said to be analogous to classification systems. We may ask then if a system of specific regions can serve the purposes that classification systems serve. In particular can such systems be productive of inductive generalizations?

When we turn to our third problem we are on less debatable ground, but one nonetheless strewn with difficulties. In taxonomy there is no doubt as to what is being classified. In regionalization the issue is less clear.

We must begin by noticing that the problem of the individual does not arise in logical division (or analytical regionalization). A class is divided and subdivided but not reduced to the parts or individuals which make up the lowest set of classes (or the infima species).[54] It is true, as Hartshorne[55] pointed out, that if subdivision of the earth's surface is continued indefinitely there comes a point where we must inquire if there is an irreducible part of the earth's surface. But in practical division this rarely arises. In classification, in contrast, we begin with the individuals and proceed to group them into classes on the basis of similarity; thus the individual must be defined. Now many of the problems of the individual diminish if we assume that there cannot be a rigorous classification of the earth's surface based on all the properties it possesses; or to put it

another way, based on the totality of the earth's surface. If we attempt such a natural classification it is clearly difficult to find individuals suitable for all the properties which geographers normally contend make up the totality of the earth's surface, such as climate, soils, vegetation, economic activity, and so forth.

But earlier we have decided that such classifications are impossible; let us now consider the problem of the individual in more limited classifications. The problem of defining an individual arises most acutely in the classifications of elements of physical geography such as climate, vegetation cover, soil types, and landforms. Discussion of what exactly the individual is in such studies has received less attention from geographers than it has perhaps merited.[56] Unstead[57] recognized the problem and called the individual "the feature," but gave little attention to the recognition or definition of such individuals. Linton[58] attempted a morphological classification; he argued that landforms are ultimately reducible to *flats* and *slopes*, and that these could be grouped together to form classes. But the recognition of these individuals seems to have been highly subjective. Bunge[59] has discussed the problem of the individual and considers "place" to be the geographical equivalent. Although this is true in a theoretical analogy, it gives little guide to the nature of the individual in a practical classification of properties of the earth's surface.

But the problem of the individual is by no means unique to geography. It arises in

54. J. A. Mourant, *Formal Logic: An Introductory Textbook* (New York: Macmillan, 1963), p. 64.
55. Hartshorne, *op. cit.*, 1939, footnote 2, p. 285.

56. For German contributions to this topic see Hartshorne, *op. cit.*, 1939, footnote 2, pp. 264-66; see also Robinson, *op. cit.*, footnote 37, pp. 49-55.
57. Unstead, *op. cit.*, 1933, footnote 25.
58. D. L. Linton, "The Delimitation of Morphological Regions," in *London Essays in Geography*, L. D. Stamp and S. W. Wooldridge (Eds.) (London: Longmans, Green, 1951), pp. 199-217.
59. Bunge, *op. cit.*, footnote 3, p. 16.

any subject where the things studied occur in a continuum or have areal expression, and we may profitably turn to the problem as it arises in other sciences. Two subjects where the individual is a matter of concern are phytosociology (phytocenology or plant ecology) and pedology. In phytosociology, plant communities are studied. It is obvious that a particular combination or plants of differing species occurs over the earth's surface; the classification of such communities is essentially areal as well as floristic, so that some individual is necessary. Much the same problems arise in classifying plant communities as arise in geographical classifications, and unfortunately there appears to be as great a confusion of method and terminology as in geography. These problems have been admirably discussed in a review article by Whittaker[60] who points out that phytosociologists are essentially seeking an equivalent, for plant communities, to the species in plant taxonomy. But botanists are split initially in two schools; those who consider that there is some particular natural unit inherent in vegetation and that the problem of the plant ecologist is to find the correct solution; and those who think natural communities are so complex that different properties may be with equal justification used as the basis of classification. This division of opinion is clearly analogous to the difference in geographical classification between those who believe the region to be a real entity and those who regard regions as simply "intellectual constructs." But whatever the approach adopted some "fundamental units," or individuals, must be grouped to form classes. In practice sampling has to be practiced and the *stand* forms the individual.

Some ecologists have adopted a more holistic approach and have attempted to classify not only the vegetation of an area but the soils and the surface morphology as well. Here the problem of the ecologist becomes even closer to that of the geographer; but for the most part the problems of classification remain unresolved. A frequently quoted example is the work of Bourne who attempted to classify landscapes. His fundamental unit he called a *site* defined as:[61]

> an area which appears, for all practical purposes, to provide throughout its extent similar local conditions as to climate, physiography, geology, soil and edaphic factors in general.

Sites are unique, but sites of the same type occur again and again; thus sites may then be grouped into regions. Bourne's ideas appear to have influenced Unstead and certainly Linton, but they were worked out only for Southeastern England. The recognition of *sites* is a highly subjective process; and again such sites would not form useful individuals for classification of the phenomena dealt with by human geographers.

Classification has recently become a major issue in soil science and a number of writers have questioned the aims and assumptions of existing systems. The most significant result has been the revision of the United States soil classification. But even this interesting work has not resolved the methodological problems of soil classification. Soils change imperceptibly and one soil type merges into another. Thus the population, as in geography and ecology, is a continuum. Pedology is further hampered by the fact that hitherto the soil profile has been used as the basis of classification. This has two consequences. Short of covering the surface of the earth with soil pits, soil classifications must be based on sampling.

60. Whittaker, *op. cit.*, footnote 42, p. 14.

61. R. Bourne, "Regional Survey and its Relation to Stock-Taking of the Agricultural and Forest Resources of the British Empire," *Oxford Forestry Memoirs*, 13 (Oxford: Clarendon Press, 1931), pp. 16-17.

Second, the soil profile is two-dimensional, whereas the classifications based upon them are three-dimensional. These problems have been partly overcome by basing classification on the principle of the modal profile. This has been explained lucidly by Cline:[62]

One may visualise a class as a group of individuals tied by bonds of varying strength to a central nucleus. At the centre is the modal individual in which the modal properties of the class are typified. In the immediate vicinity are many individuals held by bonds of similarity so strong that no doubt can exist as to their relationship. At the margins of the group however are many individuals less strongly held by similarity to this modal individual than to that of any other class.

This interpretation of soil classification will be recognized by many geographers as a process that they themselves adopt in practical classification. But it is a method which has been subject to considerable criticism.

In a recent article Jones made two searching criticisms of existing methods of soil classification. In the first place he pointed out that the soil profile, hitherto used as the basis of classification, is a "vertical section" and hence two-dimensioned. On the other hand, the soil is a continuum which is three-dimensioned, and a soil classification can hardly be based on a two-dimensioned entity. Jones also criticized the principle of the modal profile:[63]

It can easily be appreciated that the complete range of any modal quality at each level of the classification will decrease as one approaches the lower orders of the classification. It must then become extremely difficult, if not impossible, to recognize either the extremes of the modal quality or even the modal expression itself. No soil property has a discrete or circumscribed existence . . . Instead it moves immediately and imperceptibly either in the direction of greater intensity or towards complete absence. This state of affairs enforces upon our thinking a kind of calculus outlook in which we aim to build the structure of our classification from an infinite number of finite

units . . . The interval between each finite unit must be regarded as sufficiently small that in the ultimate summation the final structure will be endowed with a quality of continuity. In this manner the discrete quality of the soil profile is overcome and the three dimensional quality of the soil mass as a whole is recognized.

Jones doubted if the modal principle offers a logical basis for soil classification unless an astronomical number of profile pits are used. He concluded that it is fundamentally unsound to accept the soil profile as an:

expression of soil cover, since soil is essentially part of landscape and a soil classification must contain within itself an inherent reflection of three dimensions.

He suggested that an entirely new approach to soil classification is necessary.

It is no part of this paper to discuss the methodological problems of ecology and pedology. All that needs to be noted from the preceding paragraphs is that there is no agreement in either of these sciences on the nature of the *individual;* or at least there is no agreement at the existence of a "natural" and indisputable individual. Certainly in pedology quite fundamental disputes have arisen simply because the individual has not been clearly defined. Now this confusion may perhaps console geographers; but we cannot, however, hope to decide the nature of the geographical individual by analogy from allied sciences. The problem remains.

In fact what most geographers do in practice is to use an "operationally defined" individual;[64] here they follow the practice of most sciences which deal not with objects with a separate discrete existence but with a continuum. Such an individual does not occur in the landscape. It is dictated by the availability of statistics and clarity of defini-

---

62. Cline, *op. cit.*, footnote 7, p. 82.
63. Jones, *op. cit.*, footnote 7, pp. 196-200.

64. A term now widely used in the social sciences but derived from P. Bridgman, *The Logic of Modern Physics* (New York: Macmillan, 1927), pp. 3-32.

tion. Above all it is a function of the purpose of the classification. Say, for example, that we are interested in the agriculture of an English county. There appear to be no "natural" individuals to base our classification upon; and indeed upon reflection it will be clear that the individual in practice will depend upon both the purpose of the classification and the availability of statistics. Let up suppose we wish to divide the county into land-use regions. Although such differences can be seen, nonetheless we are likely to work from a land-use map of the county. The individual is thus dictated by the specification of the map, and the smallest clearly defined unit on a land-use map is the field. Hence for a land-use classification of the county the "field" is the individual. But a land-use classification is but a beginning. We wish to know more about the farming systems of the area and for this a classification of crops and livestock is necessary. Now agricultural statistics for English counties are available only for parishes, and each parish may contain several farms; thus here the parish must be the individual. If we wish to press our investigation further, say to discuss regional differences in farm income, then each farmer must be questioned; hence the farmer becomes the individual.

Similar principles apply to any type of areal classification. The natural individual does not exist, and must be chosen with regard to the availability of data and the purpose of the classification. The individual may in fact be a quite arbitrarily chosen unit. Thus, for example, Hammond,[65] who

wished to devise an areal classification of the landforms of the United States, took simply the squares of a grid system. In establishing climatic regions the basis of classification is not a unit of the atmosphere but the readings taken at weather stations. There are clearly hazards in adopting this type of individual. But there seems no alternative.

The last problem which is concerned with the individual also deals with location. In classification objects may be grouped into classes on the basis of some similarity. Such objects need not be near to each other, indeed they are considered in most cases quite independently of location. But we have argued that regions are areal classes. Having decided what our individual is, we select some property of the individuals and use this as a differentiating characteristic to group individuals into classes or regions. But a region must consist of contiguous individuals, otherwise a region will not be formed. Clearly such an assumption is not necessary in taxonomy. But one must immediately ask why similar individuals should occur next to each other? Now in dealing with the phenomena of the physical world soil profiles, "stands," and so forth, a metaphysical assumption is made that there is order in the world.[66] Hence in taking a number of soil profiles within a small area, we may assume that they represent soil types which are not greatly different in kind. The assumption or order assumes that distributions can be logically explained and are not merely random. To some extent such an assumption implies that we must know the causes of differences in soils before a classification can be undertaken. Now we may be entitled to make this assumption in making classifications of such phenomena as vegetation types or soil types. Is it equally valid to

65. E. H. Hammond, "On the Place, Nature and Methods of Description in the Geography of Land Forms" *(Technical Report No. 1, Contract 1202 (01), Procedures in the Descriptive Analysis of Terrain, Geographical Branch, Office of Naval Research, Wisconsin, 1957); Procedures in the Descriptive Analysis of Terrain* (Madison, Wisconsin: University of Wisconsin, 1958).

66. Cline speaks of geographic order, *op. cit.*, 1949, footnote 7.

make such an assumption when dealing with the cultural features of the earth's surface? Thus, for example, if we took every farm in England and grouped these farms into classes on the basis of some similarity, does it necessarily follow that similar farms will occur next to each other if they are then plotted upon a map?[67] This is a problem which is not easily resolved and worth more attention than is given here.

Many readers may reasonably conclude that the analogy between classification and regionalization founders upon the problem of the geographical individual. This is not a conclusion drawn by plant ecologists or soil scientists although they would surely admit that the individual and its interpretation in classifications is a considerable obstacle to progress. We will proceed on the assumption that whereas classification and regionalization are not directly analogous procedures, they are sufficiently similar for the geographer to study the principles of classification with some profit.

Principles of Classification and Division

Although this section is called principles of classification and division it should not be thought that there are inflexible rules which must be followed inexorably in practical classification. In the following list the first three principles relate to the strategy, rather than to the tactics, of classification and are general statements about the nature and purpose of classification systems which most logicians and taxonomists agree are useful guides; but they do not have the status of logical principles. Principles five, six, and seven are the principles of division established by logicians; four, eight, and nine are

simply rules which have been found by many logicians and taxonomists to be useful in constructing classification systems. The last rule follows from the preceding rules. Two cautions are necessary here. In the first place most logicians have warned of the difficulties in applying the principles of logic to practical classification.[68] The principles are counsels of perfection which are not always possible to observe. So we may claim no more than that it is rewarding to examine regional systems in the light of these principles.

Nor do we contend that regional systems have not been examined in this light before. Indeed most of the conclusions which can be drawn from a study of regional systems in this manner are conclusions which have been made before by geographers, but arguing from different premises. Such a concordance of views is doubly satisfying. It suggests first, that the principles of classification have a relevance to practical classification; and secondly, that much, but perhaps not all, existing regional theory has a secure foundation.

The principles are listed below and the relevance of each to regional systems is discussed separately later.

1. Classifications should be designed for a specific purpose; they rarely serve two different purposes equally well.[69]

---

67. M. Chisholm, "Problems in the Classification and Use of Farming-type Regions," *Institute of British Geographers, Transactions and Papers,* No. 35, (1964), p. 102.

68. Jevons, *op. cit.,* footnote 4, p. 689; M. R. Cohen and E. Nagel, *An Introduction to Logic and Scientific Method* (London: Routledge, 1949), p. 242; Chapman and Henle, *op. cit.,* 1933, footnote 14, p. 287, R. M. Eaton, *General Logic: An Introductory Survey* (New York: Scribners, 1931), p. 283.

69. Cline, *op. cit.,* 1949, footnote 7, p. 81; Simpson, *op. cit.,* 1961, footnote 5, p. 25; Gilmour, *op. cit.,* 1951, footnote 5, p. 401; Stebbing, *op. cit.,* 1963, footnote 4, pp. 107-08; Latta and Macbeath, *op. cit.,* footnote 16, p. 153; C. A. Mace, *The Principles of Logic, an Introductory Survey* (London: Longmans, Green, 1933), p. 197.

2. There exist differences in kind between objects; objects which differ in kind will not easily fit into the same classification system.[70]

3. Classifications are not absolute; they must be changed as more knowledge is gained about the objects under study. Jevons put it thus:[71]

... almost every classification which is proposed in the early stages of a science will be found to break down as deeper similarities of the objects come to be detected.

4. The classification of any group of objects should be based upon properties which are properties of those objects; it follows then that differentiating characteristics should be properties of the objects classed.[72]

5. In logical division the division should be exhaustive.[73]

6. In logical division and classification the species or classes should exclude each other.

7. In division, the division should proceed at every stage, and as far as possible throughout the division, upon one principle.

8. The differentiating characteristic, or the principle of division, must be important for the purpose of the classification.[74]

9. Properties which are used to divide or classify in the higher categories must be more important for the purpose of the division than those used in the lower categories.[75]

10. The use of more than one differentiating characteristic or principle of division produces a hierarchy of classes; the logical consistency of the hierarchy will only be maintained if rules five, six, seven, eight, and nine are observed.

The Purpose of Regional Systems

Logicians and taxonomists have all stressed the importance of considering the purpose of a classification system in both its construction and use. Geographers have also emphasized the importance of purpose in the use of regional systems.[76] The implications of this merit discussion.

It has already been pointed out that a division of the earth's surface based upon the totality of its properties is unattainable, and that such a system, which in the terminology of classification theory is a natural classification, has its expression in geography in the search for geographical regions. Such a system seems logically impossible, for it is surely implausible that all the properties of the individuals will display covariance.

But the distinction between natural and artificial classifications (or general-purpose

70. Mill, *op. cit.*, footnote 4, pp. 470-71; Cline, *op. cit.*, footnote 7, p. 87.

71. Simpson, *op. cit.*, footnote 5, p. 111; Jevons, *op. cit.*, footnote 4, p. 691.

72. Cline, *op. cit.*, footnote 7, p. 86.

73. Principles five, six, and seven are all from the same reference; see Joseph, *op. cit.*, footnote 4, pp. 117-19; Mourant, *op. cit.*, footnote 54, p. 65; Cohen and Nagel, *op. cit.*, footnote 68, pp. 241-42; Stebbing, *op. cit.*, 1963, footnote 4, p. 109. The three rules of division and their application to classification in the social sciences are discussed by P. F. Lazarsfeld and A. H. Barton, "Some General Principles of Questionnaire Classification," *The Language of Social Research*, P. W. Lazarsfeld and M. Rosenberg (Eds.) (Glencoe, Illinois: The Free Press, 1957), pp. 84-85; also by Lazarsfeld in "Qualitative Measurement in the Social Sciences; Classification, Typologies and Indices," in *The Policy Sciences*, D. Lerner and H. D. Lasswell (Eds.) (Stanford, California: Stanford University Press, 1951), pp. 115-92.

74. Mill, *op. cit.*, footnote 4, p. 468; Cline, *op. cit.*, footnote 7, p. 88.

75. Latta and Macbeath, *op. cit.*, footnote 16, p. 155; Cline, *op. cit.*, footnote 7, p. 88.

76. Hartshorne, *op. cit.*, 1939, footnote 2, p. 290; 1959, footnote 2, pp. 77-78, 139-44; P. E. James, "Toward a Further Understanding of the Regional Concept," *Annals* Association of American Geographers, Vol. 42 (1952), p. 207; E. Ullman, "Human Geography and Area Research," *Annals*, Association of American Geographers, Vol. 43 (1953), p. 58.

and special-purpose classifications) is not one confined solely to the distinction between classifications that attempt to embrace the totality of the earth's surface and those that confine themselves to a single property such as vegetation cover or type of farming. Even when considering such single property classifications of area the purpose of the system determines the construction and use. Kuchler[77] has shown, for example, that there may be many different areal classifications of vegetation, for not all the properties of vegetation may be encompassed within a single system or map. Chisholm[78] has demonstrated the importance of considering purpose when constructing type-of-farming regions. He argues that a number of workers in this field have attempted to find "objective" classifications; but the properties of the objects studied, in this case the individuals are farms, are many and no classification is likely to find covariance between such diverse properties as farm income, type of tenure, crop combination, or methods of management. Hence a classification of agriculture must, if it is to be productive of useful generalizations, be quite clear about its purpose. This does not mean that a general-purpose classification of agriculture has no value; such classifications are useful in teaching and may have some value as the basis of planning if used with caution.[79]

Clearly then the purpose of a classification must be borne in mind before attempting its construction; classifications which attempt to cover too broad a field of properties, and are often based on the assumption that there are genetic links between a diverse range of properties, lose their precision as instruments of analysis, for as Preston James has written: [80]

... the attempt to recognize combinations of several elements often has the effect of obscuring the realities rather than throwing additional light on them.

But if attention must be paid to purpose in the construction of classifications equal care must be taken in their use, for a classification constructed for one specified purpose cannot necessarily be used for an allied but different purpose. An example of this may be taken from the field of geomorphology. The classification of landforms has until recently been on the basis of origin; hence landforms have been grouped together into classes on the basis of similar genesis. Now this is perfectly valid but it is not always suitable for a study of the human geography of an area. This of course is a point now widely accepted and in recent years there have been several attempts to classify and map landforms on the basis of their observable and measurable properties, not upon their presumed origin.[81]

Once it has been realized that the purpose of a system is of paramount importance in construction, many disputes about the respective merits of different systems could be resolved. Arguments about whether one system is better than another often becomes meaningless when we realize that the respective classifications have different purposes. This point may be illustrated by considering the classification of climate. If we wish to classify climates with regard to their

77. A. W. Kuchler, "Classification and Purpose in Vegetation Maps," *Geographical Review*, Vol. 46 (1956), pp. 155-56.
78. Chisholm, *op. cit.*, footnote 67, 1964, pp. 91-97.
79. James, *op. cit.*, footnote 76, p. 109; Hartshorne, *op. cit.*, 1959, footnote 2, pp. 77-78.

80. P. E. James, "A Regional Division of Brazil," *Geographical Review*, Vol. 32 (1942), pp. 493-95.
81. Hammond, *op. cit.*, 1957, footnote 65; J. R. Van Lopik and C. R. Kolb, *A Technique for Preparing Desert Terrain Analogs* (Vicksburg: Technical Report No. 3-506, U. S. Army Corps of Engineers, 1959).

influence upon potential agricultural development, different criteria will be selected than if we are concerned with the impact of climate upon human physiology, the routes of aircraft, or the origin of climate itself.[82] It is too much to hope that one system could be devised which would serve all these purposes.

Differences in Kind

Mill,[83] although believing in the possibility of a natural classification, as did many of his contemporaries, also pointed out that there were in some cases, such great differences in kind between objects that they should not be included within the same classification system. One would recognize such a difference, for example, between plants and stones.

What relevance has this principle to regionalization? Bunge[64] pointed out that in areal classification land and sea are normally assumed to be of different kingdoms; that is they are so different that they are but rarely included within the same areal class. But the principle also adds to the argument against the feasibility of geographical regions; geographical regions assume that properties of the earth's surface, unspecified in number but including properties of both the physical and the social environment, will co-vary spatially. Here clearly objects very different in kind are included within the same classification system. James has pointed out the dangers of such a system:[85]

. . . an attempt to define regions based on phenomena produced by a variety of different proc-

esses is dangerous and could lead to serious errors of interpretation. We may find ourselves trying to add things like cabbages and kings.

Classifications and Change

It would be generally agreed that the classification of any universe of objects must be changed as knowledge about these objects becomes more complete; often as a science progresses the assumptions on which the established classifications are based become increasingly subject to criticism and the need for change becomes apparent. But a considerable problem arises here, for as Simpson has pointed out,[86] in those sciences where classification is the basis of further investigation, some compromise between stability and change is essential. The great danger is that a system will become accepted and uncriticized from sheer inertia. Kellog has written that:[87]

. . . no system of classification should ever become so sacred or so classical that the system becomes an end in itself.

This point has already been briefly discussed. But the issue of changing classifications has special problems for the geographer. First, the human geographer has a double problem, for not only does his knowledge of the objects he is studying change, but the objects themselves change.[88] This is a difficulty not faced by the biologist, although it could be perhaps argued that vegetation does change sufficiently in the short run for classifications of relatively small areas to merit revision. The problem is far greater in the classification of aspects of human activity such as manufacturing, industry, towns, or types of farming. Few classifications of agriculture at the

82. A good review of some of the problems of climatic classification is by F. K. Hare, "Climatic Classification," in *London Essays in Geography*, L. D. Stamp and S. W. Wooldridge (Eds.) (London: Longmans, Green, 1951), pp. 111-34.
83. Mill, *op. cit.*, footnote 4, pp. 407-71.
84. Bunge, *op. cit.*, 1952, footnote 3, p. 20.
85. James, *op. cit.*, 1952, footnote 76, p. 204.

86. Simpson, *op. cit.*, footnote 5, pp. 111-12.
87. C. E. Kellog, "Why a New System of Soil Classification?" *Soil Science*, Vol. 96 (1963), p. 5.
88. A point recognized by Unstead, *op. cit.*, 1916, footnote 25, p. 241.

turn of the century would have much relevance to the present world. Chisholm[89] discussed the difficulties, indeed the impossibilities, of establishing an objective (by which he means *natural*) classification of types of farming in England. He points out that few of the existing classifications take into account the changes going on in British farming. He concludes that the construction of such classification involving Herculean labors may be of doubtful value and suggests that geographers might turn to different forms of research. Although we need not necessarily accept this conclusion, his discussion does illustrate some of the difficulties of classifying the human features of the earth's surface.

But the properties commonly classified by physical geographers are also in need of constant review, on two grounds. First, classifications of features of physical geography have often been devised by workers in the allied systematic field; the classifications in these fields change as we learn more about the phenomena studied. But geographers are not always cognizant of these changes. Nowhere is this more true than in the complex field of study which attempts to interrelate climate, vegetation, and soil. Maps of types of vegetation and soil form an important part of elementary geographies, but they are not always judiciously chosen nor are they invariably the result of the most recent work in the field. A classic example of this is noted by Thornthwaite.[90] Köppen's "climatic regions" were an attempt to find meteorological limits to vegetation formations; yet the vegetation formations on which he based his work were to some extent discredited even when he wrote. Nonetheless, Köppen's work, and modified forms of Köppen's work, still loom large in geographical studies.

Second, it is by no means sure that the classifications borrowed from other fields are always really suited to the geographer's purpose. Examples of this have already been discussed and we may give one final instance. The classification of soils has been traditionally based upon genesis, and many have argued that soil classification should be based upon soil-forming factors.[91] Whether this is valid is not at issue here; more relevant is whether such a classification is useful to the geographer. Geographers are interested in soils partly because of their influence on agriculture and hence upon areal variations in economic activity. But it is by no means certain that the existing world classifications of soils are most suited to this purpose, for the properties upon which the classification is based are not in every case those which determine the suitability of a soil for various farming activities. It is a common criticism of the as yet incomplete soil classification of Britain that it is of limited value to the farmer and, incidentally, to the geographer.

The Differentiating Characteristics of Classification

In classification objects are grouped together into classes on the basis of a property they have in common called the differentiating characteristic. It might seem self-evident then that a differentiating characteristic must be a property of the objects grouped. Yet few rules are so frequently infringed.

Soil science offers an example which has been touched upon before. Much modern pedology derives from the work done in Russia in the later nineteenth century.

89. Chisholm, *op. cit.*, footnote 67, pp. 91-103.
90. Thornthwaite, *op. cit.*, footnote 21, p. 242.

91. Kellog, *op. cit.*, footnote 87, p. 4; G. D. Smith "Objectives and Basic Assumptions of the New Soil Classification System," *Soil Science*, Vol. 96 (1963), pp. 6-16; Kubiena, *op cit.*, footnote 7; Leeper, *op cit.*, footnote 7.

Pedologists were impressed by the striking differences between one natural region and another, and attributed these differences ultimately to differences in climate. Hence the major classes of soil types were not based upon properties of the soils themselves but upon climatic properties of the areas in which those soils occurred. This method of approach, which confuses climatic characteristics with empirical characteristics of the soil profile, has led to a great deal of confusion in soil classification.[92] A further example has already been cited. Whereas it is now widely accepted that classifications of agriculture should be based upon properties of agricultural systems and not on the factors that influence regional differences in such systems, agricultural regions were for long based upon differences in either climate or soil type, and some writers may still hold this view.[93]

Here we must return to a point discussed earlier. What part should genesis play in the construction of regional systems? Climate was made the basis of both soil and agricultural classifications because it was held to be the preponderant cause of regional differences in soil type and farming. Similar assumptions have been made in other classification systems. Now it can be argued that there is one overriding factor affecting the properties of objects. Where there is an obvious classification of the objects which is also a natural classification, in that the differentiating characteristic has the maximum possible number of accessory characteristics. Gilmour[94] argued that the existence of such

a powerful factor makes a natural classification possible; but that this is not the same as saying that the classification is based upon that powerful factor. Thus it might be possible to classify types of farming of the world upon the basis of the predominant crop grown. Such a property might have a large number of accessory characteristics such as the relative importance of livestock, and so forth. Such a classification might be said to be natural because it maximizes the number of accessory characteristics; the reason for this is that climate is the preponderant factor determining the distribution of crops over the earth. Hence a natural classification is possible because of the overriding importance of climate; but the classification is not based upon climate.

But having made this point it still seems clear that differentiating characteristics should be properties of the objects classed. Genetic classifications, where the differentiating characteristic will, to use regional terminology, be a factor and not an element, will in the long-run be misleading.

Are There Nonregional Areas?

Our fifth rule of classification is in fact the first principle of division in traditional logic and it simply states that any division must be exhaustive; that is, if a *genus* is to be divided upon some principle then all the constituent species must be recognized. Mourant[95] points out that in practical classification this may be impossible. Thus if roses are divided into species we can never be sure that all the roses in the world are known and hence one can never be sure that all the constituent species have been recognized. In terms of regionalization the principle can be stated as follows: if any area is to be divided or classified into regions, then the whole area must be divided or classified. This prin-

92. Basinski, *op. cit.*, footnote 47, p. 16; Manil, *op. cit.*, footnote 7, p. 9.

93. This point was discussed by Whittlesey, *op. cit.*, 1936, footnote 48, and *op. cit.*, 1954, footnote 33, p. 38. For a recent version of the older view see A. B. Lewis, *Land Classification for Agricultural Development* (Rome: F.A.O. Development Paper No. 18, 1952), pp. 31-33.

94. Gilmour, *op. cit.*, footnote 5, pp. 32-34.

95. Mourant, *op. cit.*, footnote 54, p. 65.

ciple may seem self-evident, but there are difficulties. We may conveniently recognize two aspects of this problem: first, the rule as applied to geographical regions, and second, the rule applied to generic regional systems.

If any area is to be divided exhaustively into geographical regions then a problem soon arises that has been aptly put by Barbour: [96]

> . . . a study of the *pays* of the Sudan would certainly have a number of intermediate areas that could not readily be assigned to one pays or another; and yet had no obvious name or distinctive character of their own.

Any attempt to divide an area will eventually face this dilemma; must we conclude then that there are areas which are non-regional, as Crowe[97] pertinently inquired? Some geographers have at least implied this. Jones and Bryan,[98] in the preface to their book on North America, argued that although regions exist it by no means follows that a whole continent can be divided up into well-marked areas. Now it will be apparent from previous discussions of the geographical region that an attempt to divide an area into such regions presupposes a spatial correlation between a number of properties, some which must be properties of the physical and some properties of the human environment. We have doubted whether this is logically possible. The implausibility of a set of geographical regions becomes more evident when we apply the rule of exhaustiveness to the idea, for it seems unlikely that human and physical properties of the earth's surface will co-vary continuously over any large area. We will always find areas where the relationship breaks down. The possible exceptions to this may be in relatively small areas where the dominant form of economy is agrarian, where farming techniques are backward, and where there is a close adjustment between soil type and land use. Wrigley[99] pointed out that to a large extent the great success of French regional geographers of the nineteenth century was attributed to their dealing with a society; nonetheless it would probably be difficult to devise an acceptable exhaustive set of geographical regions even for nineteenth century France, even though the delimitation and discussion of single regions carried some conviction.

The fifth principle of classification, then, is yet another means of demonstrating the logical inconsistencies of the geographical region. But when we turn to consider the rule of exhaustiveness in relation to generic regional systems important new issues arise. It will be profitable to discuss these together with the sixth principle of classification. This states that classes should be mutually exclusive as well as exhaustive. Thus if we divide Mankind into four classes, Catholic, Protestant, Muslim, and Negroid, the classes are not exhaustive because there are men who fall into none of these classes. Nor are the classes exclusive because a man can be a Catholic and also a Negro. In division care must be taken to see that classes do not overlap, whereas in regionalization regions should be mutually exclusive; to put it another way, an individual must be in one region and only one region in any given regional system.

So far the limits of classes have not been

96. K. M. Barbour, *The Republic of the Sudan, a Regional Geography* (London: University of London Press, 1961), p. 130.

97. P. R. Crowe, "On Progress in Geography" *Scottish Geographical Magazine*, Vol. 54 (1938), p. 9.

98. L. R. Jones and P. M. Bryan, *North America* (London: Methuen, 1950), p. vi; cf. Vogel, quoted in Hartshorne, *op. cit.*, 1939, footnote 2, p. 274.

99. Wrigley, *op. cit.*, footnote 31; See also G. Kimble, "The Inadequacy of the Regional Concept," in *London Essays in Geography, op. cit.*, footnote 82, pp. 164-69.

considered. When objects are grouped on the basis of some property the classification can be undertaken in two ways. In the first case objects are placed into only two classes according to whether they possess a property or not. In the second case they are grouped into a number of classes according to the degree of expression of the property. Consider an area which is classified on the basis of mean annual precipitation. The area could be classified into only two regions, one which receives no annual precipitation at all, and one which receives some precipitation. But of course a much more common procedure is to base the classes on *degrees of expression* of the property. Hence individuals could be placed in one of five classes: less than ten inches, ten inches to nineteen inches, twenty inches to twenty-nine inches, thirty inches to thirty-nine inches, and forty inches and over.

The problem is how such limits, which are also the boundaries of areal classes, should be determined. In some cases quite arbitrary classes may be chosen, as in the example above. But an attempt to find natural breaks in a statistical series should presumably be attempted. Thus if an area was being classified according to annual precipitation, of the one hundred readings available, ranging from one inch to one hundred inches, suppose twenty readings fell between five and fifteen inches, thirty between thirty and forty inches, and forty between fifty-five and sixty-five inches. Such a clustering would suggest obvious class limits. But in most cases the series would be more continuous and the problem remains. Fortunately in recent years geographers have turned increasingly to statistical methods as an aid to the determination of class or regional limits,[100] and it is to be hoped from

the present debate some recognized and generally acceptable procedures will emerge.

Where properties used as differentiating characteristics can be measured the problems of deciding class limits are minimized and classes are necessarily mutually exclusive. But in classifications of geographical phenomena where qualitatively assessed characteristics are used, the possibility of overlap is considerable. This is particularly true of classifications of world agriculture; it is impossible to base a classification on measurable properties simply because the data do not exist. Such classifications usually proceed by defining a given number of major types of agriculture and then mapping the extent of each type. A general criticism is that insufficient attention has been paid to the dangers of class exclusion in defining the types, and thus an examination of the maps and the properties of the types will so reveal parts of the earth's surface which could be in more than one class. It must, however, be admitted that such instances are often difficult to avoid given the present state of knowledge about the world.

The Use of the Principle of Division

One seventh principle, which is the third principle of traditional logic, requires first, that the division should proceed at every stage upon the same principle; and second, that as far as possible the division should proceed throughout upon one principle. Some logicians[101] have doubted whether this principle, and particularly the second

100. There is now a considerable literature on this topic: B. J. L. Berry, "A Note Concerning Methods of Classification," *Annals*, Association of American Geographers, Vol. 48 (1958), pp. 300-03; L. Zobler, "Statistical Testing of Regional Boundaries." *Annals*, Association of American Geographers, Vol. 47 (1957), pp. 83-95; O. D. Duncan, R. P. Cuzzort, and B. Duncan, *Statistical Geography, Problems in Analyzing Areal Data* (Glencoe, Illinois: The Free Press, 1961).
101. Chapman and Henle, *op. cit.*, footnote 14, pp. 287-88.

part, can be applied to practical classification; yet their consideration raises interesting problems in regionalization.

The first part of the principle is surely relevant and is indeed a corollary of previous statements. If we divide an area into regions of the same order, the basis of each region should be some degree of expression of the same property.[102] Yet in many regional systems regions of the same order are delimited on the basis of a number of different principles. To take an imaginary example we may find that a country has been divided into four major regions: the West, East, South, and North. We find that the West is defined on the basis of it being an area of young folded mountains, the East because it has a low annual rainfall, the South because it has a distinctive type of land tenure, and the North because it has the majority of the country's manufacturing industry. Now it will be readily seen that such systems are likely to have classes that overlap and, further, it will often be impossible to make the division exhaustive. It must be admitted that there is no reason why such a framework should not be the basis of a description of the geography of a country; but the system itself is unlikely to be productive of any valid generalization.

The second part of the principle is more difficult to apply rigorously; and it also requires some explanation. Stebbing expressed the rule in the following terms: the successive steps of the division must proceed by gradual stages. She illustrates this as follows: [103]

If, for example, we were able to divide university students first into science and arts students, and were then to subdivide science students into polite and impolite, and arts students into dark, fair and medium-complexioned, the division would serve no useful purpose.

Now in analytical regionalization it is customary to divide the world upon some initial principle and then further subdivide upon some different principle. Thus an area may be initially divided upon the principle of landforms, then upon precipitation, and finally upon vegetation type. Such procedure establishes a hierarchy of classes and each set or category of classes is arrived at by the use of one principle. But does the division proceed from category to category by gradual stages? Are we in fact entitled to use at each stage principles which are different in kind? Crowe expressed doubts about such a procedure:[104]

There is not the same type of connection (that is, genetic) between climate and physiography or between either of these and vegetation. We cannot build up a rational chain of climate-landform-vegetation, because of the magnitude of the missing links. The mental agility of geographers in trying to skip these gulfs has been truly remarkable, but it has usually been an acrobatic display that has just failed to come off. Regional synthesis based primarily on these three factors must ignore their incongruity and invalidate itself thereby. The popular divide of making broad divisions on one basis and then sub-dividing them according to another is no solution; it is not synthesis but arbitrary classification.

This criticism was aimed primarily at the systems of natural and geographical regions established by British geographers before the Second World War. But even if we concern ourselves with more limited classifications, dealing with, for example, climate, or vegetation, or agriculture, rather than attempts to classify the total character of the earth's surface, we are presented with similar problems. First, how do we select properties to be differentiating characteristics? Second, in division, what determines the order in which the principles selected are applied?

102. Hettner, quoted in Hartshorne, *op. cit.*, 1939, footnote 2, p. 306.
103. Stebbing, *op. cit.*, footnote 4, p. 109.

104. Crowe, *op. cit.*, footnote 97, p. 8.

The Order of Priorities

Any group of objects is likely to possess a number of properties which could be chosen as differentiating characteristics. Which of these are to be selected? Mill argued that they should be those properties which are important for the purpose of the classification. But how is *important* to be judged?

An analogy from the history of biological classification may make this point clearer. Post-Linnean classifications sought to construct classes which had the maximum correlation of properties and were based on the real essence of the things classified. With the advent of Darwin the idea of phylogenetic relationships came to dominate classification so that differentiating characteristics were selected with this in mind. The selection of properties was then weighted or influenced by a value judgment about which properties were most important. The recent rise of numerical taxonomy has attempted to avoid this preselection of properties based on assumptions about origins. The theory of numerical taxonomy is in fact a return to the principles of classification put forward by Michael Adanson before Linné. He assumed that all characters are of equal weight and that affinity, the basis of grouping individuals into the same class, is a function of the proportion of features (properties or characters or elements) in common. There is thus no assumption made about origin.[105]

The recent development of statistical methods in regionalization presents a parallel to the rise of numerical taxonomy in zoology. But as Gilmour[106] pointed out, even the use of computers cannot eliminate value judgments from the selection of differentiating characteristics. We may be able to determine statistically significant properties from a given list: but these must be initially selected on the basis of subjective judgment.

Neither logic nor taxonomy can give us any positive guide, then, to the means of selecting differentiating characteristics other than our eighth principle of classification which states quite simply that a differentiating characteristic should be important for the purpose of the classification. An example may show the relevance of this rule. Let us suppose we are studying the farms of a given area and we are concerned with the relationship between size and other characteristics of the area. Now farms, as operational units, have a great number of properties; they could be classified according to total area, number of workers, amount of fixed capital, or total annual revenue. Which of these is chosen as the differentiating characteristic will depend primarily, assuming all the requisite data is available, upon the purpose of the classification. Thus a classification based upon the total acreage of each farm would not be very helpful if our concern was to trace relationships between, say, farming intensity and crop combinations. A classification of farm size based on the number of employees would not necessarily bear any relationship to acreage, cropping, or capital inputs. The system of classification would have to be devised with the purpose in mind.

In most classifications more than one differentiating characteristic is used and hence at least two orders, or classes, or regions, are formed. In such a hierarchy the order in which the differentiating characteristics are selected is of significance. This may be most easily discussed in terms of division. If an area is to be divided into a number of regions, the whole area is first divided into a number of classes or regions upon the basis of one principle; each of these subclasses is divided on the basis of a second principle,

105. Bidwell and Hole, *op. cit.*, footnote 7, p. 58-62.
106. Gilmour, *op. cit.*, footnote 5, p. 43.

whereas the resultant classes may be further divided. What decides the order in which these principles are applied?

Hettner[107] considered this problem in his discussion of the possibilities of a natural classification of the earth's surface. He pointed out that the selection of the principles from a great number of properties is essentially subjective; he went on to indicate that a logical order of priorities could only be obtained if genetically linked properties were used as principles of division. Hartshorne, in discussing this contention, concluded: [108]

> ... that there can be no fixed order of importance of the different elements that is applicable to all parts of the world. ...

Hettner discussed a classification of the total character of the earth's surface, in such terms it is indeed difficult to see how there can be a logical and fixed order of priorities for such diverse properties as landforms, climate, vegetation, and soil type. But the problem of the order of priorities remains even if we confine ourselves to the classification of but one property of the earth's surface. The only guide that we can derive from the principles of classification is our ninth rule: that the principle used to divide in the higher categories should be more important than those in lower categories. Cline[109] gave an instance of this in soil science. In Shaw's soil classification parent material is a differentiating characteristic in a higher category and thus separates similar profiles in the lower categories. Clearly this rule again emphasizes the importance of purpose in classification. Consider a world classification of agriculture. If the highest category is divided into classes on the basis

of the degree of commercialization we would find that in the lower orders farms which are identical in terms of crop combinations, methods, and systems of land tenure are found in different classes. Conversely if the highest category is initially divided on the basis of methods of management then in the lower orders we may find farms with identical crop combinations, systems of land tenure, and degree of commercialization separated into quite different classes. Hence the purpose of the particular classification must be borne in mind when deciding the order of priorities.

One important implication of the order of priorities remains to be discussed. If classes in any given category are determined on the basis of one property alone, then the number of properties and their degree of expression determines the number of classes. The number of classes may soon become very large. Helburn,[110] for example, cited eleven properties of farms which he considers should be incorporated into a classification of types of agriculture. But as he went on to point out, if each property is considered to have only three degrees of expression then there would be some 59,000 possible classes. This problem is often avoided in practical classification in two ways. First, a category of classes may be formed on the basis of not a single property but of a number of properties. Second, many classifications are uncompleted; that is either the higher or the lower orders are omitted. Thus Whittlesey's[111] classification of agriculture claims only to deal with first-order regions, whereas as Manil[112] pointed out, some soil classifications consist only of either the higher or the lower categories.

107. Hettner, quoted by Hartshorne, *op. cit.*, 1939, footnote 2, p. 307.
108. Hartshorne, *op. cit.*, 1939, footnote 2, p. 306.
109. Cline, *op. cit.*, 1949, footnote 7, p. 88.

110. N. Helburn, "The Bases for a Classification of World Agriculture," *Professional Geographer*, Vol. IX (1957), p. 6.
111. Whittlesey, *op. cit.*, 1936, footnote 48.
112. Manil, *op. cit.*, footnote 7, p. 9.

The Hierarchy of Regions

If objects are grouped into classes and more than one differentiating characteristic is used; or if a genus is subdivided and subdivided again on some second principle, then a hierarchy of classes of different orders is formed into regions, and then these regions grouped together on the basis of some second principle, then a hierarchy of regions is formed. Such an idea has a long tradition in the history of regionalization. Hettner, Herbertson, Unstead, and others have all discussed the possibility of forming regional hierarchies.[113] But many geographers have attempted to construct such hierarchies based on the total character of the earth's surface; opinion of most geographers now is that this is logically impossible. Certainly we must agree with Hartshorne[114] that there is no way of forming a hierarchy of regions based upon total character in any way analogous to the orders of biological classifications.

But this does not mean that regional hierarchies themselves must be rejected; the great value of a hierarchy of classes or regions, is as Lazarsfeld[115] pointed out, that generalizations may be made about the same objects of study at different levels of abstraction, thus saving time in organizing and reorganizing similar material. The need for regional hierarchies is widely recognized, not only by geographers but by workers in allied fields such as soil science and plant ecology. Among geographers, Russian workers have particularly stressed the need for a hierarchial approach and a uniform nomenclature.[116]

Yet by no means are all regional systems organized upon a hierarchical basis and some regard this as a principal defect in existing regional systems. Thus Whittlesey wrote:[117]

> The general neglect of the meaning of differences of scale or degree of generalization is a lacuna in geographic thinking which . . . should be filled as soon as possible.

Whittlesey went on to suggest a standard nomenclature for regions of different orders: locality, district, province, and realm. Other geographers have suggested standard names: thus Herbertson recognized four orders: locality, district, region, and continent, whereas Unstead recognized five orders: stow, tract, subregion, minor region, and major region.[118] Russian geographers have also discussed a variety of different possible terms for regions of different orders.[119]

The need for an accepted hierarchy and nomenclature is often discussed; the thinking behind this approach is well expressed by Lebedev when discussing geomorphic regionalization:[120]

> Unfortunately they are still being compiled on the basis of different approaches and through the use of various systems of regional units, which make it impossible to compare materials covering different areas.

Presumably it is assumed that if a standardized hierarchy of regional geomorphic units could be established, the generalizations for a given order of a hierarchy for one

113. See also A. K. Philbrick, "Principles of Areal Functional Organization in Regional Human Geography," *Economic Geography*, Vol. 33 (1957), pp. 299-336.

114. Hartshorne, *op. cit.*, footnote 2, p. 128.

115. Lazarsfeld and Barton, *op. cit.*, footnote 73, pp. 84-85.

116. A. Perelman, "Geochemical Principles of Landscape Classification," *Soviet Geography*, Vol.

II, No. 3 (1961), pp. 62-63; G. V. Lebedev "Principles of Geomorphic Regionalization," *Soviet Geography*, Vol. II, No. 8 (1961), pp. 59-60; G. D. Rikhter, "Natural Regionalization," in *Soviet Geography, Accomplishments and Tasks* (New York: American Geographical Society, 1962), pp. 205-09; A. A. Grigor'yev, "Geographical Zonality," *idem*, pp. 182-87.

117. Whittlesey, *op cit.*, 1954, footnote 33, p. 47.

118. Herbertson, *op. cit.*, 1913, footnote 23; Unstead, *op. cit.*, 1933, footnote 25.

119. See footnote 116.

120. Lebedev, *op. cit.*, footnote 116, p. 59.

part of the world would be applicable to another part of the world where the standard system had also been applied. One may share Bunge's[121] skepticism of the validity of this approach. A hierarchy depends not upon any features inherent in the landscape but upon the number of differentiating characteristics chosen for the system. Whittaker, in reviewing the similar problem in plant ecology commented:[122]

> Hierarchies are not inherent in landscapes; a given landscape offers material which can be fashioned into hierarchies in innumerable ways.

But in any given classification of a given area on the basis of certain properties, a hierarchy is inevitably established. If such a hierarchy is to be a useful basis for the making of generalizations about the objects classified then the rules cited at the beginning of this section must be borne in mind, particularly principles five to nine. If such principles are grossly infringed then the system ceases to be internally consistent and the possibilities of the system producing any valid generalizations are greatly reduced. Two examples of this may be given. One of the most familiar regional systems found in textbooks of geography is where a country is divided into higher order regions on the basis of landforms, then subdivided perhaps on the basis of climatic differences, whereas the lower order regions are established on the basis of some feature of human occupance. It is these lower order regions which are used for the description of the country. Yet it will be readily apparent that the lower order regions, because the higher order regions are formed upon a principle greatly different in kind from the lower order regions, often place in different regions very similar areas of human occupance. Now admittedly such regional systems are intended not as a means

of analysis but simply as a framework of description. But not only are they valueless for the former purpose but of very limited significance for the latter aim.

The failure to maintain class exclusion is another common fault. Whittlesey's world system of agricultural regions gives instances of this.[123] Whittlesey based his classification of agricultural regions upon five properties; each of these properties may be assumed to have at least two degrees of expression. This would give at least thirty-two lower order classes in a consistent system; yet he recognized only fourteen lower order regions. Clearly there must be cases of overlapping.

But it must be admitted that there is a great gulf between the demands of logic and the expediencies of practical classification. Suppose we wish to establish a world classification of types of farming; we take as individuals, farms, and let us further suppose that statistical data on all these farms are available. Theoretically we could group these individuals into classes according to some differentiating characteristic, then group those classes upon some second characteristic, and so on. Alternatively, we may begin with the world and subdivide. In both cases a system of hierarchy of classes could theoretically be obtained; but there would clearly come a point where the system and the reality it represents would radically differ. Manil, in discussing this problem with reference to soils, doubted whether such a classification which embraced the world as the highest category and a soil profile as the individual is feasible.[124] Even if logically possible it is still a formidable task.

We hope this article has adequately demonstrated the similarity between the procedures of classification and those of region-

---

121. Bunge, *op. cit.*, footnote 3, pp. 21, 96.
122. Whittaker, *op. cit.*, footnote 42, p. 122.

123. Whittlesey, *op. cit.*, 1936, footnote 48.
124. Manil, *op. cit.*, footnote 7, p. 9.

alization. Once attention has been drawn to the differing terminologies, we can see that taxonomists and geographers are grappling with fundamentally the same methodological problems. This is most aptly shown by comparing the history of classification and that of regionalization; there is a remarkable similarity in the development of ideas on the natural system and the geographical region.

If we accept that the two procedures are similar, and it must be admitted that the problem of the geographical individual is a difficulty, then the principles of classification can be applied to the construction of regional systems, and in particular to generic regional systems. An examination of the principles confirms most of the conclusions reached independently by geographers. To a large extent these principles give negative guides to procedure; that is, they tell us what should be avoided rather than what should be done. Nonetheless we hope they will prove useful to those who are constructing systems or assessing the value of existing systems.

****

A CLASSIFICATION OF WELSH REGIONS

Christopher S. Davies

It has been argued that Wales as a whole is a "natural region" and that further subdivision is unnecessary. E. G. Bowen disagreed with the view that Wales represents a unity of any kind other than in a political sense. He consequently created a purely subjective regionalization of Wales. The objective of this paper is to analyze E. G. Bowen's regional classification of Wales.[1] By employing a concise data set and areal sample this analysis attempts to evaluate Bowen's intuitive regionalization.

This paper proceeds to group or regionalize multivariable observations. Thirteen Welsh counties are characterized by twenty-five social, economic and demographic variables which are considered to be suitable representative measures of a county. A factor analysis is performed upon an n x m data matrix (n=observations, m=variables per observation), producing a set of principal components. These components are the basic patterns of variation for the observations and variables.[2] These orthogonalized and normalized components are used as inputs into the multiple linear discriminant analysis. The discriminant analysis is performed on a regional classification of Wales which closely approximates that created by Bowen. This analysis tests the validity or logic of the classification. It determines if

1. E. G. Bowen, ed., *Wales* (London: Methuen and Co., 1957), pp. 267-515.

2. Brian J. L. Berry, "Grouping and Regionalizing: An Approach to the Problem Using Multivariate Analysis," in W. L. Garrison and D. F. Marble, (eds.), *Quantitative Geography* (Evanston: Northwestern University Press, 1967), pp. 219-51.

From "A Discriminant Classification of Welsh Regions," unpublished M.A. paper in Department of Geography, Indiana University, September 1967; also presented at the West Lakes Division of the Association of American Geographers, Indiana State University, Terre Haute, 1967. Reprinted by permission.

the assignment of observations (counties) in the predetermined regional divisions is satisfactory.[3] Finally, to further investigate Bowen's regionalization a grouping technique is used to determine a set of regions each containing counties possessing maximum homogeneity within, and maximum heterogeneity between the areal units. The resulting regions are then compared to Bowen's delimitation for possible spatial conformity.

Data constraints determine the use of discrete areas (counties) as the unit of observation (see Fig. 1). Like time, economic space is continuous and uninterrupted except when political or physical barriers are considered. However, space for measurement and planning purposes must be considered as discontinuous. The inadequate research techniques available to combat the theoretical difficulties of continuous space forces

the regionalist to perform spatial analyses upon discrete areas.[4] Since a different data set and areal sample are used, Bowen's arbitrarily drawn regional boundaries cannot be replicated. This prevents inferences as to the accuracy of his regional delineation. However, the purpose of this paper is not to dispute the validity of E. G. Bowen's regionalization of Wales, but to present either supporting evidence of his intuitive delimitation or opposing evidence which raises questions as to the accuracy of his regions. The task is to ascertain whether the end result of this analysis is similar to that of Bowen.

The commonly employed social, demographic, and economic variables are merely crude indicators of the economic and social welfare of the areas in question. These measures are secondary in nature and only available at the county level. The data are not corrected for size of the collecting area, but gross size effects are eliminated for certain variables by dividing the values of the variables 15, 16, 17, and 19 by variable 13. The remaining variables are corrected for size effects within the census material itself. (See Appendix, Table 1, for a definition of the variables.)

Regional inequalities will vary over time and change with the stages of Welsh economic development. Consequently, the results of this presentation are relevant only for a particular point in time (1960), the particular set of variables chosen, and the particular segment of space (county) used to define the units of observation.

Profiles of Selected Variables and Welsh Counties

To obtain a preliminary understanding of variations among the Welsh regional units

3. Maurice Kendall, ed., *A Course in Multivariate Analysis* (London: Charles Griffin and Co., 1957), p. 144.

WALES

Figure 1. Source: British Census 1961

4. John Friedmann and William Alonso, eds., *Regional Development and Planning* (Cambridge: M.I.T. Press, 1964), p. 77.

profiles are constructed on selected counties and variables. A 13×25 data matrix is transformed into common units of measurement (standard deviation units about a zero mean). The standard scores obtained are then used to construct the profiles shown in Figure 2, and Figure 3. Figure 2 shows the profiles of the thirteen counties characterized by the six variables mining and quarrying, density, divorce, aliens, agricultural workers, and Welsh language. These variables are chosen from the twenty-five attributes available as being a fair cross section of the social, economic, and demographic forces acting upon the counties. While Figure 2 facilitates the study of similarities and differences between the variables, Figure 3 shows the same variations for the counties.

The six selected variables are suitable indicators of the rural-urban dichotomy in Wales. The four variables mining, population density, divorce rate, and percent aliens are characteristic of industrial areas and demonstrate roughly similar profiles in Figure 2. These profiles are generally the reverse of those variables representative of rural Wales, Welsh language, and agricultural workers.

E. G. Bowen's "Core Area" counties of Caernarvonshire and Merionethshire all display similar profiles and strong positive relationships with the variables Welsh language and agricultural workers (see Fig. 3). The industrial counties of Glamorganshire and Monmouthshire display distinctly different profiles. So to a lesser degree do the minor industrial counties of Denbighshire and Flintshire. The following factor analysis provides a more succinct description of variable and county similarities and differences.

Methodology

The analysis of the regional structure of Wales begins with a data matrix X of order $n \times m$ in which twenty-five measurements (m) are assembled for each of the country's thirteen countries (n). Correlations and a principal component analysis are then computed.[5]

The problem of factor analysis is to account for the total communality variance, that is, the total variation in each variable explained by the factors.[6] Unities are placed in the principal diagonal of the X matrix as an estimate of the communalities. Only components with eigenvalues exceeding one are rotated to normal varimax position.[7]

The rotation results in U which is an $n \times r$

---

5. The sample (n) should be quite large in order to reduce the sampling errors. Data constraints preclude a large (n) value. Also, one of the assumptions of factor analysis is that all values are normally distributed. To satisfy this requirement of normality, the twenty-five variables, the majority of which are slightly skewed, are transformed by applying logarithmic transformations. Factor analysis also assumes a linear relationship among the variables which means that the orthogonal factors obtained will be independent of each other. As a test case to ascertain whether the m observed variables are linearly related the variable Welsh language is regressed separately upon four of the twenty-five variables. A linear relationship in each case is found. Due to the implied labor involved when twenty-five variables are used a visual if not a formal statistical check should be performed upon each pair of the observed variables.

6. Harry Harman, *Modern Factor Analysis* (Chicago: University of Chicago Press, 1960), pp. 382-83.

7. The aim of rotation is to obtain a set of components which has the property that any given component will be fairly highly correlated with some of the variables but uncorrelated with the rest. Each factor can then be identified with one of the clusters of variables, thereby reducing the effective number of variables to the number of components used. Thus, rotation helps to create factors that are more easily interpreted. Hubert M. Blalock, *Social Statistics* (New York: McGraw-Hill, 1960), p. 385; B. Fruchter, *Introduction to Factor Analysis* (New York: D. Van Nostrand, 1954), p. 178.

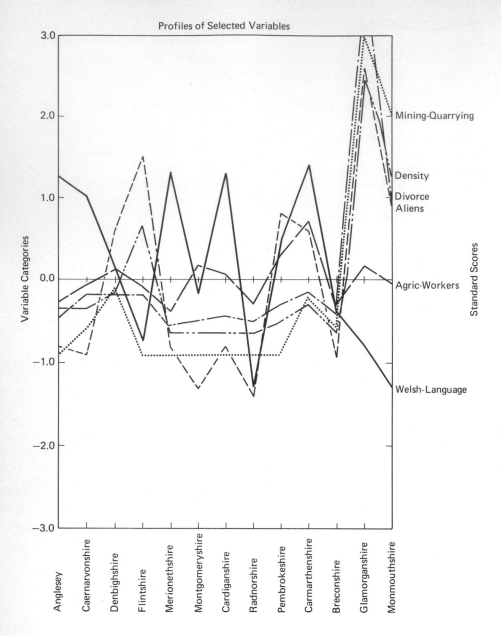

Profiles of Selected Variables

Figure 2

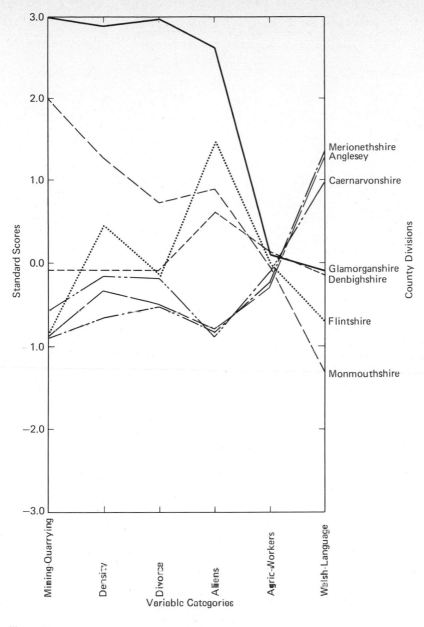

Figure 3

(13 × 5) matrix and is the result of the Q factoring of the n x m correlation matrix produced from X. The Q mode is used to examine relations among the observations (counties) used in the study. V is an r x m matrix and is the transposed result (m x r) of

Table 1   Table of Positive Eigenvalues

No.	Eigen-value	Per Cent of Communality Over			
		All (25)	Factors	5 Rotated	Factors
1	10.678	42.7	42.7	46.8	46.8
2	4.718	18.9	61.6	20.7	67.5
3	4.104	16.4	78.0	18.0	85.5
4	1.964	7.9	85.9	8.6	94.1
5	1.351	5.4	91.3	5.9	100.0
6	0.790	3.2	94.4		
7	0.600	2.4	96.8		
8	0.313	1.3	98.1		
9	0.229	0.9	99.0		
10	0.188	0.8	99.7		
11	0.045	0.2	99.9		
12	0.021	0.1	100.0		

the R factoring of the m x m correlation matrix produced from X.[8] The R mode of factor analysis is used when interest is focused upon relations among the variables. The U matrix provides scores for each observation (county) on the basic component (see Table 2) and the V matrix conjugate scores for each m (variable) on each of the r dimensions (see Table 3).

The factor analysis is applied to the n x m

8. Fruchter, *op. cit.*, pp. 176, 202-24.

data matrix and the rotated factor scores recorded on five factors for the counties and the variables. A set of components with positive eigenvalues are chosen in decreasing order of their contribution to the total communality (see Table1). Five orthogonal factors or components were extracted from the attributes. These five principal components account for 91.3 per cent of the variance leaving a small residual communality to the remaining seven factors (see

Table 2   Scores of Welsh Regions with Repect to the First Five Principal Components

Factor	1	2	3	4	5
1 Anglesey	0.319	0.035	−0.261	−0.174	−0.298
2 Caernarvonshire	0.148	0.362	−0.406	1.415	−0.263
3 Denbighshire	−0.457	−0.144	0.260	−0.984	−0.302
4 Flintshire	−0.708	−0.359	0.215	−1.747	−0.380
5 Merionethshire	0.431	0.042	−0.482	0.856	−0.205
6 Montgomeryshire	0.779	0.252	0.318	0.406	0.691
7 Cardiganshire	0.238	0.113	−0.150	0.673	−0.465
8 Radnorshire	0.494	0.123	−0.271	0.206	0.014
9 Pembrokeshire	−0.691	0.122	0.220	−0.315	2.124
10 Carmarthenshire	0.558	0.442	2.142	0.346	−0.584
11 Breconshire	0.193	0.238	0.248	−0.147	0.066
12 Glamorganshire	−1.751	0.259	0.488	−1.044	−0.445
13 Monmouthshire	0.447	−1.484	−2.321	0.509	0.048

Table 3   Loadings of the Variables in the First Five Principal Components

Variable	1	2	3	4	5
1 WELLAG	−0.027	−0.415	0.137	0.560	−0.366
2 POPCHA	0.946	0.231	0.082	−0.139	−0.013
3 DENSIT	0.659	0.715	0.081	−0.116	−0.130
4 SEAGMA	0.965	0.201	0.096	−0.064	−0.007
5 INTCEN	0.974	0.159	0.038	−0.132	−0.032
6 UPPERC	0.979	0.075	−0.030	0.044	−0.026
7 MIDDLE	0.960	0.206	0.124	−0.035	−0.022
8 LOWERC	0.960	0.178	0.020	−0.110	−0.035
9 DENOCC	−0.038	0.542	0.370	−0.706	0.097
10 HOUCOM	−0.562	0.334	0.644	−0.184	−0.013
11 SHEEPY	−0.967	−0.013	0.150	0.039	−0.047
12 TEREDU	0.530	−0.066	0.765	0.155	−0.202
13 EMPLOY	0.883	0.445	0.091	−0.010	−0.079
14 AVWILE	−0.164	0.142	0.051	0.878	0.088
15 AGRWOR	−0.004	0.178	0.880	0.141	0.243
16 INDWOR	0.255	0.940	0.159	−0.007	−0.107
17 COMNOR	0.274	0.951	0.035	−0.073	−0.047
18 HOTBED	−0.413	0.008	−0.664	0.383	−0.043
19 MINQUA	0.233	0.955	0.043	0.056	−0.080
20 DOVORC	0.063	0.989	0.016	0.024	−0.045
21 ALIENS	0.176	0.779	−0.031	−0.472	0.105
22 SANITA	−0.013	−0.193	−0.802	0.162	0.121
23 WHBAOA	0.089	0.357	−0.623	−0.205	−0.621
24 VEGETA	−0.121	−0.228	0.724	0.169	0.501
25 MIGRAT	−0.013	−0.046	0.063	−0.121	0.879

Table 1).[9] Since the five principal components account for nearly all of the variation the effective dimensions of variation have thus been reduced from 25 to 5. This makes redundant any variables which are merely duplicating the task of describing differences among the counties and illustrates the descriptive economy of component analysis. The components have separate existences and can be interpreted and identified.

Factor Interpretation

Factor I. The character of Factor I in matrix V, Table 3, is determined by its loadings on the variables. It is a factor of change. High positive loadings are found on such mobility indicators as rates of change of population, high percentage of young mothers, and strong increases in private households. An equal distribution at all skill levels of economically active males and females is also characteristic. Generally, young residents are housed in new growth areas; this explains why private household development is high, and overcrowding, as represented by household composition, low.

9. The first five factors which explain 91.3 per cent of the intercorrelation between the twenty-five variables are the most significant factors. If after 90 per cent of the total variance is accounted for and any additional factor accounts for less than 5 per cent of the total variance, then it is to be deleted. This reasoning is based upon the fact that any factor having such a small impact on the total variance could hardly have any practical significance. Harry Harmon, *Modern Factor Analysis* (Chicago: University of Chicago, 1960), p. 363.

Factor II. Factor II is considered a factor of stability. Very high positive loadings are found on industrial workers, commercial workers, mining and quarrying, aliens,[10] percentage of population divorced, and finally, density (see Figs. 2 and 3). Density and overcrowding, the latter represented by household composition, have both increased over Factor I.

Factor III. Factor III is labeled an agricultural factor. This is confirmed by the high positive correlations with agricultural workers and production of vegetables. The lack of sanitation and hotel accommodations confirm this factor's distinct agricultural or rural character.

Factors IV and V. These two factors tend to characterize the classic Welsh core. Factor IV shows a strong positive correlation with average winter leaching, a variable characteristic of an area of high relief and high aggregates of rainfall. When related to Welsh language the classic Welsh core factor acquires a distinctive meaning. It characterizes a wet, pastoral economy, a sparse population, and a strong predominance of Welsh language and culture which is more deeply rooted in this sector of pastoral tradition than in the more populous areas of the lowlands.[11]

A Graphic Representation of the Distribution of Variables and Observations on Factors I and II

The distribution of the variables that give an identification or reality to the factors is presented in Figure 4. This distribution is based upon the scores of the variables on

Factors I and II. The high positive loadings of variables 3, 13, 2, 7, 4, 8, 5, and 6 create an agglomerating effect in the upper 30° section of Figure 4. These are the variables that give credibility to the factor of change. The variables that characterize Factor II, variables 17, 16, 19, 20, 21, and 23, are also nucleated in the upper positive quadrant with high positive loadings in this case on Factor II, and low loadings on Factor I. The agricultural factor that represents areas of both the urban and mountainous core areas of Wales is typified by the position of variables 15, 25, 22, 24, and 1. Finally, the fourth group of variables is positioned in the extreme left of the graph; these are variables 11, 10, and 18. These tend to characterize the classic Welsh core or mountainous zone in Wales.

Figure 5 is a similar graph representing the distribution of counties on Factors I and II. First, note the agglomeration of counties 1, 5, 8, 7, 11, and 2, counties considered by Bowen to lie in the "Core Area" (see Table 2 and Fig. 2). Note also the extreme peripheral nature of the highly industrialized counties 12, 10 and 13; and the extreme "low left-hand" orientation of counties 4 and 3, and to a lesser degree, 9. Observation 6 (Montgomeryshire) appears something of an anomaly in this case. Although peripheral and tending toward the other highly industrialized counties it still has distinct rural traits.

To conclude, the graphs succinctly show how factor analysis reproduces known patterns. Due to the problem of dimensionality the location of counties in the remaining factor space cannot be depicted. However, it is quite clear from the previous explanation that the factors characterize the counties of Wales.

The orthogonalized and normalized scores corresponding to the first five components, accounting for 91.3 per cent of the

---

10. The high alien element is due to the in-migration of Poles, Slavs, and Hungarians after World War II and the 1956 Hungarian Revolution. Many of these people were originally from mining areas. They were re-established in the various coal districts, particularly those of South Wales.

11. Bowen, *op. cit.*, pp. 270-81.

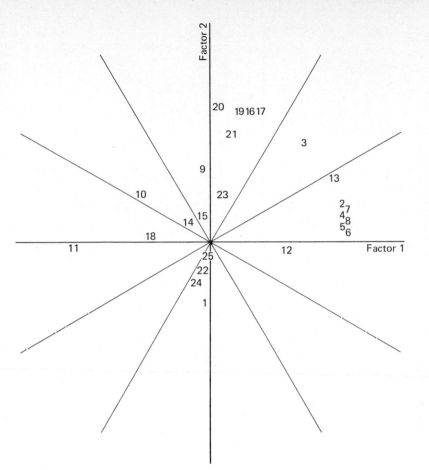

Figure 4. Distribution of variables on factors 1 and 2.

total variability, are the output of the principal component analysis and are used as input to the multiple linear discriminant program. In discriminant analysis the components (linear discriminant functions) are orthogonal only if the original data are orthogonalized and normalized.

The objective of the following discriminant analysis is to derive that combination of the five input components which will best differentiate the regional groupings. The discriminant function will test the validity and logic of a set of derived regional groups which are a close approximation of those created for Wales by E. G. Bowen. The out-

come of this valid regionalization will be a set of Regional Types, that is, areas of maximum similarity. These counties of maximum similarity may or may not be contiguous. In the former case they would comprise distinct Uniform Regions.[12]

A Discriminant Analysis of a Classification of Welsh Regions

E. G. Bowen maintains that a "Heartland" or "Core Area" exists in Wales. Bowen was

---

12. Brian J. L. Berry, "A Method of Deriving, Multifactor Uniform Regions," *Przeglad Geograficzny*, XXXIII, No. 2 (1961), pp. 263-79.

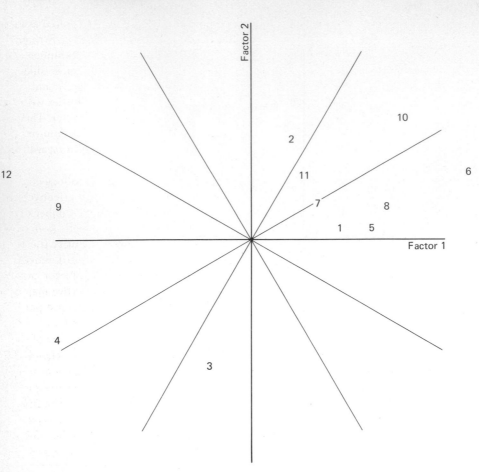

Figure 5. Distribution of observations (counties) on factors 1 and 2.

never able to prove the existence of this "Core Area" in any concise manner. He attempted by a series of map outlines to illustrate his purely subjective regionalization based upon "a long established familiarity with the land of Wales, its people and history." [13] Bowen's regionalization of Wales shows a central "Core Area" surrounded by peripheral regions. Figure 6 is a rough approximation of Bowen's regions and depicts the difference between the Core and border zones.

13. E. G. Bowen, *Wales* (London: Methuen and Co., 1957), p. 267.

To conform as closely as possible to the "Core Area" and the peripheral regions of Bowen, utilizing county units, the following three classes or regional types are constructed.

Regional Type I: Pembrokeshire(09), Montgomeryshire(06), Denbighshire(03), Flintshire(04)

Regional Type II: Radnorshire(08), Anglesey(01), Caernarvonshire(02), Merionethshire(05), Cardiganshire(07), Breconshire(11)

Regional Type III: Carmarthenshire(10), Glamorganshire(12), Monmouthshire(13)

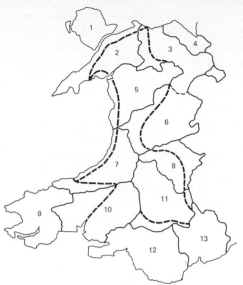

WALES

Figure 6. An approximation of Bowen's regions.
Source: United Kingdom Census 1961.

The selection of these three classifications is
supported in part by the preliminary investigation using profile analysis in which the
counties Merionethshire(5), Anglesey(1),
and Caernarvonshire(2) of Regional Type II
depict similar profiles on the selected variables. Glamorganshire and Monmouthshire
in Subset III and Denbighshire and Flintshire
in Subset I also demonstrate like within-
group outlines. Further, in component
analysis the "Core Area" counties 1, 2, 5, 7,
8, and 11 of Subset II project parallel scores
on both the first and second components as
seen in Figure 5. Counties 10, 12, and 13 in
Subset III and 9, 3, and 4 in Subset I also
present similar within-group distributions in
Figure 5.

Interpretation of the Linear Discriminant Functions

The first five principal components are used
as inputs to the discriminant analysis. The
first two components are interpreted as measuring the regional mobility and growth potential of the counties (the more similar the
scores on the components the more alike are
the county divisions—see Table 2); and
second, the position of the counties with
respect to their industrial character. The remaining components reflect the counties'
agricultural state and position in regard to
Welsh cultural traits.

The linear discriminant functions concentrate all the discriminatory effectiveness
of the original variables into a number of
linearly independent components ($l.\ d.$
$f.$'s).[14] These components identify the
dimensions which explain the differences
among the three classes. As in factor analysis
where the twelve components (five major)
account for each stage of the largest part of
the residual variability, the two $l.\ d.\ f.$'s
account for the largest possible part of the
discriminatory power among the classes. The
discriminant analysis identifies major measures of classification as factor analysis determines dimensions of variability. The first
discriminant function in one dimension
maximizes the largest power of discrimination (75.19 per cent) among the classes.

14. Emilio Casetti, "Multiple Discriminant Functions," *Technical Report*, No. 11 of ONR Task No.
389-135, contract NONR 1228 (26), Office of
Naval Research, Geography Branch, Northwestern
University, 1966.

Table 4   Welsh Regions

*Proportion of the Discriminant Power Ac-
counted for by the First Two Discriminant
Functions*

$l.\ d.\ f.\ No.$	Per Cent of Discr. Power	Cumulative Per Cent of Discr. Power
1	75.19	75.19
2	24.81	100.00

Table 5   Welsh Regions

Loadings of the First Five Principal Components
in the First Two l. d. f.s

Principal Com- ponent No.	l. d. f. No.	
	1	2
1	0.2556	0.4060
2	0.8530	0.3650
3	−0.4056	−0.1135
4	−0.1980	−0.6564
5	−0.0581	0.5081

The results of the discriminant analysis indicate that 100 per cent of the intra-class variability is condensed into two *l. d. f.*'s (see Table 4). Table 5 shows the loadings of the first five components on the two functions. In the first *l. d. f.* the principal components 3, 4, and 5 have negative loadings: and components 1 and 2 positive loadings.

The loadings on the main *l. d. f.* are positively related to the counties that display considerable population mobility and changes in economic activity (see Table 6). This tends to give positive scores as in the case of the principal components analysis (see Table 2) to counties characterized by these traits.

Negative scores are given to those counties characterized by stability and steady industrial growth (see Table 6).

The second and third principal components have the highest loadings in absolute value on *l. d. f.* number one (see Table 5). These two components demonstrate economic activity both in the industrial and the agricultural sphere. Thus, the principal component loadings on the first *l. d. f.* measure the general industrial, agricultural and social development of Welsh regions. This is substantiated by the positive scores which identify new areas of agricultural activity, while the negative scores single out the tra-

Table 6   Welsh Regions

Scores with Respect to the First Two l. d. f.s

	l. d. f. No. 1	l. d. f. No. 2
Subset I		
1. Pembrokeshire 9	−0.2229	1.0250
2. Montgomeryshire 6	0.1645	0.4568
3. Denbighshire 3	−0.1327	0.2248
4. Flintshire 4	−0.2064	0.5107
Subset II		
5. Radnorshire 8	0.2995	0.1481
6. Anglesey 1	0.2690	0.1347
7. Caernarvonshire 2	0.2464	−0.8241
8. Merionethshire 5	0.1839	−0.4210
9. Cardiganshire 7	0.1118	−0.5231
10. Breconshire 11	0.1770	0.2671
Subset III		
11. Carmarthenshire 10	−0.3838	−0.3792
12. Glamorganshire 12	−0.1920	−0.2126
13. Monmouthshire 13	−0.3136	−0.4060

ditionally stable industrial regions (see Table 6). The only anomaly to this trend is county 6, Montgomeryshire, classified as representative of Region I. The scores on this county suggest it more suitable for inclusion in Regional subset II. The distinctive character of this county is noticed in the component analysis.

The loadings on the second *l. d. f.* which account for some 28 per cent of the discriminatory power, have similar attributes to the first *l. d. f.* The signs on the scores of the counties are reversed for this second *l. d. f.* The traditionally dominant industrial counties of the South, 10, 12, and 13, still remain prominent. Region I, however, which consists of counties Flintshire, Denbighshire, and Pembrokeshire of lesser industrial strength, does not retain its distinctiveness. The signs and values of the scores in both Regions I and II change. This shows that although there is a difference between the peripheral Region I and the Core Region II of Wales, the difference is somewhat tenuous and is not so sharply defined as that found between the Core Region II and Region III. This suggests that the counties of Subset I and Subset II possess some mutual characteristics which hinder their classification into distinctive regional groupings.

A Significance Test for the Regional Groupings

Whether the discrepancies among the mean values of the three regions for the five variables are significant or whether they may reasonably be attributed to chance is determined by a significance test.

Let u_1, u_2, u_3, stand for the means of the three regions.
To test the null hypothesis: $u_1 = u_2 = u_3$ against the alternative that the three u's are *not* all the same.
Reject the hypothesis if $x^2 = x_{.05}^2$

Accept the hypothesis if $x^2 = x_{.05}^2$ with the number of degrees of freedom equaling 10. The Generalized Mahalanobis D-square = 33.05659.
The value 33.05659 can be used as chi-square with 10 degrees of freedom to test the hypothesis that the mean values are the same in all the three regions for the given five variables. Setting a level of significance of .05 we find

$$x^2 > x_{.05}^2$$
$$33.05659 > 18.307$$

The null hypothesis that there is *no* difference between the regions is rejected. The regional groupings can be considered significantly different.

The objective of this research paper, to substantiate E. G. Bowen's regional classification of Wales by employing a concise data set and areal sample, is partially satisfied by the results obtained. E. G. Bowen's regionalization of Wales which shows a central "Heartland" or "Core Area" surrounded by peripheral regions is found to exist. A spatial conformity appears to occur between the "Core Area" and the counties that comprise Regional Subset II (see Fig. 7).

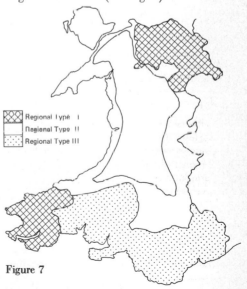

Regional Type I
Regional Type II
Regional Type III

Figure 7

The Regional Types I and II peripheral to the "Core Area" have distinctive characteristics (see Fig. 7). However, the within-group homogeneity, particulary of Regional Subset III, is not pronounced. This powerful southern block of Carmarthenshire (10), Glamorganshire(12), and Monmouthshire(13) is quite distinct from the "Core Area," and the considerable dissimilarities among these counties could define separate regional entities. The dissimilarities between Regional Type I and the "Core Area" are not so disparate. This suggests that the counties of Subset I and Subset II possess some mutual characteristics which allow the two regions to be more readily linked, but makes their classification into distinctive regional groups difficult.

The following section uses a grouping technique to obtain regional subsets of Welsh counties based upon maximum within-group homogeneity and between group heterogeneity. The resulting classification is compared with Bowen's regional delimitation for possible spatial conformity and can be considered further evidence in support of his regionalization.

Grouping for Maximum Homogeneity

A 13 x 13 distance matrix is used to group the thirteen counties into regions. This matrix of squared distances between the points (counties) is based upon three main factors. These factors account for approximately 80 per cent of the regional variation of the variables.[15] The distance function measures the "nearness" of these points in factor space. The distances between points are

indices of the degree of multi-factor similarity among the counties. The further apart the points, the more dissimilar the areas they represent. This distance similarity procedure allocates a new point (county) to a class (region) whose center of gravity in the factor space is at the shortest Euclidean distance from that county. The points in a class are clustered around their center of gravity at the same time as the center of gravity of the regions (classes) are scattered apart from each other.[16]

The objective is to search for within-region homogeneity and between-region heterogeneity. The "linkage tree" indicates that the most logical division of Wales based upon this concept of maximum similarity among counties has been reached (see Fig. 8). This linkage tree again indicates the distinct nature of the regional groupings. The individuality of Regional Type III (see Figs. 7 and 8) Glamorganshire (12), Carmarthenshire (10), and Monmouthshire (13), as compared with Regional Type I Denbighshire (3), Flintshire (4), and Pembrokeshire (9) is clearly demonstrated. The separate character of Regional Type II is also pronounced.

Evidence in support of E. G. Bowen's Welsh "Heartland" is demonstrated by the clustering of the counties of Regional Type II Anglesey (1), Radnorshire(8), Merionethshire (5), Breconshire (11), Caernarvonshire (2), and Cardiganshire (7). (See Fig. 1 and Fig. 7.) These counties, with the exception of Anglesey (1), approximate Bowen's "Core Area." Anglesey should, from the results of this analysis, be considered an integral part of the "Core Area."

Again the difficulty of placing Montgomeryshire (6) in a specific regional group is indicated in Figure 8. Montgomeryshire

15. Three factors rather than five are chosen as the determining criteria. These factors account for some 80 per cent of the regional variation. The decision on the number of factors to use roughly depends upon the percentage of regional variation they explain.

16. Brian J. L. Berry, "Grouping and Regionalizing: An Approach to the Problem Using Multivariate Analysis," *op. cit.*, pp. 233-34.

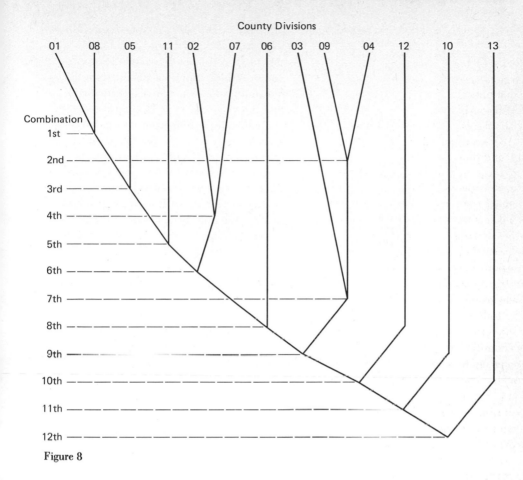

County Divisions

Figure 8

appears to have characteristics which are not easily related to other Welsh counties. E. G. Bowen did not consider Montgomeryshire a distinct part of his Core Area and this judgment is substantiated by the results of this analysis.

The loss in detail incurred as the grouping of counties of maximum similarity into regions progresses is indicated in Table 7. The variation (D^2) between the groups is suggestive of the differences among the counties. A proportion of this between-county variation is lost when regional subsets of Wales are obtained. This loss is the result of counties being considered homo-geneous members of the regional subsets. The loss in detail due to this gain in generality is given by the "within-group D^2" as indicated in Table 7.[17]

Table 7 shows how the within-group variance begins to change considerably on the seventh step and drastically on the tenth, eleventh, and twelfth steps. This suggests that the areas (counties of Regional Type II, Bowen's "Core Area") prior to the seventh step indicate similar within-group characteristics and are somewhat distinct from the

---

17. Berry, "A Method of Driving Multifactor Uniform Regions," *op. cit.*, pp. 273-74.

Table 7   Losses in Detail with Gains in Generality

	Within Group D^2	Between Group D^2	
Prior to Grouping	0.00	30.538	Perfect Detail
After 1st Grouping	0.038	30.500	
2nd	0.094	30.444	
3rd	0.153	30.385	
4th	0.286	30.252	
5th	0.512	30.026	
6th	0.865	29.668	
7th	1.394	29.139	
8th	2.039	28.494	
9th	3.510	27.023	
10th	7.300	23.232	
11th	12.568	17.965	
12th	30.538	0.000	Complete Generality

remaining Welsh counties. The tenth, eleventh, and twelfth steps add the counties of Regional Type III Glamorganshire(12), Carmarthenshire (10), and Monmouth-shire(13). Although these counties are shown to be distinctly different from the remaining counties of Wales, particularly those of Regional Type II, they also demonstrate distinct within-group dissimilarities. This disparity is also noticeable on the component scores in Table 2. These counties, especially Monmouthshire, could be considered as separate regional entities.

The focal point of Bowen's regionalization of Wales has been confirmed. The "Heartland" or "Core Area" (Regional Subset II) is distinguished from the peripheral regions (Subsets I and III) by substantial disparities. The results indicate that the two peripheral regions are not categorically homogeneous. In fact, although distinct from the "Core Area," the peripheral counties can only be considered as separate entities within themselves.

Table 1   Appendix A

	Variable	Variable Name
1.	Welsh-speaking population, percentage of population aged three and over, 1961	WELLAG
2.	Average annual rates of change of population between selected census, 1951-61	POPCHA
3.	Density in 1961: persons resident per acre, 1961	DENSIT
4.	Sex, age, and marital conditions: number of married women aged 15-44 per 1,000 females of all ages	SEAGMA
5.	Intercensal increase (1951-61) in private households (1961 Preliminary Report)	INTCEN
6.	a. 1,2,3,4,13–Upper Socio-economic classification: percentage	UPPERC*
7.	b. 5,6,8,9,12,14–Middle of occupied and retired males in	MIDDLE
8.	c. 7,10,11,15,16,17–Lower social groups	LOWERC
9.	Density of occupation: persons per room	DENOCC
10.	Household composition: percentage of households containing more than one family	HOUCOM
11.	Sheep: number of units, 1959	SHEEPY
12.	Population aged 25 and over: terminal education age 17-19 (males)	TEREDU
13.	Total economically active male and female, aged 15 and over in employment	EMPLOY
14.	Average winter leaching	AVWILE
15.	Number of agricultural workers	AGRWOR
16.	Number of industrial workers	INDWOR
17.	Number of commercial workers	COMWOR
18.	Number of hotel beds	HOTBED
19.	Number employed in mining and quarrying	MINQUA
20.	Number of people divorced; per cent of population males and females	DIVORC
21.	Aliens born outside British Isles	ALIENS
22.	Households lacking fixed baths	SANITA
23.	Wheat, barley, and oats: estimated yield per acre in each county	WHBAOA
24.	Area of vegetables for human consumption; crops under glass and flowers, at the June Census	VEGETA
25.	Migration balance for 1961: immigrants-emigrants, population per 1,000 residents	MIGRAT

* To describe the area's population, seventeen socio-economic variables have been combined by the British Census Authorities into three distinct groups. Each group contains individuals whose social, cultural, and recreational standards and behavior are similar. The approximate composition of these three broad categories is (1) employers, managers, and professional workers; (2) non-manual, skilled manual, and foremen; and (3) unskilled, semi-skilled, and agricultural workers. For this problem variable names UPPERC (6), MIDDLE (7), and LOWERC (8) represent these groupings, *European Program for National Population Census,* United Nations, Conference of European Statisticians, Geneva, 1959 (London: Her Majesty's Stationery Office, 1961).

Table 2 Variable No.

Variable No.	1	2	3	4	5	6	7	8	9	10	11	12	13	14	15	16	17	18	19	20	21	22	23	24	25
Anglesey	69.1	0.20	0.3	230	9.1	16.0	47.3	36.7	0.57	2.23	0.01	.079	19,340	16	16.0	45.0	30.0	0.02	0.02	225	2003	54.1	24.4	98	3
Caernarvonshire	63.4	-0.19	0.3	194	5.1	17.9	48.3	33.7	0.54	2.33	0.06	.071	44,320	36	9.0	46.1	51.0	0.06	3.8	624	1370	32.4	22.1	133	-2
Denbighshire	33.5	0.20	0.4	231	10.8	14.2	52.1	33.8	0.64	3.06	0.04	.052	68,630	19	8.0	40.0	44.0	0.02	8.0	768	4731	24.0	22.9	354	7
Flintshire	18.8	0.32	0.9	243	15.7	12.9	50.2	36.9	0.65	4.12	0.03	.049	61,780	10	6.0	44.0	50.0	0.02	0.01	621	5943	21.2	26.4	840	4
Merionethshire	70.4	-0.78	0.1	217	4.1	15.8	50.3	33.9	0.56	1.95	0.00	.007	15,230	27	16.0	70.0	11.0	0.06	0.03	136	1775	41.9	20.0	17	13
Montgomeryshire	31.0	-0.40	0.1	237	6.0	21.1	48.6	30.3	0.59	3.61	0.00	.004	19,060	27	31.0	50.0	50.0	0.02	0.00	130	775	46.08	28.6	40	-11
Cardiganshire	70.2	0.07	0.1	208	3.6	20.2	53.5	26.3	0.54	2.48	0.00	.075	20,141	27	26.0	45.0	28.0	0.03	0.05	201	1791	41.3	25.0	42	5
Radnorshire	04.4	-0.79	0.1	227	1.4	18.6	50.6	30.8	0.57	3.69	0.00	.006	7,830	23	36.7	2.4	5.8	0.05	0.14	65	429	43.7	25.8	42	5
Pembrokeshire	23.5	0.35	0.2	258	10.4	15.0	48.9	36.1	0.61	3.14	0.05	.081	35,760	23	18.0	38.0	44.0	0.02	0.00	447	4508	29.66	21.4	271	-5
Carmarthenshire	72.6	-0.24	0.3	253	4.1	12.0	55.2	32.8	0.60	5.43	0.05	.528	68,000	28	14.0	39.0	40.0	0.00	8.6	719	3537	29.5	18.6	170	0
Breconshire	27.5	-0.24	0.1	252	6.4	13.2	45.7	41.0	0.60	3.19	0.03	.070	23,140	31	13.0	50.0	28.0	0.01	9.0	232	1388	32.4	19.7	38	4
Glamorganshire	16.8	0.22	2.3	267	6.8	10.8	53.9	35.3	0.65	5.01	0.04	.045	302,700	29	1.9	45.0	41.0	0.03	13.0	6108	7746	28.7	28.5	1237	0
Monmouthshire	3.2	0.45	1.3	279	9.2	9.5	52.3	38.2	0.66	4.14	0.04	.040	187,560	21	3.0	42.0	40.0	0.00	10.0	2001	4902	29.8	23.9	1304	3

****

A REPORT TO THE PARENTS OF DETROIT ON SCHOOL DECENTRALIZATION

William Bunge, et al.

COMMUNITY CONTROL

The strategy of this essay is to examine the problem of a school decentralization plan afresh, as if no other plans were in existence. As a first step it is necessary to establish the criteria on which the regionalization is to be based. It is possible to optimize the interests of the taxpayer, the school system, the teachers union, the registered voter or the children. Clearly the needs of the children should receive first priority.

Protection of the Children

Black children are among the most abused children in America. It is imperative that these most endangered children receive the most protection. (The infant mortality rate of black children in the King High School area on the east side of Detroit is higher than that of San Salvador, a fact some Americans consider unpatriotic.) Therefore, a humane research strategy should be to design a plan for the schools which protects the most vulnerable children and is still in strict accordance with the law.[1] The main geographic provision of the bill is that Detroit shall be divided into 7 to 11 regional school districts with not more than 50,000 nor less than 25,000 students in each district. In addition, each of the regional school districts

will elect a single member to the central School Board. Federal law requires that each of the regional school districts be contiguous, that is, in one piece.

To meet the primary goal of protecting the most abused children, every possible legal regional combination of Detroit high school districts (over seven thousand) were ranked according to sympathetic authority to the children from most to least, the measure of sympathy used in "the total number of black children under white authority" (Appendix I). A regional school district is defined as being under white authority where a majority of voters voted for white candidates in the mayoral primary. (A man with white skin color who voted black was considered to be a "black voter" and vice versa.) Assuming short run consistency in racial voting attitudes, it can reasonably be predicted which regional school districts would be under white authority.

The easiest way to place children under sympathetic authority is to draw districts which reflect the voluntary human landscape of the city. The city's schools fall into three regions, black, integrated, and white, as shown below. In drawing the districts, a special pattern emerges when these regions are preserved. It is this general pattern which this report recommends to the community.

The plan below is our number two choice. It gives maximum control to local communities while following the black-

---

1. State of Michigan, Senate Bill No. 635, approved by the Governor, August 11, 1969.

From Discussion Paper No. 2, Department of Geography Field Notes, Michigan State University. Delivered at the Association of American Geographers meeting, San Francisco, August 1970. Reprinted by permission.

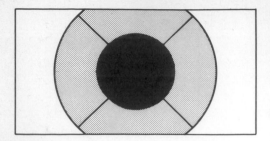

Figure 1. Generalized pattern for boundaries of child protection districts.

integrated-white pattern. It balances the number of children under the control of the opposite race. Because neighborhood control and sympathetic authority are highly correlated, it also places a great many children under sympathetic authority.

In conclusion, we recommend to the community a pattern which puts like schools together and protects the children from the battles of adults. The wisdom of the community can decide best on which of the many good possibilities will become the final plan.

Philosophy of Community Control

At this juncture the philosophy of "community control" must be briefly explained. "Community control" is another way of saying "local government" or "sub-urban units" or "homogeneous regions" or simply "democracy." The object of "community control" is to assure that all people, regardless of race, color, religion, national origin or class be given control over their own community's interests. In this case, their community's interest is sympathetic authority over their children in the public schools. The

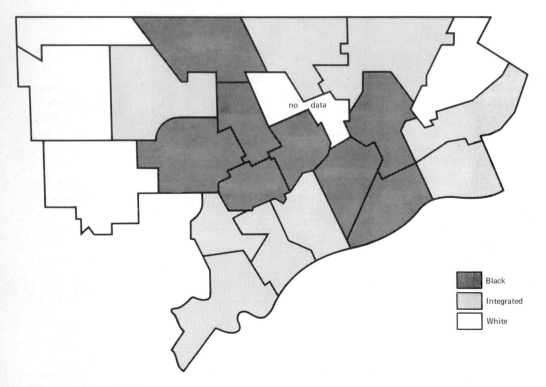

no data

Black
Integrated
White

Figure 2. The human landscape.

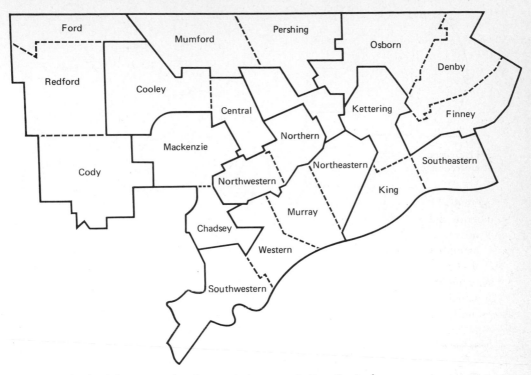

Figure 3. High school districts combined to maximize sympathetic authority.[2]

opposite of "community control" is the denial of political power to the community, and this is often accomplished by the device of "gerrymandering." "Gerrymandering" is the drawing of voting boundaries in such a fashion as to leave a group with little or no political power in spite of their numbers. Gerrymandering is geographic vote stealing.

2. The pattern of this plan is essentially the same as the one presented in the progress report, although there are several changes in the actual regional groupings. Late in the preparation of the progress report, the research team discovered inconsistencies in the data provided by the Northwest Council of Organizations. For this report, the data was recomputed correctly. The changes resulted in this slightly altered plan, which places 91.4 per cent of black children under sympathetic authority. More children could have been protected if the law did not stipulate such large regions.

The perfectly gerrymandered group is one with huge minorities in all voting districts, in theory many minorities of 49.999999999 per cent. The more voting districts of this nature the more votes the minority group has wasted. Votes are also wasted if they are near 100 per cent, so the group being gerrymandered is often given a few districts with 100 per cent votes especially in situations where the gerrymandering group cannot prevent a few regions from falling to the power of the group being gerrymandered. The gerrymandering group, on the other hand, strives to have nothing but tiny majorities, ideally 50.000000001 per cent, thus wasting not one of their votes. Notice how geographically reasonable gerrymandering can appear on the map. Both examples below of gerrymandering are in every respect legal. The voting districts in both cases are

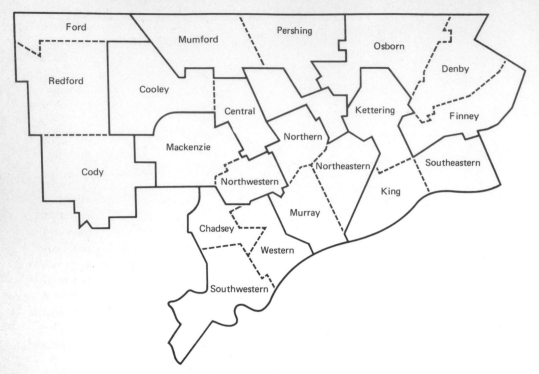

Figure 4. Maximum community control plan.

compact, contiguous, equal sized in area and equal sized in population. Yet both are severely gerrymandered. The case of Gerry-mandering by the Inner City leaves forty per cent of the people, the entire outer ring, without representation. The case of Gerry-mandering by the Outer City gives only one voting district to the Inner City and three to the Outer City in spite of the Inner City's clear majority. It leaves a total of thirty five per cent of the people, a doughnut shaped ring, without representation. To drive this

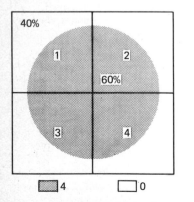

Figure 5. Gerrymandering by the inner city.

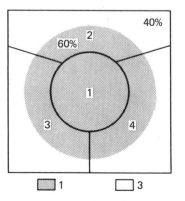

Gerrymandering by the outer city.

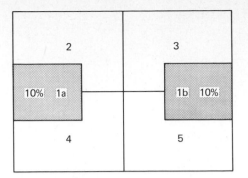

Figure 6. Region 1 is in two parts to prevent gerrymandering.

point home, it is theoretically possible that a discontiguous plan would be less gerry- mandered, though we are in no way advocat- ing such a possible illegality under existing law. The sketch below shows a case where a minority group is geographically split into two parts each representing ten per cent of the group's numbers. If the twenty per cent minority group is to have any representation under a five district plan it must be grouped discontiguously. No geographer in the world would advocate vastly discontiguous regions, but the point is made to center again on the true essence of gerrymandering and to cut through the confusion about "compact- ness," "contiguity," "equal size in area" and so forth. To repeat most forcefully, the geography of cheating voters, gerryman- dering, has only one goal and one clear meas- ure: the degree to which a group is deprived of power below its proportion of members in the total population.

The most extensively used device for achieving gerrymandering is to increase the size of the voting district just when a people is growing into a majority in a given voting district. In 1918, as black people coming up from the South were beginning to fill up eastside wards, Detroit switched to city-wide government with the power structure and its press campaigning for "governmental effi- ciency" and "modernization." The black

people of Detroit had to wait till 1957 before electing a black representative to the Common Council, a delay of thirty-nine years which made Detroit one of the last major American cities to elect a black city representative.[3] Now that the at-large voting in Detroit is about to go black, again there is much talk abroad of "efficiency," "regional planning," and a "Southeastern Michigan government" which would deny black people elected political power.

The argument that the rich suburbs added to the central city will be beneficial to the poor is deceptive. Normally in such partner- ships the poor lose political power to the affluent and do not gain economic advan- tage. Even wealth in geographic proximity to the poor is economically and politically remote to them. For instance, General Motors' headquarters on Grand Boulevard near Woodward is in the Northern High School District but what tangible advantage is gained by Northern?

The Decline of Urban Local Government

The result of centuries of gerrymandering by enlarging voter districts has left no local government in American cities. That is, the tens of millions of Americans who now have

3. "Race and Representation in Detroit and the Six County Metropolitan Region," Louis H. Masotti, John R. Krause, Jr., Sheldon R. Gawiser, Metropolitan Fund, Inc., Detroit, 1968.

Table 1. Predicted Per Cent of
Black Residences in Detroit

1970—45	1976—60
1971—48	1977—64
1972—50	1978 67
1973—52	1979—70
1974—54	1980—73
1975—57	

(Detroit Department of Health, 10/69).

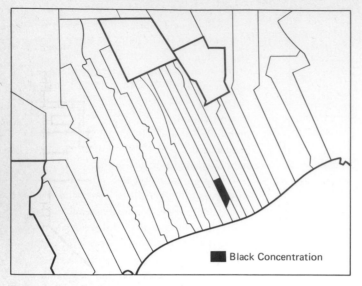

Black Concentration

Figure 7. Detroit election wards, 1915.

moved to or have been born in cities have been effectively disenfranchised out of local government representation. On the map of local governmental districts in Southern Michigan the cities show up as holes. For instance, there is no governmental unit in the cities called "townships."

The average population of townships in the State of Michigan is 2,349 people, about the same number of people as in city block clubs. In order for urban dwellers to enjoy local government comparable to that of the countryside, block clubs should be given governmental status comparable to townships. County sized units of political control have about the same number of people as suburbs on the city fringes. The city itself has no such governmental unit though "community councils" or "homeowners associations" or just plain "districts" have the right numbers of people for this natural political unit. The word "suburb" means "sub-urban," a breakdown of the huge metropolitan region into units of community control for the non-poor. The middle class "sub-urbs" in Detroit average

37,019 people, the affluent sub-urbs 11,090 people. Most sub-urbs have their own police departments, garbage collection systems, libraries, and other public services, and most pertinent to this discussion, their independent school systems. Black people will not have to move to the sub-urbs to get local government, if sub-urban units of local government are only allowed in the city. The average number of school children in the affluent sub-urban school system is 11,138. Since there are 280,000 school children in the Detroit public school system, in order for our city children to enjoy equal opportunity of local control, Detroit needs 25 school districts, the approximate size of each city high school region, not the seven to eleven regional districts for which provisions have been made. That is, to fight gerrymandering, the greater number of districts up to a high number, the better.

In schools, the human results of the lack of local control are tragic. Because neighborhoods cannot express their special characters in curriculum, the children feel like foreigners at school. The following table

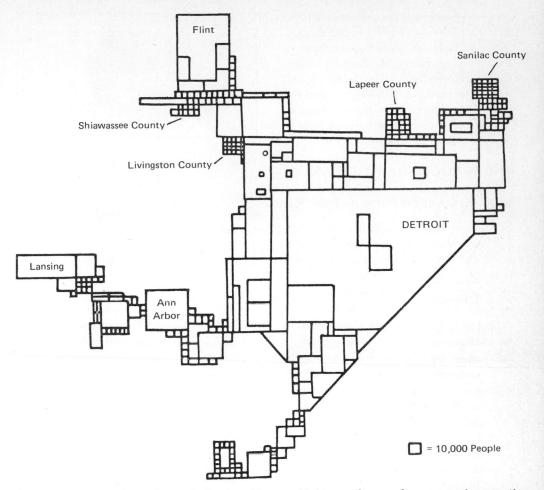

Figure 8. Cartogram of townships and cities in southeastern Michigan with areas of government in proportion to population.

Table 2

England	39
Poland	4
Italy	6
Hungary	0
Africa	7
Ireland	3
Scotland	4
Greece	0
Judaism	2

(Our Country, Eibling, King, Harlow)

indicates the number of references to various ethnic groups in a standard Detroit social studies text.

(Many less obvious groups are also left out. Only 3% of the people listed in the index were women. There were no references at all to Southern mountain culture, even though some areas of our city are heavily Appalachian.)

The first step toward expressing local cultures is to give local communities the power to set up their own curriculum. If the people of Southwest Detroit could determine the classes in Chadsey High School, they could add courses in Polish culture and start teaching students the language of their ancestors and relatives. The children could learn to be proud of themselves so that they could accept the other cultures of America calmly. But without neighborhood power, they are denied this chance.

THE SCHOOL BOARD'S PLAN

Major Error in the Pattern of the Plans

The Detroit Free Press, Sunday, December 7, 1969, released what it claimed to be the essence of the School Board's thinking. The Board's decentralization office March 3, 1970, released seven possible regional plans for public discussion. Although the plans vary greatly in actual regions, most of them are modifications of the pattern generalized below. The pattern puts unlike communities in the same region, fostering conflict. Such plans preclude local ethnic expression, local

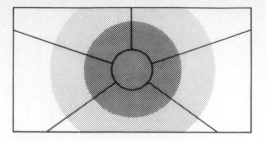

Figure 9. Generalized School Board conflict plan.

citizen participation, and local political control. Instead, the parents are divided and the children conquered.

Four of the eight published School Board Plans are illegal. Plans A, B, and B-2 use discontiguous regions, in violation of federal law. Plan F forms regions which fall below the 25,000-student minimum set by the state act. The following maps and table show the eight published plans and the percentage of black children who would fall under unsympathetic authority in each.

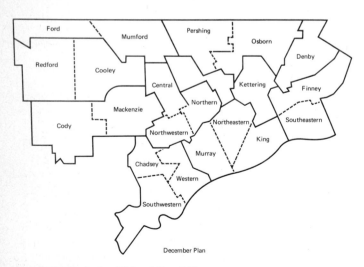

Figure 10. Analysis of School Board Plans.

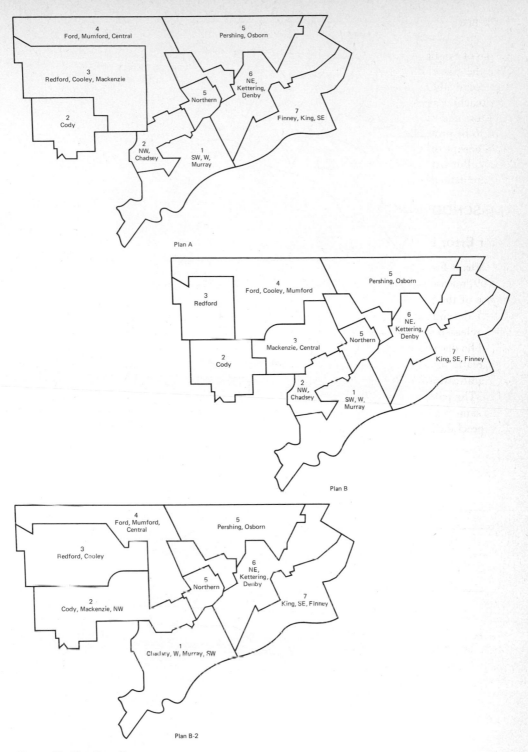

Figure 10. (Continued)

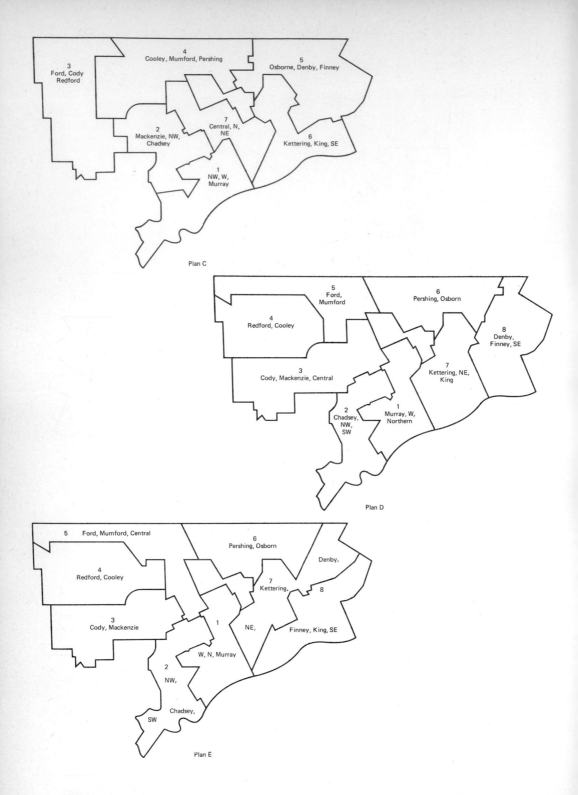

Plan C

3
Ford, Cody
Redford

4
Cooley, Mumford, Pershing

5
Osborne, Denby, Finney

2
Mackenzie, NW,
Chadsey

7
Central, N,
NE

6
Kettering, King, SE

1
NW, W,
Murray

Plan D

4
Redford, Cooley

5
Ford,
Mumford

6
Pershing, Osborn

8
Denby,
Finney, SE

3
Cody, Mackenzie, Central

7
Kettering, NE,
King

2
Chadsey,
NW,
SW

1
Murray, W,
Northern

Plan E

5   Ford, Mumford, Central

6
Pershing, Osborn

Denby,

4
Redford, Cooley

7
Kettering,

8

3
Cody, Mackenzie

1

NE,

Finney, King, SE

W, N, Murray

2

NW,

Chadsey,

SW

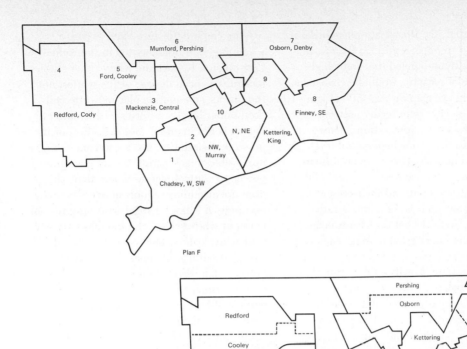

Figure 10. (Continued)

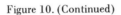

Table 3

Plan	Per Cent Black Students Under Unsympathetic Authority	No. Black-Controlled Regions	No. White-Controlled Regions
B	81	1	6
B-2	81	1	6
A	80	1	6
December	67	2	7
E	65	3	5
F	42	4	6
C	37	3	4
D	33	4	4

On April 7, the Board announced that it had chosen to implement Plan B-2. At the same time, it announced that some high school feeder patterns would be changed as indicated in the map on page 509 (Figure 10, Plan E). The change in feeder patterns supposedly "furthered integration." However, it affects only the senior high school level.[4] It also contradicts all previous School Board statements, which have stressed that children would continue to attend their present schools. It has no legal or administrative connection with the act of decentralization, although the Board tried to make such a connection by announcing the two decisions at the same time. Finally, it does not affect the power balance of the regional plan at all, since the changes were made within the proposed B-2 regions. Integration under such conditions is harmful to the children. The master and slave were geographically and physically integrated, but the master ruled. This is the type of integration the School Board proposes.

School Board public statements about their planning principles have undertones that it is protecting the white community from counter-gerrymandering by the black people. But "community control" is anti-gerrymandering, fair to all groups, it is not counter-gerrymandering. In addition, black attitudes toward white children are heavily integrationist relative to white toward black children, that is, "black authority" can not be equated with "white authority" in terms

of "unsympathetic authority." Overwhelmingly, as documented in the Kerner Commission Report and many other studies, racism is a social disease of the whites, not the blacks, so equating placing white children under black authority with counter-racism is not justified. But regardless of its possible desirability, black gerrymandering is impossible. Black people barely have enough power to control regions where their children are attending schools in overwhelming numbers. A school district with only fifteen per cent white school children has fifty per cent white voters. That is, in the crucial swing situations, the ones that determine power, each white child represents more than six times the voting power of each black child. In positions of such marginality even within their own communities, black community control can hardly afford to dilute itself at all to gerrymander control over white children. The reasons for large white voter registration relative to black are numerous and include an older white population, a white Catholic population who have no children in the black schools but have voter rights over them, and a tradition of racist law in the country making white racists feel more at home with all aspects of the governmental apparatus, including voting, than the oftentimes black victims feel with the apparatus.

Another mis-impression that some School Board statements have given is the confusion over the principle of "one-man, one vote." *Man* under the Constitution of the United States of America, does not mean a registered voter. *Man* means every human being including the newest born black infant. Representation in this country is supposed to be proportional to the total population. The placing of white voters in authority over black children under the principle of "one man, one vote" is incorrect.

---

4. It was especially hard to understand why the Board decided to re-mix two already-integrated districts, Pershing and Osborn (see map 2). Although Osborn High School is only 15% black now, the School Board's own prediction (map 3) is that within the next few years that percentage will continue to rise naturally through changing neighborhoods.

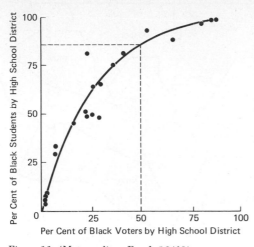

Figure 11. (Metropolitan Fund, 12/68)

The School Board Plans' Effects on Integration

If integration is defined as an attitude, "integrationist versus racist," the School Board plan places racists in the saddle of power. The truth of this assertion can be demonstrated. The key aspect of racist attitude relative to power is "Can a voter overcome his prejudices enough to vote for a man of the other race?" If voters in a given precinct vote half white and half black, they are one hundred per cent integrationists, or more sharply, if they totally vote for one race they are one hundred per cent racist. Using the primary election results of the 1969 Councilmanic race, which allows considerable extremes to register at the polls, analysis of those who voted for the top and bottom major white candidates (Ravitz and Wiezbicki) and the top and bottom major black candidates (Hood and Brown) identify patterns within the city as to degree of racist voting attitudes. Extreme voter racism exists in the totally white areas of the city, the west, northeast and southwest. (Map 1.) It is precisely these racist voters that the School Board plan places in control of integrationist

children in such examples as a Denby controlling a Kettering. Indeed, only the principle of community control allows areas like Cody to maintain their right to vote. If the School Board were consistent with its avowed principles of integration, Cody should have a regional district board totally elected by voters imposed from integrationist regions such as Northern.

The second definition of integration is not that of attitude, but rather of geographic proximity. The school board, again in the name of integration, puts geographically different regions together and arrives at a stastical integration on paper. True integration, in the sense of "geographic proximity," geographers the world over agree, means that the two races are geographically intermingled. Consider the logic of example illustrations. Case 1 is obviously one of integration. Case 2 is an example of segregation and Case 3 a mixed example of two segregated regions with a zone of integration in between. Case 3 typifies reality on Detroit's west side. The grain of the Detroit west side pattern obviously runs north and south, but the School Board pattern runs across this natural grain. The School Board plan destroys the integrated pattern and subordinates it to the racist pattern.

The only way to make the reality of the three cases appear in the statistics, a reality that is so apparent to the naked eye, is to make statistics drawn from small regions. If a huge enough region is statistically lumped together, the Planet Earth itself can be statistically "proven" to have achieved integrated brotherhood for all mankind. Even Case 2, the segregated example, comes out statistically, fifty-fifty if considered as a false whole. On the real-life earth's surface in Detroit, a high school district is the best unit to reflect this natural integration. If a high school has a fifty-fifty racial ratio, it is in fact, as well as in statistic, one hundred per

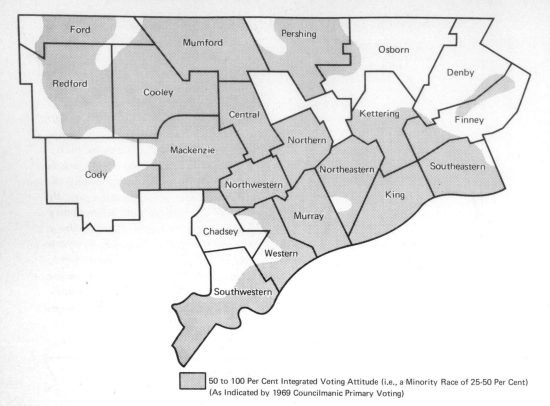

50 to 100 Per Cent Integrated Voting Attitude (i.e., a Minority Race of 25-50 Per Cent)
(As Indicated by 1969 Councilmanic Primary Voting)

Figure 12. Integration by attitude.

cent integrated. The picture of such integration in Detroit is shown on Map 2. Only community control can place these schools under integrationist authority.

Since Americans are such mobile people perhaps the geographic permanence of areas of integration is not as important as the adequate availability of integration in the general region. The metropolitan region of Detroit is growing at approximately two

yards a day. If the total urbanized city size doubles, so should the black and integrated areas. This geographic phenomenon is not the result of a pushy people aggressively invading other peoples' neighborhoods, it is simply natural proportional growth. Further, the cause of white flight from integrated areas is not necessarily simply racism. "Integration" to white too often means bad schools; and young liberal white families, the ones most likely to want to integrate, will

```
x O x O x O        x x x O O O        x x O x O O
O x O x O x        x x x O O O        x x x O O O
x O x O x O        x x x O O O        x x O x O O

  Case 1            Case 2             Case 3
Perfect Integration  Perfect Segregation  Partial Segregation
                                        and Integration
```

Figure 13.

```
x x | O x | O O
x x | x O | O O
x x | O x | O O

Community Control Districts
```

```
x x O x | O O
x x x O | O O
x x O x | O O

School Board Districts
```

Figure 14.

not do so at the expense of their children's education. The low quality of education, especially the predictable tremendous overcrowding that accompanies expanding black neighborhoods, is precisely the overwhelming factor that drives out young liberal white couples from integrated areas. The condition of the schools themselves are the most active instrument of segregation in the city today in spite of an officially proclaimed policy of integration. In neighborhoods with good schools such as the Lafayette Tower area and north of the University of Detroit, integration is showing signs of geographic stability. But such integration is only available to the highest paid black families and the middle or higher paid white ones. Modestly financed people of either race cannot buy such permanent integration assuming they so desire. Still, families of average income are achieving a mechanical integration in the northwest portion of Detroit because of the surplus housing for black people. Contrary to seeming dominant white impressions, there is not an infinite supply of black people. If the Greater Detroit Metropolitan Region were geographically integrated only less than one house in every five would contain a black family. With areas of real estate open to black families in northwest Detroit, the supply of solid housing for black people is exceeding the demand and integration has a possibility of becoming geographically fixed. As the former knife edge blurs, as can be seen again especially in northwest Detroit, rather stable geographic integration is a massive possibility. It is this sort of natural integrated community that the School Board plan injures.

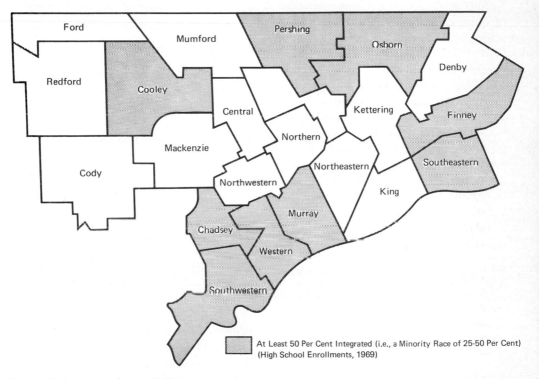

Figure 15. Integration by proximity.

Integration can be defined a third way as simply a "changing neighborhood." If integration is viewed as the time between "the first black family moving in and the last white one moving out," then the School Board plan must be considered racist in effect because breaking up these zones of change will leave black children under white control many years after the community has become black. Again, the grain of the School Board plan runs athwart the grain of coming change. To be responsive to black change, the community control plan is again clearly fair. The School Board statistician, Merle Hendrickson, has devised an accurate method of predicting racial change. It is based on the fact that neighborhoods tend to form new subdivisions with newly wed couples and about forty years afterwards the couples begin to retire and collectively sell their homes. This creates a vacuum in housing demands, and a second generation of young couples enter. The second generation in Detroit has recently always been black. Using Hendrickson's material (Map 3), clearly Osborn and Denby in the northeast side should be kept as a grouping since the slow grinding wheels of economic real estate is, regardless of the subjective attitudes of the present white residents, about to tip the whole region integrationist.[5] Thus the School Board planning violates integration defined as change and the community control plan does not.

---

5. Urban renewal of the "negro removal" sort as accorded at the Chrysler School in earlier decades was based on removing extremely poor black families and building luxury apartments on the site of their former homes and completely reversing racial balances. This luxury apartment planning has become too difficult politically so that much more modestly priced dwellings are now being constructed on urban renewal projects that keep the racial balances about the same as today, i.e., whites are no longer pouring in behind the black community downtown.

The School Board's Machinery for Making Decisions

When the Board established the Office of School Decentralization, it "encouraged" community participation in planning the new regions. More recent OSD actions, however, have caused citizens trying to participate to wonder whether this attitude was a sham. The OSD's primary ground rule for drawing regions was that high school boundaries should not be changed. The Office itself has broken this rule twice, both in the seven proposed plans and in the final plan. How can community groups participate when the ground rules change constantly? If the Board were really interested in principles other than its own, why did it never ask to see the massive computer print-out of all possible plans, or any of the research which went into this report. On a professional basis, this conduct is peculiar to say the least.

The School Board has the added advantage of controlling its own data, data that has a semi-legal status. For instance, in preparing a community decentralization school plan, the School Board can determine for itself what the legal capacities of the schools are. In 1960, Fitzgerald School was a white school and was given a listed capacity of 1,472 students. Tremendous overcrowding (the broom closet is now the violin room) produced a statistical expansion of the main building to a listed capacity of 1,760 students without the addition of a single brick of physical expansion. The School Board data control has already produced a heavily illegal school system throughout the black city of Detroit. For instance, fire regulations are normally based on the number of humans per square foot, but not in the schools. Firedoors are illegally locked, making a tragedy an increased probability, though school records indicate "safe."

In addition, the School Board itself is a

privileged group, protected from the reality of the average school and prone to have distorted images of the school system. All the School Board members live in high-income areas. (See map below.) Two of them have sent their children to private schools.

Their local schools are also privileged. Hampton Elementary School, where three of the seven Board members live, houses its children in a five year old building. At the same time, the children in the adjacent district of Fitzgerald (where no Board members live) attend classes in a building constructed between 1926 and 1930. Fitzgerald children pour out of school directly onto busy Puritan, while most Hampton children never have to cross a major street to get home. Fitzgerald's playground is strewn with broken glass; Hampton's holds a total of fourteen pieces. All of these disparities are

symptoms of a situation in which one group (Hampton) has power and another does not. It is no wonder that one Hampton PTA member opposes decentralization on the grounds that it will limit the power of her local school. She lives in a region which is already so powerful that it feels threatened by the regional power the rest of the city craves. Since the School Board members all see the system from such regions, it is no wonder that they are not realistic about their decisions.

Finally, the School Board itself stands to lose power from decentralization. Many of the problems of the Detroit school system are based on the fact that it is too large to function efficiently. In the affluent suburbs, where school systems are allowed to assume their naturally efficient size, each one serves approximately 11,000 students. In other

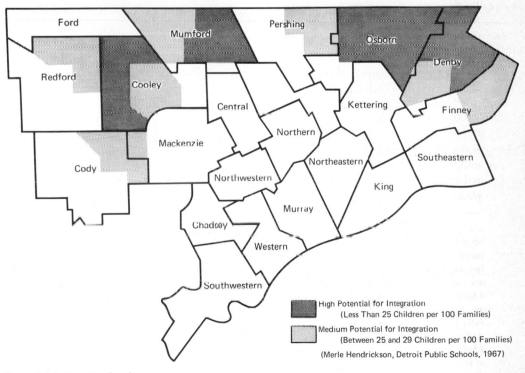

High Potential for Integration
(Less Than 25 Children per 100 Families)

Medium Potential for Integration
(Between 25 and 29 Children per 100 Families)

(Merle Hendrickson, Detroit Public Schools, 1967)

Figure 16. Integration by change.

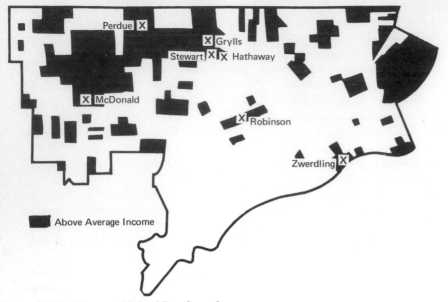

Figure 17. Residences of School Board members.

words, bigger is not always better. Most of the functions now unnaturally concentrated at the Schools Center Building could be operated at much less cost to the entire system if they were distributed regionally. As community participation increased, the value of services volunteered would also begin to lower overall costs, in addition to falling costs of antagonism (vandalism, etc.). The money saved could be invested in education instead of unnecessary administration. However, the central school board which runs the inefficient, overgrown bureaucracy has been given the power to decide whether this will happen. In such a position, it is understandable that the Board would fight for its life. No bureaucracy in the world has ever dismantled itself voluntarily. The situation is like asking a patient to take out his own appendix.

Such factors do not induce confidence in the School Board's ability to judge the question of decentralization fairly. At such a moment of crisis, only parents can be trusted to make a decision which will be good for the children. The School Board

Table 4

	Hampton	Fitzgerald
Age of Building	5 Years	40 Years
Glass on Playground	1 Pound	364 Pounds
Iowa Test Scores:	6 Months Ahead	6 Months Behind
Fourth Grade	of National Average	National Average
Traffic Accidents	None in 1969	4 in 1969
Near School		
Overcrowding	No Temporary Classrooms Necessary	11 Temporary Classrooms Necessary

plan is so technically inept that the temptation to charge cynical manipulation of a good bill badly implemented is overruled by a second possibility, just plain incompetence in the technical advice being received. The time has come for parents and competent technical help from the community to sit down and reason together with the School Board and its technicians. Only this effort may save the children from further injury.

APPENDIX I

Computer Evaluation of All Decentralization Possibilities

DR. JOHN W. SHEPHERD and DR. M. A. JENKINS

The computer analysis of the decentralization proposal was carried out in two stages, using the practical advantage of each of two different programming languages. With an APL/360 time-sharing system operated by the user with a keyboard we were able to heuristically determine a cross-section of solutions, each of them giving different political control over a decentralization scheme. Switching to the ALGOL language on the IBM 360/50 at Queen's University in Kingston, Ontario, but using the results obtained under the initial study, we were able to generate all the legal solutions and to sample a number of the pertinent ones.

The same simple approach was used to generate the amalgamation plans in the two stages. First, the set of new regions, given the constraints of (1) contiguity, (2) enrolled population of 25,000 to 50,000 students and (3) non-isolation of an illegal group,[1] is found from the twenty-one original districts. There are just over 160 possible combinations into new regions on this basis. To perform this operation is a relatively simple task using a connectivity matrix and the enrollment figures of each district.

However, to do the job efficiently, i. e. without duplication of regions, is a complex problem in graph theory. It involves the breakdown of the original set of all groups into strategic sub-groups and ordering the identification of each region in such a way that any new region is seen once and only once by the computer. This problem has not yet been solved in this instance.

Fitting the regions which were discovered together and relocating them back on the map of Detroit without over-lapping was done initially in a gerrymandering fashion. That is, we produced one set of plans with white political control dominant and the other with Black control dominant. An attempt was made to find a number of integrated solutions. Thus, in the first set of regions we grouped all the heavily black voting school districts together, thus "wasting" a large number of fair votes in "over-kill." We let the white dominated districts be grouped with the "mixed" areas in various combinations. This process forced a range of solutions from mildly white dominated plans to extremely white dominated ones.

From this analysis it was possible to obtain an idea of the proportionate dominance

---

1. An example of isolating an illegal group occurs when the computer joins Western, Chadsey and Northwestern, forming a legal region, but leaving Southwestern isolated. Since Southwestern does not include 25,000 students, it cannot be its own region legally, and we have isolated an illegal group.

for a variety of criteria in sampling the exhaustive part of the study. From an essentially similar computing algorithm, but this time using ALGOL language, no less than 7,367 maps satisfying the initial constraints were found. Of these, those that contained at least one of the following criteria were sampled.

Table for criteria:

Table I.1

Black Students under Black control — 90 per cent
White students under White control — 96 per cent
All students under Black control — 70 per cent
All students under White control — 78 per cent
All students under homogeneous control — 80 per cent[2]
All students under heterogeneous control — 44 per cent[3]

Table I.3

No. of Districts	Black	White
6	3	3
7	5	2
8	6	2
9	6	3

The results of the study were analyzed on two levels—that of the total number of districts and the political control of each. These were the important factors in the composition of the first central school board for the decentralization system.
From this analysis, it is possible to see that other things being equal, the eight district

2. Homogeneity is defined as the percentage of black under black control plus white per cent under white control, that is, a measure of fairness in the community control sense of the word.
3. Heterogeneity is defined as the percentage of black students under white control and white students under black control, a measure of integrated political control of districts and not of the composition of the individual schools.

Table I.2 Black Controlled

No. of Districts	1	2	3	4	5	6
6	4	14	1	0	0	0
7	94	824	1665	513	24	0
8	0	448	1879	1474	269	28
9	0	0	41	45	38	6

solution gives a majority of four black members on the metropolitan schoolboard, whereas a seven or nine district one gives a minority of only three blacks on the schoolboard. From Table I. 2, it is clear that there are twenty-eight sub-solutions to choose from in the eight district scheme, twenty-four in the seven district one, but only six in the nine district plan.

However, this result had to be reassessed in the light of the control over students in this system of individual new districts. The range of results is contained in the following table.

In Table I. 4, note that simply from the distribution of solutions, it is much easier to keep white children under white control (high white-under-white per cent) than it is to protect black children from white racists (high black-under-black per cent). At most the black community can protect only 91.4 per cent of its children, whereas the white community can retain control of 99.9 per cent of theirs. At worst, the white community can lose control over only 45 per cent of the white school children, although the black students can fall 75 per cent under

Table I.4

Community Control	Per Cent Category									
	0–10	10–20	20–30	30–40	40–50	50–60	60–70	70–80	80–90	90–100
BB	0	34	91	571	1254	2752	1762	209	162	32
WW	0	0	0	0	0	20	448	2478	2630	1791
AB	7	102	824	2199	2635	1340	228	32	0	0
AW	0	0	32	228	1322	2609	2227	840	102	0
HOM	0	0	0	0	56	766	4671	1842	42	0
HET	0	42	1827	4607	845	56	0	0	0	0

BB – per cent black children under "black" authority
WW – per cent white children under "white" authority
AB – per cent all students under "black" authority
AW – per cent all students under "white" authority
HOM – per cent all students under same-race authority
HET – per cent all students under opposite-race authority

white control. Also, it is much easier to gerrymander for white voters (high all-under-white per cent) than for black ones (high all-under-black per cent).

The homogeneous and heterogeneous lines complement each other. Plans which put a high number of black children under black control are also generally high on the "homogeneous" or "neighborhood power" line. Plans which place large percent-

Table I.5   Comparison of All Plans Submitted

	a	b	c	d	e	f	g	h*	i*
1.	80.0	71.2	71.2	64.1	61.8	59.5	58.6	39.4	31.4
2.	20.0	28.8	28.8	35.9	38.2	40.5	41.4	60.6	68.6
3.	20.5	15.1	15.1	14.4	19.5	22.7	10.0	4.2	20.8
4.	79.5	84.9	84.9	85.6	80.5	77.3	90.0	95.8	79.2

* High School Boundaries Altered

1. Percentage of black children under black control
2. Percentage of black children under white control
3. Percentage of white children under black control
4. Percentage of white children under white control

a. Northwest Community Organization
b. Action Committee For Education
c. Detroit Council of Organizations
d. Edison School Parents Club
e. Ad-Hoc Committee for Community Control of Schools
f. Promotion Study Success, Inc.
g. Berkowitz Plan
h. Detroit Board of Education
i. First District Democratic-Education Committee

ages of students under white control place low on the same line.

This chart, and the mountains of computer work it capsulizes, can be very valuable to the people of Detroit. Having an evaluation of every possible solution to the problem is a very valuable tool. Simply knowing how good or bad the final plan can possibly be (the range of percentages here) is a definite advantage in realistic discussions. We hope that the city will utilize the research presented here to its fullest scientific extent.

Table I.6   High School Student Capacities Located by Grade Schools

High School	Capacity	Grade School	No.
Chadsey	2006	Hanneman	62
Southwestern	1930	Beard	57
Western	1950	Maybury	54
Cody	3248	Everett	102
Northwestern	2840	Woodward	38
Mackenzie	2820	Barton	75
Redford	2710	Burt	112
Central	2350	Roosevelt	42
Cooley	2460	Burns	82
Ford	2550	Pitcher	118
Mumford	2600	Schulze	25
Pershing	2600	Atkinson	167
Northern	2230	Algar	132
Osborn	2630	Fleming	173
Denby	2480	Carleton	181
Finney	2160	Marquette	191
Southeastern	2310	Lillibridge	196
King	1910	Duffield	139
Kettering	2730	Cooper	156
Murray	2640	Edmonson	4
Northeastern	1620	Campbell 137	137

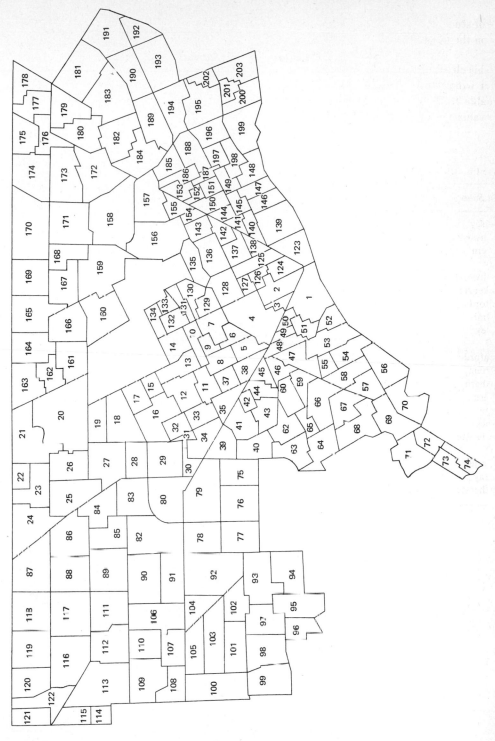

Figure I.1. Grade Schools

Table I.7

		Black Students	White Students	Austin Voters	Beck-Gribbs Voters
1.	Franklin	495	1006	152	575
2.	Burton	240	721	377	896
3.	Couzens	1234	13	598	282
4.	Edmonson	2467	674	1305	628
5.	Estabrook	788	0	598	103
6.	Goldberg	1536	48	629	63
7.	Fairbanks	869	86	616	468
8.	Thirkell	1750	0	1543	133
9.	Sanders	1362	0	940	72
10.	Crosman	2013	0	1191	133
11.	Brady	1870	0	2097	138
12.	Roosevelt	2392	0	3160	164
13.	Peck	1694	0	956	72
14.	Doty	1415	14	1804	289
15.	Longfellow	1112	11	862	36
16.	McCulloch	2628	10	3349	237
17.	Glazier	1238	0	1005	63
18.	Custer	2970	12	2371	230
19.	Hally	1372	14	1643	317
20.	Hampton	541	661	1155	2070
21.	Pasteur	37	1823	1665	952
22.	Higginbotham	837	0	931	30
23.	McDowell	1839	38	1466	407
24.	Vernor	1885	109	1773	798
25.	Schulze	1997	61	1368	943
26.	Bagley	2329	97	2267	550
27.	Fitzgerald	3941	80	2199	839
28.	Clinton	2443	156	1000	263
29.	Courtis	2737	85	1656	359
30.	Noble	1117	47	525	133
31.	Winterhalter	554	6	982	63
32.	Birney	1042	0	979	46
33.	Keidan	3016	0	1339	78
34.	McKerrow	2355	48	1173	145
35.	Angell	2176	0	1941	105
37.	Jamieson	2165	0	1891	32
38.	Woodward	1259	13	953	153
39.	Ruthruff	1710	14	834	164
40.	Sherrill	1251	1011	1506	149
41.	Pattengill	2278	0	2104	121
42.	Biddle	730	0	313	11
43.	Sampson	1382	0	1795	96
44.	Wingert	1090	0	1103	65
45.	McGraw	642	6	663	53
46.	Columbian	1613	0	994	66
47.	Craft	1086	111	589	187
48.	Chaney	849	50	301	48
49.	Kennedy (and Kennedy Annex)	1169	584	146	102

APPENDIX II

Atlas

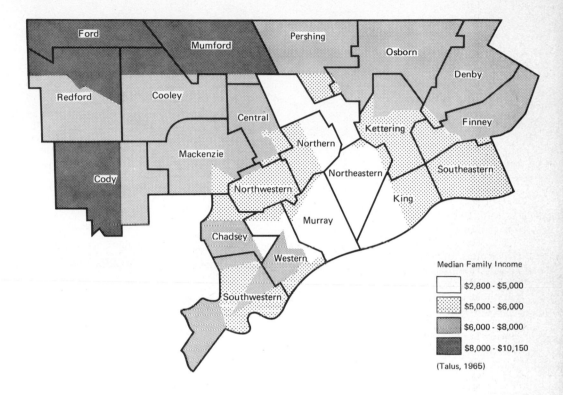

Figure II.1. Median Family Income

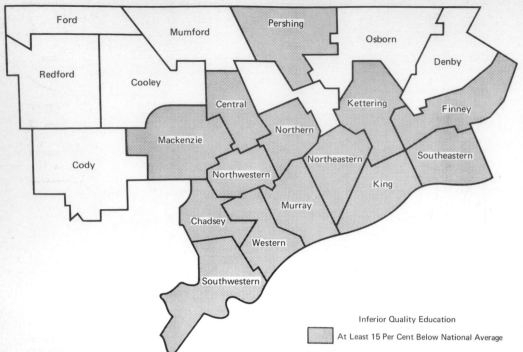

Inferior Quality Education

At Least 15 Per Cent Below National Average

(Achievement Test Scores of Pupils, Detroit Public Schools, 1969, p. 8)

Figure II.2. Inferior Quality Education

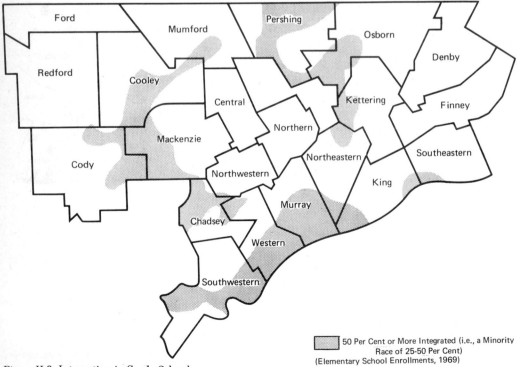

50 Per Cent or More Integrated (i.e., a Minority Race of 25-50 Per Cent)
(Elementary School Enrollments, 1969)

Figure II.3. Integration in Grade Schools

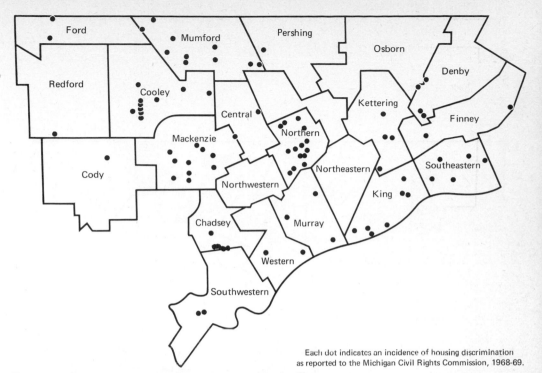

Figure II.4. Racial Tension

Each dot indicates an incidence of housing discrimination
as reported to the Michigan Civil Rights Commission, 1968-69.

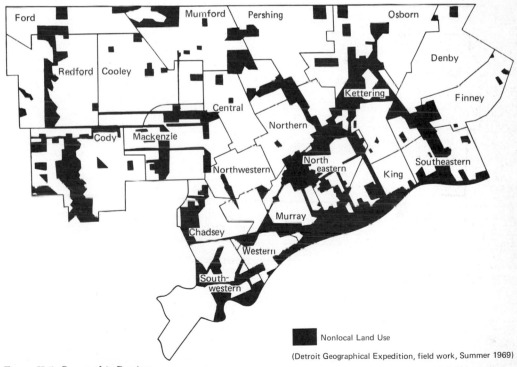

Nonlocal Land Use

(Detroit Geographical Expedition, field work, Summer 1969)

Figure II.5. Geographic Barriers

525

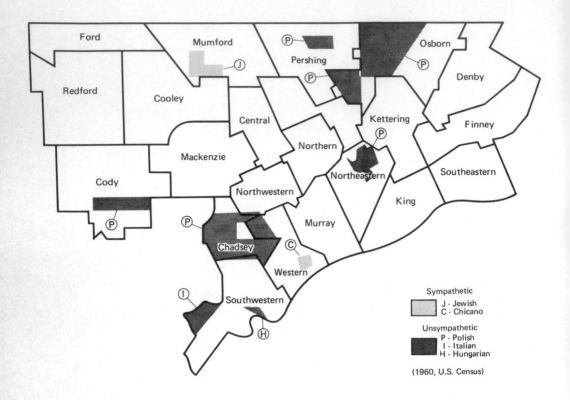

Figure II.6. Sympathetic and Unsympathetic
Ethnic Groups

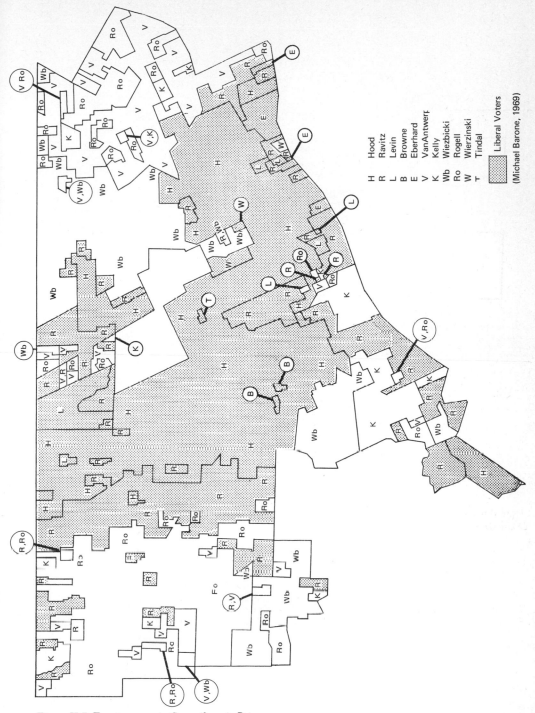

Figure II.7. Frontrunners in Councilmanic Primary

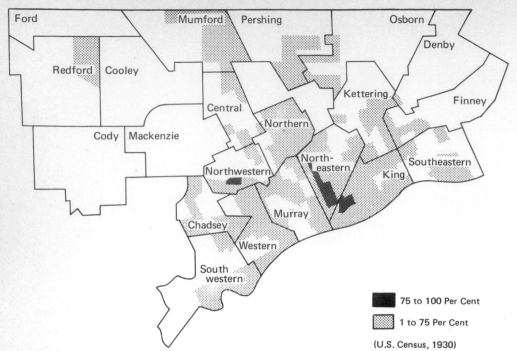

Figure II.8. Black Population, 1930

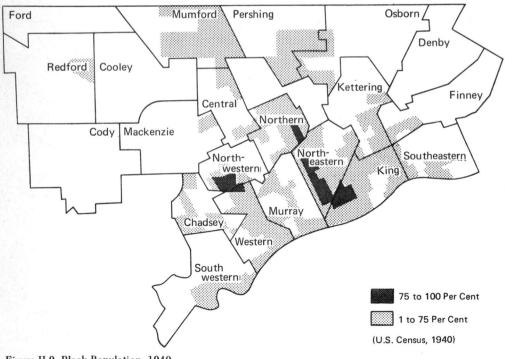

Figure II.9. Black Population, 1940

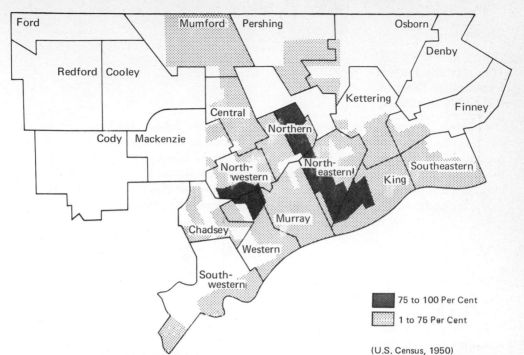

Figure II.10. Black Population, 1950

75 to 100 Per Cent

1 to 75 Per Cent

(U.S. Census, 1950)

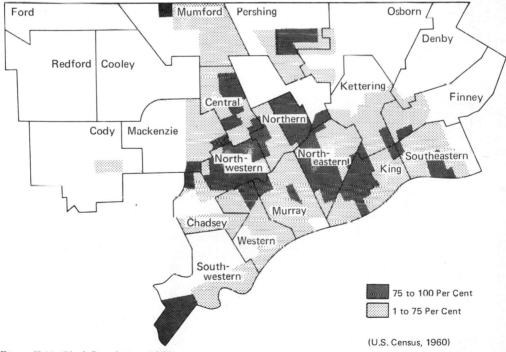

Figure II.11. Black Population, 1960

75 to 100 Per Cent

1 to 75 Per Cent

(U.S. Census, 1960)

529

APPENDIX III

Theoretically Perfect Community Control and Gerrymandering

The following diagrams analyze possible divisions of a hypothetical city in which the population is divided evenly (50-50) into two interest groups. Both segregated and integrated distributions of the interest groups are analyzed.

When the School Board plan and the plans presented in this report are graphed, the School Board pattern most closely resembles pattern Figure III.1. The child sympathy and community control plan most closely resemble Figure III.2.

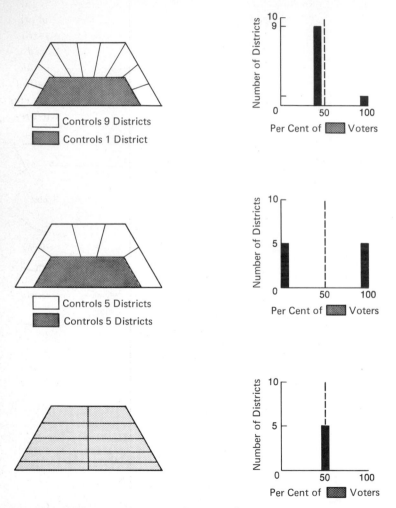

Figure III.1. Gerrymandered division of segregated area.

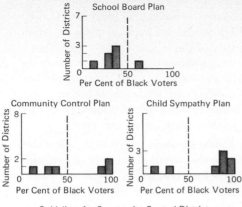

Guidelines for Community Control Districts

Figure III.2. Democratic division of segregated area.

1. It is necessary but not sufficient for perfect community control that the boundaries of the voting districts coincide with the boundaries of the community.

2. It is necessary but not sufficient for perfect community control that the proportionality of the communities be reflected in the proportion of voting districts. In terms of applied mathematics, this means a great number of voting districts.

POSTSCRIPT

Both parents and students reacted vehemently against the School Board's "integration" plan. Violence broke out in Osborn and Cooley High Schools, in addition to a walkout in the Kettering area and several other demonstrations. Opposition was so strong among parents that four School Board members were recalled in a general vote August 4. The city is now in preparation for the November elections, in which the empty Board seats will be filled and the first re-

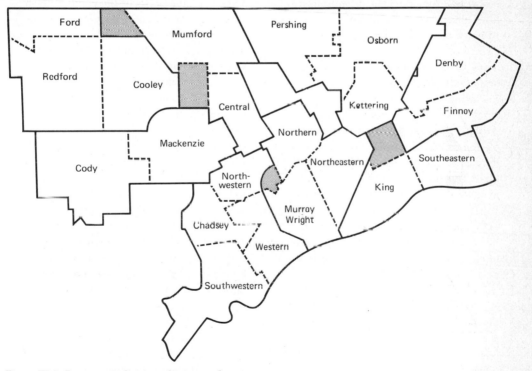

Figure III.3. Democratic division of integrated area.

gional boards elected. A dominately black organization closely associated with Mr. John Watson is using this report as the basis of its campaign strategy.

The original decentralization bill has been replaced by a new one which stipulates that the final regional plan must have eight compact, contiguous regions which are as nearly equal in population as possible. (It removes the restraints on the number of students in each region.) The three man boundary commission, appointed by Governor Milliken under this new law, released the plan below August 4. One of the most striking aspects of this new plan is that in several areas children attend schools in one district while their parents vote for officials in another. These areas are shaded on the map.

Science must rupture with law if law becomes unreal in ways such as making it illegal to assert that the earth is round, as law at one time did. The decentralization law violates the needs of children. The ratio of black to white children in the schools is two to one, but the law puts white adults in a one to one position of power. Further, the law of equal adult population results in "taxation without representation," that is tyranny, since many voters do not have voting authority over their own children. Such gerrymandering is without precedent in human geographic history! What next? Will black Detroit be allowed to vote in elections in Biafra but not in Michigan? Further, both white racism and "black pride" are strongest in "changing neighborhoods." A high school like Cooley, with 75 per cent black students likely this fall, is not only welded to a white racist hinterland which will keep the authority over the children white for decades, but it is also a high school district in which the black parents have been disenfranchised and forced to vote in a different district than the one where their children attend school. While scientists are more certain of predict-

ing eclipses of the moon than human explosions, it is certainly likely that Cooley High School will explode under the irrationality of this injustice. The pattern that emerges shows that every place where the black community is expanding it will be punished with white school boards, evidently to make sure that black people stay "in their place" in the ghetto.

Still, science is forced to be reasonable. Given that the present law is an unnatural law, a false law, what is the closest point to meeting its requirements that can be found without losing contact with the world of reality? There is no such thing as "Children Power" precisely because children are so powerless. If "only the strong" survived, all adults would have died in infancy. It is precisely the powerlessness of children that commands our concern for them. They are biologically the weakest link with life. Therefore, the needs of the children must come first, or the species (at least subsections of it) perishes. Since there are twice as many black children in the school system as white children, they must have twice the amount of sympathetic authority as white children. This means that six out of nine regions should be under black control. Since the law reads that there are to be only eight regions, the ratio must be five black to three white, even though it cheats the black child. Also, since it is classic tyranny (and might well be illegal) to have students attending a school over which their parents have no authority, existing high school boundaries are used as voting districts. Given these two restraints (three to five power and existing boundaries), the computers were set in motion still another time to keep pace with the twists and turns of the rules of the games as the power structure changes them. Within these restraints, the computer searched for the most equal total population defined as the least difference between the largest and

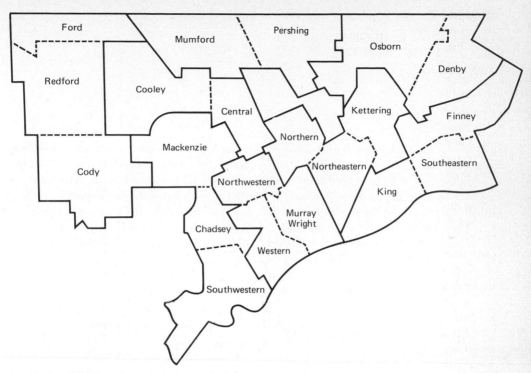

Figure III.4. Guidelines for community control districts.

smallest districts. The plan below is the best one possible, within the state law, and without straining the law of reality.

We are convinced that this plan, with only a 10 per cent deviation in population, with the voters ungerrymandered and the children protected, is more legal than the governor's plan, under both rational and human law. We urge that this opinion be tested in court by our fellow professionals in the bar association.

As scientists, we are confident that the school regions must follow the pattern presented in this report or face serious conflict as an everyday occurence. People will never cease to struggle for power over a matter so vital to them as the education of their young until they have won it.

++++++++++++++++++++++++++++++

TOPOPHILIA: PERSONAL ENCOUNTERS WITH THE LANDSCAPE

Yi-Fu Tuan

De Quincey has a story to tell of Wordsworth. One night, as happened often enough, the two of them walked from Grasmere to meet the carrier who usually brought them news of the war on the continent. They waited in vain by the roadside for over an hour. No sound came up through the winding road. At intervals, Wordsworth would stretch himself on the road and press his ear to the ground in the hope of catching the sound of grinding wheels in the distance. Once, when he was slowly rising from his effort, his eyes as he later told De Quincey caught a bright star that was glittering between the brow of Seat Sandal and the mighty Helvellyn.

The image was certainly not planned by Wordsworth. He had no time for it. The star above Helvellyn took him by surprise. Such brushes with beauty are not limited to poets and painters of landscape. They occur also with relatively earth-bound people like geographers, geologists, naturalists and farmers; people who lead a fair portion of their working hours out-of-doors. The geologist, for instance, may have clung precariously to an outcrop of the Chinle sandstone in order to measure its dip. That work—that act of concentration—done, he turns around, relaxes, and perhaps in that momentary shedding of the will—experiences the beauty of what A. N. Whitehead calls nature *in solido*. The town planner may have walked up and down Manhattan's Fifth Avenue, counting and mapping news stands and shoe stores. The work finished, it may be that he too relaxes his will and so catches for the first time that day the full impact of Fifth Avenue. His whole self, not just his mind, registers the urban scene. The color of the buildings, the traffic noises, the heat of the pavement burning through the soles of his shoes, the symphony of odors from the succession of coffee houses, shoe shops and air-conditioned department stores, together move in upon him as a coherent piece of reality.

Such encounters ought to be fairly common with people whose work takes them out-of-doors. But the evidence for it in writing is surprisingly meager. A geographer's book on the American Southwest may contain useful chapters on plant life, the motion picture industry, and even politics, but of the concrete landscape as registered by a sentient being, who has lived in it, there is little or nothing. In his publications the modern geologist likewise hides his deeper conversations with the earth; these he saves for his letters home. By way of contrast, we remember the pioneer geologists of the American West, people like Powell, Dutton and Gilbert. The prose of these men, lucid and usually unadorned, yet reveals a curious flavor of wonder and of genuine attachment to the things they study. Perhaps to modern eyes the color of their writing is here and there a touch too rich. Dutton at one place

From *Landscape*, Vol. XI, No. 1, Autumn 1961. Reprinted by permission.

characterized the vista above the Grand Canyon—with what ringing magnificence—as "cliff rising above and beyond cliff, like a colossal stairway leading from the torrid plains below to the domain of the clouds above." Even in the interest of academic stolidity we can hardly prefer a modern translation of it.

The geologist, with his more limited aims of understanding the earth, can better afford to curb his esthetic sensibility and means of expressing it than the geographer. For unlike the geologist, part of the geographer's job is to portray all aspects of those scenes (landscapes or regions) for which he has a special fondness. After all, most of us must have first felt the romance of our subject through some real encounter with the color, odor—the mood—of a place. It need not be the overpowering mood of the Himalayas; it may be the quiet mood of the hop fields of Kent, or even that of our own backyard; it may be the *gemütlich* air of southern Germany, with its dark forests and solid homes, which marks it off from the bright, denuded, Cézanne landscapes of southern France. So we are inspired to learn and write of its geography; yet how seldom our work reflects an understanding informed by attentive interest—more often perhaps a compilation that does credit to our will and industry. If nothing of the *Gemütlichkeit* comes out of our monograph on southern Germany, we ought at least not dodge the issue by declaring it nonexistent, merely something in the mind. For to do so would be to deny our experience; it is also to hide our literary shortcomings under a treacherous figure of speech—"in the mind"—and imply without justification the achievement of objectivity.

Topophilia or love of nature may prompt us to day dream over atlases, apply for Ford grants to Togoland, and to sweat over there. Our published works too often deny, intentionally or unintentionally, this enthusiasm. French geographers seem less inhibited, or fare better at expressing their communion with the land. Even the titles of some of their works appear indiscreet on the shelves of our professional literature: *La Personalité de la France, Géographie Poétique de Cinq Continents* and even *Géographie Humoristique de Paris.*

Here I should like to introduce the French writer Gaston Bachelard. He is not a geographer. He is a physicist whose attention has turned from the measurable properties of matter to those which cannot be registered by instruments other than that ultimate instrument—man. These immeasurables may haunt us like the "brooding presence of the hills," or they may infuse joy and peace by their beauty and *Istigkeit.* Bachelard has written several books on this theme. Some of them, *La Terre et les Rêveries de la Volonté,* for example, are more concerned with mapping the psychologic states of man provoked by matter than with describing properties of matter as sensed by man. There is no antithesis here but rather a difference of emphasis; although this difference, if pressed far enough, will lead to the contrary positions materialism and idealism.

Of Bachelard's books, the one I find particularly relevant to our theme is his latest: *La Poétique de l'Espace.* In it he tries to describe the images and pleasant reveries that are prompted by certain types of space, especially the enclosed space—the home. "A truly lived in home," he writes, "contains images that provide us with reasons or illusions of stability. Memory does not register concete duration—time with a certain thickness. We cannot relive abolished time. We can only think about it abstractly. It is in space that we find duration beautifully preserved and made real through long abode." Or, "The house has power to integrate our thoughts, dreams, and memories. . . . For man the house evicts contingencies and multiplies its counsels of continuity. Without it man would be a dispersed being."

In another book, *L'Eau et les Rêves*, Bachelard describes the images of water. In our contacts with nature, it does not seem that we are doing all the talking and seeing. This activity is certainly not all ours in the sense that we deliberately planned it. The feeling that mountains and lakes see, speak, and convey is at times a strong one. Viewed as the "eye" of the earth, the lake especially appears to return the human glance. (Here, I may perhaps insert an anecdote of Oscar Wilde's: Narcissus died. The lake and the flowers wept. When the flowers asked the lake whether it wept because it too missed the beauty of Narcissus, the lake replied: "No, I weep because his eyes are no longer there to mirror my beauty.") Bachelard gives other attributes of water. Among the more interesting is freshness. Water bubbling out of its source evokes the freshness of spring. Indeed in English the word for the season of renewal and for water at its source is the same. In French few vocables give a fresher, more pleasing ring than *eaux printanières*. It is curious that the epithet fresh should seem less suitable when applied to other realms of matter. A fresh wind, for instance, already carries with it the suggestion of chill.

Bachelard's *topophilia* does not appear to embrace cities. In *La Poétique de l'Espace*, he tells us how he could not sleep one night in Paris because of the ceaseless rumble of traffic. Sleep came when the city noises were transformed in his imagination into the heavy rolls of a tempestuous ocean, and his comfortable bed into a safely-anchored boat. Bachelard tells this story to illustrate how images of nature may serve as a palliative against the harangues of artifice. For me, the story also gently implies the sort of partiality that, in more strident form, is rather common among nature enthusiasts. People do not always praise wild and rustic scenes without frowning sidewise on man and his works; especially that "proud and passionate, mettlesome, mad, extravagant" work, the city. We sometimes get the impression that the poor bees and flowers are not lovable in themselves but only as palliatives against naughty man. The Chinese, for instance, are supposed to take great delight in nature. Their landscape paintings, especially those of the Sung dynasty, certainly indicate a profound awareness of natural beauty. In poetry, however, the delight in nature is frequently marred by a pathetic note. This pathos may derive from the recognition of the transience of things, or from wars, but also, less nobly, from setbacks in their official careers in the city. Chinese poets belonged to the scholar-official class. They lived in the capital and enjoyed its glories. Then came the sad day when they fell from imperial favor and were obliged to go to the wilds (i.e., the provinces), where they sang of their love for mountains and mist, children and chrysanthemums. Behind these songs, however, there lurk not too far away the sad and wistful notes of frustration and disappointment. I think that some of the poems of Tao Yuan-ming (372-427 A.D.) and even some of Tu Fu (713-770 A.D.) reflect this. But Chinese poets do not stand alone. Turning over the centuries and to another world, we find that Emerson also cannot praise "light, wave, rock and bird" without revealing in the next line his irritation with men, "the money-loving herd." It would be interesting (perhaps also depressing) to make a list of all those nature-poems, East and West, that appear to owe their original inspiration not so much to *topophilia* as to frustrations in the more demanding concourse of men.

Outside the net of purely human relations, the home is perhaps our first and strongest attachment. Bachelard has much to say on this. In the home memories and time are transfixed in concrete things—in a cot, a coffee table, a fading tea stain in one corner of the Chimayo carpet, or perhaps a bay window by which we have dreamed in solitude. Our affection for home is of course also based on its role as shelter. Thus we are apt to show a deeper awareness and appreciation of its furnishings in winter than in summer.

As we accumulate age and strength our interest and affection spread to broader landscapes outside the house to the garden, to the farms and to the hills. Historically also, both in poetry and in landscape painting, *topophilia* seems to have expanded from the humanized landscapes of gardens, farms and pastureland to wilder scenes. In that early Chinese classic *Shih Ching* (*ca.* 900-500 B.C.), poems lauded farmers who cleared brush and worked in the fields, but of landscapes loved for their own sake there was little indication until the Late Han dynasty. In the West, Homer, when he took time off from his fast-paced narrative, cast approving glances at the fat soil but only rarely at the "rosy-fingered dawn." Again in a later age it was the farm and the pastureland that received the praise of the Latin poets Virgil and Horace. In general, Western literature showed little evidence of real delight in wild nature until the later part of the 18th and in the 19th Century. By that time the Alps were open to the more intrepid English tourists. It is pertinent to recall that Wordsworth as a child received his first and deepest impressions in the relatively untrammeled Lake Country, and that later as a young man he was profoundly moved by the grandeur of the Swiss Alps. America has the more robust Walt Whitman, who claimed to have found the law of his poems in the elemental abandon of the Rocky Mountains.

The visual arts show a similar broadening of horizons. Sir Kenneth Clark traces an early expression of love for nature in the beautiful and realistic plant ornaments that began to appear on cathedral capitals, and in the margins of manuscripts in the 13th century. The sheltered garden next achieved popularity as an artistic theme. In the 15th Century the first modern landscapes appeared. Among the big names then were Hubert and Jan van Eyck; and later, in Venice, Giovanni Bellini. Of Bellini, Sir Kenneth Clark writes: "Few artists have been capable of such universal love, which embraces every twig, every stone, the humblest detail as well as the most grandiose perspective, and can only be attained by a profound humility." In the 15th Century landscapes still were not depicted for themselves. They usually illustrated a theme— "Landing of the Count of Holland," for instance—and human figures were prominent. In the 17th Century lived Jacob van Ruysdael, the greatest master of the natural vision before Constable. Ruysdael's landscapes no longer served as stages for a story or a moral. To Constable the landscape itself could convey moral ideas to the attentive painter. His works, however, show little concern with the sublime unless the cloud studies could be called such. Instead, his attention turned chiefly to ordinary scenes. *Cornfield, Willows by the Stream, A View from the Stour*, and, in his own words, to "the sound of water escaping from milldams, willows, old rotten planks, slimy posts and brickwork." In contrast, his confrère Turner was penetrated by a sense of nature's unsubduable force. He painted stormy seas, avalanches, whirlwinds and *Rain, Steam, Speed*. The last looks like high fantasy but it was in fact based on the artist's observation in torrential rain from an open train window. So we move in time from the stone flowers and tendrils on the Chapter House of Southwell Cathedral (13th Century) to Constable's slimy posts and Turner's turbulences. These images give us very different aspects of nature, but since they were all conceived in love for things as they are—not in obedience to personal fantasy or formal esthetic principles—the diversity of their message may simply reflect the awesome diversity of nature itself.

Geographers, I think, might take time off from their practical duties, and join—at least now and then—the artists and the poets in portraying the splendor of the earth. I do not mean that we should all start describing landscapes, and grimly plan on some future date when the entire earth will be covered with such portraits. We need no plan, we certainly have no obligation, to describe any area other than the one for which we have a special fondness or inexplicable fascination. Geographers have an advantage over architects, town planners and wildlife conservationists, for unlike these harassed people we are not called upon to give immediate judgment. Like poets and artists, we have greater leisure to taste the various fruits of the earth. Our chief duty is to give accurate and sensitive portrayal of their impact on us, and if a fruit, however beautiful to look at, tastes sour, we must not hestitate to say so. In other words, nature has its grim side. It is not enough to use just the palette of Renoir.

If to portray the face of the earth is a worthy aim, the problem of means remains. As a geographer, my feeling on the matter is this. To receive and then give the full flavor of a landscape we first need to concentrate on its parts; its climate, land forms, seasonal coloring, history, land use, architecture and the like. But we must not stop here as we so often are tempted to do. It seems that relaxation, a mood of attentive waiting (the French word *"attente"* best expresses this), must follow the period of concentration before the landscape will yield to us its personality. Remember Wordsworth and the star over Helvellyn. Both the hard work before and the relaxation after are necessary. A superficial, impressionistic view can only give passing pleasure to the senses. Great landscape painters in the past have paid close attention to the facts of nature. The 11th Century Chinese artist, Kuo Hsi, advocated it. The details of a Bellini landscape rendered with incredible patience, proved it. Constable's cloud studies, with his notes on wind direction and time of day, are still admired for their accuracy by British meteorologists. The fourth volume of Ruskin's *Modern Painters* contains sketches of mountains and structure that might well come out of a modern geologist's field notes. As to the poets, I am content to offer the weighty opinion of W. H. Auden. He says that if a Texas billionaire were to give him carte blanche in running a training school for poets, he would make them study—besides prosody, rhetoric and history of the language—natural history, geology, meteorology, archaeology, mythology, liturgies, and cooking. Poets too need hard facts; they also need to see nature with trained and attentive eyes. On the other hand, geographers can certainly benefit from Auden's curriculum. The course on cooking, for instance, will help us to look upon cultures and cultural landscapes with heightened appreciation. But above all, from the poets we may learn when to sit still and listen.

✦✦✦✦✦✦✦✦✦✦✦✦✦✦✦✦✦✦✦✦✦✦✦✦✦✦✦✦✦

BIBLIOGRAPHY

The Region

ACKERMAN, E. A., "Regional Research—Emerging Concepts and Techniques in the Field of Geography," *Economic Geography*, Vol. 29 (1953), pp. 189-97. An early suggestion of new directions for spatial analysis.

AMADEO, DOUGLAS, "An Optimization Approach to the Identification of a System of Regions," *Papers of the Regional Science Association*, Vol. XXIII (November 1968), pp. 25-44. The problem of minimizing variance in regionalization is related to practical considerations of budget and policy.

BERRY, B. J. L., "A Method for Deriving Multi-Factor Uniform Regions," *Przeglad Geogriczny*, XXXIII, No. 2 (1961), pp. 263-79. A pioneering illustration of the use of factor analytic techniques in regional analysis.

BERRY, BRIAN J. L., "Approaches to Regional Analysis: A Synthesis," *Annals, American Geographical Association*, Vol. 54 (1964), pp. 2-11. A three-dimensional matrix on place, characteristics, and time is developed, and ten modes of geographical analysis are suggested.

BERRY, B. J. L., "A Synthesis of Formal and Functional Regions Using a General Field Theory of Spatial Behavior," *Spatial Analysis* (B. J. L. Berry and D. F. Marble, eds.), Englewood Cliffs, N.J.: Prentice-Hall, 1968, pp. 419-28. Berry develops a general theory which relates regional attributes to regional interactions.

GILBERT, E. W., "The Idea of the Region," *Geography*, Vol. 45 (1960), pp. 157-75. Gilbert develops the view that geography is the art of recognizing, describing, and interpreting the personalities of regions. One thrust of the article seems to be that the regional novelist is a regional geographer with talent.

GRIGG, DAVID, "Regions, Models, and Classes," *Models in Geography* (R. J. Chorley and Peter Haggett, eds.), London: Methuen, 1967, pp. 461-501. Grigg extends his review of regional classification.

HAGGETT, PETER, "Regional and Local Components in the Distributions of Forested Areas in Southeast Brazil: A Multivariate Approach," *Geographical Journal*, Vol. 130 (1964), pp. 365-77.

The interrelated problem of modifiable areal units and regional generalization is examined.

HAGGETT, PETER, "Trend-Surface Mapping in the Interregional Comparison of Intra-Regional Structures," *Papers of the Regional Science Association*, Vol. XX, The Hague Congress, 1967, pp. 19-28. Trend-surface analysis is utilized in the comparison of sets of regions.

JOHNSTON, R. J., "Grouping and Regionalizing: Some Methodological and Technical Observations," *Economic Geography*, Vol. 46, No. 2 (Supplement, June 1970), pp. 293-305. The author stresses the need for a theoretically oriented methodology in regionalization, and provides a useful, relevant bibliography.

KIMBLE, G. H. T., "The Inadequacy of the Regional Concept," *London Essays in Geography*, in L. D. Stamp and S. W. Wooldridge (eds.), London, 1951, pp. 151-74. Modern industralized space seems ill fitted to the regional concept, argues the author.

LEWIS, G. MALCOLM, "Levels of Living in the North-eastern United States *c.* 1960: A New Approach to Regional Geography," *Transactions, Institute of British Geographers*, No. 45 (September 1968), pp. 11-37. An index for "levels of living" is developed using twelve demographic variables, and six regional groupings are developed accordingly.

NYSTUEN, JOHN D., and MICHAEL F. DACEY, "A Graph Theory Interpretation of Nodal Regions," *Papers of the Regional Science Association*, Vol. VII (1961), pp. 29-42. Graph theoretic concepts are utilized in deriving a method of identifying nodal regional from an "adjacency matrix."

RAY, D. MICHAEL, "The Spatial Structure of Economic and Cultural Differences: A Factorial Ecology of Canada," *Papers of the Regional Science Association*, Vol. XXIII (November 1968), pp. 7-24. National heartland-hinterland, urban hierarchy, and intermetropolitan as its patterns are produced in a factorial ecology of Canada.

ROBINSON, G. W. S., "The Geographical Region: Form and Function," *Scottish Geographical Magazine*, Vol. 69 (1953), pp. 49-58. Robinson provides a review of the concept of region in geography to 1952.

TURNOCK, DAVID, "The Region in Modern Geography," *Geography*, Vol. 52, No. 237 (1967), pp. 374-83. The concept of region is reviewed over time, suggesting simple description, environmentalism, possibilism, and probabilistic explanation as the chronological sequence.

✱✱✱✱✱✱✱✱✱✱✱✱✱✱✱✱✱✱✱✱✱✱✱✱✱✱✱✱✱✱✱✱

6
SPATIAL
ORDER

The cultural geographer is concerned with the complexity of human responses to a variety of physical environments. He may choose to examine a single human group in terms of what it has learned and transmitted over time to a progression of on-site successors. He may choose to examine and compare the differing responses of groups with similar environments. He may even explore similar responses and resulting similar communications made by groups encountering substantially different physical environments. The variety of responses available for study is in itself one of the seductively attractive elements of cultural geography. It has become increasingly evident that in order to understand human behavior over space the cultural geographer must also be concerned with the problem of common constraints placed on all cultures by the spatial context of their existence. In a recent treatise on methodology, Harvey speaks to "the principle of hidden order within chaos in human geography." But perhaps this begs a question, for it does not seem to be the chaos in human society that has attracted so many scholars, but rather the temporal continuity and sameness of communicated experience that have characterized each culture. The questions for the researcher are myriad, but two demand his special attention: (1) What are the underlying common elements of spatial order for all cultures? and (2) What response has a particular culture made to those elements of spatial order?

While it is not intended here to reargue the question of the nature of "universal laws" in geography, it is suggested that no student examining a singular culture over space and time can hope to understand fully the content of the cultural message unless he pursues those problems. He has the advantage of disciplinary support, for a central concern of geography must continue to be the development of articulate theory. It is a point of some embarrassment to note that we have not progressed particularly far in that respect. What we do know (or seem to know) often attracts the scornful label "self-evident," but at least four points should be established with respect to notions of spatial order.

1. We know that with respect to mathematical probability (a needed point of reference for questions of spatial order) human enterprises may show tendencies to be more evenly distributed spatially or decidedly more grouped than that of random spatial distribution.

By way of illustration, a Township and Range survey scheme, substantially reinforced by subsequent provisions of the Homestead Act, is known to have served to impose a particular spatial pattern of human settlement on much of the American Midwest. Some visual evidence of eveness of pattern is quite apparent there, today. Yet what is not so easily read from that scene is the evidence of the variety of spatial distributions overlying the broader rectilinear pattern. The sequential pattern of settlement, the sites of public schools, the locations of occupied dwellings in the rural areas, the surviving public transport terminals—may each reflect a substantially different non-random mathematical distribution. It is only the most meager beginning to observe that for the 1940's the rural dwellings of central Indiana illustrated a Double Poisson distribution. Indeed, it is an awkward answer without an appropriate question. Our concern for theory related to cultural process does not permit us to ignore such evidence, however, but should encourage us to extend our investigation of spatial order.

2. The widespread human proclivity for assembly in settlement groups establishes the significance of the distance-decay function over space, for most cultures.

The methodological over-kill of early quantitative efforts in using the constructs of the gravity model to demonstrate this effect should not prevent the cultural geographer from extracting two important notions from the distance-decay phenomenon.

First, is the very strong suggestion that for almost all men at most times, past or present, earth-space has been undeniably flat, not rounded. If most human interactions are necessarily constrained to the near proximity of the individual, nearest distances *perceived* as the straight line will preclude most speculation as to the spherical nature of the broader earth surface. Indeed, for a great majority of the cultures that have endured on the earth, personal concepts of earth-space as other than flat might have imposed a burden of structural inefficiency. Reaching the stage of scholarly perception of a spherical earth may be one element in a typology of cultural inventiveness, but perhaps serves as well to stamp the degree to which a culture's scholars were freed from the necessity of persistent near interaction of an economic nature.

Second, although process explanations of the distance-decay function remain elusive, an obvious opportunity exists for human geographers. For a given culture, any of several mathematical constraints might describe similarly and adequately the behavior pattern of human interaction decline with increasing distance. Although someone other than the serious student of that culture might provide the data base for analysis, only someone who has explored the cultural heritage in depth can suggest the fundamental reasons as to why the parameters of the models are what they are, for the society in question. These parameters reflect the rate of change in interaction with increases in distance, and they are often inconstant between societies, inconstant within societies reflecting marked spatial complexities, and often inconsistent over time. That they are tantalizingly constant for specific groups at specific times is an intellectual challenge for serious research.[1]

3. *Advanced cultural inventions such as urban settlement seem related to fundamental geometric properties when notions of spatial efficiency are considered.*

The best-known theoretical structures in geography are those related to central places. In considering the spatial pattern of settlement, and the spatial offering of a broad class of service functions, Christaller derived three internal geometries. Although all are based on a lattice of equidistance points, extended to a hierarchical structure of hexagons, it is imperative that the student of cultural geography not overlook an important point: fundamental relationships change when the functions change—that is to say, the market structure, the transportation structure, and the administrative structures are decidely different geometries. The Christaller theory, independently derived and extended by Lösch, is now substantially enriched to the point of mild nausea for many. Too, it is fundamentally a part of economic geography. Yet a careful reading of his text, in sections elaborating on the special case of the theory, is rewarded by numerous comments as to probable non-hexagonal regional variations over space. One finds that it is yet all too common for the novice in geography to lose the meaning of the special case in an ill-fated effort to make direct comparisons with reality. Potentially even more frustrating to him, he may dash off to race his intellectual motor over the world's inhabited flats, in search of hexagons. What would add interest to the literature on central place now would be a carefully developed set of hypotheses predicting a specific non-hexagonal geometry, building on both central place theory and an in-depth

knowledge of a non-Western culture. Too, we are in need of contributions to theories of the geometry within a culture for distances other than linear metric—over the psychological and social spaces, for instance.

4. *Many processes affecting the social organization of space exhibit elements of randomness.*

Human geographers are not alone in feeling a bit uneasy in the presence of the term, "randomness." Almost everyone who uses the notion wishes he had a better definition of it. For our purposes, we will be content to say that a random event has occurred over a space if all elements of that space which might have experienced the event had an equal and independent chance of experiencing it. The human geographer who is willing to make certain seemingly unrealistic assumptions as to the nature of events within the space-time of a culture that interests him may very well be among the first to truly understand that culture. If chance events are regularly transmitted in the form of culturally specific knowledge, it behooves the geographer to understand them. Most especially, if he wishes to be predictive with respect to the culture, he must come to grips with the probability of events. Again, to begin with the variables behaving randomly, then gradually reducing the aspect of chance by careful selection of constraints on the variables, he is to approach an estimation of *likelihood.* Although others have paved the road,[2] Hudson and Fowler's discussion of patterns is a useful guidepost to that area of concern in human geography. The article is a good example of one of the more satisfying elements in the contemporary geographic scene—the willingness and ability of two or more scholars to pool their talents in the attack on obviously long-standing problems

---

1. See David Harvey, *Explanation in Geography*, pp. 109-14, for an elaboration of this theme.

2. The pathfinder, contractor, and landscape architect is Michael Dacey, who seldom writes for the beginning student of pattern.

of definition. Their contribution is an elaboration of the properties of pattern, and they link these properties to both theoretical and empirical investigation.

In viewing race as a social characteristic, Rose examines the changing racial composition of a retail trade area in relation to changes in the spatial pattern of retail establishments in the area. Transition probabilities were established, but the researcher's ability to predict retail mix declined as the racial mix shifted from predominately white to predominately black. Although the technique utilized is not particularly successful, the author is able to go beyond his technical output to provide insights for those researchers who will take up the problem of spatial structure after him. A discipline thrives only when its proponents are able to make such contributions.

It is rare in any literature for a model to appear so fully dressed with cultural detail as is Skinner's study of marketing and social structure in rural China. The general notions of spatial arrangement within the central place framework are neatly introduced to attack several questions of particular importance to the student of China. How did a traditional tri-level hierarchy of administrative centers imposed by the state relate to the more complex system of centers whose functions were primarily economic? What was the relationship between the system of market areas and the system of social contact? Departing from formal central place constructs when necessary but always quick to use them to advantage, Skinner moves through his materials with scholarly finesse.

Spatial order is not a product of the mind, but geographers are identified by their spatial point of view. Most of us share a general curiosity as to how those favored few who make truly innovative conceptual contributions to that point of view came to do so. Walter Christaller was a gentle, warmly unassuming man much abused in the latter years of his life by governmental irrationality. As a result of those unfortunate restraints, many American geographers were denied an opportunity to meet and know the scholar who had made such a significant impact on their discipline. It is in tribute to Walter Christaller and to his contribution that we include his personal account of discovery.

It is appropriate that we close our introduction of the conceptual frameworks of landscape, environmental perception, ecosystem, spatial diffusion, the region, and spatial order with a broadly provocative article. Curry's "Chance and Landscape" is an exciting introduction to probabilistic reasoning. He points up the limitations of deterministic approaches to problems, and cites the many advantages of description in probabilistic terms. Curry reviews stochastic diffusion models including (but going beyond) the Hägerstrand approach. He exhibits his remarkable ability to develop insights in human geography from examples involving physical processes. A discussion of contingency offers a particularly intriguing view of historical process, as well. He closes with suggested applications of probabilistic reasoning in the field of decision-making.

A pertinent summary statement for this portion has been provided by Curry in the article cited above. "With regard to any particular problem or set of problems the approach of a geographer may coincide with that of a student from a neighboring discipline. But there seems to be the obligation for geography to phrase individual explanations of events in the landscape so that these may be structured into an overall articulated view of ordering in space."

🟊🟊🟊🟊🟊🟊🟊🟊🟊🟊🟊🟊🟊🟊🟊🟊🟊🟊🟊🟊🟊🟊🟊🟊🟊🟊🟊🟊🟊

THE CONCEPT OF
PATTERN IN GEOGRAPHY

John C. Hudson and Phillip M. Fowler

Under the impetus of basic research, the principal theories of geography continue to show a broadening scope, thus explaining the spatial distribution of an increasing number of phenomena. The highly stylized and abstract theory of Central Place is probably the most familiar of these logical constructs, and the hexagonal pattern of central places which results from the very restrictive postulates of this theory has stimulated considerable interest in pattern. Out of this interest there has evolved a growing awareness among geographers of the direct link between the laws and theories of location and their two-dimensional expression via pattern. In addition, it appears that the entire conceptual framework of areal association is intimately linked with pattern analysis. However, even though pattern is an important geographical concept, particularly as it expresses location theory geometrically, its role in geographical theory has been relatively minor.

Formal analysis of pattern is hampered by a lack of precision in its operational definitions. The word "pattern" is often employed loosely, which has introduced both conflicting meanings as well as confusion concerning the explicitness of any given definition. It will be shown here, however, that pattern is quite amenable to a precise definition that is intuitively satisfying as well as being geometrically reasonable. It is hoped that by lending precision to the definition of pattern, a contribution to basic research findings in the analysis of spatial distributions will be forthcoming. It is also possible that basic research into the geometric properties of pattern may lead researchers to previously unknown geographical theory which is more complex as well as more incisive.

Development of Pattern Analysis

The recent interest in pattern among geographers comes more than thirty years after plant ecologists began studying this subject. The ecologists initially assumed that plants were distributed at random, and therefore frequency counts of plant density obtained in random throws of a quadrat could be approximated by terms of the Poisson series expansion for a specified density, i.e. probability of occurrence. Since the variance and mean of the Poisson distribution are equal, values of the variance-mean ratio (variance divided by mean) provide indices of randomness. Values of the variance-mean ratio significantly greater than unity indicate clustering, whereas values significantly smaller than one indicate a more-regular-than-random arrangement. Thus, a trichotomy of pattern types evolved, based largely on technique rather than theory. Subsequent research for the most part has centered on discovering the category of pattern type in which a particular spatial distribution belongs.

Ecologists abandoned the notion that

From Discussion Paper Series, Paper No. 1, May 1966, Department of Geography, University of Iowa. Reprinted by permission.

plants were randomly distributed when it was found empirically that clustering was the most frequently occurring type of pattern. Consequently, several contagious or clustered type statistical distributions were developed which involve the use of a quadrat. Ecologists did not develop a distribution for the more-regular-than-random case, probably because of its infrequent occurrence in plant populations. However, this type of configuration does occur frequently in distributions investigated by geographers, notably central places, making this gap a serious one, even though the geographer Dacey has made several contributions in this direction.[1]

In the 1950's, Clark and Evans and others developed a means of detecting pattern type that did not involve a quadrat, which is called the "nearest neighbor" technique.[2] This involves measuring distance to nearest occurrence of a specified order from each individual in a population of known density. The methods have also been extended to higher orders of neighbors. Nevertheless, this technique, like the quadrat approach, remains dependent upon density measurement.

There remain several major shortcomings in pattern analysis in geography as it is presently carried on. First, currently available techniques which were devised for the ecologists, e.g. "nearest neighbor" and quadrat approaches, appear to have arisen partly as a result of the technical difficulties of measuring associations in the field. Thus, they do not take advantage of the geographer's access to maps from which a wide variety of relevant properties of a distribu-

tion can be easily measured via a computer. Therefore, the modern geographer need not limit himself to those types of techniques used by ecologists.

Secondly, and more important, the identification of a spatial distribution as falling into one or another category of a trichotomous classification of pattern types does violence to our intuitive notion of what pattern is. This result is due to the fact that quadrat methods assess only local aggregation of phenomena and do not in any manner measure pattern; and although nearest neighbor techniques are free of the influence of quadrat size, they are also affected by such factors as scale and density.

The Properties of Pattern

Pattern should not be confused with shape as they each represent separate geometrical or geographical properties. Such confusion can be easily eliminated by a consideration of the number of relevant dimensions of the objects being studied. Somewhat paralleling Bunge's work in shape measurement, let us say that any closed curve has a shape and any non-closed collection of points has a pattern.[3] Thus, a region has shape because its boundary is a closed curve which circumscribes an area or a space of two dimensions. By definition, however, a zero or one-dimensional object can have no shape since it is only through the addition of a second dimension that shape arises. Points circumscribed by a regional boundary are considered here, as in geometry, as being zero dimensional. Thus, to speak of the shape of an area is to deal with two dimensions; to speak of a pattern of points is to speak of zero-dimensional objects whose pattern is operationally determined via the relative

1. Michael F. Dacey, (1964) Modified Poisson probability law for point pattern more regular than random. *Annals, Association of American Geographers*, 54: 559-65.

2. P. J. Clark and F. C. Evans, (1954) Distance to nearest neighbor as a measure of spatial relationships in populations, *Ecology*, 44: 349-60.

3. William Bunge, *Theoretical Geography*, Lund Studies in Geography Series C., No. 1 (1962), Chapter 3.

distances or spacings of the objects with respect to one another. Thus, we can separate pattern and shape by the relevant dimensions of the objects being studied.

A second property is that pattern is not related to the size of area in which it occurs. Nevertheless, nearly all pattern measures found in the literature define pattern relative to the area of occurrence by requiring that the density of the distribution be computed. Thus, pattern measures currently available do not measure pattern itself, but rather measure the configuration of the distribution in relation to the area included within a particular boundary. For example, consider the two-dimensional pattern of cells of a honeycomb. The pattern is no different if it is placed in a large container or a small container of nearly the same area as the honeycomb. However, pattern measures used currently would call the former clustered and the latter regular. At the same time, we would agree that the pattern formed by honeycomb cells is the same as that of the market areas of central place theory. If the market areas of Iowa towns have a honeycomb pattern, this pattern exists whether or not we place it in a small container—Iowa—or a large container—the United States. This is not to say that the position of a set of objects in relation to a boundary around it is not important. Locating points and lines with respect to areas is a highly significant problem in geography. It is to say that this should not be confused with the pattern of the set of objects.

We are thus led to define the fundamental property of pattern as it is formally studied in Euclidean space. Two spatial distributions have the same pattern if we can pass between the two via a homothetic (or pattern preserving) transformation and a displacement.

The properties of triangles, as being similar and congruent, provides a useful

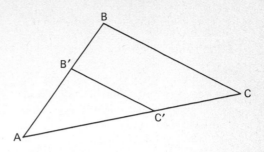

Figure 1.

analogy. Consider Figure 1. The triangles ABC and $AB'C'$ are not *congruent* because their sides are not of equal length but they are similar because their *shapes* are identical. The set of points A, B', C' and A, B, C, have the same pattern, and the two triangles have the same *shape* because their corresponding sides are parallel. We can pass between triangles A, B', C' and ABC via a homothetic transformation. Apparently, then, the study of pattern in Euclidean space should concentrate on similar angles preserved by changes in distances separating points. Thus, pattern and shape are closely related, differentiated by the relevant dimensions of the objects being studied. So called "problems of scale" are thus not part of either pattern or shape. Pattern and shape also remain unchanged under rotation, reflection, and translation—the three rigid motions or displacements of Euclidean geometry. This was first stated by Bunge, but for shape only.[4]

Another pertinent property is that a pattern is not necessarily indicative of the process which produced it. In some instances, for example, it has been felt that a pattern cannot be judged a random pattern unless generated by a random process. Yet, one does not define the shape of a cirque as being identical to that of a U-shaped valley, even though a similar process produced

4. *Ibid.*

them. On the other hand, if one found that there was no significant difference between the shapes of drumlins and the loess-deposited Palouse hills, it would seem odd to construct a measure of shape indicating the shapes were different simply because differing processes produced similar shapes. Moreover, although this is improbable, a random process may generate a regular or a clustered pattern. Thus, the process which generates a pattern is a problem quite aside from the actual geometry of the pattern itself.

Thus, pattern can be said to have the following properties: (1) It is independent of scale and density; (2) it remains invariant under the group of rigid motions of Euclidean geometry; and (3) it is expressed via the relative spacing of the individuals in the distribution. In this context, the traditional pattern trichotomy does not consider properties 1 and 3 stated above. A single distribution will have different patterns at different quadrat sizes. Pattern is thus confused with scale and density. In addition, present techniques are not capable of detecting many of the regularities present in spatial distributions. An example of the type of research that may be pursued under the approach to pattern analysis recommended here, follows.

Empirical Research in Pattern

Research by the authors on a variety of spatial distributions has established that a high degree of order is present in the spacing of individuals of a distribution even though the locations of the individuals themselves may be random.

If the distances between each individual and its 1st, 2nd, 3rd, . . .nth nearest neighbors are determined, one set of ordered distances may be used to predict another set. That is, the distance to 3rd nearest neighbor may be predicted from the distance to the 10th, and vice-versa. An example would be

the closer a town is to its second nearest neighbor, the closer it is to its tenth nearest neighbor. In some cases, over 99 per cent of the variation of certain order distances can be explained by another order of distance. The degree of explanation decreases as the orders diverge.

Putting it another way, suppose that we know the distance to the town nearest us and we know the distance to some other town, whose relative closeness is not known. We could then specify the distance order of this other town, and thus accurately predict from the series of linear equations the number of towns located closer to us than the one to which the distance is known. Such an approach to pattern analysis as this concentrates on the fundamental property of pattern because it pays no attention to the magnitude of distances separating points, but rather focuses on relationships between distances expressed by linear algebraic functions.

This high degree of regularity is partly due to the ordering properties of Euclidean geometry. As an example, consider an area occupied by a population of towns. Empirical data from various sources support the theory that as time passes the spatial distribution will rearrange itself, so to speak, as towns with a disadvantageous position decline or disappear while towns compete with each other to gain support of their common hinterlands. If each town competes with only a few others, the distances conditioned and determined by this competition completely specify all distances due to the rigid property of the triangle.

The pattern illustrated in Figure 2 is non-deformable in the Euclidean sense because it is made up of triangles. All distances in the distribution follow from the very few which are established by the competition between neighboring centers.

Thus far we have discussed pattern as it

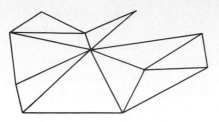

Figure 2.

exists in Euclidean two-dimensional space only. Let us introduce a third although non-geographical dimension. We shall weight each town's location according to some quantity proportional to it's population, although other magnitudes can be used as weights. The Euclidean distance function is easily extended to n-dimensions. Distances are thus measured along the hypotenuse of the triangle in 3 space formed by the original distance in the "$x-y$" plane plus the z or population coordinate.

Data on the 1960 population of the 57 Iowa cities of over 5,000 population were added to the two-dimensional distribution and it was found that the level of explanation of variation in ordered distances increased.[5] In fact all 1425 coefficients of correlation between all orders of neighbor were significant from zero. Such an approach seems to duplicate many advantages of map transformation suggested by Tobler for analyzing central place distributions, and indicates something of the amount of increase in explanation gained by transformation. The three-dimensional distance between two places is equal to the two-dimensional distance only when the two have the same z magnitude, or in this case the same

population. The distances that are increased the most are those between nearby centers of highly different population size. The effect of this is that distances are measured as if larger centers "repelled" smaller, nearby centers. Such an effect may be desirable in central place studies as a correction for the lack of empirical verification of the "vacuum" of medium-sized centers around large cities resulting from the Lösch and Christaller Central Place theories.

With the increasing development of central place theory, geographers have become more and more interested in pattern in spatial distributions. Pattern, at present, is measured largely by techniques developed by plant ecologists, but these methods do not take advantage of the geographer's access to maps, nor, more importantly, do they concentrate on the fundamental property of pattern—the attributes that remain invariant under the groups of homothetic transformations and displacements. Recent research by the authors has shown that a considerable amount of order is present in spatial distributions regardless of the regular-random-clustered trichotomy of pattern types now commonly referred to. A high degree of explanation of the magnitude of distances separating occurrences in a distribution has been achieved, showing the possibilities that exist for future applications of pattern theories. This supports the view that certain basic geometric principles, when combined with geographical theory, greatly enhance the predictive power of the research geographer. When each city in a two-dimensional distribution of cities is weighted according to its population, the degree of explanation of the spacing of cities is increased. This shows the possibilities of such an approach in solving what has been proposed as a map transformation problem.

The need for continued effort on the part

5. The z axis was scaled in thousands of persons. This was done in order to achieve an equal range of values along the three axes. The selection of units in which the z axis is scaled obviously affects the result. Thus by increasing or decreasing the relative importance of the z variable, different amounts of explanation result.

of those already involved in pattern analysis is all too apparent. There is an obvious and additional need for a broader attack, generated by an increased number of geographers who are interested in the basic geometric properties which are an inherent part of every distribution. Since formal location theory, as well as other as yet deductively unconnected locational forces, is geometrically expressed through pattern, such analysis may well provide the guidelines to new theory as well as serving as an important and basic ingredient in the underlying description of any distribution.

✦✦✦✦✦✦✦✦✦✦✦✦✦✦✦✦✦✦✦✦✦✦✦✦✦✦✦✦✦✦

THE STRUCTURE OF RETAIL TRADE IN A RACIALLY CHANGING TRADE AREA

Harold M. Rose

During the period following World War II a revolution occurred in the pattern of retail location in U.S. cities. The decline of the central business district and the subsequent rise of regional shopping centers have often been topics of in-depth research by retail location analysts. A lesser concern of researchers has been the future of unplanned shopping districts in the older neighborhoods of central cities. Of the limited attention devoted to these areas, one recent study described them this way: "Many are Sick, Many are Dying . . . What can be Done? "[1]

The most frequent death of unplanned centers is taking place within areas undergoing racial change. This has prompted a spate of statements which indicate major commercial institutions are not serving the needs of ghetto populations, and anger in the black community is frequently an outmerchants.[2] The complexity of these and other forces operating in metropolitan areas has dictated that a closer look be given at the role of race on retail structure in racially changing trade areas.

In this study race will be viewed as a social characteristic. That it is an important factor affecting retail structure was pointed out by Rolph[3] more than a generation ago. Further, Bucklin[4] has found that race, like distance, is a variable which affects one's choice of a place to shop. Yet, to date only Pred[5] among American geographers has sought to investigate this phenomenon.

2. M. C. Sengstock, "The Corporation and the Ghetto: An Analysis of the Effects of Corporate Retail Grocery Sales on Ghetto Life." *Journal of Urban Law*, 45 (1968), 673-703.
3. L. K. Rolph, "The Population Pattern in Relation to Retail Buying." *The American Journal of Sociology*, 38 (1932), 368.
4. L. P. Bucklin, "The Concept of Mass In Intraurban Shopping." *Journal of Marketing*, 31 (1967), 41-42.
5. A. Pred, "Business Thoroughfares as Expres-

1. A. Downs and J. McClean. "Many are Sick, Many are Dying—What Can be Done;" *Journal of Property Management*, 28 (1963), 132-42.

The specific objective of this study is to attempt to relate changes in retail structure to the entry of Negroes into a given trade area during the period 1950–1965. The problem of isolating changes emanating from a changing racial composition in a retail sub-system is difficult, since numerous other forces are at work which prompt change in the character and structure of a retail trade area. The problem is further compounded by the fact that retail trade areas of the type that are becoming predominantly Negro have been going through states of decline for some time, a trend which is only incidentally related to the racial character of the market. This factor was mentioned by writers assessing the possibility of commercial redevelopment along the riot ravaged commercial strips of Detroit.[6]

The Study Area

The area selected for this investigation lies approximately two and one-half miles northwest of the central business district in the city of Milwaukee, Wisconsin (Figure 1). It is a rectangular area embracing less than two square miles, and in both 1950 and 1960 it contained approximately 42,000 persons. The study area does not represent a precisely delineated trade area, but a series of contiguous neighborhoods. One assumes that the residents of the area will seek to satisfy as many of their basic retail needs as is possible from the set of commercial outlets found in close proximity to their places of residence, although there is growing evidence[7] that residents of low income areas possess a keen awareness of price differences in stores located beyond the margins of the

local neighborhood, a factor which could have a demonstrated impact upon shopping patterns.

The vast majority of retail outlets in the area under investigation are situated along four major arterials which transect the district. Two of these, North Avenue and Center Street, run east-west, while the other two, Fond du Lac Avenue and Teutonia Avenue, run to the northwest. Since many of the retail outlets which have evolved along these roads cater to the local residential market, they are more than simple string streets or ribbon developments. The retail character of the area is best reflected in the small, unplanned shopping centers found nested along stretches of the arterials. In 1950 there were seven unplanned shopping centers located along various stretches of the transecting roads. The seven individual centers were spaced at approximately one-quarter mile intervals. The spaces separating these centers were also largely commercial, generally performing urban arterial functions, although along some stretches residential land uses tended to predominate. The unplanned centers included approximately one-half of the retail establishments located along these radials. This ratio coincides with Boal and Johnson's[8] assessment of the higher importance of hierarchic functions along commercial ribbons situated in the older parts of the city. Among the seven centers or districts, there were present in the initial period a small shopping goods center, a community center, and five neighborhood centers (Figure 2).

Since the principal objective of this study is to consider the impact of the changing racial composition of the trade area on retail structure, it is useful to subdivide the trade

sions of Urban Negro Culture." *Economic Geography*, 39 (1963), 217-33.
6. *The Wall Street Journal* (July 28, 1967), 5.
7. C. S. Goodman, "Do the Poor Pay More?" *Journal of Marketing* (Jan. 1968), 23.

8. F. W. Boal and D. B. Johnson. "The Functions of Retail and Service Establishments on Commercial Ribbons," *The Canadian Geographer*, 9 (1965), 157.

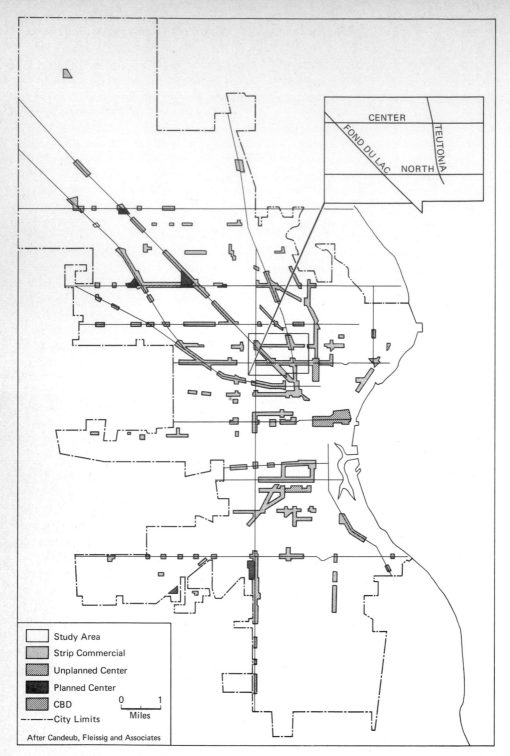

Figure 1. Pattern of retail development, Milwaukee.

552

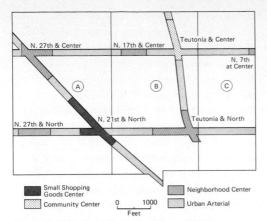

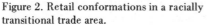

Figure 2. Retail conformations in a racially transitional trade area.

area into smaller segments in line with the community area designations developed for Milwaukee by Tien.[9] The study area embraces two complete community areas and parts of a third. These areas are designated as community areas A, B, and C in Figure 2. Only a fraction of community area C is included within the trade area, but in the initial time period it was this segment of the community that contained the only sizable number of Negro consumers in the entire market area. As recently as 1950, Negroes constituted only about seven per cent of the population in the total market area, but almost 30 per cent within community area C.

The racial composition of the population within the trade area moved from a Negro share of approximately seven per cent in 1950 to 49 per cent in 1960. If racial composition does in fact produce a significant impact on the number of operating establishments, then the racial threshold reflecting the decision of an existing operator to relocate or terminate his operation was not reached prior to 1955. This view is sup-

ported by the fact that there was only a four per cent decline in the number of establishments within the area during the initial five year interval. Berry[10] recently demonstrated the catalytic effect of racial turnover on the retail structure in several community areas in Chicago, but like others, he has pointed out the difficulty of separating race from income.

To answer the question, "what effect does the spatial development of the Negro ghetto in major central cities have on the retail structure of business clusters situated within its area," it was necessary to search for a method or technique which is sensitive to processes having an impact on retail character. Berry and his colleagues have developed models to describe changes in a given aspect of retail character as a function of certain status variables measured at some specified point in time. But these models have been found to be inadequate for predicting retail changes in small unit areas[11] and also, they do not include social variables among the independent variables. In areas undergoing racial change the models were least able to predict satisfactory results.[12]

Certain features of Markov Chain models appear to offer more satisfactory alternatives for predicting changes of the type with which this study is concerned. Markov Chain models have found only limited use among geographers although their utility has been

9. Y. Tien, *Milwaukee Metropolitan Area Fact Book—1940, 1950 and 1960.* Madison, Wisconsin: The University of Wisconsin Press, 1962.

10. B. J. L. Berry, "Comparative Mortality Experience of Small Business in Four Chicago Communities," Background Paper No. 4, *Small Business Relocation Study,* Center for Urban Studies, The University of Chicago (1966), 19-20.

11. B. J. L. Berry, "The Retail Component of the Urban Model," *Journal of the American Institute of Planners,* 31 (1965), 151.

12. B. J. L. Berry, *Commercial Structure and Commercial Blight,* Research Paper 85, Department of Geography, University of Chicago, Chicago (1963). Pp. 173-76.

demonstrated by both Marble[13] and Clark.[14] These models are used here to describe the changes of commercial structures from one retail category to another over time.

A five year interval was selected as an appropriate time period for describing shifts in retail character. Transition probability matrices were constructed which described shifts among some twelve retail categories for the set of commercial structures located along each ribbon.

These matrices demonstrate the stability or lack of stability of the various retail types. They likewise reflect the suitability, in terms of rents or character of physical facilities, which might readily allow shifts in retail types to occur. The existence of zeros in cells indicates that it is not possible for a unit in the ith state to transfer to the jth state; for example, a unit which housed an automotive service in the initial time period cannot house a clothing store at the next time period.

Depending upon one's objectives, Markov models can be employed in a number of ways. Both Marble and Clark focused their attentions solely on the transition matrix as a clue to expected behavior. Other researchers have utilized the matrix of transition probabilities to predict future outcomes. In this case, the matrix of transition probabilities is multiplied by a vector describing each category's share of the set of businesses in the present time period as a means of predicting future shares.

A matrix of transition probabilities was constructed for each of the commercial ribbons in the study area for the times 1955, 1960, and 1965. In each instance, the matrix reflects shifts in states over the preceding five years. The construction of a series of transition matrices (1950–1955, 1955–1960, 1960–1965) reflects a desire to illustrate the impact of changes taking place during the immediate past period on retail stability. A conventional Markov Chain analysis which might use only the initial transition probability matrix (1950–1955) to predict future changes would not get at this principal concern. Besides, in anticipating the impact of racial composition upon the structure of retail trade, it appears logical to expect that the dispersion of the Negro population within the trade area over subsequent five-year intervals, would distort the predicted results associated with a given transition matrix. This logic is based on recognized subcultural differences reflected in differential propensities to consume specific items[15] and the traditional behavior of white entrepreneurs engaged in the provision of social services. Eventually, the transition matrices should begin to reflect the changing racial composition of the population although the role of race cannot be precisely specified. Galloway,[16] using a Markov model, encountered a similar problem in attempting to partition the role of specified variables in explaining differences in the propensity for poverty on the basis of race.

The retail structure along all commercial

13. D. F. Marble, "A Simple Markovian Model of Trip Structures in a Metropolitan Region," *Papers, Regional Science Assoc. Western Section* (1964), 150-56.

14. W. A. V. Clark, "Markov Chain Analysis in Geography: An Application to the Movement of Rental Housing Areas," *Annals,* The Association of American Geographers, 55 (1965), 351-59.

15. M. Alexis, "Some Negro-White Differences in Consumption," *American Journal of Economics and Sociology,* 21 (1962), 11; R. A. Bauer, S. M. Cunningham, and L. H. Wortzel, "The Marketing Dilemma of Negroes,"s, Journal of Marketing, 29 (1965), 1-6; H. A. Bullock, "Consumer Motivations in Black and White," *Harvard Business Review,* 39 (1961), 89-124.

16. L. E. Galloway, "The Negro and Poverty," *The Journal of Business,* 40 (1967), 29-31.

Table 1   Transition Probabilities for the North Avenue Businesses

Retail Category	1950	1955											
		S_1	S_2	S_3	S_4	S_5	S_6	S_7	S_8	S_9	S_{10}	S_{11}	S_{12}
Professional	S_1	1.00											
Personal	S_2		.80		.05							.15	
Financial	S_3			.57	.13						.13		.17
Eating & Drinking	S_4				.95								.05
Groc. & Rel. Goods	S_5		.08			.84			.04				.04
Clothing	S_6		.10				.60		.20				.10
Auto Sales & Serv.	S_7				.04			.78	.04				.04
Multifunctionals	S_8								1.00				
Specialty	S_9		.06							.75	.06	.06	.06
Household Furnish. & Related Goods	S_{10}										1.00		
Miscellaneous	S_{11}		.07			.07					.13	.60	.13
Vacancy	S_{12}												1.00

ribbons in the study area during the period 1950–1955 can be described as stable. Some of the more important conditions leading to the retail stability were residential stability, limited change in the income characteristics of the local consumer population, and the absence of attractive alternative retail locations. These conditions are essentially related to the sub-system itself.

Tables 1 and 2, examples of the matrices of transition probabilities, demonstrate the stability that characterized retail activity in the trade area during the initial interval. Although conditions along only two arteries are shown, there was little variability within the whole area during the interval. The rate and character of change along these two arteries in the following two five-year periods, however, is quite disparate. Teutonia Avenue (Table 2) lies along the main axis of ghetto development, whereas North Avenue (Table 1) is situated at a right angle to this major direction of ghetto spread. The physical orientation of these axes accounts

Table 2   Transition Probabilities for the Teutonia Avenue Businesses

Retail Category	1950	1955											
		S_1	S_2	S_3	S_4	S_5	S_6	S_7	S_8	S_9	S_{10}	S_{11}	S_{12}
Professional	S_1	1.00											
Personal	S_2		.75							.25			
Financial	S_3			1.00									
Eating & Drinking	S_4				.95							.05	
Groc. & Rel. Goods	S_5					.80				.10	.10		
Clothing	S_6						1.00						
Auto Sales & Serv.	S_7							.91			.09		
Multifunctionals	S_8								1.00				
Specialty	S_9								.08	.50	.08	.17	.17
Household Furnish. & Related Goods	S_{10}				.07						.85	.07	
Miscellaneous	S_{11}									.09	.18	.63	.09
Vacancy	S_{12}												1.00

for far reaching changes in the later time periods.

The entries along the main diagonals of the matrices give the probabilities of remaining in the same state over the one time interval and are called the *retention probabilities*. It is clear from observing these matrices that the structures housing certain retail categories are often ill-suited to house other categories. The nature of the structures which house categories S_9-S_{11} seem to permit most readily changes of state among categories.

The development of a set of transition probability matrices for each ribbon permits one to begin to look for causal factors which would explain the differential shifts in the retail character along these ribbons. The transition matrix has been employed as a predictive device in order to test for the homogeneity of processes occurring through time (Table 3).

Along both sample ribbons, the differences between the observed and predicted shares of S_4 (Eating and Drinking) and S_2 (Personal Services) are minor. Some other differences are, in part, a function of the original retail character of the ribbons themselves. The predictive ability of the model is less satisfactory for Teutonia than for North Avenue. While a general decline in retail functions can be detected along both ribbons, the more serious decline along Teutonia is probably related to the facts that it contained fewer establishments originally, had less retail diversity, and greater residential instability during this interval.

The matrices describing shifts in the retail mix during each successive five-year interval show a general decline in the retention probabilities among states. This condition, no doubt, is basically related to the economic decline of old neighborhoods. But variations in the sensitivity of some retail categories reflect changing social characteristics.

In the transition probability matrices for those ribbons which cut across the principal axis of ghetto development, such as North Avenue and Center Street, the impact of changing racial character is less evident. Changes taking place along one stretch of the axis are masked by entry decisions occurring elsewhere on the street, since the racial factor has a less pervasive impact along

Table 3   Predicted Percentage Retail Mix, 1960, as Function of Processes Operating 1950–55

		North Avenue		Teutonia Avenue	
Retail Category		Observed	Predicted*	Observed	Predicted*
S_1	Professional	0.6	0.0	2.1	0.0
S_2	Personal	10.4	10.9	5.3	4.5
S_3	Financial	1.2	4.7	3.2	2.0
S_4	Eating & Drinking	15.3	15.3	20.2	20.2
S_5	Groceries	9.2	9.9	6.6	9.9
S_6	Clothing	3.1	9.5	4.3	10.0
S_7	Auto Sales & Serv.	9.8	10.6	8.5	10.7
S_8	Multifunctionals	4.9	6.3	3.2	4.0
S_9	Specialty	7.9	9.0	5.3	8.6
S_{10}	Household Furnish.	11.0	11.7	10.6	17.5
S_{11}	Miscellaneous	14.1	12.3	8.5	10.7
S_{12}	Vacancy	12.8	11.6	22.3	0.0

Product of 1955 state vector and transition probability matrix for 1950-55.

the total length of the ribbon in any given year.

As a means of highlighting the role of the racial composition of the trade area on retail structure, a set of transition probability matrices has been developed for the two retail conformations situated along North Avenue. Both of the conformations represent neighborhood retail centers. Since the retail changes there were minor during 1950–55, attention is focused on structural changes that took place during the 1955–1960 and 1960–1965 periods.

By 1960, the racial composition of the trade area upon which the center at 14th and North Avenue depended had become predominantly Negro. At the same time, Negro entry into the trade area served by the center at 27th and North Avenue was only nominal. Through analysis it can be demonstrated that retail entrants in the former center reflected the changing racial composition of the population while the latter center has been seemingly unaffected. Assuming that the same set of processes determined the nature of retail entry during the 1960–1965 interval as during the previous five-year interval, a first-order Markov Chain

analysis should produce a close approximation of the retail structure of these centers in 1965 (Table 4).

In both instances a general economic decline affected the predictive power of the analysis. Overprediction of shares was common for both centers. But for the 14th St. center, the analysis seriously underpredicted the proportion of retail outlets providing personal services and eating and drinking accommodations. These two categories are those which Negro businessmen are known to have a high propensity for entry. These same two categories were overpredicted for the 27th St. center. It is apparent that the process of economic decline continued within both centers and actually accelerated during the most recent period at the 27th St. center. It is likewise obvious that social factors influenced the decision of retail entrants, especially in the other center.

The retail mix of neighborhood centers characteristically reflects the cultural taste of the trade areas's residents, and a structure once initiated affects the future use of existing retail outlets. Ethnic propensities were apparent in the retail character of the two neighborhood shopping centers during the

Table 4   Retail Composition (in Percentages) of Two Neighborhood Retail Centers, 1965

Retail Category	N. Ave. at N. 14th St.		N. Ave. at N. 27th St.	
	Observed	Predicted	Observed	Predicted
Professional	3.3	3.2	2.5	0.0
Personal	26.6	16.6	12.8	16.1
Financial	9.9	3.2	10.2	1.2
Eating & Drinking	16.6	6.4	25.6	28.2
Groceries	10.0	17.2	0.0	2.0
Clothing	0.0	3.2	0.0	2.4
Automotive	6.6	5.6	0.0	0.0
Multifunctional	0.0	0.0	5.1	7.6
Specialty	10.0	9.6	7.6	10.0
Household	6.6	11.2	17.9	13.3
Miscellaneous	6.6	6.4	7.6	5.1
Vacant	13.3	19.3	10.2	2.5

initial time period. In 1950 the center at
14th and North Avenue still served a sizable
Jewish population, a fact that was evident in
the number of grocery and related activities
ocupying units there. Similarly, the *gemuet-
lichkeit* of the German neighborhood was
expressed by the importance of the German
owned drinking establishments occupying
space in the center at 27th and North
Avenue. The Negro population, representing
the most recent entrant into the area, is in
effect responsible for the superimposition of
a new retail structure upon the remnants of
a decaying structure. Although the social
and economic factors cannot always be
easily separated, while operating together
they each yield outcomes which are more
readily related to one than to the other.

Obviously, it is difficult to ascertain the
effects of racial composition on the retention probabilities of the derived matrices,
but the probability of entry is more clearly
associated with the racial composition of the
trade area. Thus, the land uses Pred[17] described as being more characteristic of Negro
commercial development appear to be widespread, showing up in commercial developments serving a Negro population in cities
throughout the nation.

Once the process of racial change is complete, there is generally less retail diversity to
be found within neighborhood centers than
previously (Figure 3). While both centers in
Figure 3 were on the decline, the center

---

17. A. Pred, *op. cit.*

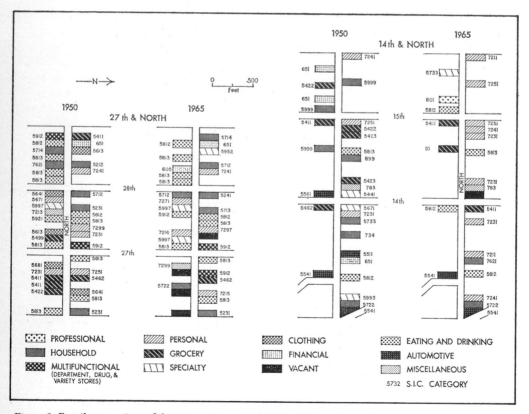

Figure 3. Retail categories and functions in two neighborhood shopping centers.

serving a predominantly white clientele provided only one less function in 1965 than it had in 1950. The center serving a predominantly Negro population, although suffering a smaller absolute decline in number of stores, provided nine fewer functions in 1965 than it had in 1950. It is evident that both of the described commercial ribbons will eventually house businesses that cater to a predominantly Negro population; it is also obvious that the probability analysis is better suited to analyze the change in retail structure which is related to race on a center by center basis.

It is apparent that competition for business space in older areas is on the decline, thereby permitting the easy entry of a multiplicity of low-order businesses. This deterioration in demand subsequently leads to the evolution of commercial blight. When one considers the relative location of commercial ribbons transecting ghetto areas one cannot be certain of the role which race plays in this situation. Yet it is apparent that race tends to serve as a catalyst which accelerates the commercial transition.

Through the use of a simplified Markov Chain analysis it was found that one could predict rather accurately the retail mix along a commercial ribbon prior to Negro entry. After Negro entry, the matrices of transition probabilities demonstrated the operation of a set of forces that were not previously discernible. The major drawback of Markov Chain analysis in this kind of study is that it does not permit one to identify precisely the roles of specific change-producing variables. Improvements in this respect might be obtained either by increasing the number of retail categories or reducing the length of the

time interval upon which the matrix of transition probabilities is based, or both.

In the evolution of the Negro business street, the dropping out of goods-supplying units is frequently observed, and this permits an increase in the relative importance of suppliers of social services. The Negro business operator along the arteries is principally engaged in operating units in this latter category. With the declining relative importance of goods outlets along commercial ribbons in Negro residential areas, the neighborhood center diminishes in importance as a source of convenience goods. At the same time, the neighborhood center becomes essentially a place for obtaining social services. This phenomenon more and more draws convenience goods shoppers into the shopping goods center, a situation that is somewhat unique.

The continuous expansion of the ghetto as an urban sub-system also means the continuous spread of commercial blight unless some stabilizing forces are intentionally introduced. As the prospective Negro business operator is by custom forced to operate within Negro neighborhoods[18] and has access to only limited risk capital, one could hardly expect him to alter this condition. If the process of commercial change which was observed within a very limited area is permitted to continue unaltered, then the problem of predicting certain kinds of commercial landscape changes, especially the intensity of blight, is a task that can be readily conducted within the context of predicting the spatial pattern of the Negro ghetto (Figure 4).

18. E. P. Foley, "The Negro Businessman: In Search of a Tradition," *Daedalus*, 95 (1966), 113.

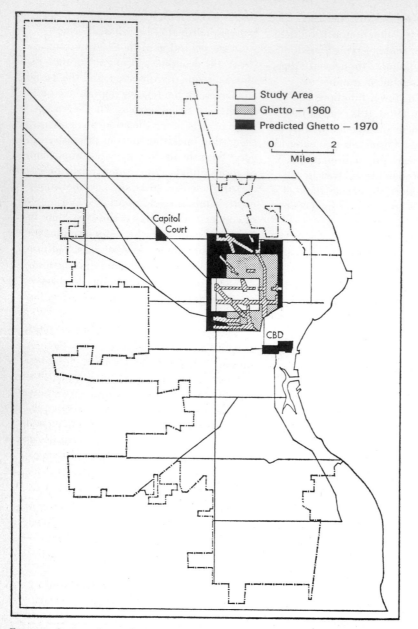

Figure 4. Projected spread of the ghetto and the spread of commercial blight.

✸✸✸✸✸✸✸✸✸✸✸✸✸✸✸✸✸✸✸✸✸✸✸✸✸✸✸✸✸✸

MARKETING AND SOCIAL STRUCTURE IN RURAL CHINA

G. William Skinner

I set forth in this paper[1] a partial description and preliminary analysis of rural marketing in China. This neglected topic has significance which ranges far beyond the disciplinary concerns of economics. It interests anthropologists in particular because marketing structures of the kind described here for China appear to be characteristic of the whole class of civilizations known as "peasant" or "traditional agrarian" societies. In complex societies of this important type, marketing structures inevitably shape local social organization and provide one of the crucial modes for integrating myriad peasant communities into the single social system which is the total society. The Chinese case would appear to be strategic for the comparative study of peasant marketing in traditional agrarian societies because the integrative task accomplished there was uniquely large; because the exceptional longevity and stability of Chinese society have allowed the marketing system in many regions to reach full maturity prior to the beginnings of modernization; and because available docu-

mentation of Chinese marketing over several centuries provides rich resources for the study of systemic development—of change within tradition.

Change which constitutes departure from the traditional system—which signals the onset of the transformation of a traditional agrarian society into a modern industrial society—can also be profitably approached through the study of rural marketing. Basic alterations in the distribution of markets and the patterning of marketing behavior provide a sensitive index of progress in modernization. Rural marketing thus deserves serious attention during each of the periods into which modern Chinese history can be divided—not excepting the contemporary Communist era. The subject takes on added significance during the most recent decade because of the correspondences which can be demonstrated between the units of collectivization and marketing systems. It is part of my purpose in this paper to suggest that an adequate interpretation of developments since 1949 in the Chinese countryside must rest on a prior analysis of premodern peasant marketing.

Although the scholarly literature on local marketing in China is relatively meagre,[2] the

1. A preliminary version was prepared for the Seminar on "Processes of Change in Chinese Society," Toronto, Nov. 1-2, 1963, organized by the Subcommittee for Research on Chinese Society of the Joint Committee on Contemporary China. A reworked and abridged version of the sections on marketing communities was given as a Public Lecture at the London School of Economics and Political Science, Feb. 10, 1964. I am grateful for both opportunities.

2. On the side of documentary research, pioneering work was done by Katō Shigeshi. He and three other Japanese scholars have begun a systematic exploitation of *fang-chih:* Katō Shigeshi, "Shindai ni okeru sonchin no teiki ichi" ["Rural Periodic

raw materials for analysis are in abundant supply. Thousands of *fang-chih*, the gazetteers prepared locally for *hsien* and other administrative units, provide information in remarkable detail about local markets and often about the marketing process itself. These and other traditional documentary sources were supplemented during the pre-Communist era of transition by the descriptions of foreign observers, information reported in local newspapers, raw data compiled through fact-finding surveys, and even bits of scholarly field work. The richest resource for the study of rural marketing in mainland China, both before and after 1949, is the large body of potential informants from the mainland now resident in Taiwan, Hong Kong, and overseas—individuals who participated over a period of years in the marketing systems to which their native places belonged. Data for the present study are drawn from my own field work in Szechwan, 1949-50[3]; intensive interviews with a handful of *émigré* informants in the United States, Hong Kong, and Singapore; a large number of *fang-chih*; and a variety of other published works.[4] I have, nevertheless, barely tapped the potential sources, and this

---

Markets of the Ch'ing Dynasty"], *Tōyō gakuhō*, XXIII, No. 2 (Feb. 1936), 153-204; Kuramochi Tokuichirō, "Shisen no jōshi ["The Local Markets of Szechwan"], *Nihon Daigaku Shigakkai kenkyū ihō*, I (Dec. 1957), 2-32; Masui Tsuneo, "Kanton no kyoshi" ["The Local Markets of Kwangtung"], *Tōa ronsō*, IV (May 1941), 263-283; Yamane Yukio, "Min Shin jidai kahoku ni okeru teiki ichi" ["Periodic Markets in North China during the Ming and Ch'ing Periods"], *Shiron* VIII, (1960), 1-52.

Chinese scholars have produced two slighter pieces on rural marketing in earlier dynasties, for which contemporary gazetteers are unavailable: Ho Ko-en, "T'ang-tai Ling-nan ti hsü-shih" ["Periodic Markets in South China during the T'ang Dynasty"], *Shih-huo*, V, No. 2 (1937), 35-37; Ch'üan Han-sheng, "Sung-tai Nan-fang ti hsü-shih" ["Periodic Markets in South China during the Sung Dynasty"], *Li-shih yü-yen yen-chiu-so chi-k'an (Academia Sinica)*, IX (1947), 265-274.

Field work on rural marketing was pioneered by Chinese sociologists. Ch'iao Ch'i-ming and Yang Mou-ch'un (Martin Yang), both trained in rural sociology at Cornell University, were the first to recognize the social significance of marketing systems. C. K. Yang's field study, conducted in 1932-33, remains a classic. Ch'iao Ch'i-ming, *Hsiang-ts'un she-hui-ch'ü hua ti fang-fa [Methods for Mapping the Rural Community]*, Chin-ling ta-hsueh, Nung-lin ts'ung-k'an, no. 31 (Nanking, May 1926); Ch'iao Ch'i-ming, *Chiang-ning hsien Shun-hua-chen hsiang-ts'un she-hui-ch'ü chih yen-chiu [A Study of the Rural Community of Shun-hua Township, Chiang-ning hsien]*, Chin-ling ta-hsüeh, Nung-lin ts'ung k'an, n.s. no. 23 (Nanking, November 1934); Yang Ch'ing-k'un (C. K. Yang),

A North China Local Market Economy, mimeo. (New York: Institute of Pacific Relations, 1944); Yang Mou-ch'un (Martin Yang), *A Chinese Village: T'ai-t'ou, Shantung Province* (New York, 1945); Yang Mou-ch'un, "Chung-kuo ti chi-chen-ch'ü yü hsiang-ts'un she-ch'ü" ("The Traditional Market-town Area as a Modern Rural Community in China"), *She-hui-hsüeh k'an*, I (Dec. 1963), 23-39.

Japanese field work in northern China has also produced a relevant literature, of which the two most important are: Chūgoku Nōson Kankō Chōsa Kankōkai, ed., *Chūgoku nōson kankō chōsa [Investigations into the Customs of Chinese Villages]* (Tokyo, 1952-1958), 6 vols; Amano Motonosuke, Nōson no kenshi shijo" [Traditional Rural Markets], Nōson shijō no kōeki" [Rural Marketing"], *Chūgoku nōgyō no shomondai [Problems of Chinese Agriculture]* (Tokyo, 1953), II, 69-174.

It remains to mention two useful field studies of marketing in Szechwan: Liao T'ai-ch'u, "The Rape Markets on the Chengtu Plain," *Journal of Farm Economics*, XXVIII, No. 4 (Nov. 1946), 1016-24; J. E. Spencer, "The Szechwan Village Fair," *Economic Geography*, XVI, No. 1 (Jan. 1940), 48-58.
3. Field work was made possible by grants from the Social Science Research Council and the Viking Fund (now Wenner-Gren Foundation).
4. Research assistance was ably provided by Stephen M. Olsen and William L. Parish, Jr., both of Cornell University. I am also indebted, for assistance of one kind or another, to Hsiao Chih and John Liu of the Union Research Institute, Hong Kong; to Joseph P. L. Jiang, University of Singapore; and to Yinmaw Kau, Ichikawa Kenjirō, John T. Ma, and William John McCoy, Jr., all of Cornell University.

essay falls correspondingly short of comprehensive treatment.

The paper appears in separate install-
ments. In this, the first part, attention is
focused on the structure of marketing systems, and the analysis is essentially syn-
chronic. The various aspects of change are
reserved for treatment in the second part, to
be carried in the *Journal*'s next issue.

Part I begins with a consideration of two
preliminary matters: the various types of
markets and the principles of market-day
scheduling. In subsequent sections, marketing structures are treated first as spatial and
economic systems and then as social and
cultural systems.

Markets and Central Places

Central places—the generic term for cities,
towns, and other nucleated settlements with
central service functions—may be classified
in a variety of ways. The approach taken
here follows the lead of Christaller and
Lösch.[5] In the analytical tradition which
stems from these scholars, a given central
place may be typed according to its position
in interlocking spatial systems, within which
economic function is associated with hierarchical level.[6] It may be suggested that
regularity in central-place hierarchies and
consistency in the alignment of function
with systemic position are enhanced by, if
they do not actually result from, a condition
of perduring "entropy"—many forces acting
on the system of central places in many
ways over a period of many centuries.[7] Be
that as it may, in the case of China at the
end of her long and relatively stable imperial
era, central places are readily analyzed on
the assumption that the economic function
of a settlement is consistently associated
with its position in marketing systems which
are themselves arranged in a regular hierarchy.

The Chinese countryside supports settlements of bewildering variety. In this attempt
to sort them into meaningful categories, I
begin with the standard market town—a type
of central place which appears to have been
common to all regions of premodern
agrarian China.

By late traditional times, markets had so
proliferated on the Chinese landscape and
were so distributed that at least one was
accessible to virtually every rural household.
They were considered essential, both as a
source of necessary goods and services unavailable in the village community and as an
outlet for local production. I term "standard" that type of rural market which met
all the normal trade needs of the peasant
household: what the household produced
but did not consume was normally sold
there, and what it consumed but did not

---

5. The two classical studies are: Walter Christaller,
Die zentralen Orte in Suddeutschland (Jena, 1933).
August Lösch, *Die räumliche Ordnung der Wirt-
schaft* (Jena, 1944); page references are to the
English translation: *The Economics of Location*
(New Haven, 1954).

6. It is convenience of exposition alone which
dictates the introduction into this paper of a central-place typology prior to the description of
systems. In fact, system analysis is prior to the
construction of an appropriate typology.

7. This hypothesis is merely an extension of the
theory put forward by Berry to account for the
fact that in certain traditional societies, China
included, the sizes of central places exhibit a rank-
size distribution. (In a distribution of this kind, the
number of cases in each ascending size class is a
regular progression from small to large, with no
deficiencies in the middle range.) The extension is
hardly daring in view of the established "compati-
bility of Christaller-Lösch type hierarchies and
rank-size distributions of city sizes." Brian J. L.
Berry, "City Size Distribution and Economic
Development," *Economic Development and Cultural Change*, IX (July 1961), footnote 4, p. 573
and p. 582. See also Martin J. Beckmann, "City
Hierarchies and the Distribution of City Size,"
Economic Development and Cultural Change, VI
(April 1958), p. 246.

produce was normally bought there. The standard market provided for the exchange of goods produced within the market's dependent area, but more importantly it was the starting point for the upward flow of agricultural products and craft items into higher reaches of the marketing system, and also the termination of the downward flow of imported items destined for peasant consumption. A settlement which is the site of a standard market (but not also of a higher-level market) is here called a "standard market town."

Settlement patterns below the level of the standard market town vary from one region to another. Nucleated villages are common throughout most of rural China, and in many areas these constitute the only settlement type below the standard market town. In some areas, however, certain "villages" support a type of market which I will here term "minor." The minor market, popularly known as a "green-vegetable market," specializes in the horizontal exchange of peasant-produced goods. Many necessities are not regularly available, and virtually no services or imports are offered. It is of negligible importance as an entry point for locally produced goods into the larger marketing system. The sporadic occurrence of the minor market in rural China, its limited functions, and its peripheral position with regard to larger marketing systems lead me to consider it apart from the regular hierarchy of central places—as a transitional type which in most cases can be interpreted as an incipient standard market. Since it leads to no confusion, I use the term "minor market" to refer both to the market and to the settlement in which it is located.

In still other parts of China, of which the Szechwan Basin is the outstanding example, neither nucleated villages nor minor markets obtain. Peasants live in dispersed farmhouses or farmhouse clusters, and the only nodes on the economic landscape below the level of the standard market town are the small clusters of shops known as *yao-tien* (literally "small shops"). The exceptional character of human ecology in the Szechwan Basin should not, however, be overemphasized. The dispersed residential units of the Szechwanese countryside form themselves into natural groupings, each focused on a single *t'u-ti miao* (earth-god shrine), which may be termed "dispersed villages." When viewed as social systems, both the dispersed village of Szechwan and the nucleated village more commonly found elsewhere in China may be considered "village communities." The *yao-tien*, which appears sporadically on the Szechwanese landscape, is in some instances simply the "general store" of the dispersed village, and thus an equivalent of the group of shops commonly found in the largest of nucleated villages elsewhere in China. Other *yao-tien*—especially those consisting of several shops and situated at crossroads equidistant from two or three market towns—are the functional equivalent of minor markets elsewhere in China. They may be seen as incipient standard markets, and indeed several examples of standard markets established *de novo* within the memory of my Szechwan informants grew out of *yao-tien*.

It will be noted that the terminology suggested here reserves the term "village" for nucleated settlements which do not support markets.[8] "Village community" is a more inclusive term for residential social systems, nucleated or dispersed, which do not involve a market of any type. No generic

---

8. The use of the word "village" to refer to towns which are the site of standard markets is, however, common enough in the general literature. Spencer, for instance, uses "village" for "market town" throughout his Szechwan study even though it requires a definition of "village" (p. 48) which he admits does not hold for other provinces.

term is proposed for minor markets or *yao-tien*, which are intermediate and transitional between village communities and standard market towns. "Market town," in the terminology used here, is limited to three types of central places positioned at adjacent levels of the hierarchical system of economic centers; each of the three corresponds to a type of market. The standard market, at the lowest of these three levels, has already been characterized. In ascending order, the other two types are here termed the "intermediate market" and the "central market." To begin with the latter, the central market is normally situated at a strategic site in the transportation network and has important wholesaling functions. Its facilities are designed, on the one hand, to receive imported items and distribute them within its dependent area and, on the other, to collect local products and export them to other central markets or higher-level urban centers. It will suffice at this point to say of the intermediate market simply that it has an intermediate position in the vertical flow of goods and services both ways. In the terminology being introduced here, a settlement which is the site of an intermediate market (but not also of a higher-level market) is termed an "intermediate market town." The "central market town" is similarly defined.

A typology of central places in the upper reaches of the hierarchy in traditional China is complicated by the distinction which can be made between "natural" economic centers and "artificial" administrative centers. The concept of urbanness has, in China, always been intimately associated with the yamen and the wall.[9] In the tradi-

tional Chinese view, a true city *(ch'eng)* is the walled seat of a *hsien* (district), *fu* (prefecture), or *sheng* (province).[10] Given the hierarchical structure of the imperial administrative system, a tripartite typology of administrative central places is virtually automatic. But what is the relation between this hierarchy of administrative centers and the upper reaches of the central-place hierarchy as determined by economic function?

Two extreme and easy answers are possible. One asserts that the two series of central places may be conjoined, the other that they are wholly distinct. Both positions are taken in the scholarly literature, and both, I believe, are wrong. Chang Sen-dou in effect gives the first answer.[11] His typology of lower-level central places is derived from the pioneering field study of C. K. Yang. After analyzing the markets found in Tsou-p'ing *hsien*, Shantung, Yang had posited three types of central places, equivalent to those which I have termed minor markets, standard market towns, and intermediate market towns.[12] The *hsien* in question happened to include no higher-level markets, and the *hsien* seat was classed, quite properly, as an

---

9. It is very nearly valid to say of traditional China that every settlement supporting a yamen was walled, but the converse—that every walled settlement supported a yamen—was never true. Especially interesting in this respect are the *wei* ("fortress town") and *so-ch'eng* ("garrison town"),

official categories of walled towns which, unlike the *hsien-ch'eng*, had no jurisdiction over territory outside the walls. I assume, however, that in these towns the headquarters of the military commander was also known as a *ya-men*.

10. *Hsien*-level units also included the *chou* (department) and *t'ing* (subprefecture). Details for the Ch'ing period are available in Ch'ü T'ung-tsu, *Local Government in China under the Ch'ing* (Cambridge, Mass., 1962), 1 7.

11. "Some Aspects of the Urban Geography of the Chinese *Hsien* Capital," *Annals of the Association of American Geographers*, LI (March 1961), 42-44.

12. C. K. Yang's typology of Chinese markets is entirely acceptable so far as it goes. His terminology, however, raises problems. The levels I term "minor" and "standard" are called by Yang "basic" and "intermediate"—terms which become anomalous in regions with few or no minor markets.

intermediate market town. Chang then accepted C. K. Yang's example as typical and proceeded to *equate* the district capital in the administrative hierarchy with the intermediate market town in the economic hierarchy.[13] Berry and Pred, in their influential critical review of central-place studies,[14] then jump to the conclusion that Chang's article has identified the "classic hierarchy" of central places in traditional China and cite a madcap typology which grafts higher-level administrative capitals onto a series of lower-level central places in the economic hierarchy.

The second of the two possible extreme answers is advanced by Fei Hsiao-t'ung.[15] There are, in Fei's analysis, two types of urban centers—the "garrison town" and the "market town"—which must be kept analytically distinct. They differ in type of site, "aspect," and function. The former are walled towns, imposed artificially on the landscape from the top and located in accordance with considerations of defense; they serve administrative functions. Market towns, by contrast, are unwalled (or at best protected by a less substantial bulwark not built as a public work), a natural growth on the landscape, and located in close congruence with the transport network; they serve commercial functions. To support his view, Fei notes that the size ranges of the two types quite overlap, with many market towns surpassing nearby garrison towns in both population and enterprise.[16]

While Fei's garrison and market towns are useful heuristic constructs, he clearly errs in suggesting that *hsien* seats and other administrative centers do not normally have commercial functions. Every *hsien* city which I have investigated in this regard supports at least one market and can be classed as a given central-place type in accordance with position in a *marketing* system. At the same time, one must agree with Fei that both administrative centers and non-administrative market towns are found at the *same* hierarchical level of economic central places, and in this respect Chang is involved in a simplistic error.

The error is well illustrated by reference to the area studied by C. K. Yang, Chang's authority on market towns. It can readily be shown that Tsou-p'ing, a *hsien* seat and an intermediate market town, is economically dependent on Chou-ts'un, a central market town with no status in the administrative hierarchy. Chou-ts'un is administratively inferior to the seat of the *hsien* in which it is located (Ch'ang-shan), whereas in economic terms, Ch'ang-shan, like Tsou-p'ing, supports only an intermediate market which is dependent on the central market in Chou-ts'un.[17] A compar-

13. Chang illustrates his hypothesis with a very atypical case—that of T'ung-kuan *hsien*, Shensi. Its district seat is unequivocally an intermediate market town, but the *hsien* is abnormally small, both its population and its area being less than one-fifth the national average. *Hsien* of average size are, of course, far more likely to have seats which support central markets.

14. Brian J. L. Berry and Allan Pred, *Central Place Studies A Bibliography of Theory and Applications* (Philadelphia, 1961), p. 153.

15. *China's Gentry: Essays in Rural-Urban Relations* (Chicago, 1953), ch. v.

16. "In the Lake Tai area in my own native district, Wukiang, the garrison town is much smaller and less prosperous than the nearby market towns, such as Chen-tse," p. 103.

17. Chou-ts'un's exalted status in the hierarchy of central places cannot be considered an anomaly resulting from the rail connections which the town has had since early in the century. To the contrary, completion of the railroad had precipitated a decline in the commercial importance of Chou-ts'un and led eventually to its economic dependence on Tsingtao and Tsinan, the railroad termini. Armstrong's comprehensive survey of central places in Shantung as of 1890 makes it clear that at that time Chou-ts'un, Chi-ning (a *chou* seat), and Wei *hsien* were all either local or regional cities in the

able illustration is provided by Chu-chou, a river port in Hsiang-t'an *hsien*, Hunan, which is also a central market town without status in the administrative hierarchy. Hua-yang *hsien*, Szechwan, to cite another relevant case, included in 1949 no less than eight intermediate market towns and one central market town, none of which served as the *hsien* seat.

The extent to which the two hierarchical series of administrative and economic centers overlap or coincide can be determined, it seems to me, only through an analysis of marketing structures in a given region; the resultant classification of the region's central places according to their economic functions and position in marketing systems may then be compared with the administrative status of each center. I have not done this with any thoroughness, but an analysis of marketing structures in several widely dispersed regions of China leads me to posit central places at two levels above that of the central market town and to offer a few sweeping generalizations. The typology and terminology proposed here may be summarized as follows:

My preliminary analyses suggest that only a minority of intermediate market towns serve as the capitals of *hsien* or higher-level administrative units, whereas a clear majority of the central places at the three highest levels have such administrative status. Urban places which served in late Ch'ing as administrative seats of *hsien* (but not also of *fu* or *sheng*) tended to be intermediate or central market towns, more often the latter. Prefectural capitals tended to be either central market towns or local cities, while most provincial capitals would need to be classed in the above hierarchy of central places as either local or regional cities.

In general, as one moves in this hierarchical typology from each type of central place to the next higher, the number of households increases[19] while the proportion of the labor force engaged in agriculture falls. In addition, as one progresses from village to central market town, each type is more likely than the last to be walled and to support the worship of *ch'eng-huang*, the urban deity par excellence. The typical intermediate market town is at least partially

Type of central market	Type of market	Maximum dependent territory
[Minor market]	[Minor market]	[Minor marketing area]
Standard market town	Standard market	Standard marketing area
Intermediate market town	Intermediate market	Intermediate marketing area
Central market town	Central market	Central marketing area
Local city	—[18]	City trading area
Regional city	—[18]	Regional trading area

economic hierarchy of central places—in positions superior to those of the provincial capital and most prefectural capitals. Moreover, at least five Shantung towns with no administrative status may be clearly identified from Armstrong's account as central market towns. Alexander Armstrong, *Shantung* (Shanghai, 1891), 57-72.

18. Central places at these higher levels usually support several markets. The complex structure of marketing in such urban centers is not treated in this paper.

19. It would appear that *within the same systems* there is seldom any overlap in the size of central places at different levels. That is, the local city normally will have more households than any of the central market towns dependent on it; each central market town has more households than any of the intermediate market towns dependent on it, etc. For instance, Chung-hsing *chen*, a central market town in Hua-yang *hsien*, Szechwan, contained approximately 2650 households in 1934. The intermediate market towns dependent on it were

walled and supports a shrine to *ch'eng-huang*. Central market towns and cities in traditional times were usually completely walled and had a full-fledged *ch'eng-huang* temple; this was true even of those centers, like Chou-ts'un, which had no formal administrative status. Thus, it can be seen that position in the hierarchical typology of central places generally correlates with urbanism, whether defined in terms of variables familiar to the urban sociologist or in the common-sense terms of the Chinese layman.[20]

Periodicity and Market Schedules

In Ch'ing China, as in most traditional agrarian societies, rural markets were normally periodic rather than continuous: they convened only every few days. This feature of traditional rural markets may be understood from several points of view.

On the side of the producer or trader, the periodicity of markets is related to the mobility of individual "firms." The itinerant peddlar, toting his wares from one market to the next with the aid of a carrying pole, is the archetype of the mobile firm in China. But equally characteristic of the traditional rural market are the wandering artisans and repairmen who carry their "workshop" about with them, and other itinerants purveying services of all kinds from letter-writing to fortune-telling. Why are these facilities mobile? In essence, because the

total amount of demand encompassed by the marketing area of any single rural market is insufficient to provide a profit level which enables the entrepreneur to survive. By repositioning himself at periodic intervals, the entrepreneur can tap the demand of several marketing areas and thereby attain the survival threshold.[21] From the point of view of the itinerant entrepreneur, periodicity in marketing has the virtue of concentrating the demand for his product at restricted localities on certain specific days. When a group of related markets operates on coordinated periodic (as opposed to daily) schedules, he can arrange to be in each town in the circuit on its market day.

The diffuseness of economic roles in traditional China is also relevant in this regard, for a firm which is at once producer and trader finds periodicity advantageous even when only one market is exploited. Again, by concentrating demand on certain specific days, marketing periodicity enables such entrepreneurs to combine sales with production in an optimally efficient manner. This advantage accrues not only to the artisan in market-town shops, but also to the peasant engaged in cottage industry, and for that matter to the housewife who occasionally has eggs to sell. Each of these producers is his own salesman.

From the point of view of the consumer, the periodicity of markets amounts to a device for reducing the distance he must travel to obtain the required goods and services. We begin here with the restricted nature of those requirements on the part of the average peasant household. General poverty, value emphases on frugality, and

---

all markedly smaller, ranging in size from 360 to 900 households. In turn, each of the intermediate market towns had more households than did any of its dependent standard market towns. The intermediate market town of Chung-ho-ch'ang, to cite just one example at this level, had 900 households in 1934, while the size of its dependent standard markets ranged from 50 to 279. *Hua-yang hsien chih,* Min-kuo 23 (1934), ch. 1.

20. A number of other distinctions among the three hierarchical types of market towns will be introduced below.

21. For a sophisticated treatment of this aspect of periodic marketing see James H. Stine, "Temporal Aspects of Tertiary Production Elements in Korea," *Urban Systems and Economic Behavior,* ed. Forrest R. Pitts (Eugene, Ore., 1962), pp. 68-78.

traditional consumption norms all contributed to a minimal definition of subsistence needs in the peasant household. Furthermore, these needs were in considerable part supplied without recourse to marketing, for the peasant household produced (or received through wages in kind) much of what it consumed; self-sufficiency was a virtue. Under these circumstances, (1) no household needed to market every day, and (2) the number of households required to support a daily market was very large. In most parts of agricultural China, especially prior to the eighteenth century when the rural population was distributed relatively sparsely on the land, the number of households required to support a daily market would have meant marketing areas so large that villagers at the rim could not manage the trip to and from market in a single day. A market meeting only once in three or once in five days, however, could achieve a viable level of demand if only one-third or one-fifth as many villages fell within its dependent area. Thus, when markets are periodic rather than daily, market towns may be distributed far more densely on the landscape so that the most disadvantaged villagers can manage the trip to market in a reasonable period of time.[22] Even when the number of households within a marketing area increases to the point where sufficient demand is present for the market to convert to a daily schedule, from the point of view of the peasant consumer such a change offers little advantage if the household's needs are such that marketing only once every five or six days is the most efficient way to meet them.

It will be noted that the level of transport is a crucial variable no matter how one accounts for the periodicity of traditional markets. It is the "friction of distance" which limits both the demand area of the firm and the dependent area of a market. Thus the periodicity of markets in traditional agrarian societies is, in the last analysis, a function of the relatively primitive state of transport.

The pulsations of economic activity which occur as both mobile firms and mobile consumers converge on rural markets define one of the basic life rhythms in all traditional agrarian societies. The marketing "week," along with the many other temporal cycles which regulate human activity in any society, may usefully be dichotomized as either natural or artificial. Cycles of the former type[23] are tied to the motions of the heavenly bodies, obvious examples being the lunar month and the various seasons of the solar year. Cycles of the latter type are units of so many days which recur in complete disregard of calendars tied to the motions of the sun or moon; when not artificial in origin, they have, like the Western month, been freed from the natural cycle which gave them birth. Most traditional agrarian societies have but one system of market schedules attuned to cycles of one or the other type. The 5-day marketing week of traditional Java and the 7-day marketing week of feudal England are typical artificial cycles, while the 10-day marketing week of Tokugawa Japan is an example of marketing rhythms tied to a natural cycle, in this case the lunar month. In China both types of marketing weeks obtain, each in a variety of versions.

It will facilitate exposition to review the whole Chinese inventory of short-term temporal cycles.[24] There were, to begin

---

22. Stine (p. 70) puts the matter succinctly: "The consumer, by submitting to the discipline of time is able to free himself from the discipline of space."

23. I except here the most basic of all the natural units—the diurnal cycle.

24. Longer-term cycles are relevant only to the scheduling of fairs, as opposed to markets. It is unfortunately the case that the English literature

with, two cycles of the type which recur in complete independence of the sun or moon. One, the *hsün* ("decade"), is ten days in duration, each day in the cycle being named after one of the ten *kan* ("stems"), which have a fixed sequence. The other is twelve days in duration, the cycle being similarly defined by the fixed sequence of the twelve *chih* ("branches"). The stems and the branches have been used ever since the Shang period as a day count,[25] and the almanacs prepared for Chinese peasants today still record the "stem" and the "branch" of each day in the lunar calendar. Another available cycle of great antiquity is provided by the twenty-four solar fortnights (*chieh-ch'i*) into which the tropical year is divided. The onset of each fortnight, all of which bear traditional names relating to the round of seasons in the north, is likewise recorded in the almanacs everywhere available in rural China. These fortnightly dates provide the fixed points in the solar year which the peasant needs to regulate the seasonal round of agricultural activities.

The remaining short-term cycles in the traditional Chinese inventory are tied to the lunar month. Since lunation or the synodic

month bears no functional relation to the rotation of the earth—on the average it is 29.53 days in length—the lunar month cannot recur indefinitely with precisely the same number of days. In China the convention is to alternate 29- and 30-day months, though in the long-run 30-day months occur slightly more often. Under these circumstances it is clear that any subdivision of the lunar month cannot continually recur with precisely the same number of days; marketing rhythms tied to the lunar month are by definition irregular.

The two conventional subdivisions of the Chinese month which have relevance here are the lunar decade, to which the term *hsün* is also applied, and the lunar fortnight. The three lunar *hsün* begin respectively on the 1st, 11th, and 21st of the lunar month; in the case of 29-day months, the third *hsün* lacks one day. The first lunar fortnight, which runs from the 1st through the 14th of the lunar month, is always shorter than the second, which is either 15 or 16 days in duration.[26]

To summarize, the traditional cycles to which marketing schedules could be tied are: the lunar *hsün* or decade (averaging 9.84 days), the independent *hsün* (10 days), the independent duodenary cycle (12 days), the lunar fortnight (averaging 14.765 days), and

on China often uses "fair" for periodic markets as well as for the festivals scheduled according to annual or other long-term cycles. At least in the case of China, the terminology should be standardized, for fairs and markets are functionally distinct, the length of their cycles do not overlap, and the Chinese themselves make a clear-cut conceptual and terminological distinction between the two. *Hui* and *miao-hui* ("temple fair") are reserved for what I term "fairs," whereas "markets" are usually called by terms involving one or more of the following: *shih, chi, hsü,* and *ch'ang. Chi* and its combinations prevail in the north, *hsu* and its combinations in the southeast, and *ch'ang* and its combinations in the southwest.

25. Joseph Needham, *Science and Civilization in China,* III (Cambridge, 1958), 396. "In the Shang period they were used strictly as a day count. The practice of using them for the years as well did not come in until the end of the Former Han ..."

26. Cornelius Osgood, on p. 88 of *Village Life in Old China* (New York, 1963), cites the case of a specialized rural market in Yunnan which suggests that market schedules could also be attuned to the 28 *hsiu* ("lunar mansions")—the zodiac-like segments of the heavens against which the motion of the moon could be measured. (See Needham, III, 233-241). Osgood writes that the town of Ma-chieh was ". . . noted for . . . its market for horses and sheep which was held on those animal days of the calendar." These refer to the animal designations of the 17th and 23rd of the 28 *hsiu* and would, therefore, coordinate with the six-day marketing week which was general in Yunnan. Analysis of this case, however, requires more details than have been supplied by the author.

the solar fortnight (averaging 15.218 days).[27] Of these, only the independent *hsün* appears not to be used in modern China as a basis for marketing schedules.[28]

The two most important families of Chinese scheduling systems are those based on the lunar *hsün* and the duodenary cycle. I shall begin with the latter, because of its regularity and relative simplicity. It provides three regular systems, yielding a 12-day, a 6-day, and a 3-day marketing week. The schedule of a market with a regular 12-day week is, of course, designated by one of the twelve *chih* (branches), that of a 6-day week by two of the *chih*, and that of a 3-day week by four. Six different schedules make up the scheduling system yielding the 6-day week. These are:

Tzu-wu	(i.e., the 1st and 7th days of the cycle)
ch'ou-wei	(2nd-8th)
yin-shen	(rd 9th)
mao-yu	(4th-10th)
ch'en-hsu	(5th-11th)
ssu-hai	(6th-12th)

Regular 3-day schedules are, in effect, combinations of two 6-day schedules: either *tzu-wu* and *mao-yu*, *ch'ou-wei* and *ch'en-hsü*, or *yin-shen* and *ssu-hai*. Thus in areas where 3-day marketing weeks are standard, only three different schedules are available for distribution among the various markets.

The three scheduling systems based on the duodenary cycle are general throughout a band which runs across southern China, broad in the west and narrowing toward the east. The line separating markets with duodenary schedules from others to the north (with schedules based on the lunar *hsün*) runs across the northeastern hook of Yunnan, roughly bisects Kweichow, crosses

northeasternmost Kwangsi, and ends in Kwangtung (just where I have not been able to ascertain). With minor exceptions, the area of duodenary schedules appears to be limited to the upper drainage basins of the Hsi (West) and the Hung (Red) river systems.[29] (Markets in the downstream plains and deltas of both river systems, in Kwangtung and in Tongking, follow schedules based on the lunar *hsün*.) In the area of duodenary schedules as a whole, the periodicity of markets becomes steadily more frequent as one moves from west to east. Twelve-day market schedules appear to be quite rare, and the only cases known to me occur in Yunnan.[30] Six-day schedules are by far the most common of the three in Yunnan and Kweichow as a whole. Three-day schedules are found only occasionally in the west, especially in and around cities, and more generally toward the east.[31] Market schedules based on the duodenary cycle occur only very sporadically outside the provinces mentioned.[32]

---

29. A definitive delimitation of the distribution of duodenary schedules would require reference to all extant gazetteers and/or interviews with informants from *hsien* near the putative boundaries of the duodenary area. The tentative generalizations given here are based on much slimmer data: a small sample of available gazetteers and the material presented by Amano (pp. 81-82) concerning market-day schedules in selected *hsien* of Yunnan and Kweichow.
30. Lo-p'ing *hsien*. Amano, p. 81.
31. Shang-lin, Kwangsi, is an example of a *hsien* all of whose markets follow regular 3-day schedules of this type. *Shang-lin hsien chih*, Kuang-hsü 2 (1876), *ch.* 4.
32. One example is provided by the capital of Ning-hai *chou* on the promontory of Shantung: five markets in and immediately surrounding the city follow five of the six possible regular 6-day schedules (Yamane, p. 500). One should also note the curious case of two markets in T'ai-p'ing *hsien*, Shansi. Their market schedules are listed in dates of the lunar month as follows: 3-9-15-21-27 and 5-11-17-23-29 (Yamane, p. 500). Six-day schedules

---

27. All figures taken from Needham, III, 390-406.
28. A singular irony may be involved here, for it is quite possible that the artificial *hsün* originated as the marketing week of the ancient Chinese. (Cf. Needham, III, 397).

The lunar *hsün* family of scheduling systems is general throughout the rest of China. Three closely related scheduling systems in this family—providing for one, two, or four market days per decade—parallel the set already described which provide for one, two, or four market days per duodenum. All schedules based on the lunar *hsün* are designated by citing the dates of markets in only the first of the three *hsün* in the lunar month. A "3 market" thus meets on the 3rd, 13th, and 23rd of the lunar month, a "3-8 market" on the 3rd, 8th, 13th, 18th, 23rd, and 28th of the lunar month. The two-per-*hsün* scheduling system which provides even spacing of market days is designated as follows: 1-6, 2-7, 3-8, 4-9, and 5-10. All but the last schedule yields six market days per lunar month. These may be combined to form various four-per-*hsün* schedules, as follows:[33]

> 1-3-6-8
> 2-4-7-9
> 3-5-8-10
> 1-4-6-9
> 2-5-7-10
> [1-3-6-8]

These schedules provide eleven or twelve market days per lunar month.

One-per-*hsün* schedules occur only rarely in China.[34] Rural markets with such sched-

ules are for the most part limited to remote mountain valleys or to such peripheral areas as the tip of the Shantung peninsula.[35] Two-per-*hsün* schedules, by contrast, are the most widespread in all of China; with the possible exception of Kwangsi, none of the eighteen provinces is without examples, and throughout most of northern China such schedules are general. Four-per-*hsün* schedules are often used by intermediate or central markets in areas where two-per-*hsün* schedules are followed by standard markets.

The other major member of the lunar-*hsün* family of scheduling systems provides three market days per decade. It consists of the following schedules:

> 1-4-7
> 2-5-8
> 3-6-9
> 4-7-10
> 1-5-8
> 2-6-9
> 3-7-10
> 1-4-8
> 2-5-9
> 3-6-10
> [1-4-7]

It can be shown that the first three schedules plus either 4-7-10 or 3-6-10 provide not only the maximum regularity in the spacing of market days but also the most efficient distribution of market schedules on the landscape. This system is general in the heart of the Szechwan basin, in the larger plains and basins of southeastern China, in the areas around major urban centers in central China, and in pockets elsewhere. Areas of three-per-*hsün* schedules appear consistently as "islands" or "continents" in a sea of two-per-*hsün* markets.

It has already been noted that scheduling systems yielding only one market day in ten or twelve are rare in China. The still longer "fortnightly" marketing weeks are corre-

---

of this kind must either be a description in lunar dates of a regular duodenary 6-day market schedule or else the conversion of such a schedule to the lunar month.

33. The various schedules in a scheduling system are set out in the form introduced here (note the integer series in each column) to point up their inner logic and to demonstrate that all schedules in the system have been exhausted.

34. John K. Fairbank, Alexander Eckstein, and L. S. Yang, in their useful survey of China's traditional argrarian economy during the first half of the 19th century, state that markets with ten-day schedules were typical. This assertion is insupportable. "Economic Change in Early Modern China: An Analytic Framework," *Economic Development and Cultural Change*, IX (October 1960), 7.

35. For examples, see Amano, p. 72, Katō, p. 21, Yamane, pp. 499-500.

spondingly rarer. I have come across only one *hsien*—Feng-shan, Taiwan, just prior to the Japanese occupation—for which schedules of one market per solar fortnight are reported.[36] As for the lunar fortnight, I am able to cite only two cases: the "great markets" held in the 1930's on the 2nd and 16th of the lunar month just inside the north and south gates of Ta-li, a *hsien* seat in Yunnan, and the market which in 1961 was being convened on the 1st and 15th of the lunar month in Ting-ssu-ch'iao, a town in Hsien-ning *hsien*, Hupeh.[37]

It remains to describe one more set of scheduling systems, namely those providing markets every other day, once a day, and twice a day. These three systems constitute a closely related group comparable to the two groups of schedules described above which provide one, two, or four markets per decade or duodenum. In each of these three families of scheduling systems, the second is a doubling of the first, and the third a doubling of the second. While it is unconventional to regard daily markets of any kind as being periodic, my Chinese sources leave no alternative. The pulsation of marketing activity does not necessarily disappear simply because the pitch of the market's periodicity becomes shorter than the diurnal cycle. It should be noted in this regard that Chinese rural markets are seldom day-long affairs; generally they last but a few hours. Certain markets are afternoon or evening markets—and these are almost always so specified in the gazetteers—but the great majority of rural markets are morning markets, no specification being normally understood in this sense. Thus, to say that a mar-

ket has a six-day schedule does not mean that it is "in session" one-sixth of the time, but rather that in every six-day period a few hours of one morning are devoted to marketing. Similarly, a market with a daily schedule is not "in session" continuously, but only for two or three hours of each morning (or afternoon or evening, in certain cases). A twice-daily market is one with two pulsations of marketing activity each day, one in the morning and one in the afternoon or evening. The pitch of its periodic cycle is simply at the opposite extreme from that of the fortnightly markets of Ta-li. When markets become "continuous," in the sense used here, then a qualitative change has occurred which takes the economic center in question outside the scope not only of periodic marketing but of the traditional economy as well. Of this, more in Part II.

Every-other-day markets are designated as *tan* ("odd") or *shuang* ("even"), which means that they meet on the odd or even days of the lunar month. Thus, at the end of a 29-day month, odd markets meet two days in a row and even markets have a two-day interval. Every-other-day market schedules have become general only in small areas which are densely populated and either highly urbanized or commercialized. Examples are the plain between Ningpo and Tz'u-ch'i *hsien* city in Chekiang, a portion of the Chengtu Plain to the west and south of the city, and a region in northern Honan between An-yang and the Yellow river. Daily and twice daily markets are for the most part limited to central market towns and cities.

The spatial distribution of marketing schedules in modern times strongly suggests that the oldest set of schedules in China— that originally adopted by the ancients in the valley of the Huang—was the one-per-*hsün* system, and that in the southwest the one-per-duodenum system was prior. As

---

36. *Feng-shan hsien ts'ai-fang ts'e*, Kuang-hsü 20 (1894).
37. C. P. Fitzgerald, *The Tower of Five Glories* (London, 1941), p. 56; *Ta kung pao* (18 February 1961). Tr. in *Survey of the China Mainland Press*, No. 2476, p. 1.

marketing structures developed, it may be hypothesized that at first higher-level markets and later standard markets "doubled" their schedules by adding one new market day; eventually these two-per-*hsün* and two-per-duodenum schedules became the most common systems in rural China.[38] At a still later stage, the highest-level markets in developing areas appear to have doubled their schedules again.

Doubling is the most advantageous means of increasing market-day frequency, for it requires no disruption of the old schedule: new market days are simply added to the old. This feature accounts for the fact that in the southwest three-per-duodenum schedules (i.e., four-day marketing weeks) never occur, even though the duodenary cycle obviously allows them. The 12-day marketing week may be halved to the 6-day week, and then halved again to the 3-day week through a simple process of adding new days to the old schedule. However, to change from a 6-day to a 4-day marketing week (i.e., from a 2- to a 3-per-duodenum schedule) necessarily involves a disruptive loss of continuity. It should now be apparent why the 4-day week, alone of all possible marketing cycles in the one-to-six-day range, is completely absent in China: The convenience of doubling plus the perfect regularity of the result inhibited the innovation of the 4-day week within the duodenary cycle. And given the module of the *hsün*, no schedule which

yields a majority of 4-day weeks is even possible.

But what accounts for the common occurrence of 3-per-*hsün* schedules? Should not the factors inhibiting 3-per-duodenum schedules also inhibit their counterpart in the lunar-*hsün* family? The difference stems, I believe, from the inherent irregularity of the 4-per-*hsün* schedules. The second doubling of schedules within the duodenary cycle yields perfectly regular 3-day marketing weeks, but the second doubling within the lunar *hsün* cycle yields very irregular spacing, namely, alternating 2-day and 3-day marketing weeks. As we shall see below, when an intermediate market doubles its schedule to 4-per-*hsün*, in effect it has merely provided a second 2-per-*hsün* schedule so as to accommodate its two functionally (though not spatially) differentiated markets: one serving its standard marketing system and one its intermediate marketing system. Thus, because of functional specialization as between market days, the irregularity of its "4-per-*hsün*" schedule presents no problem. But the situation is quite different in the case of a 2-per-*hsün* *standard* market which desires to increase market-day frequency, for in the absence of any functional differentiation, gross unevenness in the spacing of market days presents serious difficulties. While the spacing afforded by 3-per-*hsün* schedules leaves something to be desired, it is markedly superior in this regard to the 4-per-*hsün* system.[39] This advantage is coupled with another which gives the edge to the 3-per-*hsün* system: the pressures

---

38. Two-per-*hsün* schedules are standard for rural Korea in modern times. It is possible that the Koreans borrowed the Chinese system only after two-per-*hsün* schedules had become general in north China, but it seems more likely that Korea simply went through the same development as north China. One-per-*hsün* schedules were standard for rural Japan prior to modernization, suggesting that the Japanese borrowed the Chinese system at an early date when one-per-*hsün* schedules were common. It remains an interesting question just why schedule doubling never occurred in Japan.

39. The 3-per-*hsün* schedules listed earlier provide market cycles slightly more than two-thirds of which are 3-day weeks, the remainder being 4-day weeks. The innovation of 3-per-*hsün* schedules, then, follows directly from the fact that 10 is integrally divisible only by 2 and 5, and the division by 3 yields a product closer to an integer than does division by 4.

which lead to the need for more frequent
market days build up gradually, and it may
be assumed that authorities of a 2-per-*hsün*
market would, in reacting to these pressures,
favor the 50 per cent increase afforded by a
3-per-*hsün* schedule over the 100 per cent
increase of the 4-per-*hsün* schedule. Once
3-per-*hsün* schedules are established in a
given area, the disadvantages of switching
from 2- to 3-per-*hsün* schedules become
irrelevant, for new standard markets can
adopt 3-per-*hsün* schedules from the outset.

Marketing Structures as Spatial and Economic Systems

Any attempt to comprehend the social or
economic dimensions of marketing structures inevitably makes certain assumptions
about their spatial characteristics. One
reason for analyzing these structures as spatial systems, then, is to make explicit the
assumptions which underlie such remarks as
I will be able to make about the economics
and the sociology of marketing. Another
reason is to facilitate the study of change,
for as it happens the nature of systemic
change whether traditional or modern—
becomes fully apparent only when the relevant data are spatially ordered.

In order to set forth meaningful propositions about marketing structures as spatial
systems it will be necessary to have recourse
to simple models. The most radical of the
assumptions made in constructing them is
that the landscape in question is an isotropic
plain on which resources of all kinds are
uniformly distributed. Theoretical considerations based on impeccable geometry and
tolerably sound economics tell us that when
such an assumption is made, market towns
should be distributed on the landscape according to an isometric grid, as if at the
apexes of space-filling equilateral triangles.
In theory, too, the service area of each mar-

ket should approach a regular hexagon.[40]
These expectations apply anywhere in the
world—neither the geometry nor the economics is peculiarly Chinese—and it is therefore of no particular moment to report that
in six areas of China where I have been able
to test the proposition, a majority of market
towns have precisely six immediately neighboring market towns and hence a marketing
area of hexagonal shape, albeit distorted by
topographical features.[41]

But are the hexagonal standard marketing
areas discrete? That is, do the areas typically
overlap? Or, if they fit together in the
manner of hexagonal ceramic tiles, do certain of the villages lie *on* the boundary between two hexagons, oriented toward more
than one standard market? Martin Yang, the
first social scientist to map and describe a
Chinese standard marketing system, has this

40. Proof of the proposition that the regular hexagon is the most advantageous shape for marketing
areas is given in Lösch, ch. X. In common-sense
terms, it may be noted that the appropriate model
has two requirements: Markets should be so distributed that (1) the most disadvantaged villager in any
given marketing area is no more and no less disadvantaged than the most disadvantaged villager in
any other area, and (2) the distance from the market of the most disadvantaged villager in each
marketing area is minimal. The first requirement
means that all marketing areas in the model must
be of uniform shape and size. Since all parts of the
landscape must be in some marketing area, the
only possibilities are the three regular polygons
which are "space-filling," namely, equilateral triangles, squares, and regular hexagons. The second
requirement specifies that the more sides a polygon
has the more efficient it is in this regard. To put it
another way, as you move from the least advantageous position to the most advantageous position
around the rim of the marketing area, the differential is maximal for triangular areas, intermediate
for square areas, and minimal for hexagonal areas.
41. The point is worth noting, however, because
the only study of rural marketing in China which
refers to the shape of marketing areas insists that
they ". . . approach circular or square form." C. K.
Yang, p. 39.

to say: "On the whole, although there is no clear-cut line of demarcation, each market town has a definite and recognizable area, and looks upon the people of certain villages as its primary customers; in turn, it is regarded by the villagers as their town."[42] My research in Szechwan leads me to concur wholeheartedly: I had little trouble in ascertaining the limits of the standard marketing area which I was studying; the peasants within this area did the great bulk of their marketing in Kao-tien-tzu, the standard market town in question; and they considered it *their* market.[43] There are theoretical reasons, as I shall note in Part II, for expecting a standard marketing area in which new villages are being established to pass through a phase in which a small number of newly established villages are situated equidistant from two or three markets, but in a stable situation there is no theoretical reason for objecting to the assumption of essential discreteness which is supported by empirical evidence.[44]

If one assumes that standard marketing areas are in the ideal case discrete, hexagonal in shape, and dotted at regular intervals with villages, then geometric principles require an integral number of complete rings of villages around the town: either one ring (of 6 villages) or two rings (one of 6 and one of 12) or three rings (one of 6, one of 12, and one of 18), or still more. Which of these models best fits the Chinese case?

Empirical evidence clearly points to the two-ring model with its total of 18 villages. It is not that every known case of a standard marketing area has a close approximation of 18 villages. My assertion is based rather on (1) the finding that the ratio between villages and standard or higher-level markets on any sizable segment of the Chinese landscape *averages* very close to 18, and (2) the fact that variation in the ratios can be accounted for satisfactorily by a developmental model which moves from one 18-village-per-market equilibrium to another—but not by models which posit a stable equilibrium of 6 or 36 villages per market. Data relevant to the second point must await Part II; here I can appropriately do no more than cite selected averages. In the 1870's, the average number of villages per rural market was 17.9 in Hsiang-shan *hsien* and 19.2 in Ch'ü-chiang *hsien*, both in Kwangtung.[45] The classic field study of Chinese rural marketing—that of C. K. Yang in the 1930's in Tsou-p'ing *hsien*, Shantung—shows 21.4 villages per standard and higher-level market.[46] The *yin hsien t'ung-chih*,[47] compiled in 1937, one of the truly outstanding examples of Chinese gazetteer scholarship, presents detailed data which yield an average of 20.1 villages for each of its 82 periodic markets. I have been able to find records of contemporary date for the number of markets *and* villages over a really large area only in the case of Kwangtung in the 1890's;[48] the ratio of villages to rural markets for the province as a whole at that time was 19.6.

42. Martin Yang, 1945, p. 190.
43. C. K. Yang, p. 39, refers to the marketing areas of Tsou-p'ing *hsien* as ". . . economic cells, each . . . having its own boundary of operation . . ."
44. Field workers have occasionally been misled in this regard by a failure to distinguish between standard and intermediate markets. Evidence that villagers attend two different markets—one standard and one intermediate—may be misinterpreted as an indication of their membership in two *standard* marketing systems.

45. *Hsiang-shan hsien chih*, T'ung-chih 12 (1873), ch. 5; *Ch'ü-chiang hsien chih*, Kuang-hsü 6 (1800); data reproduced in Katō, p. 34.
46. Data for this computation are given on pp. 5-6.
47. *Yü-ti chih*, ts'e 3 for villages, ts'e 7 for markets.
48. Chang Jen-chun, comp. *Kuang-tung yu-ti ch'uan-t'u [Comprehensive Atlas of Kwang-tung]* Canton, Kuang-hsu 23 (1897), 2 vols.

Our model, then, which is diagrammed as the basic pattern of Figure 1, shows a hexagonal marketing area with the market town at the center, surrounded by an inner ring of six and an outer ring of twelve villages. As is empirically typical, the model calls for six major paths radiating out from the town.

These paths are at once the arteries and the veins of an economic system whose heart is the market in the town at its center. Along these paths, in the early morning hours of every market day, typically pass at least one

out of every five adults living in the whole array of dependent villages. In T'ai-t'ou, the Shantung village described by Martin Yang, "some member from almost every household in the village is in the town on market day,"[49] while in Luts'un, the Yunnan village studied by Fei and Chang, ". . . at least one went from each household each market day."[50]

49. Martin Yang, 1945, p. 191.
50. Fei Hsiao-t'ung and Chang Chih-i, *Earthbound China* (Chicago, 1945), p. 172. Households mar-

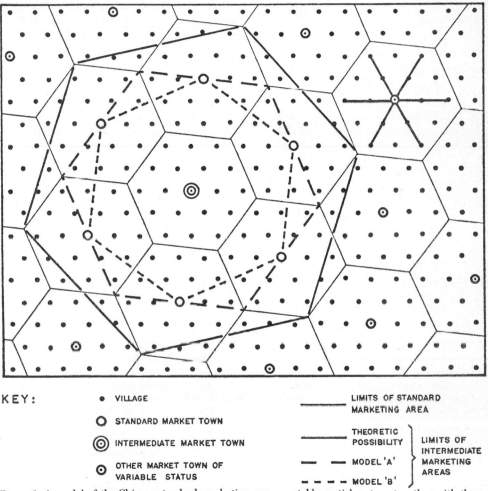

KEY:

- • VILLAGE
- ○ STANDARD MARKET TOWN
- ◎ INTERMEDIATE MARKET TOWN
- ⊙ OTHER MARKET TOWN OF VARIABLE STATUS

——————— LIMITS OF STANDARD MARKETING AREA

——————— THEORETIC POSSIBILITY
— — — MODEL 'A'   } LIMITS OF INTERMEDIATE MARKETING AREAS
- - - - MODEL 'B'

Figure 1. A model of the Chinese standard marketing area as a stable spatial system, together with three possible models of intermediate marketing areas.

During the few hours of market before the inward flow of villagers is reversed, the meagre facilities of the typical standard market town are sorely taxed. Most such towns have only one real street and lack a defined single marketplace altogether. Instead there is a multitude of petty marketplaces, one for each product. The grain market may be held in the temple courtyard, the pig market at the edge of the town, while each of the various items of perishable products and minor crafts produced locally has its customary marketing section along the main street. Even though most sellers at any standard market are likely to be itinerants, the standard market town normally has a certain minimum of permanent facilities. These typically include—in addition to the socially important tea houses, wineshops, and eating places—one or more oil shops (selling fuel for wick lamps), incense and candle shops (selling the essentials of religious worship), and at least a few others offering such items as looms, needles and thread, brooms, soap, tobacco, and matches. Standard market towns normally support a number of craftsmen as well, including most typically blacksmiths, coffinmakers, carpenters, and makers of paper effigies for religious burning. A few crude workshops to process local products may also be located in a standard market town.

The standard market functions in the first instance to exchange what the peasant produces for what he needs. The peasant needs not only goods of the kind already suggested, but also the services of tool sharpeners and livestock castrators, medical practitioners and "tooth artists," religious specialists and fortune tellers, barbers, myriad entertainers, and even, on occasion, scribes. While many of these services are not available every market day, itinerants purveying all of them occasionally visit every standard market.

The standard marketing system also has a modest financial dimension. Shops in the town extend credit to regular customers. Certain shopkeepers and landowners lend money to peasants in transactions which may take place in the town on market day. The rotating credit societies of the peasant are also usually organized in the teahouses on market day and are thereby restricted to villagers from within the system.[51] In addition, certain landlords maintain an office in the town which collects rent from tenants.[52]

With regard to transport, village communities normally include a few landless peasants, as they are usually termed, who are regularly for hire as transport coolies. (Not only the local élite but also the stratum of the peasantry which is fully "respectable" eschew such public manual labor as carrying or carting bulky produce.) These men normally cart goods along the village paths serving a single marketing area and thus

---

keted much less often in Yits'un, another of the villages studied by Fei and Chang, but this village falls in an area which is marginal to agricultural China and in which marketing areas are immense. Of this, more in the following section.

For the Szechwan Basin, Spencer (p. 55) estimates that on any given market day throughout the year, on the average every other family is represented at market—a proportion which, from my own experiences, seems low. It must also be noted that many households are represented by two or more members.

51. Ch'iao Ch'i-ming, 1934, p. 15. In this study of a marketing community near Nanking, the intervillage membership of rotating credit societies is singled out for special notice.

52. "The landlord has an office in the market-town and keeps in touch with his tenants on market-days." Li Mei-yun, *An Analysis of Social, Economic and Political Conditions in Peng-shan Hsien, Szechwan, China, Looking toward Improvement of Educational Programs,* unpublished dissertation in education, Cornell University, 1945, p. 223.

constitute another element in the standard marketing structure as a spatial-economic system.

While the activity which gives definition to the standard marketing system pulsates in accordance with the marketing week, it should not be imagined that its structure has no manifestation between market days. It is during what are in Szechwan colloquially called the "cold days" that many obligations incurred during the "hot" market day are met, and these, too, reinforce and express the total system. Grain sold to a buyer at market may be transported the next day. *Hsiao fan-tzu* ("petty commission agents") learn on market day which peasants have peanuts to sell and on the "cold days" visit their farms to make bids. Barbers travel along the village roads to give haircuts in those households which commissioned them at market. Carpenters, blacksmiths, and other artisans may also be hired at market to work in village households. These transactions all occur within the system defined in the first instance as the trading area of the standard market.

It is apparent from what has been described already that the standard marketing system, when viewed in spatial and economic terms, is but a subsystem of a larger structure. In particular, there is a regular movement both of goods and of mobile firms between the standard market town and the intermediate or still higher-level market towns to which it is immediately tied. I use the plural because in the usual case the standard market is dependent on two or three higher-level market towns rather than just one. The possibilities in this regard are presented in diagrammatic form in Figure 1. The most inclusive of the three hexagonal intermediate marketing areas shown—the only model in which the standard market town is dependent on only one higher-level market town—appears to be relevant to the Chinese

scene only where marketing systems are situated in something of a topographic cul-de-sac. Standard markets at the upper end of mountain valleys, for instance, are dependent solely on the downstream intermediate market. Even in these cases, however, the standard market towns downriver from the intermediate market are likely also to be oriented to a second intermediate market located still further downstream.

In China the great majority of empirical cases fit one or the other of the two less inclusive models labeled A and B in Figure 1, or else fall in between them. Each standard market town is dependent on two higher-level market towns in the case of Model A, and on three in the case of Model B. An actual example of a Chinese landscape whose markets are distributed essentially in accordance with Model A is depicted in Figure 2; and a comparable example fitting Model B is shown in Figure 3. Both figures are designed to show the relation between spatial "reality" as conventionally mapped and model diagrams of the kind used in this paper.

In the usual case, then, a standard market is involved in two or three intermediate marketing systems rather than a single one. This fact points up a crucial distinction between the standard marketing system, on the one hand, and intermediate and higher-level marketing systems, on the other. Whereas the former is essentially discrete with regard to the inclusion or exclusion of component settlements, the latter are not. Whereas the stable equilibrium model of the standard marketing area shows *no* villages at the boundaries (and transitional models show only a small proportion of all villages at the boundary), the regular model of the intermediate marketing area shows *all* dependent standard market towns at the boundaries, equidistant from two or three higher-level market towns. In practice, while the

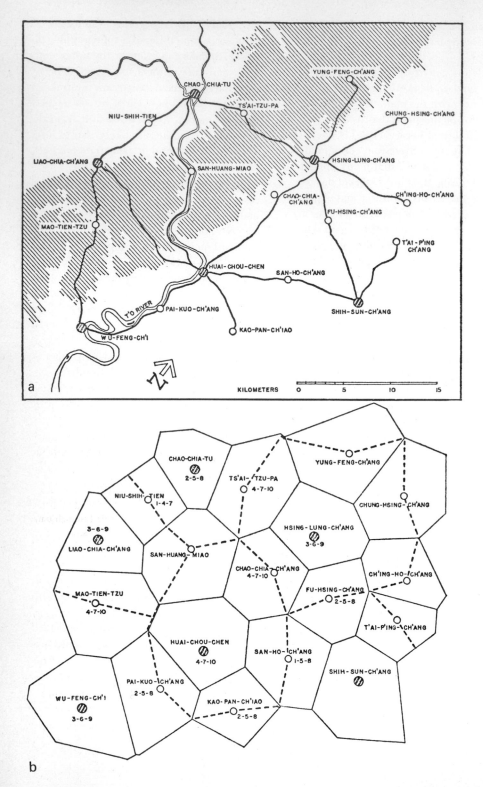

a

KILOMETERS   0   5   10   15

b

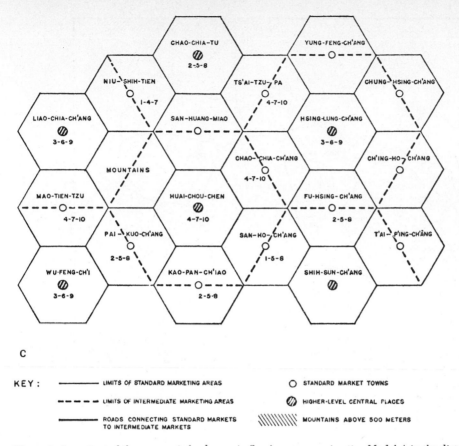

C

KEY :

———————— LIMITS OF STANDARD MARKETING AREAS

– – – – – LIMITS OF INTERMEDIATE MARKETING AREAS

———————— ROADS CONNECTING STANDARD MARKETS
TO INTERMEDIATE MARKETS

○ STANDARD MARKET TOWNS

⦾ HIGHER-LEVEL CENTRAL PLACES

\\\\\\\\ MOUNTAINS ABOVE 500 METERS

Figure 2. A portion of the economic landscape in Szechwan approximating Model A in the distribution of market towns.

Figure 2a. The 19 market towns depicted lie between 35 and 90 km. northeast of Chengtu. Five markets (Yung-feng-ch'ang, Chung-hsing-ch'ang, Ch'ing-ho-ch'ang, T'ai-p'ing-ch'ang, and Shih-sun-ch'ang) are in Chung-chiang *hsien*, the other 14 in Chin-t'ang *hsien*. The mountains shown are part of the Lung-ch'üan range. The only roads mapped are those which connect standard to higher-level market towns.

Figure 2b. First abstraction of the same landscape showing theoretic standard and intermediate marketing areas.

Figure 2c. The same reduced to diagrammatic form. Compare with Model A as diagrammed in Figure 1.

territorial overlap of intermediate marketing systems is not great, it is crucial in the sense that, apart from the nucleus itself, all the primary nodes within the system are normally not exclusive to it.

A notable feature of the intermediate marketing system concerns the distribution of market schedules within it. In the literature on periodic marketing in China, it is usually imagined that schedules are simply distributed among markets in such a way that each shares the same schedule with as

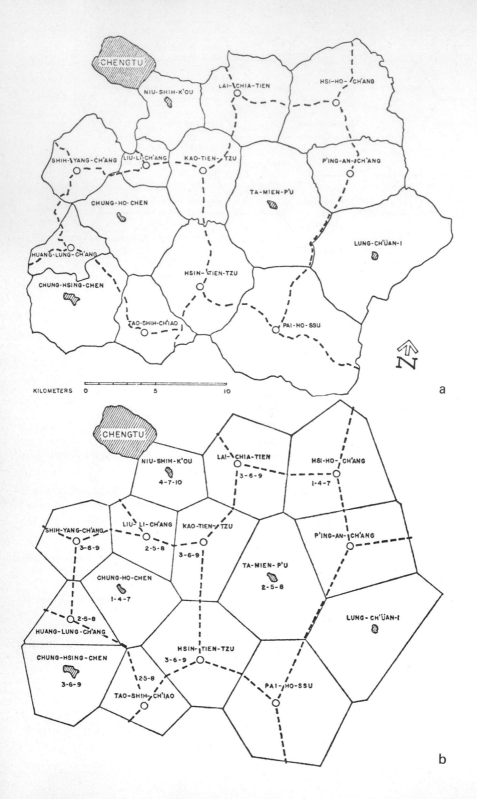

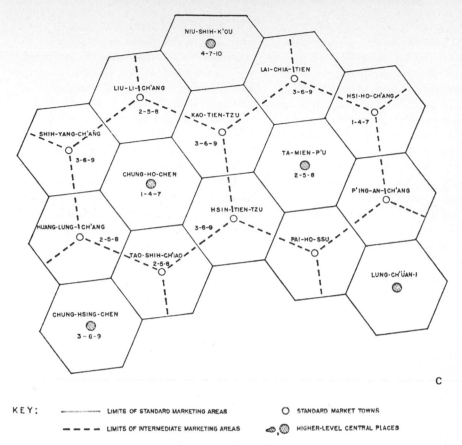

KEY: ———— LIMITS OF STANDARD MARKETING AREAS   ○ STANDARD MARKET TOWNS

━ ━ ━ LIMITS OF INTERMEDIATE MARKETING AREAS   ◍,◍ HIGHER-LEVEL CENTRAL PLACES

Figure 3. A portion of the economic landscape in Szechwan approximating Model B in the distribution of market towns.

Figure 3a. The 15 market towns depicted lie to the southeast of Chengtu within a radius of 25 km. Three markets (P'ing-an-ch'ang, Lung-ch'üan-i, and Pai-ho-ssu) are in Chien-yang *hsien*, the other 12 in Hua-yang *hsien*. The terrain varies from flat to hilly; Lung-ch'üan-i is situated at the western foothills of the Lung-ch'üan mountain range. Marketing-area boundaries are only approximate.

Figure 3b. First abstraction of the same landscape showing theoretic standard and intermediate marketing areas.

Figure 3c. The same reduced to diagrammatic form. Compare with Model B as diagrammed in Figure 1.

few of its neighbors as possible. The purpose of such dovetailing, as noted for instance by Spencer,[53] would be to make it possible for villagers to have an open market within

reach almost every day and to reduce competition among neighboring markets. However, not only have peasants little need or occasion to market more often than provided for by the schedule of their nearest standard market, but, in addition, it can be

53. Pp. 49 (Fig. 1 caption) and 51-52.

shown that schedules are not distributed in the simple manner affirmed or suggested in the literature. Rather, their distribution is designed to minimize conflict between the schedule of a given standard market and the schedules of the higher-level markets toward which it is oriented; the schedules of neighboring standard markets are essentially irrelevant. Stated another way, as new standard markets are established, a schedule will be selected which minimizes conflict with neighboring intermediate markets regardless of the schedules of neighboring standard markets.

The point may be illustrated by reference to the case of Chuan-p'eng-ssu, a market established in the Kuang-hsü reign in Chin-t'ang *hsien*, Szechwan.[54] At the time when it was established, there were four immediately neighboring markets with these schedules: 1-4-7 to the west, 2-5-8 to the northwest, 3-6-9 to the east, and 1-5-8 to the south. According to the principle of minimal conflict with all neighbors, the new market would have adopted a 3-6-10 or 4-7-10 schedule; at the very least it would have avoided any schedule including 5-8. In fact, the new market chose 2-5-8, for the simple reason that the towns to the west (1-4-7) and east (3-6-9) supported intermediate markets to which the new market would be oriented, whereas the towns with 2-5-8 and 1-5-8 schedules were standard market towns with which the newcomer would have minimal commercial ties.

As a consequence of this governing principle, neighboring standard markets often have the same schedule (note in Figure 3b Lai-chia-tien, Kao-tien-tzu, and Hsin-tien-tzu, all with 3-6-9 schedules), whereas intermediate markets usually have no scheduling conflict

with any of their dependent standard markets. This means that in areas of 3-per-*hsün* schedules, for instance, when the intermediate market has a 1-4-7 or 4-7-10 schedule, then all six of the dependent standard markets must share the only two harmonizing schedules which remain: 2-5-8 and 3-6-9. This situation is illustrated by the intermediate marketing system of which Chung-ho *chen* is the center (Figure 3b). [55]

It will be noted from Figure 1 that, in addition to portions of the standard marketing areas of all dependent standard market towns, intermediate marketing areas include one complete standard marketing area at the center. This points up the important fact that an intermediate market town functions as the nucleus not only of the larger intermediate marketing system but also of a smaller standard marketing system.[56] As C. K. Yang puts it (p. 14), the intermediate market town ". . . usually has two service areas, a primary area including nearby villages attending the market regularly or at least frequently, and a secondary area encompassing villages farther away where people come to the market only occasionally for items hard to obtain in their own . . . [standard] markets." [57]

---

54. *Chin-t'ang hsien chih*, Min-kuo 10 (1921), *ch.* 1. One of the market towns involved lies in Hua-yang, *hsien;* the schedule of its market is given in *Hua-yang hsien shih*, Min-kuo 23 (1934), *ch.* 1.

55. An equivalent example in a *hsien* where the 4-per-duodenum scheduling system is standard is provided by the intermediate marketing system centered on P̓ai-hsü (Shang-lin *hsien*, Kweichow), which has a *yin-shen-ssu-hai* schedule; its five dependent standard markets necessarily eschew P̓ai-hsü's schedule and share among them the two other possibilities. For market schedules see *Shang-lin hsien chih*, Kuang-hsü 2 (1876); data reproduced in Katō, pp. 26-27.

56. Everything which a peasant can do in his standard market can also be accomplished in his intermediate market. For those villages whose closest market is situated in an intermediate market town, the intermediate market is also the standard market.

57. The place of the intermediate market in the distribution system gives it certain economic ad-

This dual status of the intermediate market town is not infrequently reflected in the schedule of the town's market days. Throughout the areas of China where two-per-*hsün* schedules are general, many of the intermediate market towns follow a doubled schedule, with one set of two days (say 1-6) known as *hsiao-chi* ("small market") and the other (say 3-8) as *ta-chi* ("large market"). [58] In such cases, the market functions as a standard market on the *hsiao-chi* days and as an intermediate market on the *ta-chi* days. Thus, while the schedules of standard markets dependent on such an intermediate market must not conflict with its *ta-chi* schedule, it is of no consequence if they coincide with its *hsiao-chi* market days. An example is provided by K'ai-p'ing *chen* in Luan *chou* early in the nineteenth century. This town held its "large" market on a 5-10 schedule, with which none of the surrounding markets conflicted, but its "small" market was on a 2-7 schedule, which was also followed by standard markets in two of the surrounding towns.[59] Whereas the irregularity of 4-per-*hsün* schedules would be disadvantageous for a standard market, in the case of an intermediate market like K'ai-p'ing *chen*, the irregularity of the doubled sched-

ule is less apparent, for each of the regular 2-per-*hsün* schedules serves a functionally distinct market.

In general, as the above examples indicate, when the scheduling system of a higher-level market differs from that of its dependent standard markets, the schedule of the higher-level market is the more frequent.[60] All but one of the few cases known to me where the reverse is true are urban and can be accounted for in terms of complete differentiation of hierarchical function whereby intermediate markets are not also standard markets.[61]

I have made much of the fact that within intermediate marketing systems schedules are so distributed that one of the possibilities is normally monopolized by the intermediate market. Such a distribution may, in fact, be taken as circumstantial evidence of the systemic genuineness of a given cluster of markets. But just why is conflict between standard market days and intermediate market days so consistently eschewed? Clearly it is not primarily to serve the convenience of the peasantry. As the quotation from C. K. Yang's study has already noted, peasants attend their intermediate market only occasionally to make purchases which are out of the ordinary, to obtain some service which peasants do not normally demand, to secure credit on an extraordinary scale, or to attend an annual religious festival. During three months when I lived with a typical peasant family in Szechwan, whose farmstead was three *li* from one market town,

---

vantages vis-à-vis neighboring standard markets in the competition for peasant (i.e. standard-market) trade. Prices paid for local produce tend to be slightly higher, and prices charged for imported items tend to be slightly lower in the intermediate markets than in standard markets. One therefore expects standard marketing areas centered on intermediate market towns to be somewhat larger than neighboring standard marketing areas centered on standard market towns.

58. I have come across only one comparable case in 3-per-*hsün* areas of a doubled "large" and "small" market schedule: Ts'ai-lang-ch'iao, an intermediate market in Yin *hsien*, Chekiang, held its "large" market on a 3-5-8 schedule and its "small" market on a 1-7-10 schedule. *Yin hsien t'ung-chih,* 1937, *Yü-ti chih, ts'e* 7.

59. *Luan chou chih,* Chia-ch'ing 15 (1810), *ch.*2.

60. In the case of Li-ling *hsien*, Hunan, for instance, markets on a daily schedule in 1948 included all central markets, but only three of the ten intermediate markets and none of the standard markets.

61. The one exception is provided by Ta-pu *hsien*, Kwangtung, in which the two intermediate markets follow 2-per-*hsün* schedules as opposed to the 3-per-*hsün* schedules of their dependent standard markets.

Kao-tien-tzu, and five *li* from another, Niu-shih-k'ou, the household head and his wife between them marketed forty-six times at the former, their standard market, and only three times at the latter, their intermediate market. In any case, the peasant's intermediate marketing needs would have been given ample scope by any scheduling distribution which provided out of every *hsün* or duodenum one intermediate market day which did not conflict with the schedule of his standard market.

The situation was rather different in the case of the local élite. Everything which set them apart from the peasantry encouraged their attendance at the intermediate market. They were literate, and in the intermediate as opposed to the standard market they could buy books and stationery supplies.[62] Their style of life was if not exalted at least gentlemanly, and from time to time they needed to purchase foodstuffs, decorative items, or cloth of a quality which for a peasant would be sheer indulgence and hence unavailable in standard markets. They were men of comparative wealth, and the intermediate market town offered a range of opportunities for money lending and investment unmatched in their standard market towns. They were also men of leisure, and it was only in intermediate or higher-level markets that tea- and wine-houses especially equipped to fill the idle hours of leisured gentlemen were available. In short, while the

regular needs of the peasants were met by the standard market, those of the local élite were met only by the intermediate market.

If the carefully attuned schedules as between an intermediate market and its dependent standard markets were for local élite a very real convenience, for many of the local traders they were an absolute necessity. A sizable proportion of the "mobile firms" in rural China followed a circuit limited to a single intermediate marketing system; their home base was in the intermediate market town, and they needed to return there periodically to dispose of what they were buying, to restock what they were selling, and simply to rest with their families.

A reference to Figure 3c can illustrate how the intermediate market's exclusive schedule served the purposes of itinerant entrepreneurs. Take the case of the system centering on Chung-ho *chen*. A typical circuit would have the itinerant in the intermediate market for its market day on the 1st of the lunar month, in Huang-lung-ch'ang on the 2nd, Shih-yang-ch'ang on the 3rd, and back to Chung-ho *chen* for its market day on the 4th; on to Liu-li ch'ang on the 5th, Kao-tien-tzu on the 6th, and back to the central town for its market day on the 7th; then to Tao-shih-ch'iao on the 8th, Hsin-tien-tzu on the 9th, and back to Chung-ho *chen* on the 10th for a day of rest prior to entering the town's market on the 11th. Thus in each lunar *hsün* the itinerant completes a full circuit during which he has three market days at the intermediate market and one market day each at the six dependent standard markets. Those making circuits of this kind include purveyors of services with limited demand among the peasantry (the tooth artist, say, or the letter writer), artisans in crafts not usually represented among shops in the standard market town, hawkers of products imported from central markets or produced in the intermediate market

---

62. Chang Sen-dou, p. 42, asserts that the book stores of a *hsien* were found only in the capital. It may have been true that in traditional times books were ordinarily not available in intermediate market towns which were not also *hsien* seats, but central market towns other than *hsien* seats—like Chung-hsing *chen*, Hua-yang *hsien*, Szechwan—did support stationery and book stores in traditional times. As of 1949, stationery supplies and books were available in all intermediate market towns in Hua-yang *hsien*.

town, and purchasing agents, of which more below.

Central marketing systems, too, are circuited by itinerants, particularly those whose product or service is in little demand or of such a nature that too frequent exposure in the same market town is un-desirable (e.g., patent medicine salesmen and storytellers). A variety of spatial models for central marketing systems are possible; those which appear to be most commonly approached by empirical Chinese cases are four, two involving Model-A intermediate marketing systems and two involving Model-B subsystems. These are diagrammed in Figure 4. Circuits may be illustrated using Model AB and 3-per-*hsün* schedules, as in the upper right of Figure 4. By following triangular routes which bring him back to the central market for every *other* market day on its schedule, the itinerant can achieve

complete coverage in four *hsün* (39-40 days). During this period he will have spent six evenly-spaced market days in the central market, two market days each in the six intermediate markets, two market days each in the six standard markets which belong to no other central marketing system, and one market day each in the six standard markets which also belong to another central market-ing system. Central marketing systems in which schedules are perfectly attuned to one another, as in this hypothetical example, are rare. But it appears to be generally true that the *ta-chi* schedule of a central market is normally eschewed by other markets within the central marketing system. An example is provided by Chou-ts'un, the important mar-ket town in Shantung which has been cited before in other contexts. As of the early nineteenth century, its *ta-chi* schedule, 4-9, was followed by only one other market in

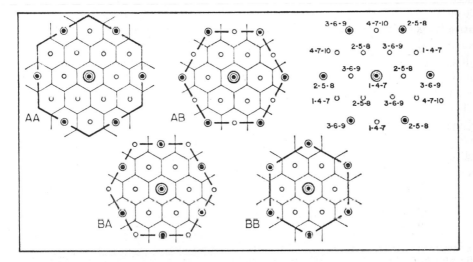

Figure 4. Four spatial models of central marketing systems. At the center of each model is, of course, a cen-tral market town. Open dots represent standard market towns, while the heavier dots around the rim of each system represent intermediate market towns. Villages are not shown. When markets at all levels are distrib-uted consistently according to Model A or Model B, the result is systems as shown in AA or BB, respectively. Systems like AB and BA involve a mixture of the two model distributions.

Markets of an AB system are shown upper right with the addition of regular 3-per-*hsun* market-day schedules.

the entire *hsien*—and that one was in the far
north, quite probably outside Chou-ts'un's
maximal marketing system.[63]

Certain itinerants, highly specialized and
relatively few in number, circuit markets
within the entire trading system of a local or
regional city, and mobile traders can also be
found who deliberately "work" a number of
adjacent marketing systems in order to
profit from the price differentials which
obtain between them. In general, however,
the mobile firm is far more important to the
intermediate marketing system than to the
larger systems at higher levels. And the proportion of itinerants to permanent firms on
market day decreases steadily as one moves
from the standard market town to central
places at each higher level in the economic
hierarchy.

Let us now look over the total complex
of nested marketing systems and survey, first
of all, the downward flow of merchandise.
Exotic goods shipped to the central market
town, and other goods produced in it, are
distributed in part through the central market itself, in part by itinerants who circuit
both intermediate and standard markets
throughout the central marketing system,
and in part to firms in the six intermediate
market towns. Merchandise received by
firms in each intermediate market town,
together with other goods produced there,
are similarly distributed: in part through the
intermediate market itself, in part by itinerants who circuit standard markets within the
intermediate marketing system, and in part
to firms in the six standard market towns.
The firms receiving goods in this downward

flow consist, in the case of standard market
towns, chiefly of small shops; in the case of
intermediate market towns they include
distributors who supply itinerants as well as
dual wholesale-retail establishments;[64] and
in the case of central market towns they
include most prominently wholesalers
equipped with warehouses. Merchandise
which is consumed by the peasantry or required by petty craftsmen flows down
through the system to every market; consumer goods for the local élite and supplies
for artisans moves no further down than the
intermediate market; while consumer goods
of interest chiefly to the bureaucratic élite,
together with industrial supplies, normally
go no further than the central market town
itself.

The flow of goods upward through the
marketing system begins when the peasant
sells his product in the standard market,
either to local consumers, to dealers based in
the standard market who process and/or
bulk the product, or directly to buyers who
are visiting the standard market from
higher-level market towns. Purchasing agents
and buyers visit standard markets from central as well as intermediate market towns;
they visit intermediate markets from local
cities as well as central market towns.
Whether the collecting firms are commercial
houses or industries which process or consume the local products, these products are
drawn up through the marketing system to
ever higher-level centers.

Amano,[65] who studied marketing in
several towns in Hopei and Shantung, makes
it clear that a hierarchy of credit arrange-

---

63. Data from *Ch'ang-shan hsien chih*, Chia-ch'ing
6 (1801). The central marketing system centered
on Ting *hsien*, Hopei, provides another example.
Sidney D. Gamble, *Ting Hsien* (New York, 1954).
From Table 88, p. 284, it is clear that 2-per-*hsün*
schedules which overlap the market days of the
hsien city's central market are underrepresented in
the lower-level markets of the *hsien*.

64. Cf. C. K. Yang, pp. 32-33: "Only four stores
in Sunchiachen and seven stores in the County Seat
[both intermediate market towns] do a very
limited wholesale business along. . . with retailing
which holds their main attention."
65. Particular cases are described in detail, pp. 129
ff.

ments parallels the hierarchical distribution and collection system, and that "mobile firms" not only operated on credit but participated in the vertical flow of goods both ways. For instance, an itinerant *fan-tzu* who in the first instance operated as a buyer for a local-products dealer in the intermediate market town, might at the same time handle goods purchased with a loan extended by that dealer; as he circuited the standard markets he both sold sundry goods and bought local products.

Yamane's research on Shantung market towns suggests that the distinction between minor and standard markets on the one hand and intermediate and central markets on the other was, during the Ch'ing period at least, fundamental with respect to the role of government. The lower-level markets (*hsiao-chi* in the usual terminology) supported only petty unlicensed brokers, and were self-regulated and self-taxed. By contrast, intermediate and higher-level markets (*ta-chi*) were officially registered, their brokerage firms were licensed by the provincial treasury, and market taxes were tapped as a source of official revenue.[66] Whether the formal distinction between *kuan* ("regulated") and *i* ("free") markets is peculiar to Shantung, and just how closely it corresponds to the dichotomy between minor/standard and higher-level markets are moot questions. But it is a reasonable hypothesis that in traditional times a given market's transactions were more likely to be regulated and taxed by bureaucratic officials the higher its position in the functional hierarchy of central places.

The association between degree of external regulation and type of market points up certain similarities between marketing and administration in traditional China. Both were hierarchical systems in which the

relevant territorial unit was larger at each ascending level. And in both, limited bureaucratic resources were concentrated at the higher levels: marketing systems below that of the central market, like administrative systems below the *hsien*, were subject to bureaucratic controls in only very attenuated form.

When, however, we consider the *manner* in which each of the two structures was articulated, a fundamental difference is apparent. Administrative units are, virtually by definition, discrete at all levels; every lower-level unit belongs to only one unit at each ascending level of the structure. Marketing systems, by contrast, are discrete *only* at the basic level, and each lower-level system is typically oriented to two or three systems at each ascending level. As a result, marketing structures, unlike administrative structures, take the form of interlocking networks. It is the joint participation of standard markets in two or three intermediate marketing systems, of intermediate markets in two or three central marketing systems, and so on, which articulates and unites the little local economies centered on each market town into, first, regional economic structures and eventually into a single society-wide economy. Thus, marketing had a significance for societal integration in traditional China which at once paralleled and surpassed—which both reinforced and complemented—that of administration.

The complexity of the whole, however, should not be taken to imply that the marketing system was either monolithic or tightly structured. Not only was there no one economic apex paralleling the administrative capital, but the flow of goods, which defined the structure, was seldom very heavy by modern standards. Moreover, as we shall see in the next section, each of the component standard marketing subsystems

---

66. Yamane, p. 502. Prior to 1726, licenses were issued by each *hsien* or *chou*.

persisted in an economic subculture all its own.

Marketing Structures as Social Systems

Chinese marketing systems have important social as well as economic dimensions. The standard marketing system in particular is a unit whose social significance for the peasantry and for peasant relations with other groups deserves major attention. In order to suggest an emphasis suited to my purpose in this section, I shall call it henceforward the standard marketing *community*. There is good reason, I believe, for attempting to analyze this type of community not only as an intermediate social structure but also as a culture-bearing unit—the locus in the Chinese case of Redfield's "little tradition." [67]

Anthropological work on Chinese society, by focusing attention almost exclusively on the village, has with few exceptions distorted the reality of rural social structure. Insofar as the Chinese peasant can be said to live in a self-contained world, that world is not the village but the standard marketing community. The effective social field of the peasant, I will argue, is delimited not by the narrow horizons of his village but rather by the boundaries of his standard marketing area.

We may begin by asking how big this area normally is and how many people the community typically includes. So as to avoid the protraction of citing numerous examples, I present a set of estimates which incorporates and reconciles data from all relevant empirical cases available to me. Table 1, based on a simple graphic model, points up the obvious but nonetheless extremely important fact that the size of standard marketing areas varies inversely with density of population. In regions where the population is sparsely distributed on the land, marketing areas must be large in order to encompass enough demand to support the market; in densely settled regions they are small. The table also reveals a relationship which common sense does not necessarily foretell—namely, that the average population of marketing communities increases along with population density *only up to a point.* As densities rise above 325 persons per square kilometer—and as standard marketing areas fall below 27 square kilometers in size—the average population of marketing systems begin to decline. A full understanding of why marketing areas come to be as small as they are in very densely settled areas must await the analysis of change in Part II, but there is nothing mysterious about the kind of relationship which Table 1 shows between the population and the area of marketing systems. Given a steady decline in the size of marketing areas as one moves from densely to very densely populated regions, it is apparent that the point must eventually be reached wherever smaller areas cannot sustain ever larger agrarian populations. In agricultural China[68] at

---

67. Robert Redfield, *Peasant Society and Culture* (Chicago, 1956), pp. 70 ff. It may, in the case of China, be only a minor distortion to conceive of the "great tradition" as unitary and homogeneous, but the variety and heterogeneity of its counterpart among the peasantry preclude any such conception. Instead of one "little tradition" there were many, and I allude here to the tendency for each to be associated with a standard marketing community.

68. As used in this paper, "agricultural China" refers to a specifically defined contiguous area inclusive for the most part of what used to be called China Proper. The line separating agricultural from nonagricultural China was drawn along *hsien* boundaries (as of 1958) so as to include in the former practically all *hsien* with population densities of at least 10 per square kilometer. In lieu of a map defining this line, its course may be briefly described (in terms of 1958 provinces) as

Table 1   Average Area and Population of Standard Marketing Communities, as a Function of Population Density, 1948 Estimates for Agricultural China*

Density: Persons per Sq. Km.	Average Population	Average Area in Sq. Km.	Average distance Traveled by Most Disadvantaged Villager (Km.)	Average Distance (Km.) Between Market Towns
10	1850	185	8.44	14.6
20	3160	158	7.80	13.5
30	4080	136	7.24	12.5
40	3800	120	6.80	11.8
50	5300	106	6.39	11.1
60	5790	96.5	6.09	10.6
70	6160	88.0	5.72	9.91
80	6500	81.3	5.59	9.69
90	6750	75.0	5.37	9.31
100	6980	69.8	5.18	8.98
125	7460	59.7	4.79	8.31
150	7870	52.5	4.50	7.79
175	8050	56.0	4.11	7.12
200	8240	41.2	3.98	6.90
225	8350	37.1	3.78	6.55
250	8570	34.3	3.63	6.30
275	8720	31.7	3.49	6.05
300	8850	29.5	3.37	5.84
325	8870	27.3	3.24	5.62
350	8790	25.1	3.11	5.39
375	8660	23.1	2.98	5.17
400	8640	21.6	2.88	5.00
450	8100	18.0	2.63	4.56
500	7850	15.7	2.46	4.26
550	7320	13.3	2.26	3.92
600	7140	11.9	2.14	3.71
650	6760	10.4	2.00	3.47
700	6370	9.1	1.87	3.24
Average for Agric. China: 111	7140	64.4		
The Modal Case: 150	7870	52.5	4.50	7.79

* The curve which graphs the relationship between size of standard marketing area and population density is closer to the axes of ordinates and abscissas the more commercialized the agrarian economy. The specific curve from which the above figures for average areas were taken was designed to represent the situation in an agrarian economy commercialized to the extent that all of agricultural China was in 1948. Its contours derive from the data plotted for 76 *hsien* in south and southeastern Szechwan, but it was positioned somewhat closer to the axes in accordance with points on the graph provided by known cases of *hsien* more commercialized than any in Szechwan as of 1948. Justification for these procedures must await the treatment of commercialization and modernization in Part II.

The next-to-last column is computed from the average area according to the following formula for regular hexagons: $A = 2.598a^2$, where A is the area of the hexagon (i.e., of the standard marketing area) and a is the distance from its center to one of the six corners (i.e., the distance to be traveled from the most disadvantaged spot in the area). The last column is computed according to the formula $b = a\sqrt{3}$, where b is the distance between the centers of two adjacent regular hexagons.

the end of the republican period, that point fell in the 300-350 density range.

Very large marketing areas of 150 of more square kilometers (at the top of the Table) occur only in mountainous regions and on the arid peripheries of agricultural China, where population is very sparsely distributed over a generally forbidding landscape. Only in such regions does one normally find marketing communities with as few as 3,000 people. At the other extreme, the very small marketing areas of 15 square kilometers or less (at the bottom of the Table) occur only on plains of exceptional fertility, situated in the typical case near major urban centers. The distribution by size of standard marketing areas in agricultural China may be summarized as follows:

advantaged villager within easy walking distance of the town—3.4 to 6.1 kilometers.[69] In the modal case (see bottom of Table 1) marketing areas are just over 50 square kilometers in size, market towns are less than eight kilometers apart, and maximum walking distance to the town is approximately 4.5 km. The average (mean) population of the standard marketing community is somewhat over 7,000.

It is clear, then, that even in the case of the typical community—1500 households in eighteen or so villages distributed over fifty square kilometers—we are not dealing with a cozy primary group structured through bonds of great intimacy or intensity. On the other hand, unused as most students of China are to thinking of marketing systems

Proportion of All Standard Marketing Communities (per cent)	Range in Average Areas (sq. km.)	Range in Densities persons per sq. km.
5	158–	–19
15	97–157	20–59
60	30–96	60–299
15	16–29	300–499
5	–15	500–

The majority of standard marketing areas, then, are of a size which puts the most dis-

as communities and given the burden of the relevant literature, we are likely to be led far

---

excluding approximately the northern third of Heilungkiang; including all of Kirin, Liaoning, Hopei, Shansi and Shensi; including a small portion of Inner Mongolia A. R., approximately two-fifths of Ningsia A. R., most of Kansu, and a few *hsien* in easternmost Tsinghai; and excluding the mountainous tracts in the west of Szechwan and Yunnan. Agricultural China (inclusive of Hainan but not Taiwan) incorporates 4,180,000 sq. km., as compared with 4,159,400 sq. km. in non-agricultural China (exclusive of Tibet and Chamdo). In 1958 there were 1791 *hsien*-level units in the former, and 260 in the latter.

In general, land productivity is so low and population so thinly settled in what is here defined as non-agricultural China that marketing systems cannot exist in the form described in this paper.

69. I see no merit in the notion that "walking distance" is in any sense a *determinant* of the size of marketing areas. Cf. C. K. Yang, pp. 14-15. If the spacing of market towns were somehow set simply to enable the most disadvantaged villager to walk to his market, carry out his business and return home during the daylight hours, then the size of standard marketing areas would vary within a narrow range. In fact, most of China's standard marketing areas are far smaller than any consideration of walking distance requires, and in areas on the periphery of agricultural China, they become so large that the one-way trip to market from disadvantageously situated villages takes more than one day. This would appear to be the case with a number of villages in the vicinity of Yits'un, Yunnan, if one may judge from the details supplied by Fei Hsiao-t'ung and Chang Chih-i, pp. 170-172.

astray in this regard. Let me illustrate with the community centered on Kao-tien-tzu, the standard market town which I studied in Szechwan. With some 2500 households in 1949-50, it was an atypically large system.[70] Did the average peasant even recognize much less *know* the members of so many households?

If Mr. Lin, the 45-year-old peasant with whom I lived, may be considered at all typical, then the answer is yes. For Mr. Lin had a nodding acquaintance with almost every adult in all parts of the marketing system.[71] He could, moreover, identify and describe the community's leading élite families, in no matter which of the dispersed villages they lived. He knew details about peasant families on the other side of the market town which most Americans would not know—and would not care to know—about their next-door neighbors. Mr. Lin's social knowledge

of Kao-tien-tzu's marketing community was more impressive, perhaps, than that of the agricultural laborer who shared his compound or the transport coolie who carted his tangerines to market, but it paled by comparison with the informed social wisdom of any leisured gentleman among the community's local élite. The long-robed landlord might nod to only a favored few, but he recognized everyone he passed on the way to market and appeared to carry in his head a full dossier on each.

But is it after all so remarkable? The peasant in Kao-tien-tzu's marketing community had, by the age of fifty, attended his standard market more than three thousand times. He had, at least one thousand times on the average, been jammed into a small area along one street with the same male representative of every other household in that community.[72] He made purchases from peasant vendors whose homes lay in all

---

70. Standard marketing systems in northwestern Szechwan were atypically large in the late republican period because the area was relatively uncommercialized. See Part II.

71. Exceptions were for the most part limited to the households of "outsiders" living on or near the highway at the northeastern rim of Kao-tien-tzu's marketing area. That part of the marketing area which lay nearest to Chengtu and through which the highway passed included in 1947 approximately 140 "downriver" Chinese, i.e., Chinese from provinces other than Szechwan, most of whom had come to the vicinity of Chengtu during World War II; and approximately 290 Szechwanese whose native place lay outside Hua-yang *hsien*. Few of these outsiders were peasants; some were shopkeepers in the *yao-tien* on the highway, others were rickshaw pullers or transport coolies who "worked" the intermediate marketing system centered on Niu-shih-k'ou, and still others were suburban residents with jobs in the city. Mr. Lin knew few of these individuals and cared little about them. "Outsiders" in the market town itself, however, were another matter. In 1947 there were 58 such individuals, including shopkeepers and schoolteachers; all were Szechwanese, and Mr. Lin knew most of them.

72. This assertion takes into account the comparative stability in the membership of Kao-tien-tzu's marketing community from one generation to the next. The social knowledge gained during each market day is cumulative over a lifetime in direct proportion to the continuity of resident households and in inverse proportion to the amount of family migration into and out of the marketing community. Of the families in Kao-tien-tzu's community in the late 1940's, the great majority were a direct continuation of families already resident there at the turn of the century; of the new households, more had been formed through segmentation of local families than had been established by in-migrants. Even in the case of the small portion of the marketing area through which the highway passed (described in Footnote 71), no less than 80 per cent of the households included no one born outside the district in which they now lived. In the much larger portion of the marketing area away from the highway—including four-fifths of the community's population—over 95 per cent of all households consisted solely of locally-born individuals. Cf. G. W. Skinner, "A Study in Miniature of Chinese Population," *Population Studies*, V (Nov. 1951), 91-103.

directions from the town, and more to the point, he socialized in the teahouses with fellow peasants from village communities far removed from his own. Nor was the peasant alone in this for in Kao-tien-tzu there was a teahouse for everyone, and few persons who went to market failed to spend at least an hour in one or two. Codes of hospitality and sociability operated to bring any community member who entered the door quickly to a table as somebody's guest. Inevitably an hour in the teahouse enlarged a man's circle of acquaintances and deepened his social knowledge of other parts of the community.

Let us pause at this point to note certain structural consequences of the fact that a peasant develops a fairly good social map of his standard marketing area whereas the social terrain beyond it is largely unexplored. It means that the services he requires—whether of a midwife, a tailor, or a hired hand—will be sought for the most part from households within the system, thereby building up a modest network of patron-client relationships all contained within the standard marketing community. It means, as noted in the preceding section, that a man in need of funds is able to look far beyond the bounds of his own village in forming a rotating-credit society.

It means, too, that daughters-in-law tend to be taken from within the marketing community. Marriage brokers—who in Szechwan operated in certain teahouses of the market town—and mothers of marriageable sons are able with considerable assurance to scan the entire standard marketing community for potential daughters-in-law; seldom, however, do they know enough to find candidates from households outside the system. There is, in short, a distinct tendency for the standard marketing community to be endogamous for the peasantry. An interesting confirmation of this point comes from Jean Pratt Watts' study of a Hakka village community in the New Territories of Hong Kong: The most active and successful marriage broker in the village was a widow of means who indeed went with exceptional frequency to her market town—Tai Po, which has a daily schedule—where she kept tabs on marriageable girls in the larger community.[73] In consequence, the arrangements whereby one lineage traditionally gives its young girls as brides to another tend to be concentrated within standard marketing communities, as are also the more nearly *ad hoc* alliances which may have no immediate precedent. The affinal bonds of the peasant thus constitute another network which spreads through the standard marketing community and gives structure to the whole.

On the agnatic side of kinship, I suspect that the standard marketing community plays a role in lineage organization which may resolve a vexing analytical problem. New villages have traditionally been founded in China either by a single family or by a small group of patrilineally related families. The households in such a new settlement consitute in effect an offshoot of the lineage localized in their village of origin, often not far away. Through segmentation of this kind over a period of centuries, certain portions of the Chinese rural landscape have come to support a number of localized lineages of the same surname, all historically related by virtue of descent from a common ancestor, but each situated in a different village or market town.[74] Why is it that in some cases

---

73. Personal communication of 8 February 1964. Also see Jean A. Pratt, "Immigration and Unilineal Descent Groups: A Study of Marriage in a Hakka Village in the New Territories, Hong Kong," *Eastern Anthropologist*, XIII (1960), 147-158.
74. Several examples from Chin-chiang *hsien*, Fukien, are cited by Father Amyot in his description of the home territory of the Philippine Chinese. Jacques Amyot, S. J., *The Chinese Community of Manila: A Study of Adaptation of Chinese Familism to the Philippine Environment*

neighboring localized lineages perpetuate or achieve organizational unity, whereas others, agnatically related through equally recent bonds, function as independent systems? My suggestion here is that, since peasant families have much social intercourse within their standard marketing community but little outside it, interlineage ties contained within a single marketing system are likely to be perpetuated whereas bonds between localized lineages sited in different standard marketing areas tend to erode with time. In the region of Szechwan where I did my research, Hakka families surnamed Lin were heavily concentrated in the three standard marketing areas centered on Kao-tien-tzu, Lai-chia-tien, and Ta-mien-p'u. The Lin households within each, however, seemed to be separately organized, with headquarters in teahouses of their respective market towns. Mizuno notes that in north China it is market towns rather than villages which normally support ancestral halls.[75] It may well be, therefore, that we should look to the standard marketing community as the usual locus of the "composite lineage."

I have another suggestive case to mention in this regard. In the standard marketing community of Kang-wei, Hai-ch'eng *hsien*, Fukien, an easy majority of the entire population belongs to a single composite lineage. The market itself was in 1948 controlled by the *ta-fang* (literally "great branch"), one of the component lineages localized in a village to the north of the market town. In the Kang-wei market the three grain measurers, the livestock agent and pig weigher, the chief of the palanquin bearers, and even the head of the beggars were all drawn from the *ta-fang*, and buyers from the *ta-fang* had special privileges at market. In this case, the ascendant social position of the *ta-fang* within the composite lineage is clearly expressed within the economic system of the marketing community. It would appear that just as the dominant branch in a localized lineage is, in appropriate circumstances, able to assert supreme power in the village community,[76] so the dominant localized lineage within a composite lineage may arrogate preponderant control in the marketing community.[77]

The case of Kang-wei also points up the fact that the power structure of a standard marketing community is, under the circumstances, unlikely to be divorced from control of the market itself. In Szechwan during the republican period, the secret societies collectively known as the *Ko-lao hui* wielded supreme power at all levels of rural society—and the standard marketing community was no exception. It was, in fact, a most crucial unit, for lodges of the society were organized by, and limited in almost every case to, a single standard marketing community. There were two lodges organized within the standard marketing community centered on Kao-tien-tzu, one "clear" and one "muddy"; both had their headquarters and held their meetings in teahouses in the town. A majority of male adults belonged to one or the other, and on almost every market day members were able to conduct business with the officers of the lodge, who could be found in a particular teahouse. In Kao-tien-tzu, as in

---

(Chicago, 1960), pp. 44-52. After noting that the villages in which lineages of the same surname are localized tend to be concentrated in a particular *hsiang* Amyot notes (p. 40): "In the usage of this area, the term *hsiang* may designate either a complex of villages and hamlets forming some kind of unity, or again, the largest village of the complex from which the latter derives its name. It is usually a market town."

75. Mizuno Kaoru, *Hokushi no nōson [North China's Villages]* (Peking, 1941), p. 171.

76. Cf. Maurice Freedman, *Lineage Organization in Southeastern China* (London, 1958), Chs. 8-9.
77. *Fang-chih* themselves occasionally provide a glimpse of the controlling power which a dominant lineage holds in a particular market. See, e.g., Kuramochi, p. 25.

many other market towns of the Szechwan Basin, the market itself was controlled by one of the secret-society lodges. The positions of grain measurers, pig weighers, livestock middlemen, and certain other commission agents were reserved for society members, and a portion of each agent's fees was claimed for the coffers of the lodge.

Elsewhere in China, control of the market may be more widely dispersed among the several founding villages. A common arrangement in Shantung rotates responsibility for market management among the participating villages; during each *hsün* of the lunar month, a given village or several villages jointly undertake to provide and subsidize public measurers to render service as honest brokers free of charge. The examples cited by C. K. Yang, however, indicate that dispersed control of this kind is limited to minor markets and less important standard markets; in the case of intermediate markets (and apparently some of the larger standard markets), authority tends to be concentrated, both because communal control by the large number of villages involved is infeasible and because the commission fees at a large and prosperous market constitute too lucrative a prize to be ignored by groups with the power to claim it.[78]

The market itself, then, constitutes one focus of social structure within the marketing community. Another, of scarcely less importance, is often provided by the major temple of the town. To begin with, the committee which runs the temple is normally composed not only of devout townspeople but also of leading citizens with religious leanings who live in village communities throughout the marketing area. The annual fair, normally held in connection with the feast day of the temple's principal deity, is,

however, too important an event to be left to the pious. In Kao-tien-tzu it was organized by a committee on which leading shopkeepers and the most powerful members of the landed élite both served. The local police unit which was formed every year at festival time to control the crowds and direct the procession, consisted in 1950 of some sixty volunteers including, again, individuals from all parts of the marketing community. Moreover, the earthly domain of the temple deity himself was seen as corresponding to the standard marketing area. Each year the graven image of Tung-yüeh, a bureaucratic official of the underworld, was carried in procession through the area of his jurisdiction. The traditional route, which followed each of the main roads radiating from town, carried him in turn to Hung-men-p'u, Sha-ho-p'u, O-o-tien, and Ta-shih-tzu—each a *yao-tien* situated at one of the corners of the marketing area. In this manner, the religious festival provided an annual reaffirmation of the community's territorial extent and a symbolic reinforcement of its town-centered structure.

The discreteness of the standard marketing community is given religious expression in yet another way. Service groups of the devout participate in religious festivals by organizing joint offerings to the deity being celebrated and by participating as a group in the procession. Over thirty such groups took part in Kao-tien-tzu's annual fair in 1950, and with the exception of three from Chengtu, each group was limited in membership to a single standard marketing community, those from outside communities being identified by the name of the market town in question. It is likely that the *hsiang-hui* ("incense societies") and *shan-hui* ("mountain societies") which conducted pilgrimages to sacred shrines in traditional times were normally organized within the standard

---

78. C. K. Yang, pp. 18-20.

marketing community, if only because the bureaucracy discouraged organized religious activity on a larger scale.[79]

These examples indicate that a variety of voluntary associations and other formal organizations—the composite lineage, the secret-society lodge, the committee on arrangements for the annual fair, the religious service society—take the standard marketing community as the unit of organization.[80] Occupational groups, too, may be organized within the standard marketing community. One teahouse in Kao-tien-tzu was the meeting place of an association of animal breeders, another the headquarters of associations of carpenters and housebuilders. Still other voluntary associations, especially those related to agricultural production (crop-watching or irrigation societies, for instance), although not coterminous with the marketing community tended to be wholly contained within it.[81]

It remains to mention that the standard marketing community is the relevant context of organized recreation for the peasantry. Standard and higher-level markets constitute the arena of professional storytellers, theatrical troupes, blind singers, purveyors of games of chance, boxers, jugglers, performing medicine sellers, and magicians. Such professionals are notably absent not only from villages but in the usual case

from minor markets as well. Just as market day brings relief from the tedium of rural life through the provision of recreational opportunities, so the temple fair affords the high point in the villagers' recreational year.

Insofar as this survey has demonstrated the structural reality of the standard marketing community, it will at the same time have provided a basis for assessing the extent to which such a community serves as a culture-bearing unit. There is in the literature a good deal of loose generalization concerning the cultural idiosyncrasy of Chinese villages. Each village, we are often told, has its own dialect, its own culinary specialties, its own version of the peasant hat, and so on. I strongly suspect, however, that when appreciable differences characterize the culture of adjacent villages, the villages in question will prove to belong to different standard marketing communities. It may well be true that in traditional times the typical peasant saw more of his fellow villagers than of all outsiders put together. But at the same time so much of his social interaction was with those from villages other than his own within the marketing community that it is difficult to imagine how cultural peculiarities of any magnitude could persist as between villages using the same standard market. By the same token, so little of the peasant's social intercourse brought him into contact with persons from outside his standard marketing community that the development of cultural distinctiveness as between marketing communities would appear inevitable. To the extent that the standard marketing community contained the peasant's life, it shaped the way he lived it. And if that community had long endured, it perforce carried on a little tradition of its own.

The most obvious case in point concerns the weights and measures associated with the marketing process itself. While they are

---

79. Cf. Hsiao Kung-chuan, *Rural China: Imperial Control in the Nineteenth Century* (Seattle, 1960), pp. 313-14.

80. An account of 1836 describes the establishment of an organization on Ho-nan island, near Canton, which can only be interpreted as a formalization of structure within a standard marketing community: "Twenty-four different villages have joined together to build a large house for purposes of general consultations; this stands at the market town. . ." *Chinese Repository*, IV (1936), p. 414. Cited in Hsiao, p. 309.

81. Hsiao, pp. 288-289, 306-308.

standardized and in fact closely regulated within any one market,[82] considerable variation occurs from one standard market to another. In eleven markets investigated in 1932, C. K. Yang found ten different standards for the *tou,* the dry measure used to portion out grain. The *ta-ch'ih* ("big rule") used to measure homespun, and the *ta-ch'eng* ("big scale") for weighing bulky products likewise varied within a wide range from one market to the next.[83] In his study of crop marketing along the Peking-Hankow railroad, Ōhashi Ikuei found that purchasing agents working out of central market towns were forced to carry with them tables of equivalence for the weights and measures used in the various local markets of the system.[84] Data of this kind point up the relative independence and isolation of the standard marketing community *qua* economic system—and thereby point to the very circumstances which underlie the cultural idiosyncrasy of each. In the last analysis, it is traditional marketing patterns of long standing which account for the fact—to cite a typical example—that the cross-stitch designs with which every Szechwan girl painstakingly adorns the hangings for her bridal bed bear the characteristic stamp of her standard marketing community.

An equally obvious case in point concerns religious folklore, and in this regard many illustrations can be gleaned from Grootaers' geographical analysis of temples and folklore in northern China.[85] One of the maps shows, for instance, that the cult of Hei Lung, the Black Dragon, is concentrated in a single circumscribed section of Wan-ch'üan *hsien,* Chahar. Reference to large-scale maps of this region strongly suggests that this particular area, in which six temples to the deity in question are extant, is in fact the standard marketing area centered on the town of Chiu-p'u. In the marketing community of Kao-tien-tzu, the lore of Tung-yueh and his hellish bureaucracy inevitably looms large in the peasant's conception of the other world, but in the religious culture of surrounding marketing communities, this deity and his court are of relative insignificance.

In the case of language, too, one expects minimal variation within a standard marketing community—in view of the massive amount of verbal interaction which takes place at market—but a degree of distinctiveness as between marketing communities. It occurred to me, when my informants in Szechwan used to discourse on the peculiarities of speech characteristic of the different markets that the minimal unit of significance to the dialect geographer of China is precisely the standard marketing area.

I have little evidence concerning the social dimensions of higher-level marketing systems in China, but there are two points I should like to make in this connection. It seems clear that in many respects Chinese social structure at the lower-intermediate levels parallels the marketing structure described in the preceding section and, like it, takes the form of a hierarchical network. Let me illustrate once again with the case of Kao-tien-tzu. This standard market town is, in accordance with Model B, oriented toward three higher-level market towns, and hence a part of three different intermediate marketing systems (see Figure 3a. Each of these structural bonds is paralleled by hierarchical arrangements involving a number of

---

82. Documents specifying the weights and measures to be used in individual markets are cited by Kuramochi, p. 24, and by C. K. Yang, pp. 18-19.
83. C. K. Yang, pp. 20-21. The situation in this regard was, as late as 1950, very similar in the Szechwan Basin.
84. Cited in Amano, p. 156.
85. Willem A. Grootaers, "Temples and History of Wan-ch'üan (Chahar), the Geographical Method Applied to Folklore," *Monumenta Serica,* XIII (1948), 209-216.

different social organizations. I restrict myself to one example apiece: (1) Liao households in the Kao-tien-tzu marketing community are, like those surnamed Lin, organized into a composite lineage with headquarters in the market town, but the Liaos consider their organization to be merely a *branch* of the far more inclusive composite lineage which maintains an ancestral hall in Ta-mien-p'u, the intermediate market town to the southeast. (2) The Chih-chung *ju-yüan* ("Confucian hall"—a benevolent society) of Kao-tien-tzu maintains close relations with a superior hall known as Chung-ho *ju-yüan* and situated in Chung-ho *chen*, the intermediate market town to the southwest. Finally (3), let me refer once again to the secret-society lodges which, while essentially independent, are nonetheless united into rather extensive federations. Kao-tien-tzu's lodge in one of these federations is tied in the first instance to its counterpart in Niu-shih-k'ou, the intermediate market town to the northwest.

It should be explicitly noted that these organizations are officered or controlled not by peasants but by leisured gentlemen, and that in general the links between organizations at the two levels are effected, if not by members of the local élite, then by the merchants who have business interests in both standard and intermediate market towns. In Kao-tien-tzu, to note a datum of similar import, peasant members of the secret society belong only to one or the other of the two lodges in their standard market, whereas merchants and members of the local élite not infrequently find it advantageous to belong to a lodge in their intermediate market town as well.

This observation leads to my second point: marketing systems at each level in the hierarchy have a distinctive significance for interclass relations. From this point of view, the standard marketing community can be seen as the locus of such intercourse as petty traders have with the peasantry on the one hand and with the local élite (primarily through the mechanism of market control) on the other. But its primary significance pertains to the relations between peasantry and "gentry." Whereas many individual villages could boast of no families which were at once landed, leisured, and literate, every standard marketing community included in traditional times a number of so-called "gentry" families. And it was in the market town that these élitist families exerted "social control," to use the usual imprecise term. Every gentleman who aspired to even informal leadership normally held court in a particular teahouse at his standard market, and disputes among peasants in different village communities were usually mediated by such leaders in the teahouses on market days.[86] It was in the market town, too, that landlords or their agents dealt with tenants, and upper-class officials of the secret-society lodge made the policy decisions which affected peasant welfare throughout the community.

The concept of the local élite as an intermediary and a buffer between the peasantry and the bureaucratic élite is—though the terminology may seem peculiar—a familiar one. And so is the view of the petty trader as a middleman between the peasantry and the merchants in higher-level central places. Both functioned as "brokers"[87] who at

---

86. Li Mei-yun, p. 212.
87. Eric Wolf refers to the Janus-faced qualities of the individuals who serve as "brokers" between community-oriented and nation-oriented groups. "Aspects of Group Relations in a Complex Society: Mexico," *American Anthropologist*, LVIII (1956), p. 1076.
88. Hsiao Kung-chuan's monograph is rich in detail concerning the interrelations between peasant villagers, members of the local élite, and bureaucratic officials. Many of these data are profitably analyzed in terms of local-élite broker-

once shielded the peasant from an outside world which he distrusted and selectively filtered and transmitted to him its products—a few necessities of exotic origin, imperial edicts as "adjusted" to local conditions, bits of the great tradition as distorted by story tellers or of élite ideology as adapted by *hsiang-yueh* lecturers.[88] My point here is simply that these Janus-faced "brokers"—whether cultural, political or economic—operated at the level of the standard market town, not the village. It was the standard marketing community which they linked to or—depending on one's perspective—isolated from the institutions of the larger society.

The social sphere of the *intermediate* market town[89] is essentially a world which the intermediaries of rural society have to themselves. Insofar as the intermediate marketing system is a social community, it is one which normally excludes both the peasantry and the bureaucratic élite. In the teahouses, winehouses, and restaurants of the intermediate market town, representatives of the local élite from the whole ring of surrounding standard marketing communi-

age between the peasantry and bureaucratic officialdom. For the *hsiang-yüeh* lecture system, see pp. 184-206.
89. As noted in the preceding section the intermediate market town served as the center not only of an intermediate marketing system but also of a smaller standard marketing system, and the town had a dual function. Each intermediate market town was, for instance, the locus, on the one hand, of interclass relations between peasants and the local élite of its *standard* marketing area and, on the other, of inter-class relations between traders and the local élite of its *intermediate* marketing system. It is nonetheless useful to keep the two functional levels analytically distinct. Certain teahouses and several of the winehouses of the intermediate market town were socially off-limits for the peasantry. These, together with the headquarters of many associations, must be seen as institutions relevant solely to the town's role as hub of an intermediate marketing community.

ties direct the affairs of the wider area served by the intermediate marketing system. The situation is comparable in the case of merchants, traders, and artisans whose business world is primarily confined within a given intermediate marketing system, for their intraclass affairs are also conducted in the intermediate market town. But perhaps the most interesting of the social relations peculiar to the intermediate marketing system are the interclass dealings between the gentlemanly élite and the merchants of the market town itself. For the crucial negotiations whereby, on the one hand, "gentry" capital is invested in the pawnbroking, moneylending, artisan manufacture, and commercial enterprise of the intermediate marketing system and, on the other, the capital of the artisan and tradesman is invested in agricultural land and translated into the coin of social respectability—these dealings, too, are carried on in the teahouses and townhouses of market towns at this level.

The interclass significance of the *central* market town is distinguished by the addition to the field of the bureaucratic élite. It may be assumed that towns at this level are the locus not only of the various intergroup relations already noted for lower-level markets, but also of the critical consultations which bureaucratic officials hold both with "gentry" leaders within their administrative jurisdiction and with leading merchants of the town. Morton Fried, describing the situation in Ch'u *hsien*, Anhwei, a small district seat and a central market town, notes that

. . . successful landlords, merchants, artisans, and officials tend to associate socially on a basis of approximate equality. Wealthy landlords associate with wealthy merchants rather than with poor landlords; successful artisans prefer the company of wealthy merchants to that of indigent co-specialists. . . . The leadership of the various guilds is often vested in a gentleman of the town, the leadership of the combined guilds is always so vested.[90]

Ho Ping-ti's discussion of the relations between merchants and bureaucratic officials in the Ch'ing period[91] suggests that the picture painted by Fried as of 1948 can hardly be dismissed as a modern deviation produced by the new forces which came into play during the republican period.

Any view of traditional Chinese social

structure which emphasizes parallels with the articulated marketing system must, increasingly at each higher level, take cognizance of the administrative system. My purpose in elaborating a somewhat unorthodox view is not to controvert earlier analyses which, following the bias of Chinese scholar-officials, assume the primacy of the administrative system. It is rather to urge balance—a recognition in future research that social structure in the middle range of traditional Chinese society is at once derivative of and enmeshed in two quite distinctive hierarchical systems—that of administration to be sure, but that of marketing as well.

---

90. Morton H. Fried, *Fabric of Chinese Society* (New York, 1953), pp. 17-18.
91. Ho Ping-ti, *The Ladder of Success in Imperial China* (New York, 1962), Ch. 2.

★★★★★★★★★★★★★★★★★★★★★★★★★★★★★

HOW I DISCOVERED THE THEORY OF CENTRAL PLACES: A REPORT ABOUT THE ORIGIN OF CENTRAL PLACES

Walter Christaller

I would like to go far back into the past. When I was at the age when one uses a school atlas, my mother suggested to our well-to-do aunt that she send me an atlas for Christmas. In my parents' house, a parsonage in the Black Forest, money was tight and the family large. Even a school atlas was quite an expense. My aunt was quite disappointed that she "just" send a "useful" gift, and not something to play with, which really would make one happy. However, it turned out otherwise: when I saw the atlas on the gift table, and its many-colored maps, I was quite bewitched. I didn't play ball, or walk

on stilts, but rather was only engrossed in the study of my atlas.

The atlas then became a plaything, not only something to look at and study. I drew in new railroad lines, put a new city somewhere or other, or changed the borders of the nations, straightening them out or delineating them along mountain ranges. Then I was given the large Debes Handatlas, which I still possess. No map in it is without traces of my entries. I designed new administrative divisions and calculated their populations—because I also had quite a passion for statistics. When I found a statistical

---

From *Geographische Zeitschrift*, Vol. 56, No. 2. Reprinted by permission of Franz Steiner Verlag, Weisbaden, Germany.

handbook advertised for about two marks, I pleaded with my father to buy it for me. He, who was only interested in literature, tried to dissuade me. From disappointment, I broke out in tears, and then, nevertheless, was given the statistical handbook. When I was wounded in the First World War at Stralsand and put in a military hospital, and my mother asked me what I would like sent to me, I wrote: a Perth Pocket Atlas. In my bed I completely painted this atlas, and I always took it with me, when I was cured and returned to the front.

Now I have dozens of atlases, large and small, planning atlases and historical atlases, English, Dutch, and French atlases. And a vast quantity of maps of all scales; also from Sweden, and the wonderful Finnish maps. I have all German maps of the 1:100,000 and 1:200,000 scales, all Alpine Club maps and road maps of all Europe.

However, I had never thought to study geography. I didn't want to become a teacher—and what other profession could one then take up as a geographer besides that of a teacher?

I would like to interpolate here: In school in Darmstadt I had an excellent geography teacher. Often we went with him through the woods and fields; suddenly he stood still and asked: What do you see here? We discovered, more or less, that the beech tree branches on one side were green with lichens, and not on the other side. And we found the explanation: on the moist windward side the lichens can grow, but on the dry lee side they cannot. Our geography teacher Völsing taught us to observe and look for causes. The geographer Hermann von Wissman came out of my class—thus two geographers from the same class!

However, back to my studies. Besides geography and statistics, I was also interested in sociology, which at that time (in 1913, when I was beginning my studies) had

begun to exist as a new scholarly discipline. So I studied national economy. Geography was almost forgotten; on the other hand I was interested in philosophy, aesthetics, and literature. At that time I witnessed the efforts of my teacher Alfred Weber in Heidelberg to create an industrial location theory.

After the First World War, I married, had to earn money, and could not proceed with my studies. In the League of German Land Reformers—Adolf Damaschke—and in construction and settlement affairs, I found an interesting activity. And so I had my first experience with planning, in particular with Berlin city planning.

In 1930 I was finally able to complete my study of economics in Erlangen. Due to personal interest, I, in addition, went to lectures of Robert Gradmann. My old love for geography awoke in all its force and drew me, as, at that time, almost a forty-year-old man, completely under its power. In Gradmann's seminar, I had to deliver a paper about two articles: by Hugo Hassinger: *Can Capital, National Wealth and National Income be Objects of Economic Geographical Importance?*[1] and by Hans Mortensen: *Tax Rate and Cultural Landscape in South Chile.*[2] I entitled my paper: "A Geography of Values." I would here like to include some paragraphs from my paper written at that time.

In Hassinger's article, there is content of especially fundamental importance. That which Hassinger proposes is not merely a stimulus, not merely a supplement for economic geographical investigations. It is much more a beginning for a completely new

1. Hugo Hassinger, Festband Eugen Oberhummer. *Geogr. Jahresbericht aus Österreich*, 14., 15. Bd. Leipzig u. Wien 1929. S. 58 ff.
2. Hans Mortensen, Geogr. Anzeiger, 30. Jgg. Gotha 1929. S. 381 ff.

orientation in economic geographical research. Indeed, besides the economic sector of geography, most other areas of geography, especially anthropological geography, have to do with the questions posed here. If the work being presented has been entitled "Geography of Values," we have already expressed that which is essential to this heading. What is to be understood by this designation will become clear in the course of the following presentation.

Hassinger comes to the conclusion: "The initially mentioned questions about whether capital, national income and national wealth can become objects of study in economic geography should be answered negatively. On the other hand it should be emphasized that it is necessary that the results of the socio-economic research on these problems should be prepared for geographical purposes and should be made useful and understandable for geography."

The initially mentioned fundamental significance of the questions posed by Hassinger becomes perhaps clearer if we state his question in a more precise, general, and comprehensive manner. We would therefore like to ask: Can economic values become an object of geographical observations? Indeed, one could extend this question still more, by formulating it as follows: Can values in general—spiritual and other values—be objects of geographical observation? Geography, predominantly oriented toward the natural sciences, only recognizes entirely material things, forces of nature, living creatures, human qualities—(physical as well as psychical)—thus everything existing in reality, mostly sure and definite elements. We can also name them "Elements of Being." Opposed to observation of elements of being we have observation of function.[3]

The most clearly expressed difference in geographical and socio-economic science is that geography treats the Being of economic facts and phenomena, whereas social economy treats their Functions. Such a task of delineation is, however, not advantageous for the discoveries made by both fields. For example: the city. Geography chiefly observes locality, outward appearance in outline and perspective, organization, and economic character. Social economy, however, chiefly takes into consideration its function in economic life:—therefore, primarily its function as a market.

Pfeifer points out, contrary to the majority of economic geographers, that in addition to "location and associations of the economic phenomenon, also its functions, the physiological processes of economic life," should be considered.[4] The economically significant factors of economic phenomena are thus merely their functions in economic life; this functional significance is that the phenomena increase, become transformed or disappear. For example: when the market function of a city (perhaps due to the founding of a competitive city) is brought to a standstill, this city dies out. Or: a city arises, where the demand for a market is present. When one, thus, undertakes to discover how an economic phenomenon functions geographically (in the manner that Hassinger determines the cultural sphere of influence), one must first of all recognize the function of the economic phenomenon; the economic function is that function which first creates and forms the external form of the phenomenon according to

3. Following Karl Muhs, Materielle und psychische Wirtschaftsauffassung. Versuch einer Begründung des Identitätsprinzips der Wirtschaftstheorie. Jena 1921. S. 5.

4. Gottfried Pfeifer, Über raumwirtschaftliche Begriffe und Vorstellungen und ihre bisherige Anwendung in der Geographie und Wirtschaftswissenschaft. In: Geogr. Zeitschr. 34. Jgg. Leipzig u. Berlin 1928. S. 321 ff. und 411 ff.

specific fundamentals of expediency; primarily in this manner the concrete outward form with its special characteristics, variations and possibilities can be understood and explained.

The study of geography, in so far as it has to do with the purely scientific sphere, has to do with laws, causalities, and functional relations, if it is to explain the phenomena of nature.[5] As soon as geography moves into the anthropological sphere, it is inclined to apply these categories of natural science predominantly. The serious geographic researcher includes the widest possible scope of historical methods also; and procures in this manner, within his result, a correct picture of the concrete specific phenomena; but he has a difficult time in discovering "laws" of an economic geographical type. He is hardly intimate with social economic categories, and thus he cannot interpret and correctly arrange sociologic and economic relations generally and correctly within the geographic picture.

For example: Alfred Weber constructs in his location theory an abstract space;[6] he is only interested in whether this space is beneficial or restrictive, i.e., its significance for economic relations. Its usefulness or injuriousness for the economic man is represented by relatively low or high transport costs. In this manner, the concrete space enters into the mind of the economic man, and becomes an "expostulated" space, and thus primarily a member in economic functional series. When one, then, in a vacuous space, so to speak, has constructed an ideal typological relation—as Alfred Weber in his location theory—one has thereby set up a schema by which it becomes possible to

explain concrete reality, to understand tendencies, clarify developments, and to predict possible future developments. All this, to begin with, determines only in the purely economic sphere, (thus not in nature), deviations, or encroachments which result from outside of the sphere of rule, or from outside the state. Or, restraints, due to attachment to tradition, stand in the way, which all more or less influence the concrete specific situation.

It is significant that economic geography, up to now, has bypassed the central chapter of economic theory, which is entitled: Value, Prices, Money, and Credit—whereas the remaining chapters of Production, Consumption, Trade, and Traffic have analogous chapters in economic geography texts. Indeed, R. Sieger said at the Geographer's Conference in Cologne, 1903: Economic geography "applies, in addition to the typical spatial point of view of geography, the economic point of view of value, as well." [7] But it is seldom that one discovers something from this in the practice of economic geographical research. Sieges says, moreover, "We must ask: What objects on the surface of the earth are of economic value?" We must go further: the economic value should not only be a selective principle for those items relevant in economic geographical observations, but it (the economic value) should itself furnish the core and foundation of observations in economic geography. So we come to a geography of values.

Let us return, by way of conclusion, to our point of departure, and let us attempt to answer the question which was asked by Hassinger and enlarged by us from the point of view that we have here derived—whether economic values can be objects of economic

5. Alfred Hettner, Die Geographie, ihre Geschichte, ihr Wesen und ihre Methoden. Breslau 1927. S. 185 ff.
6. Alfred Weber, Über den Standort der Industrien. Tübingen 1909, 2. Aufl. 1922.

7. Robert Sieger, Forschungsmethoden in der Wirtschaftsgeographie. In: Verh. des 14. Deutschen Geographentags zu Köln. Berlin 1903. S. 97 und 100.

geographical observation. We would like to answer in response to this question that evolution processes and price relations (in short, economic values) are the determining factor for human economy, and the division of their institutions and manifestations are the determining factors for their structure and variations. If economic geography wishes to elucidate an "economic picture" which it is considering, then it must understand the economic functions of the individual phenomena, as well as the entire economic mechanism and the motive powers thereof. Moreover, in addition to the methods which are generally used, the social economic method must be used; the historical method is, as a rule, indispensable as an auxiliary method for the checking of the knowledge which has been obtained. An "economic transformation" proceeds from the inner structure of the economy and its involvement with earth; not, however, from its outwardly perceptible picture. Surely, economic geography should allot greater significance to political borders than to borders of natural landscapes.

That which is difficult and problematical in economic geography—as shown by the articles of Hassinger and Mortensen—is that they would very much like to cling to the fiction of a firm basis and of concrete things, and that they would like to consider the external form of the phenomena as something which is essential. Economy, which is based on human values and human trade, is, however, much more changeable, unsteady, in eternal flux, than the surface of the earth; its phenomena and the expansion thereof can only be understood through the laws of its flow.

So much for the quotation from my seminar paper for Robert Gradmann. Gradmann was, above all, a geographer of settlement. Therefore, he not only applied the historical method, but instead, the truly geographical methods also—which can be utilized by an analysis of the phenomena of nature and of the works of man within one area, and of their causal and functional relations. Thus, he arrived at a so-called steppe-heath theory, which states that wherever a certain plant community appears, namely the steppe-heath, a type of steppe predominated during an earlier climatic period; and that these areas were free of forests or at least sparsely forested. On which account they, in earlier periods, were preferred as places of settlement—and represent the so-called Old Settlement Landscapes—in contrast to the recently settled forest landscapes—the Cleared Areas.

Thanks to my studies of economics, I have now placed the economic points of view of settlement geography into the foreground. My interest in the national economy tended to be theory-oriented, as were Alfred Weber, Max Weber, Gustav Cassel, Friedrich von Wieser, and, of course, Johann Heinrich von Thünen. The historical school, which predominated previously in economic theory, was dissolved by an economic direction of work (in the true sense of the word), which looked for economic laws or patterns—it was, however, then not yet the time of Econometrics, even if this mathematical orientation was already beginning to appear.

The problems with which I was occupied at the beginning of the 1930's in Erlangen and Nürnberg, I have formulated in the introduction to my book about Central Places in Southern Germany. My statements which were made at that time shall now follow.

How can we find a general explanation for the size, number and distribution of cities? How can we find laws?

Can purely geographical research derive them? This type of research proceeds, as a rule, from the topographic and geographic situation, and then simply explains that a city "had to appear here" and, when the site is especially favorable, that the city "had to" develop here in an especially favorable manner; it is, in this connection, not pointed out that there exist countless sites which are as favorable or more favorable, where there are no cities, and, that, on the contrary, there can be found cities in very unfavorable sites, occasionally even very large ones. The relation of the site to geographical and natural conditions can neither explain the distribution nor the number, nor the size of cities. Hettner, already in 1902, pointed out how important an investigation of the number and of the average distance apart of one city from another of similar economic character is;[8] and since his statement has been made, such calculations are rarely lacking in monographs on settlement geography; however, clear, generally valid laws have not been discovered in this fashion.

Can historical research perhaps yield a general answer? If the process of growth (from the very outset to the stage that has been reached today), of all cities were exactly researched, one could pick out certain rules from this material, which would require a specific expression, according to region and time. One can bring a specific order into variety, but the principle that brings about this order can never be found through historical research alone. This could be seen in the historical school of national economy: this school brought an extremely rich amount of factual material to light, but with the historical method, valid economic laws could not be discovered.

Last of all, can the statistical method lead further? One calculates the city density of an area, the average distance between two cities, one forms classifications of size and records the number of cities which are present in each size classification; one finds in this manner frequencies and average numerical values, perhaps certain regularities and especially frequently occurring combinations of phenomena: but the logical proof, that one is working with valid laws, can never be demonstrated by statistics alone.[9]

It is, perhaps, appropriate to elucidate the question whether "laws" determine the size and distribution of cities, and whether it is possible to recognize such laws. If settlement geography is a scientific discipline, or, rather—if it were, it would not be questionable that scientific laws would have to be the controlling factors here—for every natural phenomenon depends on such laws. We are, however, of the opinion, that settlement geography is a discipline thoroughly of the spirit (or of the arts, as opposed to the sciences). For the origin, development, and decline of cities, it is completely and clearly of crucial importance whether the residents of the city find their possibilities for livelihood there, and whether a demand for the things which the city has to offer exists. Consequently, economic phenomena are decisive for the existence of cities, and for the existence of rural settlements, the houses of which are at the same time centers of production (here economic considerations are certainly determining factors). Thus, settlement geography is a part of economic geography. The economic theory should be brought into play when the organization of the city is to be explained, especially in the field of economic geography. If there are laws in economic theory, there must be, also, laws in settlement geography, and, indeed, economic laws of a special type, to

8. Alfred Hettner, Die wirtschaftlichen Typen der Ansiedlungen. In: Geogr. Ztschr., 8. Jgg. Leipzig 1902. S. 98.

9. Following Werner Sombart, Die drei National-ökonomien. Geschichte und System der Lehre von der Wirtschaft. München und Leipzig 1930.

which one could specifically refer as economic geographic laws. The question whether economic laws are possible can, of course, not be discussed here. The author accepts this postulation decisively and thereby agrees with the greatly predominant number of national economists. These laws are certainly different from laws of nature, but on that account no less "correct." It is perhaps more appropriate to designate them as "regularities" instead of laws, because they do not operate with the same inflexibility and inevitability as laws of nature. But the terminology is not so important here, since we are not working with a recognizably theoretical investigation. It is sufficient to affirm the fact that economic laws exist which determine economic life, and, consequently, also special economic geographical laws, for example, which determine the size, number and distribution of cities. It seems therefore not foolish to look for such laws.

In Erlangen, I studied not only these more theoretical questions. At the same time, I continued my games with maps: I connected cities of equal size by straight lines, first of all, in order to determine if certain rules were recognizable in the railroad and road network, whether regular traffic networks existed, and, second of all, in order to measure the distances between cities of equal size.

Thereby, the maps became filled with triangles, often equilateral triangles (the distances of cities of equal size from each other were thus approximately equal), which then crystallized as six-sided figures (hexagons). Furthermore, I determined that, in South Germany, the small rural towns very frequently and very precisely were 21 kilometers apart from each other. This fact had been recognized earlier, but had been explained as being due to the fact that these cities were stopover places for long distance trade traffic, and that in the Middle Ages the

distance daily by a cart was about 20 kilometers.

My goal was staked out for me: to find laws, according to which number, size and distribution of cities are determined. The way to accomplish this task still remained, however, to be discovered.

One day I approached Gradmann and asked him if I could work with him for the doctorate degree on such a concept. He agreed to this, providing that we not establish a definite title and that we not arrange a plan of the layout of the work. However, after nine months had passed I presented him with the finished and neatly written dissertation. I shall always remember Robert Gradmann with great esteem. The area of his interest was completely different from mine. His orientation of research and methods were different from mine. He was a doctoral father* who was highly respected, but he tried out and recognized that which was new; and he was full of praise for my work, which was, nonetheless, very unusual for that time—1932. My investigation, as far as content and methodology are concerned, stood between national economy and geography, similar to the manner in which Gradmann's research stood between geography, botany and history:[10] on this account, most likely, he had understanding for such a work of an "outsider."

It was clear to me from the very beginning, that I had to develop a theoretical schema for my regional investigation—a schema which, as is customary in national economics, is set up by isolating the essential and operative factors. It was, thus, as in the

---

* In Germany, the man under whom one does his dissertation is referred to as a "Doktorvater." [Translator's Note]
10. For example, Robert Gradmann, Die städtischen Siedlungen des Königreichs Württemberg. In: Forsch. z. dt. Landes- u. Volkskunde, 21. Bd. Hft. 2. Stuttgart 1913, 2. Aufl. 1926.

case of Thünen's Isolated State, abstracted from all natural and geographic factors, and, also, partly to be abstracted from all human geographic factors. It had to be accepted as a symmetrical plain, without obstructions such as rivers or mountain ranges, with a uniformly distributed population, in order to then determine where, under such conditions, the site of a central city or market could form. I thus followed exactly the opposite procedure that Thünen did: he accepted the central city as already having been furnished, and asked how the agricultural land was utilized in the surrounding area, whereas I accepted the inhabited area as already having been furnished, and subsequently asked where the city must be situated, or, more correctly, where should the cities then be situated. Thus, I first of all, as is said today, developed an abstract economic model. This model is "correct" in itself, even if it is never to be found in the reality of settlement landscape in pure form: mountain ranges, variable ground; but also variable density of population, variable income ratios and sociological structure of the population, historical developments and political realities bring about deviations from the pure model. In the theoretical portion of my investigation, I thus did not satisfy myself with setting up a model for an invariable and constant economic landscape (thus, for a static condition)—but instead I also tried to show how the number, size and distribution of the central places change, when the economic factors change: the number, the distribution and the structure of the population, the demands for central goods and services, the production costs, the technical progress, the traffic services, etc.

The truly geographic aim was to be to verify the abstract theory within the reality of a specific landscape, and to show that, in reality, number, size and distribution of the central places correspond to the theoretical model to a considerable extent.

Thereupon, I had to test all available settlements, to see whether and to what extent they fulfill the central functions in their adjacent territories, and to see how far these territorial areas spread out. In any case, I could not, moreover, proceed using the legitimate concept of the city, because there also are village communities which have central functions. So I introduced the neutral and as yet not conceptually encumbered term "central place." The main problem was to find a number for this place, which would depict its significance as a central place. The mere number of inhabitants proves nothing—there are industrial cities of 50,000 or 100,000 inhabitants, which have no or almost no significance for the surrounding territory. I could have used the number of people which was active in service occupations, thus in commercial and transport enterprises, in cultural and health professions, in administration and education. That was later on done by other authors, but mostly only for less comprehensive domains. I, however, wanted to use all of Southern Germany for the field of investigation of my theory; an area where almost purely agricultural utilization of the land very much predominates [whereas in other portions of Germany industry is very widespread], where there are mountain ranges and plains, and also distinctly marked tourist traffic landscapes. Thus, I had to attempt in the simplest possible fashion to transform the quality of a place into a comparable quantity. (The quality of a place, in this instance, would be the manner in which its surrounding territory, of variable size and characteristics, would be supplied from the central place.) For all services, it is, however, of special importance to deal with the surrounding territory by telephone. So, I picked the number of telephone connections in the various places as the criterion of the central function of a settlement—related to the number of inhabitants of these places, in

order to determine the significance of surpluses (of people) in respect to the surrounding land. In addition, this was corrected by
coefficients, in order to place especially well
connected areas—such as the Rheinsfalz—on
the same level with such backward areas,
from the point of view of civilization and
technology, as the eastern border of
Bavaria. This telephone method was frequently a point attacked by the critics;
today, in view of the much greater diffusion
of the telephone, this method, of course,
could no longer be made use of.

So, I was able to assign to all central
places in South Germany value indication
numbers from 1 to 2825 (Munich): with 1
to 2, the lowest level was evaluated, with 3
and 4 the next, then with 5 to 10, the level
of the small rural towns, often already centers of administrations, with 12 to 31 the
level of the larger rural towns, up to 150 for
the medium size cities, and over that for the
levels of the larger centers. The limitations
of the evaluations of the levels are not arbitrary, but instead they are chosen according
to the model.

Henceforth, I was able to mark in the
central places in South Germany, according
to their significance as central places, on a
map, to measure the distances among them,
and to determine the rank in the hierarchy
of their "complementary areas" which
belonged to them (i.e., of their surrounding
territory). In this manner, the lowest ranked
central places have a surrounding territory
with a radius of 4-5 kilometers, and an average population of 3,000 (in the central place
and surrounding territory) and their distances from the nearest central places, which
according to the model lie within hexagonal
(six-sided) connections, amount to seven
kilometers. Within the completely regular
hexagonal system of central places, the distances of all higher ranked central places can
be derived, inasmuch as one multiplies the
distance of the next lowest ranking central

place by $\sqrt{3}$; the sequence of distances is
thus: 7-12-21-36-62-108-185. . . km. Around
a larger central place, for example, around a
12 km. ring and a 21 km. ring respectively,
are situated six central places of lower rank.

Thus, I was able to find surprising con-
currences between geographical reality and
the abstract schema of the central places
(the theoretical model) especially in the
predominantly agrarian areas of North and
South Bavaria.

It is perhaps of interest to know how I
proceeded with my investigation, especially
insofar as the deliberations in forming the
theoretical portion are concerned.

On Sundays, or also Saturday and
Sunday, I used to hike around in the
beautiful landscapes of the Frankish Alps.
While hiking, I mentally developed the progress of my work. When I found a special new
idea, I stood still and made a catch-word-
type note to myself. Thus, many an idea
which helped me progress, when I previously
would no longer know how to proceed, gave
me the happiness of a discoverer; it was
connected in my memory to some forest
path or other, just where I was, where the
sun cast its light patches through the foliage
onto the earth, or with some view or other
from a rocky height, or with some, perhaps,
field path of no importance. On the following Monday, I wrote down on paper what I
had thought about on the previous day.
Then, I was able to drink contentedly a glass
of wine in the evening in old Nürnberg. On
Tuesday, I read through that which I had
written once again, and it did not please me
at all. The greatest part of the manuscript I
crossed out, and rewrote the chapter. Together with this, to rest from my thoughts, I
proceeded with the more mechanical work
which consisted in counting up the telephone connections, the computations of
centrality, the drawing of maps of the numbers of inhabitants, and of the numbers of
telephone connections for all of South

Germany. And on the following Saturday and Sunday the thinking exercise while hiking took place. And so it went for weeks.

If I may very briefly once again describe my methodology: first of all play, paint on the maps, draw in lines and points, but in a very playful fashion—then problems suddenly emerge. Then I tried, while hiking, to elucidate them, to solve them, while hiking the thoughts are shaken back into their proper places. And, last of all, comes the completion and formulation. Thereby, the language should be of a sort that chimes, that is audible, and not just something for reading. In general, the opinion predominates that creative scholarly work is born at the desk. It must not be so. Mine was created while hiking, in nature. I, moreover, am glad to consider myself a geographer.

How is my work thought of to begin with—by geographers as well as by national economists? Some say: "that is, indeed, much too abstract, too theoretical. That is national economy, that actually has nothing to do with us." The others say: "that is, indeed, geography. As economists, we need not have anything to do with this." (It was like this, when the spatial aspect was as yet little studied in economic theory.) My hexagons were laughed at. At some banquet or other, a hexagon was drawn on my place-card. Once, when I was commenting on the numerical series of the hierarchy of central places, their numbers, and their distances, I heard one of the most prominent geographers mutter: "That's just a magic of numbers."

The breakthrough of recognition took place, actually, in America (Ullman, Harris, Berry, Bunge), in the Netherlands—where my paper, at the International Congress of Geographers, met with more rejection than agreement—and in Sweden (Kant, Hägerstrand, Godlund, Enequist). However, it has been recognized in Germany too that the functional method of observation is of crucial significance. At the Symposium on Urban Geography in Lund, in connection with the International Geographical Congress in Stockholm 1960, the "Christaller Model" (pronounced "madl") stood precisely in the focus of the discussion.[11] I was somewhat abashed, and I thought: "A Bavarian girl (madl*) would be agreeable and nice." William Bunge dedicated his book, *Theoretical Geography*, which was published in Lund in 1962, to me.[12] It is interesting that, almost simultaneously, but completely independently from my work, August Lösch in America discovered central place systems similar to mine—my book appeared in 1933, his in 1940.[13] The problem has, thus, "been in the air."

In the meantime, the theory of central places has been further extended, completed and deepened by numerous scholars in all countries. However, this no longer appertains to my topic. I would, however, like to take note of the fact that I have tried to develop a polar counterpart to the theory of central places—a theory of "peripheral places." By this I mean, primarily, resort areas, the areas of tourism and summer cottages. In addition to this, other experiments have been submitted: by Todt, Peucker and von Boventer, for example, in Germany. However, I believe that for this one cannot set up such an exact model as that of the central places. Perhaps so, nevertheless?

---

11. Proceedings of the IGU Symposium in Urban Geography Lund 1960, ed. by Knut Norborg. Lund 1962.

* Madel (or, if you wish, Madl) means "lass" in German. [Translator's note]

12. William Bunge; Theoretical Geography. Lund 1962.
13. August Lösch, Die räumliche Ordnung der Wirtschaft. Jena 1940. 2. Aufl. 1944.

++++++++++++++++++++++++++++++++

CHANCE AND LANDSCAPE

Leslie Curry

A century and a half ago the young Shelley could regard intellectual beauty as the banishing

> From all we hear and all we see,
> Doubt, chance and mutability.....

Yet by the early twentieth century in geography we find the French school discussing the sequential ordering of events in terms of contingencies, a notion taken from the contemporary mathematical probabilists.[1] Today, in the mental atmosphere of the principle of indeterminacy it is not surprising that some geographers are seeking to use the probability calculus as well as rely on its philosophical connotations. Whether this trend is only the following of a current fad which seeks to hide our ignorance and sloth or implies living boldly in one's generation, eschewing the logic of aggregation and imprecise measurement is for the future to decide. Certainly it is easy to sympathise with the resistance to regarding the earth's surface as governed by the mechanics of a roulette wheel and its development as a permanent floating crap game. The triumphs of nineteenth century science with its mechanistic cause-effect modes of thinking cannot be lightly set aside.

Yet apart from microphysics there are no a priori grounds for preferring deterministic or random formulations of physical and social behaviour. Justification lies only in aposteori results: which is most convenient, which leads to insights most readily in a particular problem, which allows greater generality should a broader view be sought. The random approach has a number of advantages. The most important is that it allows a problem to be approached with the explicit admission of considerable ignorance.

In a sense, the formulation of a random process is the reverse of a deterministic one. In the latter we specify some "causes" of certain intensity and interaction and obtain a result which will differ from reality by an "error" term. In the former we begin, at least metaphorically, with unconstrained independent random variables and, by introducing dependencies and constraints, achieve results of various likelihoods. Where nature shows only a single result, it is interpreted as the historical realisation of a process which could just as easily have produced other results but where there are a large number of realisations, their frequency of occurrence should agree with the derived probabilities. The more complex a process, the more likely we are to be ignorant of its working and thus the more we must rely on a probability calculus. One needs only consider the problem of the forces involved in a stone being moved down a river bed, let alone the development of a watershed, to realise that the task of setting down the equations governing this action in deterministic form

---

1. F. Lukermann, "The "calcul des probabilités" and the école française de géographie." *Canadian Geographer*, 9 (1965), 128-138.

From *Northern Geographical Essays in Honour of G. H. J. Daysh*, 1966, Oriel Press, Newcastle upon Tyne. Reprinted by permission.

will daunt the stoutest heart. In fact, we have skirted such problems altogether, preferring to eschew precision and concentrate on processes where vagueness of concept is possible or alternatively tackle extremely restricted problems about which we can be precise. Each problem of landscape has its appropriate time and space scale of study. Given our level of ignorance and a deterministic mode of thought, we cannot gain the level of precision necessary to tackle many of these problems. We must pick out problems of a particular scale which will allow us to use our mode of logic. These are problems which do not require rigorous formulation and imply considerable time or space scales of study or particular and relatively simple problems of limited dimensions such as the location of a factory. In the former class we have the historical evolution of landforms or the geographic zonality idea for associating climate, landforms, vegetation, soils and hydrology. It is thus likely that the probability approach will be used to open up new problems as much as re-examine old ones. Certainly there are many areas of concern to geography for which probabilistic thinking appears irrelevant. Descriptive and extremum problems in the spatial structure of the economy, of such wide interest today, do not fit this mould. The recounting of the historical development of particular areas need rarely appeal to probability reasoning except perhaps via contingency when broad enough explanatory concepts are being invoked.

In general the notion of randomness is relevant where a range of possibilities exists, implying a population of sufficient size existing either through time or over space or in the mind so that recounting these possible states of the population is of relevance to the real world. Thus, for example, it will be readily agreed that human geography has been retrospective in viewpoint with "an

express emphasis on the historical background of social behaviour." Yet to regard society as buffeted on the advancing front of a wave rather than having the ability to see some way ahead and to partially control speed and direction seems unduly fatalistic. Society is as much an organization to face the future as a product of Pavlovian conditioning. Probability analysis emphasises choice and decisions and thus aims forwards as readily as backwards.

A probabilistic formulation of a problem can lead to results which are intuitively inconceivable to our deterministically structured minds. Thus a storage system in which mean input equals mean service rate can have no change in the amount stored. In terms of random processes, however, not only must the mean output capacity be greater than mean input to constrain storage to reasonable bounds, but fluctuations in this quantity are enormous as input approaches service rate. This has obvious implications for lake levels or watertables, the characteristics of a floodplain, the operation of inventories or the heat stored in the ocean and therefore climatic change. A state of affairs can often arise via stochastic processes which has no well-defined counterpart in historical explanation: no matter what the initial state and no matter what historical course of events has occurred since, the final result is the same (at least in probabilistic terms). This "steady state" is thus independent of time so that time will not appear in the steady state equations.

Description

The ability to describe the arrangement in time and space of features of the earth's surface in probabilistic terms is clearly a first requirement of analysis. Study of the temporal variation of the atmospheric elements has led here, although the work of

Dacey[2] on two dimensional dot patterns has meant that we now have a considerable kit of tools for studying events in one and two dimensions. The fitting of standard probability series to events has had some important consequences. In the first place it has sharpened ideas on what is meant by terms such as homogeneity and heterogeneity. We can specify exactly what we mean by regular, random or clustered distributions and we realise the type and extent of dependence between events which leads to these distributions. By simply counting events per unit area or unit period and fitting a standard probability series to them, we may often infer a considerable amount of further information concerning the distances apart of nth nearest neighbors, the magnitude of variation contributed at different scales and so on. We also obtain insight into the type of process which could have produced such distributions and are thus led into explanation.

A great deal of fundamental work still remains to be done, however, on methods of description. Court, for example, discusses the problem of the form of the probability function to be fitted to the wind rose.[3] Dacey has begun work on line patterns[4] while the work of Longuet-Higgins[5] on wave statistics has still to be exploited in geography. This account could lead into the various statistical methods being used for describing surfaces numerically, for map generalization, for regionalization or for splitting continuous areal distributions into components, but this would lead us too far afield.

Although not strictly descriptive, the use of combinatorial analysis in reducing the rather perplexing ordering displayed in city sizes, the rank size rule[6] and in the branching of streams, Horton's law of stream numbers[7] may be noted here. Given all possible arrangements of a given number of things among a given number of classes, random allocation of the things among the classes provides these empirical regularities as the most probable distribution.

Diffusion

The work of Hägerstrand provides the easiest approach technically, if not conceptually, to the study of chance on the landscape.[8] Diffusion of cultural traits has long been of major concern and the tracing of such movements through historical records, physical

2. M. F. Dacey, "A compound probability law for a pattern more dispersed than random and with areal inhomogeneity." *Economic Geography*, 42 (1966), 172-9; "Modified Poisson probability law for point pattern more regular than random." *Annals*, Association American Geographers, 54, 4 (1964), 559-65; "Two dimensional random point patterns: a review and an interpretation." *Papers and Proceedings*, Regional Science Association; "Imperfections in the uniform plane." *Michigan Inter-University Community of Mathematical Geographers*, 4 (1964); "The spacing of river towns." *Annals*, Association American Geographers, 50, 4 (1960), 59-61; "Analysis of central place and point patterns by a nearest neighbour method." *Proceedings of International Geographical Union Symposium on Urban Studies*, Lund (1960), Lund Studies in Geography, B, 24, 55-76; "A note on the derivation of nearest neighbor distances." *Journal of Regional Science*, 2, 2 (1960), 81-87.

3. A. Court, "Some new statistical techniques in geophysics," *Advances in Geophysics*, V. 1, Academic Press, New York (1952), 45-85.
4. M. G. Dacey, "Description of linear patterns." Ed. W. L. Garrison, *Quantitative Geography* (forthcoming).
5. M. S. Longuet-Higgins, "The statistical analysis of a random moving surface." *Philosophical Transactions of the Royal Society*, A, 249, 321-387.
6. L. Curry, "The random spatial economy: an exploration in settlement theory." *Annals*, Association American Geographers, 54 (1964), 138-46.
7. R. L. Shreeve, "Statistical law of stream numbers." *Journal of Geology*, 74 (1966), 17-37.
8. T. Hägerstrand, "The propagation of innovation waves." Lund Studies in Geography, B, 4 (1952).

evidence and plausible inference a part of the stock in trade. Yet clearly there must always be a greater or lesser element of chance in these movements which does not yield to such methods. How far is the areal spread of agricultural innovation a matter of early chance contacts preserved in the patterns of acceptance? It was Hägerstrand who conceived the probabilistic basis of such transfers of information and the manner of analysis by simulation. For him, the contorted surface of the real world could not be represented sufficiently accurately by an abstract plane so that he eschewed mathematical formulation. Instead, he provided an initial source of information and then, assuming frequencies of contacts between people by distance were described by a normal curve, he drew randomly from this series to allow transfers of information to be made. Each person contacted a sufficient number of times became an acceptor and then a further source as the process developed. Thus patterns of spread could be built up which looked like the historical record emphasising that, in this case at least, personal contact was the dominant link rather than persuasion by the mass media. A number of studies have pursued this method of analysis although nowadays the convenience of a digital computer is commonly sought[9] rather than Hägerstrand's paper and pencil. Topics have been central places in Sweden,[10] urban growth[11] and liquid propane gas tanks[12] among others.

The main problem connected with this approach is the necessary comparison of the results of the simulation with the real world distribution it is designed to reproduce. Since the latter has in effect only a probabilistic existence, the results of a simulation will certainly not match it. How then are we to say that they are sufficiently alike that the rules we have used in the simulation may be reasonably taken as approximating the processes of the real world? It is here where the virtues of an analytic formulation are evident.

The most sophisticated analytic model of a stochastic diffusion process devised by a geographer is Culling's theory of erosion.[13] He refers to humid conditions, a permeable rock and relatively gentle slopes so that it is the efficiency of transport of eroded material via soil creep which is the limiting factor in denudation. The movements of a soil particle are regarded as independently and randomly directed so that application of the central limit theorem assures that the resulting probability distribution of its location after a number of individual displacements will be three-dimensionally normal about its original position. Gravity and gravitational soil moisture would provide a downward bias to this motion but because of the lower barrier to movement provided by the underlying solid rock, pore space would decrease in this direction so limiting displacements and thus removing the bias. Thus a steady state vertical distribution of particles will develop, probabilistically defined

9. F. R. Pitts, "Problems in computer simulation of diffusion." *Papers and Proceedings*, Regional Science Association (1962).
10. R. L. Morrill, "The development of spatial distributions of towns in Sweden: an historical-predictive approach." *Annals*, Association American Geographers, 53, 1 (1963), 1-14; "Simulation of central place patterns over time." *Proceedings, International Geographical Union Symposium in Urban Geography*, Lund (1960), Lund Studies in Geography, B, 24, 109-20.

11. W. L. Garrison, "Toward simulation models of urban growth and development." *ibid.*, 91-108.
12. L. Brown, "The diffusion of innovation: a Markov chain-type approach." Discussion Paper No. 3, Department of Geography, Northwestern University, Evanston, Ill. (1964).
13. W. E. H. Culling, "Theory of erosion on soil-covered slopes." *Journal of Geology*, 73 (1965), 230-254; "Soil creep and the development of hillside slopes." *ibid.*, 71 (1963), 127-61.

and representing a density increase and pore space decrease with depth. Density layering will be parallel to the surface and if there is no slope, no mean motion would occur although there would be a diffusion of "marked" particles. Where there is slope, an extremely slow mean motion of particles will occur depending on the density gradient and tending to replace layering parallel to the surface with horizontal layering.

Culling has a river at the foot of the slope eroding its banks and rapidly transporting the material away, so creating "pore spaces." In technical terms, an absorptive boundary for particles exists. Probabilities for upslope and downslope movement are now no longer equal, there being a bias in the general down-slope direction. An ingenious feature of the argument is that the movement of pore spaces upslope from the river is considered; this is an inverse process to that of soil particles and follows the same laws. The course of development of various landform features is followed for given boundary conditions using mathematical results obtained in heat conduction studies.

With both Hägerstrand and Culling there is a genuine attempt to describe the small-scale process leading to large-scale results. The "rules of the game" in simulation and the random displacements of the analytic model are open to empirical checking and perhaps modification in a way that aggregative deterministic models cannot match. Above all, we may perceive the large-scale ordering only after appreciating indeterminacy at the small scale.

For completeness, a word should be said about atmospheric diffusion since those geographers concerned with the heat and moisture balance at the earth's surface have had longest acquaintance with random displacements, here in terms of turbulence theory. However, so far as is known, no geographers have contributed to its development.

Development

Probabilistic reasoning has a new viewpoint to offer to the study of historical process in geography. If the development of landscape be a series of contingent events then in a certain sense the study of the historical record cannot reveal many of the generalities of process. Of course the development of particular places requires a particularistic historical account without the need for generality of concept. The ford, the shrine, the castle, the coalfield, the protestant ethic, the sea, appear in correct sequence to help explain Newcastle upon Tyne and another set of factors are used to explain another town. Mr. Morris happened to be repairing bicycles at Oxford. While true and necessary there is a lack of aesthetic satisfaction about such explanations. We would certainly feel a study of land-form development inadequate which showed how, stone by stone and particle by particle, the surface of one date became that of another.

By contingency we mean that action 1 occurred but 2 might have happened just as easily; because of 1, 3 resulted rather than 4 which would have followed 2 and so on. The odd numbers describe real history and the even a possible history which did not happen. If we cannot specify this latter sequence it is ridiculous to discuss it. However, if we classify events sufficiently broadly, events which were previously regarded as different in kind now become only differences of degree. When we can specify the probabilities of occurrence of these degrees we can write a stochastic process of which the real history described above will be only one possible sample. However, because of the generality of classification adopted, it is possible to describe the histories of a thousand towns in the same terms and these represent a thousand samples. It is then possible to say something general about all these histories—they represent a thousand realizations of the common stochastic process. Clearly this is a valid procedure; whether it is a useful one depends on the question one asks of the landscape.

Why has the American manufacturing belt retained its coherence throughout the growth of the economy? How do such regions develop and retain their differential character? Momentum and inertia in this context are vaguely suggestive words rather than attempts to describe relevant processes. Take a city, representing all cities, in which the spin of a coin determines whether a manufacturing or a "service" employee will be added to the payroll. The second employee is determined by a second toss being summed with the first and so on. We have a specialization process in which, while each increment has a random aspect, the future is being affected by the past to the extent that the past is summed up in the present, no matter how the present was arrived at. The probability distribution of the ratio of manufacturing to total employees one arrives at after a number of tosses is the U shaped arc-sine curve implying that cities will tend to be specialized in manufacturing or service with relatively few of mixed type. One can add the same type of process going on in space with adjacent cities instead of periods affecting each other so that the same probability distribution is obtained. If any uninterrupted series of manufacturing cities is called a manufacturing zone, even if there be only one city, an extremely small number of boundaries between the two types of zones can occur. We thus obtain a marked and stable regionalization. Changes are most likely at the bounds of the zones and there is a finite probability of the whole structure

changing but this is what we expect from the real world.[14]

In the previous example cities distributed in space were regarded as the sampling points of a single process. We may equally well regard time periods as samples of a process: the time perspective thus obtained is not of history unrolling but rather of a collection of periods existing simultaneously, including our own single sample. Take, for example, a stand of trees having distinct age groups visible: presumably during the life span of such trees there have been only a few occasions when natural regeneration has been allowed. We may thus speak of a probability of successful regeneration during the life span of a tree and determine probabilities of intervals of various lengths between regenerations. In many areas there will be finite probabilities that the intervals will be longer than the lifetime of a tree plus the period of viability of seeds so that the trees will die out. With an unchanging mean climate we may nevertheless expect that vegetation will change, indeed be experiencing constant change particularly at the limits of vegetation types. It is pertinent then to regard this plant cover and all plant covers as existing at some probability level. It exists because our recent period obtained a particular sample from the climatic record whereas another but unfavourable sample might have occurred just as readily. A view of the landscape as a continuously fluctuating panorama even without exogenous intervention is thus obtained.[15] The same type of argument can be applied to climate itself. In the vegetation example, the periodicity of change is clearly related to the life span of the trees which constitutes the

---

14. L. Curry, *op. cit.* (1964).
15. L. Curry, "Climatic change as a random series." *Annals,* Association American Geographers, 52, 1 (1962), 21-31.

length of "memory" of the system. In the atmosphere-earth system the oceans provide an enormous memory by storing heat: because of the stirring of the water in depth very considerable quantities can be stored there with very little overall change in temperature; furthermore, these layers are stably stratified so that the heat could be held indefinitely.[16] Now, since it is inconceivable that there should be an exact balance of heat exchange between earth and atmosphere in any one year, the oceans can be regarded as gaining heat one year and losing it another via a random process. The probabilities of the relative amounts stored and the periodicities of the fluctuations may be calculated.[17] It turns out that these are of the order of those of the ice ages. We must view climate as a very wide spectrum of conditions with any particular time period spanning a relatively narrow bandwidth of conditions. Ice ages are a normal feature of the general circulation and will, with high probability, occur again. It can be helpful to say that they occur now in a region with a certain probability.

This approach can be applied to many landscape features. The landforms of the North African desert show clearly that present forms requre recognition of an earlier wet phase.[18] But with the present concept of climate this should be taken as a normal state of affairs. To couch explanation in historical terms as a sequence of events may be useful but it is equally pertinent to analyse the landforms as mirroring a considerable part of the climatic spectrum.

---

16. C. G. Rossby, "Current problems in meteorology," *The atmosphere and the sea in motion: Rossby memorial volume*, Ed. B. Bolin, N. Y. (1959), 9-50.
17. L. Curry, *op. cit.* (1962).
18. R. Capot-Rey, "Recherches récentes et tendances nouvelles en morphologie désertique." *La géographie française au milieu du XXe siècle*, Paris (1957), 43-52.

Steady State

A feature of probabilistic processes which has been used already but not yet discussed is the notion of the steady state. Many such processes do achieve this condition. It is one without relation to any initial, i.e. conditions, with fluctuations occurring constantly but with the probabilities of the various states being independent of time. Thus, for a system in a steady state there is no need to study its history in order to understand its form or the processes going on. Such an approach does not fit well the traditional trilogy of genesis, form and function as the approaches to geographical knowledge.

This approach has been expounded most clearly in relation to landforms.[19] Genesis as secular change or history is represented by the Davisian approach which Chorley represents as closed system analysis in which the potential energy due to elevation (i.e. endogenous to the system) is being degraded until, barring upsets, a peneplain is achieved. However, where the interplay of present processes and forms is of concern and much shorter time periods are relevant, the open system viewpoint is adopted. Here a continual exogenous supply of atmospheric energy, particularly the potential energy of rain, is supplied to the land and attention is focused on the present-day equilibrium of process and form. Leopold and Langbein have shown by probabilistic arguments that an exponential form of the thalweg of rivers will result as a steady state condition; the rivers referred to are those flowing through arid areas and without tributaries.[20]

---

19. R. J. Chorley, "Geomorphology and general systems theory." *Theoretical papers in the hydrologic and geomorphic sciences*, Geological Survey Professional Paper 500-B., Washington, D. C. (1962).
20. L. B. Leopold and W. B. Langbein, "The concept of entropy in landscape evolution." *ibid.*,

DECISIONS AND BEHAVIOUR

Uncertainty is a basic fact of life for both individuals and groups of men. It matters little operationally whether this uncertainty be inherent indeterminacy or simply reflects ignorance of deterministic sets of events. Uncertainty is particularly important in connection with the future so that actions predicated on future conditions may be understood as the making of decisions within the range of possible futures. A retrospective view of society is less concerned with the decision problem since the passage of time is in a sense solving the probabilistic equations which described the future. However, it is reasonable to believe that the human landscape must to some extent mirror and be a manifestation of this uncertainty. The natural landscape must express the same principle. Three methods of adaptation appear possible although there may be others.[21] The passing of inputs through storage devices will reduce their variance, while passing them through a delay device will alter their phase and allow a conforming reaction. Finally the maintenance of a varied structure will allow adaptation to changed circumstances. The first two methods have been described for a dairy farm[22] and a central place system,[23] but other examples spring to mind.

Geological Survey Professional Paper 500-B (1962).
21. L. Curry, "Central places in the random spatial economy." (unpublished paper).
22. L. Curry, "Regional variation in the seasonal programming of livestock farms in New Zealand." *Economic Geography*, 39 (1963), 96-118. "Canterbury's grassland climate." *Proceedings*, Second N. Z. Geography Conference (1958).
23. L. Curry, "The geography of service centres within towns: the elements of an operational approach." *IGU Symposium in Urban Geography*, Lund (1960), Lund Studies in Geography, B, 24, 31-53.

The transition from individual men making decisions to groups of men which are the main concern of human geography is not an easy one and a number of methods have been used. The most obvious approach is to postulate a "representative man" and examine the choice matrix of his decisions; since goals must also be specified, the optimizing man that economic theory has provided has been used. Thus, for example, given the probabilities of herbage production as estimated from daily variations in weather throughout the year, how does the livestock farmer arrange his seasonal farm management programme to use these fluctuating uncertain supplies?[24] Note that this is an extremum problem in management of resources rather than in localization. It would be absurd to believe that economic man is really representative of any society but equally absurd to deny that considerable insights can be obtained by using him. He is extremely difficult to replace. Kates, for example, in a probabilistically stated problem of flood plain occupance has used the notion of "satisficing" man—one who goes only some way toward economic rationality.[25] However, this is more of a descriptive term for the man discovered by behaviourist studies than a concept having analytic power. Indeed it is not clear whether we cannot retain the convenience of economic man and account for non-optimality by using the perceived environment rather than the objectively described environment. That is, actions may be optimal in terms of the perception of flood hazard but not in terms of the statistical forecast of floods. The

24. L. Curry, "The climatic resources of intensive grassland farming: the Waikato, New Zealand." *Geographical Review*, 52 (1962), 174-94.
25. R. W. Kates, "Hazard and choice perception in flood plain management." Department of Geography Research Paper 78, University of Chicago (1962).

relation of perception and economic calculus in uncertainty conditions will be taken up shortly.

Wolpert, although using a representative economic man, has handled the uncertainty facing him rather differently.[26] He regards risk as fluctuation on an unchanging environment, in this case that of the Swedish farmer and obtains a deterministic "rational" allocation of these fixed resources using linear programming methods. A "risk" component is then added to explain real world departures from calculated optimality; degree of technical knowledge obtained from a Hägerstrand diffusion model is also used. It is unlikely that this formulation has general application although the use of a "certainty" equivalent for probabilistic situations does appear possible.

The other main line of attack to group decisions, i.e., to group behaviour conceived as a decision problem, is a "summation man." This "group man" represents a convolution of the situations of many individuals and the group actions he performs have fewer constraints on them than were each individual considered individually. He thus appears more like an urn scheme of the mathematical probabilist since his choices at this more general level have a considerable random component. Some examples should make this idea clearer. Consider an area of variable rainfall in which the several crops have their yields differentially affected by differing rain totals. What proportions of land should be planted to the various crops to ensure that the minimum amount of food in any year should be as large as possible? Gould has asked this question as an approach to the understanding of land utilization in Central Ghana.[27] This situation,

while having obvious affinities with the livestock farmer mentioned earlier, does not need to delve into the level of the individual farm because the problem implies a greater level of aggregation. The "group" approach is predicated here on some egalitarian sharing either of crops for consumption or of land types for individual use. The formal procedures used for choosing an optimum combination of crops are those of the theory of games—here the village is adopting a strategy against the possible plays of nature.

Marble has used a "summation man" in a study of traffic in a city.[28] His data consisted of a number of travel diaries kept by sample families in which all trips, including those having more than one purpose and thus allowing stopovers, were recorded. One possible tabulation of this data is on the basis of type, i.e. function, by origin and destination. A table was prepared showing for all origins that when a trip starts from, say, the work-place, the frequencies of destinations are, say, home 80 per cent, shopping 8 per cent, and so on. Although these frequencies are obtained from the summations of individuals trips, they may be regarded as the choice matrix of the summation man. By treating the frequencies as transition probabilities between states (i.e. home, shop, etc.) and by regarding home as an absorbing state (i.e. people do get home eventually) it is possible to conceive the travel pattern as generated by one summation man performing a random walk. The reason for doing this is that, by manipulation of the matrix, it is possible to arrive at a steady state condition describing the overall travel pattern although only the individual

26. J. Wolpert, "The decision process in spatial context." *Annals*, Association American Geographers, 54, 4 (1964), 537-58.
27. P. R. Gould, "Man against his environment: a

game theoretic framework." *Annals*, Association American Geographers, 53, 3 (1963), 290-97.
28. D. Marble, "Simple Markovian model of trip structure in a metropolitan region." *Proceedings*, Western Section Regional Science Association, Tempe, Arizona (1964).

segments of many trips were provided as data. With sufficient data, locations may also be included in the analysis. It has been seen here how the summation man is acting quite randomly, constrained only by a single probability matrix—he is an unthinking urn scheme. Yet he adequately represents the sum of the highly purposeful and specialized individual travel behaviour.

Although not concerned with statistical methods here, in discussing decision making under uncertainty it would be remiss not to mention briefly the analytic role of subjective probability in the perception-decision problem. Classical statistics is not geared to making probabilistic statements about future conditions and certainly not adapted to guiding rational decisions on the basis of subjectively held beliefs of the future course of events. Yet people in their adaptation to environment act in accordance with their beliefs about the world rather than an objectively described world. They amend their beliefs with experience as a learning process and weight them with the benefits and costs to be obtained from acting on particular beliefs; some best course of action can thus be obtained. Such a scheme is a reasonable representation of the perception-decision problem: it happens to be that provided by Bayesian statistics.[29]

A revealing example may be taken from the physical planning field: assume engineering activity is to be decided on the basis of a forecast of the population of a city. The usual forecasting procedure is to manipulate the data of past populations and come up with a single value of population for a future date for all the world as if this was an academic exercise in astronomy. Given such a

total, roads are built, sewers are laid and so on. Now, of course, it is absurd to act as though we know with certainty how big the city will be; it is equally foolish, although less obviously so, to regard a forecast on which decisions are made with attendant costs and benefits as a problem in pure science. We have some ideas about the city's future size but there is also uncertainty—a probability distribution is the best we can hope for. Let us keep gathering evidence and amending our beliefs; let us calculate the effects of these outcomes, keeping in mind their probability of occurrence. This seems to be a reasonable representation in formal terms of the way people operate; that it is not so for planners is due to the inappropriate statistics they use.

An academic discipline presumably justifies itself insofar as its individual members contribute to answering the questions we ask of nature. With regard to any particular problem or set of problems the approach of a geographer may coincide with that of a student from a neighbouring discipline. But there seems to be the obligation for geography to phrase individual explanations of events in the landscape so that these may be structured into an overall articulated view of ordering in space. Obviously no common discourse is possible for all topics studied by geographers but the formal language of probability theory does hold the greatest hope of establishing a structure of explanation to which the various parts of geography can contribute and from which they can draw. Communication can only be at a very general level but at least some co-operative building and cross-fertilization can occur.

It has been seen that there has been no real break in analytic concept throughout this essay. From the representative individual to group decisions and group be-

29. L. Curry, "Seasonal programming and Bayesian assessment of atmospheric resources." *Human Dimensions of Weather Modification*, Ed. W. R. D. Sewell, Department of Geography Research Paper 105, University of Chicago (1966).

haviour, from conscious man with his choice matrix to the movement of rock particles there is no discontinuity. Very large gaps do occur in the areas of application however and thus all assertions as to the inclusiveness of our mathematics need to be qualified. One gap which does not seem to hold promise is that of genetic climatology. It is an unfortunate fact of history, as Leighly has pointed out,[30] that studies of the causes and of the consequences of climate have tended to be organised in separate and often antagonistic camps. The statistical description of climate has generally been pursued by the functional school so that there has been little attempt to relate these statistical studies of form with the dynamics of the atmosphere. Yet there must be complete complementarity in nature allowing pursuit of the statistics back into the dynamics and forward into the landscape. Nevertheless it can be argued that statistics are but a pale reflection of the real course of events and that the meteorologist using the perfectly general deterministic equations of physics plus boundary and initial conditions can perform his integrations and produce a closer copy of the sequence of nature. It is conceivable that a model could produce hour to hour changes all over the world and, running for the computer equivalent of years on end, accumulate climatic statistics. Such a model would imply greatly expanded understanding of the physical processes involved and since the statistical measures

are but secondary rather than primary facts they do not justify separate treatment.

But does such a model allow understanding of why the statistical measures of, say, rainfall differ between stations? Here too a rigorous, quantitative, physically well-grounded theory of the atmosphere is needed. But the aim is to account for a collective rather than write a history. These statistics are primary facts as parameters of landscape and their spatial distribution should be explained directly. There are other reasons for direct probabilistic modelling of the atmosphere but that of coherence has much merit. Of course, this is not to say that such a theoretical formulation is possible, only that it does appear desirable.

To conceive the landscape as composed of elements having characteristic spectra of fluctuations in time and of differentiation in space, to depict society as an organization for facing the future and choosing among a variety of possibilities, to stress movement and development, to place uncertainty in the centre of our analysis instead of ignoring it as regrettable, all this must be welcome. That the format of the language of probabilities is equally germane to discussing both physical and human events, both spatial and temporal ordering, both retrospective and anticipatory explanations of actions, both individual and collective activities, the physical world both as exclusive of man and as the environment of man, bespeaks its versatility. A common mode of discourse thus presents itself for scientific study of the landscape, promising to promote an articulated coherent viewpoint.

30. J. B. Leighly, "Climatology." *American geography, Inventory and Prospect*, Eds. P. E. James and C. F. Jones, Syracuse, (1954).

✦✦✦✦✦✦✦✦✦✦✦✦✦✦✦✦✦✦✦✦✦✦✦✦✦✦✦✦✦✦✦

BIBLIOGRAPHY

Spatial Order

BERRY, BRIAN J. L., and D. MICHAEL RAY, "Multivariate Socio-economic Regionalization: A Pilot Study in Central Canada," in T. Rymes and S. Ostry (eds.), *Regional Statistical Studies*, Toronto: University of Toronto Press, 1966. Factor analytical structures are developed to facilitate purposive regionalization.

BERRY, BRIAN J. L., *Essays on Commodity Flows and the Spatial Structure of the Indian Economy*, University of Chicago, Department of Geography, Research Papers, Paper No. 111, 1966. Berry's general field formulation is applied to Indian district attributes and interdistrict commodity flows.

BUNGE, WILLIAM, *Theoretical Geography*, Lund: Gleerups Förlag, 1966. Stressing location as a central question in Geography, Bunge offers a major conceptual challenge to areal differentiation.

CHORLEY, RICHARD J., "Geography and Analogue Theory," *Annals, Association of American Geographers*, Vol. 54 (1964), pp. 127-37. A model for models is developed in this survey of geographical model-building.

CHRISTALLER, WALTER, *Central Places in Southern Germany* (Baskin translation), Englewood Cliffs, New Jersey: Prentice-Hall, 1966. Christaller's pioneering work on a theory of tertiary activity is carefully translated.

CURRY, LESLIE, "The Random Spatial Economy: An Exploration in Settlement Theory," *Annals, Association of American Geographers*, Vol. 54 (1964), pp. 137-46. Curry specifies an entropy model which suggests that the processes of settlement are activated by random behavior.

DACEY, MICHAEL F., "A County Seat Model for the Areal Pattern of an Urban System," *Geographical Review*, Vol. 56 (1966), pp. 527-42. A stochastic model of arrangement and distribution is developed for cities and towns over a set of counties.

DACEY, MICHAEL F., "A Probability Model for Central Place Locations," *Annals, Association of American Geographers*, Vol. 56 (1966), pp. 549-68. A random element is combined with the hexagonal point pattern of the special case in central place theory to develop a probability model.

HARVEY, DAVID, "Geographic Processes and the Analysis of Point Patterns: Testing Models of Diffusion by Quadrat Sampling," *Transactions, Institute of British Geographers*, Vol. 49 (1966), pp. 81-95. Although not coping with the problem of scale, Harvey demonstrates quadrat sampling methods and their application to the verification problem.

HORVATH, RONALD J., "Von Thunen's Isolated State and the Area around Addis Ababa, Ethiopia," *Annals, Association of American Geographers*, Vol. 59 (1969), pp. 308-23. An empirical study of spatial organization is made of the area around the Ethiopian capital.

HUDSON, JOHN C., "A Location Theory for Rural Settlement," *Annals, Association of American Geographers*, Vol. 59 (1969), pp. 368-81. The author emphasizes the processes of colonization, spread, and competition in analyzing rural settlement patterns.

ISARD, WALTER, *Location and Space Economy*, New York: John Wiley & Sons, 1956. Isard makes an attempt at posing a general location theory.

KING, LESLIE, "A Quantitative Expression of the Pattern of Urban Settlements in Selected Areas of the United States," *Tijdschrift Voor Econ. en Soc. Geographie*, Vol. 53 (1962), pp. 1-7. An early theoretical examination of settlement patterns is geared toward increased analytical objectivity.

LÖSCH, AUGUST, *The Economics of Location* (Woglom-Stolper translation), New Haven, Connecticut: Yale University Press, 1954. Lösch provides a classic early model of a space-economy operating under conditions of modified general equilibrium.

MEDVEDKOV, YU. F., "An Application of Topology in Central Place Analysis," *Papers of the Regional Science Association*, Vol. XX, The Hague Congress, 1967, pp. 77-84. Entropy measures for Ghana and Kazakhstan's urban networks are developed.

MORRILL, RICHARD L., "The Development of Spatial Distributions of Towns in Sweden: An Historical-Predictive Approach," *Annals, Association of American Geographers*, Vol. 53, No. 1 (1963), pp. 1-14. After a review of the urbanization process, Morrill develops a simulation model of an urban system.

NEWLING, BRUCE E., "Urban Growth and Spatial Structure: Mathematical Models and Empirical Evidence," *Geographical Review*, Vol. 56, No. 2 (1966), pp. 213-55. The spatial variation of urban densities over time is examined, with data from Kingston, Jamaica, and Pittsburgh, Pennsylvania.

OLSSON, GUNNAR, "Central Place Theory, Spatial Interaction, and Stochastic Processes," *Papers and Proceedings of the Regional Science Association*, Vol. 18 (1967). Olsson makes a useful contribution to a systems approach to the complexity of central place.

OLSSON, GUNNAR, *Distance and Human Interaction: A Review and Bibliography*, Philadelphia, Pennsylvania: Regional Science Research Institute, 1965. Olsson's thorough review examines the distance variable and human behavior over space.

PARR, JOHN B., and KENNETH G. DENIKE, "Theoretical Problems in Central Place Analysis," *Economic Geography*, Vol. 46, No. 4 (1970), pp. 568-86. Economic concepts are used to extend central place theory, particularly in the realm of public policy.

PRED, ALLAN, *The Spatial Dynamics of Urban Industrial Growth, 1800-1914: Interpretive and Theoretical Essays*, Cambridge: M.I.T. Press, 1966. Pred offers a thorough review of empirical evidence and theoretical constructs regarding spatial changes in urban-based industry.

RUSHTON, GERARD, "Analysis of Spatial Behavior by Revealed Space Preference," *Annals, Association of American Geographers*, Vol. 59, No. 2 (1969), pp. 391-400. A ranking of "spatial opportunities" is established from spatial behavior patterns.

SEMPLE, R. K., and R. G. GOLLEDGE, "An Analysis of Entropy Changes in a Settlement Pattern over Time," *Economic Geography*, Vol. 46, No. 2 (1970), pp. 157-60. The authors test the hypothesis of increased spatial ordering over time for the urban places of the Canadian Central Praries.

TOBLER, WALDO R., "Geographic Data and Map Projections," *Geographical Review*, Vol. 53 (1963), pp. 59-78. Map transformations are developed through geometric modification.

VON THUNEN, JOHANN HENRICH, *Von Thunen's Isolated State* (edited by Peter Hall), Oxford: Pergamon Press, 1966. Von Thunen's early model of agricultural land use for one of the basic locational contrasts.

WEBER, ALFRED, *Theory of Location of Industries* (Friedrich translation), Chicago: University of Chicago Press, 1929. This is Weber's classic on industrial location.

WOLDENBURG, MICHAEL J., "Energy Flow and Spatial Order: Mixed Hexagonal Hierarchies of Central Places," *Geographical Review*, Vol. 58 (1968), No. 4, pp. 552-74. The author suggests a lawful energy flow through hypothesized spatial hierarchies.

WOLPERT, JULIAN, "The Decision Process in Spatial Context," *Annals, American Association of Geographers*, Vol. 54, No. 4 (1964), pp. 537-58. The "satisficer" concept is used to model spatial variations of agricultural productivity in Middle Sweden.